The Global Journalist in the 21st Century

The Global Journalist in the 21st Century systematically assesses the demographics, education, socialization, professional attitudes and working conditions of journalists in various countries around the world. This book updates the original *Global Journalist* (1998) volume with new data, adding more than a dozen countries, and provides material on comparative research about journalists that will be useful to those interested in doing their own studies.

The editors put together this collection working under the assumption that journalists' backgrounds, working conditions, and ideas are related to what is reported (and how it is covered) in the various news media around the world, in spite of societal and organizational constraints, and that this news coverage matters in terms of world public opinion and policies. Outstanding features include:

- Coverage of 33 nations located around the globe, based on recent surveys conducted among representative samples of local journalists
- Comprehensive analyses by well-known media scholars from each country
- A section on comparative studies of journalists
- An appendix with a collection of survey questions used in various nations to question journalists

As the most comprehensive and reliable source on journalists around the world, *The Global Journalist in the 21st Century* will serve as the primary source for evaluating the state of journalism. As such, it promises to become a standard reference among journalism, media, and communication students and researchers around the world.

David H. Weaver is the Roy W. Howard Professor in Journalism and Mass Communication Research in the School of Journalism at Indiana University's Bloomington campus. He is widely published in journalism and political communication.

Lars Willnat is Professor in the School of Journalism at Indiana University. Before joining IU in 2009, Professor Willnat taught at the George Washington University in Washington, DC and at the Chinese University of Hong Kong. His research interests include media effects on political attitudes, theoretical aspects of public opinion formation, international communication, and political communication in Asia.

ROUTLEDGE COMMUNICATION SERIES

Jennings Bryant/Dolf Zillmann, Series Editors

Selected titles include:

- Frey: *Group Communication in Context: Studies of Bona Fide Groups, Second Edition*
- Bucy/Holbert: *The Sourcebook for Political Communication Research*
- Heath/Bryant: *Human Communication Theory and Research, Second Edition*
- Stacks/Salwen: *An Integrated Approach to Communication Theory and Research, Second Edition*
- Rubin et al: *Communication Research Measures II*
- Frey/Cissna: *Routledge Handbook of Applied Communication Research*
- Hollingshead/Poole: *Research Methods for Studying Groups and Teams*

The Global Journalist
in the 21st Century

Edited by
David H. Weaver and Lars Willnat

Routledge
Taylor & Francis Group

NEW YORK AND LONDON

First published 2012
by Routledge
711 Third Avenue, New York, NY 10017

Simultaneously published in the UK
by Routledge
2 Park Square, Milton Park, Abingdon, Oxon OX14 4RN

Routledge is an imprint of the Taylor & Francis Group, an informa business

Library of Congress Cataloging in Publication Data
The global journalist in the 21st century / edited by David H. Weaver and Lars Willnat.
    p. cm. — (Routledge communication series)
    Includes bibliographical references and index.
    1. Journalists—Biography. 2. Journalism—History—21st century. I. Weaver,
    David H. (David Hugh), 1946– II. Willnat, Lars, 1964–
    PN4820.G57 2012
    070.92—dc23
    2011035888

ISBN: 978-0-415-88576-8 (HBK)
ISBN: 978-0-203-14867-9 (EBK)

Typeset in Perpetua
by EvS Communication Networx, Inc.

Printed and bound in the United States of America by Publishers Graphics,
LLC on sustainably sourced paper.

Contents

Preface

This book is a follow-up to the 1998 *Global Journalist* book edited by David Weaver and published by Hampton Press. That original book included surveys of some 20,000 journalists from 21 different countries and territories; this new one includes studies of more than 29,000 journalists from 31 countries, 17 of which are the same as those in the earlier volume.

This book could not have been produced without the support of many friends and colleagues around the world, including the 80 chapter authors, among whom are some former students such as Young Jun Son, Sung Tae Kim, Jihyang Choi, Aralynn McMane, Mohamed Kirat, and Jason Martin. We are indebted to them, and also to former students Linda Camaj, Jason Martin, and Bill Hornaday for their help in editing the chapters. Doctoral candidate Seong Choul Hong did yeoman work compiling the author and subject indexes, and we are especially grateful for his careful attention to detail. We also thank the family of Roy W. Howard for its continued support of the chair held by David Weaver, which has provided funding for these students and other research expenses. The School of Journalism at Indiana University has also supported this project in various ways.

And we thank Linda Bathgate and her colleagues at Routledge for their support and patience after we missed our deadline for submitting the manuscript. We are pleased to be able to update the original *Global Journalist* book with so many recent studies of journalists from countries in Asia, Australia/New Zealand, Europe, Latin America, the Middle East, and North America. We regret the lack of studies from Africa, and we hope that there will be more in the future from this major region. We hope that the studies we have compiled here will prove useful to those studying and practicing journalism around the world.

1   Introduction

David Weaver and Lars Willnat

The first decade of the 21st century has seen a dramatic increase in studies of journalists and journalism, including surveys of journalists in many countries around the world. Many of these studies have been modeled on the four major surveys of U.S. journalists conducted in 1971 (Johnstone, Slawski, & Bowman 1976); 1982–1983 (Weaver & Wilhoit 1986); 1992 (Weaver & Wilhoit 1996); and 2002 (Weaver, Beam, Brownlee, Voakes, & Wilhoit 2007).

The Global Journalist (Weaver 1998) offered the first comprehensive collection of such studies by presenting surveys of more than 20,000 journalists from 21 countries and territories conducted between 1986 and 1996. This overview led to the conclusion that there were more differences than similarities between journalists from these nations, a finding that seemed to reflect social and political differences rather than the influences of media organizations, journalism education, or professional norms.

More than 13 years have passed since the first edition of *The Global Journalist,* and journalism has changed dramatically during this time. Media in most industrialized nations have been struggling with dwindling audiences, shrinking advertising revenues, reduced operating budgets, and fierce competition from new online media that have undermined the business structure of an entire industry. More and more journalists work across media platforms, often as freelancers or reporters without traditional desk jobs. Most importantly, however, the growing importance of social media in journalism has led many to question the very basic concept of who journalists are and what qualifications they should have.

The question is, of course, whether and how these unprecedented structural changes have affected the profession of journalism. Exactly how have these changes influenced the demographic composition of the profession and how have they affected the professional values and attitudes of journalists around the world?

This new book presents the findings from surveys of more than 29,000 journalists working in 31 countries conducted between 1996 and 2011 (see Table 1.1). The book includes a total of 42 survey studies conducted in Australia, Belgium, Brazil, Britain, Canada, Chile, China, Colombia, Denmark, Finland, France, Germany, Hong Kong, Hungary, Indonesia, Israel, Japan, South Korea, Malaysia, Netherlands, New Zealand, Poland, Russia, Singapore, Slovenia, Spain, Sweden, Switzerland, Taiwan, United Arab Emirates, and the United States.[1] It also includes a collection of comparative chapters on Latin American journalists, Arab journalists, political journalists working in Europe, foreign correspondents, and a chapter based on the Worlds of Journalism project directed by Thomas Hanitzsch.

As was true for the earlier book, many of these studies have been widely scattered in various papers, dissertations, articles, and reports in various languages. Here we pull together these studies in one volume and try to provide a more general synthesis of their findings across national borders and differing cultures. Given the number of new studies of journalists conducted in the past decade and the increasing interest around the world in the occupation of journalist, we believe the time is right for an updated book that takes a globally comparative perspective on the demographics, education, socialization, professionalization, and working conditions of journalists. This book is the result of our efforts to do this, with generous cooperation and help from many friends and colleagues.

Organization and Purpose

This volume groups the studies of journalists by region of the world, including East Asia, Australia and New Zealand, Europe, North America, South and Latin America, and the Middle East. Although not everyone will agree with this classification, it does illustrate that the studies come from most of the major regions, with the exception of Africa, Eurasia, and Central/South Asia. We deeply regret not including studies of journalists from these areas. We tried very hard to recruit authors and studies from them, but failed mainly because representative surveys of journalists in these countries had not been done in recent years.

Because the studies included were not planned in advance for inclusion in this book, and because inclusion depended on our knowledge of each study and the willingness of the individual authors to meet our deadlines, some countries where there have been recent surveys of journalists are not represented. We regret this as well, and we hope that future comparative studies of journalists will remedy this.

In addition to presenting the findings of each survey separately, the final concluding chapter attempts to make cross-national comparisons with respect to the basic characteristics, working conditions, and professional values of the more than 29,000 journalists included in these surveys. The aim of these comparisons, which are admittedly post hoc and based on measures that are not always as similar as they could be if preplanned, is to try to identify some similarities and differences that may give us a more accurate picture of where journalists come from, what they think about their work and their occupation, and where the differences and similarities are as we enter the second decade of the 21st century.

The major assumption, as in the earlier book, is that in spite of various societal and organizational constraints, journalists' backgrounds and ideas have some relationship to what is reported (and how it is covered) in the various news media around the world, and that this news coverage matters in terms of world public opinion and policies.

Obviously, this approach is much more inductive than deductive. Although there are various theories of journalistic socialization and professionalization that have been developed (Ettema, Whitney, & Wackman 1987; Loeffelholz & Weaver 2008; Shoemaker & Reese 1996; Wahl-Jorgensen & Hanitzsch 2009), the primary goal of this book is not to elaborate on or test such theories, but rather to discover patterns of similarities and differences that can provide a foundation of empirical data for future theorizing about the influences on journalists and their influences on the news.

Survey Evidence

Table 1.1 illustrates the sample sizes, response rates, dates, and survey methods (where reported) for the 42 surveys that form the basis for the chapters included here. In several countries and territories, more than one survey was discussed (Hong Kong, Indonesia, Switzerland, Israel,

Columbia, the United States, and the overview chapters on Latin American, Arab, political, and foreign journalists, as well as the "Worlds of Journalism" chapter).

The findings reported in this book are based on surveys of 29,272 journalists from 31 countries or territories during the years 1996 to 2011 (actually more if the overview chapters are considered). We tried to rely on representative surveys wherever possible, but made a few exceptions in cases where survey data on journalists was available for the first time (e.g., Malaysia and Indonesia). The response rates of these surveys vary from a reported low of 12% in New Zealand to a reported high of 99% among Chinese journalists. Six of the 42 surveys were done by mail; three by mail and online; one by mail, telephone, and online; eight by telephone; one by telephone and mail; two

Table 1.1   Sample Sizes, Dates, and Methods of Journalist Surveys

	Sample Size	Response Rate	Year of Study	Representative Survey*	Method(s) Used
Asia					
China	1,309	99.0%	2010/11	Yes	Personal Interviews
Hong Kong	553	62.0%	1996	Yes	Self-administered
	722	62.0%	2001	Yes	Self-administered
	1,004	55.0%	2006	Yes	Self-administered
Indonesia	385	80.0%	2001/02	No	Personal Interviews
	100	—	2007/08	No	Personal Interviews
Japan	1,011	18.4%	2007	Yes	Mail
Korea	970	–	2009	Yes	Personal Interviews
Malaysia	182	72.8%	2009/10	No	Self-administered
Singapore	447	39.5%	2009	No	Self-administered
Taiwan	1,182	72.0%	2004	Yes	Personal Interviews
Australia/Pacific					
Australia	117	—	2009/10	No	Phone
New Zealand	514	12%	2007	Yes	Online
Europe					
Belgium	682	30.6%	2007/08	Yes	Mail & Online
Denmark	2,008	44.3%	2009	Yes	Online
Finland	614	41.0%	2007	Yes	Mail & Online
France	405	87.0%	2007	Yes	Phone
Germany	1,536	72.8%	2005	Yes	Phone & Mail
Great Britain	1,238	11.5%	2001	Yes	Mail & Online
Hungary	940	—	2006	Yes	Personal Interviews
Netherlands	642	32.0%	2006	Yes*	Mail
Poland	329	—	2009	Yes	Phone
Russia	796	—	2008	Yes	All methods
Slovenia	406	29.0%	2009	Yes	Online
Spain	1,000	—	2009	Yes	Phone
Sweden	621	52.0%	2009	Yes*	Mail
Switzerland	2,020	37.1%	1998	Yes*	Mail
	449	38.8%	2006/07	Yes	Online
	657	35.6%	2007	Yes	Online
	1,403	19.0%	2008	Yes*	Mail

(continued)

Table 1.1　Continued

	Sample Size	Response Rate	Year of Study	Representative Survey*	Method(s) Used
North America					
Canada	385	21.6%	2007	Yes*	Mail
United States	1,149	79.0%	2002	Yes	Phone
	400	67.0%	2007	Yes	Phone
South America					
Brazil	506	36.5%	2009	Yes	Online
Chile	570	29.0%	2009	Yes	Online
Colombia	300	—	2006	No	Phone & Online
	217		2008	No	Phone & Online
Middle East					
Arab Journalists	601	—	2005/06	No	Self-administered & Online
Israel	209	53.7%	2002	Yes*	Phone & Mail
	200	73.8%	2004	Yes*	Phone
	333	47.4%	2008	Yes	Phone
UAE	160	32.0%	2000	No	Personal Interview & Mail
Total N	29,272				

*based on limited membership lists

by telephone and online; six self-administered; one self-administered and online; six by personal (face-to-face) interviews; seven by online; and one by using all methods.

These patterns of survey interviewing illustrate a dramatically increased tendency to use multiple interviewing methods in the same survey, and also to use online surveys, as compared with the surveys reported in the first book, where only two countries employed multiple methods of interviewing in their surveys (mail and face-to-face in Algeria, and mail and self-administered in France). None of the surveys in the first edition of *The Global Journalist* used online questionnaires. Twelve were conducted by mail, five face-to-face, and six by telephone.

Although most of these surveys were conducted independently in the various societies represented here, the task of comparing the findings was made easier by the fact that many had borrowed questions from our original questionnaire (Weaver & Wilhoit 1986), which was modeled on the first large-scale national study of U.S. journalists done by sociologists at the University of Illinois at Chicago in 1971 (Johnstone et al. 1976). But some of the surveys employed their own questions or modified the original wordings somewhat. And there is always the slippage in meaning involved in translating from one language to another and in the changing meanings of some words over time.

Nevertheless, the thousands of interviews of journalists from these 31 countries and territories constitute an excellent foundation of data for cross-national comparisons, keeping in mind the admonition of Blumler, McLeod, and Rosengren (1992) and Hallin and Mancini (2004) that things compared should be comparable.

Journalists' characteristics that can be reasonably compared in the "Conclusions" chapter of this book include age, gender, size of workforce, marital status, minority representation, education levels, and the proportions studying journalism in college. The working conditions compared include perceptions of amount of autonomy or freedom, job satisfaction (including predictors of this in a few societies), and commitment to journalism (intention to remain working as a journalist).

Professional values or orientations that can be compared include perceptions of the importance of different journalistic roles (such as reporting the news quickly, providing analysis and interpretation, investigating government claims, etc.), proportions belonging to journalistic organizations, opinions about which questionable reporting methods might be justifiable (such as revealing confidential sources, paying for information, etc.), opinions on the importance of different aspects of the job (pay, autonomy, public service, etc.), and journalists' images of their readers, viewers, and listeners.

The patterns of similarities and differences that emerge from these cross-national comparisons are not easily explained by conventional political, economic, and cultural categories, or by existing theories of mass communication, but they are striking and intriguing in their variety. We hope that future comparative studies will undertake the exciting task of trying to explain these patterns as we move through the 21st century.

Note

1. Seventeen of these countries/territories are the same as those in the earlier book, including Australia, Brazil, Britain, Canada, Chile, China, Finland, France, Germany, Hong Kong, Hungary, South Korea, New Zealand, Poland, Spain, Taiwan, and the United States. The four countries from the earlier book not included in this newer one include Algeria, Ecuador, Mexico, and the Pacific Islands.

References

Blumler, Jay G., Jack M. McLeod, and Karl Erik Rosengren. 1992. *Comparatively speaking: Communication and culture across space and time.* Newbury Park, CA: Sage.

Ettema, James S., D. Charles Whitney, and Daniel B. Wackman. 1987. Professional mass communicators. In *Handbook of communication science*, edited by Charles R. Berger and Steven H. Chaffee, pp. 747–780. Newbury Park, CA: Sage.

Hallin, Daniel C., and Paolo Mancini. 2004. *Comparing media systems.* New York: Cambridge University Press.

Johnstone, John W. C., Edward J. Slawski, and William W. Bowman. 1976. *The news people.* Urbana: University of Illinois Press.

Loeffelholz, Martin, and David Weaver. 2008. *Global journalism research: Theories, methods, findings, future.* Oxford, England: Blackwell.

Shoemaker, Pamela J., and Stephen D. Reese. 1996. *Mediating the message: Theories of influences on mass media content.* 2nd ed. White Plains, NY: Longman.

Wahl-Jorgensen, Karin, and Thomas Hanitzsch. 2009. *The handbook of journalism studies.* New York: Routledge.

Weaver, David H. 1998. *The global journalist: News people around the world.* Cresskill, NJ: Hampton Press.

Weaver, David H., Randal A. Beam, Bonnie J. Brownlee, Paul S. Voakes, and G. Cleveland Wilhoit. 2007. *The American journalist in the 21st century: U.S. news people at the dawn of a new millennium.* Mahwah, NJ: Erlbaum.

Weaver, David H., and G. Cleveland Wilhoit. 1986. *The American journalist: A portrait of U.S. news people and their work.* Bloomington: Indiana University Press.

Weaver, David H., and G. Cleveland Wilhoit. 1996. *The American journalist in the 1990s: U.S. news people at the end of an era.* Mahwah, NJ: Erlbaum.

Journalists in Asia

2 Chinese Media and Journalists in Transition

Hongzhong Zhang and Linsen Su

The Chinese media system is fundamentally different from the Western media system by definition because private ownership is prohibited by law. All news media in China are owned and operated by two parallel entities: the Communist Party of China (CPC) and the Chinese government. Further, each news media organization is stratified into four distinct levels that correspond to four levels of government: central administrative, provincial, prefectural-level city, and county governance.

However, the increasing popularity of market-oriented journalism has added commercial considerations to the traditional concern for political messaging among Chinese news media. Likewise, as Chinese journalism becomes less directly government controlled, the need to balance political, economic, and journalistic values is altering notions of journalistic self-identity in the country. This chapter uses data from a nationwide survey of Chinese journalists to describe their basic work conditions, professional self-assessments, occupational options, and daily work routines in the midst of these changes.

Chinese Media and Journalist Identity

This section provides an overview of Chinese news media, including newspapers, broadcasters, magazines, and Web sites, and concludes with a description of the two alternative professional identities available to China's journalists.

A total of 1,937 different types of newspapers were published in China in 2009. They included 225 national newspapers, 825 provincial newspapers, 871 prefectural-city newspapers, and 16 county newspapers (General Administration of Press and Publication 2010). Within the Chinese academic and media communities, newspapers are divided into four categories: party newspapers, metropolitan newspapers, specialized newspapers, and industrial newspapers.

Party newspapers are the official state vehicles, and are called the "mouthpieces" of the CPC. They serve as the chief propaganda tools for the government, mainly publishing for the institutions of the CPC and government with a low private subscription rate. *People's Daily*, founded in 1948, is a notable mainstream national party newspaper. Among all media in China, *People's Daily* enjoyed the highest administrative ranking in 2009 with a print circulation of 2.35 million (Su Nan 2009). It also has overseas and online editions.

Metropolitan dailies are an innovative new style of newspaper in China that are more market oriented, and target the public based on distribution through private subscriptions. This type of newspaper was introduced by *Western China Metropolitan Daily*, founded in 1995 in Chengdu, the capital of Sichuan Province. It is a comprehensive newspaper that includes public affairs content and even ventures into some critical reporting regarding the government within official and self-censorship limits. Soon after their introduction, metropolitan dailies became the most influential type of newspaper in China with the fastest-growing circulation and advertising revenues. Their success has changed the traditional manner of reporting style in China, and also has exerted tremendous influence on other types of newspapers.

Specialized newspapers target discrete interest groups, such as sports, finance, entertainment, and politics. Here, concern for audience preference and engagement in market competition are critical to survival and development. These newspapers are reliant upon individual subscriptions.

Industrial newspapers are usually published by a specific department or an industry association for circulation among those audiences, and are not market-oriented. They provide information only for specific industries, such as the *China Electric Power News*, the *China Gold Newspaper*, and the *China Metallurgical News*. Currently, industrial newspapers are undertaking an institutional reformation realigning how those publications relate to the government and the commercial structural base.

Electronic broadcasting encompassed 251 radio stations, 272 television stations, and 44 educational television stations in Mainland China in 2009. The comprehensive population coverage rates were 96.3% for radio and 97.2% for TV (Chinese Radio & TV Almanac Publishing Office 2010). According to the statistics from *26th Statistical Report on Internet Development in China* (2010), there were 1,310 TV programs and 139 pay-TV programs in Mainland China. National television stations include China Central Television (CCTV) and China Education Television. Each city of prefecture-level or above owns its own television station. Meanwhile, there were 2,087 county radio and television stations, broadcasting programs either produced by other stations or borrowed from other sources in the form of complete video programming.

Among all the broadcasting agencies, CCTV in Beijing enjoys the highest administrative ranking and is the largest medium of advertising in Mainland China. CCTV has 16 open-circuit TV programs, an experimental high-definition channel, 12 digital pay-TV channels, and 28 online channels, including an English-language news channel. In the southern part of China, Hunan Satellite TV is the most popular entertainment channel, mainly broadcasting entertainment programs. It is listed as the most influential satellite television station for young people.

There are two kinds of magazines in China. Again, the first type primarily serves as the government "mouthpiece." An example of this type is *Qiushi*, which is financially supported by the government. The other genre is market-oriented, such as *Finance, News Week, South Window,* and *New Weekly*. These publications offer a mixture of soft news with some reporting on sensitive topics.

The Internet is publicly accessible everywhere in Mainland China. According to the *26th Statistical Report on Internet Development in China*, which is published annually by the China Internet Network Information Center (CNNIC), in mid-2010, there were 420 million citizens in China connected to the Internet with a penetration rate of 31.8%, including 360 million broadband users and 277 million mobile smart phone users.

There are three categories of news Web sites in China. Commercial news Web sites, operated by commercial companies or individuals, have the greatest influence and are the most popular (Zhang 2009). Journalists working for commercial Web sites are not granted press cards, however, which means they cannot conduct interviews or release news. They can only reproduce news from other sources such as newspapers, television, and official news agencies. Sina, Sohu, Netease, and Tencent are the top four commercial Web sites, and all of them have become incorporated in the United States. The second category of Web sites is run by various levels of governmental departments. Some of these Web sites have the right to interview, so they can release news on the Internet directly. The final category displays an electronic version of original news from traditional media such as newspapers and broadcasters.

Table 2.1 Distribution of Journalists' Identities

	Government Agencies and Institutions	Contract System
Newspapers	Journalists of party and industry newspapers, administrators of some metropolitan newspapers & specialized newspapers	Most journalists of metropolitan newspapers and specialized newspapers
Television	Administrators, some editors and journalists	Some TV editors and journalists
Magazines	Journalists of government-funded news magazines	Journalists of market-oriented news magazines
Online	Administrators, some of the editors and journalists of government news websites	Journalists of commercial news websites

The changing identity of journalists is one of the most important indicators in the transition of China's media. Journalists are mainly divided into two groups: those under government agencies and institutions, and those who are contractual. The former enjoy the same treatment as government officials with benefits including a form of lifelong tenure and governmental stipends. By contrast, journalists under the contract system are employed on a limited basis, so they receive none of the benefits that are afforded the official journalists. Instead, their careers are marked by mobility and frequent job changes. However, they are regarded as the most active group of journalists in China, and are strongly recommended by the Chinese government. Table 2.1 displays how journalists at various media fit into these two categories.

The growing popularity of commercial content has diluted the Chinese media's political function, which had been their traditional primary aim. Market diversification also has brought about differences regarding conceptions of journalists' identities and their roles in the media. The next section describes how these professional notions are in flux among Chinese journalists.

China's Media in Transition

Chinese media are transforming themselves from being the sole government propaganda machine to being a market-based instrument under the dual influences of politics and economics. Meanwhile, the development of new technology also has affected the traditional political party-oriented mechanism, forcing the government to adopt reforms. Under pressure from political, economic, and technological advances, China's media are in a state of change. On the one hand, the development of media markets and new media demand more reformation of the traditional government and party management of media in order to face the challenges of globalization. On the other hand, the government still wants to keep tight control over the media and keep its propaganda function during this transitional period.

Historically, the political function of the Chinese media as a communist government "mouthpiece" was patterned after the model of the former Soviet Union. The news media were considered an instrument for social and political control based on the Soviet authoritarian model (Siebert 1956), and had served this function in China since the PRC was established in 1949 (Xi Chen 2006). Although commercial advertisements were introduced in the Chinese media as far back as the 1980s, the political function remained the primary purpose.

The Chinese government was substantially involved in media management even during the reform era, which means that all of the media continued to be subject to the dual supervision of government and party committees of various levels (Xi Chen 2006). These controls included government restrictions on media access and ownership (Hu 2008); exclusive rights to punishment and internal discipline; personnel choices and decisions; financial power; and other developments within the media industry. As a result, all major adjustments and reforms regarding the news media, such as media conglomeration and industrialization, have remained under the domain of government and party administrative power (Zhang 2004).

The mass media's economic role became increasingly important after Deng Xiaoping assumed leadership in the late 1970s. Paid advertisements and increased coverage of entertainment and social news were introduced, and sometimes stories about crime and corruption of government officials were even presented (Xi Chen 2006). Li Changchun, the current official in charge of news and ideology in China, remarked: "The media are 'mouthpieces' of the Party and the public institution with business management. The government should push the media to be totally market-oriented to establish an industrialization system so as to compete in the global markets" (Li 2003: 3).

In the midst of this commercialization, the most obvious change in China's media has been that media stocks have been made available for private and foreign investment, eliminating a previous requirement that all media assets had to be government owned. As part of the stepwise efforts of government to revive the industry, different forms of capital were allowed to enter the media as long as the state-owned capital remained dominant (no less than 51%) (Xi 2006). As a result, the introduction of private capital has become an important method of media expansion and reform since 2001 (Zhang 2004).

However, the opening of the media markets has created new problems. For instance, a private company like the Huashang Group, which purchased management rights in four major newspapers and more than 10 magazines, also purchased influence over hiring personnel, financial decisions, and other aspects of the media. Therefore, the relationship between entrepreneur and government has developed into a strategic game. Some scholars have labeled this dynamic "the combination of the Party and the market" (Zhao 1998) or a "tug-of-war between the authority and the market" (He 1996). Also, the process of market-oriented reform is enabling the media and private ownership to bargain with the government, which still controls the core media content (Yang & Lee 2010).

Since 1995, Internet and mobile media developments and increasing economic power have changed Chinese media in four profound ways. First, together with TV and newspapers, the Internet has become one of the three main information providers in China. It is especially welcomed by young men and highly educated people (Zhang 2010). Second, the commercial news Web sites have greatly altered the Chinese media ecology because the most popular news Web sites do not belong to the government. Third, the use of new communication sources such as blogs, microblogs, and other social media has greatly expanded news options. Hence, distribution of news on sensitive topics beyond the control of government has become possible. Fourth, foreign Web sites with audience and credibility in China, such as Yahoo!, *New York Times*, and *The Wall Street Journal* are challenging the traditional Chinese media's patterns of coverage (Zhang 2010).

Previous Studies of Chinese Journalists

As a result of the pressures of changing political, economic, and technological forces, the values of Chinese journalists are becoming increasingly diverse in spite of the fact that they continue to operate under the structure of government control.

One survey in Shanghai showed that journalists consider their responsibility to society paramount in following a moral tradition. In that survey, the majority of journalists placed professional responsibilities in front of their career choices, fame, and wage concerns (Lu & Yu 2003a, 2003b). However, another survey in Chengdu showed that journalists working for more market-oriented metropolitan newspapers emphasized individual development rather than social responsibilities

(Zhang 2002). And a third survey in Beijing produced similar findings, showing an orientation more toward individual goals (Zhang 2006). Furthermore, research shows that China's journalists are gradually accepting new and sometimes conflicting ideas of professionalism even though this is far from being a dominant domestic ideology (Pan & Chen 2005).

Several surveys in the past decade attempted to better assess the social status of Chinese journalists. One study found that journalists considered their social status and degree of specialization to be lower than the generally recognized "professional" occupations like lawyers, doctors, accountants, and professors (Pan & Chen 2005). Another survey in Shanghai showed that the journalists' personal estimations of their social status indicated they viewed themselves as being lower in rank than professors, doctors, lawyers, and engineers, but higher than middle level government officials, middle school teachers, police officers, and nurses (Lu & Yu 2003). Yet another online survey showed a similar result: journalists regarded peasants, teachers, and researchers as most respectable, with journalists ranked fourth, while workers, police, business people, nurses, and officials came after them in social status (Luan 2006).

A survey of journalists' work habits in Shanghai found that almost 82.3% journalists felt that they were suffering from the pressures of competition. Most of these pressures were coming from a media competitor; others were arising from internal competition (Lu & Yu 2003). Another study found that journalists from market-oriented newspapers and highly developed cities like Guangzhou, Shenzhen, and Beijing suffered from heavier pressures from competition than those from less developed regions. They also worked longer hours on average than those at the party newspapers (Luan 2006).

In the area of professional ethics, journalists are facing a complex predicament stemming from the conflicting concerns of transparency in news reporting, privacy in reporting, and the confidentiality of institutions (Lu & Yu 2003). Journalists in Mainland China have been found to hold high ideals, but implementing them has been found to be a difficult reality (Luo, Chen, & Pan 2001). A survey in Shanghai showed that journalists had the common view that they should respect and protect individual privacy; however, findings about attitudes toward making secret inquiries were more ambiguous (Lu & Yu 2003).

The subject of ethical attitudes and behaviors among Chinese journalists also presents a paradox: although the majority of journalists identify practices such as accepting gifts from sources or holding other jobs with conflicting interests as ethically problematic, the reality is that those occur frequently in daily life among Chinese media (Lu & Yu 2003; Yu 1998). Another survey showed that, compared to Hong Kong and Taiwan, a larger proportion of journalists from Mainland China accepted presents from informants and thought they could solicit advertising for their own media (Luo, Chen, & Pan 2001).

On the whole, the conceptions and behaviors of China's journalists are undergoing tremendous changes due to the concurrent pressures of political propaganda requirements, economic contradictions, and developing notions of professionalism.

Method

The function of China's news media has been changing from solely propaganda to a dual obligation to politics and economics, leading to changes in the identity of Chinese journalists. We attempted to better understand the impact of these changes through a nationwide survey of journalists. However, there is no existing list of Chinese journalists and the sheer geographic and population size of the nation makes truly random sampling quite difficult.

Instead, we sampled from the most influential, mainstream media located in the population centers of Beijing, Guangzhou, Chengdu, and Shanghai for three reasons. First, major cities in China are closely tied to higher political administrative levels, and so media organizations in major cities have more political and social influence. Second, the economic and technological transformation of the media began in those cities, which directly influenced the future development of media in other parts of China. Third, the advertising markets in those cities are the most sophisticated and lucrative, and therefore should produce valuable data about the impact of markets on media.

Therefore, the population of the survey is journalists working for mainstream, socially influential media organizations in Beijing, Guangzhou, Chengdu, Chongqing, and Shanghai. These five cities represent four different regions, each of them being the central city of the particular region, setting the trends for culture, economics, and regional development. Beijing, in the north, is the capital of China, and the national center of culture and politics. Shanghai, in the east, is the biggest city and the economic center. Guangzhou is the major South China city for culture, economics, and politics. Chengdu is the cultural center of West China, which gave birth to China's first metropolitan newspaper. Chongqing is the economic center and the biggest city of West China, and it is also the fourth municipality directly under the Central Government.

Next, we sampled the newspapers, TV and radio stations, news Web sites, and magazines in these five cities. For the newspapers, we sampled party and metropolitan newspapers in all five cities. Specialized newspapers in Guangzhou were chosen because they are the most dynamic newspapers in this area. Industrial newspapers were chosen from Beijing as most of them are located there. For TV stations, we selected CCTV and Beijing TV Station since they are the most influential stations in China, along with Nanfang TV Station in Guangzhou. China's most influential magazines are in Beijing, Guangzhou, and Shanghai, so they were selected for the samples. For news Web sites, we selected Sina, the largest commercial news Web site in Beijing, and the government-run Hualong in Chongqing. And for radio stations, we sampled from Beijing, where all of the nationwide broadcasts originate.

After choosing those media, we performed cluster sampling of all journalists working for those selected media and sent out 1,405 questionnaires. Using Weaver and Wilhoit's (1996) definition of journalists as persons who produce news, information, and opinion rather than those who produce fiction, drama, art, or other content, we excluded the questionnaires of logistic members, technicians and interns, and other inapplicable employees.

Therefore, the final valid sample was 1,309 completed surveys conducted from September to November 2010. The sample of news agencies was: newspapers 729, magazines 105, TV 269, radio 126, and news Web sites 80. The percentage of respondents who were working for government agencies and institutions was 41.2%, and those who were working under the contract system was 58.8%.

Findings

Demographics

Table 2.2 shows that the number of female media journalists (52.9%) exceeded males (47.1%). The greatest percentage of women worked at radio stations (63.6%), magazines (62.7%), and TV stations (59.5%). Men were in the majority only in newspapers (52.8%).

The increasing percentage of female journalists in China is a notable and consistent trend. This is the first survey that indicates that female journalists are the majority overall in China. By comparison, a national survey of journalists (Yu, Guoming, 1998) by the Public Opinion Institute of

Table 2.2   Gender Distribution of Journalists (in %)

	All	Newspapers	Magazines	TV	Radio	Online
Female	52.9	47.2	62.7	59.5	63.6	53.2
Male	47.1	52.8	37.3	40.5	36.4	46.8
Total	100.0	100.0	100.0	100.0	100.0	100.0
N	1,276	710	121	264	79	102

Note. $\chi^2 = 23.45$, sig $= 0.00$

Renmin University of China in 1997 found that men comprised 67.1% of the journalism workforce. And a 2002 survey found that males accounted for 56.7% of journalists in Shanghai (Lu & Yu 2003).

The reason for this increase in female journalists may be due to more women being enrolled in journalism schools in China's universities. For example, at the School of Journalism in Fudan University, the percentage of female graduates was 50% in 1997, but increased to 73.6% in 2002. This trend may be expected to continue for some time. At Fudan University, women made up nearly 90% of the freshmen students, and most of them indicate they would choose media as their future work (Lu & Yu, 2003). Likewise, the proportion of female students at almost every other university journalism school is nearly 90%.

The average age of journalists in China is 33.1, and they are getting younger as a group. The 1997 national survey by the Public Opinion Institution of Renmin University of China found that the average age was 37.4 (Luo, Chen, & Pan 2001). The average age in the 2002 Shanghai survey was 34.7 (Lu & Yu 2003).

The only notable difference by media type was that the average age of journalists at news Web sites is 27.6, which was significantly younger than the average age of journalists working for the traditional media. Among news Web site journalists, 81.6% are under 30, and only 3.9% are 40 or older.

Education levels are generally high among Chinese journalists (see Table 2.4). The percentage of journalists with a postgraduate degree was 93.4%. The percentage with a bachelor's degree was 72.3%, compared to 59.5% in the 1997 national survey (Luo, Chen, & Pan 2001) and 81.4% in the 2002 Shanghai survey.

Work Experience

Most Chinese journalists have been working in the field for a decade or less with the largest percentage having five years or less experience (38.6%). Only 15.9% have worked professionally for 16

Table 2.3   Average Age of Journalists (in %)

	All	Newspapers	Magazines	TV	Radio	Online
Below 30 years	48.1	47.0	41.4	40.8	54.6	81.6
30 to 39 years	31.5	33.4	39.4	32.8	21.8	14.5
40 to 49 years	15.3	13.2	15.2	22.9	17.6	3.9
50 years or above	5.1	6.4	4.0	3.4	5.9	—
Total	100.0	100.0	100.0	10.00	100.0	100.0
Average age	33.1	33.2	32.9	34.3	33.5	27.6
N	1,245	689	99	262	119	76

Note.   A Scheffe analysis indicates that there is a significant difference (p < .05) between the average age of journalists from new media and traditional media.

Table 2.4   Educational Background of Journalists (in %)

	All	Newspaper	Magazines	TV	Radio	Online
College or less	6.6	7.7	6.8	4.2	4.1	7.6
University	72.3	73.9	68.0	76.0	55.4	77.2
Postgraduate	21.1	18.3	25.2	19.8	40.5	15.2
Total	100.0	100.0	100.0	100.0	100.0	100.0
N	1,276	710	103	263	121	79

Note. $\chi^2 = 37.678$, sig $= 0.00$

Table 2.5   Work Experience of Journalists (in %)

	All	Newspaper	Magazine	TV	Radio	Online
5 years and less	38.6	35.7	43.3	34.3	36.5	76.3
6 to 10 years	28.3	33.5	28.8	19.4	24.6	16.3
11 to 15 years	17.3	15.7	15.4	26.9	13.5	7.5
16 to 20 years	8.1	6.5	6.7	12.3	14.3	—
20 years and more	7.8	8.7	5.8	7.1	11.1	—
Total	100.0	100.0	100.0	100.0	100.0	100.0
N	1,304	726	104	268	126	80

Note. $\chi^2 = 103.568$, sig $= 0.00$

or more years. The lack of experience is particularly apparent among journalists at news Web sites, where 76.3% have five years or less experience, and none had more than 15 years.

Journalists at government agencies and institutions are overall far more experienced than their colleagues who work under the contract system. A majority of journalists who have been in the field five years or less work in the contract system (74.3%) as compared to the government (25.7%). Among journalists who have 20 years or more experience, many more work for the government (84.3%) as compared to the contract system (15.7%).

Journalists working under the contract system enjoy a higher rate of job mobility than those with government agencies and institutions. A majority of contract journalists (55.9%) have worked for two or more media organizations compared to only about a third of journalists employed by government agencies or institutions (33.7%).

Most Chinese journalists were indifferent on the question of whether they would choose their jobs again given a second chance. Most respondents had no clear answer to the question (45.3%) compared to 38.8% who said yes, and 15.8% who said no.

Table 2.6   Work Experience of Journalists with Different Identities (in %)

	Government Agencies & Institution	Contract system	Total %	N
5 years and less	25.7	74.3	100.0	487
6 to 10 years	31.9	68.1	100.0	364
11 to 15 years	56.6	43.4	100.0	221
16 to 20 years	68.3	31.7	100.0	104
20 years and more	84.3	15.7	100.0	102

Note. $\chi^2 = 193.18$, sig $= 0.00$

Table 2.7   Media Organization Experience of Journalists (in %)

	All	*Government Agencies and Institutions*	*Contract System*
One media organization	53.1	66.3	44.1
Two media organizations	27.4	22.4	30.6
Three media organizations	13.0	7.4	16.8
> Three media organizations	6.4	3.8	8.5
Total	100.0	100.0	100.0
N	1,283	528	755

Note: $\chi^2 = 67.90$, sig = 0.000

Stress Factors of Chinese Journalists

On the question of the main problem facing them in their work, most Chinese journalists identified the discrepancy between professional ideals and reality (52.9%). They also said there were problems with the lack of a theoretical foundation for journalism (17.5%); the lack of information sources (16.6%); fewer chances in taking leadership in their departments (16.2%); and lack of enthusiasm for the job (11.6%).

We also investigated the stress factors affecting Chinese journalists by measuring political, market, inner relationship, and individual development factors using measures developed in a 2001 survey of Chengdu journalists (Zhang 2002). Respondents were asked to rate each factor on a scale from 1 to 5, with 5 representing a more stressful element of their jobs.

Table 2.8 shows the means of these 14 factors. "Labor wage level" is the top stress factor (3.57), followed by "development prospect of media" (3.46). These results are similar to the findings of the 2001 study in Chengdu (Zhang 2002).

Table 2.8   Stress Factors of Journalists

	All	*Newspaper*	*Magazines*	*TV*	*Radio*	*Online*	*F*	*Sig.*
Criticism from authority dept.	3.13	3.07	2.98	3.36	3.08	3.23	4.662	0.001
Labor wage level	3.57	3.58	3.40	3.67	3.29	3.83	5.468	0.000
Development of media	3.46	3.50	3.61	3.35	3.31	3.49	2.044	0.086
Working load assessment	3.32	3.34	3.05	3.32	3.27	3.50	2.904	0.021
Business state of media	3.29	3.36	3.39	3.12	3.05	3.43	5.201	0.000
Stress from marketing dept.	2.84	2.82	2.92	2.88	2.66	2.94	1.432	0.221
Job security	2.94	2.79	3.00	3.26	2.97	3.07	8.052	0.000
Attributes of the media	2.89	2.93	2.89	2.80	2.76	3.06	1.675	0.153
Leadership style	3.43	3.49	3.17	3.48	3.33	3.27	2.997	0.018
Internal competition	3.15	3.11	3.04	3.27	3.19	3.10	2.059	0.084
Interpersonal relationship	2.83	2.79	2.60	3.06	2.86	2.61	6.240	0.000
Sense of belonging	3.41	3.43	3.39	3.41	3.33	3.39	0.217	0.929
Professional development	3.38	3.36	3.25	3.41	3.41	3.53	1.049	0.380
Individual ability	3.12	3.09	3.20	3.06	3.22	3.33	1.557	0.184
N	1,309	729	105	269	126	80		

Note.   Scores based on a five-point scale where 1 represents "no stress" and 5 represents "very stressful."

Variance analysis produced five more interesting findings regarding the stresses faced by Chinese journalists across media types. TV journalists considered "criticism from authority department" as a significantly more stressful influence than was the case with journalists working at newspapers and magazines. Journalists at news Web sites and TV stations considered "labor wage level" significantly more stressful than those working at radio stations. Newspaper journalists considered "business state of media" significantly more stressful than those from TV stations. And TV station journalists considered "interpersonal relationship" significantly more stressful than journalists at the other media outlets.

From an identification perspective, journalists under the contract system showed significantly higher levels of stress than government journalists on five items: labor wage level, job security, sense of belonging, individual professional development, and individual ability. These findings show that journalists under the contract system have a greater sense of personal stress in their daily lives than those working for government agencies and institutions.

Role Perceptions of Chinese Journalists

Some scholars think that issues of political propaganda, commercialization of the media, and journalistic professionalism collectively have established a discourse system in which each of those factors conflict, affect, and reconcile with the others as journalists practice under this media transition (Lu & Pan 2002). In our survey, we chose nine roles for journalists to estimate the role played by political, commercialization, or news professionalism. These nine roles come from the most popular depictions of China's media circles in the last decades. They are measured on a five-point scale, in which 5 refers to "extremely agree" and 1 refers to "extremely disagree."

Shown in Table 2.9, Chinese journalists viewed their occupation as a collection of diverse roles. All eight items produced a mean above the 3.0 mid-point, which means that journalists see roles for themselves in most indicators, more or less. The top mean scores came from the political and market dimensions. "Wage earner" (4.25) was followed by "mouthpiece of government and party"

Table 2.9   Role Perceptions of Journalists

	All	Newspaper	Magazines	TV	Radio	Online	F	Sig.
Political Dimension								
Mouthpiece of party	4.06	4.01	3.88	4.23	4.30	3.85	5.994	0.000
Interest group spokesman	2.98	3.03	2.92	2.94	2.74	3.11	2.119	0.076
Commercial Dimension								
Wage earner	4.25	4.25	4.09	4.34	4.16	4.24	2.039	0.087
Family provider	4.06	4.07	3.87	4.16	3.92	4.11	2.597	0.035
Employer of news media	3.71	3.72	3.61	3.77	3.61	3.75	0.805	0.522
Vulnerable group of society	3.58	3.61	3.37	3.65	3.33	3.65	3.272	0.011
Professionalism Dimension								
Information disseminator	3.90	3.92	3.79	3.83	3.98	3.88	1.549	0.186
Messengers of Civilization	3.47	3.46	3.38	3.42	3.71	3.39	2.622	0.033
Humanitarian	3.28	3.28	3.12	3.32	3.56	3.04	4.744	0.001
N	1,309	729	105	269	126	80		

Note.   Scores based on a five-point scale where 1 refers to "extremely disagree" and 5 refers to "extremely agree."

(4.06) and "family provider" (4.06). Based on a paired t-test, there is a significant difference between the means of the top three indicators and the other six indicators.

From the variance analysis, we found that TV journalists regard themselves more as "mouthpieces of party and government" than their colleagues from newspapers, news Web sites, and magazines. So far as media identification was concerned, journalists under the contract system saw themselves as "employee of news media," "vulnerable group of society," "information disseminator," and "family provider" at rates significantly greater than government employees. In contrast, government journalists see themselves as "humanitarian" and "messengers of civilization" at rates significantly greater than contract journalists.

Conclusions

The effects on journalists of the transformation of Chinese media can be described by highlighting four aspects: fundamental changes in demographics; shifting conceptions of the definition of a journalism career; the tension between professional norms and ideals; and competing occupational dimensions based on swirling factors of politics, markets, and technology.

First, Chinese journalists are younger, better educated, and more likely to be female than ever before. The average age of journalists decreased from 37.4 in 1997 to 33.1 in 2010. The percentage of journalists with a bachelor's or postgraduate degree increased from 59.5% in 1997 to 93.4% in 2010. And female journalists have surpassed males as the majority for the first time.

These trends are the result of the increasingly commercialized Chinese media. The introduction of foreign and private media ownership has altered a traditional party-oriented media system. In the party-oriented system, a solid political background and being a communist were most important, and competence and education were secondary factors. However, in market-oriented media, the political standard has been minimized to include only the basic political principles, while personal aptitude and market awareness have become more critical. Thus, young people with more education and ability have more opportunities to become journalists. Also, the Chinese media industry is expanding rapidly in this market environment, and many educated young people are needed to fill the workforce.

Second, Chinese journalists increasingly consider a media career as a brief and shifting job. Our data show that about 40% of journalists have less than five years' experience, and two-thirds have worked as journalists for less than a decade. One main reason for this shift may be found in the changing notions of the profile of a journalist. In China, when media previously functioned as "mouthpieces" only, journalists were the employees of public institutions, and were treated as government staff with limited mobility. However, in the market-oriented media environment, contract journalists are employees like those hired by regular companies. In this kind of system, high mobility becomes possible, and commercial media organizations can recruit recent graduates they need. The data we gathered support this explanation. The mobility of journalists under the contract system is significantly higher than those from government agencies and institutions. More than half of the journalists under the contract system have worked for two or more media organizations while only a third of journalists from public institutions have worked for two or more media institutions. With the system of contractual employment becoming dominant, the mobility of Chinese journalists should continue to increase.

Third, Chinese journalists are increasingly confronted with the tension between their professional ideals and the difficulty of realizing those ideals under the reality of the dual political/market system. More than half of Chinese journalists think that the biggest problem in their work comes from this gap between ideals and realities, and most think it is clearly the largest problem facing the profession.

We found that journalists hired in market-oriented media obviously have more of a sense of personal crisis than those in government agencies and institutions because of low pay, job instability, and lack of the feeling of belonging. As the influence of the market on Chinese media increases, we predict that this sense of crisis will continue to exist and turn into a typical characteristic of Chinese media during the period of transformation.

Finally, the competing forces of politics and commercialism are factors that are leading to important research questions about how the identity of Chinese journalists is changing and developing. Since 2000, scholars studying this transformation have pointed out the conflicts of political propaganda, business media system, and journalistic professionalism and the influence of those factors on journalists (Lu & Pan 2001; Zhang 2006). In fact, these three factors are not in good balance. Politics and markets are playing the dominant roles while journalistic professionalism receives less attention when journalists assess their own roles. The primary role of a journalist is the role of an employee, a breadwinner in a market dimension, and the mouthpiece of the Party and government in a political dimension. The emphasis on this role reflects the dual market and political functions of the media.

Is it possible that political control will allow for more balanced considerations of journalism ideals and market consideration in China? This question deserves in-depth exploration and is of paramount importance as we continue to study the transformation of Chinese media.

References

China Internet Network Information Center (CNNIC). 2010. 26th Statistical Report on Internet Development in China. Retrieced July 14, 2010 from http://wenku.baidu.com/view/366415ec102de2bd96058854.html

Chinese Radio & TV Almanac, Editorial Board. 2010. *Chinese radio & TV almanac 2010*. Beijing: Chinese Radio & TV Almanac Publishing Office.

General Administration of Press and Publication: National Press Publishing. 2009. Basic information. Retrieved from http://www.gapp.gov.cn/cms/html/21/493/201009/702538.html

He, Zhou. 1996. From "mouth and ears" to "public opinion companies running by the party": The change of China's party newspapers. In *New views on Chinese media*, edited by Zhou He and Huailin Chen, pp. 66–107. Hong Kong: Pacific Century Press.

Hu, Jianhong. 2008. Changes and constancy of media in China within 30 years. *Media* (China) 11:26–29.

Institute of Public Opinion of Renmin University of China. 1998. Occupational ideology and ethics of journalists in China. *Journalist Monthly* 3: 10–17.

Li, Liangrong. 2003. On the double-track system of media in China. *Contemporary Communication* (China) 4: 1–4.

Lu, Ye, and Zhongdang Pan. 2002. The imagination of fame: Media professionalism in China's social transformation. *Mass Communication Research* 71:17–60.

Lu, Ye, and Weiding Yu. 2003a. Occupational state of journalists in social transition: Report 1 on the journalist survey in Shanghai in 2002. *The Journalist Monthly* 1:42–44.

Lu, Ye, and Weidong Yu. 2003b. Occupational ideals of journalists: Report 2 on the journalist survey in Shanghai in 2002. *The Journalist Monthly* 2:8–11.

Lu, Ye, and Weidong Yu. 2003c. Factors affecting the news production in social transition: Report 3 on the journalist survey in Shanghai in 2002. *The Journalist Monthly* 3:64–67.

Lu, Ye, and Weidong Yu. 2003d. Conception of journalists on media and ethics: Report 4 on the journalist survey in Shanghai in 2002. *The Journalist Monthly* 4:46–49.

Luan, Xiaolei. 2006. The report of journalist survey. *Youth Journalists* (China) 21:8–11.

Luo, Wenhui, Taowen Chen, and Zongdang Pan. 2001. Survey on the attitude and perceptions of journalists in Mainland China, Hong Kong, and Taiwan. *Mass Communication Research* (Taipei) 68:53–89.

Pan, Zhongdong, and Taowen Chen. 2004. The model change of news reform in Mainland China: A review of media models. *Mass Communication Research* 78:1–43.

Pan, Zhongdong, and Taowen Chan. 2005. Professional evaluation and job satisfaction of journalists in the process of China's reform: Survey of journalists in two cities. *China Media Report* 1:41–55.

Siebert, Fred S. 1956. *Four theories of the press*. Urbana: University of Illinois Press.

Su Nan. 2009. Circulation at the People's Daily in 2009 is more than 2,350,000. Retrieved January 6, 2009, from http://su.people.com.cn/GB/channel234/391/200901/06/22919.html

Weaver, David H., and G. Cleveland Wilhoit. 1996. *The American journalist in the 1990s: U.S. news people at the end of an era*. Mahwah, NJ: Erlbaum.

Wu, Fei, and Lin Bai. 2006. Analysis of the degree of journalists' satisfaction in their occupation. *Journal of Renmin University of China* 1:137–143.

Xi, Chen. 2006. Dynamics of news media regulations in China: Explanations and implications [Special Issue]. *The Journal of Comparative Asian Development* 5(1): 49 – 64.

Yang, Yinjuan, and Chin-Chuan Lee. 2010. Media's bargaining with the state: The case study of Guangzhou press in Mainland China. *Communication & Society (Hong Kong)* 14:47–74.

Yu, Guoming. 1998. The professional consciousness and ethics of journalists in China. *Democracy and Science* 3:10–17.

Zhang, Hongzhong. 2002. Talent demand in the competition of newspaper industry. *Chinese Journalist* (China) 181:51–53.

Zhang, Hongzhong. 2004. Selection of expansion model in China media industry. *Press Circles* (China) 1:36–38.

Zhang, Hongzhong. 2006. A research about journalist's value-orientations in the period of social transformation in China. *International Communication* (China) 144:5–9.

Zhang, Hongzhong. 2010. *Investigation on Chinese media credibility*. Nanjing, China: Nanjing Press.

Zhao, Yuezhi. 1998. *Media, market and democracy in China: Between the party line and the bottom line*. Urbana: University of Illinois Press.

3 Journalists in Hong Kong

A Decade after the Transfer of Sovereignty

Joseph M. Chan, Francis L. F. Lee, and Clement Y. K. So

Hong Kong is a media-saturated city. According to government records, there were more than 700 registered periodicals in Hong Kong in 2008, 45 of which were daily newspapers (Hong Kong SAR 2009: 333). Putting aside those that focus exclusively on special interests, about 17 newspapers can be regarded as constituting the mainstream daily press and serving the basic informational needs of a population of 7 million. In addition, several regional or international newspapers, such as the *International Herald Tribune*, the *Financial Times*, and *USA Today International*, are also printed and distributed in Hong Kong, giving newsstands in the financial districts a distinctive "international" look.

Hong Kong currently has three radio stations and two free-to-air television stations. Each of the two free television stations offers a Cantonese channel and an English channel. In addition, there are three multi-channel pay-TV service providers. Besides offering their own 24-hour news channels, pay-TV also gives the audience access to a range of international news and public affairs channels such as the BBC, CNN, NHK, CCTV, Eastern TV News (Taiwan), and Al Jazeera.

A vibrant media market, however, does not guarantee healthy journalism. The news media in Hong Kong continue to face a mix of challenges. Some of these challenges, such as political pressure from China, are unique to Hong Kong. Others are similar to what news media around the world have to face, such as the trend toward tabloidization, the challenge to keep audience attention amidst the proliferation of media and entertainment choices, and the problem of developing a feasible business model with which to exploit the Internet. Apparently, Hong Kong's news organizations have not navigated the troubled waters very successfully. In fact, research shows that the credibility of the news media has declined in the eyes of the public. In our own survey of Hong Kong journalists conducted in 2006, only three among 24 news organizations included in the questionnaire received a credibility rating of 7 or higher on a 1 to 10 scale.

Against the above background, this chapter provides an analysis of journalists in Hong Kong. It draws on three surveys of journalists conducted in 1996, 2001, and 2006. By examining to what extent and in which ways the profession has changed, we hope to gain insights into how the journalistic profession has responded to and was shaped by the changing social, political, and economic environment.

Challenges Facing Journalists and Media in Hong Kong

The relationship between the press and the political transition to Chinese rule has been one of the most important themes in the development of journalism in Hong Kong in the past decades. The Sino-British Joint Declaration signed in 1984 confirmed the return of the British colony to China in 1997. The signing of the Joint Declaration had a paradoxical impact on the city's media. On the one hand, it signaled the beginning of a 13-year transition period during which Hong Kong was influenced by Britain and China as two power centers. The "dual power structure" provided a condition in which the press enjoyed an unprecedented degree of freedom to cover and make critical comments on local matters. On the other hand, this newly found press freedom was also under threat almost immediately because the dual power structure was not meant to be permanent, and the balance of political power continued to shift toward the Chinese side as the handover approached.

J. M. Chan and Lee (1991) describe a process of paradigm shift within the media system in Hong Kong in the second half of the 1980s as many media organizations began to accommodate to the new and incoming power center. The original rightist, pro-Taiwan press declined, whereas the centrist professional newspapers have become the dominant force on the media scene. By the mid-1990s, self-censorship also became a widely observed phenomenon in Hong Kong's media organizations (e.g., C-C. Lee 1998; Schell 1996; Scuitto 1996). There were serious concerns about whether press freedom could survive the change of sovereignty.

However, media freedom did not disappear overnight. Constrained by its own promises of "one country, two systems" and a "high degree of autonomy," the Chinese government did not impose an official pre-publication censorship system onto the Hong Kong media. Instead, it resorted to several more indirect and informal mechanisms to co-opt and control the Hong Kong press. First, the Chinese government explicitly set certain "bottom lines" which the Hong Kong media cannot cross; for example, the media cannot advocate Taiwan and Tibet independence and cannot criticize the national leaders personally (P. S. N. Lee & Chu 1998). Second, the Chinese government handed out political and presumably economic rewards to the media owners. As numerous scholars pointed out, with just one or two exceptions, owners of the Hong Kong's mainstream media organizations are either people with political appointments in China (usually as members of the Chinese Political Consultative Committee or the National People's Congress) or tycoons with huge business interests on the mainland (see Fung 2007; Ma 2007).

Third, midlevel Chinese officials began to criticize publicly specific media organizations in Hong Kong. Although such criticisms usually would be met with countercriticisms from the Hong Kong media, the officials' remarks always served their main purpose by making the media aware of the reporting norms expected of them (Lau & To 2002). Finally, especially in the past few years, the Chinese government has become more active and adept in "cooperating" with Hong Kong's media by facilitating coverage of positive news stories about the nation, such as China's space missions, the Beijing Olympics, and the 60th anniversary of the People's Republic of China.

On the whole, the Chinese government's approach to controlling Hong Kong's press does not deviate fundamentally from a carrot-and-stick approach occasionally used by democratic governments when dealing with the press. But as a result of the concentration of political power and resources in the hands of the Communist Party, China's carrots can be sweeter and the sticks heavier. Because of the above described strategies of political control, many observers have argued that Hong Kong's space for free speech has been constricting, and media self-censorship has become more serious over the years. A representative survey of Hong Kong journalists conducted by the Hong Kong Journalists Association in 2007, for instance, found that 58.4% of the respondents regarded the problem of self-censorship as having become more serious 10 years after the handover ("HKJA: Freedom of speech," 2007).

This overall trend notwithstanding, other researchers argue that there have been certain counteracting forces that have prevented the media from succumbing entirely to China's political power (J. M. Chan & Lee 2007, 2008; Lai 2007; Lee & Chan 2009a). Since most media organizations in Hong Kong are commercial operations, they have to maintain their market credibility. Media organizations cannot completely avoid sensitive matters or stop criticizing the power holders, especially when there are still media outlets, such as *Apple Daily* and the public broadcaster RTHK, which dare to defy political pressure or test the boundaries of acceptability at least occasionally. Once the more daring media have spoken out, the strategic calculations of other media usually shift—not only would it be costly for them to avoid a sensitive issue (due to a potential loss in audience), but it also might become politically less risky once others have taken the lead.

Most importantly, Hong Kong journalists have maintained a high level of professionalism and a strong local orientation. As So and Chan (2007) illustrated, Hong Kong journalists have largely maintained the normative self-understanding that journalists should be autonomous professionals who are free from political and economic pressure. They still consider the quick dissemination of accurate information and the monitoring of the government and other power holders as important media functions. At the same time, Chan and Lee (2011) argue that Hong Kong journalists still see themselves serving a local public. Hence their tendency to accommodate to the power structure would be weakened when events and controversies pit the interests of China or the Chinese government against the interests of the local population, such as during the severe acute respiratory syndrome (SARS) outbreak and the poisoned-milk crisis.

Compared with media politics, the economic basis of the news media in Hong Kong has received relatively little attention from researchers, but this is no less important to an overall understanding of the media in Hong Kong. As mentioned at the beginning of this chapter, Hong Kong is a media-saturated city. The struggle for survival has arguably led to the decline of serious and high quality journalism. The publication of *Apple Daily* in 1995, in particular, marked the "re-emergence" of the tabloid press in Hong Kong (Leung 2006; So 1997, 2003). Here, the "tabloid press" refers to a group of newspapers (such as *Apple Daily, Oriental Daily, The Sun, Hong Kong Daily News,* etc.) that is marked by an emphasis on sensational news topics, a focus on sports and entertainment news, and the presence of soft pornography. These newspapers are among the most widely circulated in Hong Kong. In fact, excluding free newspapers, the *Apple Daily, Oriental Daily*, and the *Sun* combine to account for more than 70% of local newspaper circulation in Hong Kong (So 2009a).

What is even more worrying, however, is the trend of tabloidization among Hong Kong's regular press. Although there has been a lack of systematic research documenting this trend, casual observations indicate that even elite-oriented newspapers, such as *Ming Pao* and *Sing Tao Daily*, have given more emphasis to soft news topics and utilized more "tabloid" reporting styles over the years.

Besides tabloidization, economic pressure also has resulted in the emergence of free newspapers in Hong Kong since the early 2000s. Facing the effect of the Asian economic turmoil after 1997, some media organizations have experimented with the idea of publishing newspapers that are freely distributed throughout the city's mass transit railway system (So & Lee 2007). The news stories found in these free newspapers are often brief so that people can finish reading them even during a short subway ride. At the time of this writing, the city has four major free daily newspapers, three in Chinese and one in English (So 2009a). Early observations have shown that free newspapers are eating into the readership and advertising revenue sources of conventional newspapers (So 2009b). Moreover, the rise of free newspapers in Hong Kong might result in a less informed public as more and more people replace their regular newspapers with freebies that cover news inadequately.

Increasing economic competition also has had some influence on television news. Historically, the television market in Hong Kong was marked by a de facto monopoly. Although there are two free-to-air stations, TVB's market position has been (and still is) so dominant that it often captures close to 90% of the television audience. New challenges emerged, however, when multi-channel television services began to develop in Hong Kong. While pay-TV services grew slowly in the early years (Lee 2007b), 72% of all households in Hong Kong are now connected to at least one multi-channel television service (Cable and Satellite Broadcasting Association of Asia 2009).

Method

The previous section has reviewed some of the major developments and challenges facing Hong Kong's media. How did journalists respond to the changing environment? How did the changing environment shape the characteristics of the journalistic profession? To answer these important questions, we will provide an overview of the journalistic profession in the following pages by drawing upon three journalist surveys conducted in 1996, 2001, and 2006.

The first representative journalist survey conducted in Hong Kong for academic purposes was done in 1990 (see Chan, Lee, & Lee 1996). Since then, a number of surveys also were conducted by the Hong Kong Journalists Association. Those surveys, however, often aimed at generating evidence for the Association to intervene in public debates surrounding questions related to the media. The three surveys we utilized in the present chapter, in contrast, were designed to address a wide range of issues pertinent to the profession, including working conditions, professional norms, political views, and so on (see Chan & Lee, 2011; Lee & Chan 2008, 2009b; So & Chan 2007).

In all three of these surveys, the population was defined as all journalists working in mainstream daily newspapers and the news departments of television and radio broadcasters in Hong Kong. All major daily newspapers (including all general interest newspapers and financial papers) and television and radio broadcasters were included in the study. We defined a journalist as any person responsible for the production of social, political, or economic news, no matter whether the content addresses local, national, or international matters. In other words, journalists at the China and foreign news desks were included, but sports, photo-, and entertainment journalists were not. The exclusion was mainly due to our focus on journalists working on public affairs as conventionally understood. Moreover, many Hong Kong newspapers have extensive coverage of sports and entertainment news, using a lot of photographs in the process. Had sports, photo-, and entertainment journalists been included, it would have provided a sample that did not truly represent the group of professionals responsible for the production and circulation of public affairs information in the society.

Without a complete roster of journalists from each organization, we simply used news desks as "identifiers" for the individual journalists. For each of the three surveys, a group of research assistants helped distribute the questionnaire to the news organizations, usually with the help of journalists working within those organizations as contact points. To ensure a good sample size, a questionnaire was placed on every other news desk in the news organizations, resulting in a systematic sampling with an interval of two for the surveys in 1996 and 2001. In 2006, in an effort to prevent a low response rate we created two versions of the questionnaire so as to create one full length and one abbreviated. To ensure that each version of the questionnaire would be answered by a sufficient number of respondents, a questionnaire was placed on every journalist's desk with the two versions distributed on alternate news desks. In each of the three cases the journalists filled out the questionnaire in their free time. The research assistants later collected the completed questionnaires from the news organizations.

The questionnaires of three surveys overlapped, but were not exactly the same. However, most of the core questions, such as those on job satisfaction, professional norms, and beliefs about ethical behavior, remained the same across the years. All three surveys began in July and August of each year and usually ended in September. In the 2006 survey, certain news organizations were particularly difficult to "penetrate," and the fieldwork was formally completed only in November. The total numbers of respondents were 553 in 1996, 722 in 2001, and 1,004 in 2006. The response rates were 62% in 1996 and 2001 and 55% in 2006.

Findings

Demographics and Work Conditions

As Table 3.1 shows, while there were slightly more male than female journalists in our sample in 1996, the gender ratio became essentially even in the two latter years. More significantly, the educational level of the Hong Kong journalists has increased over the years. While only 44.7% of journalists had a university degree or postgraduate education in 1996, the corresponding percentage had gone up substantially to 66.2% in 2001, and 71.7% in 2006. As various local universities started to offer master's degree programs related to journalism and communication since the turn of the century, the percentage of journalists having postgraduate education has increased, and we expect that trend to continue in the future.

Among those who have at least a college education, the proportion of journalism majors has remained stable. The percentages range from 55.9% to 57.6%. There has been some increase in the percentage of journalists having taken some journalism or communication related classes, though. As a result, the proportion of college-educated journalists who have no journalism or communication education whatsoever has decreased from 32.5% in 1996 to 25.7% in 2006.

Hong Kong journalists are young. In 1996, nearly half of the journalists were under 30, with another 31.9% aged between 30 and 39. In other words, more than 80% of Hong Kong journalists in 1996 were under 40. The percentage changed only slightly over the years. In 2006, 41.2% of Hong Kong journalists were under 30, with another 35.0% between 30 and 39.

Given the age distribution, it is unsurprising that the city's journalists also are somewhat inexperienced. In 1996, 70% of journalists had fewer than 10 years of experience in the field, and only 6.8% of journalists had 20 or more years of experience. The figures improved somewhat over the next decade. By 2006, the percentage of journalists with fewer than 10 years of experience went down to 59.4%.

The above figures indirectly point to a high degree of turnover within the journalistic profession in Hong Kong. Although we do not have concrete industry statistics about this issue, the journalistic corps as a whole would not have remained largely young and inexperienced if most journalists had been staying in the field for long periods of time. Our observation is also based on the frequent feedback from media practitioners. Indeed, many of our former students are known to have deserted journalism for public relations after joining the field for a few years. So, why do so many journalists leave the field after relatively short periods of time? One possible reason might be the low salaries. Table 3.2 shows the income distribution of Hong Kong journalists in 2006. Overall, 14.2% of journalists were earning less than HK$10,000 (US$1,300) per month, while another 44.8% were earning between HK$10,000 and HK$20,000 (US$2,600) per month. When we split the sample according to years of experience, we see that even after 10 years in the field, half of the journalists still earn a monthly salary of less than HK$20,000.

Table 3.1   Demographic Background of Journalists (in %)

	1996	2001	2006
Gender			
Female	44.9	50.2	48.1
Male	55.1	49.8	51.9.
$\chi^2 = 3.51, p > .15$			
Education			
High school or below	12.3	7.2	7.6
College	43.0	26.6	20.7
University	37.4	54.4	57.3
Postgraduate	7.3	11.8	14.4
$\chi^2 = 116.82, p < .001$			
Major in journalism**			
Yes	55.9	57.6	56.8
Took some classes	11.6	15.6	17.4
No	32.5	26.9	25.7
$\chi^2 = 12.43, p < .02$			
Age			
Below 30	49.5	46.3	41.2
30 to 39	31.9	34.4	35.0
40 to 49	15.2	14.8	16.8
50 or above	3.5	4.5	7.1
$\chi^2 = 17.89, p < .001$			
Time in the field			
Fewer than 5 years	45.8	39.7	35.8
5 to fewer than 10 years	24.9	25.7	23.6
10 to fewer than 15 years	13.7	16.1	16.1
15 to fewer than 20 years	8.8	7.8	10.1
20 years or above	6.8	10.6	14.5
$\chi^2 = 32.68, p < .001$			

Note.   Only journalists with at least college education were counted for "major in journalism." Ns for the variable are 437 in 1996, 655 in 2001, and 906 in 2006. Valid Ns for the other variables range from 521 to 548 in 1996, from 663 to 720 in 2001, and from 956 to 998 in 2006. The χ^2 values were derived by cross-tabulating year of survey with the demographic variables.

Of course, the meaning of these income figures can be understood only in relation to what the journalists could earn outside the field of journalism. Here, we should be reminded that most journalists in Hong Kong obtained at least a college level education. For these journalists, the starting salary would be between HK$15,000 and HK$20,000 if they opted to become a primary or secondary school teacher. The starting salary of an executive officer in the government also would be nearly HK$20,000 per month, and most can expect a salary beyond HK$30,000 per month after 10 years of work. In short, it is reasonable to suggest that Hong Kong journalists are earning much less than they could be earning in other fields.

Table 3.2   Income by Experience in the Field (in %)

	Whole sample	By years of experience		
		Fewer than 10 years	10 to fewer than 20 years	20 years or above
2006 (N = 956)				
Below 10,000	14.2	34.0	4.5	0.4
10,000–19,999	44.8	59.9	47.4	17.5
20,000–29,999	19.7	3.7	30.9	25.1
30,000–39,999	9.8	0.9	10.7	22.0
40,000 or above	11.5	1.4	6.5	35.2
$\chi^2 = 493.95, p < .001$				

Note.   The χ^2 value was derived by cross-tabulating the "years in the field" variable with the income variable. Table lists income in Hong Kong dollars per month.

The problem of low salaries in journalism is also reflected in other parts of the survey. Table 3.3 summarizes Hong Kong journalists' level of job satisfaction. Since this set of questions was not asked in the 2001 survey, we only have the comparison between the 1996 and 2006 data. The finding shows that overall Hong Kong journalists have been somewhat satisfied with their jobs, as the mean scores for the overall job satisfaction variable were both just above the mid-point of the scale in both 1996 and 2006. But when individual job aspects were concerned, a comparison of the mean scores across different items in the same survey shows that Hong Kong journalists tend to be more satisfied with the intrinsic and relational aspects of their jobs; that is, with things such as the job's social influence, job autonomy, creativity, chance to acquire new knowledge, and relations with colleagues. The mean scores of these latter items are all above the mid-point of the 5-point

Table 3.3   Job Satisfaction of Journalists (means)

	1996	2006
Satisfaction with		
Salary	2.97*	2.72*
Fringe benefits	2.57*	2.75*
Flexibility of working hours	3.27*	2.98*
Job evaluation system	2.60*	2.74*
Chance for promotion	2.55	2.52
Sense of accomplishment	3.38	3.26
Job's social influence	3.36	3.32
Creativity involved in the job	3.28	3.21
Autonomy involved in the job	3.25	3.20
Chance to acquire new knowledge	3.28*	3.41*
Relations with colleagues	3.76	3.75
Ability of superior	2.87*	3.01*
Overall job satisfaction	3.19	3.25

Note.   All items were measured with a five-point Likert scale ranging from 1 = very dissatisfied to 5 = very satisfied. Entries are the mean scores. Items marked with * indicate that the mean scores of the two surveys differ from each other significantly at $p < .05$ in independent samples t-tests. Valid Ns range from 479 to 547 for the 1996 survey. For the 2006 survey, the overall job satisfaction item was answered by the whole sample, and valid N = 982. The other items were included in only one version of the questionnaire, and valid Ns range from 442 to 484.

scale. In contrast, Hong Kong journalists tend to score below the mid-point of the satisfaction scale for salary, fringe benefits, job evaluation system, and chance for promotion, the four items most directly pertinent to the materialistic aspects of their job.

Even more directly to the point, a set of questions in the survey asked the journalists what reasons they would have to leave the field of journalism were they to do so. The respondents were given a set of 10 reasons, plus an "others" option. They were allowed to state, in rank-ordered fashion, the three most important reasons why they would leave the field.

Table 3.4 summarizes the findings. The top half of the table summarizes the results regarding the most important reason for journalists to leave the field. In 1996, which was one year before the transfer of Hong Kong's sovereignty, "political reasons" to leave the field were often at the top of journalists' minds. About 16% of Hong Kong journalists in 1996 named "political interference" as the most important reason for them to leave the field, while another 11.2% named "no prospect

Table 3.4 Journalists' Self-Reported Reasons for Leaving Journalism (in %)

	1996	2001	2006
Most important reason to leave:			
Too much pressure	12.9	17.9	18.0
Lack of autonomy	7.8	5.5	5.2
Boring and monotonous work	7.3	7.7	5.6
Irregular working hours	4.9	7.7	5.3
Low salary	11.0	14.9	24.6
Lack of promotion chances	4.3	8.2	6.5
Lack of learning opportunities	6.7	6.6	3.5
Disagree with editorial policy	8.6	10.3	5.8
Political interference	15.9	6.5	3.9
No prospect for press freedom	11.2	5.8	4.2
Others	9.9	9.0	17.3
$\chi^2 = 206.76$, p < .001			
Mentioning the reason once:			
Too much pressure	26.9*	34.7*	33.2*
Lack of autonomy	21.9*	20.9*	16.1*
Boring and monotonous work	17.9*	20.4*	15.0*
Irregular working hours	18.4*	27.0*	24.4*
Low salary	31.6*	40.6*	50.0*
Lack of promotion chances	18.1*	27.5*	25.5*
Lack of learning opportunities	26.6*	30.0*	20.1*
Disagree with editorial policy	28.4*	24.7*	18.7*
Political interference	33.5*	17.8*	13.7*
No prospect for press freedom	39.1*	20.7*	17.2*

Note. Cell entries in the top half of the table refer to percentages of journalists stating the item as their most important reason to leave the field. Entries in the bottom half refer to percentages of journalists mentioning the item as one of their three most important reasons to leave the field. For results in the bottom half of the table, cross-tabulation analyses were conducted to see if the percentages of journalists mentioning a specific reason to leave the field would increase or decrease over the years. Items marked by ** are those which record significant changes in the three surveys. For the top half of the table, Ns are 534, 692, and 976 for the three surveys, respectively. For the bottom half of the table, missing cases were recoded as 0. Hence the Ns are the full sample sizes, which are 553, 722, and 1,004 for the three surveys, respectively.

for press freedom" as the most important reason. After the handover, however, political concerns seem to have subsided. In 2001, only 12.3% of journalists chose one of the two major political reasons to leave the field as the most important reason for them to do so. The corresponding percentage dropped even further to 8.1% in 2006.

As political reasons declined in importance, the "materialistic" reasons have gained in importance. Even in 1996, 11% of Hong Kong journalists were naming "low salary" as the most important reason for them to leave the field. The figure rose sharply over the years, reaching 24.6% in 2006. Similarly, Hong Kong journalists were also concerned with the amount of pressure they had to face at work: 12.9% of journalists named "too much pressure" as the most important reason for them to leave the field in 1996, and the percentage rose somewhat to 18.0% in 2006.

The bottom half of Table 3.4 shows the results when all three reasons the journalists named were taken into account. The pattern of the findings remains basically the same. The significance of political reasons for journalists to leave the field has gone down over the years. In contrast, in 2006 half of the respondents named "low salary" as one of the three reasons for them to leave the field. It is by far the most frequently cited reason.

Political Attitudes, Perceived Self-Censorship, and Professionalism

The previous section has shown that Hong Kong journalists have become less likely to leave the field for political reasons. But it would be wrong to conclude that these journalists do not recognize the political challenges that they and their media organizations have to face. For this reason, we included a set of items in the 2006 survey that examined journalists' political views and their perceptions of the political stances held by their news organizations.

Table 3.5 summarizes the results. Because the items were measured on a 1-to-10 scale, the midpoint of the scale is 5.5. The findings show that the average Hong Kong journalist in 2006 was strongly supportive of Hong Kong and democratization (both means = 6.8), but somewhat distant from the Hong Kong government ($M = 5.2$) and the elite class ($M = 4.9$). The mean scores for the questions related to China and Taiwan are very close to the mid-point of the scale ($Ms = 5.6$ and 5.3 respectively). These findings suggest that the average Hong Kong journalist in 2006 was a

Table 3.5 Journalists' Political Attitudes and Perceptions of Organizational Stances (means)

	Personal opinions	Organization stance	Mean difference
Specific items:			
Pro-Hong Kong	6.84	6.61	.25**
Pro-China	5.59	6.37	−.70***
Pro-upper class	4.91	5.56	−.63***
Democratization	6.83	5.82	1.01***
Close to government	5.15	5.77	−.56***
Rehabilitate June 4	6.81	5.11	1.68***
Taiwan question	5.33	4.11	1.14***
Index:			
Liberal orientation	6.04	4.99	1.04***

Note.   All items were measured with a 1-to-10 scale with 10 representing very pro-Hong Kong, very pro-China, very pro-upper class, highly supportive toward democratization, very close to the Hong Kong government, highly supportive towards rehabilitating June 4, and highly supportive toward Taiwanese self-determination. Mean differences were examined with paired-sample t-tests. Ns range from 434 to 504. *** p < .001; ** p < .01.

pro-democracy figure and considered herself as an independent social critic (i.e., distant from the government and slightly leaning toward the weaker groups in society).

Another important finding from Table 3.5 is that journalists' opinions and their perceived organizational stances differ significantly on all seven items. Journalists considered themselves as more supportive of Hong Kong than their news organizations. At the same time, they also thought of their news organizations as more supportive of China and the upper class but less supportive of democratization and Taiwanese self-determination when compared to themselves.

In short, the Hong Kong journalists generally considered themselves as more liberal than their news organizations. This is actually a phenomenon that exists in many other countries around the world (see Weaver 1998). Yet in the Hong Kong context, the relatively liberal political orientation of the journalists has implications for the notion of self-censorship. The fact that journalists perceive their organizations to be relatively conservative can be both a cause and a consequence of perceptions of self-censorship. That is, journalists may come to the conclusion that their organizations are politically conservative as a result of their perceptions that self-censorship is practiced frequently. Alternatively, journalists may believe their organizations are practicing self-censorship because of their own liberal political outlook.

In any case, most Hong Kong journalists do regard self-censorship as a growing problem. In both the 2001 and 2006 surveys, we included an item asking the journalists to evaluate the overall seriousness of self-censorship. In 2001, 13.2% of the respondents regarded self-censorship as "very serious," and 57.4% believed that self-censorship existed but was "not very serious." Only 2.9% believed that there was no self-censorship at all. In 2006, almost 27% of our respondents believed that self-censorship was "very serious," whereas 47.2% said that censorship existed but was "not very serious." As in 2001, only about 3% of the respondents believed that there was no self-censorship at all.

The 2006 survey also included a set of more differentiated items asking the respondents to evaluate how common six types of self-censorship practices were. As the bottom half of Table 3.6 shows, "toning down negative news about the Chinese government" is perceived to be the most

Table 3.6 Perceived Self-Censorship in the 2001 and 2006 Surveys (in %)

		Very serious	*Not very serious*	*A little serious*	*Not at all serious*	*Mean*
Overall existence						
Censorship in 2001		13.2	57.4	20.4	2.9	2.86
Censorship in 2006		26.6	47.2	14.0	3.2	3.07
	Frequently	*4*	*3*	*2*	*Not at all*	*Mean*
Specific Practices (2006):						
Tone down neg. news about HK gov.	9.2	25.7	31.9	17.9	4.8	3.18
Tone down neg. news about Chin. gov.	14.9	31.1	28.9	12.3	2.4	3.49$_a$
Omit neg. news about HK gov.	5.5	14.2	34.6	25.4	9.8	2.78
Omit neg. news about Chin. gov.	8.7	20.9	33.3	19.6	6.0	3.08
Bias toward HK gov. in news	9.8	25.7	36.5	13.7	2.9	3.29
Bias toward Chin. gov. in news	12.1	30.3	33.7	10.6	1.8	3.46$_a$

Note. Percentages do not necessarily add up to 100% because of the existence of "don't know" answers. For overall seriousness of self-censorship, the mean scores of the items in 2001 and 2006 differ from each other significantly at $p < .05$ in an independent samples t-test. For specific self-censorship practices, with the exception of the two items marked by the same subscript "a," the mean scores of the items all significantly differ from each other at $p < .05$ in paired-samples t-test.

Table 3.7 Journalists' Beliefs Regarding News Media Roles (means)

	1996	2001	2006
Information dissemination			
Provide news information quickly**	4.44_a	4.55_{ab}	4.39_b
Report factually**	4.55_a	4.67_a	4.45_a
Provide information to stop rumor**	4.31_a	4.36_b	4.14_{ab}
Interpretation			
Help explain government policies**	3.47_{ab}	3.76_a	3.65_b
Help public to understand policies**	3.98_{ab}	4.15_a	4.06_b
Lead public opinion**	3.30_{ab}	3.55_a	3.52_b
Discuss policies in the process**	3.87_{ab}	4.12_a	3.99_b
Advocacy			
Help public to monitor**	4.05	4.16_a	3.99_a
Serve as public's mouthpiece**	3.96_a	3.98_b	3.77_{ab}
Help social reform**	3.49_a	3.63_a	3.53
Support marginal groups**	3.00_{ab}	3.60_a	3.60_b
Adversarial			
Criticize government and officials**	3.69_a	3.89_{ab}	3.76_{ab}
Criticize business**	3.64_a	3.83_{ab}	3.71_b
Criticize social organizations**	3.61_a	3.78_a	3.69

Note.   Answers were recorded with a five-point Likert scale from 1 = very unimportant to 5 = very important. Items marked with **
have mean scores that differ from each other significantly in an ANOVA analysis. Across each row, cell entries sharing the same
subscript were significantly different from each other in post-hoc Bonferroni tests (at p < .05). Ns range from 524 to 540 in
1996, from 696 to 717 in 2001, and from 977 to 995 in 2006.

common self-censorship practice. This was followed by being "biased toward the Chinese government when reporting news" and "omitting negative news about the Chinese government."

While journalists recognized self-censorship practices in Hong Kong's media, their sense of
professionalism has remained relatively intact over the years. Table 3.7 shows how Hong Kong
journalists perceive the importance of various journalistic roles. Following Weaver and Wilhoit's
(1996) conceptualization, the survey questionnaire included items capturing the information dissemination, interpretation, advocacy, and adversarial roles. The results indicate that Hong Kong
journalists regarded all four media roles as highly important. Comparatively, Hong Kong journalists gave the greatest emphasis to the information dissemination role, as the mean scores of the
three items pertinent to this role conception are all above 4. In contrast, the mean scores of the
items pertinent to the other three role conceptions are usually lower. In the 2006 survey, for
instance, 10 of the 11 items pertinent to the interpretation, advocacy, and adversarial roles have
mean scores between 3.5 and 4.0.

When we compared the findings across the three surveys, there are indeed statistically significant changes in the mean scores of the individual items. However, the statistically significant
changes are usually not very substantive in size. One exception is whether Hong Kong journalists regarded "supporting marginal groups" as an important media role. In the 1996 survey, the
mean score of the item was only 3.0. Yet the score rose to 3.6 in both the 2001 and 2006 surveys.
However, other than this item, the other changes are not dramatic. A more appropriate overall
description of Table 3.7 is probably that, despite the changes in the social, political, and economic

environment, Hong Kong journalists have retained a relatively constant sense of what social roles the media should play in the society.

Conclusions

Despite the fast-changing social, political, and economic environment of Hong Kong, our survey findings suggest that Hong Kong journalists have not changed dramatically over the years. Among the characteristics discussed above, the one that registered the biggest change was journalists' reasons for leaving the profession. Politics has become much less important over the years, but salary and career advancement have gained weight among journalists as possible reasons for leaving the field.

We also have pointed out that Hong Kong journalists earn much less than they would earn in other fields. But what explains the low pay and benefits for journalists in Hong Kong? A full discussion of this question would require us to look into the history of the news industry in the city, as well as its changing economics over the years. But for our discussion here, it is sufficient to note that the oversaturated local media market is at least partly responsible for the low salaries. The situation is somewhat better in the broadcasting sector (and in fact the average salaries of broadcast journalists in our samples were higher than those of print journalists in all three years), but print journalists have suffered in a small market of 7 million readers that is served by no less than 17 newspapers. One consequence of the increasingly competitive media in Hong Kong is a high turnover rate in the journalistic corps. Our findings suggest that a large proportion of journalists did not stay in the field for more than 10 years. The loss of experienced journalists, in turn, might affect the news media's ability to handle issues and events competently and in an in-depth manner.

However, complaints about low salaries do not mean that Hong Kong journalists are materialistic in their orientations and do not care about their social roles. In fact, we found that Hong Kong journalists' overall job satisfaction was influenced to a larger degree by their satisfaction with the intrinsic rather than extrinsic aspects of their jobs.

On the whole, Hong Kong journalists' professional orientation is a very important counteracting force against political pressure (Chan & Lee 2007; C-C. Lee 2000; So & Chan 2007). The findings we presented above show that despite the change in power structure since the handover in 1997, there is no significant decline in journalists' emphasis on the importance of the media in disseminating truthful information to the public and criticizing the government and other power holders.

One limitation of such findings is that they only show some general or theoretical acknowledgment of the importance of journalistic roles. Underlying the apparent constancy in support of these roles may be changes that can only be observed in concrete or realistic work settings. Nevertheless, we believe that the findings are meaningful and important even if they largely represent lip service paid by the Hong Kong journalists to professional ideals. As long as journalists feel compelled to support the ideals of journalistic professionalism, unprofessional behavior cannot be openly justified and promoted. This is in line with F. L. F. Lee and Chan's (2009a) observation that, within the newsrooms in Hong Kong, the top news managers still cannot openly ask their subordinates to practice self-censorship.

Similarly, the decline in the proportion of journalists considering leaving the field for political reasons does not mean that journalists were satisfied with the political situation. On the contrary, journalists in Hong Kong held generally liberal and prodemocracy attitudes, and yet they perceived their news organizations as having become more conservative than they once were. At the same time, journalists perceived a significant degree of self-censorship going on around them and, more importantly, becoming more serious. Yet the perceived decline of press freedom did not result in stronger intentions to leave the profession.

The survey findings over time have led us to conclude that the post-handover political situation might be less problematic than initially feared by many people in Hong Kong. In the end, journalists found out that the worst-case scenario did not materialize. Instead, as long as professionalism remains a prominent force, most journalists might hope that they can still exert their influence and accomplish what they want to accomplish within Hong Kong's political constraints. It is also possible that those journalists who are most politically conscious and care the most about press freedom feel compelled to stay in order to continue the political struggle. On the whole, we believe that Hong Kong journalists remain committed to a liberal concept of journalistic professionalism. Undoubtedly, at a time when journalism faces severe economic and political challenges, professionalism is crucial to the health of Hong Kong's news media.

References

Cable and Satellite Broadcasting Association of Asia. 2009. Country facts and figures. Retrieved from http://www.casbaa.com/country_facts.aspx

Chan, Joseph M., and Chin-chuan Lee. 1991. *Mass media and political transition: The Hong Kong press in China's orbit.* New York: Guilford Press.

Chan, Joseph M., and Francis L. F. Lee. 2007. Media and politics in post-handover Hong Kong: An introduction. *Asian Journal of Communication* 17(2):127–133.

Chan, Joseph M., and Francis L. F. Lee. (eds.) 2008. *Media and politics in post-handover Hong Kong.* London: Routledge.

Chan, Joseph M., and Francis L. F. Lee. 2011. The primacy of local interest and press freedom in Hong Kong: A survey study of journalists. *Journalism* 12(1):89–105.

Chan, Joseph M., Paul S. N. Lee, and Chin-chuan Lee. 1996. *Hong Kong journalists in transition.* Hong Kong: Hong Kong Institute of Asia Pacific Studies, Chinese University of Hong Kong.

Fung, Anthony Y. H. 2007. Political economy of Hong Kong media: Producing a hegemonic voice. *Asian Journal of Communication* 17(2):159–171.

HKJA: Freedom of speech has been narrowed down after the handover. 2007, July 9. *Hong Kong Economic Times*: A30.

Hong Kong SAR Government. 2009. *Hong Kong yearbook 2009.* Hong Kong: Information Services Department.

Lai, Carol P. 2007. *Media in Hong Kong: Press freedom and political change, 1967–2005.* London: Routledge

Lau, Tuen-yu, and Yiu-ming To. 2002. Walking a tight rope: Hong Kong's media facing political and economic challenges since sovereignty transfer. In *Crisis and transformation in China's Hong Kong,* edited by Ming K. Chan and Alvin Y. So, pp. 322–342. New York: M. E. Sharpe.

Lee, Chin-chuan. 1998. Press self-censorship and political transition in Hong Kong. *Harvard International Journal of Press/Politics* 3(2):55–73.

Lee, Chin-chuan. 2000. The paradox of political economy: Media structure, press freedom, and regime change in Hong Kong. In *Power, money, and media,* edited by Chin-chuan Lee, pp. 288–336. Evanston, IL: Northwestern University Press.

Lee, Francis L. F. 2007a. Strategic interaction, cultural co-orientation, and press freedom in Hong Kong. *Asian Journal of Communication,* 17(2):134–147.

Lee, Francis L. F. 2007b. Development of pay television in Hong Kong: History, audience consumption, and challenges. *Journal of Comparative Asian Development* 4(2):247–272.

Lee, Francis L. F., and Joseph M. Chan. 2008. Professionalism, political orientation, and perceptions of self-censorship in Hong Kong. *Issues & Studies* 44(1):205–238.

Lee, Francis L. F., and Joseph M. Chan. 2009a. *Strategic responses to political changes: An analysis of newspapers editorials in Hong Kong, 1996–2006.* Occasional Paper No. 199. Hong Kong: Hong Kong Institute of Asia-Pacific Studies.

Lee, Francis L. F., and Joseph M. Chan. 2009b. The organizational production of self-censorship in the Hong Kong media. *International Journal of Press/Politics* 14:112–133.

Lee, Paul S. N., and Leonard L. Chu. 1998. Inherent dependence on power: The Hong Kong press in political transition. *Media, Culture & Society* 20:59–77.

Leung, Grace. 2006. *The apple falls: A study of Apple-zation of the Hong Kong media.* Hong Kong: Subculture Hall. (in Chinese)

Ma, Ngok. 2007. State-press relationship in post-1997 Hong Kong: Constant negotiation amidst self-restraint. *China Quarterly* 192:949–970.

Schell, Orville. 1996. Self-censorship In Hong Kong. *Media Studies Journal* 10(4):53–54.

Sciutto, James E. 1996. China's muffling of the Hong Kong media. In *Hong Kong and China: Pursuing a new destiny,* edited by Max J. Skidmore, pp. 131–143. Singapore: Toppan.

So, Clement Y. K. 1997. Pre-1997 Hong Kong press: Cut-throat competition and the changing journalistic paradigm. In *The other Hong Kong report 1997,* edited by Mee Kau Nyaw and Si Ming Li, pp. 485–505. Hong Kong: The Chinese University Press.

So, Clement Y. K. 2003. The news media under the market orientation. In *The new era for the Hong Kong media,* edited by Paul S. N. Lee, pp. 99–124. Hong Kong: The Chinese University Press.

So, Clement Y. K. 2009a, October 8–10. *Evolution of the newspaper readership: Comparing paid, free and online readers.* Paper presented at the International Media Readings in Moscow: Mass Media and Communications, Moscow State University, Moscow, Russia,

So, Clement Y. K. 2009b, May. The impact of free newspapers on Hong Kong's readership market. *Media Digest,* 2009. (in Chinese) Retrieved from http://www.rthk.org.hk/mediadigest/20090515_76_122256.html

So, Clement Y. K., and Joseph M. Chan. 2007. Professionalism, politics, and market force: Survey studies of Hong Kong journalists 1996–2006. *Asian Journal of Communication* 17(2):148–158.

So, Clement Y. K., and Alice Y. L. Lee (2007, May 24–28). *Distribution-driven journalism: The business model of free newspapers.* Paper presented at the 57th annual conference of the International Communication Association, San Francisco, CA.

Weaver, David H. (ed.) 1998. *The global journalist: News people around the world.* Cresskill, NJ: Hampton Press.

Weaver, David H., and G. Cleveland Wilhoit. 1996. *The American journalist in the 1990s: U.S. news people at the end of an era.* Mahwah, NJ: Erlbaum.

4   Journalists in Indonesia

Thomas Hanitzsch and Dedy N. Hidayat

During the past 14 years Indonesia has been experiencing rapid change. After three decades under Suharto's repressive New Order regime, journalists in the country today enjoy unprecedented press freedom, which makes Indonesia one of the most vibrant media systems in Asia. *Freedom House*'s 2009 press freedom survey rates Indonesia's media as "partly free," with a press environment that has slightly improved since 2006.[1] Reporters Without Borders (2009) even lists Indonesia as one of the two freest countries in the region, after East Timor and before the Philippines.[2]

The controversial re-election of Suharto in March 1998 marked the beginning of a "fascinating chapter" in Indonesia's media history (Hidayat 2002: 174). Just one year later, the media started to cover the first free elections in the post-Suharto era in a way that reminded many observers of U.S.-style election coverage (Manzella 2000). Indonesia's "golden age of press freedom" (Dharma, Pane, Nurkholis, & Mustafid 2003: 5) began shortly after Abdurrahman Wahid came into power in 1999. At the same time, the abolition of political restrictions on the media triggered an explosive demand for young and qualified journalists as the number of news outlets sharply increased. The number of print outlets alone skyrocketed from 289 in May 1998 to 1,536 in August 1999, and to 2,033 in 2001 (Mursito 2000; Siregar 2002).

Press freedom not only equipped Indonesia's journalists with unparalleled independence from state intervention, but it also constituted a serious challenge to professionalism (Arismunandar 2002; Eisy 2002). Many observers believe press freedom in Indonesia has led to malpractices and excesses in journalism (Dharma et al. 2003; Loeqman 2003). Criticized is a loss of accuracy, objectivity, neutrality, completeness, and depth in national and local news coverage (Abar 1998; Ma'ruf 1999). These problems were aggravated by ineffective journalism education and weak press self-monitoring mechanisms (Dharma et al. 2003; Hanitzsch 2001; Manzella 2000). Furthermore, as long as bribery continues to be widespread among Indonesian journalists (Hanitzsch 2006), efforts to improve professional awareness will largely remain ineffective.

It is common for politicians to accuse the media of being "slanted" and "manipulative". Many among the political elites expressed concerns about a press law that is, in their view, too liberal. Partly as a result, in November 2002 the parliament passed a highly restrictive broadcasting law that was feared would "give birth to a new authoritarianism" (Sudibyo 2003). Six years later, Indonesian press freedom was offset by the use of criminal defamation laws to restrict reporting, overly strict broadcast licensing requirements, and continued attacks against journalists. Today, violence against and intimidation of journalists continue to be an issue.

At the same time, Indonesia's journalists were repeatedly found "biased," "partisan," and "provocative" in their reporting and labeled as "lapdogs" rather than "watchdogs" (Anwar 2001: 42; Dharma et al. 2003: 51; Loeqman 2003: xiii). Anwar (2001: 42–43) described the press as "heartless," "entertainment-oriented," as well as lacking ideology, vision, and mission. This picture, however, is quite different from the self-perception of Indonesian journalists who see themselves as "watchdogs," "agents of empowerment" and "nation-building," but not as "entertainers" (Romano 2003: 57). It is in this context that surveys of journalists in a transitional democracy such as Indonesia produce important and interesting insights into the state of public communication.

Media in Indonesia

Indonesia's media will remain a highly contested field in the foreseeable future. This political and economic power struggle involves various actors, including elements of civil society, market forces, media owners and managers, as well as journalists. In the transitional context of Indonesia, the media constitute a political-economic entity that is constantly reconstituted and altered in response to the ever changing socio-economic environment, new information technologies, as well as both local and global market conditions.

During the rule of President Sukarno, a left-leaning nationalist in the 1960s, the media largely functioned as partisan outlets. Defined as a "tool of revolution," they were responsible for energizing and mobilizing public opinion (Hill 1994: 140). The Old Order regime even required all newspapers to be formally affiliated with a political party or organization. When Suharto's New Order regime seized power in 1966, however, the media gradually became depoliticized. The subsequent expansion of the market economy allowed a rapid growth of the media industry. Private television was introduced in 1988, which shortly became the dominant force in Indonesia's media system, both in terms of agenda-setting influence and a growing orientation toward commercial values.

During the New Order regime, Indonesia's media were commonly viewed in their capacity to serve as "free but (socially) responsible press" (Assegaff 1983: 12), but literally all news outlets were in fact subject to tight government control on various levels (Hill 1994). At the content level, control was largely exercised by informal means, which the journalists' vernacular often referred to as "telephone culture." Editors often received phone calls from the authorities who warned them against publication of "sensitive" issues. At the individual level, all journalists were obliged to join the only officially recognized union of journalists, the Indonesian Journalists Association (*Persatuan Wartawan Indonesia*). At the organizational and industrial levels, the regime retained control by means of licensing, thus creating political barriers for market entry. General Suharto was very effective in having members of his own family and close friends buy into the media (Vatikiotis 1993).

The collapse of the New Order regime in 1998 brought a relatively abrupt and substantial transformation of Indonesia's media industry and the profession of journalism. The most significant changes were, at the institutional level, the liquidation of the Ministry of Information, the establishment of an independent regulatory body for the broadcasting industry, and a relatively liberal press law.

After the abolition of publishing licenses, the number of media outlets soared from around 300 to more than 1,000 newspapers and from 700 to more than 1,000 radio stations during the first year after the collapse of the Suharto regime. In addition, five national commercial television stations entered the market, competing with the five already existing ones (Johannen & Gomez 2001; South East Asian Press Alliance 2000). The Indonesian Broadcasting Commission estimates the number of local commercial television stations at 97 throughout the country (Komisi Penyiaran Indonesia 2010).

However, Indonesia's liberated media industry still struggles with the maintenance of a diversity of public voices. First and most importantly, there is a tendency toward concentration of ownership, most notably in the television industry, but also in the print media sector (Piliang 2002; Sen & Hill 2000). Second, it has become obvious during the past few years that the state has tried to consolidate its power to regain regulatory authority (Freedom House 2009).[3] The government, for instance, regained direct control over the broadcasting industry after a revision of the broadcasting law in 2004. Third, large media corporations resisted all attempts to decentralize broadcasting operations, a policy that was aimed at creating a market niche for independent local television stations. Fourth, the newly gained press freedom in Indonesia also prompted strong opposition from parts of Indonesia's multi-ethnic and multi-religious society. Even today, news organizations and journalists across the country are well-aware of potential mob attacks that might be triggered by the coverage of sensitive issues, such as anything related to Islam or the small but wealthy minority of Indonesia's Chinese community. Most news editors avoid covering these controversial issues since neutrality is the best option for safely navigating Indonesia's multi-cultural space. To compensate, many Indonesian journalists make excessive use of official sources (Ishak 2002; Qodari 2000; Sudibyo 2000).

Method

This chapter reports findings from two surveys of Indonesian journalists conducted in 2001 and 2008. The first study was fielded between August 2001 and February 2002 with a sample of 385 journalists (see Hanitzsch 2005). One half of the sample was drawn from the capital province Jakarta in West Java, and two regional sub-samples (each 25%) were obtained from the provinces of Yogyakarta in Central Java and North Sumatra. This largely reflects the overall structure of Indonesia's media system in which roughly three out of four news organizations operate from the main island Java and half from the capital Jakarta. The three regions were selected according to the various degrees of industrialization, affiliation to center/periphery, and composition of ethnic groups.

The original sample of 480 randomly selected journalists yielded 385 completed and valid interviews, representing a response rate of 80%. The questionnaire consisted of 59 questions, many of which resembled questions used in similar survey projects throughout the world (e.g., Weaver & Wilhoit 1991, 1996; Weischenberg, Löffelholz, & Scholl 1998). They included aspects of the journalists' backgrounds, their professional views, media use, work patterns, interactions with sources, and reporting practices. The interviews were conducted face-to-face with the help of independent teams of local researchers in each of the three regions.

The second study was a sub-sample of the cross-national research project, *Worlds of Journalism* (see Hanitzsch et al. 2010). Field research was conducted between November 2007 and January 2008. As in all other countries that participated in this project, the survey employed a sample of 100 journalists working in 20 news organizations. The sample structure was standardized across all countries. The local team first selected 20 news organizations, with the selection being organized along two first-level dimensions: The first layer distinguished between types of media, as well as between national and local/regional media. The second level stratified print newsrooms into quality and popular (tabloid) media, and electronic media according to ownership in primarily public media, state-owned media, and private channels.

Five journalists were randomly selected in each newsroom, wherever possible. Within the news organizations, the selected journalists were further stratified according to the extent of their editorial responsibility. Ideally, one journalist was selected from the highest level of the editorial hierarchy (strategic leadership: e.g., chief editors and their deputies), one from the middle level (operational decision-makers: e.g., senior editors and desk heads), and three from the lowest level of the editorial hierarchy (e.g., reporters). The selection of journalists thus slightly oversampled senior editors.

The questionnaire used in the second study was a translation from a collaboratively designed master questionnaire. It included 46 questions that asked respondents about their role perceptions, ethical views, professional autonomy, factors influencing their work, and other aspects of their practice. As in the previous survey, the interviews were conducted personally. All newsrooms that were selected participated in the study and none of the selected journalists refused to be interviewed.

Findings

Basic Characteristics, Education, and Training

The "typical" journalist in Indonesia is male, in his mid-30s, and has worked in the field of journalism for 9 to 10 years (see Table 4.1). Women constitute a minority in editorial offices throughout Indonesia, though their percentage has grown over the years. A high percentage of male journalists in Indonesia has also been found in previous studies that looked at gender distributions in professional organizations of journalists (e.g. Budiyanto & Mabroer 2000), but the share of women is not as small as these data sources suggest (see Table 4.1).

One of the reasons for the small number of women among Indonesia's journalists is, as Romano (2003: 109) argues, that they seem to find public relations work more attractive than journalism. Furthermore, the results indicate that female journalists tend to be younger and have less professional experience than their male colleagues, and that they enter the profession at an earlier stage in their lives. Obviously, combining career and family appears to be difficult for women journalists, given the fact that family is culturally defined as their first duty in Indonesia (Romano 2003). As news work often requires total dedication and commitment to "immediate" demands of nonroutine work, it is often detrimental to the maintenance of a healthy balance between family and career (Lavie & Lehman-Wilzig 2003: 21).

Most Indonesian journalists are members of at least one of the many journalists' unions in the country. On the one hand, this fact might be traced back to a practice of the former New Order regime during which membership in the Indonesian Journalists' Association was mandatory for all journalists. After the collapse of the Suharto regime in 1998, the number of journalists' associations skyrocketed to 43 in 2003, 26 of which agreed on a common standard code of

Table 4.1   Basic Characteristics, Education, and Training

	2001 (N = 385)	2008 (N = 100)
Age (median)	34	35
Percentage of Woman journalists	22.1%	33.0%
Work experience (years)	9.0	10.3
Member of a journalists' union	58.1%	58.6%
Holding college degree	80.2%	87.8%
Majored in journalism	10.8%	53.5%
Professional training	37.0%	77.1%

ethical conduct (*Kode Etik Wartawan Indonesia*). Although the Indonesian Journalists' Association "has repeatedly failed to support journalists' actions against ministerial intervention, particularly arbitrary withdrawals of publication permits" (Sen & Hill 2000: 55), the association is still the largest of its kind in Indonesia. Younger journalists, however, seem to be less keen to join a professional association.

In terms of education and training, the data indicate a steady professionalization of journalism in Indonesia. In 2007, roughly eight of nine journalists said that they held a college or university degree. Six years before, it was only four of five. Journalists clearly constitute an "educated elite," as they are, on average, far better educated than members of the overall population. Younger journalists tend to have more formal education than their older colleagues.

Even more striking are the differences in the percentages of journalists who have studied journalism and who went through professional training. While in 2001, only one of nine journalists said that he or she had studied journalism, the share of journalism graduates rose to more than 50% in 2008. Similarly, the percentage of those who went through professional training roughly doubled to more than 77% during these years. Thus, it seems that the booming media industry in Indonesia introduced a whole new generation of well-educated youngsters into the profession. This is a result of a substantial growth in the number of academic schools offering journalism and mass media degrees. These institutions started to flourish shortly after the collapse of the New Order regime.

Working Conditions

One important indicator of the perceived quality of working conditions is job satisfaction. According to the 2001 study, 22.6% of the interviewed journalists said they were very satisfied, 54.4% were satisfied, 21.8% indicated they were unsatisfied, and only 1.2% said they were very unsatisfied. This suggests a relatively high level of job satisfaction among Indonesian journalists. These findings are further corroborated by the journalists' commitment to the profession. Of all journalists interviewed in the 2001 study, only 1.6% indicated that they planned to move to public relations or another field. Altogether, 81.7% of the journalists said that they did not plan to leave the profession in the foreseeable future.

There are several factors that contribute, although quite unevenly, to job satisfaction, the two most important of which relate to pay and job security (see Table 4.2). More than 80% of the interviewed journalists in the 2001 study said that these factors were "very important." Fringe benefits that constitute another facet of the material remuneration of journalists rank in third

Table 4.2   Job Factors (2001, $N = 385$, % of journalists saying "very important")

Pay	85.4
Job safety	82.5
Fringe benefits	67.2
Editorial policy	66.1
Job freedom	61.6
Career opportunities	60.2
Opportunity to specialize	59.1
Opportunity to influence public opinion	44.1
Opportunity to help people	42.0

Table 4.3   Perceived Autonomy (2008, $N = 100$, in %)

	I have a lot of control over the work that I do.	I am allowed to take part in decisions that affect my work.
Strongly agree	16.5	24.2
Somewhat agree	62.9	65.7
Neither agree nor disagree	9.3	6.1
Somewhat disagree	9.3	3.0
Strongly disagree	2.1	1.0
	100.0	100.0

place. Altogether, this suggests that in a society that is characterized by widespread poverty, low wages, and precarious employment conditions, journalists—as is probably true of members of many other professions—give priority to conditions that ensure that they can, in a sustained manner, make a living from their work. Under such circumstances it is hardly surprising that factors that are more intrinsic to the profession—such as editorial policy, as well as opportunities to help people and influence public opinion—are not among the top priorities of Indonesian journalists. Job freedom, career opportunities, and having an opportunity to specialize in a particular area were perceived to be of moderate importance.

The extent to which journalists think that they can work autonomously was among the dimensions measured in the 2008 study. Somewhat surprisingly, the vast majority of the interviewed journalists indicated a considerable amount of perceived professional autonomy (see Table 4.3). Only slightly less than 80% of the news workers said that they have a lot of control over the work that they do, and almost 90% of the respondents agreed that they are allowed to take part in decisions that affect their work. These results, however, do not necessarily mean that journalists enjoy exceptionally great professional autonomy. In the political-economic context of Indonesia, journalists often seem to actively anticipate the limits of their freedom by shaping the news in a way that preemptively complies with the interests of owners and politicians.

The two indicators of job freedom correlate fairly strongly (Spearman's $\rho = .56$, Cronbach's $\alpha = .68$), and together they constitute an index measure of perceived professional autonomy. This new variable was subsequently used in a regression analysis in order to establish the main determinants of professional autonomy in the Indonesian context. The resulting model included five predictors and explained about 22% of the overall variance. Table 4.4 shows that organizational determinants are the strongest predictors of professional autonomy. According to the results, journalists feel substantially less autonomous in state-owned media organizations, including the

Table 4.4   Predictors of Perceived Autonomy (2008, $N = 100$)

	b	Beta	p
Constant	4.916		.000
News production	.007	.258	.044
Editorial coordination and management	.007	.340	.010
College education	−.476	−.240	.045
Advertising, share of revenue	−.173	−.449	.031
State-owned medium	−.864	−.593	.005

Corr. $R^2 = .217$; Backward method ($p_{in} = .01, p_{out} = .05$)

national news agency ANTARA, as well as the broadcasting body that produces the programs of Televisi Republik Indonesia (TVRI) and Radio Republik Indonesia (RRI). This finding sheds interesting light on the TVRI and RRI's aspirations to become true public broadcasters. Hierarchical structures and political influence seem to remain salient even ten years after the collapse of the Suharto regime.

Private ownership, on the other hand, is not significantly related to perceived autonomy. Here, once again, it would be dangerous to conclude that private owners do not exert influence on editorial content. During the national convention of the Golkar party in 2009, for instance, two candidates for the party chairman, Surya Paloh and Aburizal Bakrie, were owners of large media corporations. Both candidates actively used their media channels, most notably *MetroTV*, to promote their candidacy, which prompted a warning issued by the Indonesian Broadcasting Commission.[4]

Another strong indicator of professional autonomy is the media organizations' dependence on advertising. The higher the share of revenue that originates from advertising, the less autonomous journalists feel in Indonesia. This indicates that journalistic freedom in Indonesia is increasingly restricted by economic considerations, and it signifies a trend toward commercialization within the newsrooms of privately owned media.

On the individual level, perceived professional autonomy is significantly related to the journalists' work profiles. Those who spend more time with news production, editorial coordination, and management feel that they have more job autonomy than others. This group of journalists mostly consists of people who populate higher echelons in the editorial hierarchy and who have more editorial responsibilities. Another individual-level predictor is education, or more specifically, whether or not journalists hold a college degree. Journalists with college degrees seem to feel less autonomous than their colleagues. Counter-intuitive as this might be, it only indicates that better educated journalists may have a greater need for autonomy and, consequently, a stronger sense of the lack of it.

The level of editorial autonomy is one important indicator of the quality of the professional environment; perceived influences on news work is another. In the 2008 study, we asked journalists to indicate the extent to which they feel their work is affected by various sources of influence. According to the results, the journalists' work is mostly influenced by professional and procedural factors (see Table 4.5). Procedures and standards of news making, as well as conventions of the profession in general and the newsrooms in which the journalists work, are by far the most important perceived sources of influence. The omnipotent power of pressing news deadlines, the restrictions imposed by limited newsroom resources, and ever-changing new media technologies also belong to this category.

The audience and their sensibilities, together with the limits set by media laws, form another group of substantial influences in the journalists' views. The audience constitutes, by the very nature of mass communication, an essential reference for journalists, and the importance of media laws stems from the fact that they provide the legal ground on which journalists operate. This hardly comes as a surprise. The significance of the audiences' sensibilities, however, is a very specific feature of Indonesia's media system. While Indonesia has initially greeted press freedom with great enthusiasm, there are numerous examples in which journalists and their media organizations were attacked by groups of religious or political radicals who felt their sensibilities offended by certain media coverage (Haryatmoko 2002). This is one of the reasons why the influence of religious leaders is perceived to be relatively strong. Especially when they have to cover sensitive topics, such as religious affairs and corruption, journalists and editorial decision makers tend to be

Table 4.5   Influences on News Work (2008, $N = 100$)

	Mean	SD
Procedures and standards	3.75	1.03
Newsroom conventions	3.72	.98
Professional conventions	3.68	.91
Market and audience research	3.52	.91
Sensibilities of the audience	3.42	.80
News deadlines	3.36	.85
Readers, listeners, or viewers	3.31	.94
Media laws	3.28	.74
Shortage of resources	3.19	.85
New media technologies	3.14	.77
Management	3.08	.88
Competing news organizations	3.08	.93
Ownership	3.06	1.03
Supervisors and higher editors	3.03	.91
Media watch organizations	3.00	.97
Religious leaders	2.94	.70
Journalism unions	2.89	.83
Profit expectations	2.85	.96
News sources	2.81	1.03
Advertising considerations	2.51	1.12
Peers on the staff	2.29	1.18
Advertisers	2.27	.96
Colleagues in other media	2.22	1.11
Government officials	2.12	1.00
Censorship	2.10	1.08
Friends, acquaintances, family	2.10	1.08
Politicians	1.97	.90
Public relations	1.92	.99
Business people	1.90	.84

Scale range: 5 = "extremely influential"; . . . 1 = "not influential at all"

very cautious not to provoke the anger of radicals. This practice often leads to self-censorship as a means of anticipating the potential for intimidation or physical violence.

Table 4.5 also shows that the direct influence of politicians, government officials, and censorship, as well as of businesspeople and public relations, is perceived to be of little relevance. While it is quite common in Indonesia for politicians and business people to use their power to receive favorable media coverage, their influence is often channeled through editorial decision makers and insiders within the media. As such, these influences mostly operate behind journalists' backs and rarely become the subject of direct experience by ordinary reporters.

Economic imperatives are perceived to be of higher importance than political factors, but they are still less significant than professional, procedural, and organizational aspects. In the view of the interviewed journalists, profit expectations, advertising considerations, and advertisers themselves do not belong to the major sources of influence. Only market and audience research seems to have a substantial impact by introducing economic considerations into journalists' work. Organizational factors, including management, owners, and supervisors are perceived to be of less importance.

Role Perceptions and Epistemological Views

The 2008 study was based on a conceptualization that identified three major dimensions of role perceptions (Hanitzsch 2007): (1) Interventionism reflects the extent to which journalists pursue a particular mission and promote certain values. The distinction tracks along a divide between two ideal types of journalist—the one interventionist, involved, socially committed, assertive, and motivated; the other detached and uninvolved, dedicated to objectivity, neutrality, fairness, and impartiality. (2) Power distance refers to the journalist's position in relation to locations of power in society. The critical pole of the continuum captures a kind of journalism that openly challenges those in power, while opportunist journalists tend to see themselves in a collaborative role, as "partners" of the ruling elites. (3) Market orientation reflects the two principal ways of addressing audience members, primarily in their role as citizens or consumers.

In the following paragraphs we will try to synthesize the findings from the two studies along the three dimensions (see Table 4.6). The results, however, are difficult to compare because only a few items used similar wording. Furthermore, the two studies used different response scales, a 4-point scale in the 2001 survey and a 5-point scale in the 2008 study.

With respect to the distinction between interventionist vs. passive reporting, the 2008 data indicate a slight preference for interventionist reporting among Indonesian journalists. Influencing public opinion and advocating for social change were perceived to be of higher importance than a passive understanding of journalists as detached observers. Among the journalists interviewed in 2001, 40% actually rated supporting disadvantaged people as "extremely important," which makes this news function the top priority among Indonesia's news people. Setting or influencing the political agenda, which was of little appeal to journalists in 2001, has become slightly more important in 2008 (see Table 4.6).

Interventionist journalism can go along with both critical and opportunist reporting. Here, the traditional Western understanding of journalism as the Fourth Estate of power is also deeply embraced by Indonesian journalists. Among the top priorities of journalists listed in the 2001 study were criticizing bad states of affairs; monitoring politics, business, and society; and investigating claims and statements of the government. However, they did not see themselves as adversaries of the government or the business world. The journalists' critical impetus changed little in the 2008 survey. Opportunist journalism, on the other hand, is of only little relevance. Only a few journalists find it extremely important to support official policies to bring about prosperity and national development, and even fewer are interested in conveying positive images of political and business leadership (see Table 4.6).

The results regarding the prevalence of professional traits that could be related to a journalistic philosophy relating to national development are fairly ambivalent. On the one hand, Indonesian journalists see the need for a more assertive and interventionist mode of reporting in the context of the country's ongoing political transition and economic development. On the other hand, any affirmative attitude toward policymakers and business leaders is clearly disapproved of by the majority of Indonesian journalists (see Table 4.6). Despite its normative appeal and the presence of journalism education, there seems to be no particularly developmental orientation shared by

Table 4.6   Role Perceptions (% of journalists saying "extremely important" or "strongly agree")

	2001 (N = 385)[1]	2008 (N = 100)[2]
Interventionist vs. passive reporting		
Get information to the public quickly	35.7	—
Be an absolutely detached observer	—	21.6
Support disadvantaged people	40.0	—
Convey positive ideals	24.6	—
Present new trends and convey new ideas	16.4	—
Discuss national policy while it is still being developed	12.7	—
Set/influence the political agenda	12.5	19.2
Influence public opinion	—	27.3
Advocate for social change	—	33.3
Critical vs. opportunist reporting		
Criticize bad states of affairs	37.5	—
Monitor politics, business, and society	26.8	—
Investigate claims and statements of the government	29.4	—
Serve as adversary of the government through skepticism	9.0	—
Serve as adversary of business through skepticism	6.6	—
Act as watchdog of government	—	39.4
Act as watchdog of business elites	—	33.7
Support national development/official policies to bring about prosperity	22.1	9.1
Convey positive image of political and business leadership	—	3.0
Market-oriented vs. citizen-oriented reporting		
Concentrate on news that is of interest for/will attract the widest audience	27.3	40.8
Provide most interesting information	—	47.5
Refer to intellectual and cultural interests of the public	17.2	—
Provide help in everyday life issues	24.3	—
Provide entertainment and relaxation	13.7	—
Give ordinary people the chance to express their views	23.5	—
Motivate people to participate in civic activity	—	43.4
Provide citizens with information needed to make political decisions	—	51.5

1 Scale range: 4 = "extremely important"; ... 1 = "not important"
2 Scale range: 5 = "extremely important"; ... 1 = "not important"

Indonesia's journalists. This finding concurs with results from Romano's (2003) survey of Indonesian journalists, and also with studies from developing countries in Africa and Asia (Chaudhary 2000; Murthy 2000; Ramaprasad 2003; Rampal 1996).

In terms of the distinction between citizen-oriented vs. market-oriented reporting, the results reveal no general tendency among Indonesia's journalists. The political information function of journalism, as well as its potential to motivate people to participate in civic activity and political conversation, does not seem to contrast with an orientation toward the audience and market imperatives. In the view of journalists, the function of journalism to fuel political debate is in fact slightly more appreciated than providing interesting information and attracting the widest audience (see Table 4.6). Furthermore, providing entertainment and relaxation for an audience ranks very low among journalists' priorities. This finding is somewhat inconsistent with the realities of Indonesia's news media that are very much saturated with celebrity news and sensational stories.

With respect to their epistemological beliefs, Indonesian journalists very much seem to follow the path of their Western counterparts. This is not surprising after four centuries of Dutch colonial rule during which Indonesia's mass media were established and began to prosper. Although the struggle for independence brought about an era of "partisan journalism" during the 1940s, this trait seems to have vanished shortly after Suharto came into power in 1966.

Table 4.7 shows that Indonesian journalists are strongly oriented toward some of the "classical" Western journalism values such as impartiality, neutrality, factual accuracy, verification, and credibility. Almost 60% of the interviewed journalists in the 2008 study "strongly agreed" that they make claims only if they are verified by evidence and reliable sources. In the 2001 survey, a majority of news workers found it "extremely important" to get information to the public neutrally and precisely, which made this statement the highest priority among the journalists interviewed in the first wave.

One reason for this similarity to journalists in the West is the relatively strong orientation of Indonesian journalism education toward Western values and models (Hanitzsch 2001). In a similar vein, Indonesian journalists said that their personal beliefs and convictions do not influence reporting and that they rather stay away from stories with content and information that cannot be verified. The moderately strong orientation toward depicting reality "as it is" suggests a still widespread belief in the media functioning as a "mirror" of reality.

Providing opinion, analysis, and interpretation to the audience, on the other hand, is clearly not among the priorities of Indonesia's journalists. In fact, it seems that providing analysis and interpretation has lost its appeal among journalists during recent years, indicating an even stronger orientation toward what are commonly believed to be "typical" Western professional values. Few journalists interviewed in the 2008 study felt committed to the practice of providing orientation in the political conversation about controversial issues: Only 4% of the journalists "strongly

Table 4.7   Epistemological Beliefs (% of journalists saying "extremely important" or "strongly agree")

	2001 (N = 385)[1]	2008 (N = 100)[2]
Get information to the public neutrally and precisely	53.5	—
Remain strictly impartial	—	29.6
Do not allow beliefs and convictions to influence reporting	—	43.9
(Journalists can) depict reality as it is	40.0	33.7
Facts speak for themselves	—	19.2
Stay away from stories with unverified content / from information that cannot be verified	38.5	43.4
Make claims only if verified by evidence and reliable sources	—	58.6
Provide analysis and interpretation	20.6	9.2
Provide opinion to the public	11.2	—
Always make clear which side has better position	—	4.0

1 Scale range: 4 = "extremely important"; ... 1 = "not important"
2 Scale range: 5 = "strongly agree"; ... 1 = "not agree"

Table 4.8   Controversial Reporting Practices (2001, $N = 385$, % of journalists saying "may be justified")

Pretend another opinion or attitude	80.1
Claim to be somebody else	70.2
Use hidden microphones and cameras	68.3
Pay people for confidential information	67.3
Get employed in a firm or organization to gain inside information	62.1
Use confidential government documents without authorization	31.7
Use personal documents without permission	29.2
Badger unwilling informants to get a story	17.6
Agree to protect confidentiality but not doing so	8.1

agreed" that making clear which side in a dispute has a better position is always part of their reporting (see Table 4.7).

Ethical Views

Indonesian journalists' ethical orientations were measured differently in the two studies. The 2001 survey used a widely applied set of questions that tapped into the way Indonesia's journalists justify methods of reporting that are often perceived to be controversial. Here, evidence points to a two-faceted structure (see Table 4.8). It seems that most Indonesian journalists justify controversial reporting practices based on harmless deceptions. It is especially interesting that four of five journalists would pretend to have another opinion or attitude if this helps them to get critical information. And more than 70% would claim to be somebody else in such a case. This seems to be the easiest way to navigate the sometimes difficult territory of obtaining sensitive information.

Using hidden microphones and cameras, paying people for confidential information, and getting employed in a firm or organization to gain inside information are also justified by a majority of Indonesian journalists. These methods may be seen in the context of the practice of investigative reporting. In addition, the justification for providing money in return for sensitive information is also very much supported by a journalistic culture in which journalists accept "envelopes" in return for favorable coverage (see Table 4.8).

Using confidential government documents without authorization, on the other hand, was disapproved by more than two-thirds of the journalists, but there are notable differences. Among those working for national quality newspapers, about 71% actually approved this practice. The results generally point to a much stronger endorsement of investigative journalism among news workers from elite newspapers that are nationally distributed and have an excellent reputation. Similar differences also exist between journalists working in the country's capital, Jakarta, and those based in the more remote provinces of North Sumatra and Yogyakarta. While 47% of Jakarta's journalists generally justified the use of confidential documents, the percentage was much lower among their colleagues in North Sumatra (28%) and Yogyakarta (30%).

At the same time, only a few Indonesian journalists said that they justified reporting practices that might be considered unscrupulous. These methods often involve serious offense and harm. The vast majority of journalists in Indonesia would not consider badgering unwilling informants as proper reporting methods, even if this means they would not get the story. Even fewer journalists would guarantee confidentiality to sources but then not keep their promise (see Table 4.8). As in most other places in the world, such a practice would seriously undermine a journalist's

Table 4.9   Ethical Views (2008, N = 100, % of journalists saying "strongly agree")

There are ethical principles which are so important that they should be followed by all journalists, regardless of situation and context	31.3
There are situations in which harm is justifiable if it results in a story that produces a greater good	31.3
Ethical dilemmas in news coverage are often so complex that journalists should be allowed to formulate their own individual codes of conduct	24.5
Journalists should avoid questionable methods of reporting in any case, even if this means not getting the story	15.2
What is ethical in journalism varies from one situation to another	6.1
Reporting and publishing a story that can potentially harm others is always wrong, irrespective of the benefits to be gained	5.1

Scale range: 5 = "strongly agree"; … 1 = "not agree"

credibility. Using personal documents without permission seems to be a borderline case. Three out of 10 journalists interviewed said that they would justify this reporting method under certain circumstances.

In the 2008 study, the measurement of ethical beliefs followed a different and more abstract approach. It was argued that the fact that certain reporting practices are justified in some countries, while in others they are not, does not necessarily indicate that journalists in these countries are less professional. Such behavior may in fact be related to general cultural beliefs about morality and ethical conduct in these societies. The journalists' ethical views were therefore measured by using six abstract indicators that were based on the work of Forsyth (1980).

Table 4.9 shows some interesting results. Most supported was the statement that "there are ethical principles that are so important that all journalists should follow them, regardless of situation and context." A situational approach to ethical decision making, indicated by the statement, "what is ethical in journalism varies from one situation to another," was far less supported by journalists. Somewhat in contrast to the strong disapproval of a situational approach, Indonesian news people also felt that ethical dilemmas in news coverage are often so complex that journalists should be allowed to formulate their own individual codes of conduct (see Table 4.9). This relatively strong subjectivist orientation of Indonesia's journalists may be related to the fact that they have to cope with a legal and moral environment that is characterized by a high degree of volatility, uncertainty, and unpredictability. Under these circumstances, it makes sense that Indonesian journalists try to retain at least some latitude in situations where they confront ethical dilemmas.

This conclusion corresponds with the journalists' attitudes toward the (potential) consequences of using questionable methods of reporting. About one-third of the interviewed "strongly agreed" with the statement that there actually "are situations in which negative consequences for particular individuals or groups are justifiable if the resulting story produces a greater good for the community or society at large." By way of contrast, very few journalists felt that "reporting a story that can potentially harm others is always wrong, irrespective of the benefits to be gained" (see Table 4.9). This again points to journalists' need for flexibility in the often complex circumstances of ethical dilemma situations.

Conclusions

The evidence reported in this chapter clearly suggests that journalism in Indonesia is the domain of an educated, primarily male elite. One indication of the steady move toward professionalization is the relatively high degree of organization among Indonesian journalists. Similar to what has been found in many other national surveys, despite low pay and often difficult working conditions, job satisfaction and professional commitment remain reasonably high.

Another indication of growing professionalism is the considerable amount of professional autonomy reported by the majority of Indonesia's journalists. Journalists in state-owned media organizations feel substantially less autonomous than their colleagues in private media where commercialization has become an important driving force. Altogether, journalists feel that their work is influenced by professional, procedural, and organizational factors more than by political and economic forces. One specialty of Indonesian journalism is the relatively strong influence of religious leaders, a tendency that reflects the country's multiethnic and multireligious society.

In terms of their professional views, Indonesian journalists turned out to be remarkably similar to their counterparts in the West. They very much embrace the idea of journalism serving as the Fourth Estate in democracy, and they are strongly oriented toward impartiality, neutrality, factual accuracy, verification, and credibility. The partisan style of journalism that endured during Sukarno's regime seems to have vanished from Indonesia's newsrooms. It is only their slightly greater appreciation of interventionist reporting—that is, to influence public opinion and advocate for social change—which sets Indonesian journalists somewhat apart from media workers in Western countries. And although most journalists in the country were socialized into the ideology of the media as being "free but responsible" (Assegaff 1983: 12), there seems to be no particularly developmental orientation shared by Indonesia's news people.

Like many of their colleagues in the West, most Indonesian journalists justify controversial reporting practices based on harmless deceptions, but only a few of them would consider methods of investigation that involve serious offense and harm. One striking difference from Western journalists is the relatively strong subjectivist orientation among Indonesia's journalists when it comes to the way they go about professional ethics. These differences may reflect the rather weak legal and moral environment, as well the high degree of uncertainty that comes with it. The evidence reported in this chapter, however, shows that despite the often ambiguous context and political conditions in which Indonesia's journalists carry out their work, there are positive signs of growing professionalism.

Notes

1. See http://freedomhouse.org/template.cfm?page=16.
2. See http://en.rsf.org/press-freedom-index-2009,1001.html.
3. See http://www.freedomhouse.org/inc/content/pubs/pfs/inc_country_detail.cfm?country=7626&year=2009&pf.
4. See http://www.kpi.go.id.

References

Abar, Akhmad Z. 1998. Pers reformasi [Reform press]. *Bernas*, July 22, 4.

Anwar, H. Rosihan. 2001. Pers nasional: dunia macam apa [The national press: What kind of a world]. *Gamma,* January 31, 42–43.

Arismunandar, Satrio. 2002. Dicari, pers yang berpihak dan prorakyat: tanggapan untuk Agus Sudibyo dan Solahudin [Wanted, a press that takes sides and stands up for the people: Response to Agus Sudibyo and Solahudin]. *Kompas*, February 4, 4–5.

Assegaff, Dja'far H. 1983. *Jurnalistik masa kini: pengantar ke praktek kewartawanan* [Journalism today: Introduction to the practice of journalism]. Jakarta: Ghalia.

Budiyanto, Rochman, and Mabroer M. S. 2000. *Kesejahteraan jurnalis antara mitos dan kenyataan: potret sosial ekonomi jurnalis Jawa Timur* [Journalists' wealth between myth and reality: A social-economic portrait of journalists in East Java]. Surabaya: AJI.

Chaudhary, Anju G. 2000. International media images: Is development news ignored in Western and Third World newspapers?, *Media Asia* 27(4):212–219.

Dharma, S. Satya, Neta S. Pane, M. Nurkholis, and A. Mustafid. 2003. *Malpraktek pers Indonesia: dari somasi BJ. Habibie ke tuntutan Tomy Winata* [Malpractices of Indonesia's press: From the B. J. Habibie summons to the lawsuit against Tomy Winata]. Jakarta: AWAM Indonesia.

Eisy, Muhammad R. 2002. Menegakkan kemerdekaan pers [Building press freedom]. In *Direktori pers Indonesia 2002–2003* [Indonesia press directory 2002–2003], edited by Serikat Penerbit Suratkabar, pp. 22–30. Jakarta: SPS Pusat.

Forsyth, Donelson R. 1980. A taxonomy of ethical ideologies. *Journal of Personality and Social Psychology* 39(1):175–184.

Hanitzsch, Thomas. 2001. Rethinking journalism education in Indonesia: Nine theses. *Mediator* 2(1):93–100.

Hanitzsch, Thomas. 2005. Journalists in Indonesia: Educated but timid watchdogs. *Journalism Studies* 6(4):493–508.

Hanitzsch, Thomas. 2006. Selling the autonomy of journalism: The malpractice of corruption among Indonesian journalists. In *Issues and challenges in Asian journalism*, edited by Hao Xiaoming and Sunanda K. Datta-Ray, pp. 169–188. Singapore: Marshall Cavendish Academic.

Hanitzsch, Thomas. 2007. Deconstructing journalism culture: Towards a universal theory. *Communication Theory* 17(4):367–385.

Hanitzsch, Thomas, Maria Anikina, Rosa Berganza, Incilay Cangoz, Mihai Coman, Basyouni Hamada, Folker Hanusch, Christopher D. Karadjov, Claudia Mellado, Sonia Virginia Moreira, Peter G. Mwesige, Patrick Lee Plaisance, Zvi Reich, Josef Seethaler, Elizabeth A. Skewes, Dani Vardiansyah Noor, and Kee Wang Yuen. (2010). Modeling perceived influences on journalism: Evidence from a cross-national survey of journalists. *Journalism & Mass Communication Quarterly* 87(1):7–24.

Haryatmoko. 2002. Etika media dalam situasi konflik [Media ethics in conflict situations]. *Kompas*, February 4, 4–5.

Hidayat, Dedy N. 2002. "Don't worry, Clinton is Megawati's brother": The mass media, rumours, economic structural transformation and delegitimization of Suharto's New Order. *Gazette* 64(2):157–181.

Hill, David T. 1994. *The press in New Order Indonesia*. Needlands: University of Western Australia Press.

Ishak, Otto S. 2002. Konstruk berita: kaum cap kaki tiga [The news construct: Tribe of the "three-legged brand"]. In *Luka Aceh, duka pers* [Aceh hurt, mourning for the press], edited by J. Anto, pp. 198–209. Medan: Kippas.

Johannen, Uwe, and James Gomez. 2001. *Democratic transitions in Asia*. Singapore: Select.

Komisi Penyiaran Indonesia. 2010. *Laporan tahunan 2009* [Annual report 2009]. Jakarta: KPI.

Lavie, Aliza, and Sam Lehman-Wilzig. 2003. Whose news? Does gender determine the editorial product? *European Journal of Communication* 18(1):5–29.

Loeqman, Lobby. 2003. Melihat wajah pers di Era Reformasi [Looking at the face of the press in the Reformation Era]. In *Malpraktek pers Indonesia: Dari somasi BJ. Habibie ke tuntutan Tomy Winata* [Malpractices of Indonesia's press: From the B. J. Habibie summons to the lawsuit against Tomy Winata], edited by S. Satya Dharma, Neta S. Pane, M. Nurkholis, and A. Mustafid, pp. ix–xviii. Jakarta: AWAM Indonesia.

Manzella, Joseph C. 2000. Negotiating the news: Indonesian press culture and power during the political crises of 1997–8. *Journalism* 1(3):305–328.

Ma'ruf, Ade. 1999. Media massa untuk transformasi budaya [Mass media for cultural transformation]. *Bernas*, January 5, 4.

Mursito, B. M. 2000. Industri pers: tumbuhan dalam tekanan dan kebebasan politik [The press industry: Growth in the context of political pressure and freedom]. *Jurnal Ikatan Sarjana Komunikasi Indonesia* (5):17–29.

Murthy, D. V. R. 2000. Developmental news coverage in the Indian press: An analysis of four dailies. *Media Asia* 27(1):24–29/53.

Piliang, Narliswandi. 2002. Televisi di kantong segelintir pemilik: temali bisnis televisi keluarga Soeharto dan Liem Sioe Liong Mengait ke pendatang baru [Television in the pocket of a handful owners: Business links between the Soeharto family, Liem Sioe Liong pulls newcomer]. *Pantau* 4:12–19.

Qodari, Muhammad. 2000. Minim pemberitaan versi Kristen [Little coverage from a Christian angle]. *Pantau* 9:3–12.

Ramaprasad, Jyotika. 2003. A profile of journalists in post-independence Tanzania. *Gazette* 63(6):539–556.

Rampal, Kuldip R. 1996. Professionals in search of professionalism: Journalists' dilemma in four Maghreb states. *Gazette* 58(1):25–43.

Romano, Angela. 2003. *Politics and the press in Indonesia: Understanding an evolving political culture*. London: Routledge.

Sen, Krishna, and David T. Hill. 2000. *Media, culture and politics in Indonesia*. Victoria, Australia: Oxford University Press.

Siregar, Amir Effendi. 2002. Membangun dekokrasi: tantangan politik, ekonomi, dan media [Creating democracy: Political, economic and media-related challenges]. In *Direktori Pers Indonesia 2002–2003* [Indonesian Press directory 2002–2003], edited by Serikat Penerbit Suratkabar, pp. 2–9. Jakarta: SPS.

South East Asian Press Alliance. 2000. *Attacks on Indonesian journalists: January–October*. Jakarta: SEAPA.

Sudibyo, Agus. 2000. Republika antusias memberitakan seruan jihad [Republika enthusiastically reports on calls for jihad]. *Pantau* 9:26–34.

Sudibyo, Agus. 2003. Menimbang kembali KPI [Reconsidering KPI]. *Kompas*, December 15, 4.

Vatikiotis, Michael R. J. 1993. *Indonesian politics under Suharto: Order and pressure for change*. London: Routledge.

Weaver, David H., and G. Cleveland Wilhoit. 1991. *The American journalist* (2nd ed.). Bloomington: Indiana University Press.

Weaver, David H., and G. Cleveland Wilhoit. 1996. *The American journalist in the 1990s*. Mahwah, NJ: Erlbaum.

Weischenberg, Siegfried, Martin Löffelholz, and Armin Scholl. 1998. Journalism in Germany. In *The global journalist: News people around the world*, edited by David H. Weaver, pp. 229–255. Cresskill, NJ: Hampton.

5   The Japanese Journalist in Transition
Continuity and Change

Shinji Oi, Mitsuru Fukuda, and Shinsuke Sako

Japanese journalism embraces the principles of societal service, press freedom, editorial independence, and, like its Western counterparts, is undergoing substantial change. Throughout the past two decades, newspapers and broadcasters have had diminished sales and advertising profits. Internet news is more popular than ever—especially among the younger generation—and technological advancements have rapidly spread media that are available on personal computers and mobile phones. While 70% of the Japanese public rates their nation's press as reliable and satisfying (National Opinion Survey on the Media 2010), a better understanding is necessary of how these economic and technological changes affect journalism in Japan.

So far, most research on Japanese journalists has focused on professional accounts or normative journalistic practices. This chapter presents findings about what Japanese journalists think about their changing environment based on research conducted by *Shimbun Gaku Kenkyujo* [the Institute of Journalism & Media Studies; IJMS] at Nihon University in 2007.

The Japanese Media

Although Japan has one of the world's most advanced media systems, the structure of its news media differs from those in other democracies in three important ways. First, while newspaper readership and revenues have declined in recent years, Japanese newspapers still have greater reach than in most other industrialized nations—due largely to the concentrated ownership of five daily publications that each serve more than 1 million readers. Second, five commercial television networks, closely affiliated with the five major newspaper companies, dominate local affiliate programming. As a consequence, most of Japan's news and entertainment media are controlled by only a few large newspapers and television stations that cooperate closely.

Third, news coverage in Japan depends heavily on the *Kisha* (journalist) club system, which tightly controls access to news sources and press conferences. The *Kisha* clubs operate as a kind of cartel for news based on close relationships between journalists and their sources. This brings about traditionally bland and homogenous journalism (Feldman 1993; Freeman 2000; Kim 1981), which combined with the limitations of the *Kisha* system, leads to both an absence of investigative reporting and the public's distrust of the media.

Freedom of the press is guaranteed by Japan's constitution. There are rules against cross-ownership of media, as well as regulations that limit newspaper holdings in broadcasting. However, the government controls the free flow of news and information and suppresses free expression of news media through the *Kisha* clubs. While a few national newspaper companies have close relationships with several national broadcasters through stock holding and interlocking directorships (Cooper-

Chen 1997), the broadcasters have built national TV networks and dominated local affiliates as well as their programming. Both large cross-media ownership and concentrated ownership are characteristics of Japan's media structure, compared to the media structures of other Western nations.

The Japanese press was born in the late Shogunate (1603–1868) and early Meiji (1868–1912) eras, which were influenced by the Western press system. The Meiji government adopted a policy of *fukoku kyohei* (enrich the country and strengthen the military) and subsequently guaranteed freedom of the press under the Meiji constitution (1889). During the Taisho era (1912–1926), the press grew into a mass-circulation medium and fostered a boom in democratic thought and party politics. In 1926, however, Japan fell under military rule. The militaristic government of the early Showa era gradually intensified press censorship during World War II and forced Japanese newspapers and radio stations to cooperate with the war effort.

At the end of World War II, the U.S.-led Allied occupation forces immediately abolished all press restrictions. Since then, Japanese journalism has been heavily influenced by the American model. As the Japanese media accepted their role as a cornerstone of a democratic society, Japanese journalists quickly adopted the principles of objectivity, impartiality, detachment, and the separation of fact from opinion. In addition, under the guidance of the Allied occupation forces, several universities established departments and institutes of journalism to prepare students to enter the occupation and to improve the quality of Japanese journalism.

Today, Japan has 121 daily newspapers with a total circulation of about 50.4 million copies per day, according to a 2009 survey by Nihon Shimbun Kyokai [the Japanese Newspaper Publishers and Editors Association; NSK]. Japanese newspapers are divided into national, block, local, and sports publications. On average, each Japanese household consumes nearly one newspaper (0.95) each day. The five largest newspapers are *Yomiuri Shimbun, Asahi Shimbun, Mainichi Shimbun, Sankei Shimbun,* and *Nihon Keizai Shimbun,* all based in Tokyo, which reach millions of readers daily. *Yomiuri Shimbun,* for example, has a daily circulation of 10 million. These newspapers are nationally circulated and their combined circulation (26.8 million) accounted for slightly more than half of the total daily newspaper circulation (50.4 million) as of April 2009.

Local newspapers dominate local markets. In addition, Japanese newspapers have a comprehensive, nationwide delivery network, with about 94% of circulation depending on this system. Japan has two major news agencies, Kyodo News and Jiji Press. Kyodo is similar to the Associated Press in being a non-profit, cooperative news service that serves domestic media outlets. Jiji provides economic information to the government and to private corporations, including publishing firms.

The Japanese TV broadcasting system, which is composed of both public and commercial channels, was established in the 1950s. The public broadcaster is Nippon Hoso Kyokai [Japan Broadcasting Corporation; NHK], which is comparable to the United Kingdom's BBC in terms of quality and the size of its operations. For example, in addition to terrestrial TV (54 local stations), NHK operates satellite TV and radio networks across the country. Like other public broadcasters, NHK depends on a subscription fee for its revenue, which was about 670 billion yen in 2010. NHK also operates various media businesses, including program production companies, a publishing firm, and a symphony orchestra.

Along with NHK, the five largest commercial television networks are Nihon TV, TBS TV, Fuji TV, TV Asahi, and TV Tokyo. They respectively provide various television programs for their local affiliates. The penetration rate for television is 99% in Japan, which makes it a truly national medium. Four of the five commercial broadcasters have formed large, cross-media ownership groups with newspapers—Nihon TV with *Yomiuri*, TV Asahi with *Asahi*, TV Tokyo with *Nihon Nikkei*, and Fuji TV with *Sankei*. These relationships allow newspapers to have close links with TV stations, both in stock and human relations, reflecting a historical situation in which newspaper companies led the establishment of the nationwide broadcasting system after World War II (Yada 2007). Although highly concentrated news industries do not automatically lead to dictatorships, the situation does pose real dangers to basic democratic tenets (Bagdikian 2000).

Weekly newsmagazines, or *shukanshi*, in Japan comprise a genre of news media without any real parallel in the Western world. According to circulation data of the Nippon Zasshi Kyokai (Japan Magazine Publishers Association; JMPA), in 2010, *Shukan Bunshun* had a circulation of 720,000, and *Shukan Sincho* had a circulation of 610,000. As these weekly newsmagazines are not permitted to join the *Kisha* clubs, they take a different approach to news coverage in both content and style from the mainstream media. Were it not for the *Kisha* clubs, these magazines could not exist in their current form (Gamble & Watanabe 2004).

While the Internet in Japan plays a complementary role to newspapers and TV for audiences, it is also gradually superseding the role of mainstream media. Younger generations in Japan increasingly obtain news through the Internet. According to the White Paper on Information and Communication in Japan (Ministry of Internal Affairs and Communication of Japan 2010), the Internet reached about 94 million people by the end of 2009, an increase of 47 million from 2000, with a penetration rate of 78%. The 2009 figures are twice those of 2000. Among younger age groups, the penetration rate is high, reaching 97% for those in their 20s and 96% of those in their 30s.

As in other nations, Japanese mass media have been shaken by the digitalization of information and communication technology that began in the mid-1990s. Traditional news media have lost audiences to online media and quickly lost sales and advertising revenue. Yet the dominance of the Japan's big five newspaper and TV networks have kept audience erosion and competition from new media (such as citizen-based news media) from being as severe as in the United States and other industrialized nations.

Previous Studies

Most Japanese journalism research is difficult to compare cross-nationally because of the objectives and methods of the studies. Because most Japanese media generally have national audiences, most research has focused on specific aspects and practices within the country. Research that uses surveys similar to other countries, or work that places Japanese journalism in an international context, is less common.

The first study on Japanese journalists was conducted in the early 1980s by Kim (1981). In *The Japanese Journalist,* Kim studied a limited number of reporters and government officials, largely through interviews and field research. Kim made it clear how reporters depend on official news sources in news production. He discussed not only the highly competitive entrance examination and on-the-job training, but also role conceptions and other orientations of Japanese reporters.

Feldman (1993) used surveys and interviews to analyze interrelationships between members of the Diet and political journalists. He found that the nature of political reporting was affected by these interrelationships, and concluded that *Kisha* clubs were the ultimate factor to be considered in any attempt to understand how Japanese journalists covered political events.

Cooper-Chen (1997) explored various characteristics of Japanese mass media, with particular importance placed on the insularity, homogeneity, and harmony that characterize Japanese media. She also found that homogeneous journalism as an institution in Japan exerted a great influence on journalistic practices and pointed out how the *Kisha* system limited independent activities.

Yada (2007) analyzed Japanese media between the mid-1980s and 2005, and found that the most conspicuous change was the simplification and trivialization of hard news. He concluded that journalists did not sufficiently provide their audience with a range of news that enabled them to effectively think about and understand their society and history.

More recently, Takeshita and Ida (2009) researched the Japanese system of political communication. They pointed out that understanding the relationship between politics and the media hinges on three unique characteristics: the *Kisha* clubs, the editorial policy of neutrality, and differences between public and commercial news broadcasts.

While these studies have contributed greatly to a better understanding of Japanese journalism, none were based on representative survey data. However, two large surveys of newspaper and broadcasting journalists were conducted in the mid-1990s. The first true survey of Japanese journalists was carried out in 1994 by the NSK and was based on a national sample of 1,735 newspaper journalists. The second was conducted in 1996 by *Nippon Minkan Hoso Remmei* (National Association of Commercial Broadcasters in Japan; NAB) and focused on a national sample of 865 commercial broadcast journalists. Both surveys were based in part on the research carried out by Weaver and Wilhoit (1986) regarding American journalists.

This chapter discusses the findings of the most recent survey by the Institute of Journalism & Media Studies (IJMS) at Nihon University in 2008. It not only shares a number of interests and topics with the NSK and NAB surveys, but also the recent survey of U.S. journalists by Weaver and colleagues (2007).

Method

The IJMS survey defined Japanese journalists as news people—reporters, editors in news organizations, and directors for TV news programs—responsible for the production of news. The 2007 *Japanese News Media Directory*, which is considered the most representative list of journalists in Japan, was used to create a sample of 5,494 randomly chosen journalists for the study. The sample included reporters and editors from organizations of various sizes in Japan, but the majority was composed of executive staff, managing editors, city editors, copy editors, news directors, and similar positions. The average age of the sample was older than that of journalists in general, and the percentage of female journalists was less than that of the overall workforce of journalists.

The survey was conducted by mail from February 13 to March 9, 2007. A total of 1,011 valid questionnaires were returned, for an overall response rate of 18.4%. Respondents were asked questions that focused on: (1) the demographic backgrounds of journalists; (2) perceived roles of journalists; (3) journalistic practice; (4) the perceived self-image of journalists; (5) the perception of journalistic professionalism; (6) the recognition of environmental changes in journalism; (7) the perceived impact of online journalism; (8) problems in journalistic practice; (9) objectivity; (10) journalists' opinions of their audiences; (11) journalists' political inclinations; and (12) journalists' relationships with news sources.

Findings

Basic Characteristics

The vast majority of respondents to the IJMS survey are male (97.6%) with an average age of 53.3 years. Most graduated from college (89.5%), while only 3.8% finished graduate school and less than 5% did not go to college at all (see Table 5.1).

Table 5.1   Demographic Background of Journalists (*N* = 1,011)

Characteristic	Percent	Frequency
Male	97.6	987
Female	2.1	21
NA	0.3	3
Age		
Under 30	2.8	28
30–39	4.4	44
40–49	16.7	169
50–59	60.2	609
60 or older	14.6	148
NA	1.3	13
Years Employed as Journalist		
Under 10	34.7	351
10–19	7.5	76
20–29	17.1	173
30–39	33.4	338
More than 40	4.3	43
NA	3.0	30
Education		
Junior High School Grad	0.2	2
High School Grad	4.3	43
Vocational College Grad	0.6	6
College Graduate	89.5	905
Graduate Degree	3.8	38
Other	0.8	8
NA	0.9	9
Employment		
Newspaper Companies	82.2	831
TV Stations	6.0	61
Wire Service	5.4	55
Freelance Journalists	1.6	16
Other	3.3	33
NA	1.5	15
Experience as Reporter?		
Yes	79.2	801
No	20.1	203
NA	0.7	7

The majority of journalists in the survey worked for newspapers (82.2%), while 6% worked for TV stations, 5.4% worked for wire services, and 1.6% worked as freelance journalists. This distribution reflects the actual situation in Japan quite well. The average job experience was 20.3 years, suggesting a well-seasoned group of news people (see Table 5.1).

It should be noted that, according to NSK data, the total number of employees in Japanese newspaper companies and news agencies was 46,433. The average age was 42.1 years, with 14.4% being female. Yet data from the National Association of Broadcasters in 2010 show that the total number of employees in broadcasting companies was 24,709 (average age 41.2 years, 21.5% female). NHK had 10,582 employees (average age 40.3 years, 13.5% female) in 2010.

Roles of Journalism

The goals and responsibilities of Japanese journalists have been affected by dramatic changes in the media environment. This includes technological, political, economic, and cultural forces, as well as the cultural and historical context of the profession itself. To analyze perceptions of journalistic roles, respondents were asked which three roles Japanese journalists should adopt. As Table 5.2 indicates, two roles were considered most important: "providing accurate information" (42.0%) and "serving as a watchdog of the government" (40.3%). The role of "seeking social justice" (11.7%) was a distant third.

However, such findings suggest that the journalistic practices and duties considered important by most journalists are not necessarily put into practice (see Table 5.3). Responses indicate, for example, that while most journalists believe that "getting information to the public quickly" is something Japanese media are good at (90.8% strongly or somewhat agree), they also believe they are not very successful at "investigating the activities of the government" (29.8% strongly or somewhat agree). Although the watchdog role is considered an important media function, only about one-third of Japanese journalists believe they actually fulfill this role.

Table 5.2   Journalists' Role Perceptions (in %, $N = 1,011$)

What are the three most important roles of journalism?	*First*	*Second*	*Third*
Providing accurate information	42.0	18.5	18.6
Watchdog of government	40.3	26.5	15.6
Quest for social justice	11.7	21.7	17.0
Rousing public opinion	1.5	11.3	9.4
Agenda setting of social issues	1.4	7.5	8.7
Speaking for the distressed	0.6	6.6	13.8
Proposal of policy	0.5	1.8	1.8
Education and enlighten	0.3	1.9	4.3
Creation of social consensus	0.3	0.7	2.2
Providing entertainment	0.2	0.5	2.0
Providing forum for discussion	0.2	2.3	5.5
Other	0.7	0.3	0.4
N/A	0.4	0.5	0.7
Total	100.0	100.0	100.0

Table 5.3   Perceived Actual Role Performance of Journalists (in %, N = 1,011)

	Strongly agree	Somewhat agree	Somewhat disagree	Strongly disagree	Don't know	Total %
Concentration on interesting news	33.8	57.0	8.2	0.3	0.7	100.0
Getting information to the public quickly	33.5	57.3	7.7	1.0	0.5	100.0
Avoiding unconfirmed information	31.9	45.0	17.2	4.5	1.4	100.0
Advocacy on social issues	13.9	51.5	30.8	3.0	0.8	100.0
Proposal of national policy	13.6	59.6	23.1	3.3	0.4	100.0
Providing interesting stories	12.3	56.9	26.7	3.1	1.0	100.0
Watchdog of government	8.4	69.0	19.5	2.9	0.2	100.0
Providing entertainment and relaxation	9.6	58.7	27.8	3.5	0.4	100.0
Analysis of complicated issues	6.2	52.2	36.3	4.6	0.7	100.0
Relief for the socially distressed	2.9	41.4	46.2	9.1	0.4	100.0
Investigation of government claims	2.5	27.3	54.9	14.7	0.6	100.0

The Changing Media Environment

As mentioned above, Japanese journalism has been affected strongly by recent economic and technological changes. So how do Japanese journalists feel about them?

Table 5.4 provides an overview of factors Japanese journalists consider to be most important in influencing their profession. Laws about protecting personal information (66.2% considered this item extremely influential); the Internet's impact (56.4%); and decreasing readership and audiences (43.2%) were cited as the three most influential factors. While the Internet's impact on traditional journalism and declining media audiences has been observed in other industrialized nations, nearly half the respondents (48%) think the Internet and news media in Japan coexist and fulfill a separate function. About one in five (18.8%) perceive the Internet as having a complementary role. Above all, the focus on privacy laws is uniquely Japanese because few other countries have laws with similar provisions. For example, the Protection of Personal Information Act of

Table 5.4   Journalists' Perceptions of Audiences (in %, N = 1,011)

	Extremely Influential	Somewhat influential	Not very influential	Not influential at all	Don't know	Total %
Protection of personal information law	66.2	28.2	4.2	0.4	1.0	100.0
Diffusion of internet in daily life	56.4	32.0	9.2	0.9	1.5	100.0
Decreasing readership & audiences	43.2	36.8	16.5	1.9	1.6	100.0
News production by digital technologies	35.3	38.1	21.1	4.3	1.2	100.0
Increasing damage by media coverage	35.0	55.4	7.9	0.3	1.4	100.0
Development of Web journalism	33.6	39.3	23.4	2.4	1.3	100.0
Other industries' entry into media	22.8	40.1	30.9	4.8	1.4	100.0
Conservative swing of media	22.7	44.7	26.9	4.1	1.6	100.0
Move toward entertainment in media	18.2	41.1	34.8	4.2	1.7	100.0
Self-regulation of media	15.8	48.7	32.4	1.6	1.5	100.0
Tighter controls of jobs & costs	13.9	44.7	35.5	4.2	1.7	100.0
Social pressure against *kisha* clubs	4.8	36.4	49.6	7.2	2.0	100.0

2003 originally stipulated media organizations as private businesses that must protect private information. This aspect of the law was met with strong opposition from the press until finally the law was approved with some exceptions (Yamada 2004).

Because this law could violate freedom of the press and expression guaranteed by Japan's constitution, the NSK continues to seek to revise it. As might to be expected, once in effect the revised law not only has been stretched, but has been applied more arbitrarily and excessively than in Western nations. As a result, various journalistic practices, such as the identification of victims, have been impeded.

Interestingly, Japanese journalists seemed less concerned about more entertainment in the media (18.2%), the growing trend toward self-regulation (15.8%), and tighter cost controls (13.9%), all of which were considered the least important factors.

Relationships with News Sources

Although the *Kisha* system has a significant and controversial influence on newsgathering in Japan, the 2007 IMJS survey did not include questions about it. Instead, the survey focused on the broader context of journalists' relationships with government news sources. Those findings show that about 6 out of 10 Japanese news professionals believe that the relationship between journalists and government sources is "very" (7%) or at least "somewhat" cooperative (58.4%). Only a small minority rates this relationship as "very" (1%) or "somewhat" hostile (13.5%). This suggests that most Japanese journalists believe their relationship with government sources is symbiotic rather than antagonistic.

Views of Audience and Self-Image of Journalists

The 2007 survey also asked journalists what kind of images they had of the general public. Table 5.5 shows these evaluations based on seven perspectives. The first four are related to audiences' trust, expectations, anxieties, and the belief in the necessity of journalism. The remaining three questions sought journalists' assessments of their audiences' ability to make rational judgments, understand important issues, and level of media literacy.

About 42% of the journalists "strongly agreed" that audiences recognize the necessity for journalism, and 27.1% thought that audiences trust and hold high expectations of journalism. However, only about 14% of journalists strongly agreed that audiences actually believe in journalism, and fewer thought that audiences use rational judgments (7.2% strongly agreed) or understand important issues (2.6%).

Table 5.5   Journalists' Perception of Audiences (in %, N = 1,011)

	Strongly agree	Somewhat agree	Somewhat disagree	Strongly disagree	Don't know	Total %
Audience recognizes necessity of journalism	41.9	50.8	5.9	0.4	1.0	100.0
Audience has high expectations	27.1	60.9	10.7	0.3	1.0	100.0
Audience believes in journalism	14.0	69.5	14.4	0.9	1.2	100.0
Audience has anxiety about journalism	10.1	61.2	25.8	1.5	1.4	100.0
Audience uses rational judgment	7.2	52.1	35.9	3.5	1.3	100.0
Audience has media literacy	4.5	56.5	34.0	1.7	3.3	100.0
Audience cannot understand issues	2.6	40.0	48.8	7.3	1.3	100.0

Such mixed results may reflect ambivalence on the part of journalists toward their audiences. Generally speaking, Japanese journalists are elite, well-educated, and high-income earners compared with ordinary citizens. Because journalists belonging to *Kisha* clubs, for example, often spend most of their waking hours working sources, it is difficult for them to keep in personal touch with the public on a daily basis. Such factors may contribute to journalists' low estimation of their audiences.

Questions about how Japanese journalists saw themselves compared to the general public provided additional information. While journalists viewed themselves as professionals (47.7%) and opinion leaders (37%) with a strong sense of justice (60.4%), they also felt that the public sees them as arrogant (60.6%), impudent (58.2%), and elitist (39.9%). In sum, Japanese journalists perceive themselves positively, but do not necessarily think the public sees them in such terms. Although the reasons vary, it seems clear that while journalists are confident that they accomplish their mission, they feel that journalistic credibility and trust is deeply eroded by a series of scandals that include false or fabricated stories and inaccurate quotations (Tase 1994).

The Principle of Objectivity

According to recent findings from comparative studies, the principle of journalistic objectivity is widespread in liberal democracies and countries with a strong journalistic partisanship (Oi 2003). Japanese journalism has embraced the principle of *fuhen futo* ("principle of neutrality") since the Meiji era, which is slightly different from the concept of objectivity. As noted, Japanese journalism was heavily influenced by the American model of journalism after World War II. Although the principles of objectivity, impartiality, detachment, and separation of fact from opinion were quickly adopted, they have been modified gradually in accordance with the spirit of *fuhen futo*. Objectivity is an assertion that facts should be reported fairly and in as balanced a way as possible (Knowlton & Freeman 2005). The principle of *fuhen futo* demands more. It states that journalists not only should be impartial observers or bystanders of events, but also should not take sides in analytical or editorial stories (Takeshita & Ida 2009).

A clear majority of Japanese journalists cite "accurate news reporting based on facts" (83.3%), "a fair and impartial attitude" (63.5%), and "facts separated from opinion" (57.8%) as meaningful reflections of objectivity in Japanese journalism. The "spirit of *fuhen futo*," however, is mentioned by slightly less than half of respondents (47.5%).

Although these findings may seem to show that most Japanese journalists see objectivity in much the same way a Western journalist would, Japanese concepts about objectivity are often varied and lack accurate definitions (Oi 2003, 2008). Since the Meiji era, *fuhen futo* has been used to justify numerous journalistic roles and sometimes has been employed to support military governments. In the best cases, *fuhen futo* led to an editorial policy that was, as the term indicates, "objective and fair." In too many cases, however, it was used to justify criticizing only the safest targets, such as issues and individuals that met with government disapproval or those that other papers already criticized without serious repercussion (Gamble & Watanabe 2004).

To grasp the perceived meaning of objective reporting in more detail, respondents also were asked whether it was permitted to insert interpretation into factual reporting. Most journalists (72%) thought it was all right to do so if facts are clearly separated from opinions, while 62.3% said it was permissible in news commentary and 39.7% said it was permissible if there is a byline (Oi, Sako, & Miyawaki 2009).

One of the IJMS survey's goals was to compare the attitudes of Japanese and American journalists regarding ethical dilemmas. Based on questions developed for U.S. studies conducted by

Table 5.6　Journalists' Willingness to Use Reporting Methods (in %, N = 1,011)

	May be justified	Not sure	Cannot be justified	Don't know	Total %
Using documents without permission of government, business, or organizations	55.8	34.3	9.1	0.8	100.0
Badgering unwilling informants to get story	14.6	55.7	28.8	0.9	100.0
Using hidden cameras and microphones	7.1	40.6	51.7	0.6	100.0
Paying for information	6.0	29.4	64.0	0.6	100.0
Using personal documents such as letters and photographs without permission	2.2	21.8	75.3	0.7	100.0
Claiming to be somebody else	1.7	12.1	85.7	0.5	100.0
Agreeing to protect confidential sources and not doing so	1.5	16.3	81.5	0.7	100.0

Weaver and his colleagues (2007), the survey asked journalists to indicate whether they believe certain reporting methods may be justified under special circumstances.

As Table 5.6 shows, the only reporting method accepted by most Japanese journalists was "using documents without permission"—55.8% said it may be justified. Badgering unwilling informants to get a news story was justified by 14.6%, and using hidden cameras by only 7.1%. Paying for information was considered justifiable under special circumstances by only 6%, with other questionable methods receiving even less support. Such findings exemplify bland, uncontroversial journalism in Japan that offends neither readers nor advertisers. Moreover, because Japanese journalists believe it is their task to help defuse conflict rather than reflect it, much remains unreported (van Wolferen 1993: 439).

Problems in Japanese Journalism

Problems cited by Japanese journalists as urgent matters of concern are listed in Table 5.7. The biggest concern was the growing conformity and uniformity in news reporting (75.4%), which

Table 5.7　Perceptions of Main Problems in Japanese Journalism (in %, multiple answers permitted, N = 1,011)

Perceived Problems	Percentage
Too much uniform, conformist news reporting	75.4
Too many press releases	64.0
Tendency to make passing news reporting	63.9
Less in-depth media coverage	53.5
Sensationalism	44.7
Lack of critical spirit	38.2
Important facts may not be covered	32.3
Accommodation to the public needs	30.5
Mixture of fact and opinion	27.6
There is no constructive proposal	20.6
Collusive relationship with the news sources	14.8
Too much news that disregards human rights	9.2
Too many anonymous sources	9.0
Other	1.5

references a common criticism that Japanese journalists work in step with their colleagues and decline distinction by trying not to break news first. The next biggest concern was an over-reliance on government and organizational press releases (64%), followed by a preference for "temporary" news reporting (63.9%). The fourth most selected problem was a lack of in-depth reporting and superficial event coverage (53.5%).

Respondents also were asked how to improve Japanese journalism, and what was necessary to enrich and refine journalistic practices (see Table 5.8). Most journalists (82.9%) noted that there is a clear need to improve journalism education and training in Japan. A majority (52.2%) also thought journalism could be improved by encouraging free expression without organizational restraints (52.2%) and giving broader power to editors and sub-editors (50.5%). Journalism training in Japan remains unstructured, largely based upon on-the-job training or apprenticeships (Gaunt 1992). Accordingly, almost all journalists receive on-the-job training in the organizations that employ them. The virtual absence of schools of journalism in Japan might be recognized as a serious problem (Oi 2009a, 2009b).

Journalists were asked to evaluate the journalistic practices of organizations they work for. The vast majority found that practices were either "very good" (20.1%) or "good" (60%). Only about one in five journalists offered a "fair" (14.7%) or "poor" (3.9%) evaluation. More than half were satisfied with their jobs, with 4.8% claiming to be "very satisfied" and 44% of them "somewhat" satisfied. However, a significant number of journalists also said that they were either "somewhat" (38.7%) or "very dissatisfied" (3.6%).

To determine what factors might influence the job satisfaction of Japanese journalists, a multiple linear regression analysis was performed that tested the impact of journalists' years in the occupation, education, evaluation of journalistic practices, relationships with government news sources, and relations with the government in general.

The results suggested the most influential predictor of job satisfaction was their evaluation of journalistic practices at their news organizations ($b = .37$, $p < .001$), followed by relationships

Table 5.8 Perceived Solutions of Problems in Japanese Journalism (in %, multiple answers permitted, $N = 1,011$)

Perceived Solutions	Percentage
Enrich education and training for journalists	82.9
Encourage free expression	52.2
Give broader power to editors	50.5
Increase personnel	43.7
Ensure autonomy for journalists	31.8
Alter lack of understanding of business managers	30.8
Reduce outside pressure on journalism practice	23.5
Strengthen cooperation with branch offices	21.3
Upgrade hardware of news reporting	18.2
Reduce pressure from business manager	15.1
Improve system of foreign news reporting	12.9
Expand effective outsourcing	8.8
Increase the number of full time workers	6.6
Other	1.8

with the government in general ($b = .09$, $p < .02$). All other associations, including demographic factors, were insignificant.

Conclusions

Entering the second decade of the 21st century, Japanese journalism has been shaken by the digitalization of information and communication technologies, and the emergence of Internet news outlets that increasingly have attracted younger generations. Traditional news media seek a new way to suitably fulfill their mission. Yet Japan's five largest newspapers and five largest TV networks still hold dominant positions, and it is no exaggeration to say they constitute monoliths of Japanese journalism.

In these changing times, Japanese news media face several problems. Above all, they are confronted not only with declining circulation and advertising revenues, but shrinking credibility with audiences. In addition, the convergence of new media outlets is transforming the quality of journalistic work and the traditional mode of on-the-job journalistic education. To see how these changes affected Japanese news professionals, this chapter focused on the results of a 2007 survey conducted among 1,011 journalists. Among the key findings was that Japanese journalists identify accuracy and watching the government as the chief roles. However, these findings also suggest that practices and duties considered important by most journalists are not necessarily put into practice. For example, while most journalists believe that "getting information to the public quickly" is something Japanese media are good at, they also believe they are not very successful in "investigating the activities of the government."

As for the image of journalists, differences appear between self-image and the image they perceive their audiences to have. For example, many journalists think they are perceived by most of the public as arrogant or impudent, yet most journalists see themselves as having a strong sense of justice, or as opinion leaders. Journalists also have a low opinion of the public's intellectual faculties. This seems to stem from the fact that journalists do not stay in touch with the public because they are part of the elite, well-educated, and high income earners. Most journalists are university graduates, compared to about 10% of Japan's total population, according to the nation's 2005 census.

Japanese journalists tend to move in step with their colleagues and, as a result, rarely achieve distinction by breaking news. A trend of overly conformist and uniform reporting is a major concern. This may be due to an over-reliance on government and organizational press releases, but it also could be a symptom of the *Kisha* club system of reporting. Most Japanese journalists spend the entire day with fellow *Kisha* members, and generally have little contact outside this environment. Their club makes collective decisions on what members may or may not report, and occasionally determines even the tone of their report (van Wolferen 1989). The *Kisha* system makes for cozy relationships with sources, whose activities and aims *Kisha* members are expected to investigate and report. There is little incentive for journalists to investigate anything independently, and there is no reward for presenting a case in a manner that offends their colleagues.

Along with roles and performance, another concern among Japanese journalists is that government has placed various restrictions on public information, which affects reporting practices. Although the Protection of Personal Information Law recognizes that citizens have the right to control information about themselves, including details of incidents withheld by police authorities, such laws present numerous obstacles for Japanese journalists. Such findings may suggest that relationships between journalists and government are hostile or adversarial, but cozy links between them are the rule rather than the exception. Likewise, relationships between journalists and public officials, as well as government, are highly cooperative and harmonious. Although watchdog journalism is rated highly in Japan, journalists' actual relationships with public relations staff and government seem to be symbiotic.

Japanese journalists consider education the most important way to improve the quality of journalism in the country. So far, training has been based mainly upon on-the-job experience, while institutions for tertiary education play only limited roles. However, the system of life-long employment in the media industry is gradually breaking down and workforce mobility is rising. In addition, credibility and trust in journalism is deeply eroded by scandals that include false or fabricated stories and inaccurate quotations. These factors may contribute to rethinking the training and education of Japanese journalists.

To resolve the most important problems of Japanese journalism, most journalists contend that more freedom of expression within news organizations and greater authority for editors is needed. Economic conditions surrounding the news industry also have taken a turn for the worse, and most journalists face cost-cutting pressures and staff reductions.

Although web-related media have shaken the existing order of traditional mass media in other industrialized countries, they are considered less of a menace in Japan. This is largely because an established and concentrated commercial media industry controls the country's five largest newspapers and TV networks. Yet according to the NHK data from 2005, as well as NSK data from 2010, TV viewing time has leveled off since 2000. Audience ratings are gradually declining and total newspaper circulation has decreased after peaking in 2001.

Under such unfavorable conditions, Japanese journalists should reaffirm their democratic mission and improve their performance. Moreover, they must sweep away the public's distrust of media and *Kisha* clubs, which are a target of criticism at home and abroad, as they adopt an open-door policy toward the outside world.

References

Akao, Mitsushi. 1994. Gendai shimbun kishazo [The profile of the newspaper journalists in Japan]. *Nihon Shimbun Kyokai Kenkyujo Nempo* [Annals of Institute of the Japan Newspaper Publishers and Editors Association] 12: 1–91.

Bagdikian, Ben H. 2000. *The media monopoly.* Beacon Press. Boston: Beacon Press.

de Beer, Arnold S. 2008. *Global journalism: Topical issues and media systems,* 5th ed. Boston: Allyn & Bacon.

Cooper-Chen, Ann, with Miiko Kodama. 1997. *Mass communication in Japan.* Ames: Iowa State University Press.

Esser, Frank, and Barbara Pfetsch. (eds.) 2004. *Comparing political communication.* New York: Cambridge University Press.

Feldman, Ofer. 1993. *Politics and the news media in Japan.* Ann Arbor: University of Michigan Press.

Freeman, Laurie Anne. 2000. *Closing the shop: Information cartels and Japan's mass media.* Princeton, NJ: Princeton University Press.

Gamble, Adam, and Takesato Watanabe. 2004. *A public betrayed.* Washington, DC: Regnery.

Gaunt, Philip. 1992. *Making the newsmakers: International handbook on journalism training.* Westport, CT: Greenwood Press.

Institute of Journalism & Media Studies (IJMS). 2008. Nihon no journalist 1000 nin chousa [A survey of Japanese journalism: The profile of 1,000 journalists]. *Journal of Journalism & Media Studies* 1: 85–122.

Kasza, Gregory J. 1988. *The state and the mass media in Japan, 1918–1945.* Berkeley, CA: University of California Press.

Kim, C. Young. 1981. *The Japanese journalists and their world.* Charlottesville, VA: University Press of Virginia.

Knowlton, Steven R. and Karen L. Freeman. (eds.) 2005. *Fair & balanced.* Northport, AL: Vision Press.

National opinion survey on the media. 2010. Retrieved from http://www.chosakai.gr.jp/notification/index2.html

Ministry of Internal Affairs and Communications of Japan. 2010. *The 2010 White Paper on Information and Communications in Japan.* Retrieved from http://www.soumu.go.jp/johotsusintokei/whitepaper/eng/WP2010/2010-index.html

Nihon Shimbun Kyokai (NSK). 2007. Shimbun Jinmei Roku (Japanese News Media Directory), in the 2007 Nihon Simbun Nenkan (Japan Newspaper Annual, 2007). Tokyo: Dentsu.

Nippon Minkan Hoso Renmei Kenkyujo. 1996. Minpo Terebi Hodo Tanto-Sha Chousa [Survey on news people of the commercial TV broadcasting companies]. In *Shuzai no jiyu to kouteki kisei wo kangaeru,* [Considering freedom of news-gathering and regulation], edited by Nippon Minkan Hoso Renmei Kenkyujo, pp. 101–170. Tokyo: Nippon Minkan Hoso Renmei Kenkyujo.

Oi, Shinji. 2003. Komyunikeishon to janarizumu [Communication and journalism]. In *Komyunikeshon no seijigaku* [Politics of communication], edited by Makoto Tsuruki, pp. 127–141. Tokyo: Keio Gijuku Diagaku Shuppan-Kai.

Oi, Shinji. 2008. Nihon no journalist zo [A profile of the Japanese journalist]. *Asahi Soken Report* 212: 27–58.

Oi, Shinji. 2009a. Journalism kyoiku [Journalism education]. In *Shintei shimbun-gaku* [Journalism studies: A new edition], edited by Junichi Hamada, Yasuhiko Tajima, and Keiichi Katsura, pp. 162–172. Tokyo: Nippon Hyoron-Sha.

Oi, Shinji. 2009b. Media, journalism kyoiku [Media and journalism education]. In *Media kenkyu to journalism 21 seiki no kadai* [Media studies and journalism: Challenges in the 21st Century], edited by Toshihiro Tsuganezawa, Takesato Watanabe, and Hideo Takeichi, pp. 300–323. Kyoto: Minerva Shobo.

Oi, Shinji, Shinsuke Sako, and Takeshi Miyawaki. 2009. Jizoku to henka no naka no media hyogen no jiyu [A survey of press freedom in Japan: Continuity and change]. *Journal of Journalism & Media Studies* 2: 151–174.

Takeshita, Toshio, and Masamichi Ida. 2009. Political communication in Japan. In *Political communication in Asia*, edited by Lars Willnat and Annette Aw, pp. 154–175. New York: Routledge.

Tase, Yasuhiro. 1994. *Seiji journalism no tsumi to batsu* [The crime and punishment of political journalism]. Tokyo: Shincho-Sha.

Tsuruki, Makoto. (ed.) 1999. *Kyakkan hodo: Mou hitotsu no journalism Ron* [Objective journalism: An alternative theory]. Tokyo: Seibun Do.

Weaver, David H. 1998. *The global journalist: News people around the world.* Cresskill, NJ: Hampton Press.

Weaver, David H., Randal A. Beam, Bonnie J. Brownlee, Paul S. Voakes, and G. Cleveland Wilhoit. 2007. *The American journalist in the 21st century: U.S. news people at the dawn of a new millennium.* Mahwah, NJ: Erlbaum.

Weaver, David H., and G. Cleveland Wilhoit. 1986. *The American journalist: A portrait of U.S. news people and their work.* Bloomington: Indiana University Press.

Wolferen, Karel van. 1989. *The enigma of Japanese power: People and politics in a stateless nation.* New York: Alfred A. Knopf.

Yada, Yoshikazu. 2007. Journalism in Japan. In *The future of journalism in the advanced democracies*, edited by Peter J. Anderson and Geoff Ward, pp. 175–189. Burlington, VT: Ashgate.

Yamada, Kenta. 2004. Mass media issues. In *Japan's mass media*, edited by the Foreign Press Center/Japan, pp., 117–124. Tokyo: Foreign Press Center.

6 Korean Journalists in the 21st Century

Young Jun Son, Sung Tae Kim, and Jihyang Choi

Just as South Korean society changed dramatically after democratic reforms in 1987, so has South Korean journalism. Before that date, the nation had been ruled by a series of authoritarian regimes. Journalists worked either as "enlightened intellectuals" for the society-at-large, or as "lapdogs" for the politically powerful ruling class. When the last non-democratic regime collapsed in 1987, various new journalistic ideals emerged, such as the "professional journalist" and "government watchdog," and press freedom expedited Korea's democratization (Yang 2007).

In addition to this historical context, the present state of South Korean journalism can be better understood when keeping several factors in mind. First, there is the fierce competition that prevails in Korea. The late-1980s liberalization of media led to more outlets and unprecedented competition to capture audiences. For example, the number of daily newspapers jumped from about 30 to about 100 between 1987 and 1992. During the early 2000s, when competition reached its peak, national dailies even enticed readers with gifts in return for subscriptions (H. H. Cho 2002).

On a related note, the competitive atmosphere prompted a polarization of media, particularly between the conservative print and broadcast press and their progressive adversaries. Although Korean media gained autonomy after the reform, major newspapers still allied themselves with political power factions to protect their interests in the competitive market (Sa 2009). As a result, the progressive TV network MBC, the liberal newspapers *Hangyereh* and *Kyunghyang,* and the left-of-center online news site OhmyNews, for example, are extremely critical of the three conservative newspapers, *Chosun, JoongAng*, and *Donga*. As Park (2007: 186) has pointed out, a variety of inter-media conflicts erupt in Korea due to a lack of "rules of the game" that might mediate those clashes.

However, it is also true that these conflicts are a natural consequence of the expanded ideological spectrum in Korea. After the collapse of authoritarian rule, the ideological spectrum was broadened by successive conflicts between the political left and right in almost every realm of Korean society.

As in many other countries, a third factor concerning Korean journalism is that mainstream media (daily newspapers, magazines, and broadcast television stations) have been losing audiences and experienced huge profit declines. As a result, advertisers have emerged as the most influential element that affects journalists' news selection.

The increase in advertisers' importance reflects the financial distress that the Korean media is enduring. According to the Korea Communications Commission (2009), Korea's total advertising spending in 2007 stood at 8.11 trillion won (US$7.05 billion), which represents a 17% increase from five years ago, whereas advertising sales in newspapers and magazines declined by 11%, from 2.56 trillion won ($2.22 billion) to 2.26 trillion won ($1.96 billion)during the same period. Advertising totals for broadcast television also dropped 13%, from 2.45 trillion won ($2.13 billion) to 2.11 trillion won ($1.83 billion).

Lastly, the perceived role of the "professional journalist" in Korea is becoming blurred. In recent years, the news media have provided more opportunities for citizens to file, record, change, and amend news from their own perspective. While technological changes certainly bring something new to journalism, professional journalists struggle to maintain a traditional role that separates them from self-described journalists writing online.

These current trends in Korean journalism may not be totally new. They might be better understood by comparing them with past conditions, and may bear similarities to or differences from trends found within the larger framework of global journalism. The main purpose of this study is to examine how Korean journalism has changed over time and to provide information that contributes to understanding broader global trends.

Previous Studies

Surveys conducted after democratic reforms in South Korea indicate that the perceptions of Korean journalists have changed over time in accordance with social, economic, and political transformations that likewise have come to pass.

One study focused on journalistic freedom, a collateral boon of the democratic reform. In 1989, journalists were asked to rate their perceived autonomy on a 10-point scale that ranged from 1 ("barely autonomous") to 10 ("almost absolutely autonomous"). The findings (mean = 6.2) indicated that Korean journalists believed they enjoyed a fairly high level of freedom (Korean Press Institute [KPI] 1989). In subsequent years, such ratings remained comparable, with means of 6.0 (KPI 1991) and 7.0 (KPI 1993). As Heuvel and Dennis (1993) observed in a Freedom Forum survey on East Asian media, the Korean press during this period enjoyed unprecedented freedom to criticize government and expanded without restraint. Job satisfaction was also high. In 1991, 37.4% of Korean journalists were "satisfied" with their job, with only 7% "dissatisfied." Another indicator of job satisfaction—journalists' commitment to journalism—was also relatively high. The percentage of those who considered leaving the field was as low as 10.9% (KPI 1991).

This "golden age" for Korean journalists proved to be short-lived. As the number of media outlets increased, competition grew more intense—and journalists' workload increased. In 1997, Korean journalists wrote an average of 11.5 stories a week, and 72.2% considered their workload to be "too much" (KPI 1997). Professional commitment also waned. In 1997, 21.5% of journalists responded that they planned to leave the profession for other jobs—twice the number who responded similarly in a 1991 survey.

In the early 21st century, one of the most distinctive survey findings was a decline in Korean journalists' perceptions of credibility of the press. It should be noted that a tax investigation and audit by the National Tax Service between 1999 and 2001 led to the arrest and detention of four prominent newspaper owners. During their battle with the government, the media tended to frame the issue favorably toward themselves, rather than to report objectively. Criticism of the "privatization of news space and electronic waves" also erupted among journalists themselves (Keum 2001). In the first survey of perceived press credibility, Korean journalists only offered a 5.86 rating out of a 10-point scale, indicating that perceived credibility was not very high (Korea Press Foundation [KPF] 2001).

Another interesting characteristic of Korean journalists is their emphasis on securing a specialty within their profession. Korean journalists have consistently listed the opportunity to specialize as one of the most significant aspects of their job. When respondents were asked in 2007 to rate 10 aspects of their job on a 4-point scale (1 = "not important," 4 = "extremely important"), the top three aspects were the chance of "developing a specialty" (mean = 3.25), "job autonomy" (3.22), and "job security" (3.19). The "chance for advancement" (2.60) and "salary" (3.03) received were deemed less important. The finding that a number of Korean journalists pursued postgraduate courses also reflected their desire to develop a specialty. In 2005, 21.9% of respondents finished or were pursuing a master's degree (KPF 2005).

The surveys also reveal a slight fluctuation over time in perceived importance among 10 different media roles (Oh 2005). The perceived importance "to be a neutral reporter" and "to get information to the public quickly" declined, while "accurate reporting of facts" has consistently been the most important media role. The perceived importance "to be a neutral reporter" dropped from a mean of 3.67 (1999: 2nd rank) to 3.25 (2003: 3rd rank); and again to 3.04 (2007: 4th rank), when evaluated on a 4-point scale. Considering the long-held appreciation of prompt reporting by journalists, the decay in importance of quickly getting information to the public seems to illustrate a significant change. That category has consistently declined from a mean of 3.34 (1999: 4th rank), to 2.89 (2003: 5th rank), to 2.79 (2007: 7th rank).

As the proportion of female journalists has steadily increased, researchers also conducted surveys regarding gender discrimination in the newsroom. Based on a survey of 230 TV journalists, Sohn and Kim (2004) found that females tend to have a higher standard of professionalism and self-evaluation than males, which implies that female journalists struggle to overcome significant social hurdles in their profession. Another survey of 266 female journalists also revealed that perceived gender discrimination increased as females advanced to higher ranks (Hong 2010).

Method

The main goal of this study is to provide a comprehensive analysis of full-time journalists in Korea. Based on a similar study in 1993 (Auh, Lee, & Kang 1998), this research focuses on how Korean journalists have changed during the past two decades. Similar to the 1993 study, this analysis is based on a national survey by the Korea Press Foundation (KPF) in 2009.[1]

Both studies employ similar definitions of journalists and use identical sampling methods, although some measurement methods have been modified and new questions have been added to track changes over time. Combined, these surveys allow changes among Korean journalists during the past 16 years to be tracked.

As with the 1993 survey, journalists for the 2009 survey were chosen through stratified sampling that randomly selected respondents based on location, type of media, beat, and rank. Both studies gathered samples from the *Directory of Korean Journalists* (1993, 2009). Yet the 2009 survey differed from the earlier survey because it was based on personal interviews, while the 1993 survey used questionnaires mailed to journalists. Overall 970 journalists completed the survey in April and May of 2009. Most respondents were employed by daily newspapers (51.4%), followed by TV networks and cable television stations (26.7%), business newspapers (14.4%), wire services (4.7%), and sports newspapers (2.7%).

Basic Characteristics of Korean Journalists

Age and Gender.   The average Korean journalist in 2009 was 38.6 years old, compared to 36.7 years in 1993. This slight rise seems to derive from an increased number of journalists in their 40s. That ratio has grown from 18.7% in 1993 to 39.3% in 2009 (see Table 6.1).

Table 6.1   Age Distribution of Journalists (in %)

Age	1993 (N = 721)	2009 (N = 970)
20–29	16.4	13.2
30–39	54.3	40.1
40–49	18.7	39.3
50 and older	10.6	7.4
Total	100.0	100.0
Mean age	36.7	38.6

The proportion of women journalists in 2009 was low at only 17.8%. While this was more than double the 8.2% found in the 1993 study, the proportion of female Korean journalists remains far lower than in other professions (Organization for Economic Co-Operation and Development [OECD] 2010). In addition, far fewer female journalists were married compared to their male colleagues (female: 35.8%; male: 80.1%).

Education.   The vast majority of journalists (97.1%) held at least a bachelor's degree, somewhat higher than the 94% found in 1993. The most popular major was journalism and mass communications (21.9%), an increase over 13.5% in 1993. This was followed by the humanities and literature (20.7%), social sciences (14.6%), politics and law (14.3%), and business and economics (11.2%).

What stood out in 2009 was the number of graduate diploma holders. A quarter of all traditional journalists (25.1%) held at least a master's degree and 42.4% of those held diplomas in journalism and mass communications. This was followed by politics and public administration (18.9%), and business and economics (11.9%).

Professional Training.   While almost all journalists (98.2%) mentioned the importance of continued education or training, only about a quarter (25.2%) of them had ever participated in such a program. Considering the fact that 30% of journalists had formal training in 1993, professional training among Korean journalists seems to become less common.

When asked about the kind of training needed, 59.6% of journalists chose some sort of specialized knowledge, which reflected their general desire to develop their own specialties. Instead of relying on formal training programs, most Korean journalists (64.1%) try to develop specialized knowledge on their own. Of that amount, 48.7% subscribed to academic or professional journals related to their beat assignments, 13.4% participated in related professional seminars, and 8.8% pursued graduate work.

Political Attitudes.   To measure political orientation, Korean journalists were asked to rate their political views on an 11-point scale that ranged from 0 ("very progressive") to 10 ("very conservative"), and 5 indicating the moderate or neutral center point. The findings indicate that Korean journalists mostly consider themselves slightly progressive (mean = 4.62). Compared to an average of 5.03 in 1993, this indicates a slight move to the political left during the past 16 years.

There was an interesting, though small, discrepancy between journalists' political attitudes and the perceived political attitudes of their employer. When asked to rate their company's political views, most considered their media company to be slightly conservative (mean = 5.72), which implies that journalists tend to consider they are more liberal than the news outlet for which they work.

Table 6.2   Perceived Freedom of Journalists (in %)

Level of Freedom	1993 (N = 727)	2009 (N = 970)
Almost absolutely free	23.2	14.8
Somewhat free	65.2	76.1
Barely free	10.2	9.1
Never free	1.3	—
Total	100.0	100.0

Working Conditions

Workload and Stress.   In the 2009 study, Korean journalists worked an average of 10 hours and 37 minutes per day. Such long and stressful time demands induced 61% of respondents to say that their workload was "too much."

Various issues were mentioned as potential stress factors. When asked to rate factors on a 4-point scale (1 = "strongly disagree," 4 = "strongly agree"), the requirement to "display creativity" in their jobs was named as most important (mean = 3.04). Other key factors were a "lack of professional training" (2.88), "increased workload" (2.84), and an "unfair promotion system" (2.66). Factors such as a "lack of cooperation from colleagues" (2.54), "lack of value-pursuing opportunities" (2.45), and "lack of their right to make decisions" (2.19) were cited less often.

Perceived Freedom.   More than 90% of the respondents said they had reasonable autonomy to select and present the stories they cover. As shown in Table 6.2, 14.8% of journalists in 2009 said they felt "almost absolutely free" and 76.1% considered themselves "somewhat free." Only 9.1% thought they were "barely free." This differs little from the findings in 1993 and implies that perceived press freedom has improved vastly since the transition to democracy and remained at a high level since 1993.

Journalists also were asked to choose three factors that significantly impair their freedom when covering news (see Table 6.3). Findings suggest that advertisers were seen as the most salient fac-

Table 6.3   Factors Impairing a Free Press (in %)

Factors	1993[a] (N = 727)	2009[b] (N = 970)
Advertiser control	9.2	60.8
Government control	15.1	56.7
Newsroom manager	15.3	51.8
Media owner	—[c]	44.3
Lack of media effort	57.4	35.6
Media law and policy	—	19.7
Audience	—	15.1
Interest group	2.6	10.2
Labor union control	0.4	—
Total	100.0	—

[a] In 1993, the question was about "factors impairing a free and responsible press."
[b] Respondents were asked to provide up to three factors impairing a free press (multiple choices).
[c] Indicating the factor was not included in the study.

tor restricting news selection and presentation (60.8%). This reflects the increasingly competitive media market in Korea, as well as the viewpoint that journalism is primarily driven by business interests. The influence of political power was another important factor (56.7%), followed by influence from newsroom managers (51.8%) and media owners (44.3%). About a third of the journalists blamed themselves by mentioning lack of media effort (self-censorship or their newsroom's hierarchical decision-making process) as a factor that impairs press freedom (35.6%).

The results of 1993 and 2009 cannot be compared on exactly equal terms because in 1993, the question was concerned with "factors impairing a free and responsible press." However, one can detect a few notable changes over time. For example, only 9.2% of journalists in 1993 listed advertisers as the most important factor impairing a free and responsible press. At that time, the survey did not include the category of "media owner" as a potential factor in restricted freedom, which implies that the media market was not as commercialized then.

Evaluation of Journalism Activities.   The 2009 survey also sought evaluations of the current state of Korean media on a 5-point scale that ranged from 1 ("strongly disagree") to 5 ("strongly agree"). Findings revealed the belief that "diversity" (mean = 3.14) and "freedom" (3.07) in news coverage characterize Korean media today. Yet journalists also were concerned about "journalistic performance" (2.84), "professionalism" (2.8), and "job satisfaction" (2.7). Fairness rated lowest (2.62) among the six trends surveyed. When asked about the perceived level of fairness within Korean journalism, 3.4% and 44.6% of respondents said "never fair" and "barely fair," respectively, while those who view Korean journalism as "fair" was as low as 13.2% ("somewhat fair": 12.9%; "almost absolutely fair": .3%). In general, journalists' overall perception of Korean journalism is more negative than positive.

Job Satisfaction.   In 1993, most Korean journalists were "fairly satisfied" (58.7%) or "very satisfied" (16.7%) with their jobs. Notably fewer were "somewhat dissatisfied" (21.1%), or "very dissatisfied" (2.8%). As Table 6.4 shows, the proportion of satisfied journalists in 2009 dropped significantly compared to 1993. Those who were "very satisfied" shrank to 5.9% and those who were "fairly satisfied" also declined to 46.2%. At first glance, it seems that journalists in the dissatisfied group also declined when compared to 1993, as 13.9% and 2.2% of respondents answered "somewhat" and "very dissatisfied" with their jobs, respectively. However, this was not the case, as a new category, "neither satisfied nor dissatisfied," was added in 2009. The new category absorbed respondents who previously said they were "fairly satisfied" or "somewhat dissatisfied."

Table 6.4   Job Satisfaction (in %)

Rating	1993 (N=727)	2009 (N=970)
Very satisfied	16.7	5.9
Fairly satisfied	58.7	46.2
Neither satisfied/dissatisfied	—[a]	31.9
Somewhat dissatisfied	21.1	13.9
Very dissatisfied	2.8	2.2
Don't know	0.7	—
Total	100.0	100.0

[a] This answer category was not included in the 1993 study.

Table 6.5   Perceived Importance of Job Aspects

Job Aspects	1993[a] (N = 727)	2009[b] (N = 970)
Job security	93%	3.29
Job autonomy	97%	3.23
Developing a specialty	96%	3.20
Salary	89%	3.12
Welfare	—[c]	3.11
Editorial policy	88%	3.06
Retirement plan	—	3.05
Helping people	95%	2.97
Public duty	—	2.95
Chance to advance	59%	2.69

[a] Numbers indicate percentage saying "important" or "very important."
[b] Numbers indicate means based on a 4-point scale: 1 = "not important at all," 4 = "very important."
[c] This category was not included in the 1993 study.

In terms of job satisfaction, 36% of Korean journalists said they planned to stay in the profession, which is a considerable drop from 53% in 1993. Such sentiments were particularly low among journalists at sports newspapers, with only 3.8% saying that they want to remain in journalism. Journalists at TV networks indicated the highest level of commitment, with 57.9% answering that they would stay.

Importance of Job Aspects.   Korean journalists were asked to indicate the perceived importance of 10 job-related aspects on a 4-point scale, including autonomy, a chance for advancement, job security, salary, and a chance to develop a specialty. As Table 6.5 shows, journalists chose "job security" (mean = 3.29) as most important, followed by "job autonomy," (3.23) "developing a specialty" (3.20), and "salary" (3.12).

There were key similarities between the 1993 and the 2009 results. First, "job autonomy" and "developing a specialty" consistently were seen as significant factors. Likewise, journalists in both surveys saw the chance to advance as least important.

Yet considerable changes over time were also clear. The perceived importance of job security leaped from fourth to first place—and was notably high among journalists at sports newspapers (mean = 3.54), with local newspapers (3.34) tagging along. Given that their level of commitment to journalism was the lowest of all journalists, one possible interpretation would be that sports journalists' low level of job satisfaction is related to their focus on job security.

Professionalism

Media Roles.   Korean journalists were asked to answer 10 questions about the importance of professional media roles. As Table 6.6 shows, most viewed their professional roles as multifaceted, rather than limited to one or two aspects. A large majority (80.1%) thought it was extremely important for journalists to report facts accurately. At the same time, more than half (54.5%) felt it was extremely important to avoid coverage that contains unverified rumors.

Table 6.6   Importance Journalists Assign to Various Media Roles (% saying "extremely important")[a]

Media Roles	2009 (N = 970)
Accurate report of the facts	80.1
Avoid stories with unverified content	54.5
To be a neutral reporter	40.8
Serve as a watchdog of public servants	40.0
Investigate government claims	32.8
Serve as a watchdog of business	32.6
Provide enough analysis of major issues	23.4
Get information to the public quickly	17.5
Let people express views	16.5
Provide open forum for national issues	16.0

[a] This question was not asked in 1993

The special attention placed on accuracy seems to be in line with their evaluations of journalistic activities. One possible interpretation is that Korean journalists' dissatisfaction with the level of fairness has led them to pay more attention to reporting accuracy.

Other notable findings were that only a minority of journalists thought it was extremely important to "investigate government claims" (32.8%) and "provide enough analysis of major issues" (23.4%). Given the traditional analytical and "watchdog" roles that media serve, this pattern requires careful review in terms of a potential shifting relationship between the public, government and journalists.

Reporting Practices.   Korean journalists have debated professional ethics for many years. To measure such values, respondents were asked to rate whether seven controversial reporting practices were "justifiable," "unjustifiable," or whether reporters were "not sure" about their stance (see Table 6.7).

Between 1993 and 2009, there was a slight decline in journalists who under certain circumstances felt it may be justifiable to pay for secret information, use business or government documents without permission, claim to be someone else, use personal documents without permission, or get a job in order to gain insider information. Yet significantly more journalists over

Table 6.7   Justifiability of Various Reporting Practices (% saying "may be justified")

	1993 (N = 727)	2009 (N = 970)
Pay for secret information	27.3	15.9
Use business/government documents without permission	49.8	48.8
Claim to be someone else	58.7	44.2
Reveal confidential source	9.2	15.1
Badger or harass news sources	17.0	66.2
Use personal documents without permission	49.8	48.8
Get employed to gain inside information	36.8	33.6

time were willing to "harass their news sources for information" (a huge increase, from 17% in 1993 to 66.2% in 2009), or "reveal confidential sources" (9.2% in 1993 compared to 15.1% in 2009).

The increased justification for harassing news sources is worth special attention. This pattern could possibly be attributed to Korean journalists' increased dependence on official news sources, combined with an ever-more-competitive media environment. Although the survey did not directly ask why journalists think harassing news sources can be justified, the answers to related questions provide clues to the reasons behind their opinions. When journalists were asked how heavily they depend on certain news providers, the top-ranked supplier was "press release by news sources" (77.4%), followed by "news wire" (56.1%), and "Internet information" (33.0%).

In another ethics-related question concerning reasons for "infringing on human rights in news stories," journalists listed the "excessive competition to scoop" as most critical. Although that is still not a definitive answer, one could infer that the sudden leap in justification for harassing news sources might be related to an increased dependence on sources and the excessively competitive environment in which journalists work.

Internet Use

Running Blogs.   Given the variety of new online technologies in journalistic work, several questions about online activity were added to the 2009 study. The findings indicate that about 23% of journalists have their own blogs. TV journalists (32.6%) and local newspaper staffers (26.7%) were more likely to use blogs than local broadcasters (14.3%) or journalists for national newspapers (22.2%).

The main motivation for Korean journalists to blog seems related to their personal hobbies (35.1%), rather than journalistic activities. Yet journalists increasingly use blogs to "collect information about issues they are interested in" (22.2%), to "offer their personal opinions about journalism and current issues" (14.7%), and "write about stories that do not make the regular news" (6.7%).

Perception of Internet News Sites' Influences on Traditional Media.   While online news sites have drawn audiences from traditional media outlets, most media have embraced new technologies to complement their original print or broadcast products. So how do Korean journalists perceive the influences of Internet news portals on traditional media?

When asked to rate such factors on a 4-point scale, Korean journalists considered the "production of more sexual and brutal news stories" (3.21) and "influence on editing strategies of traditional media" (2.89) to be the most significant impacts (see Table 6.8). This suggests a sense of crisis concerning the possibility that new channels for news presentation would destroy the existing ecosystem of journalism by promoting more sensational news, by changing editing strategies, or by weakening the authority of media.

A closer look at the survey's results reveals mixed views on the impact of Internet-based news. While Korean journalists mostly focused on negative aspects, they also admitted to positive effects by agreeing that it raises "issues that traditional media do not cover" (2.67) and provides "audiences with diverse perspectives" (2.58).

Table 6.8   Perceived Impact of Internet News Sites on Traditional Media (in %)[a]

Perceived Impact	2009[b] (N = 970)
Induce production of sexual and brutal news stories	3.21
Influence on editing strategy of traditional media	2.89
Raising issues that traditional media do not cover	2.67
Weakening authority of traditional media	2.63
Providing audiences with diverse perspectives	2.58
Destructing news values of traditional media	2.57
Help increase profit	1.93

[a] This question was not asked in 1993.
[b] Numbers indicate means based on a 4-point scale: 1 = "strongly disagree," 4 = "strongly agree."

Conclusions

A comparison of contemporary Korean journalists with those of 1993 reveals consistencies and inconsistencies alike. The proportion of female journalists more than doubled from 8.2% to 17.8%. Female journalists are less likely to marry than male journalists (35.8% to 80.1%, respectively). This seems to reflect the consistently male-centered makeup of Korean media, and it seems to imply that journalism is not yet a friendly field for married women. S. Cho and Davenport's study (2007) of gender discrimination in Korean newsrooms provides some clues to this trend. Their findings, based on a survey of 102 female journalists, showed that 60% of those with children said they were denied assignments not only because of their gender, but their role as a parent.

Also noteworthy is the struggle for Korean journalists to maintain their professionalism. Even though it is still debated whether journalism is a true profession, the idea of professionalism is long-cherished among Korean journalists (Lee & Kim 2006). Yet it seems obvious that some sort of shift has occurred regarding their occupational perception.

Job security and salary have suddenly become matters of greater importance. Given that journalists' priorities previously had been either "autonomy" or "developing a specialty" since the Korea Press Foundation began biennial surveys in 1989, this change suggests a very interesting trend. Even in the 2007 survey, Korean journalists listed "developing a specialty" as their most important consideration (3.25 on a 4-point scale) with autonomy (3.22) close behind. Traditionally, Korean journalists have been less likely to consider salary as an important part of their job. In the 1993 survey, "salary" was the fifth most important aspect out of seven choices offered.

Given that "autonomy" and "ability to develop a specialty" are viewed more as professional aspects than a "salary," "job security," or the "chance to advance" (McLeod & Hawley 1964), it can be inferred that Korean journalists' once-robust perception as belonging to a true profession is wavering. Although further study may be needed to clarify what prompted this trend, it might also be indicative of the current general state of journalism's instability.

The survey also reveals journalists' ambivalence toward the Internet. The Internet has had significant effects on journalism because of its immediacy and convergence of its multimedia features. The rapid diffusion and use of online media has transformed Korean journalism and helped create online journalism as a new field (J. H. Cho & Ban 2007; Kim 2008).

As emerging technology has expanded the reach of media—forcing traditional practitioners to adapt and change—most Korean journalists use the Internet to gather information and keep in touch with audiences (Kim 2008). Yet some also view the Internet negatively, believing that it promotes sensational news, transforms editing strategies, or weakens the authority of traditional news outlets. According to one Internet user survey (KPF 2007), online news portals have become the most important news source for the Korean population. About 60% of the respondents said they access such sites as Naver, Daum, Yahoo Korea, and Nate at least once a week for news. Moreover, they prefer portal sites to other types of news media, including newspapers and broadcasting. This presents the possibility that the impact of Internet news sites on traditional media could become even further pronounced.

The main goal of this chapter was to follow up on a 1993 survey of Korean journalists and analyze how Korean journalism changed as it entered the 21st century. About two decades ago, Korean journalists seemed to be on the brink of a golden age with the liberalization of its media. Instead, what followed was a period of fierce competition, ideological polarization, and challenges from a proliferation of media channels. Throughout this period Korean journalists have felt that they enjoy a reasonable amount of autonomy in their jobs. Yet this latest research suggests that they have felt increasingly stressed and professionally insecure. Korean journalists are therefore at a crossroads.

These findings also raise intriguing points to be addressed in future studies. Further research about the dynamic relations between Internet use and traditional journalism is needed. Better understanding is also required concerning changes in the perceived importance of certain aspects of journalists' jobs, and the importance reporters assign to various media roles. By addressing this, the dynamics of modern journalists and journalism can be better understood.

Note

1. This survey is part of a series of "Journalists' perception surveys," carried out by the Korea Press Foundation every other year, beginning in 1989. Until 1997, those surveys were conducted by Korean Press Institute, which was consolidated into KPF in 1999. Among those biennial surveys, the 1993 survey was conducted in collaboration with KPI and the Newspaper and Broadcasting Institute of Korea University, and the result was published in a previous edition of *The Global Journalist: News People Around the World* (Weaver 1998).

References

Auh, Taik Sup, Chang Keun Lee, and Myung Koo Kang. 1998. Korean journalists in the 1990s. In *The global journalist: News people around the world*, edited by David H. Weaver, pp. 55–69. Cresskill, NJ: Hampton Press.

Cho, Hyun Ho. 2002. Newspaper business is being destroyed. *Media Today* July 11. Retrieved from http://www.media-today.co.kr/news/articleView.html?idxno=17568

Cho, Jeong Hyun, and Hynn Ban. 2007. Who are the portal news readers: Focusing on their motivation and attitude. *Korea Journalism Review* 1(2):113–129.

Cho, Sooyoung, and Lucinda D. Davenport. 2007. Gender discrimination in Korean newsrooms. *Asian Journal of Communication* 17(3):286–300.

Heuvel, J. V., and E. E. Dennis. 1993. *The unfolding lotus: East Asia's changing media*. New York: Freedom Forum Media Studies Center, Columbia University.

Hong, Eun-Hee. 2010. The study on gender differences in leadership among reporters' recognitions: Focus on the perception of promotion and leadership. *Media, Gender & Culture* 13:115–154, 184.

Keum, Chang Hwan. 2001. Journalists' perceived credibility. *Newspaper & Broadcasting* 369:12–18.

Kim, Sung Tae. 2008. *Internet communication research*. Seoul, Korea: Nanam Press.

Korea Communications Commission. 2009. *The advertisement change among diverse medium*. Seoul, Korea: KCC.

Korea Press Foundation (KPF). 2001. *The Korean journalists: The 7th biennial survey of newspaper, broadcasting and wire service reporters*. Seoul, Korea: KPF.

Korea Press Foundation (KPF). 2005. *The Korean journalists: The 9th biennial survey of newspaper, broadcasting and wire service reporters.* Seoul, Korea: KPF.

Korea Press Foundation (KPF). 2007. *The Korean journalists: The 10th biennial survey of newspaper, broadcasting and wire service reporters.* Seoul, Korea: KPF.

Korea Press Foundation (KPF). 2008. *National internet user survey.* Seoul, Korea: KPF.

Korea Press Foundation (KPF). 2009. *Directory of Korean Journalists 2008/2009.* Seoul, Korea: KPF.

Korean Press Institute (KPI). 1989. *Journalists' responsibility and ethics: The 1st national journalists' perception survey.* Seoul, Korea: KPI.

Korean Press Institute (KPI). 1991. *Journalists' responsibility and ethics: The 2nd national journalists' perception survey.* Seoul, Korea: KPI

Korea Press Institute (KPI). 1993. *Directory of Korean Journalists.* Seoul, Korea: KPI.

Korean Press Institute (KPI). 1993. *Journalists' responsibility and ethics: The 3rd national journalists' perception survey.* Seoul, Korea: KPI.

Korean Press Institute (KPI). 1997. *Journalists' responsibility and ethics: The 5th national journalists' perception survey.* Seoul, Korea: KPI.

Lee, Jung-Hoon, and Kyun Kim. 2006. The historical formation of professional identity among Korean journalists. *Korean Journal of Journalism and Communication Studies* 50(6):59–88, 490.

McLeod, Jack M., and Searle E. Hawley Jr. 1964. Professionalization among newsmen. *Journalism Quarterly* 41:529–538, 577.

Oh, Su Jeong. 2005. Responsibility, freedom and values of journalists. *Newspaper & Broadcasting* 414(June):30–37.

Organization for Economic Co-Operation and Development [OECD]. 2010. Korea country report. Retrieved from http://www.oecd.org/country/0,3377,en_33873108_33873555_1_1_1_1_1,00.html

Park, Hong-won. 2007. Inter-media conflict in post-democratization era and its implication. *Korea Journalism Review* 1(3):183–192.

Sa, Eun Suk. 2009. The press and democracy in South Korea. *Asian Social Science* 5(6):19–39.

Sohn, Seung-Hye, and Eun-mee Kim. 2004. Gender differences among the employee of broadcasting systems: Perception of professionalism and organizational socialization. *Korean Journal of Journalism and Communication Studies* 48(6):196–224, 432–433.

Weaver, David H. 1998. *The global journalist: News people around the world.* Cresskill, NJ: Hampton Press.

Yang, Seung-mock. 2007. Korea's democratization and the role of the media. *Korea Journalism Review* 1(3):168–172.

7 Malaysian Journalists

Ezhar Tamam, Sony Jalarajan Raj, and Manimaran Govindasamy

Journalism in Malaysia remains torn between a free press and government control despite tremendous growth this century and the introduction of the first newspapers in this Southeast Asian nation. Government intervention and political party ownership of Malaysian mass media have limited the concept of free, fair, and fearless journalism. From the government's perspective, news media should be catalysts for national development. While this model of journalism is increasingly challenged by digital and market-driven media, most Malaysians still consume the traditional pro-development print and broadcast sources (Mustafa 2000).

While Malaysian media have been subject to economic and technological changes similar to those in other nations, the changes have not necessarily led to improvements in journalistic standards or quality. In fact, one of Malaysian journalism's pioneers, Tan Sri Samad Ismail, commented that it is "dull" (BERNAMA 2006), while Mustafa (2006) noted that during the past few years the nation's media seemed to have lost vigor and spontaneity in reporting and analyzing important issues. Specific trends that have affected Malaysian journalism and how its practitioners view their roles and practices include: (1) the consolidation of media ownership, (2) growth in online and independent media, and (3) the expansion of an already regulated and controlled media environment.

Various government restrictions undermine press freedom in this mostly Muslim nation (Faruqi & Ramanathan 1998). A recent press freedom survey by Freedom House (2010) ranked Malaysia's media 143 out of 195 countries worldwide. Many political and cultural issues go unmentioned in its mainstream media, or only are discussed online if at all. For example, although the Malaysian government does not promote any particular religion, the media have always steered clear of religious and racial issues. Zaharom (2007) argues that the mainstream media in Malaysia, with a few notable exceptions, have been emasculated through political buy-outs and undemocratic laws that have been in force since the country gained its independence more than 50 years ago.

Despite many journalism studies in Malaysia (e.g., Mohamed & Khalib 2006; Mustafa 2006; Ng 2004; Wong 2004), none has focused on the personal and work-related attitudes of its journalists. This chapter describes the findings of a survey of 182 Malaysian journalists conducted between October 2009 and January 2010. It starts with a brief introduction of Malaysia and its media, followed by a brief description of its media infrastructure, ownership, control mechanisms, and the state of the nation's journalism education. The next section explains the survey's methodology. The findings and discussion section is divided into eight themes: basic characteristics, job benefits, job satisfaction, role perceptions, journalistic freedom, perceptions of journalism quality, journalists' perceptions of their audience, and controversial reporting practices. The conclusion interprets the main findings and addresses future trends and changes.

The Media in Malaysia

Malaysia is a multi-ethnic, multi-religious country of about 27 million people and has practiced parliamentary democracy since its independence in 1957. Some political scientists have categorized the Malaysian system as a "semi-democracy" (Case 1993) that perches uneasily between democracy and authoritarianism. The ruling political party is the Barisan Nasional (BN), a coalition of 13 parties closely aligned with Malaysia's three main ethnic groups (Malay, Chinese, and Indian). The BN has been in power since 1957.

Malays and other indigenous groups represent 65% of the total population, Chinese 26%, and Indians 8%. Islam is the official religion, and 60.4% of the population is Muslim. Buddhism is the second-largest religion, followed by Christianity and Hinduism. In addition to the right to practice any religion, Malaysia's constitution, as stated in Article 10, provides each citizen with "the right to freedom of speech and expression." However, this right is not absolute. Clause (2) of Article 10 allows parliament to restrict press freedom in areas such as freedom of expression.

The beginnings of Malaysian journalism can be traced to 1806 and the publication of the *Government Gazette* in Penang (Mohd Safar 1996). During the pre-independence period, the country witnessed the birth of several daily newspapers published in English, Malay, Chinese, and Indian. As in many other developing countries, the central role of journalism in Malaysia has been to disseminate national policies, educate the masses, and foster economic growth and stability (Hachten 1996).

The Malaysian press system experienced tremendous growth during the first four decades of political independence. At present, Malaysia has 72 daily and 16 weekly or biweekly newspapers (English, Malay, Chinese, Tamil, and Punjabi) in Peninsular Malaysia, Sabah, and Sarawak, with a total circulation of about 4.65 million (Audit Bureau of Circulation 2008). The best-known English newspapers in Malaysia are *The Star, The Straits Times, Malay Mail, The Borneo Post, The Sun,* and *Edge.* The prominent Malay newspapers are *Utusan Malaysia, Berita Harian, Harian Metro, Sinar Harian,* and *Kosmo.* There are also seven audited Chinese newspapers (*China Press, Guang Ming Daily News, Kwong Wah Yit Poh, Mun Shang Poh, Nanyang Siang Pau, New Life Post,* and *Sin Chew Jit Poh*) and three Tamil newspapers (*Malaysian Nanban, Makkai Osai,* and *Tamil Nesan*).

The first Malaysian radio stations were established in 1920. Until the early 1960s, broadcasting in Malaysia was controlled by state-run radio stations, which mostly provided information and news for national development and supported the ruling government's ideology and policies. Currently, there are more than 20 private and public 24-hour radio stations (Media Guide 2008).

Television in Malaysia began in 1963 with one state-run channel (TV1) operated by Radio and Television Malaysia. A second channel (TV2) was launched in 1969. As with radio, television in Malaysia was guided by the same directives, which included the propagation of government information and policies, promoting Malaysian art and culture, educating the Malaysian population, and the spread of entertainment. To this day, both state-run television channels have continued to support the dominant ideology and policies of the ruling political elite (Muhammed 2009).

Privatization policies introduced in 1984 allowed the establishment of the first privately owned television station (TV3) in Malaysia, ending the government's 20-year monopoly over broadcasting. Additional commercial television stations were added in a deregulation period after 1995. These included three terrestrial stations (NTV7, 8TV, and TV9) and one satellite station

(ASTRO, All Asia Television and Radio Company). All four terrestrial stations (TV3, NT7, 8TV, and TV9) are owned by Media Prima Berhad, the nation's largest media conglomerate. Media Prima Berhad, which is controlled by one of the leading political parties in Malaysia (United Malays National Organisation; UMNO), also owns the national newspapers *The New Straits Times* and *Berita Harian*.

During the 1990s, online journalism began to make a significant impact on Malaysia's press environment. While mainstream media continue to dominate the nation's audience, with television and radio reaching more than 90% of the population and newspapers 54%, online journalism has grown substantially. *Malaysiakini* and *Malaysian Insider* are examples of successful independent online news sites with substantial numbers of Malaysian subscribers. Of course, the emergence of independent online news media has challenged state-controlled media and undermined government propaganda efforts (Kenyon & Marjoribanks 2007). Access to online news media, however, has been limited by the relatively low penetration rate of the Internet, which now reaches about 20% of Malaysia's general population (Nielsen Company 2008).

Media Control

While Malaysia's news media are diverse and highly developed, important principles of journalism often are compromised. Press freedom, independence, autonomy, objectivity, and truthfulness frequently have been sacrificed to protect the government, the ruling party, religious groups, or the monarchy. These sacrifices often are mischaracterized by the Malaysian government as necessary, pro-development measures that protect the nation's welfare. Modern Malaysian media are largely the product of two major historical developments. The first was the May 1969 ethnic riots between Malay and Chinese groups, which were blamed on failed earlier attempts to address economic imbalance (Abdullah 1997) and followed by waves of censorship. After the riots, the government suspended the publication of all newspapers for two days in an attempt to curb the spread of violence. Major newspapers later were allowed to publish again, but with the provision that the government could censor items deemed dangerous to national security.

In the second development, the government introduced new laws in 1971 to further restrict press freedom on issues such as citizenship rights, Malay special rights, the power of Malay rulers, the status of Islam, and Malay as the sole national language (Wang & Zaharom 2004). The government also amended the Control of Imported Publications Act (1958) in 1972, which enabled the Ministry of Home Affairs to ban or censor imported publications deemed prejudicial to public order, national interest, morality, or security (Zaharom 1994).

While it is fairly unusual for political parties to own media businesses, their involvement in Malaysian media is commonplace (Gomez 1994). Through a complex web of companies and investments, Malaysia's political parties have become the nation's largest shareholders of media (Wang 2001), and the liberalization policies instituted by Mahathir Mohamed in the early 1980s strengthened this relationship (Zaharom 1994). As previously mentioned, Malaysian conglomerate Media Prima Berhad has direct links with the ruling UMNO party, which, in turn, also controls shares in Utusan Melayu Berhad. Huaren Holdings Sdn Bhd, the investment arm of the political party Malaysian Chinese Association (MCA), owns the newspapers *The Star, Nanyang Siang Pau,* and the *China Press*. Other important media groups include Karangkraf, Nexnews Bhd, Pemandang Sinar, and the KTS Group of Companies, all of which are owned by individuals closely linked to the main political parties.

In sum, Malaysia's media are inextricably linked to the government and controlled through ownership structure, security-related laws, and a nurtured fear of political instability. Its journalism can be described as a mixture of Asian, value-based development journalism, and so-called cue journalism that frequently takes cues from government before reporting on issues or events (Mustafa 2006). Diversity is limited by legislation that curtails press freedom and concentrates media ownership within ruling parties or their close allies.

Journalism Education and Training

Journalism education in Malaysia started in the early 1970s at the Universiti Sains Malaysia (USM) and the Universiti Teknologi Mara (Idid 2000; Lent 1973; Mustafa 2005). Prior to this, such training and education was based on short courses conducted by press and broadcasting institutions such as the South East Asia Press Center and the National Broadcasting Training Center in Kuala Lumpur (Lent 1979). The general agenda of communication and media education was and still is to train practitioners who primarily will serve a national agenda of developing the economy (Zaharom 2003).

Almost all public universities and many of the private colleges currently offer communication programs with the option of majoring in journalism, broadcasting, public relations, mass communication, advertising, or interpersonal communication. While journalism has been a popular field of study in Malaysia since the early 1970s, none of the programs offered are actually located in independent journalism schools. Instead, students take basic journalism courses as electives or as a core component of other communication majors. On occasion, media organizations and associations such as the Malaysian Press Institute and the Public Relations Institute also offer continuing education programs for practicing journalists. Yet formal training is not required for Malaysian journalists to enter the profession, and media organizations often hire graduates from other disciplines.

The 2009 Journalist Study

The 2009 journalist study was designed to analyze the demographic profile of Malaysian journalists, and how they perceive their profession and their journalistic responsibilities toward society. Most prior studies in Malaysia focused on media content, historical development, performance, control, and ownership (e.g., Mohd Safar 1996; Mohd Sani 2004, Mustafa 2006; Ng 2004; Wong 2004; Zaharom & Mustafa 1998). While such studies enriched the local media literature, this survey addressed the following questions: What is the demographic and work-related profile of Malaysian journalists? How do they rate various job-related benefits, and how satisfied are they with their jobs? What roles do Malaysian journalists believe media should fulfill, and how do they rate these roles? What do they think of their readers or viewers, and how do they evaluate journalistic quality at their organizations? How do Malaysian journalists rate their freedom to select stories and emphasize certain aspects of coverage? And to what extent do Malaysian journalists justify controversial reporting methods?

Method

The study used a cross-sectional survey research design based on a standardized paper questionnaire. The data were collected between October and November 2009 and in January 2010. The questionnaire adopted, with modifications where necessary, some questions from *The American*

Journalist survey (Weaver & Wilhoit 1991). The questionnaire was pretested by two editors and two journalists prior to data collection to see if respondents would be able to answer the questions, which were written in English. Although most journalists in the pretest understood and answered the questions without problems, small changes were made after the pretest.

Because of a lack of basic data about Malaysian journalists and media organizations, a multi-step sampling design was used to select respondents. First, a list of Malaysian news media was created based on information obtained from a 2008 Media Guide. The list was confined to prominent news groups with outlets registered as members of the Malaysian Press Institute. The list also included two independent online portals in order to include online journalists. A total of 13 news groups (media companies and conglomerates) were included, from which 21 mainstream print, broadcast, and online media were selected based on large audiences and geographic locations. Because of a lack of resources, media in Sabah and Sarawak were excluded, and the survey was conducted in Kuala Lumpur and Selangor only.

Next, selected media outlets were contacted for consent to conduct the survey. Surveyors visited the media outlets, briefed editorial officers about the project, and then asked them to randomly distribute questionnaires to their editorial staffs. The term *editorial staff* was defined as those who perform professional roles related to the "core" of journalism, such as investigating, selecting, writing, and editing news. Depending on an organization's size, the contact persons were instructed to issue questionnaires to at least one senior editor, at least five editors or sub-editors, and at least five journalists of different news beats. A total of 250 questionnaires were distributed and 182 were returned for a 72.8% response rate. Although the sample size is small, all types of media (print, broadcast, online, private, government, and semi-government) and journalists (managerial and non-managerial) were represented.

Table 7.1   Sample Breakdown by News Groups and Media Outlets

News Group	Media	Distributed Questionnaires	Completed Questionnaires
Media Prime Group	New Straits Times	12	9
	Berita Harian	10	3
	TV3 and TV9	20	14
Utusan Group	Utusan Malaysia,	15	11
	Kosmo	10	5
Karagkraf Group	Sinar Harian	15	14
Sin Chew Group	Nanyang Siang Pau	10	6
	China Press	20	14
	New Life Post	5	2
Star Publication	The Star	15	13
National News Agency	Bernama	25	23
Radio and Television Malaysia	RTM	35	29
Oriental Daily Sdn Bhd	Oriental Daily	10	8
Tamil Nesan Sdn Bhd	Tamil Nesan Daily	10	8
Penerbit Sahabat Sdn Bhd	Malayan Nanban	10	3
The Edge Communication Sdn Bhd	The Edge Weekly	8	6
Malaysiakini	Malaysiakini	10	7
Malaysian Insider	Malaysian Insider	10	7
Total *N*:		250	182

Findings

Demographic and Work Profile

The "typical" Malaysian journalist is about 35 years old, a full-time professional who is likely to be married, has worked in journalism for about nine years, and earned a monthly income of about 3,000 ringgit (about $857). He or she is likely to remain in journalism for the next five years and work for the same type of outlet.

Male journalists tend to be older and slightly better paid than their female colleagues. They also are more likely to be married. No significant differences were found concerning the number of years they worked in journalism. While a slight majority of the media workforce is female (55.5% compared to 44.5% male) slightly more males (13.6%) work online than females (7.2%). Nevertheless, the proportions by gender across different media types are not significantly different.

The high percentage of female journalists suggests that Malaysia's media are not as male-dominated as in many other Asian countries. For instance, in neighboring Indonesia, women journalists are still a small minority (21.1%) (Hanitzsch 2005). It is also important to note that Malaysian journalism is not dominated by any racial group. As shown in Table 7.2, about 45% of journalists are Malay, suggesting that non-Malay journalists are not working in media outlets that cater only to racial minorities.

Findings regarding participation in union and professional associations show low levels of involvement. As indicated in Table 7.2, only 27.3% of respondents are union members and 39.6% are part of a professional journalism or communication association. No significant difference is found in union or association membership across gender. The lack of participation in unions is partly explained by the fact that Malaysian labor law does not allow managerial-level journalists to join a union. The reasons behind low participation in professional associations remain unclear.

Table 7.2   Journalists' Basic Demographic and Work Characteristics

Socio-Demographic Attributes	Men (N = 81) 44.5%	Women (N = 101) 55.5%	Total (N = 182) 100%
Average age (years)	35.1	31.3	32.9
Has worked in journalism (years)	8.8	7.2	8.8
Average salary (Malaysian Ringgit)	3,365	2,741	3,005
Married	51.9%	35.3%	42.6%
Full-time	91.3%	98.0%	94.0%
Race (Malay)	48.1%	43.1%	45.4%
Print media	53.1%	54.9%	54.1%
Broadcast media	23.5%	25.5%	24.6%
Online media	13.6%	7.8%	10.4%
Management level	38.3%	27.5%	32.2%
Member of journalist union	25.9%	28.4%	27.3%
Member of journalism or communication organization	40.0%	39.2%	39.6%
Like to be in news media in the next five years	74.1%	72.5%	71.1%

Table 7.3   Journalists' Education and Training Background (in %)

	Men (N = 81)	Women (N = 101)	Total (N = 182)
Holding college or university degree	87.6	94.1	91.2
Major in journalism or broadcast journalism at undergraduate level	32.8	28.6	30.4
Did take courses in journalism	64.1	74.4	70.0
Non-journalism or communication graduate	34.4	26.2	29.7
Major in journalism at graduate level	32.8	45.2	39.9
Had short courses, sabbaticals, workshops, or fellowship	77.0	76.1	76.5
Need additional training	83.3	82.5	82.9

Education and Training Profile

Table 7.3 addresses education and training. The typical Malaysian journalist is a university graduate with additional professional training. More than 91% have university degrees and 70% have taken journalism courses. However, only about 30% majored in journalism during their graduate studies. While this percentage is low, Table 7.3 also shows that about 77% of the journalists received professional training organized by their organization or relevant institutions. Yet a large majority (82.9%) felt they needed additional training. An analysis of responses to a related open-ended question also shows that many journalists would like to take additional courses to enhance their skills or managerial competence.

Job-Related Benefits and Job Satisfaction

To measure how journalists think about their jobs, respondents were asked to rate the importance of eight job-related benefits and their overall level of job satisfaction. Malaysian journalists value especially "job security" and "pay" as the most important benefits (66.3% and 57.5%, respectively, saying these are "very important"). This was followed by "the chance to develop a specialty" (53.3%), "the chance to help people" (52.2%), "fringe benefits" (45.9%), "the chance to influence public affairs" (47.8%), "the chance to get ahead in the organization" (45.8%), and "job autonomy" (33.9%).

As Table 7.4 shows, most respondents were very (18.1%) or fairly (62.6%) satisfied with their jobs as journalists. Only about 2 in 10 journalists (19.3%) reported that they were somewhat or very dissatisfied. A slightly higher percentage of females (21.6%) were dissatisfied with their jobs compared to males (16.2%). Qualitative data revealed that journalists especially valued flexible

Table 7.4   Perceived Level of Job Satisfaction by Gender (in %)

	Men (N = 81)	Women (N = 101)	Total (N = 182)
Very satisfied	25.0	12.7	18.1
Fairly satisfied	58.8	65.7	62.6
Somewhat dissatisfied	15.0	21.6	18.7
Very dissatisfied	1.2	—	0.6
Total	100.0	100.0	100.0

working hours and the opportunity to meet interesting people. Low salaries were the main reason for job dissatisfaction.

Journalistic Freedom

Because the press in Malaysia is only "partly free" (Freedom House 2010), questions related to journalists' perceived job autonomy are especially relevant. Only a small percentage of Malaysian journalists said that they have almost complete freedom to "select the stories to work on" (16.3%) or "decide which aspects of the story should be emphasized" (17.4%). In addition, Malaysian journalists are expected to exercise self-censorship and "responsible" journalism. This is clearly evident in responses to an open-ended question about limits to journalistic freedom. While responses were varied, many acknowledged the expectation of self-censorship and that they report "sensitively" about racial, religious, and political issues. A few specifically mentioned that they did not want a police case filed against them for writing "insensitive" articles—particularly on race or religion issues.

Journalistic Roles

Journalists were asked to indicate the importance of 15 typical roles used in previous studies (Weaver & Wilhoit 1991). As shown in Table 7.5, most Malaysian journalists (78.3%) considered "getting information to the public quickly" as extremely important, followed by "providing analysis and interpretation of issues and problems" (62.8%), and "investigating claims and statements made by the government" (62.2%). Being an "adversary" of government (21%) or business (19.4%), or being able to "set the political agenda" (18.3%), were considered least important. These findings indicate that

Table 7.5   Perceived Importance of Journalistic Roles

Communication Goals	N	Mean[1]	Saying "extremely important"
Get information to the public quickly	182	3.77	78.3%
Provide analysis and interpretation of issues and problems	182	3.55	62.8%
Investigate claims and statements made by the government	182	3.52	62.2%
Concentrate on news that's of interest to the widest possible audience	182	3.35	50.5%
Develop intellectual and cultural interests of the public	182	3.28	42.3%
Provide analysis and interpretation of international developments	182	3.28	42.9%
Stay away from stories where factual content cannot be verified	179	3.27	48.0%
Give ordinary people a chance to express their views on public affairs	182	3.26	43.4%
Motivate people to get involved in public discussion of important issues	182	3.22	43.7%
Point people toward possible solutions to society's problems	182	3.17	38.8%
Discuss national policy while it is still being developed	182	3.16	37.2%
Provide entertainment and relaxation	182	2.96	27.2%
Be an adversary of government through skepticism	176	2.64	21.0%
Be an adversary of business through skepticism of their actions	176	2.60	19.4%
To set political agenda	180	2.35	18.3%

1 Higher scores equal greater importance. Perceived importance is measured on a four-point scale (4 = extremely important, 3 = quite important, 2 = somewhat important, 1 = not really important).

Malaysian journalists see themselves and the news media mostly as information disseminators and interpreters, not as critical observers of government and business.

The 15 journalism roles were subjected to a factor analysis to examine possible connections between the various roles. As Table 7.6 shows, the analysis extracted five separate role dimensions from the data, which account for 68% of the total variance. The first was labeled the "watchdog role," and included such items as being the adversary of the government or business. The second factor, labeled as the "mobilizer role," included such items as giving ordinary people a chance to

Table 7.6   Dimensions of Journalism Roles ($N = 182$)

Communication Goals	Mean[1]	Factors and Factor Loadings				
		I	*II*	*III*	*IV*	*V*
Watchdog	2.55					
Be an adversary of government through skepticism		.890				
Be an adversary of business through skepticism of their action		.914				
To set political agenda		.603				
Mobilizer	3.22					
Give ordinary people a chance to express their views on public affairs			.799			
Motivate ordinary people to get involved in public discussion of important issues			.826			
Point people toward possible solutions to society's problems			.718			
Interpreter	3.45					
Provide analysis and interpretation of issues and problems				.626		
Investigate claims and statements made by the government				.739		
Provide analysis and interpretation of international developments				.861		
Disseminator	3.36					
Get information to the public quickly					.789	
Provide entertainment and relaxation					.605	
Concentrate on news that's of interest to the widest possible audience					.711	
Analytical-Objective	3.24					
Discuss national policy while it is still being developed						.585
Develop intellectual and cultural interests of the public						.661
Stay away from stories where factual content cannot be verified						.721
Eigenvalue		4.71	1.78	1.46	1.28	1.02
% of variance explained [2]		31.7	11.87	9.72	8.52	6.79

Note. Principal Component Analysis Varimax rotation with Kaiser Normalization, KMO = .748; Bartlett's Test of Sphericity, p < .001.
1 Higher scores equal greater importance. Perceived importance is measured on a four-point scale (4 = extremely important, 3 = quite important, 2 = somewhat important, 1 = not really important).
2 Total percentage of variance explained = 68.29%.

express their views, or motivating them to get involved. The third was called the "interpreter role," and involved the analysis and interpretation of issues and problems, along with investigating government claims or statements. The fourth factor reflected the "disseminator role" of journalists, which included getting information to the public quickly, or concentrating on news of interest to the widest possible audience. The final factor captured the "analytical-objective role" of journalists. This included such items as discussing national policy, developing intellectual and cultural interests of the public, and avoiding news stories without factual content.

A look at the mean scores for the role scales shows that Malaysian journalists are especially supportive of the "interpretive" ($M = 3.45$) and "disseminator" roles ($M = 3.36$). This suggests that the role perceptions of Malaysian journalists are not that different from those of journalists in other parts of the world. Even while working in a restrictive environment, journalists in Malaysia consider spreading and interpreting information to be their primary functions. Yet the findings also indicate that Malaysian journalists are much less supportive of the traditional "watchdog" role. Their ability to serve in that role is constrained by the various laws and regulations that limit press freedom in Malaysia.

Views of Journalism Quality and the Public

What do Malaysian journalists think of the quality of news coverage at their organizations, and what are their beliefs about the general public? As shown in Table 7.7, they harbored mixed views of their media organizations. While a substantial majority believed that journalistic quality had risen at their outlet during the past few years (58.3% strongly or somewhat agreed), a small minority thought their organizations value profit more than good journalism (34.6%), or that newsroom resources have shrunk (30.9%).

While Malaysian journalists are somewhat critical of their news organizations, perceptions of their audiences are quite positive. Only a small percentage believed their audiences had little interest in social problems (33.7%), or are easily fooled (16.4%). However, most journalists (70.8%) thought that the public is more interested in breaking news than analysis.

Table 7.7   Journalists' Beliefs about Their Organizations and the Public ($N = 182$)

	Mean[1]	Saying "strongly and somewhat agree"
The quality of journalism at my news organization has been rising steadily over the past few years.	3.60	58.3%
My news organization does a lot of audience research to learn what kinds of information our audience wants or needs.	3.22	39.5%
At my news organization, profits are a higher priority than good journalism.	2.96	34.6%
At my news organization, newsroom resources have been shrinking over the past few years.	2.90	30.9%
The public (readers/viewers/listeners) are more interested in the day's breaking news than in analysis.	4.14	70.8%
The majority of public (readers/viewers/listeners) have little interest in reading about/viewing/ listening to social problems.	2.78	33.7%
The public (readers/viewers/listeners) are gullible and easily fooled.	2.16	16.4%

1 Larger means indicate higher levels of agreement. Agreement is measured on a five-point scale (5 = strongly agree, 4 = somewhat agree, 3 = neutral, 2 = somewhat disagree, 1 = strongly disagree).

Table 7.8   Controversial Reporting Practices (in %, N = 182)

Reporting Practices	Justified on occasion	Would not approve	Not sure
Using hidden microphones or cameras	54.6	34.4	11.0
Using confidential business or government documents without authorization	39.4	52.1	8.5
Paying people for confidential information	38.6	48.0	13.3
Disclosing the names of rape victims	27.0	61.6	11.4
Claiming to be somebody else	26.8	60.8	12.4

Controversial Reporting Practices

Upon measuring the acceptance of controversial reporting practices, it is probably safe to say that Malaysian journalists generally do not approve of methods that go beyond the standard interview with sources. As Table 7.8 shows, only a slight majority (54.6%) thought the use of hidden microphones or cameras might be justified on occasion; paying people for confidential information (38.6%), disclosing the name of rape victims (27%), or claiming to be somebody else (26.8%) proved considerably less acceptable.

Conclusions

Malaysian journalists are mostly young, well-educated, married, full-time professionals who earn reasonable salaries, with a slight female majority across the profession. They have relevant academic and professional qualifications, are fairly committed to their profession, and generally satisfied with their jobs. They mostly see themselves as disseminators, facilitators, and interpreters of news within a highly controlled and monitored media system. They feel their capacity to operate as free and fearless journalists is compromised by external and internal pressures that are the byproduct of draconian regulation. Despite this, they practice ethical reporting and disapprove of methods that go beyond conventional or standard newsgathering methods.

Unlike countries with more liberal media systems, where journalists often feel they contribute to a vibrant public sphere, Malaysian journalists are acutely aware their autonomy is restricted. They are more or less "lapdogs" of government and political bureaucrats, which makes them a prime example of restricted media. As a result, their job satisfaction is largely income-based and less tied to civic mindedness and altruism. The core values, ideology, and responsibilities of the profession are marginalized so that journalism is regarded more as a means to a financial end. As a consequence, disseminating and interpreting news is viewed as a journalist's main responsibility, while other roles such as watchdog, investigator, analyst, critic, political communicator, activist, and mobilizer are downplayed.

The Malaysian Sedition Act, the Internal Security Act, the Official Secrecy Act, the Printing Presses and Publications Act, and the Communications and Multimedia Act restrict the professional freedom and independence of Malaysian journalists. The government frequently uses these policies to discourage the rise of a vibrant, investigative, and critical press. The multiethnic, multiracial and multireligious nature of Malaysian society adds another layer of restraint.

The government and the establishment in Malaysia argue that a controlled and 'restrained' news media is conducive to a development-oriented and socially responsible media ecology. Reporting on matters related to race and religion is approached with a fair degree of caution. Asian values also are used to justify a journalistic culture that is "sensitive" to controversy and supportive of national objectives. Censorship, arrests, license non-renewal, official enforcement raids, unlawful detainment, human rights violations, and harassment are constant threats. For Malaysian journalists, freedom of speech, expression, information, and communication is always in peril.

References

Abdullah, Firdaus. 1997. Affirmative action policy in Malaysia: To restructure society, to eradicate poverty. *Ethnic Studies Report* 15(2): 189–220.

Audit Bureau Circulation Report. 2008. *Audit report: Analysis of print media audited by circulation by Media Specialist Association for Audit Bureau of Circulation (Malaysia.).* Retrieved from http://www.abcm.org.my

BERNAMA. 2006, February 21. Malaysian media dull, says veteran journalist. Retrieved from http://www.access-mylibrary.com/article-1G1-142667658/malaysian-media-dull-says.html

Case, William. 1993. Semi democracy in Malaysia. *Pacific Affairs* 66(2): 183–205.

Faruqui, Shad Saleem, and Sankaran Ramanathan. 1998. *Mass media laws and regulations in Malaysia.* Singapore: AMIC.

Freedom House. 2010. *Freedom of the press.* Retrieved from http://www.freedomhouse.org/template.cfm?page=251&country=7869&year=2010

Gomez, Edmund Terence. 1994. *Political business: UMNO's involvement of Malaysian political parties.* Townsville, Australia: James Cook University of North Queensland.

Hachten, William A. 1996. *The world news prism: Changing media of international communication.* 4th ed. Ames: Iowa State University Press.

Hanitzsch, Thomas. 2005. Journalists in Indonesia: Educated but timid. *Journalism Studies* 6(4): 493–508.

Idid, Syed Arabi. 2000. Bidang (penyelidikan) komunikasi di Malaysia—Realiti kini atau masam muka [Communication research field in Malaysia—Current realities and future]. In *Pasca sidang seminar penyelidikan komunikasi* [Communication research conference], edited by Latifah Pakwanteh and Mazni Buyung, pp. 1–18. Bangi, Selangor: Universiti Kebangsaan Malaysia.

Kenyon, Andrew T., and Tim Marjoribanks. 2007. Transforming media market: The case of Malaysia and Singapore. *Australian Journal of Emerging Technologies and Society* 5(2): 103–118.

Lent, John A. 1973. Malaysian students prefer rewrites to news gathering. *Journalism Educator* 28(3): 12–15.

Media Guide. 2008. *Media planning guide Malaysia.* Kuala Lumpur, Malaysia: Perception Media Sdn Bhd.

Mohamed, Ramli, and Aini Haryati Khalib. 2006. Engaging and applying new communication technology; a case study of the usage of internet as a search practice among BERNAMA journalists. *Kajian Malaysia* 24(1&2): 73–96.

Mohd Safar, Mohd Hashim. 1996. *Akhbar dan kuasa: Perkembangan sistem akhbar di Malaysia sejak 1806* [Newspapers and power: The development of the newspaper system in Malaysia since 1806]. Kuala Lumpur, Malaysia: Universiti Malaya Press.

Mohd Sani, Mohd Azizuddin. 2004. Media freedom in Malaysia. *Journal of Contemporary Asia* 35(3): 341–367.

Muhammed, Mokhtar. 2009. Television history and development in Malaysia: From analogue to digital. *Forum Komunikasi* 7(1): 2–5.

Mustafa, K. Anuar. 2000. Malaysian media and democracy. *Media Asia* 27(4): 183–190.

Mustafa, K. Anwar. 2005. Journalism, national development and social justice in Malaysia. *Asia Pacific Media Educator* 19(9): 63–70.

Mustafa, K. Anwar. 2006. "Cue journalism": Media should stop playing follow-the-leader. *Asia Pacific Media Educator* 17(8): 97–101.

Nielsen Company. 2008. Mainstream media continues to lead Malaysia media scene. Retrieved from http://www.acnielsen.com.my/news/index.shtml

Ng, Kit Yoong. 2004. *From the first line to the byline: Malaysian journalists' learning in practice under the power of media ownership.* Unpublished doctoral dissertation, University of Georgia, Athens.

Wang, Lay Kim. 2001. Media and democracy in Malaysia. *Journal of the European Institute of Communication and Culture* 8(2): 67–68.

Wang, Lay Kim, and Nain Zaharom. 2004. *Who owns the media? Global trends and local resistance.* London: Zed Books.

Weaver, David H., and G. Cleveland Wilhoit. 1991. *The American journalist*, 2nd ed. Bloomington: Indiana University Press.

Wong, Kokkeong. 2004. Coverage of the 1999 general elections in Malaysia: Asian-based development journalism and political elections. *Gazette* 66(1): 25–40.

Zaharom, Nain. 1994. Commercialisation and control in a "caring society": Malaysian media "Towards 2020." *Journal of Social Issues in Southeast Asia* 9(2): 178–199.

Zaharom, Nain. 2003. Media role in a k-economy: Transforming media education in Malaysia. *Asia Pacific Media Educator* 14(13): 156–165.

Zaharom, Nain. 2007. Bloggers and bullies. *Aliran for Unity* 27(6): 4–6.

Zaharom, Nain, and K. Anuar Mustafa. 1998. Ownership and control of the Malaysian media. *Media Development* 14(4): 9–17.

8   Singapore Journalism
Buying into a Winning Formula

Xiaoming Hao and Cherian George

Professional journalists in Singapore are an enigma because the context within which they operate does not fall neatly into any familiar category. While Singapore lacks the press freedom and civil liberties of liberal democracies, the state has not completely commandeered the media in the style of totalitarian regimes. Justifications for Singapore's press model stress nation-building, with echoes of the 1970s development journalism proposition associated with the Third World. Yet, the country is an advanced industrial economy with among the highest living standards in the world. Singapore journalists are able to operate in a safe and secure environment, free from the deprivation and corruption that plague the profession in many less developed societies. But, they do not inhabit a political culture that values media freedom enough to guarantee the right to access information or to express ideas freely.

Singapore has been variously classified as an "electoral autocracy" (Diamond 2002), "illiberal democracy" (Zakaria 2003), and "semi-democracy" (Case 2002) to highlight its hybrid political status. Since 1959, Singaporeans have chosen their governments through regular elections contested by multiple parties, and every election since then has been won decisively by the People's Action Party (PAP). Singapore's remarkable socio-economic progress is widely credited to the competent and non-corrupt rule of the PAP. The PAP also has been the single most powerful influence on the evolution of Singapore's brand of professional journalism since the 1960s. Its interventions have been apparent on several fronts.

First, it cracked down on media that it considered threatening to its nation-building project. Singapore is a multi-ethnic, immigrant society made up of Chinese (74%), Malays (13%), Indians (9%), and others (3%) (Singapore Department of Statistics 2010). There is no majority religion: the Chinese are mainly Taoist, Buddhist, or Christian; Malays are almost exclusively Muslim; Indians are mainly Hindu, Muslim, Sikh, or Christian. Singapore's Inter Religious Organization—reputedly the world's oldest inter-faith NGO—represents 10 religious groups. The British colonial authorities made virtually no attempt to integrate Singapore's various ethnic groups, but the PAP came to power with a determined multi-racial and secular platform. Most newspapers at the time continued to serve separate ethnic communities, putting the press on a collision course with the new government. The PAP used repressive laws inherited from the British to close down publications and detain journalists—without trial, and, in some cases, for several years. While each of the main linguistic communities (English, Malay, Chinese, and Tamil are Singapore's four official languages) has its own newspapers and broadcast stations, the PAP has made it clear that overly assertive championing of any sub-group's interests will not be tolerated.

Second, by the 1970s, the PAP had developed a media doctrine with an illiberal twist on the classic formulation of press freedom. While not denying the value of independently owned newspapers, the PAP rejected the notion of the press as the Fourth Estate with an adversarial watchdog role. It argued that an elected government was the embodiment of citizens' democratic wishes and that the press, as an unelected institution, had no authority to obstruct the government's work. According to the PAP, this was especially the case in a small, new, and vulnerable republic. "In such a situation, freedom of the press, freedom of the news media, must be subordinated to the overriding needs of the integrity of Singapore, and to the primacy of purpose of an elected government," said the country's first Prime Minister Lee Kuan Yew (1971). The PAP said the press should instead play a positive role in good governance. Again, dissenting newspapers were suspended or banned, and journalists were detained to force compliance with the PAP's vision.

In addition, through the Newspaper and Printing Presses Act introduced in 1974, the government effectively gained the power to name the boards of directors of newspaper companies, thus indirectly getting a say in the appointments of chief editors and the setting of editorial direction. As radio and television began as government services, the PAP never saw the need to institute a BBC-style independent public service broadcasting model. Annual government permits, which can be suspended or revoked at any time without court approval, are required for broadcasters and publishers of newspapers and magazines. In addition to serving as an omnipresent "Sword of Damocles" dangling above the media, the licensing regime combined with Singapore's small market has resulted in a paucity of alternative media in print or broadcast formats.

Third, unusually early for a post-colonial state, the PAP understood that a media's profit orientation was not necessarily in conflict with its political objectives; on the contrary, a profitable and secure media industry could serve as a stable partner for a pro-business government. Therefore, the government progressively re-organized the national broadcaster to operate as a commercial entity. Furthermore, the PAP never nationalized the ownership of newspapers but left them in private hands. Its 1974 press law ingeniously required companies to be publicly listed with shares thinly spread out, so that directors would have a fiduciary responsibility to focus on shareholder value and not be swayed by the whims of any politically motivated press baron. It also engineered newspaper mergers, ultimately grouping almost all the local newspapers together to form the Singapore Press Holdings Limited in 1984 to ensure that vernacular newspapers remained on a sound financial footing. While respecting the profit motive as an incentive for news production, the government was suspicious of market competition, believing that publishers become more irresponsible when competition is unbridled.

The resulting news media landscape has a duopolistic structure. Singapore Press Holdings (SPH) is the dominant newspaper and magazine publisher. Its flagship is the English-language daily, *The Straits Times*, which was founded in 1845. SPH publishes two other English dailies, the country's three Chinese dailies, one bilingual English-Chinese daily, and the national Malay and Tamil dailies. Singapore's other media giant is MediaCorp, which evolved from the state broadcaster. MediaCorp runs all free-to-air television stations, including the country's single all-news station Channel News Asia, as well as most radio stations. It owns a free newspaper, *Today*, which is the only local daily not controlled by SPH. Singapore is also a regional hub for several international news organizations, such as Reuters and CNBC Asia.

Virtually since its establishment in 1984, every chairman of SPH has been a former senior civil servant or cabinet minister. Chief executives have also been drawn from similar establishment sources. Editors are experienced journalists appointed from within the newsroom, though in recent years they have included some who started their careers in the civil service. There is press accreditation but no licensing system for journalists, and the government is not known to interfere in hiring decisions. Most SPH and MediaCorp journalists are Singaporeans or citizens of neighboring Malaysia, but newsrooms have always been topped up with expatriate staff. Initially drawing their staff from Australia, Britain, and the United States, English-language media are now more likely to hire Indian nationals. Chinese-language media include journalists from the Greater China region.

PAP government leaders regularly remind journalists not to ape the West, but instead to develop a press system suited to Singapore. As one former prime minister put it:

> Even though Singapore is now more developed and our population better educated, it remains crucial for Singapore to maintain our own unique and tested system of political governance and media model. They have worked well. We should improve them from experience and by learning from others. Accept what has worked and reject what has not, whether they are from the East or West. But we must be bold enough to evolve our own model of a responsible, lively and credible media (Goh 2005).

Structurally, Singapore's news media clearly deviate from the liberal norm in terms of the legal framework within which they operate. However, the normative signposts that matter to Singapore journalists have always been harder to identify. Where do they stand relative to professionals elsewhere in their interpretation of news values, their public mission, and their professional ethics, for example? Leaders of the profession have said that they are ultimately guided by Singapore's long-term interests and that there is no shame in supporting good government:

> Who, after all, can argue with wanting Singapore to succeed? Patriotism has a large following in Asia and needs no intellectual justification. In Singapore's case the followers in the press have had a much easier time because its leaders have received such overwhelming endorsement from the people over the last 30 years, and with demonstrated success to boot (Han 1995, p. 100).

Additional evidence of what matters to Singapore journalists is provided by the journalistic honors that they consider relevant. SPH and MediaCorp journalists compete against professionals from other countries for international honors, such as the Society of Publishers in Asia awards for editorial excellence, which also draw entries from the likes of Hong Kong's *South China Morning Post* and regional editions of powerhouses such as *Time* and *Financial Times*. Singapore journalists and their organizations take obvious pride in whatever successes they achieve in these competitions. This suggests that while perhaps accepting Singapore's particularities, they also see themselves as part of a global profession.

Other than a survey of journalists with the Singapore Press Holdings in regard to their ethical decision making (Yew & Hao 2002), there have been no systematic and comprehensive studies of Singapore journalists as a profession. This study is the first of its kind to survey local journalists and examine their professional values and attitudes toward various issues related to their job.

Method

This study is based on a 2009 survey of journalists working for SPH and MediaCorp, who make up more than 95% of Singaporean journalists. We did not include a small number of Singaporean journalists who work for international media operating in Singapore. They may face the same press environment in Singapore but with different newsroom and organizational cultures.

Due to the concentration of journalists in SPH and MediaCorp, we first contacted the management of the two companies to seek their permission to allow us to survey their journalists through our contacts in various newsrooms. SPH agreed to allow us access to their journalists, but MediaCorp refused. As a result, we had to approach MediaCorp journalists individually through personal contacts.

For SPH, we tried to reach every journalist in the newsroom of every newspaper owned by the company. We distributed a total of 930 questionnaires and collected 330 completed questionnaires. Without the support of MediaCorp's management, we were not able to obtain a complete list of the 300-plus journalists in the company, and neither could we have direct access to journalists in the newsroom. As a result, we managed to contact only about 200 MediaCorp journalists through personal connections. We eventually received about 100 responses from the 200-plus MediaCorp journalists we contacted. Discarding some incomplete questionnaires, we ended up with a total of 447 completed responses, including 305 respondents who identified themselves as journalists from SPH, 91 from MediaCorp, and 51 who declined to name their institution. For SPH, all the newspapers are represented. For MediaCorp, we missed a small number of journalists working for MediaCorp Radio and those working for *Today*, a free newspaper published by Mediacorp. Of the 447 respondents who completed the questionnaire, 84 hold managerial positions in the newsroom as editors, deputy editors and assistant editors, and others.

Findings

Basic Background Characteristics

The respondents' ages range from 23 to 63 years old and their work experience as journalists ranges from less than 1 year to 41 years (see Table 8.1). There are more females (60%) than males (40%), and females make up the majority of the junior journalists, accounting for 74% of those with five years or less of journalistic experience but only 40% of those with more than 20 years of journalistic experience. However, among those holding managerial positions in the newsroom, half of them are men and half are women.

The multi-racial and multi-religious characteristics of Singapore society are well represented by the ethnic and religious diversity of the journalists in our sample. Of the three major ethnic groups, Malays make up 8.2% of the respondents which is less than the proportion of Malays in the total population (13%). On the other hand, the Chinese account for 79.4% of the respondents, whereas their proportion in the national population is 74%. Indians make up 10% of the respondents, close to the proportion of Indians in the national population (9%) (Singapore Department of Statistics, 2010). Of the 68% of respondents who have a religious belief, Christians (37.4%), Buddhists (17.7%), and Muslims (9.5%) make up the majority.

Table 8.1   Journalists' Ages and Years of Professional Experience

Age	
30 years or younger	37.6%
31–40 years	30.1%
41–50 years	20.9%
51 years or older	11.3%
Years as Journalist	
5 years or less	39.6%
6–10 years	20.5%
11–20 years	26.0%
21 years or more	13.9%

Journalism education at the university level started in Singapore only in the early 1990s when a school of communication studies was founded at one of the local universities. It is therefore no surprise that the overwhelming majority of respondents have university degrees in other disciplines. Those with secondary and pre-university education account for only 11.1% of the respondents. About 63% of the respondents have an undergraduate degree and more than a quarter of them have studied at the graduate level. Those with a master's degree account for 18.8% of the respondents, while four of the respondents have Ph.D. degrees. A university degree has increasingly become an important qualification for journalists in Singapore. Of the 156 respondents who joined journalism in the last five years, only five did not have an undergraduate degree. Among the more recent recruits are also recipients of scholarships offered by the media who joined the work force after completing their studies at leading overseas universities.

The majority of respondents (63.4%) joined journalism because of personal interests and passion. Many of them love writing and consider journalism a dream job. However, about 10% of the respondents became journalists simply because the job was available, or they were attracted by the scholarship offered by media organizations. Other reasons mentioned include personal talent and being trained for the job (5.5%), the desire to inform others of what has happened (5.2%), desire to learn and face challenges (5.2%), the chance to meet people (4%), and the impact of journalism on society (3.3%).

Working Conditions

Job Satisfaction.   The overwhelming majority of the respondents are satisfied with their job, with 12.2% of them feeling very satisfied and 63.4% feeling fairly satisfied. Those who feel somewhat dissatisfied make up 21.8% of the respondents while a tiny minority (2.6%) feels very dissatisfied. Job satisfaction correlates with some demographic variables such as age and income. Younger journalists and those who are better paid are more likely to find the job satisfying but education and number of years spent as a journalist did not affect this issue.

Job satisfaction also correlates with respondents' assessment and expectations of the roles played by the news media. Those who are happy with their own institution's performance in informing the public are more likely to be satisfied with their job or vice versa. Those who feel they have greater freedom in choosing what subjects to cover, what stories to write, and what aspects of a story to emphasize are also more likely to be satisfied with their job. On the other hand, those who find it important for the news media to be adversaries of public officials and business, set the public agenda, motivate ordinary people to get involved in discussion of important issues, and develop the public's intellectual and cultural interests are less likely to find the job satisfying. However, these correlations are weak despite their statistical significance (see Table 8.2).

Of the various factors considered important in assessing a job as a journalist, the respondents find the editorial policy of a news organization the most important, with 45.9% of them citing it as very important. This is followed by developing a specialty (44.9%), autonomy on the job (43.1%), helping people (40.3%), job security (38.4%), pay (36.8%), getting ahead in the organization (35.4%), influencing public opinion (32.5%), and job benefits (16.2%). Print and broadcast journalists do not differ much in their assessment of the importance of these factors, but more broadcast journalists (48.8%) than print journalists (32.3%) think that pay is very important. This is not a surprise given the fact that print journalists are better paid than broadcast journalists in Singapore.

Table 8.2   Correlations between Job Satisfaction and Various Variables

Variables	Job Satisfaction
Rating of own institution in Informing public	.34**
Able to cover a subject	.18**
Freedom in selecting stories	.17**
Freedom to choose aspects to emphasize in story	.16**
Set public agenda	−.16**
Motivate people for public discussion	−.12*
Develop intellectual and cultural interests of public	−.12*
Be adversary of public officials	−.11*
Be adversary of businesses	−.12*
Age	.13**
Income	−.11*
Years spent as a journalist	−.08
Education	.08

Note.   The correlations are measured with Spearman's rank correlation coefficient.

Autonomy.   Despite the fact that the overwhelming majority of respondents believe that the amount of autonomy they have is very or fairly important to their job satisfaction, they are not completely free in doing their jobs. Journalism remains a supervised and scrutinized profession in Singapore, especially for those who are new in the field. About a quarter of the respondents receive regular comments on their work from their superiors, news sources, and the audience, and about half of them receive such comments occasionally. While comments from supervisors reflect the institutional assessment of the work of a journalist, comments from news sources (many of whom are government officials and powerful people from other institutions0 and the audience reflect external assessment of the work of a journalist and may indirectly affect the institutional assessment of his or her work as well. The length of service as journalists does not change how often journalists receive (or perceive receiving) feedback on their work from superiors, news sources, or the audience. According to our findings, even journalists with more than 20 years of experience may still receive comments on their work from their superiors as often as junior journalists. At the same time, print journalists receive comments from news sources more often than their broadcast counterparts. This could be due to the fact that print news stories are more accessible for scrutiny by public relations officers working for various government agencies and businesses.

About half of the respondents feel they have either complete freedom (11.1%) or a great deal of freedom (43.6%) in deciding what stories to work on. About the same proportion of respondents feel they have complete freedom (10.3%) or a great deal of freedom (41.1%) in deciding which aspects of a story to emphasize. However, a small percentage of respondents feel they do not have any freedom to choose the stories they would like to work on (10%) or to select the aspects of a story they would like to emphasize (5.6%). In addition, a majority of the respondents (72.9%) feel that when they have good story ideas, they are usually able to cover them.

Despite the fact that a considerable number of respondents feel that they enjoy a certain level of journalistic freedom, the overwhelming majority of the respondents also feel that there are clear limits to this freedom. Of the various limits to freedom cited by the respondents, the most

Table 8.3 Major Limits to Press Freedom as Seen by Journalists (% in parentheses)

	Ordinary Journalists	*Journalists in Management*
Government and politics	67 (27.8)	23 (41.1)
Editorial policies	85 (35.3)	12 (21.4)
Self-censorship and OB markers	25 (10.4)	10 (17.9)
Laws and regulations	7 (2.9)	3 (5.4)
Commercial interests	20 (8.3)	1 (1.8)
National, public, and community interests	11 (4.6)	5 (8.9)
Others	26 (10.8)	2 (3.6)

common limit seems to come from the news organizations themselves. One-third of the respondents (32.8%) feel that their freedom as journalists is limited the most by the newsroom culture, the editorial policies of their institutions, and the preferences of their editors. The second most significant limit, mentioned by 30.4% of the respondents, comes from the government and political authorities.[1] Such a limit may not necessarily express itself in the form of direct censorship. Instead, journalists might be asked to cover certain government activities, or government agencies might monitor press coverage and provide critical feedback to the news media when undesirable or critical content is spotted. The next most often mentioned limits (11.7%) are self-censorship as a result of so-called OB (out-of-bounds) markers, a term used in Singapore to denote the informal limits of political discourse. The term is adopted from golf, where an out-of-bounds marker denotes the area beyond which playing is not allowed (Koh, Auger, Yap, & Ng 2006).

Commercial interests, such as not offending advertisers and the pursuit of high ratings for TV news, were mentioned by 7% of the respondents. The pressure to protect national, public, and community interests, such as by avoiding controversial ethnic and religious issues, was considered a significant limit by 5.4% of the respondents. Law (especially defamation) and other regulations were cited by 3.3% of the respondents as a major limit to their journalistic freedom.

Journalists differ in their perceptions of what constitutes the most significant limit to their freedom as journalists depending on their position. On the one hand, 41% of the journalists holding managerial positions consider the government and political authorities the most significant limit to their journalistic freedom, while only 21.4% cite the newsroom culture and editorial policies of their organizations as the most significant limit. On the other hand, 35.3% of the journalists who do not hold managerial positions cite the newsroom culture and editorial policies of their organizations as the most significant limit, while 27.8% of them cite the government and political authorities as the most significant limit.

Finally, the work experience of journalists also makes a difference. Those who have been journalists for less than 10 years tend to see the newsroom culture and editorial policies of the news organizations as the most significant limit to their freedom, while those who have worked longer tend to think that the government and political authorities pose the major limit to journalistic freedom.

Perception of Audience and News Institutions

The majority of respondents strongly (22.1%) or somewhat (38%) agree that their readers, viewers, and listeners are more interested in breaking news than analysis. Most of them also believe that their audiences are interested in social problems (74.2%) and cannot be easily fooled (79.4%).

Most journalists also feel that their news organizations either are doing a fair (18.5%), a good (41.6%), very good (32.8%), or an outstanding (5.8%) job of informing the public. Only very few of the interviewed journalists (1.4%) think that their own news organizations are doing a poor job. This perception is fairly consistent among the various types of journalists represented in our study. The only significant difference was found between journalists who hold managerial positions in the newsroom and those who do not. Among the former, 15.6% believe that their institution is doing an outstanding job in informing the public, only 10.4% of them rate their institution as doing a fair job, and none of them rates their institution as doing a poor job in informing the public. For journalists not holding managerial positions, only 3.7% believe that their institution is doing an outstanding job, but 20.4% and 1.7% of them rate their institution as doing only a fair or poor job in informing the public respectively.

Professionalism

Perceived Media Roles.   We also asked the journalists to comment on the importance of various roles the news media are expected to perform in Singapore. Of all the tasks, they value most the role of informant. The majority of respondents rated it as extremely important to get information to the public. This was followed by the role in analyzing and interpreting complex problems. Journalists holding managerial positions rank the tasks a bit differently from journalists holding no such positions. For example, journalists holding no managerial positions rated investigating government claims as a much more important task for the news media than those who held managerial positions.

Table 8.4   Rank-Order of Tasks Rated by Journalists as "Extremely Important" (% in parentheses)

	Rank-Order by All Journalists	Rank-Order by Journalists not Holding Managerial Positions	Rank-Order by Journalists Holding Managerial Positions
Informing public quickly	1 (58.6)	1 (55.7)	1 (70.4)
Analyzing complex problems	2 (45.0)	2 (40.0)	2 (67.1)
Outlets for people on public affairs	3 (40.1)	3 (37.7)	3 (50.6)
Investigating government claims	4 (35.6)	4 (37.5)	11 (29.3)
Motivating people for public discussion	5 (33.1)	5 (30.7)	4 (44.6)
Analyzing international development	6 (29.4)	6 (27.9)	7 (36.6)
Discussing national policy	7 (28.4)	7 (27.7)	8 (32.5)
Focusing on popular news	8 (27.6)	9 (24.1)	5 (43.4)
Developing public intellectual interest	9 (26.3)	8 (25.7)	10 (29.6)
Staying away from non-verified stories	10 (24.7)	12 (20.6)	6 (42.5)
Solution of social problems	11 (24.1)	10 (23.7)	12 (24.1)
Entertainment and relaxation	12 (23.8)	11 (22.5)	9 (30.1)
Being adversary of public officials	13 (10.7)	13 (11.2)	14 (8.8)
Being adversary of businesses	14 (10.5)	14 (10.8)	13 (10.0)
Setting public agenda	15 (5.9)	15 (5.6)	15 (7.3)

Sources of Influence on News Values.   As noted earlier, tertiary programs in journalism first became available in the 1990s in Singapore. As a result, many of the journalists working at SPH and MediaCorp acquired their news values on the job rather than through formal education. Of the various potential influences on their concept of what is newsworthy, the journalists rated their supervisor and journalistic training as the most influential, averaging 4.0 for both on a 5-point scale, which ranges from not at all influential (1) to very influential (5). They are followed by news sources (3.8), priorities in news presentation by large newspapers and local competing news media (both 3.6), findings of audience research and public opinion polls (both 3.5), peers within the news organization (3.4), friends/acquaintances, wire service budgets and priorities of TV network news (all 3.2), priorities of independent online news sites, and priorities of cable network news (both 3.1).

Ethical Standards.   Among a number of ethically questionable journalism practices, the journalists found "disclosing the names of rape victims" the most objectionable and "using a hidden camera" the least objectionable. Significant differences were found between the veterans and the less experienced journalists and between journalists who hold managerial positions and those who do not in terms of their assessment of these ethically questionable journalistic practices. Those who have worked as journalists for more than ten years are more likely to disapprove of practices such as unauthorized use of confidential government documents, claiming to be somebody else, using personal documents without permission, and using hidden microphones or cameras. Those who have worked for ten years or less as journalists, on the other hand, are more likely to disapprove of breaching a promise of protecting confidentiality. Overall, it is clear that those with more journalistic work experience also have higher ethical standards. Those holding managerial positions in the newsroom also seem to be less tolerant of certain questionable journalistic behaviors compared with those not holding such positions (see Table 8.5).

Table 8.5   Ethically Questionable Practices Disapproved by Journalists (in %)

	All Journalists	*Less Experienced Journalists (10 years or less)*	*Seasoned Journalists (more than 10 years)*	*Journalists not Holding Managerial Positions*	*Journalists Holding Managerial Positions*
Disclosing name of rape victim	97.0	98.7	94.1	97.1	92.7
Breaching promise of confidentiality	84.5	88.4	78.1	85.8	80.5
Using personal docs without permission	71.8	67.7	78.5	72.7	73.8
Claiming to be someone else	70.5	62.8	85.1	67.0	85.3
Employed in a firm for information	68.9	67.2	71.8	65.8	77.3
Paying for information	66.2	62.6	72.6	63.7	80.0
Unauthorized use of government documents	63.0	56.5	73.8	59.7	78.3
Badgering informants	53.7	54.3	52.8	52.0	55.1
Dramatization of news by actors	49.8	47.5	53.3	46.3	63.3
Hidden camera	31.7	25.7	43.2	31.6	43.2

Note.   Percentages in the cells represent those who would not approve these acts under any circumstances.

Table 8.6   Perceived Factors Influencing Journalism Ethics (in %)

	Extremely Influential	Quite Influential	Somewhat Influential	Not Very Influential
Day-to-day newsroom learning	35.3	40.4	20.9	3.4
Senior reporters/editors	24.2	46.3	21.7	7.8
Decisions by respected news org.	22.1	34.4	30.1	13.4
Family upbringing	21.1	38.4	22.5	17.9
Religious training	15.5	19.1	20.5	44.9
Seminars on ethics	13.2	26.4	32.7	27.6
Experiences with college media	11.5	24.3	25.3	38.8
High school and college teachers	11.0	26.5	26.8	35.7
Publishers and managers	9.3	19.3	29.6	41.8
Web resources	9.3	16.3	34.1	40.2
Professional/trade publications	7.8	20.3	35.6	36.3

Note.   The list is rank-ordered by what the respondents found extremely influential in shaping their ideas in matters of journalism ethics.

The greatest influence on journalists in handling ethical issues comes from the newsroom, where journalists learn through daily routines and interaction with senior journalists. Newsroom coaching is followed by ethical decisions made by respected news organizations and personal upbringing. Please see Table 8.6 for the rank-order of various factors that influence journalists' ethical decision making (see Table 8.6).

Influence on Public Opinion.   Our findings also indicate that the journalists as a group feel that the media have a rather significant influence on the formation of public opinion. On a scale from 0 (no influence) to 10 (very great influence), the respondents gave the media an average score of 7.3. But when they were asked how strong they think the media's influence on public opinion should be, the average score is 6.7. In other words, the respondents as a group think that the media should have a bit less influence on the formation of public opinion than what the respondents think they have. No significant differences were found between those who hold and do not hold managerial positions in the newsroom, and between junior and more seasoned journalists.

Commitment to Journalism.   When asked whether they plan to work in the news media during the next five years, more than half the respondents (55.5%) said that they want to stay on the job. While 19.7% said that they were not entirely sure whether they wanted to pursue another career, only 17.4% were sure that they wanted to work somewhere else within the next five years. As expected, the younger journalists, those who have worked in journalism for shorter periods, and those who were dissatisfied with their jobs said that they are more likely to leave journalism. The most cited reasons for wanting to leave the profession were to get better pay (27.4%), to change career (26.2%), and to pursue personal interest and self-improvement (22.6%).

English- vs. Asian-Language Journalists.   Although they are housed inside the same company, the Asian-language news media (Chinese, Malay, and Tamil) serve specific ethnic communities while the English news media cut across ethnic divisions. Lee (2000) even argued that English-language journalists are more Westernized and have different cultural values compared with their colleagues working in Asian-language media. To see if these two groups of journalists hold different views about journalism as a profession, we compared the answers to our survey questions from respondents working for English- and Asian-language newspapers.[2] The findings show that the two groups share common views on most topics, but some differences do exist between them.

Journalists working for English-language newspapers are more likely than their colleagues at Asian-language newspapers to plan to leave journalism to work somewhere else (21.4% vs. 15.4%) or to feel undecided about whether they will still work for the news media in five years (26.2% vs. 14.4%). More Asian-language journalists joined the news media due to their interests and passion for journalism than their English-language counterparts (68.2 vs. 46.4%).

Journalists working for English-language newspapers tend to receive higher pay than their Asian-language counterparts. The latter are more likely to consider pay (43.1% vs. 23.2%), benefits (20.7% vs. 9.3%), and job security (44.7% vs. 29.3%) very important in judging journalism jobs. Also, more journalists working for the Asian-language newspapers find the job somewhat or very dissatisfying (33.0% vs. 18.0%) than their colleagues at English-language newspapers.

No significant differences were found between the two groups in their assessment of journalistic freedom in Singapore, except that more English-language journalists find government and politics to be a major limit on their professional freedom (42.4% vs. 28.8%). As for their views on various ethically questionable journalism practices, more English- than Asian-language journalists believe that "unauthorized use of business or government documents" (53.2 vs. 23.7%) may be justified on occasion, "badgering unwilling informants to get a story" (66.2 vs. 48.3%), and "using recreation or dramatization of news by actors" (64.1 vs. 41.4%). At the same time, English-language journalists are more likely to disapprove of "paying people for confidential information" (74.7 vs. 56.4%) and "breaking a promise of confidentiality" (97.4 vs. 78.9%).

Conclusions

Journalists' attitudes, as revealed in this survey study, are clearly influenced by the way their profession has evolved in Singapore. They share with their colleagues globally a strong sense of professional responsibility to inform the public and to help citizens express their interests. However, Singapore's journalists are circumspect about where the press stands in relation to the state and society. Most do not see their profession as the Fourth Estate or adversary of government. What the survey cannot answer, however, is the degree of normative acceptance of this position. It is possible that journalists, having had direct experience of a government with a strong record of clean and competent administration, may genuinely agree that Singapore does not need the press to play the role of an adversarial watchdog. Alternatively, journalists who disavow such a role may be simply accepting the reality of politically imposed limits on the press. The institutional memory of the news media in Singapore is of a government that countenances measured criticism of its policies, but that brooks no challenge to its ultimate authority.

Also noteworthy is that journalists in the aggregate seem to desire slightly less influence on public opinion than they claim to have (this may not be true for many individual journalists). This group discomfort with the role of actively shaping public opinion or setting the political agenda is again apparently in line with the circumscribed role of the press in the PAP model. Yet, the classic "nation-building" role of the press—described in the "development journalism" model as well as in some of the PAP's own thinking—encourages a more active role for the press as an educator. Indeed, Singapore's national news media have always been called upon to support and amplify various public education campaigns, on topics ranging from personal hygiene to staying economically competitive. The journalists' aggregated responses about media influence on public opinion and public agenda setting suggest no great enthusiasm for such a function. Instead, they seem to be more comfortable with the detachment of a reportorial role, in line with the routine of professional objectivity.

Singapore journalists' acceptance of a political role that is narrowly interpreted may help explain one of the most surprising findings of the survey: their sanguine attitude toward government controls. Almost three-quarters said that they are able to work on the stories that they want to. Only one-quarter are dissatisfied with their work, while a negligible proportion feel that their news organizations are doing a poor job of informing the public. These figures are difficult to reconcile with Singapore's low press freedom ratings. The most plausible explanation is that government actions to limit freedom of speech mainly affect forms of communication that most journalists do not see as part of their work, such as political advocacy and dissent. Similarly, the government's use of discretionary licensing to restrict entry into the newspaper and broadcast industries does not adversely affect journalists working for the companies that already have licenses.

Although most analyses of Singapore's media focus on government–press relations, the organizational level deserves some scrutiny. This is especially the case in Singapore, with its highly concentrated industry structure: few journalists work outside of Singapore Press Holdings and Mediacorp. This has important implications. Journalists are simultaneously members of a profession with a set of high-minded norms as well as employees of or freelancers for media outlets with an interest in commercial success. It could be argued that professional standards are easier to maintain when the organization is spared the excesses of cut-throat competition, as in Singapore's duopolistic media industry. On the other hand, when professional norms are in conflict with corporate priorities, the absence of alternative employers may weaken professionals' bargaining position, leading to journalists being forced to compromise professional standards under management pressure.

When the data from Singapore are examined, there is no evidence that industry concentration has had a negative effect on journalists' professed professional ethics. The majority of SPH and MediaCorp journalists expressed disapproval for the questionable practices probed in the survey. Longer-serving respondents, as well as those with supervisory roles, profess stricter ethical standards. Journalists cite the newsroom and their peers as the biggest influences on their ethical orientation. Together, the data suggest that although the profession as such is weak in Singapore in terms of its degree of organization and solidarity, newsrooms have contributed to the nurturing of professional standards, including ethics.

One other possible area of concern is the difference in perceptions between more junior journalists and their seniors. Newsroom supervisors tend to identify external, political controls as the main limit on journalists' autonomy, while lower-level journalists tend to attribute the lack of freedom to internal constraints. This perception gap probably results from the opacity of government influence on editorial decision making. Supervisors on the receiving end of behind-the-scenes government pressure usually keep such communications confidential, leaving their staff to assume that the resulting editorial decisions were made independently. In a more overt censorship regime, journalists at all levels, and their readers, are united in their knowledge of where and when censorship is exercised. Such knowledge can be a source of professional solidarity and of a concerted reaction against unwarranted repression (Curry & Martin 2003).

In Singapore, however, the government has passed the buck to gatekeepers within the media to predict and pre-empt government intervention in lieu of external censorship. This is a mixed blessing. On the one hand, it has spared today's press from the bans and lengthy detentions that occurred in the 1960s and 1970s. On the other hand, the internalization of political considerations within the newsroom places newsroom supervisors in an awkwardly ambiguous position and makes it difficult to gauge—even for insiders, as shown by the survey—where professional judgment ends and self-censorship begins. In press systems that are more overtly repressive as well as in those that are more free, journalists have a clear us-and-them attitude toward the powers that be. Singapore's hybrid regime denies the profession such a clear self-identity.

Note from the Authors

We would like to thank the management of Singapore Press Holdings for agreeing to allow us access to journalists working for the company. However, the views expressed in this article are entirely our own.

Notes

1. Many journalists cited the most significant limit to their freedom as the "government," "government agencies," "government control," "politics," and "politicians." Considering the local context, we find it difficult to separate these categories as they are often used interchangeably. Therefore, we combined them into this broad category of government and political authorities.
2. MediaCorp journalists were not included in this analysis as we do not have information on whether the MediaCorp respondents work for the English news or news in Asian languages. The analyses were based on 274 SPH journalists, including 147 respondents from the English newspapers and 127 from the Asian-language newspapers.

References

Case, William. 2002. *Politics in Southeast Asia: Democracy or less.* Richmond, England: Curzon.

Cialdini, Robert B., Carl A. Kallgren, and Raymond R. Reno. 1991. A focus theory of normative conduct: A theoretical refinement and reevaluation of the role of norms in human behavior. *Advances in Experimental Social Psychology,* 24: 201–234.

Curry, Jansen, Sue Curry, and Brian Martin. 2003. Making censorship backfire. *Counterpoise,* 7(3): 5–15.

Diamond, Larry. 2002. Thinking about hybrid regimes. *Journal of Democracy* 13(2):21–35.

Goh, Chok Tong. 2005. Speech by Mr Goh Chok Tong, Senior Minister, at the 5th Anniversary Dinner of TODAY Newspaper, October 31. Retrieved from http://stars.nhb.gov.sg.

Han, Fook Kwang. 1995. The Lee way and the ST. In *The Straits Times: 1845–1995, 100.* Singapore: Singapore Press Holdings.

Koh, Tommy, Timothy Auger, Jimmy Yap, and Wei Chian Ng (eds.). 2006. *Singapore: The encyclopedia.* Singapore: Editions Didier Millet/National Heritage Board.

Lee, Kuan Yew. 1971. *The mass media and new countries.* Address to the General Assembly of the International Press Institute at Helsinki, June 9. Retrieved from http://journalism.sg/lee-kuan-yews-1971-speech-on-the-press/.

Lee, Kuan Yew. 2000. Managing the media. In *From third world to first: The Singapore story 1965–2000,* pp. 212–225. Singapore: Singapore Press Holdings and Times Editions.

Singapore Department of Statistics. 2010. Singapore residents by age group, ethnic group and sex, end June 2009. Retrieved from http://www.singstat.gov.sg/pubn/reference/mdscontents.html#Demography

Yew, Roseline, and Hao, Xiaoming. 2002. Journalism ethics: Mainstream versus tabloid journalists. *Asia-Pacific Media Educator,* 12–13:139–155.

Zakaria, Fahred. 2003. *The future of freedom: Illiberal democracy at home and abroad.* New York: W.W. Norton.

9 Journalists in Taiwan

Ven-hwei Lo

Taiwan has one of the freest and most competitive media environments in Asia. An island nation situated about 100 miles off the southeast coast of Mainland China, Taiwan has a highly diversified media system with 2,039 newspapers, 5,883 magazines, 174 radio stations, five terrestrial television stations, 64 cable television system operators, and 98 satellite broadcasting program providers (Government Information Office 2009).

As of 2009, Taiwan's population was estimated at 23.1 million. About 98% of Taiwanese people are Han Chinese, and the remainder are mostly Malay-Polynesian aborigines who reached the island thousands of years ago (Government Information Office 2009). In the early 1950s, Taiwan was a poor, rural society with a per capita GDP of less than US$100. In 2008, however, Taiwan's GDP surpassed that of most other Asian countries with a per capita GDP of US$17,083 (Government Information Office 2009).

In recent years, Taiwan has been marked by its political reforms and media transformations. The country's political reforms began with the lifting of martial law in 1987. Prior to 1987, Taiwan was a one-party state. The Nationalist Party, also known as the Kuomingtang (KMT), was Taiwan's only legal, active political party. No opposition party was allowed to form, although non-KMT members had contested seats in elections at various levels.

As a result of the lifting of martial law, many political parties emerged. In 2008, a total of 136 political parties had registered with the government, but only six were significant in electoral politics: the KMT, the Democratic Progressive Party, the New Party, the People First Party, the Taiwan Solidarity Union, and the Nonpartisan Solidarity Union (Government Information Office 2009).

Taiwan's Media

The lifting of martial law also has profoundly influenced Taiwan's news media industry. Before 1987, all news media in Taiwan were under direct or indirect control of the government, which imposed a ban on the number of newspapers and on the establishment of new television and radio stations. Before the lifting of martial law, there were only three terrestrial television stations, 33 radio stations, and 31 daily newspapers in Taiwan (Wang & Lo 2000).

Through the media ban, the government had effectively restricted freedom of the press by facilitating government control over the news media and by preventing media ownership from falling into the hands of the opposition leaders. Consequently, all three television stations were controlled by the government. In addition, 12 of the 33 radios stations and 14 of the 31 daily newspapers were owned by the government and the ruling KMT.

Since the end of the newspaper ban in 1988, the number of newspapers has increased drastically. By May 2009, there were 2,039 registered newspapers, but only 30 were published regularly

(Government Information Office 2009). The largest and most prestigious newspapers are the *Liberty Times*, the *Apple Daily*, the *United Daily News*, and the *China Times*. These four privately owned newspapers dominate the daily newspaper market and account for more than 89% of the total daily newspaper circulation in Taiwan (Chang & Liao 2009).

The 22-year ban on the establishment of new television stations was lifted in 1993 when the government enacted a law legalizing the cable industry. In 1994, when cable television was in its embryonic stage, the three terrestrial stations dominated the market. Since 1994, television in Taiwan has grown rapidly. In 2007, there were five terrestrial television companies, 66 cable television companies and 155 satellite broadcasting channels (Government Information Office 2008). About 84% of Taiwan's television households subscribed to cable television services, with many operators offering more than 90 channels of information and entertainment programs (Chang & Liao 2009).

Before the emergence of cable television, Taiwan was served by three terrestrial television stations. The Taiwan Television Company was controlled by the Taiwan Provincial Government. The China Television Company was primarily owned by the KMT, the ruling political party. The Chinese Television System was owned by the Ministry of Defense and the Ministry of Education. Therefore, the three television stations were virtually owned and controlled by the triple alliance of the government, the military, and the governing party. In 2006, the government passed a media reform law freeing the terrestrial television stations from the control of the government and political parties. Under the media reform law, the government-controlled Chinese Television System was incorporated into the Taiwan Public Broadcasting System. The China Television Company, owned by KMT, was sold to the China Times media group, a private media organization. The government-controlled Taiwan Television enterprise was acquired by Unique Satellite Television and became a private station in 2007. Before the media reform law was enacted, the three television stations' political coverage was overwhelmingly pro-government or pro-KMT. After the change of ownership, however, the three stations provided more balanced coverage of election campaigns and political events (Lo & Huang 2010).

At present, about 15 channels broadcast regular Chinese-language news programs, including seven all-news cable channels. Most cable news channels have their own staffs of reporters and editors and offer news in various forms including breaking news reports, interviews, financial news, public affairs shows, and call-in programs around the clock. From the Taiwanese viewers' perspective, television news has never been so diverse or easily accessible (Lo & Chang, 2006).

The stringent control of radio stations also was eased when the government lifted the ban on new radio licenses in 1993. In 1994, there were only 33 radio stations in Taiwan. By mid-1998, the number of radio stations soared to 80. By May 2009, Taiwan had 174 radio stations, of which only 29 were in operation before 1993 (Government Information Office 2009). It is apparent that Taiwan's broadcast industry has entered a new phase, which is marked by unprecedented competition and broader freedom in news coverage.

With their enormous news holes, cable news channels have provided their audiences with significantly more content diversity by offering more news reports, more interviews, and more analyses of current affairs. As a result, the audience for television news has increased significantly. Past studies indicated that respondents who watched television news almost every day had increased from 63.6% in 1992 to 79.6% in 2008 (Lo 1993; Chang & Liao 2009). On the other hand, newspaper readership has declined sharply. The Taiwan Social Change surveys found that those who claimed to read a newspaper almost every day had declined dramatically from 61.9% in 1993 to 38.5% in 2008 (Chang & Liao 2009).

As a result, newspapers' advertising revenue decreased substantially and most newspapers suffered serious financial difficulties (Hsu & Lo 2009). In 1995, newspapers had a 36% share of the total media advertising revenue, which dropped to 12.2% in 2007 (Government Information Office 2008; Wang & Lo 2000). The declining readership and advertising revenue levels have been accompanied by staff layoffs, cost cutting, content reduction, and even the closing of newspapers. In 2006 alone, five newspapers were shut down, including the *Central Daily News*, the *Min Sheng Daily,* and the *Great China Daily News*. Thus, as in most other industrialized nations, Taiwanese newspapers are experiencing financial difficulties and are facing an uncertain future.

Although radio news listenership has not increased in recent years, radio news programs have diversified to include news and current events, traffic updates, stock market reports, regular features, studio and telephone interviews, as well as call-in programs.

The rapid growth of electronic media and the development of new media inevitably led to heavy competition. This competition and the struggle for audience growth and retention have led newspapers and television stations to place a greater emphasis on sensationalism, entertainment, and soft news to boost circulation figures or ratings and increase revenues. Consequently, soft news has been on the rise and the distinction between news and entertainment is increasingly obscure (Ma 2003). It therefore comes as no surprise that the news media have been widely criticized for trivializing news and intermixing news with entertainment. The major concern of Taiwan's media critics is no longer the lack of press freedom, but the increasingly confused ethical principles and level of media independence from commercial sponsors (Ma 2003; Wang & Lo, 2000). Overall, the quality of the news media in Taiwan is declining and is slowly losing the public's confidence (Lo 2004).

Previous Studies

Surveys of journalists were rare in Taiwan until the 1990s. Most of the early studies of journalists were based on convenience samples with small sample sizes. For example, in a 1986 study of newspaper, television, and radio reporters, Cheng (1988) found that reporters in Taiwan were predominately male—75.8% were male and 24.2% were female. This study also found that 95.7% of Taiwan reporters had received at least some college education with 18.7% having pursued graduate studies. Among college degree holders, 53.4% majored in journalism. The same study also revealed that about 90% of the reporters surveyed were less than 40 years old with most (69.4%) falling between the ages of 26 and 35.

In the 1990s, two national surveys of journalist were conducted (Lo 1998; Lo & Chan 2004). The surveys found that the average age of Taiwanese journalists changed very little between the two survey periods: from 35.8 years in 1994 to 35.0 years in 1996. Both surveys also found that Taiwanese journalists tend to be under 45 years of age, with most falling between the ages of 25 and 44. The largest group is between 25 and 34 years old, followed by the 35 to 44 age group. There are, however, very few journalists under the age of 25 or over the age of 55.

With regard to gender, the studies revealed that Taiwanese journalists were predominately male (62.3% in 1994 and 59.4% in 1996). However, the proportion of women in journalism had increased from 37.7% in 1994 to 40.6% in 1996. In terms of education and training, the two surveys found that in 1994, 93.5% of Taiwan journalists had received at least some college education and 15% of them had pursued graduate studies. In 1996, 98% had received at least some college education and 14.4% had graduate training. Among college graduates, 52.2% majored in journalism or communications in 1996, compared to 57.5% in 1994.

Method

This study is based on a 2004 national survey of working journalists in Taiwan. The purpose of the survey was to examine journalists' basic characteristics, their education and training, working conditions, professional values, and ethics in 2004. In this study, we followed the definition of journalists used by Weaver and Wilhoit (1986). We also adopted many of the questions originally asked by Weaver and Wilhoit (1986), although some of the questions were altered to make them more suitable for the Taiwanese respondents.

Following Weaver and Wilhoit (1986: 168), we defined journalists as those "who have editorial responsibility for the preparation or transmission of news stories or other information." However, our definition of journalist also includes researchers, photographers, and camera operators. In other words, the population of our survey is full-time editorial personnel including all reporters, editors, wire editors and translators, correspondents, columnists, researchers, news announcers, photographers, and camera operators employed by Chinese-language radio and television stations and daily newspapers in Taiwan.

To obtain a representative sample, we used a multi-stage sampling plan. For the first stage, we compiled a list of all Chinese-language daily newspapers, radio, and television stations in Taiwan. For the second stage, we drew a random sample of individual newspapers, radio, and television stations from that list. For the third stage, we obtained lists of all journalists working for the selected newspapers, radio, and television stations. The final stage was to draw a random sample of individual journalists.

Before formal interviews were conducted, we sent a letter to each of the journalists in our sample telling them the purposes of the study and asking for their cooperation. Face-to-face interviews were conducted in November 2004. Of the total 1,642 journalists contacted, 1,182 (or 72%) completed the questionnaires, including 100 (8.4%) radio journalists, 436 (36.8%) television journalists, and 646 (54.7%) daily newspaper journalists.

General Characteristics of Journalists

Age and Gender.   The survey indicates that the average age of Taiwan journalists is 35.9 years old. As Table 9.1 shows, Taiwanese journalists tend to be under 45 years old, with most falling between

Table 9.1   Age and Gender of Journalists (in %)

	Radio (N = 100)	Television (N = 436)	Newspaper (N = 643)	Total (N=1,179)
Age				
Under 24	–	8.1	1.1	3.7
25–34	32.3	61.9	30.9	42.5
35–44	47.5	27.8	45.3	39.0
45–54	19.2	1.9	21.7	14.1
55–64	1.0	0.2	1.0	0.7
Mean	38.3	32.0	38.3	35.9
Gender				
Male	40.0	60.6	58.3	57.5
Female	60.0	39.4	41.7	42.5

the ages of 25 to 44. The largest age group is 25 to 34 years old, followed by the 35 to 44 age group. Only a few journalists are under 25 or over 55.

The age distribution shows that television journalists are considerably younger than their counterparts in radio and newspaper. The average age for television journalists is 32.0 years compared to 38.3 in radio and newspapers. Overall, these findings suggest that journalism in Taiwan tends to be a young occupation and that most journalists leave it relatively early. They also suggest that Taiwan's news media may experience a considerable exodus of their most experienced journalists. Compared to research conducted by Lo and Chan in Mainland China and Hong Kong (2004), Taiwanese journalists are younger than Chinese journalists, but older than their Hong Kong counterparts.

The findings also show that Taiwan journalists are predominately male (57.5%). However, it is clear that there is considerable variation in the extent to which the different types of news media are dominated by male journalists (see Table 9.1). About 60% of those working in radio are women, compared to only 42% female journalists at daily newspapers and 39% at television stations. More significantly, the proportion of female journalists between the ages of 25 and 34 is higher (49.2%). In fact, more than 50% of all journalists under the age of 34 are female, suggesting that most women leave journalism in their early 30s.

Education and Training.   In general, Taiwan journalists tend to be well educated. Table 9.2 reveals that almost all (96.5%) of Taiwanese journalists had at least some college education. Specifically, 16.1% of the journalists hold junior college degrees, 79.2% hold bachelor's degrees, and 19.7% hold graduate degrees.

Among the college degree holders, 59.2% majored in journalism or communications. This illustrates that although journalism and communications are the most popular fields of study for Taiwan journalists, the news media employ a large number of journalists whose college preparation is in other fields. The humanities are the second most popular field, followed by other social sciences.

Table 9.2   Education and Training of Journalists (in %)

	Radio (N = 100)	Television (N = 436)	Newspaper (N = 643)	Total (N = 1,179)
Highest Education				
High school grad	2.0	7.6	1.7	3.5
Junior college grad	26.0	13.3	16.6	16.1
Some university	3.0	0.9	0.9	1.1
University grad	41.0	54.4	53.4	52.7
Some grad school	8.0	8.3	5.7	6.8
Master's	20.0	15.5	22.3	19.7
Major in College				
Journalism	19.4	28.0	31.9	29.5
Communications	34.7	35.5	25.4	29.7
Others	45.9	36.5	42.7	40.8
Major in Grad School				
Journalism	55.0	30.9	22.2	27.4
Communications	25.0	42.6	27.1	31.2
Others	30.0	26.5	50.7	41.4

The proportion of journalists who had majored in business, sciences, and law, however, is very small. No significant differences in types of college degrees were found when television, radio, and daily newspaper journalists were compared (see Table 9.2).

Working Conditions.   The most important indicator of working conditions is salary (Weaver & Wilhoit 1986). Our survey indicates that in 2004, Taiwanese journalists' salaries averaged US$1,733 per month. Less than 1% of the respondents report monthly incomes of less than $667, while 18.6% said they made more than $2,333. Most journalists (40.5%) earn between $1,000 and $1,667 per month and about a third (35.5%) make between $1,667 and $2,333. However, Taiwanese journalists usually receive one or two months' salary as a bonus at the end of each year. Therefore, the average annual income of a typical Taiwanese journalist is about $23,400. Of course, journalists' salaries varied significantly by medium. Journalists at daily newspapers earned the most ($1,833), followed by those working for television ($1,633) and radio stations ($1,533).

There is also a significant salary discrepancy by gender. Male journalists have an average monthly income of $1,767, compared to $1,667 for female journalists. Most of the disparity can be explained by length of employment. On average, male journalists have about two more years of work experience than female journalists (11 vs. 9 years).

Perceived Autonomy.   Another indicator of working conditions is perceived autonomy. Our survey indicates that levels of perceived work autonomy among Taiwanese journalists are fairly high. Half of all journalists claimed to have "almost complete" (8.3%) or "considerable" freedom (41.7%), while slightly more than a third (37.5%) claimed to have at least "some" freedom. Only 5.9% said that they had "almost no freedom at all." Considerable differences in perceived autonomy also appeared among journalists from the various news media. About 55% of the daily newspaper journalists, 71% of the radio, and 39% of the television journalists claimed to have complete or considerable freedom in their work. Thus, radio journalists appear to have the highest level of perceived autonomy, while television journalists tend to have the least (see Table 9.3).

Job Satisfaction.   Our survey also asked respondents to indicate their levels of job satisfaction by answering the following question: "All things considered, how satisfied are you with your present job—would you say you are very satisfied, satisfied, dissatisfied, or very dissatisfied?" The results reveal that although very few Taiwan journalists say they are very satisfied with their jobs, a majority appeared to be satisfied. While 64.4% of the respondents say they are satisfied with their jobs, less than a third say that they are either dissatisfied (22.6%) or very dissatisfied (4.6%).

Regression analysis shows that several factors are significant predictors of job satisfaction. Journalists who rate their news organization more highly in informing the public or who claim more autonomy in their jobs tend to express higher levels of job satisfaction. In addition, those who earn higher

Table 9.3   Perceived Autonomy of Journalists (in %)

	Radio (N = 100)	Television (N = 435)	Newspaper (N = 641)	Total (N = 1,176)
Almost complete freedom	14.0	4.6	10.0	8.3
Considerable freedom	57.0	34.3	44.5	41.7
Some freedom	25.0	45.3	34.3	37.5
Almost no freedom	1.0	10.1	3.7	5.9
No opinion	3.0	5.7	7.5	6.5

Table 9.4   Job Satisfaction of Journalists (in %)

	Radio (N = 100)	Television (N = 436)	Newspaper (N = 636)	Total (N=1,172)
Very satisfied	4.0	6.0	5.3	5.5
Satisfied	73.0	51.4	61.8	58.9
Dissatisfied	16.0	27.4	20.4	22.6
Very dissatisfied	3.0	7.1	3.1	4.6
No opinion	4.0	8.1	9.3	8.4

salaries or who have higher levels of education are more likely to express greater job satisfaction. Age and gender, on the other hand, are not significant predictors of job satisfaction (see Table 9.4).

Journalists' Rating of Their Organization.   While only a small percentage of Taiwanese journalists (8.1%) think their media organizations are doing an outstanding job of informing the public, a majority (68.2%) think that their organizations are doing a "very good" or at least a "good" job in news reporting. Only a few journalists (7.9%) think that their organizations are doing a "poor" job. The findings also indicate that radio journalists are more likely to rate the public performance of their media organizations highly than newspaper or television journalists.

Employment Aspirations.   About 46% of the journalists say that they want to work for the same media organization in five years, while 11% say that they want to work for different news organizations, and 20% are planning to leave the field of journalism completely within five years. Interestingly, about a quarter (24%) of the journalists are undecided regarding this question. In 1994, only 12% of surveyed journalists said they planned to leave the field of journalism in five years. Similar to the high exodus rate among female journalists, the relatively high proportion of journalists who plan to leave the field during the next five years is disturbing because it may indicate a coming shortage of experienced journalists.

Considerable media differences emerge with regard to journalists' future employment aspirations. Radio journalists (54%) are the most likely to say that they planned to work for the same media organization in five years, followed by newspaper (52%), and television journalists (34%). Discriminant analysis reveals several factors that are important for distinguishing those who want to work for the same media organization in five years and those who plan different jobs or are undecided. The analysis shows that job satisfaction is the most important factor in distinguishing between these two groups. Journalists who claim higher levels of job satisfaction are more likely to say they want to work for the same organization in five years. Other influential factors that correlate positively with journalists' willingness to stay in the profession are higher ratings of media organizations as information providers, higher levels of perceived work autonomy, more years of work experience, and higher levels of education.

Perception of Journalistic Roles.   Following Weaver and Wilhoit's (1986) study of American journalists, we asked the journalists in our sample to rate the importance of 11 media roles on a scale ranging from 1 ("not really important") to 4 ("extremely important"). Table 9.5 shows that most Taiwanese journalists consider three journalistic roles as extremely important: "reporting the news accurately" (71%), "avoiding stories with unverified content" (52.5%), and "getting information to the public quickly" (47.2%). While these roles indicate that Taiwanese journalists value the information dissemination function of the media, a significant number of journalists also consider

Table 9.5   Perceptions of News Media Roles (% saying "extremely important")

Report news accurately	71.0
Avoid stories with unverified content	52.5
Get information to public quickly	47.2
Provide analysis of complex problems	43.1
Develop intellectual/cultural interests	40.4
Discuss national policy	36.0
Investigate government claims	32.9
Concentrate on widest audience	32.1
Provide entertainment	25.5
Serve as adversary of government	9.0
Serve as adversary of business	6.2

the interpretative and investigative functions of the media as extremely important: "providing analysis of complex problems" (43.1%), "discussing national policy" (36%), and "investigating government claims" (32.9%). Only a small number of journalists consider the roles of "adversary of government" (9%) or "adversary of business" (6.2%) as extremely important (see Table 9.5).

Ethical Perceptions of Reporting Practices.   Another indicator of professional values is journalists' perceptions of various reporting practices. Our survey asked the respondents to indicate their agreement with eight statements adapted from previous research concerning various reporting practices (Weaver & Wilhoit 1986). The results suggest that Taiwanese journalists tend to disagree with all eight reporting practices. Taiwanese journalists oppose especially two reporting practices: "divulging confidential sources" (81.6%) and "using personal documents without permission" (74.3%). Somewhat less opposition is found for "badgering sources" (62.4%), "using hidden microphones" (59.4%), and "using confidential documents" (55.9%). The least opposition is found for "using false identification" (53.7%), "paying for confidential information" (53.5%), and "employment under false pretenses" (52.8%) (see Table 9.6).

Conclusions

This study examined Taiwanese journalists' basic demographics, their education and training, their working conditions, and their professional values and ethics. The results show that the

Table 9.6   Ethical Perceptions of Various Reporting Practices (in %)

	Agree or Strongly Agree	*Disagree or Strongly Disagree*
Using false identification	38.9	53.7
Employment under false pretense	37.4	52.8
Using confidential documents	36.3	55.9
Paying for confidential information	35.4	53.5
Using hidden microphones	32.8	59.4
Badgering sources	29.9	62.4
Using personal documents without permission	19.3	74.3
Divulging confidential sources	15.5	81.6

average journalist in Taiwan is a married (50.3%) male who has a bachelor's degree, is 36 years old, earns about $1,700 per month, works for a daily newspaper, likes his job, and plans to stay with the same news organization for another five years.

Compared with Hong Kong and Chinese journalists (Lo & Chan 2004), Taiwanese journalists are more likely to hold a graduate degree and to major in journalism or communication. They tend to be younger than Mainland Chinese journalists, but older than their Hong Kong counterparts.

Another significant finding is that although Taiwanese journalists are predominately male, women are a growing force in the newsroom. The proportion of women in journalism increased from 37.7% in 1994 to 42.5% in 2004. However, this study also reveals that women are more likely to leave journalism jobs than are men. They are more likely than men to desire to work for a different news organization or to leave journalism within five years. It appears that male journalists will continue to dominate the newsroom if the news media cannot retain more experienced female journalists.

In fact, retaining the best and brightest journalists, both men and women, will be the most difficult challenge faced by the news media in Taiwan. This study clearly indicates that many of the most experienced journalists plan to leave the field relatively early because of low job satisfaction, limited autonomy, low pay, and a lack of esteem for the organization they work for. The findings leave little doubt that the news media have to make significant improvements in the working conditions of their editorial staff by increasing their salaries, improving their job satisfaction, providing them with more autonomy, and helping them advance in order to retain seasoned journalists. Thus, future studies need to examine the problems and obstacles journalists face during their professional careers.

References

Chang, Ly-Yun, and Pei-Shan Liao. 2009. *The basic survey project of Taiwan social change.* Taipei: Academia Sinica.

Cheng, Jei-Cheng. 1988. *Examining mass media.* Taipei: CommonWealth.

Government Information Office. 2008. *The Republic of China yearbook 2008.* Taipei: Author.

Government Information Office. 2009. *The Republic of China at a glance.* Taipei: Author.

Hsu, Jung-Hua, and Ven-hwei Lo. 2009. The problems of Taiwan newspapers. In *The reconstruction of Taiwan media,* edited by Foundation for Distinguished Journalism Award, pp. 153–176. Taipei: Chuliu.

Lo, Ven-hwei. 1998. The new Taiwan journalist: A sociological profile. In *The global journalist: News people around the world,* edited by David H. Weaver, pp. 71–88. Cresskill, NJ: Hampton Press.

Lo, Ven-hwei. 1993. *News media credibility.* Taipei: National Science Council Research Report.

Lo, Ven-hwei. 2004. Selective credibility. *Mass Communication Research* 80:1–50.

Lo, Ven-hwei, Jei-Cheng Cheng, and Chin-Chuan Lee. 1994. Television news is government news in Taiwan. *Asian Journal of Communication* 4(1): 99–110.

Lo, Ven-hwei, and Joseph Man Chan. 2004. *The changing journalists in China, Hong Kong and Taiwan.* Taipei: Chuliu.

Lo, Ven-hwei, and Chingching Chang. 2006. Knowledge about the Gulf Wars: A theoretical model of learning from the news. *The Harvard International Journal of Press/Politics* 11(3):135–155.

Lo, Ven-hwei, and Yi-Chia Huang. 2010. Television coverage of the 2008 presidential election in Taiwan. *Communication and Society* 11:165–189.

Ma, Ringo. 2003. Status of media in Taiwan. In *Encyclopedia of international media and communications,* edited by Donald H. Johnston, pp. 329–339. Boston: Academic Press.

Wang, Georgette, and Ven-hwei Lo. 2000. Taiwan. In *Handbook of the media in Asia,* edited by Shelton A. Gunaratne, pp. 660–681. New Delhi: Sage.

Weaver, David, H. 1998. *The global journalist: News people around the world.* Cresskill, NJ: Hampton Press.

Weaver, David H., and G. Cleveland Wilhoit. 1986. *The American journalist: A portrait of U. S. news people and their work.* Bloomington: Indiana University Press.

Journalists in Australia
and New Zealand

10 The Australian Journalist in the 21st Century

Beate Josephi and Ian Richards

Australian journalism is practiced in an environment that is contextualized by a number of forces. One of these is the historic division between government and non-government media. Australia's first newspapers were, in effect, official information sheets servicing the needs of the administration of the six British colonies, which later united to form the nation of Australia.

The earliest newspaper was the *Sydney Gazette*, established in the colony of New South Wales in 1803 by Governor Philip Gidley King to promulgate government orders and decrees (Lloyd 2002). While most early newspapers were dominated by administrative content, it has been claimed that there were examples of good journalism right from the beginning. For example, according to one study, the founder of *The Gazette* was "a marvelous journalist" and "his accounts of hangings and public events in Sydney of the highest standard" (Lloyd 2002: 6). With time, private individuals began establishing newspapers as businesses intended to make money, and thus a second theme emerged which remains influential today—the drive for commercial profit.

Business considerations have played a major part in shaping the development of the Australian media, which for much of the last century have been dominated by a small number of media corporations and two media moguls—Rupert Murdoch and the late Kerry Packer. Today the level of concentration of media ownership in Australia is higher than in most other countries (Richards 2005). One side effect of this situation has been intermittent but ongoing tension between public and private media, especially since the establishment of the Australian Broadcasting Commission (later Corporation) in 1932, and the Special Broadcasting Service in 1978.

Background

The style of journalism that evolved in Australia was strongly influenced by the colonial inheritance from the United Kingdom and, as in that country, can be described as an Anglo style of journalism that places considerable emphasis on the adversarial role (Deuze 2002). Australia's colonial inheritance also led to the emulation of the British practice of on-the-job training of new recruits via internships rather than university study, although this has changed in recent decades.

Geography has also been an important shaping influence on Australian journalism, most notably through what has been labeled "the tyranny of distance." This term refers both to Australia's remote location in relation to Europe and North America, and to the vast size of the continent, which means distances between population centers can be extensive. While Australia is as large as the continental United States, its population is little more than 21 million, located largely along the coastline. The pattern that developed was of five media hubs based in the metropolitan centers of Sydney, Melbourne, Brisbane, Perth, and Adelaide, and a far smaller, mostly coastal, regional media covering smaller towns and hamlets. This pattern of development led to some differences in outlook between urban and rural journalists, as the latter have tended to be more concerned with their relationship to their local community than in the case of those based in bigger cities (Bowd 2009).

Traditionally, the Australian journalist workforce has been heavily unionized, most notably through membership of the Australian Journalists' Association (AJA). Formed in 1910, the AJA was for many years able to achieve a membership in most media workplaces exceeding 90%. However, this level of membership has decreased dramatically in recent years for a number of reasons, including the effects of industrial legislation brought in by previous federal governments; dissatisfaction over the AJA's amalgamation with Actors' Equity to form the Media, Entertainment and Arts Alliance; and a wider social trend which has seen a dramatic decline in union membership in Australia generally. The increasing employment of women has been a feature of many newsrooms in Australia over the past two to three decades, but this has not been accompanied by a corresponding extension of female influence at the senior management level in media organizations.

As has happened elsewhere, with the rise of the Internet, technological change has become one of the strongest forces shaping contemporary Australian journalism. There have been many consequences from the new media, from the breakdown of traditional media business models to the rise of blogging and the need for journalists to develop their skills base so as to be equipped to handle images, audio and video, as well as write. Although the recent global financial crisis had less impact in Australia than in most countries, the associated decline in media profits and in newspaper circulations, in particular, have contributed to a general decline in the job market for journalists in Australia, and several media organizations have fired journalists in recent years.

Australia's Definition of Journalists

Journalists customarily have been hard to define. The data and definitions used in this study are based on the Australian Bureau of Statistics (ABS) 2006 census (ABS 2008), and the Australian and New Zealand Standard Classification of Occupations (ABS 2006).

Under the specification of "journalists and other writers" are listed copywriter, newspaper or periodical editor, print journalist, radio journalist, technical writer, television journalist, as well as journalists and related professionals "not further defined" and journalists and other writers "not elsewhere classified." The last group comprises bloggers, critics, editorial assistants, and essayists. As the ABS gives a breakdown of each occupation in its census, copywriters and technical writers can be eliminated from the data. The number of journalists steadily increased in the ten years from 1996 to 2006.

Although most Australian newspapers have lost sales over the last decade, they have not experienced the decline in circulation seen in the United States. Australian newspaper circulation figures for 2001 to 2009 show a decline for Saturday and Sunday papers of between 5% and 6%, and a drop of weekday papers of 3.6% (Australian Newspaper History Group Newsletters (ANHG) 14 2001; ANHG 39 2006; ANHG 54 2009) (see Table 10.1).

Table 10.1   Circulation of Australian Papers

	2001	2006	2009
Audit period	1/1–6/30/2001	1/1–6/30/2006	4/1–6/30/2009
Monday–Friday papers	2,336,189	2,296,571	2,256,436
Saturday papers	3,142,459	3,047,027	2,955,791
Sunday papers	3,469,141	3,497,959	3,297,584

In its 2008 Annual Report on the State of the Australian News Print Media, the Australian Press Council observed that, despite sharp increases in the number of readers accessing newspapers via the Internet, the weekday circulation of broadsheets was generally holding steady, while there had been a decline in tabloid circulation, and also steep falls in circulation in the magazine market (Australian Press Council 2008). However, newspaper advertising revenue had dropped significantly, although again not as sharply as in the United States. Although Australia was the only industrialized country not to have gone into recession in the recent global financial crisis, Australian journalists appear to be very aware of the changes and challenges that lie ahead.

Previous Studies

John Henningham's study published in *The Global Journalist: News People Around the World* (1998: 91–108) was the only major study of Australian journalists since the 1970s. Henningham's report, which provides a major point of comparison, was based on a large national telephone survey conducted in 1992 and a smaller survey in 1994.

A second comprehensive study of Australian journalism, titled *Sources of News and Current Affairs*, was commissioned by the Australian Broadcasting Authority (ABA) and carried out by Mark Pearson and Jeffrey Brand (Pearson & Brand 2001). Among other things, Pearson and Brand looked at attitudes and characteristics of news producers, agenda setting, ethics, accuracy, and credibility.

More recently, Hanusch (2008) surveyed 100 Australian journalists for a large cross-national study. He asked for journalists' conceptions of their institutional roles and ethical principles. The questions were phrased differently from the Henningham study; for example, with regard to power distance, market orientation, and truth claims. In terms of Australian journalism culture, Hanusch concluded that Australian journalists could be characterized as following the traditional values of the media as the Fourth Estate, seeing their role as non-partisan, adversarial reporters mainly focusing on facts but also trying to provide analysis of events and issues.

In October 2008, Australia's trade union for journalists, the Media Entertainment and Arts Alliance, surveyed its members online about the changes in their jobs (The Future of Journalism 2008). Questions centered on workload and work–life balance, pay, quality of output, training, and morale. A majority of 70% reported an increased workload, with only 14% being compensated for the extra hours worked. About 37% saw the quality of their work affected negatively while 43% saw no change and 20% considered there had been an improvement. Similarly, about 40% saw the expansion into new media as affecting the traditional media either somewhat or very negatively, with 35% being worried about jobs in the future.

Method

The results for basic characteristics of Australian journalists are based on data taken from the Australian Bureau of Statistics 2006 census (ABS 2008). The results for education and training, working conditions and professionalism are based on telephone surveys carried out between November 2009 and February 2010 with 117 journalists in metropolitan and regional areas in all Australian states and territories, and referred to as the 2010 survey. The research was supported by a grant from the Centre for Research in Entertainment, Arts, Technology, Education and Communications at Edith Cowan University and a grant through the University of South Australia. The questionnaire used in this survey was adapted from the one provided by Weaver, Beam, Brownlee,

Voakes, and Wilhoit (2007), covering all essential areas, including working conditions, perceived autonomy, reporting methods, views on public opinion, peer influence, and professional values.

Although the sample size for the 2010 survey is small compared with Henningham's 1992/94 study (1998), it is representative in that it interviewed journalists from national, metropolitan, suburban, and rural newspapers, and public and commercial broadcasting organizations operating at national, metropolitan, and local levels in all Australian states and territories. Of the journalists surveyed, 30% worked in the electronic media, 60% in the print media, and the remainder online, which closely replicates the balance of the Australian journalistic workforce between different media.

Importantly, the 2010 survey is the first to reflect an even gender balance in Australian journalism. In the 2010 study, 56% of journalists interviewed were female and 44% were male. In comparison, 33% of respondents in Henningham's study, and 40% in Hanusch's study were female. The mean age of respondents in the 2010 study was 39, which corresponds to the mean age for print journalists reported in the 2006 census. This compares with Hanusch's finding that the median age of Australia's journalists in 2008 was 37 years, up from 32 years in the early 1990s.

Findings

Basic Characteristics

Size of Workforce.   According to the ABS (2008), the number of journalists and other writers increased steadily from 12,152 in 1996 to 15,560 in 2006. Within this group, the number of print, television, and radio journalists rose from 7,455 in 1996 to 8,033 in 2006 (ABS 2008). The 2006 figures, though, predate the changes that occurred in the newspaper market following the onset of the global financial crisis.

Age.   There are considerable differences in the median age between print, radio, and television journalists. In 2006, the median age of print journalists was about 38 years. The single largest age group of print journalists was 55 years and older, while the second largest was those between 25 and 29 years old (ABS 2008). The picture is different in radio and television journalism where the group 30 to 34 was the largest. The overall median age was 35, three years older than in Henningham's (1998) earlier study, but in line with the median age of journalists globally (Josephi 2009).

Gender and Income.   Australian journalists achieved virtual gender balance by 2006 (ABS 2008). This result represents a considerable change from the 67% male and 33% female workforce recorded by Henningham (1998) in the early 1990s (see Table 10.3). According to the ABS data, 70% of print journalists and 73% of radio journalists work full-time, whereas 80% of television journalists work full-time. The average yearly income for print, radio, and television journalists in 2006 was about Australian $52,000 (approx. U.S.$55,000) per year (ABS 2008).

Table 10.2   Number of Australian Journalists

	1996	2001	2006
Journalists and other writers	12,152	13,973	15,560
Print, TV, and radio journalists only	7,455	7,108	8,033

Table 10.3　Gender Distribution of Journalists

	1996		2001		2006	
	Male	*Female*	*Male*	*Female*	*Male*	*Female*
Print journalist	3,238	2,585	2,933	2,589	3,201	3,103
Radio journalist	344	295	283	335	309	362
Television journalist	517	476	517	451	526	532
Total	4,099	3,356	3,733	3,375	4,036	3,997

Ethnic and Racial Origins.　The ABS (2008) data break down those born in Australia into indigenous and non-indigenous categories, and those born overseas into English- and non-English-speaking countries. According to the data, 77.6% of print journalists are Australian-born, and of these only 0.5% are indigenous. Of overseas-born print journalists, a further 70% come from English-speaking countries, primarily the United Kingdom, the United States, New Zealand, Ireland, and South Africa. Only 6.5% of the total number of print journalists are from non-English speaking countries. Among radio journalists, 76% are Australian-born. However, only 37% of overseas-born radio journalists were from English-speaking countries. This result is a reflection of the impact of Australia's second public broadcaster, the Special Broadcasting Service (SBS), which provides radio programs in original languages for Australia's many migrant communities, and also the rise of local community radio stations, which often broadcast in languages other than English. In television, on the other hand, 84% of journalists are Australian born, and only 2.3% come from non-English speaking countries. The number of indigenous journalists in radio and television is barely above 1%.

Religion and Political Leanings.　The largest proportion (42%) of Australian journalists stated that religion was "not at all important" to them, and a further 23% indicated that it was "not very important" (ABS 2008). This finding is in line with Henningham's previous findings.

The results on political leanings come from the 2010 survey and show that, since the 1992 study, Australian journalists have moved to the left (see Table 10.4). In the context of Australian politics, "left" generally refers to the policies of the Australian Labor Party and the Greens, while "right" generally refers to the policies of the Liberal and National parties. For political leaning, the 2010 data give a mean of 45.3, which puts Australian journalists slightly to the left of center. On the other hand, Australian journalists judged the editorial policy of their organizations to be a little right of center with a mean of 54.3.

Table 10.4　Political Leanings of Journalists (in %)

	1992[a]	*2008*[b]	*2010*[c]
Left of center	39.0	55.8	50.2
Middle of the road	41.0	27.4	28.4
Right of center	16.0	16.8	13.8
Declined answer	4.0	—	7.6

a Henningham (1992)
b Hanusch (2008)
c Josephi & Richards (2010)

Table 10.5   Education Levels of Journalists (in %)

	1992/1994	2010
Highest education level		
High school	45	16
Some undergraduate	20	4
Undergraduate degree	31	66
Some graduate	2	4
Graduate degree	2	10
Major at university		
Journalism/Broadcast Journalism	33	35
Communication/ Mass Communication	8	13
Other majors	59	52

Education and Training

Major shifts in educational levels of journalists can be observed in comparison to Henningham's 1992 study. Whereas in 1992/1994 almost half of the journalists had only a high school diploma, in 2010 the vast majority (84%) had a university degree (see Table 10.5).

Equally significant is the fact that the percentage of working journalists that graduated with an undergraduate degree in journalism has risen by only 2% from 33% in 1992 to 35% in 2010. Of those who completed an advanced degree in graduate or professional school, 61% did so in journalism or broadcast journalism, and a further 6% in communications.

Working Conditions

Of the journalists surveyed, 74% regularly undertook reporting duties and a further 11% did so occasionally. These were split equally between those who covered a specific beat and those who did not. While the notion of autonomy can be understood in many ways, most journalists in the 2010 survey interpreted it as the freedom to determine the approach to the stories on which they work. Ninety percent of the journalists said that they could "almost always" or "more often than not" follow up their story ideas. Similarly, 82% said that they had "almost complete" or "a great deal of freedom" in choosing the stories they worked on, and more than 90% stated they had "complete" or "a great deal of freedom" in deciding which aspects of a story should be emphasized. Consistent with the long-established Australian practice of using sub-editors (copy editors), 70% of journalists said that their work got some editing from others.

Job Satisfaction.   Although this survey was conducted at a time of widespread uncertainty in journalism, Australian journalists appeared to be only marginally less satisfied with their jobs than they were 18 years ago. In 2010, 76% of the journalists reported being very or fairly satisfied, while 24% were somewhat or very dissatisfied. This compares with the findings from 1992 that found 80% of journalists being very or fairly satisfied, while 20% were somewhat or very dissatisfied (Henningham 1998).

This data is corroborated by the fact that more than 70% of the respondents in 2010 saw themselves still working in the news media in five years, with 20% intending to work somewhere else and the remainder expecting to retire. Of those who still saw themselves working in the news media in five years, 20% expected to be working online. On the other hand, more than half of the respondents reported that the size of the newsroom staff in their organization had shrunk during the past few years.

Media Organization Perception.   Job satisfaction is often closely tied to the perception of the performance of the employer for whom the journalist is working. Asked whether their media organization was doing an "outstanding, very good, good, fair or poor job," 52% said that their organization was doing a very good job, and a further 18% said that it was doing an outstanding job. Only 3% thought that their organization was doing a poor job.

Audience Perception.   Overall, Australian journalists have a positive picture of their audience or readership. Only 6% believe that the public is gullible and easily fooled, with 56% strongly rejecting this suggestion. They also credit their audience with an interest in social problems, with 72% rejecting the notion that the audience does not want to hear or read about matters such as poverty or racial discrimination. Their position on whether the public is more interested in breaking news than in analysis is more evenly spread. Fifty-eight percent of the journalists agreed with this proposition, while 31% disagreed (somewhat or strongly for both).

Professionalism

A significant shift in union membership has occurred since Henningham's research. While in 1992, 86% of Australian journalists were union members, this survey found that the level of membership had dropped to 56% in 2010.

Media Roles.   Table 10.6 provides a comparison of Australian journalists' attitudes toward different media roles in 1992 and 2010. The data come from Henningham's 1992 survey and our 2010 study of Australian journalists. These findings suggest that the "watchdog" role is regarded more highly than any other, and that serving the public interest is highly regarded by many Australian

Table 10.6   Perceptions of Media Roles (% considering each role "extremely important")

	1992	2010
Get information to public quickly	74	80
Provide analysis of complex problems	71	72
Provide entertainment & relaxation	28	20
Investigate government claims	81	90
Analysis of international developments	—	60
Avoid stories with unverified content	45	35
Concentrate on widest audience	38	29
Discuss national policy	56	55
Develop cultural/intellectual interests	37	33
Serve as adversary of government	30	35
Serve as adversary of business	27	32
Set political agenda	—	15
Give people chance to express views	—	43
Motivate people to get involved	—	53
Point toward possible solutions	—	30

Table 10.7   Perceptions of Reporting Practices (% saying "may be justified on occasion")

	1992	2010
Paying for confidential information	31	25
Using confidential business/government documents without authorization	79	81
Claiming to be somebody else	13	11
Agreeing to protect confidentiality and not doing so	4	3
Badgering unwilling informants	55	40
Making use of personal documents without authorization	39	44
Getting employed in a firm to get Inside information	46	41
Use hidden microphones or cameras	—	52
Use re-creations of news by actors	—	70
Disclose name of rape victims	—	7

journalists. For example, 53% considered it was extremely important to motivate people to get involved in public discussions of important issues, and 61% considered helping people to be a very important part of their job. Somewhat surprisingly, only a third reported that they consider the adversarial role extremely important.

The second highest priority was placed on getting information to the public quickly. Providing analysis of complex problems also continues to be important. On the other hand, the media are seen to be less of a provider of entertainment and relaxation and less of a stimulant of cultural and intellectual interests than in 1992.

Reporting Practices.   Reporting practices are widely considered to be one of the most important indicators of ethical standards in journalism. They also reflect levels of professionalism. The figures below indicate what percentages of respondents indicated that the practice nominated "was justified on occasion" (see Table 10.7).

Using confidential government or business documents without authorization was overwhelmingly considered to be acceptable, while agreeing to protect confidentiality and then not doing so was the least acceptable practice. Australian journalists are strongly opposed to disclosing the names of rape victims (93% disapproval) and almost evenly divided on the use of hidden microphones and cameras (52% in favor). Gender cross-tabulation indicates that, while female journalists are consistently less likely to approve of questionable practices than their male counterparts, the difference between gender responses is minor.

Influences on Ethics.   In Australia, newsroom learning as well as guidance by senior reporters, editors, or news directors is considered to be of highest importance (85% each). For Australian journalists, the idea of what is newsworthy is most shaped by news sources. Seventy-five percent named these as influential, followed by journalistic training (72%) and supervisors (64%). Peers on the staff and friends are also judged as influential, with 55% and 50% respectively.

Public Opinion.   The public's view of journalist ethics remains low (Media Credibility Survey 2004). Newspaper journalists were seen at the same level as state politicians, with a 10% rating for honesty and ethical standards. Television journalists were rated at 16%, in contrast with doctors who rated 81%.

Table 10.8　Perceptions of Workplace (in %)

Importance of ...	1992 Very important	2010 Very important
Pay	23	19
Fringe benefits	7	7
Editorial policies of the organization	55	67
Job security	58	52
Chance to develop a specialty	40	50
Amount of autonomy	51	64
Chance to get ahead in the organization	51	43
Chance to help people	44	61
Chance to influence public affairs	—	58

As in previous studies, journalists think that the media are highly influential in the formation of public opinion. Similar to 1992, journalists gave the media's influence a median rating of 7.9 (previously 8, with 10 indicating very great influence). Similarly, when asked how strong the media's influence should be, their median rating was 6.5 (previously 6). When asked how frequently they got reactions from readers or listeners, more than half of the journalists indicated "regularly" and only 15% said that they heard seldom or never from their readers or audience. Similarly, 75% of journalists received regular or at least occasional feedback from their news sources.

Professional Orientations.　While pay continues to be fairly important to Australian journalists, it is notable that in 2010 fewer rated it as very important compared to 1992 (see Table 10.8). In relation to other issues, however, professional orientations appear to have shifted considerably, and gender cross-tabulation suggests that the rise in the proportion of female journalists has contributed significantly to this change. Job security is considered very important by women (60% compared to 42% of males) as is the chance to get ahead (53% compared to 28% males). The importance accorded to autonomy has also increased (up 13%), and was rated equally highly by male and female journalists. The responses of female news workers (75% very important compared to 58% males) were a major reason for the increased weight given to the editorial policies of the organization (up 12%). Female responses also contributed to the increased commitment to public service—the rating which has changed most of all—with 63% of female respondents rating this as very important compared to 48% of male journalists. Together, the responses to professional orientations suggest that the freedom and variety of their work is more important to Australia's journalism practitioners than ever before, and that this change is largely attributable to the increase in the proportion of females in the journalistic workforce.

Conclusions

It seems clear that Australian journalists have changed considerably since Henningham's survey in 1992. They are no longer a set of predominantly young and fairly well educated men, but a more mature group in which women slightly outnumber men. The reasons for the change in gender balance are not immediately apparent, but it coincides with an extended period during which female students have substantially outnumbered male students in Australian university journalism programs (Grenby, Kasinger, Patching, & Pearson, 2009). Levels of education have increased and more Australian practitioners than ever have university degrees. While the percentage of industry practitioners with journalism undergraduate degrees has not altered greatly, the number with postgraduate journalism qualifications has increased notably.

With regard to their professional roles, Australian journalists see themselves first and foremost as a watchdog on government. However, while they aspire to influence public affairs in ways that serve the public interest, they claim not to want to set the political agenda. At the same time, a decreasing number of journalists want to serve the widest possible audience, a development that appears to be a product of audience fragmentation and the breakdown of the media market into an increasing number of niche publications.

The increased concern with autonomy in the workplace and a greater emphasis on employers' editorial policies, which is carried in particular by the female side of the workforce, can be interpreted as an indicator of quality journalism and professional standing, while a decreased emphasis on pay, job security, and getting ahead in the organization might partly be a response to ongoing uncertainty in the industry in relation to employment and anxiety about the media's future directions. All the same, the fact that most Australian journalists consider the performance of their media organization to be very good or outstanding suggests that most are satisfied with the degree of autonomy they are given by their employer.

There is little doubt that the greatest challenge faced by Australian journalists at the time of the survey was the demand from new media and the continuing transfer of journalism to the digital platform. Having said this, though, their responses indicate that many, if not most, regard this as a challenge that can be overcome and consequently they share a fundamentally optimistic outlook. It remains to be seen whether this stance will be justified in the longer term.

References

Australian Bureau of Statistics. 2006. Australian and New Zealand standard classification of occupations, first edition: Unit group 2124 journalists and other writers. Retrieved from http://www.abs.gov.au/AUSSTATS/ABS@.NSF/Product+Lookup/1220.0~2006~Chapter~UNIT+GROUP+2124+Journalists+and+Other+Writers

Australian Bureau of Statistics. 2008. Employment in culture in Australia. Retrieved from http://www.abs.gov.au/AUSSTATS/abs@.nsf/DetailsPage/6273.02006?OpenDocument

Australian Newspaper History Group. 2001. Newsletter 14. Brisbane: University of Queensland. Retrieved from http://espace.library.uq.edu.au

Australian Newspaper History Group. 2006. Newsletter 39. Brisbane: University of Queensland.

Australian Newspaper History Group. 2009. Newsletter 54. Brisbane: University of Queensland.

Australian Press Council. 2008. State of the news print media. Retrieved from http://www.presscouncil.org.au/snpma/snpma2008/index_snpma2008.html

Bowd, Kathryn. 2009. Did you see that in the paper? Country newspapers and perceptions of local "ownership." *Australian Journalism Review* 31(1):49–62.

Deuze, Mark. 2002. National news cultures: A comparison of Dutch, German, British, Australian, and US journalists. *Journalism and Mass Communication Quarterly* 79(1):134–149.

Future of Journalism, The. 2008. *Life in the clickstream.* Redfern, NSW: Media Entertainment and Arts Alliance.

Grenby, Mike, Molly Kasinger, Roger Patching, and Mark Pearson. 2009. Girls, girls, girls. A study of the popularity of journalism as a career among female teenagers. *Australian Journalism Monographs 11.*

Hanusch, Folker. 2008. Mapping Australian journalism culture: Results from a survey of journalists' role perceptions. *Australian Journalism Review* 30(2):97–109.

Henningham, John. 1998. Australian Journalists. In *The global journalist: News people around the world*, edited by David H. Weaver, pp. 91–108. Cresskill, NJ: Hampton Press.

Josephi, Beate. 2009. Journalists: International profiles. In *Global journalism: Topical issues and media systems*, edited by Arnold de Beer and John Merrill, pp. 143–152. Boston: Pearson.

Lloyd, Clem. 2002. Th historical roots. In *Journalism: Investigation and research,* edited by Stephen Tanner, pp. 2–19. Frenchs Forest, NSW: Pearson Education Australia.

Media Credibility Survey. 2004. Why Australians don't respect the media. Retrieved from http://www.roymorgan.com/resources/pdf/papers/20040903.pdf

Pearson, Mark, and Jeffrey Brand. 2001. *Sources of news and current affairs.* Sydney: Australian Broadcasting Authority.

Richards, Ian. 2005. *Quagmires and Quandaries: exploring journalism ethics.* Sydney: University of New South Wales Press.

Weaver, David H., Randal Beam, Bonnie J. Brownlee, Paul S. Voakes, and G. Cleveland Wilhoit. 2007. *The American journalist in the 21st century.* Mahwah, NJ: Erlbaum.

11 Journalists in New Zealand

Geoff Lealand and James Hollings

The concluding remarks about the state of New Zealand journalism 10 or so years ago, in Weaver (1998), described New Zealand journalists as "well educated, well trained and, in many cases, possess[ing] considerable power and influence in shaping public debates about New Zealand political and social life" (Lealand 1998: 122). A number of subsequent surveys of New Zealand journalists (Hollings, Lealand, Samson, & Tilley 2007; Lealand 1994, 2004) support and reiterate these broad generalizations, but significant changes and trends over the past decade also mean that such conclusions are in need of revision and reassessment.

Many of the changes in journalism in the past 10 years have global ramifications beyond their impact on journalism in a small South Pacific nation of 4 million people. Such changes include the impact of technological innovation on both workplace practice and continuing viability of the mainstream media (newspapers and magazines, in particular), intensified financial pressures on media institutions both large and small, the changing nature of audiences and their media consumption, the emergence of transparently partisan journalism, and the proliferation of quasi-journalistic online news sites.

It is the latter phenomenon, loosely defined as "citizen journalism," which quite possibly has had the most significant impact on notions of journalism as a profession. Certainly the aggregation of media ownership across the globe—and the subsequent closures of news outlets and layoffs of news workers—have had a visible impact on journalism, but it is the arrival of blogs which pose the fundamental question of what it is that defines the field of journalism in 2011. As the British journalism educator Bob Franklin puts it, "What is a journalist? These days, it is an existential question" (Franklin 2009).

It is probably the intrusion of blogs into the public sphere that has polarized the mainstream journalism community more dramatically than any other aspect of change. Blogs are usually criticized for lacking formal editing, for replacing research with opinion or conjecture, or for being too transparently partisan or aligned to a particular worldview. They present a challenge to the traditional structures of journalism training and professional practice because they sweep aside the long-established gatekeeping roles of formal training and newsroom experience.

Blogging and other forms of "new journalism" (such as cell phone or video camera reportage of public disorder or disaster) suggest that *anyone* can do journalism these days. In many ways a new ideological divide is developing between newsmakers and citizens: whilst Rupert Murdoch as head of News Corp is telling the world that "There's no such thing as a free news story" (Murdoch 2009) academics and critics argue that journalism should not be seen as a professional practice but as a human right (see Hartley 2009).

As in other countries, New Zealand's quasi-academic blogs (such as publicaddress.net) have become part of the media mix but, as elsewhere, they continue to be regarded with a great deal of ambivalence—regarded with disdain by many mainstream journalists but also mined for breaking stories or news-ready capsules of opinion.

In the meantime, most mainstream media have drifted toward media convergence, merging their Internet-based news media with websites, video streaming, archived or extended content, and forums for feedback and discussion. In New Zealand, for example, the two leading online news media are now owned by a duopoly of news corporations (stuff.co.nz is owned by Fairfax Australia, and nzherald.co.nz is owned by Australian-based APN News & Media).

Technological innovation re-shapes many aspects of contemporary media. Indeed, the British commentator Mark Fisher suggests that new forms of journalism have resulted in the mainstream media becoming over-defensive and intent on self-preservation, "[t]he best blogs … have bypassed the mainstream media, which, for the reasons described in last year's Flat Earth News, has become increasingly conservative, dominated by press releases and PR" (Fisher 2009: 44).

There are exceptions to such a broad generalization, but it is possible to discern similar shifts toward a more overt conservatism in the New Zealand media. This conservatism can be seen in a cautionary attitude toward controversy, a new emphasis on the salacious and titillating, and a focus on the bottom-line—further accentuated by the continuing global recession. In New Zealand, through the first decade of the 21st century, the print industry has outsourced editorial processes and closed down some evening newspapers, concentrating instead on morning and omnibus weekend editions. Television further privileges the ratings discourse and imperatives aimed at maximizing advertising revenue, whilst a crowded commercial radio market has become even more cut-throat.

A similar conservatism prevails in journalism training in New Zealand. Drawing on her own research, journalism educator Ruth Thomas notes that "journalism training in New Zealand, controlled by the New Zealand Journalists Training Organisation, still resembles that of 20 years ago, despite increasing numbers of students learning as part of degree programmes." (Thomas 2008: 3). Thomas continues, "students are trained for the media through a method described as 'learning by doing' … journalism educators see themselves as journalists and they were teaching the students in the same way as they had learnt themselves" (Thomas 2008: 5).

In the main, the emphasis remains on training journalists in programs of traditional skills and practices, even though the world of news-gathering and consumption is rapidly changing around us. The assumption is that, for the foreseeable future, there will be a continuing need for such skills, and ready employment for the hundreds of graduates from the 10 tertiary training courses in New Zealand each year. There are, however, some signs of change. The Whitireia Journalism School, for example, introduced a Certificate in Multimedia Journalism in 2010 as a pathway to the National Diploma in Journalism (Multimedia), and other institutions are beginning to incorporate elements of new media into their programs as well. However, journalism training in New Zealand remains largely "old-school" and this is reflected in the ways journalism is subsequently performed across all areas of the media.

The New Zealand Media Environment

Despite various uncertainties, the media environment in New Zealand certainly displays more stability than those in many other countries. New Zealand remains a media-saturated nation, with high levels of overseas ownership of major media institutions and corresponding dependence on imported technology, programming, and ideas. Nevertheless, the combination of a small population and geographic isolation generates circumstances that support stability rather than hasten fragility. The lack of viable local television and radio markets means that the advertising spending is directed to national channels, whilst newspapers and magazines can more easily target local readership and advertising. Meanwhile, the New Zealand online population has grown rapidly, with access to online connections equivalent to 83% of the population (Smith et al. 2009: 2).

There are no fully national newspapers in New Zealand and even the largest circulation daily (the *New Zealand Herald*, at about 195,000) is essentially geared toward a parochial Auckland readership. Even though profit margins in the print media shrank in 2009, the decline in newspaper readership has not been as dramatic as in other countries. According to 2008 figures, 1.6 million New Zealanders read a daily newspaper, and more than 70% of all New Zealanders 15 years or older read at least one newspaper each week (Nielsen Media Readership Survey 2008). More than 4,000 magazine titles circulate, with around 150 of these being New Zealand-published titles (Nielsen Media Research National Readership Survey 2008).

Television viewing was also up in 2010, with the mix of nine free-to-air channels (state-owned Television New Zealand TV1 and TV2; Australian-owned TV3 and C4; pay-TV Sky owned Prime; state-funded Freeview TVNZ6 and TVNZ7, and two channels operated by the Maori Television Service), pay-TV (dominated by Sky Network, with more than 80 channels) and regional channels, providing unprecedented options for New Zealand viewers.

Even though the majority of programming comes from overseas sources, New Zealand generated programming contributed 31.7% of local content on the six major free-to-air channels in 2010 (New Zealand on Air, 2009), the great majority of news journalism on television remains locally generated and consistently registers in the top ten rating programs. Despite the dominance of imported content, which has been a characteristic of New Zealand television since its beginnings in the early 1960s, locally made programming has always been the most popular viewing choice. In 2008, for example, news and current affairs programming increased to an unprecedented 3,660 broadcast hours of the 11,600 hours of local programming screened on the six national free-to-air channels (NZOA 2009).

The radio spectrum is particularly crowded, with more radio stations in the Auckland market (close to 50 FM stations) than in the much larger Sydney market, and a thriving public radio network provided through Concert FM and National Radio.

The 2007 Journalist Survey

New Zealand journalists work in a cultural and political milieu that provides both continuity and relentless change. The most recent stock-taking of the profession—"The Big NZ Journalism Survey"—took place in 2007 (Hollings et al. 2007). There have been more recent surveys but these have adopted a much narrower focus. Concentrating on the public trust of the news media, and broad public opinions about the value of journalism, they have produced rather predictable outcomes suggesting that public trust in the media generally is in decline, with journalists now regarded as only marginally better than car salesmen and politicians (Ethical Martini 2009). The present study is based on the survey of New Zealand journalists conducted by Hollings et al. in the year 2007.

Method

The 2007 survey provided New Zealand journalists with opportunities to report on education and training, working conditions, judgments on matters of professionalism, and on issues of ethics and the general state of journalism in New Zealand. The 2007 questionnaire was drawn up using questions from previous surveys, including the 2004 Pew Research Center for the People and the Press survey of attitudes about the American media (Pew 2004) together with questions devised by the authors of the 2007 study (e.g., Hollings et al. 2007). The survey included a mixture of closed questions on demographic and personal characteristics, such as age, gender, income, years in journalism, qualifications and whether working part-time or full-time, attitudinal questions using Likert-scales on issues as similar as possible to those covered by Pew, such as pay, levels of newsroom support and mentoring, freedom to report as journalists saw fit, commercial pressures, and the quality of general, local, political, foreign, sports and lifestyle coverage. It also included open-ended questions inviting comment from respondents on issues such as the watchdog role of the New Zealand press, the relationship with public relations, the impact of foreign ownership, and what they wanted to know more about in future surveys.

The survey was pilot tested on a small group of journalists ($N = 12$) in order to identify the most useful questions for a broad questionnaire. The survey was supervised and analyzed by the authors as part of their academic research program, with no external funding or sponsorship. To create a representative sample of journalists, a distribution list of print, broadcast, and Internet news organizations was drawn up from published media guides, the researchers' industry knowledge, and media associations. Key people at each—mostly chief reporters or editors—were identified and invited to forward a link to an online questionnaire to their staff. Follow-up phone calls at one day and one week later were made to ask if the email had been received and passed on. Survey responses were monitored as they arrived, and areas with low response rates were prompted with follow-up calls and attempts to target respondents from these groups.

A reasonably good response rate ($N = 514$) from the 4,000 estimated NZ journalists (New Zealand Census 2007) was achieved, with a fairly even spread of gender and job position. Since respondents were self-selecting to participate in the survey, the sample should not be regarded as truly representative of all New Zealand journalists. Nevertheless, a comparison of basic demographic characteristics with national census data from the previous year (Hollings 2007) and two other non-representative surveys within the previous four years, suggest that this particular survey reflects a reasonably similar profile group. For example, the median age, income, and gender split do not vary more than about 5 percentage points across the four surveys.

Our intention has been to gather and record the experiences and opinions of a wide range of New Zealand journalists, and we feel reasonably confident that we have neither misreported nor misrepresented the profession in the information provided here. Thus, we believe that the general conclusions of this study provide reasonably accurate reflections of the profession as a whole.

Findings

The survey produced a range of findings that overall gave a comprehensive, in-depth picture of New Zealand journalism. It extended and updated the portrait developed by previous surveys of the demographic characteristics of NZ journalists. But for the first time it also fleshed out and colored that image by capturing journalists' own views on the quality of coverage they provide, on everything from sport, politics, foreign affairs, and lifestyle news to crime and local news and on their own ethics and standards. Also for the first time, and somewhat controversially in the conservative NZ newsroom environment, it gathered journalists' opinions on the quality of their workplaces, including questions on newsroom resourcing, pay, training, support, and mentoring. It also captured rich qualitative data on issues pertinent to journalism, such as the level of

Table 11.1   Journalists' Main Occupational Sub-Groups (*N* = 514)

	Frequency	Percent
Reporter full time	219	43
Sub-editor full time	43	8
Photographer full time	18	3
Newsroom middle manager full time	118	23
General manager/publisher full time	11	2
Newsreader full time	1	—
Reporter part time/freelance	56	11
Sub-editor part time	4	1
Newsroom middle manager part time/freelance	11	2
General manager/publisher part time	3	1
Category missing	15	3
Total	514	100

plagiarism, the usefulness of the New Zealand media as a watchdog, the relationship with public relations, and commercial pressures on journalists.

To attain a suitable sample size, job status was divided into three categories (reporters, sub-editors, and managers) for full-time employees only (see Table 11.1). "Managers" included all categories from chief reporter/sub-editor up through deputy editor, editor, general manager, and publisher. It should be noted that in New Zealand, "editor" is a title given only to those in charge of a news organization; the equivalent U.S. title would be managing editor. Open-ended questions inviting comment were analyzed thematically using a qualitative, grounded theory methodology (Glaser 1992), and coded according to whether they could be classified as positive, negative, or ambivalent indicators.

The Characteristics of New Zealand Journalists

Age and Gender.   In line with the findings of earlier surveys, female journalists greatly outnumbered male journalists in younger age groups (up to 35 years old), then were progressively outnumbered in older age groups. More than half the female respondents were younger than 35 (56%) and nearly two-thirds (64%) under 40 years. In many ways, such a bias can be regarded as a mirror image of the current composition of journalism courses, where the female intake is consistently higher than the number of male students. Table 11.2 shows the proportions of male vs. female in each age group, as a percentage of the total for each age group.

Ethnicity.   Previous survey studies have established that journalism in New Zealand is dominated by working journalists of European origin, and there was little to contradict this assumption in our 2007 study. Eighty-six percent of the journalists indicated they had European roots, with considerably smaller numbers of journalists indicating Maori origins (4.3%), Pacific Island or Asian ancestry (0.6% in both cases), and "other" ethnicities (8%). This distribution certainly does not reflect the current ethnic composition of the New Zealand population, with the 2006 New Zealand Census recording the following ethnic groupings: European 67.6%; Maori 14.6%; Pacific Island origins 6.9%, and Asian ethnicity 9.2%.

Table 11.2   Journalists' Gender by Age (in %, N = 514)

	Male	*Female*
Under 20	—	100
21–25	17	83
26–30	40	60
31–35	35	65
36–40	51	49
41–45	48	52
46–50	55	45
51–55	56	44
56–60	53	47
61–65	56	44
Over 65	67	33

The number of Maori-oriented media outlets has increased in the past two decades, with the development of a state-funded *iwi* (tribal based) radio network, the arrival of print publications such as the *Mana* magazine, and, most importantly, the setting up of two state-funded television channels operated by the Maori Television Service. Nevertheless, there is dissatisfaction with the mainstream media's treatment of the Maori language (one of the official languages of New Zealand), and its failure to acknowledge or appreciate the formal obligations between the Maori people and the New Zealand government. There is also considerable criticism of representations of Maori issues in the mainstream media, where an undue emphasis on negativity persists. Certainly, the under-representation of Maori-speaking journalists working in major news institutions in New Zealand is a factor in this. Similar complaints are now echoed in respect to other ethnic groupings in New Zealand, as the country increasingly moves toward a multi-cultural and increasingly diverse population.

Experience and Income.   Sub-editors had been working in journalism for the longest periods, followed by those now in management roles. News photographers and reporters, on the other hand, had worked for the shortest periods in journalism. More than half the full-time reporters in our sample (58%) had worked for less than five years in journalism, and three quarters (75%) for less than 10 years, and only 16% for 15 years or more. Overall, almost half (49%) of full-time sub-editors had been in journalism 21 years or more, suggesting that they could be well established in the profession and, in some cases, possibly nearing the end of their working careers.

When placed beside the evidence of a high proportion of relatively inexperienced reporters, there is a real possibility that journalism in New Zealand could face a serious shortage of journalists with mid-range experience in coming years, with considerable knowledge, institutional history, and learned experience being lost as more and more senior journalists retire. Table 11.3 illustrates the relative experience in years for each occupational sub-group.

As expected, there were significant differences in income in respect of the position held in news organizations. Overall, managers earned more than reporters and subeditors, with television journalists earning most, followed by journalists working for national weeklies, magazines, daily newspapers, and radio. A greater proportion of male journalists tended to be in the higher income categories than their female counterparts (see Table 11.4 and 11.5).

Table 11.3   Journalists' Professional Experience by Main Occupational Sub-Groups (in %, N = 344)

	Reporter	Sub-Editor	Newsroom Manager
Under one year	15	2	—
2–5 years	43	9	11
6–10 years	17	14	17
11–15 years	9	7	17
16–20 years	5	19	15
21+ years	11	49	40
Total	100	100	100

Education and Training.   Journalism in New Zealand has traditionally been taught as a trade, but is increasingly becoming a university qualification. Employers are increasingly asking fresh graduates who want to enter the media business to have a nationally recognized journalism degree, and more and more of New Zealand's students are turning to one of the country's seven journalism schools to gain one. In the 2007 survey, 39% of the journalists held a university degree or post-graduate qualification, with a further 29% holding a diploma (usually a one-year course not requiring a

Table 11.4   Journalists' Income by Main Occupational Sub-Groups (in %, N = 317)

Income	Reporter	Sub-Editor	Newsroom Manager
Under 20,000	1	3	—
21–30,000	13	6	—
31–40,000	33	14	7
41–50,000	23	28	10
51–60,000	13	14	14
61–70,000	5	19	20
71–90,000	9	14	27
Over 90,000	3	3	22
Total	100	100	100

Note.   Income listed in NZ dollars.

Table 11.5   Journalists' Income by Gender (in %, N = 486)

Income	Male	Female
Under 20,000	2	6
21–30,000	4	13
31–40,000	13	29
41–50,000	14	19
51–60,000	14	13
61–70,000	13	7
71–90,000	24	6
Over 90,000	16	7
Total	100	100

Note.   Income listed in NZ dollars.

Table 11.6   Journalists' Educational Qualifications by Main Occupational Sub-Groups (in %, N = 490)

	Reporter	*Sub-Editor*	*Newsroom Manager*
None	19	44	37
College diploma	29	42	31
College degree	18	7	14
Post-graduate diploma	32	7	11
Post-graduate degree	2	—	7
Total	100	100	100

bachelor's degree or higher as an entry qualification) from a recognized journalism school. Most New Zealand journalism schools teach journalism as a one-year "diploma" course. There is a significant difference in quality among these courses, with the top three (Auckland University of Technology, Massey University, and Canterbury University) consisting mostly of university graduates, and the rest drawing mostly on non-graduates. Nearly one-third (31.5%) reported that they had no formal journalism qualification—mostly older journalists who instead received on-the-job experience or training. Table 11.6 shows the numbers in each occupational sub-group and what kind of qualification each has. One way of summarizing the above information is to draw on an article describing the outcome of the survey, published in the New Zealand journal Pacific Journalism Review (Hollings et al. 2007), where the primary characteristics of the typical New Zealand journalist were summarized as young, European, female, formally educated, earning a mid-range salary, and relatively new to journalism.

Working Conditions and Professionalism

New Zealand has been more exposed to the forces of globalization than many other countries. Virtually all of New Zealand's newspapers, most magazines, and more than half the broadcast media have passed into foreign hands in the past 40 years. The 2007 survey shows that New Zealand journalists feel the pressures of globalization, manifested in increasing commercial demands, tabloidization, and technological change. Nevertheless, local journalists continue to model their working practices on mainstream conventional Anglo-American journalistic ethics and norms. In terms of journalistic ethics and attitudes, New Zealand's journalists are probably situated somewhere between North American and British journalists. They believe in the watchdog role of the press, that the news media should provide analyses of important issues, but also think that the media should report without embellishments. Table 11.7 provides the percentages of responses to ethical questions. The questions were based on a Likert-scale from 1 to 5, where 1 was agree strongly, and 5 disagree strongly.

According to our 2007 study, journalists are fairly happy with the level of media freedom in New Zealand (see Table 11.7), with more agreeing the local news media are free to tell the truth as they see it (58% agree, 23% disagree) and to make decisions based on journalistic rather than commercial or political values (43% agree, 36% disagree). Not surprisingly for a country consistently near the top of press freedom rankings (Reporters Without Borders 2009), journalists generally agree that the limits on media freedom in New Zealand are "about right" (43% agree, 20% disagree). As in many other countries with a recently deregulated media environment, most journalists also agree that sensationalism is a growing problem (65% agree, 18% disagree). However,

Table 11.7   Journalists' Ethics and Standards (in %, N = 440)

	Agree	Neutral	Disagree
NZ media should provide analysis of important issues	97	2	2
NZ media has a responsibility to record important events	97	2	1
Sensationalism is a growing problem in NZ media	65	17	18
Current ethics codes are adequate	67	24	9
NZ media should report simply without embellishment	60	17	22
NZ media perform their watchdog role well	57	28	15
NZ journalists are free to tell truth as they see it	58	19	23
NZ journalists do not knowingly omit/distort facts	52	25	23
Limits on NZ media freedom are about right	43	37	20
NZ media needs to be regulated for higher standards	26	33	41
News media should stick to more traditional roles	17	20	63
NZ journalists' story choices are driven by journalistic values	43	21	36

more regulation is not seen as the answer to ensure higher journalistic standards (26% wanted more regulation, 41% did not).

No study yet has measured bribery or payments to journalists for stories, and this survey did not specifically ask about this issue either. Anecdotally, the general consensus among New Zealand journalists is that it is minimal or non-existent. One possible exception is travel features, which are nearly always sponsored by the subject of the story (an airline or accommodation provider, for example). While this would be disturbing to some journalists in other countries, there is little or no questioning of it locally. This level of satisfaction with their own ethics is reflected in the majority (67%) who feel current ethics codes are adequate (vs. 9% who don't, with 24% stating no opinion).

While New Zealand's journalists feel that they have retained their ethical moral ground in the face of globalization, they are less sanguine about the impact of commercial pressures. More than half (55%) reported that newsrooms had been pressured to do a story because it related to an advertiser, owner, or sponsor. Half thought commercial pressures were hurting the way news organizations functioned, while a further 22% agreed they were "just changing" the way things were done. Their biggest concerns are those pressures that have become synonymous with media globalization: low pay and long hours, reductions in staffing, and consequently high staff turnover and a lack of mentoring and training. Less important, but still a concern, is the high level of foreign ownership, as in the following typical comment: "From my 30-odd years in journalism it now appears that the news is money-driven ... the return on shareholder's funds has now become uppermost in the metropolitan newspapers owned by overseas corporations, to the detriment of coverage" (Hollings et al. 2007: 191).

These commercial pressures also are reflected in journalists' attitudes toward watchdog journalism. The survey found that while most journalists still think the news media in New Zealand perform the watchdog role well (57% agree vs. 15% disagree), many are concerned about the levels and quality of resourcing. Table 11.8 shows the mean responses to resourcing questions, based on a Likert-scale where 1 was poor and 5 was excellent. The dissatisfaction with pay was the most clear-cut of all responses to resourcing questions. The disgruntlement over pay may partially explain the mildly left-wing political orientation of these journalists (44% considered themselves

Table 11.8   Journalists' Perceptions of Resourcing Adequacy (in %, *N* = 430)

	Poor	*Below Average*	*Average*	*Above Average*	*Excellent*	*Total*
Number of senior staff	19.9	28.6	38.8	12	0.7	100
Number of reporters	23.0	37.2	34.7	5.1	—	100
Mentoring and training	32.0	40.0	22.4	5.4	0.2	100
Counseling and support	34.1	38.5	23.8	2.4	1.2	100
Pay	41.3	35.0	21.7	1.9	0.2	100

left or strongly left; a further 42% neutral; and only 13% right). However, most believe the NZ news media is slightly left-leaning (42%) or neutral (36%) with only 19% considering it right-leaning. Interestingly, despite the very high foreign ownership of the New Zealand media, most journalists (53%) consider their own organization to be neutral, with smaller numbers considering their organization left (20%) or right (25%) (see Table 11.9).

While the above sections generated useful hard data, some of the more colorful insights came in response to the open-ended questions. One question "What do you think of public relations?" drew a roughly even number of responses for and against, but with some vitriolic language flavoring those against: ("loathsome," "paid liars," "peopled by sell-out scum") (Hollings et al. 2007: 189–90) A thematic analysis of another question, asking those who thought that the media was not doing its watchdog role well what they thought should be done about it, showed the most frequent concern was resourcing (47% of responses mentioned this). Most of the journalists also say that there are too few journalists, with too little time to do anything in-depth, compounded by management focused on quick copy at the expense of complex analysis. The next most common theme, mentioned by only 15%, was the need for more analysis in stories.

Another question asking what the survey should have asked produced some of the most interesting responses of all. A theme analysis of overall patterns showed the most frequent areas of comment related to motivation and recruitment issues, pay, and conditions. "More than anything else, respondents wanted us to ask them why they became a journalist, why they stayed in the job, whether they were happy and why, and whether they were planning to 'get out' and if so why or why not" (Hollings et al. 2007: 190). Several journalists also expressed puzzlement as to why the public perception of the performance of journalists is so negative, when they felt they provided the New Zealand public with good, comprehensive news coverage at little cost. Nevertheless, many respondents also said they loved the adventure and excitement of the job, and some said the quality of coverage had improved greatly in the past 40 years: "It is way better than it was when I started in journalism in the 60s … much greater range in subject matter being covered, much

Table 11.9   Journalists' Perceptions of Personal, Employer, and Media Political Orientation (in %, *N* = 406)

	Journalist	*Journalists' Organization*	*NZ Media Overall*
Strongly left	5	1	2
Left	39	20	42
Neutral	42	53	36
Right	13	25	19
Strongly right	1	1	1
Total	100	100	100

better coverage of politics and analysis, and much more racial inclusiveness—though there is still a way to go on this last" (Hollings et al. 2007: 192).

Conclusions

More than 10 years ago, an overview of journalism in New Zealand offered the following predictions:

> Journalism in New Zealand will continue to change and be shaped and reshaped by market forces and the evolving demographics of the workforce, but it will also be affected in the near future by changes in the workplace, as new technology defines what is news, how news is gathered, and how news is disseminated. (Lealand 1998: 123)

Certainly, these predictions have become a reality for New Zealand's journalists in the past years. But, as our 2007 findings show, these dramatic changes in journalism have not discouraged journalists. Instead, responses demonstrated a vibrant curiosity about the state of journalism in New Zealand. One young and enthusiastic journalist summed up this pointedly by declaring: "Bring me the people! Bring me the stories! Bring me the excitement of seeing my words and name in print! It's the best job I've ever had. I finally feel like I've got a purpose" (Hollings et al. 2007: 192).

Even though the 2007 survey concentrated on mainstream journalists and journalism-as-we-know-it rather than journalism-as-it-might-become, many journalists also were interested in speculating about the impact of technological convergence and innovation on modern journalism. In some cases, such change was regarded with cautious optimism: "Slowly we are edging ahead [but] not as swiftly as overseas organizations but at a pace with the other key players in this country" (Hollings et al. 2007: 193). Other judgments were less positive: "a true understanding of the internet, for example, and its impact on society, education, and culture is still generally not appreciated or understood. There are still only a dozen or so people in this country who can write authoritatively beyond the hype of gadgets and gizmos and entertainment distractions, to comment on the wider picture" (Hollings et al. 2007: 193).

Of course, the immediate effects of these changes are a reality for most journalists in most places. For New Zealand's journalists, the reality of globalization is with them every day. They work in smaller, more pressured, more multi-media newsrooms, on stories about people they have less time to meet in person, for readers increasingly distracted by an explosion of news choices. While many still hold to traditional journalistic ethics and standards, many feel these are under more threat from employers increasingly likely to be based overseas and a burgeoning army of public relations practitioners trying to manipulate access to news sources. Most seem to feel newsroom management has not kept pace with change, with consequent deep levels of unhappiness about pay and working conditions. Yet, there is still among many a satisfaction with the craft itself that has not dimmed. The information gathered in the surveys cited here suggests that New Zealand journalists face particular challenges in respect of changing work practices and larger structural shifts in the industry, as well as the consequences of broad social change. Some of these challenges are local (such as demographic trends towards a more multi-cultural New Zealand) but many are the same challenges faced by journalists around the globe.

References

Ethical Martini. 2008. *We don't trust the news media—So where's the news in that?* Retrieved from http://ethicalmartini. wordpress.com/2009/10/08/we-dont-trust-the-news-media-so-wheres-the-news-in-that/

Fisher, Mark. 2009. Running on empty. *New Statesman* May 4, 43–44.

Franklin, Bob. 2009. *Opening remarks.* Future of journalism conference, Cardiff University, Wales, September 9.

Glaser, Barney. 1992. *Basics of grounded theory analysis.* Mill Valley, CA: Sociology Press.

Hartley, John. 2009. *Journalism as a human right.* Presentation to Centre for Law, Justice & Journalism, City University, London.

Hollings, James. 2007. Still European and female, but older: Profiling the New Zealand journalist. *Pacific Journalism Review* 13(1): 183–193.

Hollings, James, Geoff Lealand, Alan Samson, and Elspeth Tilley. 2007. The big NZ journalism survey: Underpaid, under-trained, under-resourced, unsure about the future—but still idealistic. *Pacific Journalism Review* 13(2): 175–199.

Lealand, Geoff. 1988. *A national survey of New Zealand journalists 1987: A report for the New Zealand Journalists Training Organisation.* Wellington: NZ Journalists Training Organisation.

Lealand, Geoff. 1994. *A national survey of New Zealand journalists 1994: A report for the New Zealand Journalists Training Organisation.* Wellington: NZ Journalists Training Organisation.

Lealand, Geoff. 1998. Journalists in New Zealand. In *The global journalist: News people around the world,* edited by David Weaver, pp. 109–124. Cresskill, NJ: Hampton Press.

Lealand, Geoff. 2004. Still young and female: A (modest) survey of New Zealand journalists. *Pacific Journalism Review* 10(2):173–196

Murdoch, Rupert. 2009. *There's no such thing as a free news story.* Guardian Online. Retrieved from http://www.guardian.co.uk/media/2009/dec/01/rupert-murdoch-no-free-news.

Nielsen Media. 2008. *Nielsen media readership survey 2008.* Auckland: Author.

New Zealand Journalists Training Organisation. 2006. *National survey of journalists 2006.* Wellington: NZ Journalists Training Organisation.

New Zealand On Air. 2011. *New Zealand television local content 2010.* Wellington: New Zealand On Air.

The Pew Research Center for the People and the Press.2004. Bottom line pressures now hurting coverage, say journalists. Retrieved from http://people-press.org/reports/display.php3?ReportID=214

Reporters without Borders. 2009. World press freedom index 2009. Retrieved from http://en.rsf.org/IMG/pdf/classement_en.pdf

Smith, Philippa, Nigel Smith, Kevin Sherman, Ian Goodwin, Charles Crothers, Jennie Billot, and Alan Bell, 2010. *World internet project: The internet in New Zealand 2009.* Auckland: Institute of Culture, Discourse & Communication, AUT University

Statistics New Zealand. (2007). Census of population and dwellings statistics. Available at: http://www.stats.govt.nz/Census/2006CensusHomePage.aspx

Thomas, Ruth. 2008. *The making of a journalist: the New Zealand way.* Paper presented at the Journalist Educators Association of New Zealand (JEANZ) conference, Christchurch.

Weaver, David H. 1998. *The global journalist: News people around the world.* Cresskill, NJ: Hampton Press.

Journalists in Europe

12 A Survey of Professional Journalists in Flanders (Belgium)

Karin Raeymaeckers, Steve Paulussen, and Jeroen De Keyser

Belgium became an independent state when it seceded from the Netherlands after the 1830 revolution. A number of journalists played a prominent part in this revolution and even collaborated on writing the Constitution, which was very progressive for its time and guaranteed freedom of the press. Since the first constitutional step toward federalization was taken in 1970, Belgium has evolved toward a state structure that divides the country into three communities—Dutch-, French-, and German-speaking—and three regions. The largest region is Flanders, the northern Dutch-speaking part of Belgium with about 6.2 million inhabitants. The French-speaking community comprises about 3.5 million Belgians, most of them living in the Walloon region. The third region, the officially bilingual Brussels-Capital region, has about 1 million inhabitants (Statistics Belgium 2010a).

The current Belgian federal state structure is reflected in the country's media landscape, which roughly consists of two language-based markets. Since media policy is under the authority of the individual communities, we can observe some differences between the two markets with limited intertwining between then. Only recently we have observed examples of cross-participation between Flemish and Walloon media firms and concentration trends that traverse the language sphere. The newspaper market in Flanders is dominated by three media groups: Corelio, De Persgroep, and Concentra. Together they publish 10 Dutch-language daily newspapers. Roularta is a large media group that has interests in the commercial broadcasting as well as in the magazine markets. The French-language newspaper market is controlled by the Walloon media groups Rossel and IPM. The interests of foreign investors in the Belgian media market are demonstrated in the magazine market, where the Finnish media group Sanoma has become one of the major players.

Newspaper readership is slowly declining, although the decline is more prominent in Wallonia than in Flanders. With 160 readers per thousand, Belgium ranks between high and low newspaper consumption in comparison with other European countries. The total audit circulation figures of print paid-for dailies published at least five days a week in 2007–2008 were 1,117,628 in Flanders (1,250,740, including the free daily *Metro*) and 558,268 in Wallonia (680,680, including *Metro*). The Belgian newspaper industry has suffered from the financial crisis of 2008, which marked the start of a profound economic crisis. Advertising revenues were shrinking; media that were largely dependent on advertising revenues became highly vulnerable. Media companies introduced plans to reduce staff. Some reduced newsroom staff by one third.

Belgium has a strong tradition in public service broadcasting. Commercial broadcasting was introduced in 1987 in Wallonia and two years later in Flanders. The most important commercial broadcaster is VMMa, in which two Flemish media publishing groups, De Persgroep and Roularta, each hold half of the shares. Foreign investors for Flemish commercial broadcasting are minor players. They recently sold their niche channels to a new Finnish competitor, Woestijuvis, thus introducing a thrid powerful actor in the Flemish broadcasing landscape. The Walloon commercial broadcasting market is dominated by the German-Luxembourgian media group RTL/TVi. Public broadcasters in Flanders (Vlaamse Radio- en Televisie-omroep [VRT]) and in French-speaking Belgium (Radio-Télévision belge de la Communauté française [RTBF.be]) operate independently from each other, as media policy and media legislation belong to the institutional and legal authority of the regions.

Belgium's online news market is dominated by the traditional media companies. When it comes to visitors, *HLN.be* is the most popular online newspaper in Flanders. Although it is a part of the same media group and uses the brand name of the popular paper *Het Laatste Nieuws*, an autonomous editorial staff produces the Web site. The same editorial staff also provides content for *7sur7.be*, the French-language counterpart of *HLN.be*, which tops the list of most popular news Web sites in the French-speaking part of Belgium. Newspaper Web sites have their own editorial staff, but the number of online editors is mostly small due to limited profitability. Most of the Flemish online newspapers are still running at a loss. The main competitors of the commercial online newspapers are the Web sites of the public broadcasters.

The 2008 Flemish Journalist Survey

Research on journalism in Belgium is well-established and has been conducted for more than 25 years. In 1983, media scholar Els De Bens was the first to interview Flemish journalists in a survey that included 250 professional journalists from print and broadcasting media, as well as freelancers (De Bens 1983). This survey investigated social-demographic, work-related, and political-ideological features of Flemish journalists, but contained no questions concerning their professional roles. In 1992, the survey was repeated, but excluded freelancers (De Bens 1995). In 1999 and 2001, these studies were complemented with two surveys on gender issues in journalism (De Clercq 2001, 2003).

In 2003, a team of researchers from Ghent University in collaboration with the Association of Flemish Professional Journalists (VVJ) conducted the first large-scale study of the entire population of professional journalists in Flanders (Paulussen & De Clercq 2005). The survey included a total of 1,026 respondents, or about 45% of the entire population of journalists in Flanders. The original questionnaire, which was adopted from the 1992 survey study, was expanded with items gauging the professional and ethical views of journalists and their use of the Internet. This brought the questionnaire more in line with similar questionnaires used in the United States, Germany, and the Netherlands (Deuze 2002a; Scholl & Weischenberg 1998; Weaver & Wilhoit 1986, 1996).

The 2003 Flemish journalist survey, in combination with the aforementioned previous surveys of 1983, 1992, 1999, and 2001, yield a detailed picture of the socio-demographic, work-related, professional, and political-ideological characteristics of Flemish professional journalists. First, the data show the continuing gender imbalance in the profession, although the number of female journalists rose from 9% in 1983 to 30% in 2003. A second pattern is the increasing level of education, with 57.5% academically educated journalists in 2003, compared to 33% in 1983 and 53% in 1992. Further, the Flemish journalist surveys all revealed a high degree of job satisfaction, a high perceived importance of autonomy, and a politically progressive self-perception among professional journalists (Paulussen & De Clercq 2005).

In 2008, the research team of the Center for Journalism Studies at Ghent University decided to repeat the 2003 survey with a sample of journalists from Flanders. In view of the fundamental changes that have taken place in journalism in the past 10 years (see Dahlgren 2009), we thought it relevant to investigate to what extent recent economic and technological developments in the media have influenced journalism in Belgium. Our 2008 survey was carried out in collaboration with the Association of Flemish Journalists (VVJ) and targeted all professional journalists in Flanders. A detailed report of the results was published as a book in 2010, in Dutch (Paulussen, & Raeymaeckers 2008).

Method

This analysis is based on the above-mentioned survey, which was conducted among 682 Flemish journalists between December 2007 and January 2008. As in the 2003 survey, all active professional journalists in Flanders were invited to complete the questionnaire. The questionnaire was distributed along with the December issue of *De Journalist*, a journal that is mailed monthly to all members of the association. The small percentage of Flemish professional journalists who are not members of the VVJ (15%) and consequently did not receive its journal, were sent a personal letter. Overall, 2,230 Flemish journalists received an invitation, which represents almost the entire population of journalists in Flanders (the database contained a total of 2,356 journalists, 126 of whom were listed with incomplete or obsolete contact information and thus were excluded from the survey).

The journalists were offered a choice to complete the questionnaire either in a printed form or on a Web site that was secured with a password. The questionnaire comprised 68 questions, divided into 11 modules. It was pretested with 10 journalists. After one month, during which two reminders were sent to all journalists, 682 journalists had completed the questionnaire. This amounts to a response rate of 30.6%. Most journalists completed the questionnaire in printed form, while 245 respondents opted for the online version.

A comparison of the cohort in our survey with the complete VVJ database shows that it is representative of the entire group in terms of gender, seniority, status, and distribution among the various media sectors.

Findings

The total number of professional journalists in Flanders continues to grow. In 1983, there were 698 recognized Flemish journalists (De Bens 1983: 7). Twenty years later, in 2003, their number had grown to 2,257 (Paulussen & De Clercq 2005). The VVJ database shows that between 2003 and 2008 the number of professional journalists in Flanders further increased to 2,356.

The majority of these journalists are employed in the print media sector: 38% work for a daily newspaper and 27% for a weekly or monthly magazine. Television broadcasters employ about a third (29%) of the respondents. Our survey further indicates that 17% of Flemish professional journalists work in radio broadcasting, 8% for a photo or press agency, and 10% for online media. The total percentage exceeds 100% because an increasing number of journalists work in several media sectors simultaneously. While in 2003 as few as 23% of journalists worked in two or three sectors at the same time, by 2008 this number had risen to nearly 30%: 18% work for two media sectors, and 10% in three media or more.

A closer look at the specific functions exercised by the journalists who participated in the survey reveals that 55% of the respondents work as journalists, editors, reporters, or correspondents. Of all Flemish journalists, 22% have an executive function, either as (deputy) editor-in-chief (7%), or as section or editing chief or as editor-in-chief/coordinator (15%).

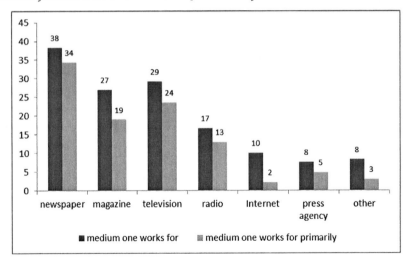

Figure 12.1 The Media Employing Journalists (in %)

One in 10 journalists work as copy editors, 7% work as cameramen/camerawomen or photographers, and 6% have a variety of other functions. Women are markedly underrepresented in the executive functions; only 11% of the editors-in-chief or deputy editors are female. However, significantly more female journalists work as copy editors: 41% are female.

Basic Characteristics of Flemish Journalists

The average Flemish journalist is a white, 42-year-old, highly educated male (see Table 12.1). We shall analyze the educational level of Flemish journalists in the next section. First, we briefly discuss the journalists' age, seniority, ethnicity, ideological views, and family situation.

Age and Seniority.   The average age of the Flemish professional journalist rose from 39 to 42 between 2003 and 2008. This is surprising as it goes against the common perception that media newsrooms increasingly prefer less costly, younger workers. Also, the average seniority of the group has increased significantly over the past five years. In 2003, the average work tenure was 11.5 years, while by 2008 it had risen to 15 years. Job mobility, on the other hand, measured by the number of employers they have worked for in the course of their careers, has remained unchanged since 2003. The average Flemish journalist has worked for three different employers,

Table 12.1   Demographic Background of Journalists in 2003 and in 2008

Background Characteristics	2003* (N = 1,026)	2008 (N = 682)
Number of professional journalists	2,257	2,356
Percentage of females	29.8%	27.8%
Average age	39	42
Average seniority (as a professional journalist)	11.5	15.1
Individual or (one or both) parents born outside the EU–25	2.8%	1.3%
Percentage with further or higher education degree	89.8%	90.4%

Source: Paulussen & De Clercq, 2005

and half of all respondents worked in a different profession before they took up journalism. While Flemish journalists tend to work a relatively long time for one employer, we will show later that a considerable number of journalists still worry about job security.

Gender and Ethnicity.   It is remarkable that the number of female journalists has not increased in the past 20 years (De Clercq 2003). Indeed, compared with 2003, the share of female journalists in 2008 has decreased slightly from almost 30% to almost 28%. This may be partly explained by the fact that the number of older journalists who left the profession has been lower than the number of younger journalists who entered it. Indeed, in the younger age categories, the division between men and women is more balanced: in the under-35 group, 42% of the journalists are female. The gender proportion is most unequal among those employed by press and photo agencies—barely 16% of press agency journalists are female. Women are also underrepresented in online media (20%), newspapers (22%), and TV journalism (25%). In weekly and monthly magazines (36%) and in radio broadcasting (46%), the gender division is more balanced.

While women remain underrepresented in media organizations overall, journalists of foreign descent prove to be rare in the Flemish media landscape: 96% of respondents were born in Belgium and a further 2% in the Netherlands. As far as the religious convictions of journalists are concerned, nearly all respondents are either atheists (61%) or Christians (38%).

Most Flemish journalists can be found on the "left" or "progressive" side of the political spectrum. A clear majority considers itself either "very progressive" (33%) or "moderately progressive" (41%). Fifteen percent situate themselves in the political center and the remaining 11% call themselves "moderately conservative." Half of the professional group (48%) find themselves more progressive than the medium for which they work. On the other hand, only about 7% of journalists consider themselves more conservative than their employers, and the remaining 44% situate themselves on the same ideological line as the media organization for which they work.

Turning to marital status, 44% of the respondents are married, 14% are single, nearly one-third (32%) live with a partner, and 7% claim to have a partner with whom they do not live. Forty-one percent of the journalists said that the profession of journalism is hard to combine with family life. Interestingly, though, 62% of the female journalists believe that children impede their career, while only 38% of male journalists agree with this statement. These findings might explain why Flemish journalists have a relatively low average number of children (1.3) as compared to the Flemish average of 1.7 (Statistics Belgium 2010b).

Education and Training of Flemish Journalists

As in most European countries, it was not until after the World War II that Belgian universities started to organize degrees in journalism. In the 1990s, Flemish "colleges of higher education" also started to offer degrees in journalism. In Flanders, a master's degree in journalism can be received from three colleges or from Ghent University, whose Department of Communication Sciences includes a journalism section. Furthermore, three Flemish colleges offer a one-year program in journalism and various organizations supply specific master classes.

Our data show that Flemish journalists are highly educated. Overall, 9 of 10 journalists have a higher education degree: 62% of the respondents have a university degree and 28% have attended a college of higher education. In 1983, these percentages were 33% and 26%, respectively (De Bens 1983: 18). While in 2003 half of all professional journalists had a degree in journalism or communication sciences, this percentage rose to 58% in 2008. Sixteen percent of Flemish professional

Table 12.2   Perceived Importance of Journalistic Skills (in %)

Skills	(Very) Important	Neutral	(Very) Unimportant	Total %
Linguistic skills	99	1	—	100
Critical, analytical skills	96	4	—	100
Social skills	97	3	—	100
Research skills in general	89	10	1	100
Online research skills	90	9	1	100
Multimedia skills	80	18	2	100
Technological skills	77	20	3	100
Statistical skills	54	36	10	100
Data Management skills	40	48	12	100
Graphical skills	14	48	38	100

journalists have a master's degree in communication sciences, and another 7.5% of respondents have attended university courses in media or journalism studies. Furthermore, 15% of the journalists have a bachelor's (8%) or master's (7%) degree from a college of higher education. Finally, an increasing number of Flemish journalists have attended further master classes and training courses—6% have attended a course at the Journalism Institute (organized by the Association of Journalists), while 12% of the respondents indicate that they have received further training on the job.

These figures point to the increasing significance of having a journalism degree. Half of all respondents recognize that professional training is important for future journalists, while only 18% disagree with this statement and the remaining 32% have a neutral opinion.

The survey also focused on the skills of present-day journalists. Respondents were asked not only to indicate how important these skills were—most skills were considered important to very important—but they were also requested to indicate the top three skills required. Overall, Flemish journalists judge linguistic skills as the most important skill—half of all respondents place knowledge of language, writing, and communicative skills at the top of their lists. Critical and analytical skills are considered the second most important skills, and social skills are placed third. It is notable that general research skills are not mentioned among the top three by three-quarters of respondents, and only 2% put these skills at the top of their lists.

Although the Flemish survey suggests the growing importance of education and training, a degree in journalism in itself does not directly provide entry into a career in journalism. When asked about the factors that had played a decisive part in their being recruited, Flemish professional journalists rank training only in fourth place, after journalism skills, general knowledge, and a flexible attitude. The academic degree comes fourth. What respondents apparently want to emphasize is that formal training remains secondary to actual knowledge and skills. Thirty-one percent of respondents admit that their training played a part in being recruited as a journalist. It is noteworthy that mainly journalists with a university degree consider their degree decisive in getting employment. Only a quarter of (non-university) college graduates agreed with this statement.

Working Conditions

Our findings show that 9 of 10 journalists are employed full-time. In the radio and magazine sectors, 18% and 15% journalists work part-time, respectively. These percentages are significantly lower than in other sectors, where the number of part-time working professional journalists remains under 10%.

However, the global economic crisis has also had an impact on the Flemish media sector. In 2009 it resulted in waves of restructuring in various newsrooms. Although primarily a consequence of the financial crisis, the layoffs have been predicted for some time (De Bens & Raeymaeckers 2010).

The Internet has had an especially large impact on the position, role, and even survival of the traditional media. As digitalization and convergence have thoroughly reshaped newsrooms and news practices, the skills required from journalists also have changed (Deuze 2007; Lewis, Williams, Franklin, Thomas, & Mosdell, 2008). This is clearly shown in the increasing significance of multi-media journalism, a growing need for flexibility, a rising workload, and a trend toward desk journalism. At the same time, experienced journalists are worried about their job security. In this section we examine to what extent the Flemish survey provides empirical evidence for these trends. Furthermore, we shall pay attention to the general job satisfaction of Flemish journalists.

Multi-Media Journalism. The academic literature has pointed out that convergence usually leads to multi-media journalism. Multi-media journalists producing content for print media, radio, television, and the Internet are becoming more and more common. Although our data indicate that this trend has reached the Belgian media, it appears to be still relatively weak in Flanders.

The fact remains that more than 7 of 10 Flemish journalists still work in a single media sector, and only about 2% of all journalists work exclusively for online media. Yet the number of multi-media journalists is rising. In 2003 only 23% of Flemish journalists were active in two or more media sectors, but by 2008 this percentage had risen to 28%. More specifically, 18% of respondents work in two media sectors and 10% in three or more. Our data indicate that 45% of print journalists also work for online media. For television, radio, and press agency journalists, these percentages are 15%, 13%, and 5%, respectively.

Flexibility and Workload. Media convergence is accompanied by an increasing demand for flexibility and an expansion of job duties. Convergence allows the fusion, the abolition, or the rationalization of certain professional profiles, all of which reorganize the range of duties in the newsrooms. Thus, when applying for a new position in journalism, a candidate's flexibility increasingly will be taken into account (Hollifield, Kosicki, & Becker 2001; International Federation of Journalists [IFJ]/ International Labour Office [ILO] 2006). In fact, our survey found that 41% of Flemish journalists agree that their flexible attitudes played a major part in their recruitment.

The need for flexibility is also reflected in the journalist's work schedule. Flemish professional journalists say they work an average of 45.5 hours a week. More than three-quarters regularly work evenings and two of three journalists regularly work on Sundays and holidays.

Shifting the focus from how much Flemish journalists work to where they work, we find that 78% work in the newsroom regularly or all the time. Fifty-seven percent of the journalists regularly do fieldwork, but one of five journalists rarely if ever leave their desks. Finally, 38% say they regularly or always work at home.

The growing amount of deskwork has also influenced the journalists' use of sources. At best, journalists have contact with their sources through the telephone and email, but often even that is no longer the case, and journalists simply consult press releases and secondary sources. According to Boczkowski (2009), an increasing use of such secondary sources results in thinner and more uniform news reporting. Some data from our survey support that concern. Even after excluding text editors working in the print media, nearly one-third (32%) of the interviewed journalists are occupied daily with editing texts written by colleagues. For about 11% of the journalists text-editing is among the three main daily tasks. In addition, 22% of journalists edit press releases every day.

The increasing amount of deskwork and the pressures of cost-efficiency apparently force Flemish journalists to use sources that are easy to consult, such as press releases and material from public relations agencies. Our analysis finds that journalists who spend more time in the newsroom are more likely to consult these information sources ($p < .05$). The importance of this relationship is illustrated by the fact that there is only one other significant connection between work location and use of sources: journalists who do more field work conduct more interviews of their own ($p < .05$).

Use of New Media Technologies.   The trend toward a more "sedentary journalism" (Baisnee & Marchetti, cited in Boczkowski 2009: 59) naturally is also connected with the new possibilities offered by the rapidly developing new media environment. Our data suggest that the more the journalists become office-bound, the more likely they are to use new media technologies for newsgathering and production. As expected, the survey data confirm that journalists who regularly work in the newsroom are also more likely to surf the Internet, use search engines, and consult online dictionaries and encyclopedias.

Nevertheless, the use of the Internet by Flemish journalists is mostly restricted to basic online applications such as email and search engines: 96% of respondents use email on a daily basis and nearly as many use a search engine at least once during a working day (95%). Fifty-four percent of journalists use sites with contact information on a daily basis and about 39% make daily use of online dictionaries and encyclopedias. However, other online applications are used less frequently. For example, one in five journalists (20%) visit blogs and one in eight (12%) search for videos online on a daily basis. Other, more advanced online applications that may be important tools in newsgathering appear to be less common. At the time the survey was conducted, nearly one-quarter of the interviewed journalists (24%) did not know what "social bookmarking" was, one-fifth (20%) had never heard of RSS feeds, and more than one in 10 journalists (11%) did not know what "social networking sites" were for.

Job Security.   A further consequence of media convergence is that the career of a journalist is increasingly marked by contingency. A 2006 study by the International Federation of Journalists and the International Labour Office shows that jobs in media newsrooms are increasingly characterized by "atypical" working conditions (IFJ/ILO 2006). That study shows that a growing proportion of journalists are on a temporary contract and are more frequently forced into freelance work (see also Deuze 2009; Dupagne & Garrison 2006). However, our own comparison with the 2003 data shows that the proportion of freelancers has remained virtually stable over the last five years—more than a quarter of journalists (27%) are fully or partly self-employed. In the weekly and monthly press the proportion of freelancers (30%) is significantly higher than in the other media sectors. In the daily newspaper and television sectors, nearly one of five journalists has a self-employed status, while in radio and the online media freelancers are absent.

Comparing freelancers with their salaried colleagues, we find that the latter worry more about their job security. Among the freelancers who participated in the survey about a quarter (24%) say they are satisfied with job security; 41% say they are dissatisfied; and 35% take a neutral standpoint.

Table 12.3 Job Satisfaction of Journalists (in %)

Elements of Job Satisfaction	(Very) Satisfied	Neutral	(Very) Dissatisfied	Total %
Employment status	87	9	4	100
Function	89	8	3	100
Pay	46	28	26	100
Possibilities to outline specialties	56	33	13	100
Chance of promotion	26	48	26	100
Job security	64	22	14	100
Work pressure	35	33	32	100
Working hours	46	34	20	100
Variation (concerning content)	89	8	3	100
Intellectual challenge	76	17	7	100
Creativity	78	17	5	100
Abundance of contacts	83	14	3	100
Individual freedom	76	18	6	100
Social/civil commitment	59	36	5	100
Status among professional group	61	33	6	100
Social status	71	27	2	100

Job Satisfaction. Overall, job satisfaction among Flemish journalists is relatively high. For most of the items shown in Table 12.3, more journalists are satisfied than dissatisfied. The one exception is promotion prospects, where we find that 26% of the respondents are either satisfied or dissatisfied and the remaining 48% are neutral. Further analysis shows that dissatisfaction with career opportunities is significantly higher among female journalists (35% dissatisfied), freelancers (37% dissatisfied), and—unsurprisingly—journalists who have not had any promotion yet (50% dissatisfied). More than half of the respondents (54%) do not foresee any opportunity for promotion in the next two years, while 29% believe they will get some promotion during the next two years.

Just as in 2003, the Flemish journalists are most dissatisfied with their promotion prospects, workload, and income. However, their dissatisfaction with job security has decreased from 26% in 2003 to 14% in 2008. Similarly, their discontent with the long and irregular working hours has decreased from 29% in 2003 to 20% in 2008. Respondents show the highest satisfaction with the diversity of content in the media, the high number of social contacts, and the creative aspects of journalism. It is quite remarkalble that so far as job satisfaction is concerned, there are only a few significant differences between freelance and salaried journalists. Although freelancers are clearly less satisfied with their legal status (13% dissatisfied), this appears to have little impact on their general job satisfaction. Only the lack of career opportunities and job insecurity, two factors that are implied in the status of freelancer, seem to cause more worries among self-employed journalists. Furthermore, 3 of 10 freelancers also are dissatisfied with their income and workload, but not to a degree that is significantly different from their salaried colleagues.

In view of the high job satisfaction levels among Flemish journalists, it should come as no surprise that most respondents wish to remain in journalism. No fewer than 97% said that they would like to work in journalism in the next two years. When asked to look five years ahead, 88% of the journalists said they would like to remain in journalism for that time.

Professionalism

Freedom of the press implies that journalists can act and take decisions completely independently. However, common journalistic ethics also state that freedom and independence imply a number of responsibilities. Similar to journalist surveys conducted in other countries (see Weaver 1998), we probed for journalists' perceptions about autonomy, professional roles, and ethical norms.

Autonomy.   Our findings confirm that journalists attach much importance to the individual freedom that their jobs offer them. In fact, individual freedom was a major motivation for choosing a job in journalism for 34% of the respondents. Overall, 76% of the Flemish journalists said that they are satisfied with their individual freedom (see Table 12.3). Only a minority expressed serious concerns about the internal and external commercial pressures on newsrooms. Indeed, in comparison with 2003, dissatisfaction with editorial autonomy has slightly decreased. In 2003, 18% of the respondents said they were dissatisfied with the commercial pressure on newsrooms, and 22% were dissatisfied with the internal pressure from the marketing department or the editor-in-chief. In 2008, these percentages had dropped to 14% and 17%, respectively.

Professional Role Perceptions.   Flemish professional journalists are also fairly unanimous in their opinions about the importance of reliable (objective) information. A clear majority of the interviewed journalists said it is important that information is distributed with adequate analysis and interpretation (93%) and as fast as possible (80%). Although 70% consider the watchdog function of the press important, not all of them want to influence public opinion or set the political agenda—less than a quarter believe journalism should play such a role. Moreover, 40% of journalists say that they do not need to function as spokespersons for certain groups in society. We also found that more than three-quarters (77%) of the respondents want to reach as wide an audience as possible. More than half of professional journalists (57%) believe that it is important to stay in touch with the public, which is up 8% from 2003. On the other hand, it is clear that respondents consider it less important to offer a platform for the public to express their views. In 2003, 46% agreed that it was an important journalistic duty, but by 2008 this figure had fallen to 39%.

Ethical Norms.   As far as journalistic deontology is concerned, the results of the 2008 survey are in line with those of 2003, although the degree of tolerance for questionable reporting methods appears to have increased. The percentage of journalists who completely object to going undercover, using hidden microphones or cameras, or badgering unwilling informants, has decreased slightly since 2003. On the other hand, more than 90% of the respondents agree that journalists should never accept any money from a source, and 60% state that accepting gifts from a source is equally inadmissible.

Table 12.4 shows that journalists find that some practices are acceptable under certain circumstances. This suggests that journalists usually make fine distinctions when thinking about ethical issues. These results mirror findings from similar international studies. Based on a comparative analysis of data from Australia, Germany, the Netherlands, the United Kingdom, and the United States, for example, Deuze (2002b: 86) concluded that journalists apparently make a distinction "between active and passive impersonalization; between 'lying' and 'not telling'" (see Table 12.5), In other words, not identifying yourself as a journalist ("not telling") might be ethically less problematic than posing as someone else ("lying"). Also, the distinction that journalists appar-

Table 12.4   Importance of Journalistic Goals (in %)

Journalistic Goals	(Very) Important	Neutral	(Very) Unimportant	Total %
Provide the public with reliable (objective) information	99	1	—	100
Provide analysis and interpretation of complex problems	93	6	1	100
Disseminate information as quickly as possible	80	17	3	100
Reach the widest possible audience	77	17	6	100
Be a watchdog for democracy	69	23	8	100
Signal new trends and ideas	58	30	12	100
Staying in touch with the public	57	34	9	100
Take the public's feedback into account	50	36	14	100
Provide entertainment	40	34	26	100
Give ordinary people a chance to express their views	39	42	19	100
Be a spokesperson for certain groups in society	27	33	40	100
Set the political agenda	23	41	36	100
Influence public opinion	22	44	34	100
Create a good environment for advertisers	8	25	67	100

ently make between confidential business/government and personal documents is relevant in this context. Journalists in our survey believe that they should proceed with more caution when the private sphere is concerned as opposed to the public sphere. This finding also is consistent with Deuze's (2002b) international findings.

The Present and Future State of Journalism in Flanders

At the end of our survey, we presented the journalists with 10 statements that gauged their opinions on recent developments in journalism. Two statements were concerned with the rise of citizen

Table 12.5   Ethical Opinions Held by Journalists (in %)

	Always justified	Justified on occasion	Would not approve	Not sure	Prefer not to say	Total %
Being paid by a source	—	6	91	1	2	100
Using personal documents	1	24	70	4	1	100
Claiming to be someone else	—	26	70	3	1	100
Accepting gifts from a source	2	32	58	5	3	100
Paying people for information	—	42	48	7	3	100
Not presenting yourself as a journalist	2	51	43	3	1	100
Using confidential business/gov't documents	2	57	33	6	2	100
Badgering unwilling informants	16	52	27	3	2	100
Using hidden microphones or cameras	4	72	19	2	3	100
Go undercover	13	76	6	2	3	100

journalism. Although 26% of respondents agreed with the statement that "ordinary citizens and semi-professionals will increasingly produce news," only 19% believed that "bloggers and other citizen journalists constitute a threat to the professional journalist."

Furthermore, a majority (83%) of respondents agreed with the statement that "sensationalism of the news has increased over the past five years," and 45% believed that "the global quality of journalistic news reporting has been declining." Interestingly, though, only a small percentage of the journalists agreed with the statements that "the mainstream media provide less and less space for news coverage of foreign affairs" (17%) or for "thorough investigative journalism" (10%).

Flemish journalists also hold strong views concerning their working conditions. According to 79% of the respondents, the duties of the journalist have increased over the past years, and 72% say that media editors demand more from their journalists. Forty-four percent of the respondents also think that journalists will be increasingly forced to work as freelancers (even though 38% have a neutral view on this issue). Two-thirds of the respondents (67%) believe in a further growth of multi-media and cross-media journalism. When asked whether they believed that the number of jobs in journalism will decline, journalists were less sure: 34% believed this will be the case, but 26% did not, and the remaining 40% replied in a neutral way.

Conclusions

In this chapter we presented a summary of the research data on journalists that are available in Flanders from profile studies of journalists. Our analysis put the emphasis on the most recent data, while giving a more longitudinal perspective whenever possible.

A general conclusion we can draw from the data is that the profile of the Flemish professional journalist remains fairly stable. The average journalist can be described as a white man, about 40 years of age, working full-time in permanent employment in the traditional print media sector.

Obviously, we can discern a number of trends as well. We see, for example, that the proportion of women in journalism has increased since 1983, although men continue to be strongly over-represented—more than seven in 10 Flemish journalists are men. Moreover, women have difficulty gaining access to senior positions in the media. Even more remarkable is the ethnic disparity in the profession; professional journalists of foreign descent remain virtually absent from the Flemish media sector.

If we look at the data about the journalists' professionalism, we notice few changes compared to 2003. The data from 2008 indicate a fairly wide consensus among journalists on their roles and their ethics. Editorial independence is considered of equal importance. Politically and ideologically, journalists call themselves progressive and situate themselves predominantly on the left of the political spectrum. This lies, once again, fully in line with previous studies in Flanders and abroad.

Most indications of change can be found in the data on working conditions. The Belgian figures indicate that Flemish journalism, too, is subject to the international trends of multi-skilling, flexibility, and increased job mobility. These findings need to be put in the right perspective, though, since not all professional journalists are equally affected by these trends. For one, the survey shows that a vast majority of professional journalists in Flanders, including younger journalists, work for one single media sector. Comparably, most professional journalists have been working with their current employers for a fairly long time already, despite the increasing demand for flexibility. The data confirm the increasing workload in journalism and point to specific problems of the freelance status. On the other hand, the less favorable working conditions do not seem to induce overall job dissatisfaction within the profession. It must be noted, however, that the most recent survey was conducted before the onset of the latest economic crisis, which resulted in many job losses in general including in Flemish newsrooms.

References

Boczkowski, Pablo J. 2009. Materiality and mimicry in the journalism field. In *The changing faces of journalism: Tabloidization, technology and truthiness,* edited by Barbie Zelizer, pp. 56–67. London: Routledge.

Dahlgren, Peter. 2009. The troubling evolution of journalism. In *The changing faces of journalism: Tabloidization, technology and truthiness,* edited by Barbie Zelizer, pp. 146–161. London: Routledge.

De Bens, Els. 1983. *Het profiel van de beroepsjournalist in Vlaanderen* [The profile of the professional journalist in Flanders]. Brussels: VUB Uitgaven.

De Bens, Els. 1995. Het profiel van de Vlaamse dagbladjournalist [The profile of the Flemish newspaper journalist]. In *Communication, culture, community: Liber amicorum James Stappers,* edited by J. G. Stappers, E. H. Hollander, Paul Rutten, and Coen van der Linden, pp. 263–277. Nijmegen: Bohn Stafleu Van Loghum.

De Bens, Els, and Karin Raeymaeckers. 2010. *De pers in België* [The press in Belgium].4th ed. Leuven: Lannoo.

De Clercq, Mieke. 2001. Vrouwelijke journalisten:Nog steeds een zeldzaam fenomeen? [Female journalists: Still a rare phenomenon?]. *Kluwer Mediagids Boek en Pers* 8:1–16.

De Clercq, Mieke. 2003. Van onze correspondent(e) ter plaatse. Over de vrouwelijke ondervertegenwoordiging op de Vlaamse nieuwsredactie [From our field reporter: On women's underrepresentation in Flemish newsrooms]. In *Verslagen van het Centrum voor Genderstudies—UGent* nr. 12, pp. 29–54. Ghent: Academia Press.

Deuze, Mark. 2002a. *Journalism in the Netherlands: An analysis of the people, the issues and the (inter)national environment.* Amsterdam: Arant.

Deuze, Mark 2002b. National news cultures: A comparison of Dutch, German, British, Australian, and U.S. journalists. *Journalism and Mass Communication Quarterly* 79:134–149.

Deuze, Mark. 2007. *Media work.* Cambridge, England: Polity Press.

Deuze, Mark. 2009. Technology and the individual journalist. In *The changing faces of journalism: Tabloidization, technology and truthiness,* edited by Barbie Zelizer, pp. 82–97. London: Routledge.

Dupagne, Michel, and Bruce Garrison. 2006. The meaning and influence of convergence: A qualitative case study of newsroom work at the Tampa News Center. *Journalism Studies* 7:237–255.

Hollifield, C. Ann, Gerald M. Kosicki, and Lee B. Becker. 2001. Organizational vs. professional culture in the newsroom: Television news directors' and newspaper editors' hiring decisions. *Journal of Broadcasting & Electronic Media* 45:92–117.

International Federation of Journalists (IFJ)/ International Labour Office (ILO). 2006. *The changing nature of work: A global survey and case study of atypical work in the media industry.* Research report of the International Federation of Journalists supported by the International Labour Office. Retrieved from http://www.ifj.org/assets/docs/068/112/3fbf944-95ebe70.pdf.

Lewis, Justin, Williams, Andrew, Franklin, Bob, Thomas, James and Mosdell, Nick (2008, February 1). *The quality and independence of British journalism: tracking the changes over 20 years.* Retrieved December 26, 2011, from http://www.mediawise.org.uk/www.mediawise.org.uk/files/uploaded/Quality%20%26%20Independence%20of%20British%20Journalism.pdf.

Paulussen, Steve, and Mieke De Clercq. 2005. Eigen berichtgeving. Bevindingen en beperkingen van sociologische enquêtes bij journalisten [Their own reporting: Findings and limitations of sociological surveys among journalists]. In *De media in maatschappelijk perspectief* [The media from a societal perspective], edited by Hans Verstraeten and Frieda Saeys, pp. 69–90. Ghent: Academia Press.

Paulussen, Steve, and Karin Raeymaeckers (Eds.). 2010. *Journalisten: Profiel van een beroepsgroep* [Journtalist: Profile of a profession]. Lenven: Lannoo Campus.

Scholl, Armin, and Siegfried Weischenberg. 1998. *Journalismus in der Gesellschaft: Theorie, Methodologie und Empirie* [Journalism in society: Theory, methodology and empiricism]. Wiesbaden: Westdeutscher Verlag.

Statistics Belgium. 2010a. *Structure de la population* [Structure of the population]. Retrieved from http://statbel.fgov.be/fr/statistiques/chiffres/population/structure.

Statistics Belgium. 2010b. *Vruchtbaarheidscijfers volgens verstreken leeftijd van de moeder* [Fertility figures according to the mother's birth age]. Retrieved from http://statbel.fgov.be/nl/statistieken/cijfers/bevolking/geboorten_vruchtbaarheid/vruchtbaarheidscijfers/verstreken.

Weaver, David H. (Ed.). 1998. *The global journalist: News people around the world.* Cresskill, NJ: Hampton Press.

Weaver, David H., and G. Cleveland Wilhoit. 1986. *The American journalist: A portrait of U.S. news people and their work.* Bloomington: Indiana University Press.

Weaver, David H., and G. Cleveland Wilhoit. 1996. *The American journalist in the 1990s: U.S. news people at the end of an era.* Mahwah, NJ: Erlbaum.

13 Media Professionals or Organizational Marionettes?

Professional Values and Constraints of Danish Journalists

Morten Skovsgaard, Erik Albæk, Peter Bro, and Claes de Vreese

In February 2006, the Danish embassy in Damascus and the Danish Consulate General in Beirut were set on fire by mobs of enraged protestors. Elsewhere in the Middle East, the Danish flag was burned at demonstrations, threats against Danish citizens forced them to flee, and Danish commodities were boycotted. For a month, Denmark was shaking under the international pressure and the newspaper *Jyllands-Posten* was the epicenter.

The violent reactions were set off by *Jyllands-Posten*'s decision to explore alleged self-censorship in regard to Islam in Western societies by publishing a number of cartoons depicting the Prophet Muhammad. The "cartoon crisis," as it was named, left no doubt that news decisions made by journalists even in a small country can have not only a national but also a major global impact.

In the aftermath of the crisis, reflections and debates among journalists revolved around their societal and public responsibility and the norms of their occupation. The debate was an indication of the widely shared norms and the professionalization of journalists, which have developed since the turn of the 20th century when newspaper articles were typically written by politicians, novelists, and students, news writing being a part-time hobby or occupation (Søllinge 1999a).

The debate about the cartoons also made clear that journalists do not work in a void. Even though the individual journalist holds the microphone, types the words, and asks the critical questions, journalists are, to some extent, constrained by the organization in which they work. In the aftermath of the cartoon crisis Danish newspapers were accused of producing news that was politically biased in favor of their own political leaning. The alleged bias was ascribed to the values of the news organizations and not to the personal or professional values of the individual journalists.

Knowledge about who Danish journalists are and which professional norms and values they hold is limited. Little is known about the interplay between professionalism and organizational context, and whether certain journalists with certain professional values are employed at certain types of media organizations.

The cartoon crisis stressed the need to know more about Danish journalists as it made clear that journalists may, on occasion, ignite riots or violence in other parts of the world. The results presented here originate from the most extensive survey of Danish journalists to date.

Background

The formation and development of the Danish media system and the professionalization of its journalists resemble those in the surrounding countries in Northern Europe. A high literacy rate in these countries formed the base for early mass circulation newspapers and a tradition of widespread news consumption (Hallin & Mancini 2004). In Denmark, democracy was introduced with the enactment of the constitution in 1849, and in subsequent years newspapers emerged and became increasingly popular.

At first, newspapers were largely a political enterprise (Thomsen 1972). They were either owned by, or closely affiliated with, the four most significant political parties and served as enthusiastic party supporters as well as communication channels to the voters. The system of nationwide networks of newspapers affiliated with the four major political parties became known as the "four paper system"; i.e., four newspapers, each supporting one party only, competed in every provincial town of a certain size (Søllinge 1999a).

At the turn of the 20th century, journalism in Denmark slowly began to develop into a regular occupation. With inspiration from the United States and the United Kingdom, journalistic reporting methods such as the inverted pyramid evolved along with the popularization of reportage and interviews (Kolstrup 2005). Political opinion pieces were toned down in favor of news stories and a broader selection of topics. This was an attempt to gain new readers among a population in which newspaper readership (distribution) was already approaching 100% (Søllinge & Thomsen 1989). This trend, in turn, increased the demand for full-time journalists, and, as a sign of dawning professionalization, a trade union of provincial journalists was formed in 1900. Four years later, a corresponding union for Copenhagen-based journalists was founded. The two unions merged into the Danish Journalism Union in 1961.

Through the first part of the 20th century, the journalistic profession grew stronger and more coherent. State-controlled radio news was introduced in 1926 and television news in 1965. Broadcast news was edited according to statutes and rules of neutrality and a public service obligation, which meant that politically independent journalism gained popularity (Søllinge 1999b).

Newspapers also began to liberate themselves from explicit affiliation with the political parties, but, to some extent, remained political in their story selection and framing. However, the economic problems for the smaller newspapers after World War II and the economic boom that started in the late 1950s eroded the foundation for political news selection. The significant increase in living standards for blue-collar workers throughout the 1960s blurred the traditional class lines in society. The electorate became much more volatile and the economic and ideological pillars that used to characterize the newspaper market crumbled and eroded reader loyalty toward the party newspapers (Nissen 1991; Søllinge & Thomsen 1989).

This left editors and management with little choice but to tone down or eliminate their already waning political partisanship and emphasize their independence in order to appeal to a broader audience. As a result, most newspapers that were affiliated with the old political parties folded. What remained were newspapers that catered to all citizens with politically neutral news (Jensen 2003).

In 1970 the education of journalists was reformed to emphasize vocational training at the Danish School of Media and Journalism in the city of Århus rather than apprenticeships at media organizations. This further fueled the development toward a more coherent journalistic profession, and in 1998 two universities introduced journalism education at bachelor's as well as master's level in competition with the original journalism program in Århus.

Research on the professionalization of Danish journalists is quite limited. However, some research suggests increased professionalization from 1970 and onwards. Previous surveys show substantial support among Danish journalists for neutrality as an important ideal as well as for a journalistic obligation to encourage citizens' engagement in societal affairs. This indicates that Danish journalists share professional norms (Kristensen 2003; Lund 2001).

A longitudinal analysis of political journalism in Denmark shows that it has become more independent and more active through the latter part of the 20th century. The political news coverage has become increasingly similar in four national newspapers, indicating that news selection is based on professional rather than political criteria (Pedersen & Horst 2000).

The signs of increased professionalization throughout the 20th century do not mean that professionalization should be considered a linear process with a progression toward the perfect profession. The professional journalistic norms and ideals in Denmark—and elsewhere—are under pressure from profit demands and the Internet's dismantling of journalists' monopoly on access to mass audiences. These pressures can potentially undermine the professional norms of journalists and their professional legitimacy.

The key foci of this chapter are the characteristics of Danish journalists, their professional norms, and how these norms interact with the organizational context in which the journalists work. Role perceptions, objectivity, and news selection are the *sine qua non* for the journalistic profession. We have limited knowledge of how widely and strongly these professional norms and ideals are held and how they are interpreted among Danish journalists. We also have limited knowledge about how professional norms and ideals are connected to the organizational context, including the amount of autonomy journalists have to exercise their professional preferences. We tried to answer these questions with a large-scale survey of Danish journalists in 2009.

Method

The survey was conducted in close cooperation with the Danish Union of Journalists (*Dansk Journalistforbund*) during June and early July 2009. The total population of Danish journalists who were working full-time in media organizations or as freelancers (excluding journalists working in public relations and those who were unemployed) was extracted from the Union's member records by choosing relevant media categories; e.g., magazines, daily newspapers, radio, television, and Web media, those employed full-time as well as freelancers, amounting to a total of 5,519 journalists. The Danish Union of Journalists estimates that today membership includes around 90% to 95% of regular Danish journalists. This gives a unique opportunity to survey that population. We were given permission to send an e-mail invitation including a link to the online questionnaire to all 5,519 journalists in the Union's directory.

A total of 327 of the potential respondents turned out not to belong to the population and 664 questionnaires were not delivered correctly and thus never reached the respondent. 2,008 respondents completed the questionnaire, which represents a 44.3% response rate of the total population—a sound result compared to similar surveys in other countries (Weaver 1998).[1]

The union had information on variables such as gender, age, place of residence, and media type, which made it possible to compare respondents and non-respondents and see that the two groups are largely similar. However, the proportion of women is a bit larger among the respondents than among the non-respondents. In the sample women are overrepresented by only three percentage points compared to the total population.

Findings

Basic Characteristics

In many ways, Danish journalists constitute a rather homogenous group and are overwhelmingly of Danish origin. Some 99% of them have Danish citizenship, the rest are from Western countries. Among the general population, 93% have Danish citizenship and 3.5% non-Western citizenship.

With 46% women in Danish journalism, gender is more balanced today than it was in most other countries a decade ago (Weaver 1998: 457–458). When the Danish economy boomed through the 1960s and the welfare state expanded, women were included in the workforce to a greater extent in Denmark than in comparable countries. More women than men work in the public sector, in health care, education, and social institutions. Since many women also choose journalism, the gender distribution of journalists resembles the gender distribution in the general population more than the gender distribution in most other Danish occupations.

In terms of socio-economic background, Danish journalists are less representative of the general Danish population. About 56% of Danish journalists have one parent with at least three years of higher education and 30% of journalists have two parents in this educational bracket. For the general Danish population aged 45 to 69, only about one in five has completed a higher education of at least three years' duration. Thus, journalists' parents tend to be better educated than the general population of their age.[2]

Journalists are also quite homogenous in terms of education. Most of them have a degree from the Danish School of Media and Journalism, which is equivalent to a bachelor's degree. For almost 30 years this was the only formal journalism education, and therefore, a bachelor's degree in journalism is the ticket to jobs in the media industry. As a result, 65% of Danish journalists hold such a degree. In addition, 5% hold a master's degree in journalism and another 13% have learned journalism either by apprenticeship or through special journalism programs designed for people who have already completed another type of education and want to become journalists. All in all, more than 83% of Danish journalists have some sort of journalism education, which is high in comparison to journalists in many other countries now and a decade ago (Weaver 1998).

For journalists below the age of 30, 95% have a formal journalism education at the bachelor's level or higher. The younger the journalists, the more common it is to take this straight route to jobs in journalism. Supply seems to be no problem. In recent years, more than three in four applicants to the Danish journalism programs have been turned down due to limited slots in these programs.

There is also limited access to jobs in journalism for people with no formal journalism education. Thus, the journalistic profession in Denmark de facto resembles the traditional professions such as law and medicine (Soloski 1989).

So far as journalists working in the different types of media organizations are concerned, younger and less experienced journalists tend to work in online media and television. One explanation may be that these media types often rely on fast news dissemination, which may prove stressful and make some journalists change to other types of media outlets later in their career. Another explanation might be that online media are relatively new media that have to recruit young and recent journalism graduates.

The daily newspapers have the highest proportion of journalists with a formal journalism education (see Table 13.1). Not surprisingly, the lowest proportion of people with a formal journalistic education (61%) is found among freelancers who are not on the permanent staff of a news organization. Apart from these differences, the basic characteristics of the journalists generally look alike across all types of media organizations.

Political Convictions

Just as in other nations, the personal political convictions of journalists have been widely debated in Denmark (Hopmann 2009b). In the United States, claims of liberal and conservative bias in the

Table 13.1   Demographic Background of Journalists

	Dailies (N = 590)	Tabloid (N = 66)	TV (N = 266)	Radio (N = 135)	Web (N = 92)	Freelancer (N = 453)	Other[3] (N = 369)	Total (N = 1,971)
Age[4]	46[1]	46	41[2]	45	39[2]	47[1]	44	45
Journalistic experience[4]	18[1]	19	14[2]	18	11[2]	18[1]	16[2]	17
Gender (female)	42%[2]	31%[2]	43%	46%	30%[2]	56%[1]	49%	46%
Journalists with Bachelor's level education	79%[1]	75%	71%	68%	69%	61%[2]	68%	70%

1 The score is significantly higher than the mean score for all the other media types at the .05 level.
2 The score is significantly lower than the mean score for all the other media types at the .05 level.
3 The 'other' category contains journalists from news agencies, weekly magazines, weekly newspapers, and union magazines.
4 Average years.

media have been debated and studied extensively (for an overview see D'Alessio & Allen 2000). Some claim that media content is politically biased due to the political beliefs of individual journalists (e.g., Patterson & Donsbach 1996). Others argue that journalists are constrained by news organizations and that media content is instead politically biased due to the political standpoints and beliefs of the news organizations (e.g., Altschull 1995). Accordingly, media content has claimed to have a liberal bias stemming from journalists' own political beliefs and to have a conservative bias stemming from the news organizations, which are most often right-of-center business corporations (see D'Alessio & Allen 2000, for an elaboration).

The results from the Danish survey provide some ammunition to both camps. Like their colleagues in most other countries, Danish journalists on average report themselves to be slightly left of center (Deuze 2002a; Patterson & Donsbach 1996). On the other hand, most journalists place their own media organization slightly to the right of center.

This is similar to results from a survey among the general Danish population, asking whether the journalistic content in Danish newspapers showed any political leaning. The respondents placed some of the newspapers to the left of the political center and others to the right. Most respondents, however, identified a majority of slightly right-leaning newspapers (Hjarvard 2007).

Systematic content analysis of political bias in Danish newspapers is limited. An exception is a study of news about the war in Iraq in 2003, which found political bias in the war coverage that correlated with editorial opinions in the analyzed newspapers (Hjarvard 2007). The weakness of this analysis, of course, is the exclusive focus on one event. A recent and more comprehensive study of Danish television news during election campaigns over the last 15 years showed no systematic political bias in terms of appearances of or tone toward political actors (Hopmann 2009a). This result supports the notion that professional norms and values have a counterbalancing role against possible influences from individual journalists' personal beliefs and convictions as well as from organizational policies and conditions (Preston 2009). It is therefore important to study professional norms and values and their role within the organizational context (see Table 13.2).

Professional Ethics, Roles, and News Values

Scholars have pointed out that education is an important first socialization to the norms, ideals, procedures, and goals of the profession (Soloski 1989). On the other hand, some studies have shown that the first years in a newsroom have a bigger impact on journalists' views of their profes-

Table 13.2   Political Leaning of Journalists and Their Organizations

	Dailies (N=534)	Tabloid (N=57)	TV (N=237)	Radio (N=115)	Web (N=76)	Freelancer (N=406)	Other (N=317)	Total (N=1,366)
Journalist's self-placement[1]	4.11	4.25	4.18	3.78	3.88	3.86	3.89	3.99
Media organization the journalist works for[1]	6.35[2]	5.16[3]	5.45[3]	5.07[3]	5.68	—	5.23[3]	5.73

1 Journalists were asked: In politics people often talk about the political right and the political left. On a scale from 0 = 'furthest to the left' to 10 = 'furthest to the right' and 5 = 'center' please indicate where you would place yourself, and where you would place the news organization you work for. The scores are mean scores on this 11 point scale.
2 The score is significantly higher than the mean score for all the other media types at the .05 level.
3 The score is significantly lower than the mean score for all the other media types at the .05 level.

sion and its values than the education that preceded the first job (Bjørnsen, Hovden, & Ottosen 2007).

Denmark seems to be a good case study for this interplay between professional socialization through education and early socialization in the workplace. A substantial proportion of journalists have a formal journalism education and most of them have a bachelor's degree from the Danish School of Media and Journalism in Århus. Even though the universities in Odense and Roskilde now offer journalism courses as well, there is little diversity in the socialization Danish journalists have received through their education, especially compared to other countries. The idea of strong educational socialization would lead us to expect only small differences in the professional norms and ideals held by Danish journalists.

Journalists do not work in a void, however. They go on to work in different media organizations with different structures, audiences, routines, and goals. This may lead to the opposite expectation that journalists working in different types of media organizations differ substantially in their perception of their work and their professional norms and ideals, even though to a large extent, they have been exposed to the same educational socialization.

Contrary to the case in other countries (e.g., the United States, Canada, Belgium, Spain, Germany, or the former communist countries in Eastern Europe), no ethnic, language, or generational divides disturb the coherence of the journalistic profession in Denmark. Thus, if variations are found in journalists' professional norms and ideals, they may be attributed to variations in socialization across types of media organizations. Consequently, the following discussion of Danish journalists' professional norms, values, and ideals is framed by the type of media organization they work for.

Public Service Obligation.   An important aspect of professionalization is journalists' sense of public obligation (e.g., Deuze 2005; Hallin & Mancini 1994: 36; Tumber & Prentoulis 2003). To get a better idea of how journalists feel about "public obligation," we asked the journalists in our sample to whom they feel accountable in their work. They overwhelmingly indicated "citizens" in general, closely followed by their "sources," and to a lesser degree "colleagues" and "superiors." They feel least accountable to "advertisers" and the "owners of the media organization" in which they work.

It is important to note that there is practically no variation in responses across types of media organizations. This indicates that the obligation to the public (or citizens in general) rather than to colleagues, media owners, and advertisers is a strong professional and widely held norm among Danish journalists.

Journalistic Role Perceptions.   How journalists are to fulfill their obligation toward citizens is not clearly defined. But by asking a battery of questions about the roles journalists may potentially perform, we were able to track whether journalists employed at different types of news organizations have different perceptions of the roles they should perform in society.

Three factors that may be interpreted as three distinct role perceptions emerge from the analysis: the *critical-active* role, the *public mobilizing* role, and the *breaking news* role.[3] For the critical-active role, the journalist finds it important to be a representative of the public, to be skeptical, and to be critical of people with either political or economic power. The role also includes the importance of helping the public analyze and interpret complex issues.

For the public mobilizing role, journalists find it important to engage citizens in the public democratic debate, to give them a platform on which to express their views, and to help them find solutions to societal problems. This journalistic function gained popularity in the public journalism movement, which blossomed in the United States in the early 1990s and also found an audience among Danish journalists and editors in later years. Proponents argued that this movement was a reaction to overly critical and superficial journalism, which had shown too little regard for a public obligation to air democratic issues (Bro 2004).

In the breaking news role, emphasis is on the immediacy and the speed of the information dissemination. It is important to get information to the public quickly and it is important to break a news story. A competitive element is also embedded in this role perception.

Other studies have shown that journalists' role perceptions are not one-dimensional and that journalists can adhere to several roles at the same time (Deuze 2002b; Weaver & Wilhoit 1996; Weaver, Beam, Brownlee, Voakes, & Wilhoit 2007). The interesting question, then, is to ask whether Danish journalists put more emphasis on one role than another and whether this varies across type of media organization.

The most emphasized role is the critical-active role in which journalists act as the citizens' representatives by asking critical questions on their behalf and investigating claims made by elected public officials (see Table 13.3). This comes close to being a classic watchdog role.

The critical-active role is emphasized more by journalists than the other two roles, but the latter are by no means considered unimportant. The average score for both roles is 2 on a scale from 0 to 3. There are no significant differences in the emphasis put on the critical-active role across

Table 13.3   Journalists' Role Perceptions

	Dailies (N = 565)	Tabloid (N = 60)	TV (N = 249)	Radio (N = 124)	Web (N = 79)	Freelancer (N = 426)	Other (N = 338)	Total (N = 1,845)
Critical-active role[1]	2.5	2.4	2.5	2.4	2.4	2.5[2]	2.5	2.5
Public mobilizer role[1]	2.1[2]	1.8[3]	1.9[3]	2.1	1.8[3]	2.0	2.0	2.0
Breaking news role[1]	2.1[2]	2.3[2]	2.1[2]	2.0	2.2[2]	1.8	1.9[3]	2.0

1 The scores are the mean score on a scale from 0 to 3.
2 The score is significantly higher than the mean score for all the other media types at the .05 level.
3 The score is significantly lower than the mean score for all the other media types at the .05 level.

the various types of media organizations.[4] This indicates that the critical-active role is a strongly held professional norm among Danish journalists regardless of which type of media organization they work for.

Statistically significant differences are found for the other two roles. So far as the breaking news role is concerned, it seems that the most competitive journalists work at tabloids and for online media, which are both highly competitive due to fluctuating audiences. It also makes sense that freelancers emphasize the breaking news role the least. Tabloid and online journalists also adhere least to the public mobilizing role.

Thus a competitive media environment appears to moderate journalists' sense of obligation to create a public debate for ordinary citizens. It should be noted, though, that although these differences are statistically significant, they are rather small. The largest difference for the public mobilizing role across media type is 0.3 and for the breaking news role 0.5 on a scale from 0 to 3. This implies that differences in the organizational context only have a small impact on the journalistic role perceptions.

The Objectivity Norm.   The objectivity norm is key in analyses of the professionalization of journalists. It has been called the "defining norm of modern journalism" (Patterson 1998: 28) and the key that legitimates the professional ethics of liberal journalism (McNair 1998: 65).

At the same time, it has been rejected on epistemological grounds as a utopian illusion. Still, journalistic practice is very much based on the idea of objectivity, one reason being that it creates trust and legitimacy. However, objectivity is an ambiguous concept. Journalistic practice therefore largely relies on different proxies for objectivity; i.e., balanced and factual accounts containing references to credible sources and rigorous separation of commentary and reporting (e.g., Chalaby 1998; Tuchman 1972; Westerståhl 1983).

Danish journalists' own view of the disputed norm of objectivity reflects its ambiguity. When confronted with the statement "selection and exclusion in journalistic work means that the journalistic product can never be objective," more than three in four journalists agree to some extent. On the other hand, when asked how important it is for a journalist "to be as objective as possible," almost half of the respondents said "very important," representing the highest possible degree of importance, and three in four agree in one of the two highest categories of agreement on a seven point scale. Furthermore, four in five respondents agree to some extent that "striving for objectivity makes the journalistic product trustworthy" (see Table 13.4).

Though disputed and largely acknowledged by journalists not to be fully attainable, objectivity is still a strong professional norm among Danish journalists, perceived to be an important tool for creating trustworthy journalistic products and providing legitimacy for the journalistic profession.

Is the norm so strong that it crosses the walls between the different types of media organizations? Again, journalists working at tabloids stand out. They ascribe substantially less importance to objectivity than their colleagues in other types of media organizations. This does not seem to be driven by a more disillusioned notion of the possibility of achieving objective reporting. On the question whether objectivity in journalism is possible there are no statistically significant differences between journalists at tabloids and their colleagues elsewhere. However, in general their colleagues at other media tend to believe more strongly than tabloid journalists that striving for objectivity creates a more trustworthy journalistic product.

Apart from journalists working at tabloids, the differences reported in Table 13.4 are again rather small. Disregarding tabloid journalists, the difference between the highest (journalists at dailies) and the lowest scores (freelancers) on the importance of objectivity is only 0.37 on a 0 to 6

Table 13.4   Journalists' Perceptions of the Objectivity Norm

	Dailies (N = 558)	Tabloid (N = 58)	TV (N = 249)	Radio (N = 124)	Web (N = 80)	Freelancer (N = 421)	Other (N = 338)	Total (N = 1,830)
Importance of objectivity[1]	5.18[2]	3.98[3]	5.12[2]	5.08	4.96	4.81[3]	4.83	4.97
Selection makes objectivity impossible[1]	4.26	4.45	4.06[3]	4.27	4.43	4.49[2]	4.33	4.31
Striving for objectivity creates trust-worthiness[1]	4.61[2]	3.88[3]	4.61[2]	4.60	4.67	4.27[3]	4.35	4.46

1 The scores are the mean score on a scale from 0 to 6. In 'Importance of objectivity' 0 = 'Not important at all' and 6 = 'Very important'. For 'Selection makes objectivity impossible' and 'Striving for objectivity creates trustworthiness' 0 = 'Disagree very much' and 6 = 'Agree very much'.
2 The score is significantly higher than the mean score for all the other media types at the .05 level.
3 The score is significantly lower than the mean score for all the other media types at the .05 level.

scale. The differences for the two other categories are equally small, indicating substantial agreement in journalists' view of this central norm across different media.

News Selection.   Journalists incessantly make decisions on what is and what is not news. The world depicted by journalists is not an objective one-to-one representation of reality. This makes news selection an important part of journalistic work.

This is why news criteria or news values are an essential part of any journalism education program. Here, future journalists learn how to select news both in theory and practice. However, journalists graduate and proceed to work in different media organizations with different conditions for production, and different target groups and business strategies. News selection can be expected to be adjusted in accordance with such organizational needs. Thus, even though the news criteria are taught in journalism courses, there may be variations across different types of media organizations (e.g., Allern 2002; O'Neill & Harcup 2009).

News becomes news for different reasons. A given event may be important and have an impact on many people: It may appeal to the readers' curiosity or it may, as a story, fit into the setup of the news organization. An event may more likely become a news story when there are journalists available to process the news story in the newsroom or when the story is easy for a journalist to approach. This can be summarized into three categories: *relevance, dramatic appeal,* and *organizational conditions.*

We asked the journalists how important, in their experience, a number of parameters are in actual selection, and how important the same parameters, in their opinion, should be in the ideal news selection process. A factor analysis of the responses shows "dramatic appeal," "relevance," and "organizational conditions" to be important in news selection.[5]

Table 13.5 shows that most journalists prefer to select important rather than dramatic stories. Only tabloid journalists put greater emphasis on dramatic appeal than relevance in their perception of ideal news values. They also rate dramatic appeal significantly higher than their colleagues at other types of media organizations.

We also asked the journalists how important these parameters are in their actual news selection. The answers indicate that journalists at tabloids are more likely to choose stories with dramatic

Table 13.5 Journalists' Assessment of Actual and Ideal News Selection[1]

	Dailies (N = 528)	Tabloid (N = 54)	TV (N = 224)	Radio (N = 110)	Web (N = 74)	Freelancer (N = 387)	Other (N = 306)	Total (N = 1,683)
Dramatic appeal (actual news selection)	3.59	3.82[2]	3.57	3.49	3.61	3.61	3.51[3]	3.58
Dramatic appeal (ideal news selection)	3.07[2]	3.29[2]	2.88	2.86	3.06	2.79[3]	2.84[3]	2.93
Difference (actual-ideal)	.52[3]	.59	.69	.63	.55	.82[2]	.67	.65
Organizational conditions (actual news selection)	2.31	1.78[3]	2.05[3]	2.31	2.34	2.49[2]	2.32	2.30
Organizational conditions (ideal news selection)	1.08	.98	1.13	1.13	1.01	1.17	1.12	1.11
Difference (actual-ideal)	1.23	.80[3]	.92[3]	1.18	1.33	1.32[3]	1.20	1.19
Relevance (actual news selection)	2.76[2]	2.44	2.61	2.83[2]	2.50	2.42[3]	2.62	2.62
Relevance (ideal news selection)	3.30	2.85[3]	3.21	3.43[2]	3.16	3.33	3.30	3.28
Difference (actual-ideal)	−.54[2]	−.41	−.60	−.60	−.66	−.91[3]	−.68	−.66

1 The scores are the mean score on a scale from 0 = 'No impact' to 4 = 'Very big impact'. The differences are the score for the ideal news selection subtracted from the scores for actual news selection in the three categories.
2 The score is significantly higher than the mean score for all the other media types at the .05 level.
3 The score is significantly lower than the mean score for all the other media types at the .05 level.

appeal compared to journalists at most other types of media organizations. This is not surprising since tabloids are known for giving priority to spectacular stories about crime and conflict.

This being said, it is again worth noting that differences are quite small. The differences on ideal news selection across types of media organizations are no more than 0.58 on a scale from 0 ("should have no impact") to 4 ("should have very big impact"). Disregarding tabloid journalists, differences across the rest of the media types are even smaller, which implies that journalists across media organizations hold very similar news values.

Across media organizations, journalists agree that organizational conditions should play a small role in news selection. However, regardless of their place of employment, journalists find that organizational conditions do play too big a role in actual news selection while relevance has too little priority. Thus, it is fair to conclude that there is a significant gap between journalists' views of ideal news values and actual criteria for news selection (see Table 13.5).

A recent Danish study demonstrates that this gap between ideals and practice in journalism has a negative impact on job satisfaction, since constraints preventing enactment of ideals create frustration (Pihl-Thingvad 2010). This could prove an important problem for the perceived working conditions in the media industry and might lower the attractiveness of the profession to potential newcomers.

Autonomy and Working Conditions

In terms of their adherence to journalistic norms, ideals, and values, there seems to be a strong professional coherence among Danish journalists. Nevertheless, journalists work under different conditions in different organizations, and this may create variation in their ability to implement professional decisions (Hallin & Mancini 2004).

Since news production demands a number of rapid decisions, news organizations cannot set up bureaucratic rules to fully control the behavior of journalists. To some extent, news organizations have to rely on the professional decision making of reporters and editors, which gives the latter considerable autonomy in news selection and processing (Soloski 1989: 208). Other scholars point out that routines and standard operating procedures (SOPs) both enable and constrain news production and limit the autonomy of journalists without them necessarily realizing it (Gans 1979; Tuchman 1978).

Hallin and Mancini (2004) point out that professional autonomy among journalists varies over time, across media systems, and across media organizations. Table 13.6 shows that journalists working in different types of media organizations do not believe they have the same degree of autonomy in their journalistic work. In general, journalists at daily newspapers have a greater sense of autonomy than journalists at other types of news media, while television journalists, on the other hand, report less autonomy. This is no surprise since a more structured, routine, and controlled production is needed to obtain a high degree of predictability of outcome for planners of broadcast news. The technical demands of broadcast news make it difficult (and expensive) to replace a story that turned out different than expected.

Overall, the results show that even though journalists do enjoy some professional autonomy, it is constrained by organizational context. Interestingly, journalists in all types of media organizations perceive the freedom to choose sources as more extensive than the freedom to either choose or frame a story. Apparently superiors exercise control in the initial selection and framing of stories, but leave extensive discretion to journalists when it comes to more detailed decisions about the story, such as source selection. This means that journalists do exercise professional discretion, but it is more constrained in the initial choices that set the course for the news story

We also asked the journalists how much several different factors affect their work. The findings show that the influence from advertisers, sources, and owners or stakeholders is rather limited, while immediate pressures from deadlines, competition, audience figures, editorial policy, and budget cuts exert more influence on the journalists' work and their professional autonomy (see Table 13.7). This finding fits well with the notion that influence from owners or advertisers is

Table 13.6   Journalists' Sense of Professional Autonomy (% saying "almost complete freedom")

	Dailies (N = 428)	Tabloid (N = 42)	TV (N = 207)	Radio (N = 109)	Web (N = 53)	Freelancer (N = 453)	Other (N = 224)	Total (N = 1,516)
Free to choose story	52[1]	31	22[2]	46	43	43	41	42
Free to choose framing	61[1]	36	25[2]	51	51	37[2]	50	45
Free to choose sources	72[1]	57	39[2]	54	59	47[2]	59	56

1 The score is significantly higher than the mean score for all the other media types at the .05 level.
2 The score is significantly lower than the mean score for all the other media types at the .05 level.

Table 13.7   Influential Aspects in Journalistic Work

	Dailies (N = 584)	Tabloid (N = 65)	TV (N = 266)	Radio (N = 132)	Web (N = 92)	Freelancer (N = 435)	Other (N = 362)	Total (N = 1,507)
Time pressure/deadlines[1]	6.9[2]	6.6	7.0[2]	7.3[2]	7.0[2]	5.0[3]	6.3	6.4
Competition with other media[1]	5.7[2]	6.9[2]	5.9[2]	4.9	6.3[2]	3.4[3]	5.2	5.1
Editorial policy of own media[1]	4.9[3]	5.1	5.2	4.9	5.5	—	5.5[2]	5.1
Audience figures[1]	4.8	6.3[2]	5.8[2]	5.2	6.9[2]	3.6[3]	5.1	4.9
(Risk of) Budget cuts[1]	4.5	3.8[3]	4.5	4.2[3]	4.7	5.3[2]	4.7	4.7
Owners/stakeholders[1]	2.8[3]	2.6	2.7[3]	2.8	3.4	—	4.1[2]	3.1
Pressure from sources[1]	2.6	2.0[3]	2.4	2.2[3]	2.6	2.4	3.1[2]	2.6
Advertisers[1]	2.6[2]	1.9	1.6[3]	.5[3]	2.7	2.5	3.1[2]	2.4

1 Scores are mean scores on a scale from 0 = 'Not influential at all' to 10 = 'Very influential'.
2 The score is significantly higher than the mean score for all the other media types at the .05 level.
3 The score is significantly lower than the mean score for all the other media types at the .05 level.

seldom overt and thus not felt directly by journalists (Breed 1955; Hallin 2000). Instead, their influence works through the indirect pressure on journalists to reach high audience figures, the demand for a competitive product, and cuts in available resources for producing journalism.

As expected, time pressure is reported to have the most substantial impact on journalistic work. News work is very much about timeliness, and frequent deadlines are a fact of life in this kind of work. While journalists who work for daily newspapers, radio, television, or online media report significant levels of influence as a result of time pressure and deadlines, tabloid journalists are more influenced by media competition. This makes sense since tabloids are primarily sold to non-subscribers who decide whether or not to buy a newspaper every single day. Thus, tabloid journalists especially fear competition and are highly dependent on daily readership figures.

Freelancers report the least influence from audience figures but the biggest influence from budget cuts. They sell their products, which are not always directed toward a mass audience, and they are the most flexible part of the work force, so when budgets are being cut they are a natural first choice for elimination.

Overall, there are clear limitations to the autonomy of journalists, and the type of media organization does have a significant influence on the amount of autonomy in journalists' daily work.

Conclusions

Since Breed (1955) wrote his classic piece on social control in the newsroom, media scholars have debated the extent to which journalists internalize the values of their news organizations. The influences that shape journalistic values range from the journalist's individual background, his or her educational socialization, to the cultural and political developments in the society in which the journalist is embedded (e.g., Plaisance & Skewes 2003; Schultz 2002; Zhu, Weaver, Lo, Chen, & Wu 1997).

The Danish case cannot resolve this complex question, but the fact that Danish journalists are exceptionally homogenous in terms of educational background means that the findings presented in this chapter can provide some insight.

Overall, Danish journalists report very similar views on professional norms across different types of news media organizations. They have a strong sense of public obligation, and they strongly adhere to objectivity and relevance rather than dramatic appeal in news selection. Significant differences are found between journalists at different types of media organizations, but for the most part these differences are rather small. In short, professional values seem to transcend differences in organizational context among Danish journalists.

This finding is in line with Cook (2006), who, from an institutional perspective, emphasizes that despite considerable variation in audiences and formats, news reports are similar across media organizations. News is produced according to distinctive roles, routines, rules, and procedures, which cut across differences in the type of media organization.

Our findings could indicate two things. First, that educational socialization does have an impact, and second, that even though media organizations have different goals, audiences, and production conditions, there is a core of journalistic values that are a part of the organizational socialization process. The results could also indicate a relationship between educational and media organization socialization such that both contribute to a strong, coherent journalistic profession.

It is important to note that these findings only inform us about the professional norms, ideals, and values, and not the actual journalistic practice. Danish journalists' views of ideal versus actual news selection suggest a discrepancy between their professional news values and how they perceive the daily practice of story selection within their media organizations. This indicates that there are organizational constraints that moderate journalists' professional autonomy. Thus, even though Danish journalists are media professionals, they are also, at least to some degree, organizational marionettes.

As the debate that followed the cartoon crisis illustrated, journalistic norms and values are not carved in stone. They are subject to interpretation and debate, which constantly shape and reshape them. Two important points can be learned from the cartoon crisis. First, traditional media still have a potential impact in society and can serve as engines for debate. Second, the Internet with its free flow of information and a blogosphere that picks up information from traditional media can strongly amplify the dissemination and interpretation of information outside the control of professional journalism. The question is whether this Web of free flowing information will erode the foundation of the journalistic profession or whether the journalistic profession will become even more important in a global society in which people need trustees who, on their behalf, can sort out and decode an endless stream of information.

Notes

1. Response rate 2 in accordance with the standard definitions from The American Association for Public Opinion Research (see The American Association for Public Opinion Research. 2009. *Standard Definitions: Final Dispositions of Case Codes and Outcome Rates for Surveys*. 6th ed. Orlando, FL: Author). We had a threshold for completed questionnaires which means that some respondents did not fill in the entire questionnaire. This explains why, in the following analysis, the N in most cases is lower than 2,008.
2. Based on numbers from *Statistics Denmark*.

3. The respondents were asked: "Here is a list of things that the media do or try to do today. How important do you think each of the following things should be in journalistic work?" *The critical-active role* consists of the items: (a) Investigate claims and statements from the government. (b) Be the devil's advocate vis-à-vis public officials. (c) Provide analysis and interpretation of complex problems. (d) Be the devil's advocate vis-à-vis business. (e) Be a representative of the public and ask questions on its behalf. (f) Discuss policy proposals while they are still being developed. Cronbach's alpha = .79. Scale mean = 2.46. *The public mobilizer role* consists of the items: (a) Motivate ordinary people to engage in the public debate on important societal issues. (b) Give ordinary people a chance to express their views on public affairs. (c) Lead people toward solutions to society's problems. Cronbach's alpha = .64. Scale mean = 2.00. *The breaking news role* consists of the items: (a) Get information quickly to the public. (b) Be the first to get a news story out. Cronbach's alpha = .56. Scale mean = 1.98.

4. The comparison does show that freelancers are significantly different from journalists in other media types. However, the difference is so small that it makes no sense to interpret it.

5. The respondents were asked: "Various things determine whether an incident is picked up by a news medium. We want you to answer to which extent the following things, in your experience, are significant in determining whether an incident is turned into a journalistic story, as well as to which extent, in your opinion, it should be." Based on a factor analysis we created six scales. *The dramatic appeal in actual news selection* consists of the items: (a) The incident is sensational and unexpected; (b) the incident interests many people; (c) the incident is dramatic and exciting. Cronbach's alpha = .73. Scale mean = 3.58. *The dramatic appeal in ideal news selection* consists of the same items, but assessed from a normative rather than a descriptive perspective. Cronbach's alpha = .73. Scale mean = 2.93. *The organizational conditions in actual news selection* consist of the items: (a) There is a good press release; (b) there is a journalist available to cover the incident; (c) there is a journalist who takes a special interest in the incident. Cronbach's alpha = .59. Scale mean = 2.30. *The organizational conditions in ideal news selection* consist of the same items, but assessed from a normative rather than a descriptive perspective. Cronbach's alpha = .64. Scale mean = 1.11. *The relevance in actual news selection* consists of the items: (a) The incident increases the citizens' insight into and knowledge about the world surrounding them; (b) the incident informs the citizens about inconsistencies in society; (c) the incident has consequences for the everyday life of the citizens. Cronbach's alpha = .74. Scale mean = 2.62. *The relevance in ideal news selection* consists of the same items, but assessed from a normative rather than a descriptive perspective. Cronbach's alpha = .78. Scale mean = 3.28.

References

Allern, Sigurd. 2002. Journalistic and commercial news values: News organizations as patrons of an institution and market actors. *Nordicom Review* 23(1–2):137–152.

Altschull, J. Herbert. 1995. *Agents of power: The media and public policy.* London: Longman.

Bjørnsen, Gunn, Jan Fredrik Hovden, and Rune Ottosen. 2007. Journalists in the making. *Journalism Practice* 1(3):383–403.

Breed, Warren. 1955. Social control in the newsroom. *Social Forces* 33 (May): 326–335.

Bro, Peter. 2004. *Aktionsjournalistik* [Action journalism]. Odense: Syddansk Universitetsforlag.

Chalaby, Jean. 1998. *The invention of journalism.* New York: St. Martin's Press.

Cook, Timothy E. 2006. The news media as a political institution: Looking backward and looking forward. *Political Communication* 23(2):159–171.

D'Allesio, Dave, and Mike Allen. 2000. Media bias in presidential elections: A meta-analysis. *Journal of Communication* 50(4):133–156.

Deuze, Mark. 2002a. National news cultures: A comparison of Dutch, German, British, Australian, and U.S. journalists. *Journalism & Mass Communication Quarterly* 79(1):134–149.

Deuze, Mark. 2002b. *Journalists in the Netherlands.* Amsterdam: Aksant.

Deuze, Mark. 2005. What is journalism? Professional identity and ideology reconsidered. *Journalism* 6(4):442–464.

Gans, Herbert. 1979. *Deciding what's news: A study of CBS Evening News, NBC Nightly News, Newsweek, and Time.* New York: Pantheon Books.

Hallin, Daniel. 2000. Commercialism and the professionalism in the American news media. In *Mass media and society.* 3rd ed., edited by James Curran and Michael Gurevitch, pp. 218–237. London: Arnold.

Hallin, Daniel, and Palo Mancini. 2004. *Comparing media systems: Three models of media and politics.* Cambridge, England: Cambridge University Press.

Hjarvard, Stig. 2007. Den politiske presse: En analyse af danske avisers politiske orientering [The political press: An analysis of Danish newspapers' political leaning]. *Journalistica* 5: 27–53.

Hopmann, David. 2009a. *Politically biased coverage of national election campaigns? Studies on Danish television news.* Ph.D. thesis, Centre for Journalism, Department for Political Science, University of Southern Denmark, Odense.

Hopmann, David. 2009b. Public service og politisk balance: En typologi [Public service and political balance: A typology]. *Journalistica* 3(1): 5–27.

Jensen, Klaus Bruhn (ed.). 2003. *Dansk mediehistorie I-IV* [Danish media history I–IV]. Frederiksberg: Samfundslitteratur.

Kolstrup, Søren. 2005. Telling the news. In *Diffusion of the news paradigm 1850–2000,* edited by Svennik Høyer and Horst Pöttker, pp. 105 - 122. Gøteborg: Nordicom.

Kristensen, Nete Nørgaard. 2003. *Udfordringer i journalistikken i lyset af kildernes professionalisering—slinger i valsen?* [Challenges in journalism in the light of the professionalization of the sources]. Ph.D. thesis, Copenhagen University.

Lund, Anker Brink. 2001. *Forskning om medier og demokrati* [Research on media and democracy]. Danske Dagblades Forenings debatserie no. 16. København: Danske Dagblades Forening

McNair, Brian. 1998. *The sociology of journalism.* London: Arnold.

Nissen, Henrik S. 1991. *Gyldendal og politikens danmarkshistorie bind 14: Landet blev by 1950–1970* [Gyldendal og politikens danmarkshistorie 14: The countryside turned into city 1950–1970]. Copenhagen: Politikens Forlag.

O'Neill, Deirdre, and Tony Harcup. 2009. News values and selectivity. In *The handbook of journalism studies,* edited by Karin Wahl-Jorgensen and Thomas Harnitzsch, pp. 161–174. New York: Routledge.

Patterson, Thomas E. 1998. The political roles of the journalist. In *The politics of news the news of politics,* edited by Doris Graber, Denis McQuail, and Pippa Norris, pp. 23–39. Washington, DC: CQ Press.

Patterson, Thomas E., and Wolfgang Donsbach. 1996. Journalists as partisan actors. *Political Communication* 13: 455–468.

Pedersen, Ove K., and Maja Horst. 2000. Den selvstændige journalistik: Udviklingen af den politiske journalistik fra 1958 til 1998 [The independent journalism: The development of the political journalism from 1958 to 1998]. In *Politisk journalistik* [Political Journalism], edited by Ove K. Pedersen, Peter Kjær, Anders Esmark, Maja Horst and Erik Meier Carlsen, pp. 145–168. Århus: Forlaget Ajour.

Pihl-Thingvad, Signe. 2010. *Selvledelse og psykisk arbejdsmiljø i det grænseløse arbejde.* [Self-leadership and psycho-social work environment in modern flexible work]. Ph.D. thesis, University of Southern Denmark, Odense,

Plaisance, Patrick Lee, and Elisabeth Skewes. 2003. Personal and professional dimensions of news work: Exploring the link between journalists' values and roles. *Journalism & Mass Communication* 80(4): 833–848.

Preston, Paschal. 2009. *Making the news: Journalism and news cultures in Europe.* London: Routledge.

Schultz, Tanjev. 2002. Does education matter? Characteristics of journalists who went to graduate school. *Journalism* 3(2): 223–238.

Soloski, John. 1989. News reporting and professionalism: Some constraints on the reporting of the news. *Media, Culture and Society* 11: 207–228.

Søllinge, Jette D. 1999a. Danish newspapers. Structures and developments. *Nordicom Review* 20(1): 31–76.

Søllinge, Jette D. 1999b. Historien om den politiske journalistik—et drama i flere akter uden slutning [The history of the political journalism—A drama in several acts without ending]. In *Magt og fortælling. Hvad er politisk journalistik* [Power and narratives. What is political journalism], edited by Erik Meier Carlsen, Peter Kjær, and Ove K. Pedersen, pp. 76–95. Århus: Forlaget Ajour.

Søllinge, Jette D., and Niels Thomsen. 1989. *De danske aviser 1634–1989* [Danish newspapers 1634–1989]. Copenhagen: Dagspressens Fond/Odense Universitetsforlag.

Thomsen, Niels. 1972. *Dagbladskonkurrencen 1870–1970* [The competition of daily newspapers]. Copenhagen: Gads Forlag.

Tuchman, Gaye. 1972. Objectivity as strategic ritual: An examination of newsmen's notions of objectivity. *The American Journal of Sociology* 77(4):660–679.

Tuchman, Gaye. 1978. *Making news: A study of the construction of reality.* New York: Free Press.

Tumber, Howard, and Marina Prentoulis. 2005. Journalism and the making of a profession. In *Making journalists,* edited by Hugo de Burgh, pp. 58–74. London: Routledge.

Weaver, David. 1998. Journalists around the world: Commonalities and differences. In *The global journalist: News people around the world,* edited by David Weaver, pp. 455–480. Cresskill, NJ: Hampton Press.

Weaver, David, Randal Beam, Bonnie Brownlee, Paul Voakes, and Cleveland Wilhoit. 2007. *The American journalist in the 21st century: U.S. news people at the dawn of a new millennium.* Mahwah: Erlbaum.

Weaver, David H., and G. Cleveland Wilhoit. 1996. *The American journalist in the 1990s: U.S. news people at the end of an era*. Mahwah, NJ: Erlbaum.

Weischenberg, Siegfred, Maja Malik, and Armin Scholl. 2006. *Die Souffleure der Mediengesellschaft. Report über die Journalisten in Deutschland*. [The Prompters of the Media Business: Report on Journalists in Germany].Konstanz: UVK.

Westerståhl, Jörgen. 1983. Objective News reporting. General premises. *Communication Research* 10(3): 403–424.

Zhu, Jian Hua, David Weaver, Ven-Hwei Lo, Chongshan Chen, and Wei Wu. 1997. Individual, organizational, and societal influences on media role perceptions: A comparative study of journalists in China, Hong Kong, and the United States. *Journalism & Mass Communication Quarterly* 74(1): 84–96.

14 Finnish Journalists

The Quest for Quality amidst New Pressures

Jyrki Jyrkiäinen and Ari Heinonen

Finland is highly industrialized, technologically advanced, and sparsely inhabited, with a population of 5.3 million in an area of 338,000 square kilometers or about the size of Germany. Officially, Finland is a bilingual country with a Swedish-speaking minority of 5.4%. In Lapland, a province in the north of Finland, there is a constitutionally protected minority of 7,000 Sámi people, of whom 1,600 speak Sámi. In addition, some people (156,000) speak other languages as their mother-tongues (Finland in Figures 2010).

Newspaper and periodical publishing, along with news agencies and radio and television, covered nearly one-third (32.7%) of the gross value added from culture in the 2006 national economy. When books, motion pictures, and other publishing activities were included the share of mass media rose to over half (53.5%) of the cultural gross value added, with mass media accounting for 1.7% of the Finnish GDP (Cultural Statistics 2007).

In this culturally homogenous though rapidly diversifying environment, journalism is practiced in a typically Western European framework in both political and economic terms. Freedom of expression is guaranteed in the Constitution, media laws are permissive along the lines typical in the European Union (EU), and the self-regulatory mechanism also is solid with an independent press council and a code of journalistic ethics approved by the profession and recognized throughout the field. The principal law governing the media is the Exercise of Freedom of Expression in Mass Media Act (2004), which applies to all forms of mass communication from print to broadcast to online publications. However, this law does not actually regulate online publications by individuals, and there are also some gray areas with regard to online discussion forums within established media.

The mass media landscape in Finland is relatively rich and varied with the print media still dominant in economic terms. While the total market volume of mass media in 2008 was €4.4 billion (U.S.$6.5 billion), newspaper revenues were about €1.2 billion (U.S.$1.9), those of broadcasting €1 billion (U.S.$1.5), and the magazine sector €800 million (U.S.$1.1 billion). The Internet sector (excluding online operations of the established media) was €158 million (U.S.$232 million). The annual growth from 2007 was biggest in the Internet sector (34%), but also broadcast, newspaper, and even magazine revenues grew, albeit modestly (8.5%, 2.4%, and 1.1% respectively; Finnish Mass Media 2009).

In 2008 the average daily radio listening time was 3 hours 15 minutes. Daily television viewing increased slightly to 2 hours 57 minutes in 2008. The Finns read newspapers for an average of 34 minutes and magazines 18 minutes daily in 2008 (Finnish Mass Media 2009). Like the other Nordic nations, the Finns have long been avid newspaper readers ranking first in the EU and third in the world in circulation of dailies with 483 copies per 1,000 persons in 2008. The number of newspapers was at its highest at 252 titles in 1990. In 2008, a total of 201 newspaper titles were published with an aggregate circulation of 3.1 million copies (down from 3.3 million in 1999). There are 53 dailies (published 4–7 times a week) with a circulation of 2.1 million copies. Two major publishers, Sanoma and Alma Media, account for 55% of the aggregate circulation of the dailies (Finnish Mass Media 2009).

It is characteristic of the Finnish newspaper scene that there are only a few nationwide newspapers, but the regional daily press is very strong. Since the 1950s, most towns have become single-paper places, and competition among daily newspapers is today almost non-existent. The strength of newspapers in Finland continues to be that they are home-delivered early in the morning and that they are mostly subscribed to on an annual basis. However, advertising was 54% of revenues, while subscriptions and single copy sales were 45% of the newspaper's revenues in 2008 (Finnish Mass Media 2009). As a reaction to the steadily, but so far slowly, declining economic and circulation situation, newspapers have made structural changes by discontinuing unprofitable operations and taking cost-saving measures, such as outsourcing journalistic work to freelancers or favoring short-term employment. There has been a considerable increase in editorial cooperation between newspapers, even across corporate borders.

The total number of magazines in Finland was 3,300 in 2008. Nearly half of the titles were trade, business, and other specialized magazines, while there were 400 consumer magazines. The total circulation of magazines was 13.8 million in 2008 (Finnish Mass Media 2009). The biggest players in this field are Sanoma Magazines and Yhtyneet Kuvalehdet. Unlike the newspaper market, there are foreign companies like Aller and Bonnier operating in the Finnish magazine sector.

Turning to broadcast media, it is noteworthy that radio has maintained its popularity in Finland. Almost all (95%) Finns listen to radio every week, and it is particularly interesting that in 2009 radio was more popular among young people (age group 15–24 years) than 10 years earlier (Finnpanel 2010). In 2008, there were five national radio stations of which four were public service and one commercial. The national public broadcaster YLE is a BBC-style full service, non-commercial media company with radio programs in Finnish, Swedish, and Sámi (and, as a curiosity, weekly current news in Latin). On the commercial side, there are a total of 33 operators, but only one radio station that is nationwide. The rest operate locally or regionally, but belong to larger chains that are mostly part of some international company. In 2009, the public broadcaster YLE had a share of 52% of listeners, with the remainder divided between the commercial operators.

The major operators in television are the public broadcaster YLE, the commercial MTV Media (owned by the Swedish Bonnier media company), and Nelonen Media (owned by the Sanoma group). Each has several channels, and in addition there are channels operated by smaller companies. Measured by viewing time, YLE is the leading television company with a share of about 44% followed by MTV Media (32%) and Nelonen Media (15%) (Finnpanel 2009).

Because about 70% of Finnish households had broadband Internet access in 2008 (Finnish Mass Media 2009), online media use is taken for granted. Practically all newspapers have some kind of an online version, and many are constantly being developed. However, as the Finnish print newspapers are still doing relatively well economically, online versions are not their priority, at least not yet. The emphasis is on breaking news; otherwise the content consists of material originally produced for print versions (Heinonen & Kinnunen 2005). At the same time, the broadcast media also are offering their programs online. Besides editorial content, Finnish media have in the 2000s introduced various interactive features to their online outlets with the aim of engaging audiences more actively in their own realm. These strategies by the established media clearly reflect the recent challenges posed by the social media (Heinonen 2008).

With regard to trends in the professional culture of journalism in Finland, the major perceived challenges relate to the economic and technological aspects of media work. In a recent study of newspaper editors, it was found that journalists feel that economic competition in the media field has intensified, and subsequently business thinking has become omnipresent in news work. In addition, technological change requires adaptive measures for how journalism is carried out. These issues, along with cultural and political changes, have forced the profession to re-negotiate its ideals and practices. However, amidst all the turmoil in and around journalism, it is believed that basic elements of journalistic work will endure (Kunelius & Ruusunoksa 2009).

Previous Studies

In Finland, representative studies of professional journalists typically use the membership of the Union of Journalists in Finland (UJF) as their population. This is fully justified in this country as practically all professionals in journalism are members of this labor organization. From the late 1980s onwards, the UJF membership has been used for research by several empirical studies—relatively late considering the long history of journalism studies in Finland (Heinonen 1998). Most notable in the context of this article are two representative mail surveys carried out in 1987 and 1993 in collaboration with the UJF on, among other issues, basic characteristics of journalists and their working conditions (Kehälinna & Melin 1988; Melin & Nikula 1993). The questionnaires of the two surveys contain several identical questions, which allow for timeline comparisons. Some of them were also included in the most recent journalist survey, which is the basis of the data used in this chapter.

Other relevant studies are two thematic mail surveys (Harju 2002; Heinonen 1995), which focused on the ethical attitudes of Finnish journalists, and which used partly the same design. Besides these, the UJF has quite regularly carried out its own studies on labor market, wage trends, and equality for its own internal use. Useful background for this article also comes from a portrait of Finnish journalists (Heinonen 1998), which was published in Weaver's *The Global Journalist* (1998), and a brief overview of the Finnish media landscape to be found in Jyrkiäinen's *Media Moves* (2008b).

These previous studies have shown that Finnish journalists are conscious of and appreciate the social role of the profession, while at the same time individual reasons (such as a desire to express oneself) are important in their career choice. The studies have also indicated a growing concern about anticipated deterioration of journalism's quality and working conditions.

Method

The main data source for this chapter is the representative Finnish Journalist Survey 2007 (Jyrkiäinen 2008a). The aim of the study was to gain information on how journalists keep up with changes in and around media, and how they cope professionally with the intensive economic, technological, and production pressures within the media industry. The study was carried out in 2007 by the Journalism Research and Development Centre of the University of Tampere as a joint research project with the Union of Journalists (UJF) in Finland. The two main data gathering methods were mail survey and diary. The study population was the membership of the Union currently working in the profession.

The UJF had 14,794 members at the end of 2006. Because the focus of this study was on actively working journalists, retired, student, and unemployed members were excluded, as were those located in the autonomous province of the Åland Islands and members who worked abroad. Thus, the population consisted of 10,820 active working journalists representing 73.1% of the total membership of the Union and, in effect, the full active journalistic workforce in the country.

According to the register of members, the active working members of the UJF fall into three main media areas: the newspaper and publishing sector (49%), magazines (19%), and radio and television broadcasting (32%). A random sample of 1,500 was constructed to represent the relative share of each sub-group of the whole membership. In each sub-group every seventh member was randomly chosen. The sample was built by relative quotas according to the breakdown of members in the register. The sample groups represented their relative share of the total membership.

The questionnaire's 170 questions were divided into four main themes: 1) issues of content and current problems in work, 2) changes in work tasks and their effects, 3) working methods and practices, and 4) attitudes and concepts regarding Finnish society and selected value statements. The questionnaire contained structured, semi-structured, scaled, and open-ended questions. The respondents could choose to use either a printed questionnaire or an online version.

The data were gathered between March 23 and June 1, 2007. Overall, 614 or 41% of the contacted journalists responded. The great majority of those answered via the Internet, (only 44 printed forms were returned). Women were slightly overrepresented and broadcast journalists slightly underrepresented among the respondents. The majority of respondents represent the core groups of the profession (writing, reporting, and editing journalists or sub-editors).

Nearly half of the respondents in the 2007 survey had a university degree (48%), almost a fifth had some university studies (18%), and a tenth had a polytechnic degree (10%). More than half of the respondents worked in the metropolitan (Helsinki) area (54%), a quarter in major provincial towns (25%), and about a fifth in smaller cities or municipalities (21%). On average, the respondents had spent 9.5 working years in their present jobs and had worked 16 years in journalism.

In addition to the data from the 2007 survey, other data sources for this chapter include UJF internal surveys, other related studies on the state of the journalistic profession and media in Finland, and also specifically elicited details from informed sources in the field.

Findings

Most Journalists in Print Media

As previously stated, the membership of the Union of Journalists offers a valid basis for describing the journalistic workforce in Finland. According to UJF's own Labor Market Report (SJL 2008), its membership has been increasing, contrary to the general trend of decreasing membership in trade unions in Finland. In 2009, the total number of UJF members was about 15,500 (Table 14.1). Of these, about 11,000 (72%) were active journalists.

According to the UJF information, during the past few years the share of magazine journalists has increased. The formerly observed increase in broadcasting, however, turned into a decline three or four years ago because of reforms in the public service and commercial broadcasting companies. In the television sector, only the independent production houses show an increase. The main increase in the number of members is concentrated in the metropolitan area, although there has been a slight increase in such important regional centers as the cities of Tampere, Turku, and Oulu.

The number of freelance members does not show any clear developmental trend, because it is not as dependent on the fluctuations of the economy as are other membership categories. The relative percentage of freelance journalists has recently stabilized after rising for some time. Accord-

Table 14.1 Categories of Membership in the Union of Journalists in Finland, 2009

	Number	Percent
Employed under contract	8,981	58
Retired	2,801	18
Freelance	1,549	10
Student	1,063	7
Radio and TV freelance	590	4
Unemployed	528	3
Others	17	0
Total	15,529	100

Source: The Union of Journalists in Finland.

ing to UJF estimates, the percentage of retired members will increase markedly in the next few years.

The distribution of active journalists (retirees and students excluded) across media sectors reveals the significant role of the print media in the Finnish media market. In 2008, 54% of journalists worked in newspapers and magazines, 30% in broadcasting, 12% freelanced either for print or electronic media, and 4% worked as editors in publishing (SJL 2008).

In 1995, the percentage of female journalists exceeded 50% for the first time in Finland and thereafter the figure has increased annually. In 2009, the percentage of women stood at 56.7%. Most notably, in all of the six youngest age groups (from 20 to 49 years), women were in a clear majority, 75% of the age group 20 to 24 and 55% of the age group 45 to 49. Among the older journalists of more than 50 years of age, the gender ratio was close to 50-50, with only slight variations. The percentage of journalists over 60 years old has strongly increased, which is also seen in the growing number of retirees. The percentage of the 60 to 69 age group stood at 7.7% in 1998 and 17.5% in 2009. The only other growing age group during the same period was 20 to 29 (8.3% in 1998 and 9.4% in 2009).

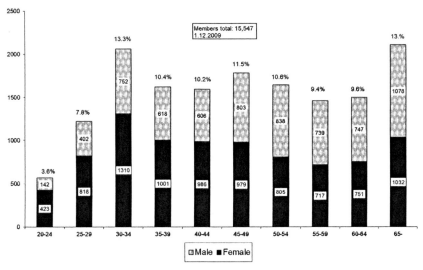

Figure 14.1 Age and Gender of Journalists, 2009 ($N = 614$)

Source: The Union of Journalists in Finland.

Well-Educated Professionals

Journalism education has a fairly long history in Finland. The first formal journalism program was established in 1925 at the then Helsinki Civic College. The program gained more prestige in the late 1940s, when the first professorship in journalism was established at the college. The Civic College moved from the capital to the city of Tampere in 1960 and became a university with the Department of Journalism and Mass Communication as one of its flagship schools (Salokangas 2009).

Today, journalism education is offered at three universities in Finland. In addition to the University of Tampere, another journalism program has been offered since 1987 at the University of Jyväskylä. In these programs, prospective journalists can take bachelor's, master's, and doctoral degrees. In addition, since 1962 the Swedish School of Social Sciences (part of the University of Helsinki) offers a journalism program leading to a bachelor's degree. University journalism programs are a mixture of practical journalism training and communication theory, with additional elements from a variety of minor subjects ranging from social sciences through humanities to economics. Despite almost universal tensions between journalism academics and practitioners, university-educated journalists are well appreciated in the media industry and their employment rate has been consistently high (Lappalainen 2009; Raittila, Olin, & Stenvall-Virtanen 2006).

In the 2000s, according to the official student register of the Finnish universities, 72% of new journalism students in the universities were female, which has continued the development observed earlier. The share of women among student members of the Union of Journalists is also roughly 70%. Both figures are higher than the share of females among the membership of the Union (Figure 14.2). The fact that the media recruit others besides university students balances the gender distribution in the profession.

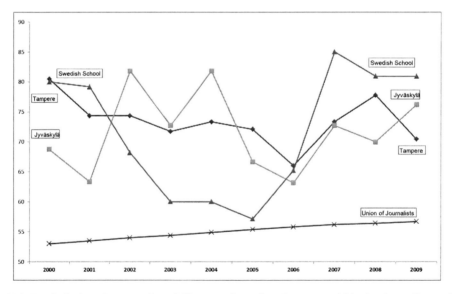

Figure 14.2 Female Students Beginning Finnish University Journalism Programs and Membership in Union of Journalists, 2000–2009 (Female, %)

Sources: The student figures were provided by the three universities in question and are based on the statistical data on universities and fields of education by the Ministry of Education. Figures on journalists are provided by the Union of Journalists in Finland.

Journalism continues to be an open profession in Finland without any formal educational or other requirements. As a consequence, much of the workforce enters newsrooms with other than journalism studies as their background. However, the share of journalists having a journalism education has steadily risen. According to the latest labor market study by the UJF from 2008, 18% of the active working members had at least a bachelor's degree in journalism from a university and 9% had a polytechnic (college) degree in a media subject. Thirty-two percent had a university degree in a major subject other than journalism, which included members with a minor subject in journalism or media studies, and 13% had polytechnic degrees in subjects other than journalism or another media subject. In addition, 13% of the members had unfinished studies at a university or polytechnic. In all, 27% of active working journalists had at least a bachelor's degree in journalism from a university or a polytechnic degree in a media subject in 2008 (SJL 2008).

All in all, the educational level of Finnish journalists has risen. In the 1987 journalist survey, 33% had a university degree (40% of women and 29% of men) (Kehälinna & Melin 1988) and in the 1993 survey 41% did (48% of women and 35% of men) (Melin & Nikula 1993). In the 2007 survey, 50% had at least a bachelor's degree (54% of women and 42% of men) (Jyrkiäinen 2008a). According to the membership register of the UJF in 2008, 50% of members had at least a bachelor's degree (SJL 2008). Compared to the general educational level in Finland, journalists are a well-educated workforce. In 2008, the share of population with at least bachelor's level qualifications was 17% (Educational Structure of Population 2008). The trend of rising education level of journalists is likely to continue as the older age cohorts retire and younger, better-educated recruits replace them.

Freedom at Work Still Appreciated

A conventional, even traditional, image of a professional journalist can be distinguished from how Finnish journalists described the most important aspects of their work. In the 2007 survey, top-ranked aspects were the opportunity to use one's own competencies diversely (89% called this very or fairly important), the chance for self-expression and self-fulfillment (86%), and the opportunity to influence one's own work schedules (77%). Similar comments that emphasized the freedom and the self-expressive nature of the work, real or assumed, were reported in a study in the 1990s when Finnish journalists described their reasons for entering the profession (Heinonen 1998: 178).

However, Finnish journalists also valued more mundane aspects of their jobs. In the 2007 survey, 81% of respondents reported that a permanent job is important and 67% reported that the salary is important. On the other hand, only 36% reported that prospects of career advancement are important. These findings can be interpreted to reflect a correct assessment of the working environment in the media industry: As the media companies are streamlining their workforces, holding on to one's job is all the more important, even more important than high income, much less promotion.

Social dimensions of journalistic work are slightly less valued than self-centered and financial aspects. However, 72% of the journalists in the 2007 survey reported that the opportunity to follow what is happening in the world is important in their job, and 54% mentioned as important the opportunity to influence society.

When asked (in an open-ended question) to elaborate on the desirable characteristics of a professional journalist, Finnish journalists appeared to see professionalism as being largely based on mastery of different skills. In all, 631 different abilities or skills and 273 qualities or talents were mentioned. Among the skills, particularly the ability to write, versatility, creativity, and innovativeness stand out. Somewhat surprisingly, terms like *analytical, critical,* or *questioning* were mentioned as seldom as technical know-how (in about 2% of all mentions).

When asked how they could foster their strengths in the job, Finnish journalists reported that they would like to pay more attention to the quality of their assigned tasks and have more time to do their work. They also expressed the wish to have more education and training, even though media companies have cut back further training opportunities. It is also telling that journalists reported that they long for more feedback, encouragement, and recognition for their work. These comments may reflect unsatisfactory atmospheres and management in newsrooms.

Turning our attention to the social attitudes of Finnish journalists, we can say generally that journalism professionals were critical of big business and sympathetic toward private individuals. In the 2007 survey, respondents reported that big business or large companies have too much power in society followed interestingly enough by advertising and marketing, afternoon (tabloid) papers, banks, and the European Union. Big business and banks were also reported to have too much power in the 1987 survey. At the other end of the scale, those having too little power were private individuals, families, and civic organizations, possibly reflecting the journalistic ideal of defending the underdog. But Finnish journalists seem to agree less on whether nature conservationists had an appropriate amount of power (see Figure 14.3).

Most Finnish journalists (82%) agreed that media in general have an appropriate amount of power in society. However, journalists criticized both the afternoon papers and particularly advertising and marketing for having too much power (61% and 74% of respondents, respectively). It is interesting to note that in a nationally representative survey in 2006, as many as 64% of Finns claimed that the mass media in general have too much power (Haavisto, Kiljunen, & Nyberg 2007). It seems that journalists as media insiders assess the situation very differently from their audiences.

Comparing journalists' opinions on social power holders in the surveys of 1987 and 2007, we can detect some interesting changes. The most important observation is that in 20 years, opinions

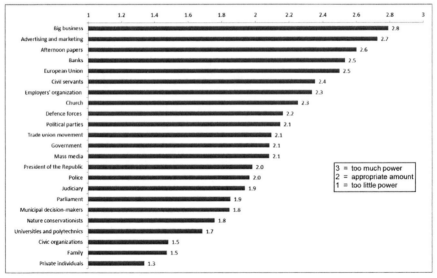

Figure 14.3 Journalists' Perceptions of the Power of Societal Forces (mean, scale = 1-3)

Source: Jyrkiäinen 2008a.

that most social agents (like judiciary, government, media, police, the president) have an appropriate amount of power increased significantly in all 14 categories included in both surveys. This finding indicates a development toward a more uniform opinion climate among journalists about social power holders. An interesting question is whether this is reflected in reporting, and if so, in what way.

From another perspective, we note that in the 2007 survey the majority of journalists reported that big business and banks have too much power, whereas in the 1987 survey the majority of journalists also included civil servants, employers' organizations, political parties, and the church in this category. In 2007, 77% of journalists believed that political parties have an appropriate amount of power, while in 1987 only 32% did.

Thus, on the surface, it would seem that journalists have become more aware of social power. However, the situation is more complex than that. In the 1980s it was observed that professional identity increasingly brought a more critical attitude toward power holders (Aula 1991), and this ethos still prevails among journalists. But, in a small country, journalists (particularly chief editors and political correspondents) are part of the social elite networks with political and economic policymakers. Especially younger generations both in media and the power elite largely tend to have similar educational and cultural backgrounds and understand each other's thinking, which includes the fact that media and power holders need one another (Kunelius, Noppari, & Reunanen 2009). This does not necessarily mean less critical reporting by journalists, but it may imply that the relationships in general are based more on shared value systems than professional or ideological controversies.

A Satisfied but Stressed Workforce

Finnish journalists are unanimous in saying that they enjoy their work. Both in the 1993 survey and the 2007 survey, the overall job satisfaction was considerable and the great majority was at least fairly satisfied. When asked in both surveys "How satisfied are you with your present job?" there appeared only a slight change in the course of almost 15 years: in 1993, 77% reported that they were satisfied, whereas 84% reported so in 2007. However, from the early 1990s to the late 2000s, job dissatisfaction also increased slightly as 10% were dissatisfied in 1993 and 15% in 2007. The percentage of respondents responding "difficult to evaluate" was decidedly greater in 1993 (16%) than in 2007 (1%). These changes may indicate a growing polarization within the profession.

In 2007, the youngest age group of 20 to 35 years was slightly more satisfied (88%) than the older groups of 36 to 55 years (80%) and 55 years and older (84%). Women were more satisfied (87%) than men (78%). This is interesting, as the debate about the obstacles to women's career development in journalism has been a fairly constant topic in Finland (Torkkola & Ruoho 2009: 7–9). Among the various media, the overall satisfaction in 2007 was higher among the print journalists (85%) than among radio and television journalists (79%). However, in the broadcast media 25% were very satisfied and in the printed media 19%.

When asked about problems in the workplace, more than half of the journalists (69%) reported the biggest problems being haste and time pressure (see Table 14.2). A considerable majority (59%) also reported that their salaries do not correspond to the demands of the work.

On the brighter sides of the job, the majority of the journalists said that they could regulate their own working hours (73%), and most were content with their work (63%) and the working conditions (59%). The majority of the journalists also trusted other workers (71%) and did not regard competition (70%) or authoritarian management style (54%) to be a big problem.

Table 14.2   Perceptions of Severity of Workplace Problems (in %, N = 614)

	Very big	Rather big	Difficult to say	Rather small	Very small
Competition between workers	2	10	17	40	30
Workers' lack of confidence in each other	3	12	14	35	36
Chance to influence one's own working hours	4	12	11	42	31
Chance to influence work content	4	17	16	42	21
Chance to influence working conditions	6	19	16	37	22
Too hierarchic job structures	10	23	19	31	17
Workers' inequality	11	19	19	34	17
Authoritarian management style	12	21	14	27	27
Bad organization of work	15	29	18	28	10
Haste and greater time pressures	22	47	10	18	2
Salary does not correspond with demands	23	36	18	20	3

Source: Jyrkiäinen 2008a.

In the 2007 survey, there were two issues in particular that brought at least some joy and satisfaction to the journalists' jobs: the chance to influence one's own working hours (75%), and the atmosphere in the work community (73%). Many respondents derived almost as much satisfaction from the chance to influence their own working conditions (65%), and to travel and move about related to the work (60%). Learning new work methods and technologies was also considered as a satisfactory feature in the job (59%). From the other viewpoint, there were three features in the work that seemed not to produce joy for the majority of respondents—being a supervisor ("boss") (66%), being continually available or reachable (63%), and being visible or in the public eye (50%).

Concerning the negative job factors, more than half (58%) of respondents reported that the number of assignments was annoying them. Among other considerable sources of annoyance were some aspects that were also mentioned as positive aspects of the job, including things like the atmosphere of the work community (42%), the need to be continually reachable (41%), the requirement to learn new work methods and technologies (39%), and the inability to influence one's own working conditions (36%).

Despite some obvious problems with the job, Finnish journalists seem to be fairly committed to their work. About one-third of the journalists reported that their commitment toward their work department (35%), their professional identity (33%), and their work community (31%) had increased in recent years. Their commitment to the whole company or conglomerate, however, was reported to have decreased (36%) rather than increased (24%).

Constant Change Dominates

The characteristic that is perhaps most illustrative of the journalistic profession in Finland has been the accelerating pace of constant change. Earlier it was noted that journalists feel that they have to carry out their tasks at excessive speed, and that they long for more time to better focus on their assignments. When reflecting on past and future trends in the profession, journalists again pointed at the ever-changing nature of news work and the increasing pace of production in particular (see Table 14.3).

There seem to be several aspects of journalistic work that have lately become more demanding. Compared to the situation a couple of years earlier, journalists reported in the 2007 survey that

Table 14.3   Perceptions of Change at Workplace Since 2005 (in %, N = 614)

	Increased very much	Increased somewhat	Difficult to say	Decreased somewhat	Decreased very much
Number of editorial staff in relation to total content produced	2	11	35	40	13
Number of characters or words in the stories (length, duration)	3	9	47	33	8
Story exchange between own and other companies or conglomerates	5	11	79	3	2
Acquisition of stories from outside the editorial office	6	31	47	13	3
Aiming the stories at special target groups	8	37	50	5	0
Number of stories a week for each editor	11	45	36	7	0
Story exchange inside the same company or conglomerate	13	31	53	2	1
Making of stories for more than one medium	22	44	31	2	1

Source: Jyrkiäinen 2008a.

the greatest increase was in the demands for creating stories for more than one medium (66%). It was also noted that the number of stories processed by the editorial staff each week had increased (56%), as had aiming stories at special target groups (45%), and story exchange within the same company or conglomerate (44%). Conversely, the greatest decrease was in the number of editorial staff in relation to the total amount of content produced (53%) and in the number of characters or words in the stories (41%).

It seems that fewer journalists write more but shorter stories than was the case until recently. However, it is noteworthy that identifying concrete issues that were either on the increase or decrease was rather difficult for the respondents. In no less than five of eight issues the most common single reply was "difficult to say."

Looking closer at the perceived rush in Finnish newsrooms, we can see in Table 14.4 that journalists blame the Internet (e-mails) and administrative aspects for their increasing workload. According to the respondents, the workload has increased most because of the ever growing

Table 14.4   Perceptions of Change in Workload during Past Year (in %, N = 614)

	Increased very much	Increased somewhat	Unchanged	Decreased somewhat	Decreased very much
Number of meetings during a working day	3	23	63	9	2
Number of calls during a working day	5	24	54	13	3
Responsibility for business results	6	19	71	2	2
Bringing work home	8	27	56	6	2
Time used for meetings	8	30	46	11	5
Responsibility for extra assignments	11	29	54	3	3
Pressure to work overtime	12	33	46	7	2
Bureaucracy related to my work	12	33	49	4	1
Disruptions in the editorial office	15	31	47	6	2
Number of e-mails during a working day	30	44	23	2	1

Source: Jyrkiäinen 2008a.

Table 14.5   Perceptions of Change in Time Use of Total Working Hours during Past Few Years (in %, N = 614)

	Increased very much	Increased somewhat	Remained unchanged	Decreased somewhat	Decreased very much
Time to be used for one story	2	6	40	38	14
Writing, photographing, editing	6	30	44	15	4
Ideation and design	9	31	29	22	9
Acquisition & processing of material	9	35	36	17	3
Multimedia work	11	34	48	4	2

Source: Jyrkiäinen 2008a.

number of e-mails that have to be answered each day (74%). In the second place there were three issues with almost the same percentage: the disruptions in the editorial office (46%), the amount of compulsory bureaucracy related to the management of one's work (45%), and the pressure to work overtime (45%).

The most significant change in the use of time within different work stages was the diminished time available for each story, and there also seems to be less time to muse over ideas in newsrooms. More than half of the respondents reported that the time for an article or output had decreased (52%) and about a third (31%) said the time for brainstorming and designing had decreased somewhat or a lot. On the other hand, as Table 14.5 shows, things that seem to take more time than before were most notably multimedia work or working with multiple outlets. Almost half (45%) of the respondents brought this up. More time is also devoted to acquiring and processing of news material (44%).

Despite the increased pressures at work, Finnish journalists tend to believe that they can meet the requirements, at least from a skills point of view. In the 2007 survey, more than half (53%) of the respondents estimated that the demands for their skills have remained unchanged in relation their own competence. About a quarter (23%) considered that the demands were nowadays a little greater and also about a quarter (23%) estimated that the demands were slightly or considerably well within their own competence.

An open-ended question revealed that the new skills requirements deal particularly with new technology. These included IT applications, working for multiple media outlets, the Internet in general, online publishing, and the electronic media. More than half (53%) of all 518 mentions were in these areas. More than a quarter of the mentions (27%) dealt with managing, controlling, and using new information technology and the expertise in information technology.

The journalists also noted that technical know-how not only requires command of modern equipment but also a need to keep up with rapidly changing technology. Thus, the respondents reported that online publishing and multiple outlets require additional education, new skills, and perhaps also a new attitude in editorial work.

Concern about Future Quality

Finnish journalists are not very optimistic about the future of journalism, as Table 14.6 shows. There is clear concern among journalists about the effect of the increasing commercialization of the media, which it is feared will override quality in journalism. In the 2007 survey, as many as 85% agreed with the statement that "commercial objectives would supersede ethical values in journalism," and the same share agreed with the statement that "large audiences will be pursued

Table 14.6 Perceptions of Trends in Media (in %, N = 614)

	Extremely good	Quite good	Difficult to say	Quite bad	Not at all
The quality of Finnish journalism would not decline even if the Council of Mass Media were abolished	4	10	30	34	22
Journalist's instructions often help to solve ethical problems in my work	6	38	32	19	5
The number of the stories will be emphasized at the expense of quality of content	11	51	24	12	2
Local or regional news gathering will decline because of production costs	11	48	24	15	3
Ordinary people can express their views in the media on socially important matters too seldom	13	33	26	26	2
More and more journalism will be directed to special target groups and not to a social discussion	15	59	17	10	0
Marketing and PR material will be included in the news more often because of a decrease in news gathering resources	15	47	24	13	1
The growth of the entertainment material in the media supply will weaken people's active desire to influence matters	25	43	21	9	2
Factual journalism will become more entertaining and "difficult and heavy" subjects will be ignored	27	55	10	7	0
Large audiences are sought at the expense of the quality of content	32	53	9	5	0
Commercial objectives will be increasingly preferred to journalistic ethical values	35	50	10	4	1

Source: Jyrkiäinen 2008a.

at the expense of quality of contents." Almost as many (82%) agreed that "factual journalism will become more entertaining, while difficult and heavy topics will be pushed aside." In addition, a clear majority (74%) of the respondents said that journalism would be directed more at special target groups instead of serving the general social debate, and that marketing and PR material will be included in news more often because of the decline in news gathering resources (62%). Perhaps somewhat contradictory to the journalists' assessments of social power holders, almost half (46%) of the respondents estimated that ordinary people can too seldom express their views in the media on socially important matters.

Comparing the survey answers in 1993, 2002, and 2007 with regard to appreciation of journalistic work ("How will the appreciation of journalistic work develop in the future?") the share of those predicting a decrease in appreciation was clearly greater in 2007 (48%) and in 2002 (47%), than in 1993 (26%).

The respondents were also asked how different issues related to the journalistic profession will change in the future, as Table 14.7 shows. More than half of the respondents assumed that in the future journalists' independence and autonomy (61%), analytical and critical ability (60%), adherence to the professional ethics of journalism (57%), and the difference between journalistic and other content production (51%) will decrease. In all these four areas, the percentage of those who estimate that the elicited matter "will clearly decrease" is distinctly greater than that of those who estimate that it "will clearly increase."

Table 14.7   Estimates of Future Trends (in %, N = 614)

	Clear decrease	Slight decrease	Difficult to say	Slight increase	Clear increase
Analytical and critical journalism	18	42	22	17	2
Journalists' independence & autonomy	15	49	26	10	1
Following rules of professional ethics	14	43	36	7	0
Diff. between journalistic & other content production	14	37	30	14	5
Appreciation of journalistic work	9	39	32	18	3
Social significance of own work	4	20	49	25	3
Significance of journalists in society	3	28	29	34	6
Economic accountability in own work	1	2	36	50	12
Experientialism & entertaining in journalism	1	3	6	50	41
Management of editorial organization as business	0	1	19	47	33

On the other hand, a fifth of the respondents estimated that the difference between journalistic and other content production will increase. Likewise a fifth of the respondents believed in the increase in the appreciation of journalistic work in the future.

Journalists seem to be uncertain about the public image and influence of their profession and their work. Nearly half (49%) answered "cannot say" when asked how the social significance of one's own work would develop in the future. Two-fifths (42%) estimated the significance of journalists in the society would increase and correspondingly less than a third (31%) estimated it would diminish.

Here it is interesting that the respondents seem to make a distinction between the profession in general and one's own journalistic work. When the social significance of the individual's own work was raised, the share of those who answered "cannot say" was distinctly greater than when the significance of journalists in society was the focus. The vast majority (91%) estimated that entertainment in journalism would increase. Likewise, most (80%) believed that the management of the editorial organization as a business would increase and that responsibility for business results from one's own work (62%) would increase.

As an important subject related to the status of journalism in society and also to professional life, it is noteworthy that Finnish journalists seem to be increasingly pessimistic about professional ethics. In all surveys (1993, 2002, and 2007), the percentage of those anticipating less respect for ethical codes has been larger than the share of those expecting a more optimistic view. The percentage of those predicting that following ethical instructions would *increase* in the future decreased by half from an already low 14% in 1993 to a meager 7% in 2007. At the same time, the share of those saying that this is "difficult to evaluate" grew from 27% in 1993 to 29% in 2002 and to 36% in 2007.

Conclusions

At the dawn of the second decade of the 21st century, Finnish journalists seem to perceive their profession as one experiencing exceptionally grave changes. Journalism has always been a field where almost by definition constants are rare and everything is in flux on a daily basis, but the situation at the moment is felt to be somewhat different. Journalists in Finland are still fairly content with their jobs, but at the same time especially the effects of economic and technological factors are perceived to threaten the satisfaction that the job in principle creates. In addition, Finnish journalists are insecure, even pessimistic, about the future of their profession as quality journalism and professional ethics seem to be endangered aspects of news media work.

It is noteworthy that Finnish journalists describe the positive dimensions of their work largely in terms similar to those used in the 1990s. Most joy and satisfaction were derived from the chance to influence one's own working hours and from the atmosphere of the work community, both of which are usually important satisfaction factors in working life. The journalists trust their co-workers and do not regard competition or authoritarian management style as a big problem.

Also, the biggest problems experienced by journalists are familiar from earlier years, but their intensity seems to be growing. Schedule pressures, accelerated working pace, and excessive workload are common complaints among journalists. The most significant change in the use of time in recent years has been the diminishing amount of time that can be devoted to one item. As this trend coincides with a decrease in the size of the editorial workforce, the result is "more with less," which in the case of journalism causes justified concern about the quality of the output. In spite of all this, the Finnish journalists' commitment to their work has remained high during the past few years.

Journalists' concern about the future of journalism should serve as a warning signal to media executives and also to media policymakers. According to the majority of journalists, in the future journalism will feature less independence and autonomy as well as less analytical and critical reporting. On top of that, the journalists' forecast for the future of journalism is gloomy as they believe that the importance of ethical codes in the profession will decrease. Instead, it is anticipated that entertainment journalism will accelerate in the media, and that newsrooms will be treated even more like a business than they are today.

Journalists in Finland are thus a profession working amidst intensified pressures, but preserving traditional journalistic values, at least in their minds. In a way, today's journalists need to be able to function in almost schizophrenic circumstances. There are journalistic values that are transmitted from earlier generations to contemporary ones by professional education and tacit knowledge in the workplace. There is rapidly developing technology constantly challenging journalists' practical skills, and there is media convergence shaking traditional media-related job descriptions. And, as if this were not enough, business logic has become a permanent resident in newsrooms instead of residing somewhere out there in the corridors of marketing departments.

In addition to these internal trends, there are the new communications practices of ordinary citizens and amateur journalists evolving in the online environment outside established media and professional journalism. Thus, it may be fully justified for journalists to feel insecure about the future nature of their work and the social status of their profession.

References

Aula, Maria Kaisa. 1991. *Poliitikkojen ja toimittajien suhteet murroksessa?* [Relationship between politicians and journalists in transition?] Helsinki: Yleisradio, tutkimus-ja kehitysosaston raportti 5/1001.

Cultural Statistics 2007. 2009. *Culture and the media.* Helsinki: Statistics Finland.

Educational structure of population 2008. 2009. Helsinki: Statistics Finland. Retrieved from http://www.stat.fi/til/vkour/2008/vkour_2008_2009-12-04_tie_001_en.html

Finland in figures. 2010. Statistics Finland. Retrieved from http://www.stat.fi/tup/suoluk/suoluk_vaesto_en.html

Finnish Mass Media. 2009. *Culture and the media.* Helsinki: Statistics Finland.

Finnpanel. 2009. *Results from the TV audience measurement: Viewing distribution by channel, year 2009.* Retrieved from http://www.finnpanel.fi/en/tulokset/tv/vuosi/share/viimeisin/

Finnpanel 2010. *Press bulletin 21.1.2010.* Retrieved from http://www.finnpanel.fi/en/tulokset/radio.php

Haavisto, Ilkka, Pentti Kiljunen, and Martti Nyberg. (2007). *Satavuotias kuntotestissä: EVAn kansallinen arvo- ja asennetutkimus 2007* [Centenarian in a fitness test—EVA's 2007 attitude and value survey]. Helsinki: Taloustieto. Retrieved from http://www.eva.fi/wp-content/uploads/2010/06/satavuotias_kuntotestissa.pdf; http://www.eva.fi/wp-content/uploads/files/1806_EVA_2007_Attitudes_english_summary.pdf

Harju, Auli. 2002. *Journalistisen työn säätely ja ammattietiikka* [Regulation on journalistic work and professional ethics]. University of Tampere, Tampere Journalism Research and Development Centre. Retrieved from http://www.uta.fi/jourtutkimus/journalistiliitto.pdf

Heinonen, Ari. 1995. *Vahtikoiran omatunto* [Conscience of the watchdog]. University of Tampere, Department of Journalism and Mass Communication. Publications A 84. Retrieved from http://tampub.uta.fi/tiedotusoppi/951-44-5322-0.pdf

Heinonen, Ari. 1998. The Finnish journalist: Watchdog with a conscience. In *The global journalist: News people around the world,* edited by David H. Weaver, pp. 161–190. Cresskill, NJ: Hampton Press.

Heinonen, Ari. 2008. *Yleisön sanansijat sanomalehdissä* [Letting the audience have a say in newspapers]. University of Tampere, Department of Journalism and Mass Communication. Publications A 108. Retrieved from http://tampub.uta.fi/tiedotusoppi/978-951-44-7551-1.pdf

Heinonen, Ari, and Terhi Kinnunen. 2005. Finland: Cautious online strategies. In *Print and online newspapers in Europe: A comparative analysis in 16 countries,* edited by Richard van der Wurff and Edmund Lauf, pp. 117–130. Amsterdam: Het Spinhuis.

Jyrkiäinen, Jyrki. 2008a. *Journalistit muuttuvassa mediassa* [Journalists in the changing media]. University of Tampere, Department of Journalism and Mass Communication. Publications B 50. Retrieved from http://tampub.uta.fi/tulos.php?tiedot=233. Data available at the Finnish Social Science Data Archive from http://www.fsd.uta.fi/aineistot/luettelo/FSD2361/

Jyrkiäinen, Jyrki. 2008b. *Media moves.* Retrieved from http://finland.fi/public/default.aspx?contentid=162833&contentlan=2&culture=en-US

Kehälinna, Heikki, and Harri Melin. 1988. *Tuntemattomat toimittajat. Tutkimus Suomen Sanomalehtimiesten Liiton jäsenistä* [The unknown journalists]. Helsinki: Suomen Sanomalehtimiesten Liitto.

Kunelius, Risto, Elina Noppari, and Esa Reunanen. 2009. *Media vallan verkoissa* [Media in the webs of power]. University of Tampere, Department of Journalism and Mass Communication. Publications A 112. Retrieved from http://tampub.uta.fi/tiedotusoppi/978-951-44-7891-8.pdf

Kunelius, Risto, and Laura Ruusunoksa. 2009. Mapping professional imagination: On the potential professional culture in the newspapers of the future. In *The future of newspapers,* edited by Bob Franklin, pp. 33–49. New York: Routledge.

Lappalainen, Elina. 2009. Vastaako koulutus työelämän tarpeita [Does education meet the needs of working life?] In *Suomen Lehdistö,* 8–9, pp. 16–19. Finlands Press. http://www.sanomalehdet.fi/index.phtml?s=170

Melin, Harri, and Jouko Nikula. 1993. *Journalistit epävarmuuden ajassa: Tutkimus Suomen Journalistiliiton jäsenistä 1993* [Journalists in a time of uncertainty: Organizational survey of the Union of Journalists]. Helsinki: Suomen Journalistiliitto.

Raittila, Pentti, Nina Olin, and Sari Stenvall-Virtanen. 2006. *Viestintäkoulutuksen nousukäyrä* [The growth curve of communication education]. University of Tampere, Department of Journalism and Mass Communication. Publications C 40.

Salokangas, Raimo. 2009. The Finnish journalism education landscape. In *European Journalism Education,* edited by Georgios Terzis, pp. 120–129. Bristol, UK: Intellect.

SJL 2008. Suomen journalistiliitto. Journalistien koulutustausta [Union of Journalists in Finland. Educational background of journalists]. Retrieved from http://www.journalistiliitto.fi/liitto/liiton_jasenet/ammatti_yhdistaa/ Information from the Union of Journalists in Finland.

Statistics Finland. 2009. Retrieved from http://www.stat.fi/tup/tilastotietokannat/index_en.html.

Torkkola, Sinikka, and Iiris Ruoho. 2009. *Subscribing to a woman editor-in-chief? Female and male editors' views on the impact of gender on careers.* University of Tampere, Department of Journalism and Mass Communication. Publications B 54. Retrieved from http://tampub.uta.fi/tiedotusoppi/978-951-44-7851-2.pdf

Weaver, David H. (ed.). 1998.*The global journalist: News people around the world.* Cresskill, NJ: Hampton Press.

15   The French Journalist

Aralynn Abare McMane

French journalists of the early 21st century work in an environment of both advantage and limitation, the heritage of a long and complex past. Legally, journalists are protected by a century-old defamation law that puts most of the liability for misdeeds on the director of the news organization. However, other parts of the law continue to leave French journalists unable legally to reveal information that is routinely reported in many other Western countries.

Journalists have been protected ethically since 1935 by a "conscience clause" in the National Work Code that allows them to leave, with substantial severance pay, when a news organization is sold or greatly changes its editorial line. Economically, French journalists enjoy a tax exemption that reduces their taxable income by a substantial amount, but at the start of the 21st century they have faced the same general threat to their livelihood as their cohorts elsewhere as the overall economy of news work has shifted.

In France as in many other places, newspapers, by far the largest employer of journalists, have experienced a gradual loss of advertising to television and of large amounts of advertising altogether after the 2008 worldwide economic crisis (World Association of Newspapers and News Publishers [WAN-IFRA 2009]). Many newsroom staff had lost their jobs by 2008, including 60 journalists among the 103 staff members who accepted buyouts at *Le Monde* (Mediapart 2008). A growing digital environment provides both opportunities and threats for journalists. Even though it increases the potential for reaching and interacting with audiences in new ways, we still lack evidence that digital platforms can raise enough revenues to support quality journalistic enterprises (WAN-IFRA 2009).

French journalists also work in a setting that mixes long tradition with accelerating change. As early as the 18th century, France had developed a literary press of opinion in Paris, along with a less interpretive, more information-giving regional press that would thrive later. The two traditions crossed paths in history, notably when the Paris press produced mass-circulation newspapers in the late 19th century, but the distinction remained largely intact even as late as the early 1970s when the very opinionated new paper *Libération* emerged from the social protest movement of 1968 to become a notable part of the Paris newspaper world. Soon thereafter, in 1976, the Paris press lost its circulation dominance, and a regional daily in Rennes, *Ouest-France*, took the lead (McMane 1989b). By 2009, the most-read Paris daily was the compact, fact-filled free paper, *20 minutes*, co-owned by the Norwegian Schipsted group and *Ouest-France* (WAN-IFRA 2009).

The overall number of daily newspapers rose in the early 21st century thanks to the development of such free newspapers. The number of dailies remained stable at 24 national titles and 85 regional and local titles in the first years of the century. In the meantime, the free dailies, which arrived on the French market with *Metro* in 2002, rose to 24 titles by 2008, including regional editions of the two leaders, *Metro* and *20 Minutes*. Indeed, while France ranked 68th in the world for per-capita consumption of paid newspapers, ahead of only Spain, Italy, and Portugal in Europe, it ranked fifth in total circulation among the 56 countries with free newspapers (WAN-IFRA 2009).

At the beginning of the 21st century, France continued to rank very high for both numbers of titles and readership of magazines. However, these circulations have slightly declined recently. In 1999, France (with 95.9%) ranked second only to the Netherlands (96.8%) and just ahead of the United States (95%) for average magazine readership among adults and counted 1,250 consumer magazines, putting it sixth in the world behind the United States, the United Kingdom, Japan, Germany, and Poland. By 2008, France produced more than 4,000 consumer magazines, fewer than only the United States and Russia. Nearly all adults (96.8%) reported that they read magazines every month in 2008. However, magazine circulation declined 3.7% between 2008 and 2009, even as newspaper circulation remained stable, with the news magazine *Le Nouvel Observateur* alone losing 8.7% of its audience (Audipresse 2009; Federation Internationale de la Presse périodique [FIPP] 1999, 2009, 2010).

In broadcast journalism, the 1980s privatization process brought new opportunities and competition. Since the inception of the state's monopoly broadcast system, directors of the state-run stations had routinely held or lost their jobs depending on the desires of the government in power. The sale of one of the state-run television channels, TF1, in 1987, started a new era of market dependence for television and debates about newscasters as highly paid TV stars (McMane 1989b). By the 1990s, France had become the home for two all-news television stations—the joint-European venture Euronews and LCI, the offshoot of the private French TF1 channel. In 2005, the owners of Radio Monte Carlo launched the all-news BFM television station, and Canal Plus converted its paid-for I-Télévision to the free I-Télé. In 2006, the government created France 24, a cluster of three linked news operations in English, Arabic, and French (Tailleur 2008).

France had experimented with doing journalism on a widespread digital communication channel long before much of the rest of the world, but was slow to develop Internet news services. The Minitel project had begun in 1983 and put a terminal in homes throughout the nation in a project led by the national telephone company, with users charged as part of their telephone bills. Newspapers were the sole purveyors of interactive services, which produced considerable revenues. Journalism on the Minitel, however, produced less success. Journalism schools offered courses beginning in the 1980s about how to write the very short stories the technology required, but audiences preferred the sexy "Minitel rose" chat rooms to reading news (McMane 1993). Further, the wide presence of low-cost Minitel terminals in the home stalled the purchase of home computers and online news services. In 1998, France had 6.2 Internet users per 100 inhabitants, compared to more than 30 per 100 for Sweden, the United States, New Zealand, and Australia. In Europe, only Greece, Italy, and Spain had lower rates (International Telecommunications Union [ITU] 1998).

Basic newspaper Web sites began to appear in 1995, notably for *Les Dernières Nouvelles d'Alsace, Le Monde,* and *Libération.* By 2001 most other newspapers had launched online editions. Participant journalism hit radio first in France. In 2002, Skyrock began offering Skyblog.com, which encouraged its mainly young audience to create their own blogs. In 2005, two information technology scientists created Agoravox.com to allow French citizens to publish unknown news, submit commentary on stories, and even collaborate in investigative reporting (Eveno 2001; Polomé 2009).

By 2008, France had caught up and, in some ways, joined the world's media technology leaders. The skyblog.com service had grown to become Europe's third most popular social site, ranking ninth among such sites worldwide (Comscore 2008). No other medium in France came even close to such a level of audience participation. Also in 2008, the skyblog.com host site, skyrock.com, ranked first among audited Web sites within France with 196 million visits in September of that year, higher than the main online telephone directory. The French media audit bureau (OJD) notes that other media sites in the French top 10 were those of *Le Monde*, third with 38 million visits, *Le Figaro* (6th), *Libération* (8th), *20 Minutes* (9th), and the newsmagazine *Le Nouvel Observateur* (10th) (Association pour le contrôle de la diffusion des medias [OJD] Internet 2008).

Though France still ranked relatively low among European countries in 2008 for number of Internet users per 100 inhabitants, ahead of Portugal and Greece but behind Spain and most other European countries, it ranked 11th in a worldwide ranking of broadband subscribers per 100 population, behind only the Nordic countries, the Netherlands, Switzerland, Iceland, South Korea, Luxembourg, and Canada (ITU 2008).

Meanwhile, online news sites had begun to develop outside established news operations, such as Rue89.com, founded in 2007 by a journalist formerly with *Libération*, and Arretsurimages.net, also founded in 2007 by the presenter of a television show of the same name that analyzed audiovisual images. In late 2009, leaders of seven such online news services created a new union, le Syndicat de la presse indépendante d'information online en France (SPIIL). The union required that members have at least one "professional" journalist on staff (someone with a national press card) and insisted on the same treatment as traditional media. One of its first efforts was to successfully lobby for the same tax and subsidy advantages accorded other news media (SPIIL 2020; Polomé 2009; Ternisien 2009; Wauters 2009).

However, Desportes and Rampazzo (2008: 52) cautioned about the extent to which the French press had advanced online compared to other countries:

> One doesn't need to go to the United States to find a richness of multimedia content. *La Republica* [in Italy], with 20 sites, shows what is possible to do. In Spain or Denmark as well, sites have little resemblance to what does, or doesn't happen, in France. In terms of overall structure and the place of interactivity along with video and audio content, the gap is widening. The "French exception" is glaring and it is not in our honor but is a collective defeat.

Who is a Journalist?

In 1935, the French legislature amended the National Work Code to grant journalists special consideration. The law and various related decrees that followed it created a "professional" French journalist who worked full-time in the gathering of news for a salary and who would have a national press identification card to prove it. A decree a year later created the Commission de la Carte d'Identité des Journalistes, with an equal number of news organization directors and journalists. The commission was granted the power to decide each year who would receive such national press cards and to oversee their distribution.

The law changed in 1974 to allow freelancers to have national press cards if they earned a monthly salary of at least minimum wage from journalistic work, and it was changed again in 1985 to include broadcast journalists, who had been government employees until the 1980s. Journalists working for Web or mobile telephone news operations were added in 2009. Foreign nationals working in France can also have a national press card (Marquis 2010; McMane 1989b, 1998).

The national press card is not supposed to be a license to practice journalism, but it is far more than a perk of the job. Discussions in France typically include a disclaimer that the press card verifies, but does not grant, the status of a journalist, and that a person can do newsgathering without having a journalist's card. However, national agreements between media owners and journalists have long stipulated that an owner cannot employ for longer than three months someone who does news work without having a card or having applied for one.

The Training and Role of the Journalist

Debates about the proper training and role of the journalist began early in France. The efforts to make the newsgathering practices recognized as professional date at least from the late 1800s, when anti-Semitism and other excesses in the coverage of the treason court martial of Alfred Dreyfus prompted some Paris journalists to found the country's first journalism school. In 1945, *Le Monde* journalists created a Societé des Rédacteurs (Society of Journalists), arguing that they had a moral right to safeguard the professional values of the newspaper by participating in its management.

By 1970, about 20% of French journalists had joined one of 33 journalist societies. Such groups prompted one of the earliest of modern qualitative studies of journalists by the government's Lindon Commission. The commission argued against codifying the groups, and conflicts with national unions helped speed the decline of the movement, but the study was one of the earliest to examine closely the values and role of journalists (Lindon Commission 1970). Freiberg (1981) also studied the associations of journalists as part of his qualitative inquiry into the continuing failed efforts of highly idealistic post-war journalists to dominate a commercial press.

Meanwhile, French researchers had begun regular charting of the demographic profile of all holders of French journalists' cards, a broad population that included people in both full-time and part-time reporting as well as other journalistic jobs (Centre d'Etudes et de Recherche sur les Qualifications [CEREQ] 1974; Commission de la Carte d'Identité des Journalistes Professionels 1967, 1986, 1995; Institut Français de la Presse 1991).

The 1980s saw several important qualitative studies of journalists. For his examination of journalists who produced the "elite" French news media, Rieffel (1984) interviewed 120 journalists at two national television channels, two major radio stations, three Paris dailies, and four newsmagazines. He concluded that his interviewees tended to support three roles for journalists: as explainers, as organizers of facts, and as teachers.

Voyenne (1985) provided a thorough, largely historical portrait of the changes in the working situation of French journalists. Padioleau (1985) offered a highly detailed comparison of journalists at *The Washington Post* and *Le Monde* and found that journalists at both dailies shared a strong sense of their newspaper's social and political mission, but that practices differed and notions of professional role at *The Post* were more clearly expressed and codified than at *Le Monde*. Balle (1987) used a historical perspective for most of his analysis and relied heavily on comparisons with the United States. He argued that the role of the journalist in France was limited by both an inability to breach highly suspicious public and private institutions and by the limited financing of and audience for newspapers.

McMane (1989b, 1992b, 1993, 1998) compared responses from a random national sample of full-time French journalists to those of their counterparts in the United Kingdom, Germany, and the United States. This study indicated that French journalists who worked full-time for news operations tended to be predominantly male with women over-represented in younger age groups and under-represented in management. They tended to be married if male and single if female. They were more likely than the French labor force in general to have college educations, to come from a white-collar background, and to be members of a union. They tended to see themselves as slightly left of center and their organizations as slightly right of center. They highly valued independence in their jobs, but were not sure as a group that they were free from outside pressures. Similar to journalists in the United Kingdom, the United States, and Germany, more than 9 of 10 journalists thought they should keep a promise of source confidentiality. Most were satisfied with their work and expected to remain in journalism.

In his analysis of press card holders, Charon (1993) argued that although they were more numerous and better trained than in the past, French news people had lost prestige and political clout, and had also seen a weakening of the classic conception of their role as key elements in the democratic process. He argued that two less critical alternative roles were emerging with the journalist acting as the connector between a market society and its isolated consumers or as a connector among individuals with common interests. He saw neither alternative as preferable to the classic role and called upon journalists to engage in a thorough re-examination of the situation in order to find a new unity and legitimacy for the profession.

In the early 2000s, journalists and communications scholars continued to examine the potential threats and opportunities for French journalistic practice. Rieffel (2005) described the evolution of eight key characteristics of French journalism based on studies two decades apart that he helped conduct at the Institut Français de Presse (Institut Français de Presse 1991; Devillard, Lafosse, Leteinturier, & Rieffel 2001). He noted that French journalism was (1) a very male occupation but becoming more and more feminized, (2) an occupation with young practitioners moving toward an older profile, (3) seeing an increase in the level of education, (4) increasing in its proportion of freelancers, (5) increasing in its proportion of white collar workers ("cadres"), (6) retaining a pattern of the journalistic workplace as working mostly in the print sector, (7) experiencing a continuing concentration of journalists in the Paris region, and (8) experiencing a continuing disparity between different media sectors in terms of salaries, with the national daily press paying the highest salaries, followed by general interest magazines, television stations, and news agencies.

Method

The following quantitative findings about French journalists are based on secondary analysis of two sets of data. Attitudinal findings emerge from results of the 2007 telephone survey with a representative national sample of 405 journalists conducted by CSA for the *Les Assises du Journalisme pour Journalisme et Citoyenneté*. Results were weighted for gender, job description, and medium based on statistics about the population of French journalists furnished by the French Press Card Commission. The survey was conducted between February 19 and 23, 2007. Demographic assessments for 2008 come from analysis of data from the population of all holders of national press cards gathered by the French Press Card Commission.[1]

The 2008 demographic data included full-time workers who had either a permanent or temporary contract plus part-time workers on all journalistic platforms, including news operations, Internet, the specialized periodical press, and weekly newspapers. Unless otherwise noted, when findings refer to "journalists," they will refer to these "card-carrying" journalists in France.

When appropriate, comparisons will be made with the results of the following studies: (1) two studies described above that explored the demographic progression of card-carrying journalists between 1990 and 2000 (Devillard et al. 2000; Institut Français de Presse 1991); (2) the study by Christine Leteinturier (2010) that compared first-time card holders in 2008 to those of 1998 and 1990; (3) results from a 1988 survey with a national random sample of 412 French journalists reported in the previous edition of *The Global Journalist* and in McMane (1989, 1992a,b,c,d, 1993).

Table 15.1   The French Journalistic Workforce

Period	Journalistic workforce growth	French labor force
1980–1990	60.14%	5.50%
1990–2000	25.17%	6.95%
2000–2006	11.68%	4.59%
2000–2001	4.45%	0.88%
2001–2002	2.24%	0.86%
2002–2003	1.46%	0.71%
2003–2004	1.07%	0.55%
2004–2005	0.84%	0.63%
2005–2006	1.62%	0.88%
2006–2007	0.84%	NA
2007–2008	0.19%	NA

Source: INSEE 2008, CCIJP 2009.

Findings

Basic Characteristics

Size of Journalistic Workforce.   As they had for centuries, most French journalists worked in print in 2008. That sector accounted for nearly two-thirds (62.26%) of the surveyed population, followed by television (14.0%), radio (7.6%), and press agencies (6.6%). Pure "Web" journalists accounted for under 1% of journalists.

Magazines and regional newspapers led as employers of print journalists, followed by the specialized press and national daily newspapers. Neveu (2001/2004) observed that the most salient feature of French journalism was its expansion, noting that the profession had tripled its workforce between 1960 and 2000, with most of the growth in the 1980s when the number grew by 10,000 workers (see Table 15.1).

Historically, the growth rate for the journalistic workforce had been far greater than that of the general population of working age. Between 1980 and 1990, the increase was a massive 60% among journalists versus a progression of only 5.5% for the French labor force. This rate slowed in the next decade, when the journalistic workforce grew 25%, while the overall labor force increased 7%).

The growth rate from 2000 to 2008 was 12.7% for all journalists with 37.5% for television journalists, 21% for radio journalists, and 7% for print journalists. Among journalists working in print, regional newspapers had a larger growth in staff (15%) than did the Paris national daily press (4.4%). Magazines and the specialized press saw a growth rate of between 3% and 4%. The corps of news agency journalists declined 3.7% in the period, while the staff for the country's free newspapers grew from 8 to 150 journalists.

By 2008, the growth rate essentially stopped, having slowed considerably since the start of the century. Card-carrying journalists numbered 37,738 in 2008—just 73 more news people than in 2007. This represented an increase of 0.2% and an all-time low in the growth rate for this workforce. The number of print journalists, who are the bulk of French news people, actually decreased 0.67%.

Age and Gender.   The journalistic profession in France continues to age while the proportion of women in its ranks is increasing. The mean age of journalists in 2008 was 42.2 years old with nearly 4 in 10 over age 45. This represented an increase from a mean age of 40.5 years in 2000.

An aging trend among journalists had already become clear in the last decade of the 20th century. From 1990 to 1999, the corps of French journalists went from nearly a quarter of journalists under age 30 in 1990 to only 14% in that age range by 1999 and from 11.5% of journalists over age 50 in 1990 to nearly twice that percentage (21.5%) in 1999 (Devillard et al. 2000).

Disparities existed for age in 2008 based both on gender and type of work contract. Female journalists were younger than men, with a mean age of 40.6 years compared to 43.4 for men. More than a third of female journalists (35.4%) were under age 35 in 2008, versus a quarter (25.4%) of male journalists. For both males and females, the proportion under age 35 was higher in 2000 (40% for women and 30% for men).

Journalists in insecure jobs (those on short-term contracts and freelancers) tended to be younger as well. Journalists on short-term contracts had an average age of 31 years with freelancers averaging age 39.5 years, compared to age 42.5 years for journalists working on a long-term contract. Freelancers accounted for 18.1% of the journalistic workforce.[2]

The 2008 statistics showed continued trends concerning women in French journalism. Female journalists still earned less than men, and the proportion of women in journalism increased, with underrepresentation at the top levels of news organizations and slight overrepresentation at the bottom of French journalism in precarious and lower-paying jobs.

Women accounted for 43.8% of all French journalists in 2008, up from 39.9% in 2000 and 33% in 1990 (Devillard et al. 2000). Historically, as elsewhere, French women have not held management positions in French news media organizations. The female journalists in the 1988 survey were as likely as their male colleagues to note that they did reporting or editing "regularly," but males were far more likely, by nearly 3 to 1, to report that they "regularly" had influence in hiring and firing (McMane 1989b, 1992a, 1998) (see Table 15.2).

According to a 1994 tally done by the national press card commission, about 1 in 10 (11.8%) directors at media operations was a women (Commission de la Carte d'Identité des Journalistes Professionels [CCIJP] 1995). In 2008, the proportion of women among top editors (editors in chief, deputy editors in chief, and managing editors) was 3 in 10 (31.8%). However, when one

Table 15.2   Women in French Journalism

	Women	Men
All journalists	43.8%	56.2%
New card holders	54.3%	45.7%
Top editorial managers (all media)	31.8%	68.2%
Top newspaper editorial managers	18.1%	81.9%
Top broadcast editorial managers	21.3%	78.7%
Freelancers	51.3%	48.7%
Journalists out of work (2010)[1]	58.2%	41.8%
Average age	40.6 years	43.4 years
Average monthly salary	€3,145	€3,694

1 Figures available only for 2010 from Centre national de reclassement des journalistes (CNRJ). All other figures from CCIJP—Observatoire des métiers de presse, 2008.

considers only regional and national newspapers or radio and television, the entities accounting for most of the traditionally "hard news" journalistic population, the proportion dropped in each case to about 2 in 10.

Women remained somewhat over-represented in the precarious job of freelancer, accounting for slightly more than 4 in 10 of all journalists but more than half (51.3%) of freelancers. The proportions have risen about 10 percentage points in the past two decades. In 1990, women represented 33.3% of all journalists and 41.6% of freelancers (Devillard et al. 2000).

Male journalists, whether freelancers or on staff, received between 16 and 17% more in salary than their female counterparts in 2008. Overall, the average gross monthly salary was €3,694 (US$4,630) for men versus €3,145 (US$3,943) for women. More than half of female journalists received less than €3,000 (US$3,760) per month, compared to 41% of male journalists. The difference was proportionally similar in 2000.

Christine Leteinturier (2010) examined the profile of journalists who got their first national press card in 1990, 1998, and 2008 and found some important trends including the beginnings of a feminization of French journalism and a change in where journalists secure a first job. Among the 2,010 first-time card holders in 2008, women were in the majority (54%), which had not been the case in 1990 or 1998. The shift had first occurred in 2002 when women represented 50.9% of new card holders, according to CCIJP/*Observatoire des Métiers de la Presse* figures (Barret 2009b). Leteinturier found that a much higher proportion of new card holders (70.4%) were under age 30 than had been the case a decade earlier, up nearly 10 percentage points. She attributed at least part of that rise to the abolition of military service, which allowed men to enter the profession earlier.

The sectors most likely to hire those new to the profession were local media, notably regional dailies, and the specialized press. However, the print sector as a whole saw a decrease as a haven for new journalists, still ranking first in 2008 with 56% but down from the 72.6% level of 1998. Television continued to rank second, six percentage points higher than a decade earlier, and Web enterprises were outdoing radio in hiring first-time card holders (11.8% versus 10.91%). In addition, all new card holders in 2008 had more previous journalistic experience than the three months required before they could get a card, and a quarter of them had done as many as six internships or short-term contracts (Leteinturier 2010).

Education of Journalists

Beginning in 1976, the Commission Paritaire Nationale de l'Emploi des Journalistes, a national commission on the employment of journalists formed by an equal number of representatives from unions of publishers and those of journalists, gave some French journalism schools a sort of accreditation. It first "recognized" five, then seven, journalism schools, whose reputations were based on producing a highly controlled number of graduates—about 300 nationally per year by the 1980s—who had been "professionally" trained (McMane 1989a).

By 2008, France had 12 such "recognized" schools of journalism producing 440 graduates a year. Most programs lasted two years and cost about €1,400 (US$1,755) per year. Acceptance rates ranged from a high of 10% to a low of just under 3%, with as many as 1,700 candidates vying for 50 spots in an incoming class. Private schools have also emerged, notably the two-year journalism program started in 2004 at the prestigious public institution, l'Institut d'Études Politiques de Paris (Paris Institute of Political Studies), which used to serve instead as the first academic stop for many budding journalists before they attended one of the accredited schools. Its annual tuition in 2008 was about €12,000 (US$15,000) (Brigadaudeau 2009; Volker 2010).

A diploma from a "recognized" journalism school or just a journalism diploma at all, is not a requirement for working as a journalist. Indeed, in 2008 only 14.8% of all journalists with national press cards had graduated from one of the recognized schools, up slightly from the 2000 level of 12.2% (Barret 2009a; CCIJP/Observatoire des Métiers de la Presse 2009).

However, the new card holders studied by Leteinturier (2010) showed a different profile. They were far more likely to have journalism degrees than the general journalistic population in 2008. Four in 10 had journalism degrees, nearly equally from the 12 schools that were "recognized" by the profession (21.6%) and from the more than 80 schools that were not (19.6%). This was a substantial rise from a decade prior, when just over 2 in 10 had such degrees. Leteinturier (2010) credits the increase partly to the establishment of recognized schools, which have tough entrance requirements for the master's programs they offer, and the growth of private schools targeting a broader, younger student base. New card holders also had more education in general, with just over half (50.3%) having master's degrees, compared to just over 40% (42.8%) in 1998 and 37.9% in 1990.

Continuing education for journalists was institutionalized when the people who had run the resistance press during World War II set up a training center in 1946 to learn about the new values and skills they would need to run commercial newspapers. For journalists and most other workers in France, continuing education became routine after 1971, when all workers got the legal right to such study paid for by their employer from an obligatory budget. However, financing is limited and while workers can request a topic of study, they ultimately must abide by the employer's preference (McMane 1989a).

The organization Médiafor collects the funds that must go to continuing education for the French press and manages the delivery of continuing education for about half the press enterprises. While Mediafor's statistics do not take into account in-house training or other kinds of training a media operation does, they do offer a useful snapshot of the main trends in continuing education for journalists. According to Mediafor, 19.5% of journalists covered under the system took some sort of course in 2008. That year, journalists most often studied multimedia, journalism itself, languages, political science, and business economics (Barret 2009a, 2009b).

Two decades earlier, four-fifths of a national sample of news people said they would like continuing education, most frequently mentioning journalism (35%) and language (14.4%), with other topics such as history, art, and political science mentioned by fewer than 10%. Two-fifths reported having already participated in continuing education in the previous three years, with more than half having studied a journalistic topic, such as writing and editing. Electronic editing (including layout) was mentioned most frequently—by 11.8% of those who mentioned a specific topic. Videotext journalism (the era's online journalism) was mentioned by nearly as many (10.8%) (McMane 1989a).

Working Conditions

Job Satisfaction and Plans to Stay in Journalism.   Most French journalists in the 2007 survey by CSA indicated they were happy to be doing their job, but less satisfied with their job conditions. Most felt that the profession itself was declining but expected to remain in journalism all of their working lives (see Table 15.3).

More than 9 in 10 journalists agreed they were either somewhat or very happy to be a journalist. Women were slightly more likely to say they were happy than men (94% for women versus

Table 15.3   Journalists' Attitudes toward Work and Working Conditions (in %, N = 405)

	All	Men	Women	<29	30–35	35–45	46–55	>56	Freelancer
Happy to be a journalist?									
Very happy	38	41	33	18	34	53	42	23	32
Somewhat happy	54	49	61	81	65	42	50	41	41
Somewhat unhappy	5	4	6	1	1	3	5	13	9
Very unhappy	3	5	—	—	—	—	—	23	16
Did not answer	<1	—	—	—	—	—	3	—	2
Satisfied to be journalist?									
Very satisfied	6	5	7	–	8	9	1	5	–
Somewhat satisfied	64	66	61	76	68	61	79	34	59
Somewhat unsatisfied	23	19	31	23	22	23	17	35	12
Very unsatisfied	7	10	1	1	2	7	3	26	22
Did not answer	—	—	—	—	—	—	—	—	—
How much professional freedom?									
Total freedom	27	27	26	11	34	34	27	13	17
Some freedom	61	60	64	80	60	59	59	50	60
Little freedom	12	13	10	9	6	7	14	37	23
No freedom at all	—	—	—	—	—	—	—	—	—
Has profession evolved positively or negatively?									
Positively	30	31	27	17	37	30	46	11	20
Negatively	63	61	67	77	52	60	52	88	67
Did not answer	7	8	6	6	11	10	2	1	15
Will leave journalism before retirement age?									
Yes	30	33	25	38	40	23	17	38	40
No	67	63	73	61	53	74	79	62	60
No answer	3	4	2	1	7	3	4	—	3

Source: CSA, 2007. Questions: Today, are you very happy, somewhat happy, somewhat unhappy or very unhappy to be a journalist? Today, are working conditions very satisfactory, somewhat satisfactory, somewhat unsatisfactory or not satisfactory at all; According to you, in the last few years, has the exercise of your job as a journalist evolved somewhat positively or negatively? Do you see yourself leaving journalism before you reach retirement age?

90% for men). Overall, the level decreased slightly with age, but remained positive for more than 90% of respondents, except among those over age 55 among whom 64% characterized themselves as "happy."

Although still in a clear majority, fewer respondents were satisfied with their working conditions with 7 in 10 journalists somewhat or very satisfied. Nearly 7 in 10 journalists expected to remain in journalism for the rest of their careers.

The level of job satisfaction was similar two decades earlier as was the level of commitment to stay in journalism. In 1988, 87% of a national sample of journalists said that they were either somewhat satisfied (72%) or very satisfied (15%) with their jobs. As for the future, 77.5% of respondents expected then to still be in journalism in five years (McMane 1989b).

In 2007, 6 in 10 (63%) believed the profession was in decline ("evolving negatively"). The youngest and the oldest journalists were least optimistic, with 77% and 88% agreeing that the situation had declined. Women were slightly more likely than men to perceive a decline (67% versus 61%).

Table 15.4   Main Perceived Threats to the Quality of a Journalist's Work (in %, N = 405)

Perceived Threats	Percentage
Insufficient material and human resources	44
Insufficient time	40
Conformity in newsrooms	38
Economic pressures (profit, advertisers, etc.)	38
Precariousness of one's status	24
Editorial marketing (based on the demands of readers)	24
Tendency to follow the herd ("suivisme editorial")	22
Insufficient ethical rigor	14
Self-censorship	10
Criticism by superiors	6
Political pressure	5
None of these	—
No answer	—

Source: CSA (2007). Question: What do you think most threatens the quality of your work? Total is more than 100 % because respondents could give up to three replies.

When asked to choose three items from a list of possible elements that could threaten their work, fewer than half picked anything, and most who did selected primarily the ubiquitous journalistic complaints of insufficient material and human resources (44%) and time (40%). Nearly equally important, chosen by 38%, were the notions of conformity in the newsroom and the economic pressures from profit and advertising. Such economic pressures have also been a recurring concern in surveys of the public with slightly fewer than 6 in 10 in 2008 believing journalists resisted them (La Croix-TNS-SOFRES 2009). The notion of political pressure ranked last among possible threats, chosen by only 5% of the journalists (see Table 15.4).

Perceived Autonomy.   Among the eight statements proposed to a national sample in 1988 about what was important in a job, the two that addressed the importance of personal autonomy drew by far the highest support among French respondents, more so than for the U.K., U.S., and German samples (McMane 1989b, 1992b, 1993, 1998). Nearly 20 years later, only 12% of the journalists surveyed in 2007 felt they generally lacked freedom to do their work with 61% saying freedom to do their work was "mostly the case" and 27% saying it was totally so (see also Table 15.3).

Perceptions of Media Ownership

Two sets of questions addressed the effect of media ownership on journalists' working conditions. In the first list, journalists had to decide whether a given phenomenon was a threat or an opportunity for the evolution of journalism in France (see Table 15.5). "Media concentration" topped the list, with nine out of 10 perceiving this tendency as a threat. In a separate question, about 6 in 10 (57%) supported "measures against media concentration."

The movement toward fewer companies owning more media began in the 1970s and 1980s, prompting a 1986 law forbidding any company from owning more than 30% of the daily press. It emerged again in the early 21st century with the growth of non-press organizations owning

Table 15.5   Threats and Opportunities for Journalism in France (in %, N = 405)

	More of a threat	*More of a benefit*	*No answer*
Media concentration	90	8	2
Tools for measuring audience	52	40	8
Tools for citizen journalism	45	43	12
Free newspapers	43	53	4
Multimedia journalism	34	62	4
Blogs	31	58	11
Media "on demand"	30	60	10
Methods for determining and analyzing the desires of the public	27	67	5

Source: CSA (2007). Question: What are the priorities for improving your professional practice in terms of ethical codes and practices? Total for each item is 100 percent

media. A new group of owners had emerged in the 1980s, composed mainly of industrialists for whom media were part of a much larger portfolio. In the 1990s, non-French multimedia companies entered the picture, especially for magazines, notably the German company Gruner & Jahr.

Digital Technologies

The rapidly changing technologies that allow ordinary citizens to share news and commentary are the newest challenges faced by journalists in France and worldwide (see Table 15.6). The 2007 CSA survey asked several questions about such citizen participation in the journalistic process. Nearly all French journalists (96%) declared themselves open to citizen criticism of journalistic work, including in electronic comments. They were also open to blogs, with 55% seeing blogs as an opportunity in the evolution of journalism. Respondents were evenly split about the effects of the tools that allowed citizens to take digital photos and videos, with 4 in 10 seeing this capability as a threat and an equal number seeing it as an opportunity for French journalism.

Professionalism

Memberships in Professional Organizations.   France's first journalism union, the Syndicat National des Journalistes (SNJ), is its largest with about 3,000 members, according to Eric Marquis, who is its representative on the national press card commission (Marquis 2010). The SNJ emerged in

Table 15.6   Digital Platforms and "Citizen" Journalists (in %, N = 405)

	Agree	*Disagree*	*No Answer*
Possibility for all citizens to criticize the work of journalists in the medium in which that work appeared	96	4	—
It would be better to distinguish what is in the domain of journalism versus free expression or commentary	95	4	1
It is a good thing that citizens who are not journalists develop editorial content on their blogs	70	28	2
It is a good thing that journalists develop their own blogs	55	40	5

Source: CSA (2007) Question: Do you agree or disagree with these opinions?

1918 amid a turbulent post-war journalistic environment that accentuated both the precariousness of journalistic work and an interest in professionalization (Bellanger Godechot, Guiral, & Terrou 1976). The most recent union was formed in 2009 by a group of online news organizations.

Although union membership declined among journalists starting in the mid-1970s (Mermet 1988), unions themselves continued to play a strong role in shaping the working conditions of all journalists. The 16 members of the French journalists' card commission are still elected from slates of candidates provided by unions of journalists and publishers. Also, the national and regional contracts that set salary and vacation minimums were negotiated only between unions of owners and of journalists but apply to all journalists.

Among the 1988 national sample, 37% of respondents belonged to a union. French workers in general have been less unionized than other Western Europeans, although the general level of unionism in France had progressed until 1975. By the time of the 1988 study about 10% of all French wage earners were unionized, and by 2003, this "density" figure had dropped to 8.3% (Mermet 1988; Visser 2006).

Ethical Standards.   French journalists have dealt with their ethical standards in a formal way for nearly a century. France's first journalism union, the Syndicat Nationale des Journalistes (SNJ), created an ethical code in 1918 that called on journalists to, among other things, refrain from seeking the position of a colleague by offering to work for less. The code also told journalists to keep professional secrets and to refrain from posing as someone else. The code retained those elements when it was revised in 1938, but lost bans on promoting "games of money" and on accepting appointments or gratuities that might present a conflict of interest. The later version also eliminated a threat of sanction by a union disciplinary council (Friedman 1988; Syndicat Nationale des Journalistes 1918).

Ombudsmen entered the picture in the 1990s with *Le Monde* establishing the post of "media-teur" in 1994, and Radio France International and the two French public service stations established the post in 1998 (Civard-Racinias 2003). *Ouest-France, Le Monde,* and the France 2 national TV station are among news organizations with an internal code of ethics.

The 2007 survey asked journalists to assess the ethical performance of their colleagues, and nearly seven in 10 said that journalists did well or very well (see Table 15.7). Highest support (81%) came from the oldest journalists (over 56). There was no significant difference by gender.

The survey also asked journalists to note up to three priorities for improving professional practice "in terms of ethical codes and practices" and to choose up to "three priorities for defending journalism." Respondents put protecting anonymous sources at the top of the list of "priorities for defending journalism," with 58% favoring that practice (see Table 15.8). This attitude was

Table 15.7   Journalists and Ethical Practices (in %, N = 405)

	All	Men	Women	<29	30–35	35–45	46–55	>56	Freelance
Very well	2	2	2	—	1	3	3	2	—
Somewhat well	66	65	67	68	63	63	64	79	79
Somewhat badly	27	27	28	32	32	26	29	16	19
Very badly	3	4	1	—	3	4	3	2	2
Did not answer	2	2	2	—	1	4	1	4	—

Source: CSA (2007). Question: In terms of ethical codes and practice, do you think journalists do very well, somewhat well, somewhat badly or very badly?

Table 15.8   Priorities for Improving French Journalistic Ethical Codes and Practice (in %, N = 405)

Priorities	Percentage
Collective action (unions, editors' societies)	35
Adoption of an ethical charter for all newsrooms	32
Adopting tools for continuing education about these themes	29
Including editorial rights in the statues of press enterprises	26
Better consideration of the topic in journalism schools	25
A regulatory body such as those in Italy and Canada	16
Establishment of ombudsmen	12
None	2
Did not answer	1

Source: CSA (2007). Question: What are the priorities for improving your professional practice in terms of ethical codes and practices. Total is more than 100% because respondents could give up to three answers.

even stronger two decades ago when more than 9 in 10 journalists in surveys in France, the United States, and then Western Germany rejected the idea of betraying a promise of anonymity (McMane 1889b, 1993, 1998).

The notion of continuing education to address the matter of ethical practice was assessed with two questions, ranking third in both listings of priorities for defending journalism (41%) and for improving respect for ethical codes and practices (29%). A quarter of respondents supported better consideration of the topic in journalism schools.

Both batteries of questions also asked about including editorial rights in the statutes of news enterprises, with respondents ranking the concept fourth in each set of questions (37% and 26%). Support for an ethical charter in all newsrooms was in the same range with 32%. Support was low (under 20%) for both the re-establishment of some sort of ethical regulatory body, specifically "such as those in Italy and Canada," and the establishment of ombudsmen.

Journalists used the original results of the attitudinal CSA survey to inform deliberations about the future of their profession during the first Assises du Journalism national conference at the University of Lille in 2007. A draft charter for a national code, adopted in 2008 at a follow-up, international version of the "assises," described itself as the direct descendent of the ethical code of the French Syndicat National des Journalistes (1918) and of an international declaration of the "rights and duties of journalists" (1971) that was later supported by the International Federation of Journalists and by several European journalism unions.

The new draft French charter would move the emphasis of ethical responsibility from just one kind of actor (journalists) to the entire media team, including top management. It would keep the emphasis on honesty and independence present in the two earlier ethical codes, but would require more attention to needs and criticism of the public. Proponents of the charter hoped to make it part of the national collective agreement between media enterprises and journalists, which already sets out, notably, minimum wages for the categories of work and basic work rules and benefits (Agnes 2010; Bouvier 2008; Syndicat national des journalists [National union of journalists; SNJ], Confédération nationale du travail [National association of labor unions; CGT], Confédération française démocratique du travail [The French democratic association of labor unions; CFDT] 2009).

Conclusions

The overall demographic portrait of French news people is one of a relatively stagnant, aging workforce that operates mostly in print. Women remain a minority, mostly in the margins, with less pay and away from the levels of power. The profile changes somewhat when one examines those most recently entering the field and obtaining their first national press card. Such a new-comer is far more likely to have a journalism degree than is the general journalistic population, with a shift to more females than males. While most new journalists still work in print, the proportion in other media has increased, with new hires having had more internships before a first job than in the past.

Most journalists are happy in their jobs and expect to stay in journalism throughout their careers, despite a perception that the profession itself is in decline. Media ownership, especially media concentration, is a concern to French journalists, but fewer than half of those surveyed feel that anything in particular threatens their own jobs. Economic and political pressures are perceived to play a very small role, though time and resource constraints are a concern to some. Fully 9 in 10 feel totally or mostly free to do their work. Few belong to a union.

New technologies present both a threat and opportunity to French journalists, with a large majority welcoming citizen criticism of their work, including in electronic comments, and a smaller majority interested in doing blogs. However they are split about the potential of citizen-created videos and photographs. Those who take continuing education courses are most likely to have studied multimedia topics.

French journalists continue a long-held belief that professional ethics are important, and most believe their colleagues do well in this area. They have a strong sense that they should be able to protect anonymous sources but are less unified on the notion of strengthening or changing ethical codes and adding a system for their regulation, or increasing consideration of ethics in journalism schools or establishing more ombudsmen.

In future quantitative comparative studies of journalists, it might be useful for scholars elsewhere to consider some of the attitudinal questions asked only of French journalists in 2007 to further enrich the international portrait beyond mostly U.S. notions of what is worth asking. For example, offering respondents the chance to categorize a set of possible developments as threats or opportunities fits well with modern management concepts and thinking, and offers interesting nuances in positioning of those developments.

Notes

1. The author warmly thanks Eric Marquis, president of the commission, for his guidance toward several useful sources and Nathalie Barret of the Observatoire des Métiers de Presse (Observatory of Occupations in the Press), whose 2009 report served as a precious point of departure and whose assistance in further analysis of the raw data was crucial.
2. These figures do not include the freelancers who have not earned enough income through journalistic work, the equivalent of minimum salary, to obtain a national press card.

References

Agnes, Yves. 2010. Enfin une charte d'ethique de l'information? [Finally an ethical charter for information?]. *Dossier Pédagogique—La Semaine de la Presse*. Paris: Clemi, p. 25.

Albert, Pierre, and Fernand Terrou. 1985. *Histoire de la presse* [History of the press], 4th ed. Paris: Presses Universitaires de France.

Audipresse 2009. *L'étude AEPM. 2008-2009*. Retrieved from http://www.audipresse.fr/media/document/aepm0809/docs/Dossier_de_presse_AEPM_08-09_Communique.pdf

Bailly, Christian. 1987. *Théophrast Renaudot*. Paris: Le Pré aux Clercs.

Balle, Francis. 1987. *Et si la presse n'existait pas* [And what if the press had never existed]. Paris: J. C. Lattès.

Barret, Natalie. May 2009a. *Photographie de la profession des journalists: Etude des journalists détenteurs de la carte de journaliste professionel de 2000 à 2008* [Snapshot of the journalistic profession: Study of journalists who held a national press card from 2000 to 2008]. Paris: Observatoire des métiers de la Presse.

Barret, Nathalie. 2009b. *Statistics from 2000 through 2008 and 2009*. Paris: Commission de la Carte d'Identité des Journalistes Professionels (CCIJP)/Observatoire des Métiers de la Presse.

Belanger, Claude, Jacques Godechot, Pierre Guiral and Fernand Terrou, eds. 1976. *Histoire générale de la presse française* [A general history of the French press]. Paris: Presses Universitaires de France.

Bouvier, Jérôme. 2008, 28 May. Une charte pour la qualité d'information [A charter for information quality]. *Le Monde*. Retrieved from http://www.journalisme.com/images/stories/pdf/revue_presse_assises08/lemonde_240508.pdf

Brigadaudeau, Anne. 2009. *Report for France 2 Television Channel*. November 24. Retrieved from http://www.france2.fr/info/dossiers/france/2291953-fr.php

Centre d'Etudes et de Recherche sur les Qualifications (CEREQ). 1974. Les Journalistes: Étude statistique et sociologique de la profession [The journalists: A statistical and sociological study of the profession]. *Dossier Number 9*. Paris.

Charon, Jean-Marie. 1993. *Cartes de Presse: Enquête sur les Journalistes* [Press cards: A study of journalists]. Paris: Stock.

Civard-Racinias, Alexandrine. 2003. *La déontologie des journalists: Principes et Pratiques* [Journalists' ethics: Principles and practice]. Paris: Ellipses.

Commission de la Carte d'Identité des Journalistes Professionels (CCIJP). 1967. *Enquête Statistique et Sociologique* [A statistical and sociological study]. Paris: Author.

Commission de la Carte d'Identité des Journalistes Professionels (CCIJP). 1986. *50 Ans de la Carte Professionnelle: Profil de la Profession, Enquête Socioprofessionnelle* [Fifty years of the professional card: Profile of the profession, socioprofessional study]. Paris: Author.

Commission de la Carte d'Identité des Journalistes Professionels (CCIJP). 1995. *Chiffres de 1994*. Paris: Author.

Comscore. 2008. Social networking explodes worldwide as sites increase their focus on cultural relevance. Press release, August 12. Retrieved from http://www.comscore.com/Press_Events/Press_Releases/2008/08/Social_Networking_World_Wide

Desportes, Gérard, and Nata Rampazzo. 2008. *L'avenir de la presse? Une affaire de volonté* [The future of the press? A matter of will]. *Revue Médias*, Winter: 51–61.

Devillard. Valérie, Marie-Françoise Lafosse, Christine Leteinturier, and Remy Rieffel. 2000. *Les Journalistes Français à l'Aube de l'An 2000* [French journalists at the dawn of the year 2000]. Paris: Panthéon Assas.

Eveno, Patrick. 2001. *Le journal Le Monde, une histoire d'indépendance* [The newspaper Le Monde, a history of independence]. Paris: Editions Odile.

Federation Internationale de la Presse périodique (FIPP) [International Federation of the Periodical Press]. *World Magazine Trends 1999–2000, 2008–2009 and 2009–2010*. London: FIPP.

Freiberg, J. W. 1981. *The French press: Class, state and ideology*. Eastbourne, England: Holt-Sanders.

Friedman, Michel. 1988. *Libertés et Responsabilités des Journalistes et des Auteurs* [Freedoms and responsibilities of journalists and authors]. Paris: Editions CFPJ.

Institut Français de Presse. 1991. *Les Journalistes Français en 1990: Radiographie d'une Profession* [French journalists in 1990: X-ray of a profession]. Paris: La Documentation Française.

International Telecommunication Union. 2008. *Statistical tables from 1998 and 2008*.

Leteinturier, Christine. 2010. Les Journalistes nouveaux titulaire de la carte de presse 2008. [New National Press Card holders in 2008]. *Cahiers du journalisme* No. 21.

Lindon Commission. 1970. *Rapport sur les problèmes posés par les sociétés de rédacteurs* [Report on the problems posed by companies' editors]. Paris: La Documentation Française.

Marquis, Eric. (President of La Commission de la Carte d'Identité des Journalistes Professionels [CCIJP]). March 15, 2010, interview with the author.

McMane, Aralynn Abare. 1989a. Les journalistes français et le perfectionnement [French journalists and their further development]. Advisory research report. Paris: Centre de Perfectionnement des Journalistes.

McMane, Aralynn Abare. 1989b. *An empirical analysis of French journalists in comparison with journalists in Britain, West Germany and the United States.* Doctoral dissertation, School of Journalism, Indiana University, Bloomington, Indiana.

McMane, Aralynn Abare. 1992a. *Journalism and gender in France.* Paper presented to annual meeting of Association for Education in Journalism and Mass Communication, Montreal, Canada.

McMane, Aralynn Abare. 1992b. *Vers un profil du journalisme 'occidental': Analyse empirique et comparative des gens de presse en France, au Royaume-Uni, en Allemagne et aux Etats-Unis* [Toward a profile of "western" journalism: An empirical, comparative analysis of news people in France, the United Kingdom, Germany and the United States]. *Reseaux* 51: 67–74.

McMane, Aralynn Abare. 1992c. L'indépendence et le journaliste: Comparaison France et les Etats-Unis [Independence and the journalist: A comparison of France and the United States]. *Médiaspouvoirs* 26: 5–14.

McMane, Aralynn Abare. 1992d. French lessons. *Editor and Publisher* 126: 66–70.

McMane, Aralynn Abare. 1993. A comparative analysis of standards of reporting among French and U.S. newspaper journalists. *Journal of Mass Media Ethics* 8(4): 207–218.

McMane, Aralynn Abare. 1998. The French journalist. In *The global journalist: News people around the world*, edited by David H. Weaver, pp. 191–212. Cresskill, NJ: Hampton Press.

McMane, Aralynn Abare. 2009, October. "Play Bac." In *Publishing to targeted audiences, SFN Strategy Report 9.1.* Paris: World Association of Newspapers and News Publishers.

McMane, Aralynn Abare, and M. Kent Sidel. 1995. Western Europe. In *Global journalism: Survey of international communication*, 3rd ed., edited by John C. Merril, pp. 123–152. New York: Longman.

Mediapart. 2008. 103 départs au "Monde". Retrieved from http://www.mediapart.fr/journal/economie/economico/010708/103-departs-au-monde-il-ne-faut-pas-se-rejouir-trop-vite-previent-

Mediasig. (2009). *MÉDIASIG: L'essentiel de la presse et de la communication* [The essentials of the press and communications]. Paris: La Documentation Française.

Mermet, Gérard. 1988. *Francoscopie: Les Français, Qui Sont-Ils? Ou Vont-Ils?* [The French, who are they, where are they going]. Paris: Larousse.

Neveu, Eric. 2004. *Sociologie du journalisme* [The sociologie of journalism]. La Découverte (Repères), Paris (2nd ed.). Retrieved from http://novovision.fr/?Crise-des-generations-dans-le (Original work published 2001)

OJD Internet. October 8, 2008. *Pour la premiere fois l'OJD détaille la frequentation internet site par site* [For the first time, the OJD gives details of Internet use site by site]. Press packet.

Padioleau, Jean-Georges. 1985. *Le Monde et Le Washington Post.* Paris: Presses Universitaires de France.

Pecquerie, Bertrand. 2008. Que faut-il sauver: Les journaux ou le journalisme? [What must be saved: Newspapers or journalism?] *Médias*, Winter:39–47.

Polome, Pierre. 2009. *Les medias sur Internet* [The media on the Internet]. Paris: Milan.

Rieffel, Rémy. 1984. *L'élite des journalistes* [The elite of journalists]. Paris: Presses Universitaires de France.

Rieffel, Remy. 2005. *Sociologie des Médias* [Sociology of the media]. Paris: Ellipses.

Rieffel, Remy. 2009. *Que sont les medias* [What are the media?]. Paris: Folio Actuel.

SNJ, CGT, CFDT. 2009. *Letter ouverte à President Nicolas Sarkozy* [Open letter to President Nicolas Sarkozy]. November 3.

Syndicat de la presse indépendante d'information en ligne (SPIIL). [Union of the independent online information press]. n.d. Information retrieved on April 19, 2010, from http://www.spiil.org

Syndicat Nationale des Journalistes (SNJ). 1918. Les devoirs et les droits professionnels [Professional responsibilities and rights]. *Bulletin Mensuel* 1, December, 2.

Tailleur, Jean-Ternisien. 2008, 16 July. *France media guide.* Report for the Open Source Center.

Ternisien, Xavier. 2009. *Les editeurs de presse en ligne se repartissent-20 millions-d euros d'aides* [Online publishers will share €20 million in aid]. December 30. Retrieved from http://www.lemonde.fr/actualite-medias/article/2009/12/30/les-editeurs-de-presse-en-ligne-se-repartissent-20-millions-d-euros-d-aides_12859'32_3236.html

Visser, Jelle. 2006. Union membership statistics in 24 European countries. *Monthly Labor Review*, January, 38–49. Retrieved from http://www.trabajoyequidad.cl/documentos/temp/UnionDensityStat14counties.pdf

Volker, Bernard. 2010, 23 February. Director of the journalism program at Institut d'Études Politiques de Paris. E-mail message.

Voyenne, Bernard. 1985. *Les journalistes français* [French journalists]. Paris: CFPJ.

Wauters, Corentin. (October 21 2009). Association of online publishers to lobby government in France. *European Journalism Centre Magazine.* Retrieved from http://www.ejc.net/magazine/article/association_of_online_publishers_to_lobby_government_in_france/

Weaver, David H., and G. Cleveland Wilhoit. 1986. *The American journalist: A portrait of U.S. news people and their work.* Bloomington: Indiana University Press.

World Association of Newspapers and News Publishers (WAN-IFRA). 1995 through 2009. World Press Trends. Tatiana Repkova, Editor. /

16 Journalism in Germany in the 21st Century

Siegfried Weischenberg, Maja Malik, and Armin Scholl

Journalism research in Germany is celebrating its centenary. In 1910, sociologist Max Weber presented a complete research program at the first German Convention of Sociology on the situation of the media in general and of journalism in particular. This research program was elaborate and comprehensive with respect to the relevant research topics in this field and therefore it is still worthy of discussion today. It included questions of power relations between journalists and their sources, institutional influences on journalists' work, journalistic professionalization, the quality of journalistic coverage, relevant characteristics of journalists, and even media effects.

Weber, who was already well known for his analysis of modern society's development being a result of rationalization and disenchantment (*Entzauberung*), planned a vast and fundamental research project on journalists in order to disenchant the world of media, too. He insisted on international comparisons and on cooperation with media practitioners, both of which are very modern and relevant for social research today (Weischenberg 2012: 78f).

Weber's outline also included the well-known problems concerning the economic basis of newspapers, which at that time did and still do jeopardize not only newspaper journalism but all journalism in Western-type social systems. U.S. communication scholar Hanno Hardt (1979: 183f.) appreciated Weber's project as pioneering: "His ideas [...] anticipated many developments in the research patterns as they developed particularly in the United States some decades later." However, the ambitious project failed for several reasons. Weber's research ideas could neither be realized by himself nor by anybody else in the early 20th century because World War I, financial shortages, and in particular his legal dispute with the press stopped its implementation.

Background and Previous Studies

After World War II, communication research in Germany had to recover from the ideological legacy of the Nazi regime. Media research in West Germany was now interested in the subjective dimensions of journalism (e.g., journalists' role perceptions and political attitudes) as well as its objective dimensions (e.g., structure of newsrooms, autonomy of journalists). In numerous empirical studies, researchers examined "what journalists think and how they work" (Kepplinger 1979) and considered specific research questions of whether certain journalistic roles (such as sports reporters, or local reporters, or editors-in-chief) and gender exert an influence on role perceptions or on working conditions. These studies (Weiß, Frantz, Räder, & Uekermann 1977) included observations of the structures of media organizations within the general context of how the media system has developed (Rühl 1969).

In the 1980s, computerization of newsrooms became relevant for journalists' editorial work, and its consequences were examined and discussed in journalism research. Journalists more and more became responsible for technical and administrative tasks, too, at the expense of their core task, which is investigating information and checking facts (for an overview, see Weischenberg, Löffelholz, & Scholl 1998: 229f.).

After the fall of the Berlin Wall in 1989 and German reunification in 1990, the media in East Germany were restructured and East German journalism adapted the structure and professional norms of Western journalism. In order to analyze this structural shift from socialist to liberal journalism in the unified Germany and to document the social and professional consequences for East German journalists, the study *Sozialenquete* [Social Investigation] (1992) included two representative samples of permanently employed journalists in the former West Germany (*N* = 983) and the former East Germany (*N* = 585). The authors found differences between Eastern and Western German journalists' role perceptions, which could be explained by the different societal situations in East and West Germany at that time, but which were not as serious as could have been expected with respect to their completely different professional socialization (Schönbach, Stüzebecher, & Schneider 1998).

The study *Journalism in Germany* (1993) then collected representative data about the population of all segments of German journalism in the re-unified country. Its purpose was a theory-driven analysis of German journalism following ideas developed by German sociologist Niklas Luhmann (Görke & Scholl 2006), drawing on the empirical tradition of Max Weber's project (Weischenberg, Löffelholz, & Scholl 1998; Weischenberg 2012). It adapted parts of survey questionnaires developed in the United States by Johnstone and Weaver in the 1970s and 1980s (Johnstone, Slawski, & William Bowman. 1976; Weaver & Wilhoit 1986, 1996). The sample consisted of 1,498 journalists, who were interviewed face-to-face. Unlike a study of the 1980s, which blamed German journalists for a missionary role perception (Köcher 1986), the study substantiated that German journalists approve of professional norms, such as objective reporting, which are commonly accepted in Western journalism.

The 1990s brought fundamental changes to the structure of journalism. In Germany, newsrooms were restructured by degrading the structure of individual editorial departments (such as politics, business, culture, etc.) toward a news desk structure integrating the formerly separated departments. The reasons were mainly economic to save money by means of rationalizing workflow and reducing the number of staff. Several observational studies examined the processes of editorial coordination of workflow (Altmeppen 1999), different cultures of newsroom organization between English and German media (Esser 1998), the new structures of newsrooms, such as replacing editorial departments by news desks (Blöbaum 2008, 2009), or the elementary job activities of Internet journalists (Quandt 2005).

Another far-reaching change in journalism was caused by the development of the Internet. Not only has the Web given journalists the opportunity to investigate issues faster and in much more detail, but it has also allowed non-professional or semi-professional competitors (i.e., bloggers) to challenge the traditions of professional journalism at its core.

Analyzing online journalism today challenges journalism research for two reasons: On the one hand, information provided by professional journalists' coverage should be distinguished from other content on the Internet such as that provided by hidden public relations organizations or by private citizens, and on the other hand, new kinds of online journalism, such as participatory journalism or blog-based journalism. Two recent studies tried to find online journalism within the Internet environment, separating it from information provided by non-journalistic sources. Methodologically, they had to cope with the challenge of circular argumentation which defines journalism and journalistic coverage in a conservative manner by simply adapting (professional) criteria of offline journalism to online journalism. From this perspective one will hardly find journalistic coverage on the Internet. However, their definition of journalism should not be too inclusive by incorporating every content-producing source, because that risks also including public relations content (Quandt, Löffelholz, Weaver, Hanitzsch, & Altmeppen 2006; Neuberger 2009; Neuberger, Neuernbergk, & Rischke 2009). Both studies identified independent journalistic media coverage beyond the traditional media's Web coverage on the Internet but also provided evidence that professional journalists could clearly be separated from non-professional journalists by considering their professional norms.

A third challenge to journalism research is the growing need for internationally comparative journalism research, as we live in a globalized (media) world today, which may cause both the need for harmonizing professional norms and the need for specifying locally or regionally specific news values. In the 1980s the first study that involved German journalists compared British and German journalists' professional and political attitudes (Köcher 1986). In the 1990s, the comparison was broadened to five countries (Donsbach & Patterson 2004), and in the 2000s 17 countries were included (Hanitzsch 2008, 2009). These studies share a methodological preference for cross-cultural comparisons with one common questionnaire, in contrast to the Global Journalist study (Weaver 1998), which is based on post hoc comparisons between 21 national-based studies. All these studies illustrated many differences and commonalities between journalists in different countries, which partly could be explained either by theory or post hoc, but which also showed inconsistent or unexplainable results.

We should remember, though, that the search for journalism within a new medium or within different societies cannot be arbitrary or conventional. What is needed is a theoretical framework to distinguish the societal phenomenon of journalism from other communicative phenomena in a globalized world society, such as public relations information or private information (identification between variances), and to observe its structural variety (diversification within variances) (Rühl 2008; Weischenberg & Malik 2008).

Method

The following discussion is based on a representative survey study of 1,536 German journalists conducted by the authors in 2005. The study replicates a previous survey that was carried out in 1993 with a sample of 1,498 German journalists (Weischenberg, Löffelholz, & Scholl 1998). The data from these two studies allow us to describe the current structure of journalism in Germany as well as the structural changes that took place between 1993 and 2005.

The study starts with a comprehensive definition of journalism that is characterized by three distinct levels. At the *societal* level, journalism is defined as a social system that enables society to observe itself, as it provides the public independently and periodically with information and issues that are considered newsworthy, relevant, and fact-based. Thus, it can be distinguished from public relations, which is neither independent nor necessarily relevant or fact-based in all cases (Scholl 1996; Scholl & Weischenberg 1998).

At the *organizational* level, journalistic media and newsrooms institutionalize formal rules as well as specific processes of acting, communicating, and decision making. Journalistic organizations can be distinguished from other organizations by their contribution to journalistic coverage—which has been determined as material that is newsworthy, relevant, fact-based, independent, current, and periodical. This definition of journalistic media includes media which are (1) independent units, (2) not published by political parties, associations, trade unions or other unions, or public authorities, (3) produced (mostly) by professionals, (4) published periodically and at least six times a year, and (5) contain journalistic coverage (not only advertising, fiction, music, games, puzzles, etc.). This definition excludes non-periodical media (e.g. books, quarterly published journals), fictional media (e.g., paperback novels, motion pictures, etc.), public relations media, and media that have limited public relevance because of small distribution numbers.

Third, at the *individual* level journalists are conceptualized as the system's actors. They work in professional roles for which they are prepared by training and their work in newsrooms. Journalistic roles are defined by their main activities and duties within the process of producing journalistic coverage whether as full-time employees or freelance staff. A member of a newsroom is considered a journalist if he or she is predominantly engaged in producing journalistic coverage and thereby influencing the content of the media. This includes TV news show anchors and editors of online news, as well as magazine freelancers. Excluded are technical occupations, secretaries, interns, publishers and managers, photographers, and camera crews. Although they are necessary to produce media, they are not mainly occupied with news making in the sense of determining newsworthiness, relevance, and facts, which have been defined as the central characteristics of journalism (Malik 2005; Scholl 1996). Freelancers are considered professional journalists only if they work for journalistic media more than half of their working hours. Otherwise they are considered non-professional freelancers or non-journalists working in public relations, advertising, or entertainment.

Following this definition of journalism, the population for the current survey study was identified in four steps. First, we determined the universe of journalistic media in Germany by collecting all print, television, radio, and online news media as well as news agencies and media services in Germany using several catalogues and registers as sources. Overall, 2,890 journalistic media organizations were identified in Germany. Next, a stratified random sample of 1,768 media organizations was surveyed with a written questionnaire about the number of journalists working as full-time employees or as freelance journalists, the number of male and female journalists, and the number of journalists working for various editorial departments and in various hierarchical positions. Based on this information, we then estimated the total population of professional journalists working in Germany at 48,000. Finally, a multi-stage stratified random sample of 3,534 journalists was drawn from this population.

The stratification was carried out on the level of different media types (e.g., small and big regional daily newspapers, nationwide daily newspapers, small and big weekly newspapers), employment status (employed vs. freelance journalists), position in newsroom hierarchy, gender, and editorial departments (such as politics, economics, sports, culture, local/regional departments). After subtracting ineligible respondents (e.g., those not journalists according to our definition, wrong telephone numbers) a sample of 2,111 respondents remained. A final sample of 1,536 journalists was interviewed by telephone between February and April 2005, which represents a response rate of 73%.

The survey included questions about professional status and professional career, role perceptions, ethics of reporting, image of the journalists' audience, perceived influences on journalists, job satisfaction, and socio-demographic characteristics. The interviews were conducted by the German polling firm Ipsos, in Hamburg and lasted about 40 minutes on average.

Findings

Basic Characteristics

Most German journalists are male (63%), middle aged (41 years on average), well educated (69% hold a university degree), married (44%), earn a monthly net income of €2,300 (approx. US$3,140), have a middle class origin (67% of journalists' fathers are officials or employees at least in a middle or advanced position or self-employed) and slightly lean toward a liberal political position (mean value of 38 points on a scale from 1 = "extremely left" to 100 = "extremely right").

In 2005, about 48,000 journalists worked for about 2,900 media organizations in Germany. Around 12,000 of them were professional freelancers, whom we define as journalists either deriving more than half of their income from journalistic work (rather than from public relations activities) or spending more than half of their working time on journalistic tasks (rather than for public relations or any other tasks). If we compare the data with the earlier study in 1993, we can observe an increase in the number of media organizations but a decrease in the total journalistic workforce. While the number of full-time journalists remained stable at 36,000, the number of professional freelancers decreased from 18,000 to 12,000. In 1993, more than half of the freelancers worked for one or two media only; in 2005 more than two out of three of them worked for up to three media. Obviously, freelancers had to struggle harder in 2005 to earn enough money from their work.

We can conclude from these findings, first, that the journalist's job has become more stressful because fewer journalists do more coverage for more media. Second, an unknown number of non-professional freelancers or of journalists with hybrid roles (working both as journalists and as public relations practitioners) hide behind the decreasing number of professional freelancers, compensating for the increase in media and journalistic media coverage.

Still, more than a third of all German journalists (including the professional freelancers) work for daily or weekly newspapers, followed by those working for broadcast media and magazines. Less than 5% are employed at online media, which shows that professional online journalism is still the business of a small minority in Germany.

Most German journalists cover local or regional issues (27%) or politics (15%). One in ten journalists covers culture (10%) or special-interest issues (10%). Fewer journalists specialize in lifestyle (8%), sports (6%), and business (5%). In addition, there are a considerable number of journalists who cannot be assigned to a specific beat (18%). Overall, these findings show a deep structural change in German media organizations, which have reorganized their more decentralized or

Table 16.1 Number of Journalists by Type of Media Organization*

Type of Media Organization	Number of Journalists	Percentage
Daily and weekly newspapers	17,113	35.4
Freesheets	2,876	5.9
Magazines	9,419	19.5
News agencies and media services	1,428	3.0
Public and commercial radio	8,003	16.5
Public and commercial television	7,215	14.9
Online media	2,325	4.8
Total	48,379	100.0

* Included are full-time staff and (professional) freelancers.

autonomous editorial departments to match the typical news desk organization of Anglo-American journalism.

The number of female journalists had increased from 31% to 37% between 1993 and 2005. The higher the position in newsroom hierarchy, the lower is the percentage of female journalists. Women still have less income, which is not only due to their lower position but also depends on which medium they work for. They are well represented in commercial broadcast media or in free periodicals, both offering lower payment. In contrast to the vertical segregation the horizontal segregation has decreased significantly—women often work for lifestyle magazines, but they are also reporting on political and economic issues and even the former male domain of sports.

Although female representation in journalism has improved, German journalists as a whole do not mirror demographically the German population as a whole: They usually belong to the middle class, tend to hold political attitudes that are more liberal than those held by the general population (mean value of 38 points on a scale from 1 = "extremely left" to 100 = "extremely right"), and often favor the Green party (35% vs. 10% in the population in 2005).

It should be mentioned that having a liberal political attitude does not necessarily imply that journalists favor liberal politicians or parties and are more critical of conservative politicians or parties. In general, the work of journalists is much more influenced by organizational rules, publishers' guidelines, and professional values than political attitudes or personal biases (Shoemaker & Reese 1996).

Education and Training

More than two-thirds of German journalists have a university degree and an additional 15% have at least an incomplete university education. Most journalists studied a variety of university subjects that ranged from humanities (30%) or social sciences (32%) to history (8%), economics (8%), law (4%), and natural sciences (10%). The journalists' training on the job often starts with an internship (a couple of months practical training) and usually is followed by a traineeship (a two-year practical training period), which is still considered the most common way to get employed as journalist in Germany. It is interesting to note that compared to 1993 the number of journalists having completed one or more internships has increased greatly from 32% to 69%. This finding suggests that age has a significant impact on the likelihood of getting an internship (*eta* = .42), which means that younger generations of journalists are more likely to start their career with an internship.

Other ways of journalism-specific training beyond internship and traineeship are chosen by fewer German journalists. Only 14% have completed a non-academic journalism school (e.g., Axel Springer Akademie, Henri-Nannen-Schule, Freie Journalistenschule), while another 14% attended an academically focused journalism program. To understand these findings, it is important to know that in Germany only a few universities offer journalism studies (*Journalistik*) as an academic subject. It is more common to study social scientific communication science (*Kommunikationswissenschaft*) or the humanities oriented media studies (*Medienwissenschaft*), which actually 17% of the journalists do, but both subjects do not immediately and directly prepare one to work as a journalist.

In order to increase their chances to successfully enter the job market, many budding journalists combine a study of these subjects with more practical training. Almost two of three journalists started their jobs by combining two or more journalism-specific training programs (such as internship, traineeship, journalism school, journalism study, study of communication science, and the like); a quarter of them had only one kind of training, and less than 9% of the journalists had

Table 16.2   Type of Journalistic Education/Training (*N* = 1,536)

Journalistic Training*	In %
Internship	69
Traineeship	62
Journalism school (non-academic)	14
Study of journalism	14
Study of communication science or media studies	17
Other ways of training and advanced training	14

*Multiple responses

no journalism-specific training at all to get into the job. There is an inverse correlation between age and the number of journalism-specific training programs attended (*r* = −.26), indicating that younger journalists tend to be slightly more likely to combine various journalistic training programs than do older journalists.

To sum up our findings on journalism education and training, it is safe to conclude that while the paths into the profession are diverse, German journalism has become more "academic" over the years. It is also clear that those who want to become journalists in Germany cannot simply follow a predetermined educational path, but must instead combine university studies with different kinds of practical training opportunities.

Working Conditions

Workload.   If it is true that journalists are more stressed because fewer of them have to produce more coverage for more media, this should be reflected in their attitudes about their working conditions. Contrary to our expectations, however, journalists reported an average workload of 45 hours per week in 2005, which is almost the same as in 1993.

While the average work time did not increase between 1993 and 2005, there seems to be a significant shift in time spent for specific journalistic activities. Most striking are two results: On average, German journalists spent 23 minutes less a day on investigating and gathering information in 2005 as compared to 1993. The amount of time spent on administrative (organizational) and technical tasks, on the other hand, has increased, as Table 16.3 shows.

Table 16.3   Journalists' Workload (*N* = 1,536)

Journalistic Activities	Time Spent (minutes per day 2005 (1993)
Investigating and gathering information	117 (140)
Writing and editing own texts	120 (118)
Selecting texts (from press material)	33 (49)
Editing texts provided by agencies	33 (37)
Editing colleagues' texts	55 (39)
Organizing and administrative tasks	78 (69)
Technical tasks	84 (50)
Communication with readers, spectators etc.	26 (*)
Marketing activities for own media organization	9 (*)

*Not included in the questionnaire of 1993.

These overall results must be differentiated by the type of employment and by the position of each journalist in the newsroom hierarchy. Editors, for example, spent much more time than senior editors or editors-in-chief (executive journalists) on investigating and gathering information (124 vs. 91 minutes per day) or writing stories (129 vs. 85 minutes per day). Unsurprisingly, higher-ranking journalists were more likely to be responsible for editing their colleagues' stories (75 vs. 49 minutes per day) or for organizing and administrative tasks (125 vs. 63 minutes per day).

We also found that freelancers, on average, spent more time than full-time staff on investigation (133 vs. 112 minutes per day) or on writing stories (136 vs. 115 minutes per day). Full-time journalists, on the other hand, are more often responsible than freelancers for selecting stories from agencies and press material (35 vs. 28 minutes per day), editing incoming material (37 vs. 24 minutes per day), editing colleagues' stories (65 vs. 24 minutes per day), and organizing and administrative tasks (80 vs. 61 minutes per day). In a way, these observed relationships between full-time staff and professional freelancers correspond with the typical Anglo-American relationships between editors (full-time staff) and reporters (freelancers) with respect to typical job activities.

These findings on time spent on various journalistic tasks were observed in the 1993 study as well (Weischenberg, Löffelholz, & Scholl 1998). However, there are some significant differences between the two studies that can be summed up as follows: First, some of the journalists' *core tasks* (like investigating and gathering information, selecting texts) have decreased in their importance for the job of journalists, but other core tasks (like writing texts) are still as important as they were 12 years earlier. Second, *additional tasks* (like technical, organizational, and administrative tasks) have considerably increased. Third, journalists' *routine tasks* (like editing incoming press material) are stable, while the importance of *controlling tasks* (like editing colleagues' texts) has increased.

Overall, our findings about the new newsroom structures and the shift from journalistic core activities toward more technical and administrative tasks suggest that journalism in Germany is moving from a focus on "news making" to a more business-oriented emphasis on "news management."

Job Satisfaction.   Journalists reflect these trends in a way when they are questioned about their satisfaction with various aspects of their jobs. On the one hand, only about half of them are satisfied with the time available for investigation (48%), their income (54%), their job security (50%), or with their daily workload (48%). On the other hand, the vast majority are satisfied with the quality of their journalistic training (72%), with the possibility of organizing their work independently (75%), and with their relationships with colleagues (88%). It seems that those aspects related to job satisfaction that journalists can manage or influence themselves (training, atmosphere within newsroom, self-organizing daily work) are seen as positive by more journalists. Factors that are determined by the organization (income, job security, daily workload), however, are perceived as satisfying by fewer journalists.

Counterchecking Practices.   Another practice that characterizes German newsrooms is counterchecking. Although we might expect that media organizations want to minimize the time needed to check the work of their journalists, this newsroom practice is very common. Two of three journalists (66%) said that their stories are usually checked by others. Counterchecking is most often practiced by immediate superiors, such as senior editors (73%), colleagues (59%), editors-in-chief (41%), and even trainees (20%). We interpret this common practice not only as a measure by superiors for controlling journalists but also as a quality check of the coverage. By comparing these findings with the results of the time spent on editing colleagues' stories (which has increased since 1993) and with the time spent on investigating information (which has decreased), it seems reasonable to argue that a certain amount of journalists' work has shifted from activities outside the newsroom to activities within it, and consequently to an increased orientation toward the colleagues of one's own newsroom.

Perceived Autonomy.   We measured perceived autonomy in an indirect way by asking the journalists about the impact of several persons, groups, or associations on their jobs. Factors within newsrooms seem to be more influential than factors from outside when it comes to the journalists' daily work. About a third of the journalists consider editors-in-chief (32%) or senior editors (39%) as having a strong influence on their work. The impact of colleagues (23%) or the top management (12%), on the other hand, is considered influential by notably fewer journalists.

External influences seem to be of less importance, except for the audience's influence that is perceived to be important by about a quarter (23%) of the journalists. Business and private contacts with family, friends, and acquaintances are mentioned by only one in ten journalists (9%) as important sources of influence. Political parties (3%), sports associations (6%), churches (3%), or trade unions (2%) are mentioned by even fewer journalists.

It would be a mistake, though, to infer from these results that journalists are free from external influences and constraints. Even the internal influence of superiors and particularly editors-in-chief is affected by external influences. In addition, external influences might be stronger among certain types of journalists. For example, political parties are known to exert considerable influence on local journalists covering politics, while businesses often exert influence on business coverage (Weischenberg, Malik, & Scholl 2006).

Professionalism

Role Perceptions and Role Performance.   Journalists' professionalism is closely related to their journalistic roles, which can be measured both in an objective and in a subjective dimension. In order to combine subjective role perception with (the estimation of) objective role performance we asked journalists about their professional goals and whether they think that they are able to attain them. By asking these questions, we not only hope to identify the main professional goals in journalism, but also whether journalists believe that these goals are merely professional "ideology" or real practices that can be achieved.

As we argued in an earlier publication (Scholl & Weischenberg 1998), different role perceptions should not be considered mutually exclusive. Rather, they seem to be hierarchically ordered and complex. It is no contradiction, for example, for a journalist to try to be both a neutral disseminator of information and a critical observer of state affairs.

The most relevant group of items refers to the key concept of *objective reporting*. Theoretically, we suggest considering *objective reporting* as a four-dimensional construct: The first dimension can be called *substantial* because information will be objective (reflecting reality), neutral, and precise; the second dimension is more *formal* because information will be presented in a simple (complexity reducing), analytical, and interpretative way; the third dimension is *temporal* because information will be disseminated quickly; and the fourth dimension is *social* because information will be of interest for the broadest possible audience or public.

The survey findings provide strong evidence for the theoretical and practical importance of *objective reporting* in German journalism (see Table 16.4). Most journalists supported related role items such as "getting information to the public neutrally and precisely" (89%), "providing analyses

Table 16.4   Aimed and Realized Role Perceptions (N = 1,536)

Professional role items	Aimed role (in %)*	Realized role (in %)**
Get information to the public neutrally and precisely	89	76
Provide analyses and interpretations of complex problems	79	75
Get information to the public quickly	74	79
Present reality as it is	74	67
Concentrate on news which is of interest to widest possible public	60	74
Criticize bad states of affairs	58	43
Give ordinary people a chance to express their views on public issues	34	57
Stand up for the disadvantaged population	29	43
Control politics, business, and society	24	27
Influence the political agenda and setting issues on the political agenda	14	39
Present new trends and convey new ideas	44	58
Convey positive ideals	44	43
Help people in their everyday lives	44	69
Present one's own opinion to the public	19	67
Provide entertainment and relaxation	37	79

*   Percentage of respondents who entirely agree or mostly agree with a professional role item.

** Percentage of respondents who entirely agree or mostly agree with a professional role item and who entirely agree or mostly agree that they are able to realize this role in their jobs.

and interpretations of complex problems" (79%), "getting information to the public quickly" (74%), "presenting reality as it is" (74%), or "concentrating on news which is of interest to widest possible public" (60%). Moreover, the majority of those who approve of these role items also thought that it is possible to accomplish these journalistic ideals. Finally, it is interesting to note that the support of these various roles was more widespread in 2005 than in 1993 (Weischenberg, Löffelholz, & Scholl 1998).

Another group of role items was used to operationalize *advocacy journalism*. Journalists were asked whether they would want to "criticize bad states of affairs," "stand up for a disadvantaged population," "control politics, business and society," or "influence the political agenda." Here, too, we can theoretically distinguish between different dimensions of *advocacy journalism*: *critique*, *advocacy*, and *control*. The order of these three dimensions represents an order of commitment. As *criticism* is rather unspecific, it can be applied to all kinds of phenomena. *Advocacy*, on the other hand, is clearly related to certain populations (disadvantaged people) but still is an everyday phenomenon. *Control* should demand the highest commitment because it requires an oppositional attitude toward powerful people and groups.

The findings in Table 16.4 show that the approval of the *critique* dimension does not necessarily correlate with approval of advocacy and control dimensions. While more than half of German journalists say they would criticize grievances (58%), for example, only about one-third would give ordinary people a chance to express their opinions about issues of public interest (34%) or stand up for a disadvantaged population (29%). Even fewer journalists would like to control politics, business, and society (24%) and only a small minority says that they would like to influence the political agenda (14%). This low approval of some journalistic role items can be partly explained by the sample of journalists itself—it includes not only typical news journalists but also lifestyle, entertainment, and society journalists. Indeed, local journalists and journalists covering political issues are somewhat more interested in criticism, advocacy, and control (between 5 to 10% higher than the overall sample).

A third cluster of items consists of roles that do not seem to be core demands of journalism but clearly belong to a modern understanding of journalism. Again, these roles can be described theoretically in more than one dimension. The first dimension is labeled *lifestyle* journalism and includes items like "convey positive ideals" and "present new trends and convey new ideas." The second dimension is labeled *service* journalism and includes items such as "help people in their everyday lives" and "present one's own opinion to the public." The latter dimension should not be interpreted in the context of political debates but as orienting the audience and performing a kind of service in everyday matters. The third dimension reflects *entertainment* journalism and is represented by the item "provide entertainment and relaxation."

The findings indicate that *lifestyle journalism* is approved of by almost half of German journalists. About 44% of journalists say they want to present "new trends and ideas," while 40% say that they would like to convey "positive ideals." With respect to *service journalism*, German journalists are split, as Table 16.4 shows. Again, 44% of the journalists approve of "helping people in their everyday lives," but only 19% want to "present their own opinion to the public." Finally, more than one-third of journalists (37%) would like to "entertain and relax their audience."

Again, these results are partly due to the broad definition of journalism employed in this study, which includes lifestyle magazines and other entertainment media. We find that journalists who work for magazines or cover soft news are more likely to approve the service, lifestyle, and entertainment roles compared to the overall sample. It should be noted, though, that journalists in 2005 do not assign higher approval levels to any of these roles as compared to journalists in 1993 (Weischenberg, Löffelholz, & Scholl 1998; Weischenberg, Malik, & Scholl 2006).

German journalists also seem convinced that they can actually accomplish these roles in their work, as Table 16.4 indicates. While most seem to think that they can entertain (79%), help people in their everyday lives (69%), and also present their own opinions (67%), fewer journalists think that they can successfully convey new trends and ideas (58%) or positive ideals (43%). Obviously, it is more difficult to influence the audience with coverage in these two latter areas than it is in the areas of entertainment and service-oriented news.

Image of the Audience.   Media coverage is largely dependent on the audience's expectations, and journalists have more or less concrete and precise assumptions of what their audience demands of them. We measured the journalists' images of their audience by using a five-point semantic differential scale that includes nine items (politically interested/politically not interested; progressive/conservative; educated/uneducated; influential/not influential; information-oriented/not information-oriented; entertainment-oriented/not entertainment-oriented; rich/poor; young/old; and politically left/politically right).

Overall, journalists perceive their audience to be mostly educated, information-oriented, politically interested, and older, as Table 16.5 indicates. However, these perceptions differ by the type of journalist asked. Journalists working for online media (2.3) or news agencies (2.3) or those who cover political (2.5), cultural (2.5), or economic issues (2.6) assess the audience's political interests as being above average, whereas journalists working for magazines (3.1) or free periodicals (3.2) or those who cover entertainment and lifestyle (3.1) are convinced that their audience is not much interested in politics.

Table 16.5   Journalists' Images of Their Audience* ($N = =1,497–1,532$)

the audience is …		the audience is …
politically interested (1)	2.7	(5) politically not interested
progressive (1)	3.1	(5) conservative
educated (1)	2.5	(5) uneducated
influential (1)	3.0	(5) uninfluential
information oriented (1)	2.2	(5) not information oriented
entertainment oriented (1)	2.6	(5) not entertainment oriented
rich (1)	2.9	(5) poor
young (1)	3.3	(5) old
politically left (1)	3.0	(5) politically right

*Scores based on five-point scale with left expression = 1 and right expression = 5

Similar results were found for perceptions of the audience's information and entertainment needs. Journalists working for online media (1.8) or news agencies (1.9) were more likely than other journalists to think that their audience is interested in information. And while journalists covering lifestyle issues (2.3) or sports (2.3) think that entertainment is relevant to their audience, journalists working for online media (3.0) or news agencies (3.0) or those covering economics (3.4) are less likely to do so.

Reporting Practices.   If professional goals represent what journalists want to do, ethical considerations are indicators of what journalists are allowed to do. Ethics can be observed with the help of reporting practices because they are both specific with respect to certain cases and situations and general in terms of overall rules for "do's and don'ts."

Overall, the survey findings indicate that German journalists are very cautious when it comes to using "unusual reporting practices" in their jobs, as Table 16.6 shows. In fact, most of the interviewed journalists thought that "claiming to be somebody else" (60%), "paying people for confidential information (67%), "using hidden microphones or cameras" (67%), "badgering unwilling informants to get information" (87%), "agreeing to protect confidentiality and not doing so" (96%), and "making use of personal documents without permission" (92%), were not justified under any circumstance. On the other hand, the use of "confidential government documents without authorization" (16%), "getting employed in a firm or organization to gain inside information" (40%), and "pretending another opinion or attitude to inspire an informant's confidence" (44%) were rejected by fewer journalists as unacceptable reporting techniques.

As in 1993, we find a clear-cut distinction between methods German journalists assess as aggressive but legitimate in principal and methods considered unscrupulous and therefore illegitimate. However, in comparison to the data from the 1993 survey these findings document a significant loss of courage or ethical sensitivity depending on whether one regrets or appreciates this development (Weischenberg, Löffelholz, & Scholl 1998). As the justification of unusual reporting practices partly depends on the journalists' age—younger journalists tend to be more accepting of unusual reporting practices (correlations of .15 $< r <$ .25 for seven of the nine items)—the overall decrease of their justification in comparison with 1993 may depend on the overall growing age of journalists (from 37 years on average in 1993 to 41 years on average in 2005).

Table 16.6   Approval of Unusual Reporting Practices (*N* = 1,536)

Reporting Practices	Justify entirely/ mainly (in %)	Depends on circumstances (in %)	Do not justify mainly/entirely (in %)
Using confidential government documents without authorization	25	59	16
Getting employed in a firm or organization to gain inside information	11	49	40
Pretending another opinion to inspire an informant's confidence	11	45	44
Claiming to be somebody else	8	32	60
Paying people for confidential information	6	27	67
Using hidden microphones or cameras	5	28	67
Badgering unwilling informants to get information	1	12	87
Agreeing to protect confidentiality and not doing so	1	3	96
Making use of personal documents without permission	<1	8	92

Conclusions

German journalism is diminishing in size: The number of professional journalists has decreased from 54,000 in 1993 to 48,000 in 2005, which is due to a decrease in the number of professional freelancers but not of full-time staff. As the number of media organizations has increased and therefore the amount of journalistic media coverage, the journalists' daily or weekly workload has not increased simultaneously. Therefore we assume that non-professional or part-time freelancers fill in for them.

There are *stabilities* with respect to media types, as the number of online journalists is still small, and *changes* with respect to a decomposition of the traditional editorial departments (politics, business, sports, culture, etc.) in favor of a more centralized news desk structure, as a considerable number of journalists are not assigned to a specific department or beat.

German journalists have shifted the center of their job activities slightly from journalistic core activities (such as information gathering) to additional tasks (such as administrative or technical tasks). It is not surprising that only half of them are satisfied with the time available for investigation, with the daily workload, with job security, or with their income. On the other hand, most of them are satisfied with their independence in self-organizing their daily work or the relationship with their colleagues. This finding corresponds with journalists' perception of their autonomy: the impact of superiors or colleagues on the journalists' daily work outranks external forces (such as the impact of politicians, business, public relations, etc.).

Although the media have changed dramatically since the 1990s, we do not observe any dramatic shifts in journalists' professional attitudes and performances. The vast majority of journalists still approve of the role of objective reporting. A slight decrease of advocacy journalism can be observed. However, in addition to the subtle transformation *in time*, there are differences *between* various segments of journalism. Advocacy journalism can be found primarily in political media and political beats, whereas lifestyle journalism is preferred by journalists working for magazines.

The same pattern is true for the assessment of unusual reporting practices and for the journalists' image of their audience: There is a subtle decrease of approval for aggressive or unscrupulous methods between 1993 and 2005 and a difference with respect to age—younger journalists seem to be a bit more courageous. With respect to different segments of journalism, the image of the audiences varies: Journalists working for media with more political coverage, for example, ascribe a higher amount of political interest to their audience.

Taking all the results together we observe a decrease of professionalism in the *structure* of German journalism (regarding the number of journalists and non-professional freelancers) but a stabilization regarding the *function* of journalism for society (role perceptions and perceived autonomy).

References

Altmeppen, Klaus-Dieter. 1999. *Redaktionen als Koordinationszentren: Beobachtungen journalistischen Handelns* [Newsrooms as centres of coordination: Observing journalists' actions]. Opladen/Wiesbaden: Westdeutscher Verlag.

Blöbaum, Bernd. 2008. Wandel redaktioneller Strukturen und Entscheidungsprozesse [Change of newsroom structures and the processes of decision-making]. In *Seismographische Funktion von Öffentlichkeit im Wandel* [The seismographic function of a changing public sphere], edited by Heinz Bonfadelli, Kurt Imhof, Roger Blum, and Otfried Jarren, pp. 119–129. Wiesbaden: VS Verlag für Sozialwissenschaften.

Blöbaum, Bernd. 2009. Journalistic media content in transformation. Paper presented at the 59th Annual convention of the International Communication Association (ICA) on "Keywords in Communication," Chicago.

Donsbach, Wolfgang, and Thomas E. Patterson. 2004. Political news journalists: Partisanship, professionalism, and political roles in five countries. In *Comparing political communication: Theories, cases, and challenges*, edited by Frank Esser and Barbara Pfetsch, pp. 251–270. New York: Cambridge University Press.

Esser, Frank. 1998. *Die Kräfte hinter den Schlagzeilen: Englischer und deutscher Journalismus im Vergleich* [Powers behind the headlines: Comparing English and German journalism]. Freiburg/München: Alber.

Görke, Alexander and Armin Scholl. 2006. Niklas Luhmann's theory of social systems and journalism research. *Journalism Studies* 7(4): 644–655.

Hanitzsch, Thomas. 2008. Comparing journalism across cultural boundaries: State of the art, strategies, problems, and solutions. In *Global journalism research. Theories, methods, findings, future*, edited by Martin Löffelholz and David Weaver, pp. 93–105. Malden, MA: Blackwell.

Hanitzsch, Thomas. 2009. Comparative journalism studies. In *Handbook of Journalism Studies*, edited by Karin Wahl-Jørgensen and Thomas Hanitzsch, pp. 413–427. London: Routledge.

Hardt, Hanno. 1979. *Social theories of the press: Early German and American perspectives*. Beverly Hills, CA: Sage.

Johnstone, John W. C., Edward Slawski and William Bowman. 1976. *The news people. A sociological portrait of the American journalists and their work*. Urbana: University of Illinois Press.

Kepplinger, Hans Mathias. (Ed.). 1979. *Angepaßte Außenseiter: Was Journalisten denken und wie sie arbeiten* [Conformist outsiders: What journalists think and how they do their job]. Freiburg/München: Alber.

Köcher, Renate. 1986. Bloodhounds or missionaries: Role definitions of German and British journalists. *European Journal of Communication* 1(1): 43–64.

Malik, Maja. 2005. Heterogenität und Repräsentativität: Zur Konzeption von Grundgesamtheit und Stichprobe der Studie "Journalismus in Deutschland II." [Heterogeneity and representativeness: Population and sampling procedure in the study "Journalism in Germany II"]. In *Auswahlverfahren in der Kommunikationswissenschaft* [Sampling methods in communication science], edited by Volker Gehrau, Benjamin Fretwurst, Birgit Krause, and Gregor Daschmann, pp. 183–202. Köln: Halem.

Neuberger, Christoph. 2009. Internet, Journalismus und Öffentlichkeit: Analyse des Medienumbruchs [Internet, journalism and the public sphere: Analyzing media changes]. In *Journalismus im Internet: Profession—Partizipation—Technisierung* [Journalism in the Internet: Profession—participation—technologization], edited by Christoph Neuberger, Christian Nuernbergk, and Melanie Rischke, pp. 19–105. Wiesbaden: VS Verlag für Sozialwissenschaften.

Neuberger, Christoph, Christian Nuernbergk, and Melanie Rischke. 2009. Journalismus neu vermessen: Die Grundgesamtheit journalistischer Internetangebote—Methode und Ergebnisse [Journalism realigned: The universe of journalistic coverage on the internet—method and results]. In *Journalismus im Internet: Profession–Partizipation—Technisierung* [Journalism on the internet: Profession—participation—technological development], edited by Christoph Neuberger, Christian Nuernbergk, and Melanie Rischke, pp. 197–230. Wiesbaden: VS Verlag für Sozialwissenschaften.

Quandt, Thorsten. 2005. *Journalisten im Netz: Eine Untersuchung journalistischen Handelns in Online-Redaktionen* [Journalists on the Web: Observing journalists' actions in online newsrooms]. Wiesbaden: VS Verlag für Sozialwissenschaften.

Quandt, Thorsten, Martin Löffelholz, David Weaver, Thomas Hanitzsch, and Klaus-Dieter Altmeppen. 2006. American and German online journalists at the beginning of the 21st century: A bi-national survey. *Journalism Studies* 17(2): 171–186.

Rühl, Manfred. 1969. *Die Zeitungsredaktion als organisiertes soziales System* [The newsroom as an organized social system]. Bielefeld: Bertelsmann Universitätsverlag.

Rühl, Manfred. 2008. Journalism in a globalizing world society. In *Global journalism research: Theories, methods, findings, future*, edited by Martin Löffelholz and David Weaver, pp. 28–38. Malden, MA: Blackwell.

Scholl, Armin. 1996. Sampling journalists. *Communications: The European Journal* 21(3): 331–343.

Scholl, Armin, and Siegfried Weischenberg. 1998. *Journalismus in der Gesellschaft: Theorie, Methodologie und Empirie* [Journalism in society: Theory, methodology, and empirical results]. Opladen, Wiesbaden: Westdeutscher Verlag.

Schönbach, Klaus, Dieter Stürzebecher, and Beate Schneider. 1998. German Journalists in the Early 1990s: East and West. In *The Global Journalist: News People around the World*, edited by David H. Weaver, pp. 213–227. Cresskill, NJ: Hampton Press.

Shoemaker, Pamela J., and Stephen D. Reese. 1996. *Mediating the Message: Theories of Influence on Mass Media Content* (2nd ed.). White Plain, NY: Longman.

Weaver, David H. (Ed.). 1998. *The global journalist: News people around the world*. Cresskill NJ: Hampton Press.

Weaver, David, and G. Cleveland Wilhoit. 1986. *The American journalist: A portrait of U.S. news people and their work*. Bloomington, IN: Indiana University Press.

Weaver, David, and G. Cleveland Wilhoit. 1996. *The American journalist in the 1990s: U.S. news people at the end of an era*. Mahwah, NJ: Erlbaum.

Weischenberg, Siegfried. 2012. *Max Weber und die Entzauberung der Medienwelt: Theorien und Quereleneine andere Fachgeschichte* [Max Weber and the disenchantment of the media world: Theories and quarrels—an alternative history of the field]. Weisbaded: Springer VS.

Weischenberg, Siegfried, Martin Löffelholz, and Armin Scholl. 1998. Journalism in Germany. In *The global journalist: News people around the world*, edited by David H. Weaver, pp. 229–256. Cresskill, NJ: Hampton Press.

Weischenberg, Siegfried, and Maja Malik. 2008. Journalism research in Germany: Evolution and central research interests. In *Global journalism research: Theories, methods, findings, future*, edited by Martin Löffelholz and David Weaver, pp. 158–171. Malden, MA: Blackwell.

Weischenberg, Siegfried, Maja Malik, and Armin Scholl. 2006. *Souffleure der Mediengesellschaft: Report über die Journalisten in Deutschland* [Prompters of media society: Report on the journalists in Germany]. Konstanz: UVK.

Weiß, Hans-Jürgen, Wolfgang Frantz, Georg Räder, and Heinz Uekermann. 1977. *Schlußbericht Synopse Journalismus als Beruf: Forschungssynopse* [Final report on the synopsis: Journalism as a profession]. Unpublished report, Munich, Germany.

17 British Journalists

Karen Sanders and Mark Hanna

Throughout the 20th century Britain developed a news industry that, generally speaking, flourished. In the early 21st century, the country's news agenda continues to be set mainly by national newspapers, which are more highly competitive, in terms of breaking news "exclusives" and readership figures, and more truly "national" as a media sector, than their counterparts in other large European countries and in the United States (Tunstall 1996: 2–3, 7). They cater to the entirety of the British media market, distributed in the four main constituent nations of England, Scotland, Wales, and Northern Ireland that comprise the United Kingdom of Great Britain and Northern Ireland, to give the country its official title, with a combined population of 61.8 million (Office for National Statistics 2010).

Whereas Britain's newspaper industry is not subject to statutory regulation (except in some aspects of anti-monopoly law), the other major structural characteristic of Britain's news culture is a broadcast industry legally bound to be accurate and impartial in its journalism, to comply with ethical codes, and to fulfill a number of other public service commitments, including provision of news as a contribution to democratic debate, in the context of Britain's centuries-old parliamentary system. As we explain below, the British Broadcasting Corporation (BBC) dominates the landscape of the British broadcast industry. Since its foundation, having endured periods of fierce criticism by each of the main political parties—Labour and Conservative, particularly when each was in government—the BBC has built a reputation for accuracy, and now enjoys a wide political consensus that it should continue to exist in, broadly speaking, its current, publicly funded form. In opinion polls, the British public has consistently expressed a greater trust in the BBC's journalists regarding the capacity to "tell the truth" than they have in the journalists of national newspapers (Barnett 2008: 7–8).

Newspapers, free to be partisan in their viewpoints, remain the crucible for the highly competitive reporting traditions that have shaped British journalism. From the left-liberal Guardian, owned by the independent Scott Trust, to the highly partisan and populist Sun, part of Rupert Murdoch's News International, newspapers at a national and regional level have sought to maintain maximum freedom of the press. At the best of times, this produces challenging and rigorous reporting; at the worst of times, reporting is scurrilous and invasive and newsgathering techniques are frequently condemned as immoral or illegal. Despite circulation decline, Britain continues to have one of the highest levels of newspaper readership in the world (Ofcom 2007a).

In the first edition of The Global Journalist, Henningham and Delano (1998: 155–159) noted that British news journalists, compared with journalists in the United States and Australia, were "far more 'gung ho' in ethical areas" and "less concerned with ethical niceties." This culture, they suggested, arose from the strongly competitive newsgathering environment in Britain and from Britain's relatively late introduction of professional education in journalism. Henningham and Delano (1998: 153, 160) also found there was an "adversarial mindset" in the British journalism workforce which, they suggested, arose from the lack of a supportive legal environment (compared with the freedoms set out in the U.S. First Amendment).

For some commentators, British journalism's more "gung ho" culture—as exhibited in particular by its national newspaper industry—may be a social price worth paying to preserve democratic freedoms. Speaking to parliamentarians, The Guardian editor Alan Rusbridger stated his view that "it is good in Britain that you have a highly-regulated BBC at the heart of the broadcasting industry, and a ... broadcasting industry which can be set against the more wild west of the printed word. That tension is good" (House of Lords Select Committee on Communications [HLCC] 2008: 46).

The Press Complaints Commission (PCC), the ethical watchdog of Britain's newspaper and magazine industries, announced in its 2007 review that, for the first time, it had received more complaints referring to articles published online than those published in print form. In both 2007 and 2008, it received a record number of complaints, facilitated by the use of email, and made a record number of rulings about intrusion into privacy (Press Complaints Commission 2008, 2009). These statistics illustrate that the British journalism workforce, while increasingly publishing in "new media" platforms, retains a traditional capacity to enrage, offend, and stir up controversy—traits particularly associated with those working for the mass-circulation national newspapers, as illustrated by the closing of the *News of the World*.

In the first decade of the 21st century, British media analysts, educators, and journalists debated developments such as the blogosphere, social media, and user-generated content (UGC) and their effect on the nature of journalism itself (see, for example, Newman 2009). From 2007, mainstream media began to take more seriously the new media phenomena; they launched training and awareness courses, appointed social media editors, and began using Twitter both to monitor events and to attract readers. News editors discovered through events such as the 2004 Asian Tsunami and the 2009 Iranian election protests that breaking news was no longer a salaried journalist's prerogative (Newman 2009).

In this chapter we provide a sketch of the British journalism landscape, and a portrait of the British journalistic workforce, detailing where journalists work, their changing educational background, and some key aspects of their journalistic careers. Finally, we briefly consider some relevant characteristics of British journalism students, the group from which much of the next generation of British journalists will be drawn, and speculate about their possible impact on British journalistic culture.

The British Journalism Landscape

The BBC dominates the British media landscape with a mission defined by one of its former director generals as being to "make the good popular and the popular good" (cited in Thompson 2002). It has remained a benchmark for high standards in British journalism notwithstanding the intensified recent debates about the future of public service broadcasting or of its funding mechanism, and about the BBC's unfair competitive position or the quality and impartiality of its journalism.

The BBC has eight national TV channels, 10 national radio stations, 40 local radio stations and, in BBC Online, a national and worldwide Internet platform. The vast majority of BBC journalists work in Britain. The BBC has for some years been reducing its workforce, partly because the funding agreement it reached with the Labour government was smaller than expected (BBC 2005, 2007, 2010a; BBC Trust 2009b; Tryhorn 2009). In 2007 it employed 7,200 journalists, including those in 40 news bureaus around the globe. That year it announced plans to cut its total journalism workforce by 400 (HLSCC 2008). Nevertheless, the BBC, founded by Royal Charter in 1927 (BBC 2010b), continues to draw on huge resources, compared to those of its competitors, because it is primarily funded by a license fee—a form of annual tax—levied on every British household which owns a television set. The fee per household in 2009 was £142.50 (approx. U.S.$214.75), which equates to a household tax of around 39 pence (approx. U.S.59 cents) per day (BBC Trust 2009a). In the 2008–2009 financial year the BBC spent £3.4 billion (approx. U.S.$5.1 billion) on making programs and other activities, and continued to dominate other broadcasters nationally as regards audience reach in TV viewing and radio listening (BBC Trust 2009a). In 2008–2009, BBC News Online reached around 10 million "unique users" in Britain each week (BBC Trust 2009a: 73). The international BBC World News television service attracted 74 million viewers globally a week (BBC Trust 2009a). The BBC World Service, which had 177 million radio listeners globally in 2008–2009, was funded separately by a grant administered by the British Government, but will be funded within the license fee system from 2014 (Foreign and Commonweatlh Service 2010).

Most British media organizations employing journalists are, with the obvious exception of the BBC, commercial enterprises funded by advertising and consumer-derived revenue. As in other nations, in Britain their revenue streams were hit hard by the economic slump that began in 2007 and by structural changes we mention below. Under the regulation system, four British national commercial TV networks have some "public service broadcaster" (PSB) obligations regarding news provision. These broadcasters, which include ITV1, Five, and Channel 4, saw net advertising revenue decrease 8% in 2008 to £2.2 billion (approx. U.S.$3.3 billion) (Ofcom 2009).

Britain has around 340 commercial radio stations, almost all local. Most have some regulatory PSB obligation to provide news. In 2009, the chief executive of RadioCentre, the body that represents this industry, said that revenues for 2009 were projected to be down by 11%, after an 8% fall in 2008, and up to 50 of these stations could "go bust" within two years (House of Commons Select Committee for Culture, Media and Sport 2010). This remark should be taken in the context that radio companies, and regional and local newspaper groups, were lobbying for relaxation of anti-monopoly law to allow cross-media "consolidation" of ownership.

Britain has 10 daily newspapers indisputably defined as national as well as eight Sunday nationals. The number of British adults reading at least one national daily newspaper on an average day fell by 19%, from 26.7 million in 1992 to 21.7 million in 2006. The total average daily circulation of these national daily newspapers in 2009 was around 11 million, a decrease of 2 million since 1995, although some titles have in recent years gained circulation, including the Daily Mail, the Times, and the Financial Times (Currah 2009). Data from mid-2010 showed that all of the British national papers had lost circulation in the previous 12 months, with some suffering a severe drop in sales (Ponsford 2010). The leading British newspaper Web sites in 2009 were those produced by the Guardian and the Daily Telegraph, each attracting over four million unique British visitors every month (Ofcom 2009).

British newspapers' advertising revenue fell by 10% in 2008, accelerating a decline that began in 2004 (Ofcom 2009). Advertising revenue for regional and local newspapers fell by 15.8% in 2008, and was forecast to fall by 28% in 2009 (House of Commons Select Committee for Culture, Media and Sport 2010; Ofcom 2009). But despite the economic difficulties, there continues to be a significant regional and local newspaper market of 1,269 newspapers that, according to its trade body, are read in print by more than 40 million adults (69% of Britain's population) and are accessed online by more than 37 million users (Newspaper Society 2010).

The magazine sector in Britain includes more than 3,000 consumer magazines and almost 5,000 business magazines (Periodicals Publishers Association [PPA] 2009). Our survey of British journalism students (see below) showed that shortly before graduation, 29% described the magazine sector as their career goal, 19% national newspapers, 16% television, 9% radio, and 4% the regional and local press (Hanna & Sanders 2007). The magazine sector, too, is adjusting to new economic realities. According to the Periodical Publishing Association (PPA), for the first six months of 2009 the total average circulation for all magazines fell to 657.5 million compared to 683.6 million in the same period in 2008 (PPA 2009), and advertising revenue for British magazines fell by 10% in 2008 (Ofcom 2009).

By early 2010 the economic future of journalism in Britain appeared difficult in general, except for journalism produced by the publicly funded BBC. It seems that at least 3,500 editorial/journalism jobs have been lost in Britain since 2006 in television, radio, and in the regional and local newspaper sector (Newspaper Society 2008, 2009; The Sector Skills Council for Creative Media [Skillset] 2004–2009), as a result of the economic downturn. The loss of journalism jobs was also due to the longer-term effect of structural changes on media organizations including the migration of advertising to the Internet; continuing decline in national newspaper readership; and audience fragmentation, a factor in the decline of viewing of channels which are the main providers of TV news (HLSCC 2008; Ofcom 2009; Printing Industry Research Association [PIRA International] 2002). Developments such as aggregated news sites and news distribution through social networks began to impact on the way news is consumed.

By 2009, the business model underpinning the news industry, the danger of a "deficit" in news provision, and therefore a deficit in the workings of democracy, as well as journalistic identity itself had become subjects of keen debate in Britain, as in other countries (see, for example, Currah 2009; Journalism 2009; Journalism Studies 2010; Newman 2009; Ofcom 2007a, 2007b).

Previous Studies of British Journalists

Since Henningham and Delano's 1995 survey (1998), there has been only one systematic survey of the British journalism workforce, carried out in 2001 by the Journalism Training Forum (2002). This was an ad hoc body, backed by industry and editors' organizations, which sought to assess the composition of the nation's journalism workforce and whether it was being equipped with the skills it needed. Its research covered quite different ground to the 1995 survey omitting, for example, a study of perceptions of news media roles or views of ethical practices.

In this chapter we supplement the Forum's findings with more recent data from a range of industry and government sources, necessary to outline changes in the British media industries since 2001. For example, the Forum study reported that work patterns suggested a relatively stable profession and referred to industry forecasts that an additional 20,000 jobs for journalists would be created by 2010 (Journalism Training Forum 2002). It may be that thousands of such additional jobs were created—as we explain below; however, discerning changes in the size of Britain's journalism workforce is not a straightforward task.

How Many British Journalists Are There?

Establishing the size of the British journalistic workforce is one of the key challenges for those seeking to survey it. There is no generally accepted definition of what defines a journalist, nor does any central organization in Britain hold all the relevant data. Therefore, trends in the size and composition of this workforce by media sector are not easily identified.

Estimates made by Henningham and Delano (1998) in their 1995 survey of the British newspaper and news broadcasting sectors, and by Delano (2001) from a second survey completed in April 1997 on magazine journalists and "non-news" journalists in the British broadcast sector, suggest that during the period 1995 to 1997 there was a total of around 31,596 British journalists. The Forum study, on the other hand, estimated that during 2001 Britain had a much higher total number of journalists, ranging between 60,000 and 70,000. Around 50,000 to 60,000 journalists based on the Forum sample claimed to work in the publishing sector (i.e., newspaper and magazine) and 10,000 in broadcast journalism (Journalism Training Forum 2002).

It seems unlikely that the British journalism workforce would have nearly doubled in size between 1995–1997 and 2001, and therefore it is probable that Henningham and Delano underestimated its size or that the Forum survey over-estimated it. However, it should be kept in mind that there were methodological differences between these surveys (Frith & Meech 2007) as well as differences in their scope and categorization. For example, respondents in the Forum survey included journalists who defined themselves as working in the book publishing sector (1% of the respondents) and some who said they were in the public relations sector (1%).

Henningham and Delano's survey did not cover either of these two sectors. Henningham and Delano had a response rate of 81% from the 1995 fieldwork (1998), and Delano had an 84% response rate from the subsequent survey of magazine and non-news broadcast journalists (2001). Moreover, Henningham and Delano gathered data through telephone interviews. The Forum survey, on the other hand, was based on self-completion questionnaires, of which 10,737 were sent out by post, and the questionnaire was also made electronically available on a Web site and through distribution by email, producing a return of 1,238 valid questionnaires.

As regards the magazine sector, in 1997 Delano estimated that 20% of British journalists worked for business, professional, trade, or technical publications, and 10% for entertainment or consumer magazines (2001: 50). Using a similar categorization for its 2001 data, the Forum study concluded that 15% worked for business magazines, 8% for consumer leisure magazines, and 2% for other types of magazine (Journalism Training Forum 2002).

So far as can be established from the limited data available, in the 10 or so years to 2008, journalism employment probably grew overall for some of this period in television, radio, and the regional and local newspaper sector (Newspaper Society 2008, 2009; Skillset 2004–2009). In 2007 or early 2008 several national newspaper editors stated that their journalism workforces were the same size or larger than they had been 10 years previously (HLSCC 2008; Preston 2008).

The National Union of Journalists' (NUJ) president stated, in late 2007, that compared to the 20 previous years, there were more journalists overall with substantial growth in the broadcasting and magazine sectors, but that by late 2007 some 2,000 media editorial jobs had been lost in the previous 3 years (HLSCC 2008). By May 2009 the NUJ had recorded more than 1,500 job losses in newspapers in the previous 12 months (House of Commons Culture, Media and Sport Select Committee 2010). In 2010 there was a further blow when the Trinity Mirror group, the owner of three national newspapers, announced that 200 editorial staff (25% of these papers' journalists) were to be made redundant (Greenslade 2010). Data from the creative industries' census (Skillset 2004–2009, 2010) suggests that 1,750 journalism jobs in the TV and radio sector, 15% of the total, were lost from 2006 to 2009.

General Characteristics of British Journalists

Age and Gender. The Forum survey found that the majority of the British journalistic workforce was younger than 34, with 55% falling into this age bracket. In findings similar to those in Henningham and Delano's 1995 fieldwork, the Forum survey recorded that national newspapers in 2001 had a higher proportion of older journalists, while regional and local newspapers and radio had a higher proportion of young people under 25 years, 25% and 18% respectively.

A comparison of the Henningham and Delano data from 1995 to 1997 (Delano 2001) with the data from 2001 (Journalism Training Forum 2002) shows that during this relatively short time period women achieved numerical parity with men in the British journalism workforce.

Delano (2001) reported from the data collected in 1995 to 1997 that nearly 40% of British journalists were women. The Forum study found in 2001 that 49% were women, with a greater proportion of females among the younger journalists (see Table 17.1). With regard to national, regional, and local newspapers, Delano (2001) found that in 1995 only 23% of their journalists were women, while the Forum study found in 2001 that 45% of journalists in these media outlets were women.

British magazine journalism has long been a bastion of female employment. Delano (2001) reported that the female majority in this sector was 56%, and the Forum study stated it to be 55%. Delano (2001) found that 41% of journalists in television and radio were women. The Forum research reported that 54% of television journalists and 49% of radio journalists were women. The 2009 census of journalists in the television and radio sectors conducted by Skillset (2010) found that 46% of journalists were women.

Britain's Labour Force Survey (LFS) annual data for the time period between 2001 and 2009 provide broad corroboration of this increasing female representation among British journalists, and suggest that in some of these years, females outnumbered males (Office for National Statistics. 2009). Although the statistically "rounded" nature of LFS data prevents precise calculation of the male/female ratio in the journalism workforce in 2001—which could be expected to include most of the journalist respondents—the ratio was around 59% male and 41% female, and by 2009 it was 52% male and 47% female.

We can surmise that a factor in progress toward numerical gender equality in the journalism workforce was the increase in journalism education programs at British universities (see Table

Table 17.1　Age Distribution of Journalists in 2001 (in %)

Age	All	Men	Women
19–21	2	2	3
22–24	12	10	14
25–29	23	19	26
30–34	18	15	21
35–39	14	13	14
40–49	19	23	14
50–59	11	15	6
60+	2	3	2
N	1,220	621	598

Source: Journalism Training Forum 2002.

17.3). British undergraduate (bachelor) journalism programs have consistently enrolled more females than males since they began to develop within the university sector from 1994 (Hanna & Sanders 2007). We reported in 2007 that the gender disparity within these journalism programs peaked in 2001–2002, with 60% female compared to 40% male, and by 2004–2005 this ratio was 57% female and 43% male (Hanna & Sanders 2007).

Socio-Economic Background.   By 1995 journalism was already an occupation dominated by workers from a middle-class background, as indexed by parental occupation, with 45% from homes whose parents held professional or managerial positions (Henningham & Delano 1998). This trend was confirmed by the Forum 2001 data that showed that 68% of new entrants to journalism had a parent who was from a professional occupation, or who was a manager or senior official; whereas only 24% of Britain's employed population (i.e., all occupations) held jobs in these categories (Journalism Training Forum 2002). A survey has shown that at a time when only around 37% of the British working population (all occupations) could be deemed to fall into either "professional" and "managerial or technical" categories, around 67% of journalism undergraduates and 81% of journalism postgraduates were from such family backgrounds (Hanna & Sanders 2009).

In some quarters there is concern that Britain journalists are increasingly likely to be from higher socio-economic classes (Wilby 2008). Factors in this trend are the cost of "pre-entry" education and skills training, and the practice of some media employers of requiring unpaid internships that may last several months. These requirements discriminate against those who cannot draw on parental financial support, and the low wages in journalism deter some young people whose families cannot help by funding them in the early stages of their careers (Hanna & Sanders 2009; Journalism Training Forum 2002; Sutton Trust 2006).

Changes to student funding and support in Britain since the 1990s have exacerbated the problem of debt for all those graduating from universities. The Forum survey found that 68% of new entrants to journalism had debts ranging from £300 (U.S.$452) to £25,000 (U.S.$37,600), with a median value of £4,750 (U.S.$7,156) against an average debt for all students of £7,400 (U.S.$11,149) (in 2008 prices) (Bolton 2009; Journalism Training Forum 2002). By 2007, the average debt for all graduating students was around £12,500 (U.S.$18,833) (Nat West 2007).

Marital Status and Ethnicity.   In 2001, 59% of journalists were married or in a long-term relationship, compared to 72% who were married or living with a partner in 1995, a reflection of wider social trends, and in 2001 41% journalists were single, widowed, or divorced and 77% had no dependent children (Henningham & Delano 1998; Journalism Training Forum 2002).

Ninety-six percent of respondents to the 2001 Forum survey were white, a figure 2% higher than the figure at that time for the total British population (Journalism Training Forum 2002). The under-representation of ethnic minority groups can be seen as starker when it is considered that much of the journalism industry is based in London. For example, Skillset (2004–2009) found in its 2006 census that 11% of broadcast journalists were from ethnic minorities, yet in London at that time around 24% of the working population (all occupations) was from ethnic minorities. In 2003–2004, 14% of British university students enrolling in journalism postgraduate programs and 9% enrolling in journalism undergraduate programs classed themselves in an ethnic minority or as being of mixed ethnicity (HESA 2003–2004).

Table 17.2   Breakdown of Job Titles Self-Ascribed by Journalists (in %)

Roles	%
Writers/reporters (newspapers/magazines)	35
Editorial management (editor, chief sub-editor, exec. producer)	28
Production (sub-editor, producer)	16
Broadcast reporters	13
Section heads (e.g. sports editor)	6
General management (managing director, station manager)	1
Other	2
Total	100%

Source: Journalism Training Forum 2002: 16 (Percentages rounded).

Distribution of Journalists by Job Title

The Forum survey questionnaire asked "What job title do you normally use to describe what you do?" The responses were grouped into six broad categories that reflected levels of seniority and were further analyzed by age and gender (see Table 17.2).

Those classifying themselves as writers/reporters together represented 48% of the total sample. This category was subdivided to show those working for newspapers and magazines and those working in the broadcast sector. The first group provided the largest number of journalists: 35% described themselves as newspaper/magazine writers and reporters with similar numbers of men—34% of the male sample; and women, 37% of the female sample (Journalism Training Forum 2002). This category also had the greatest proportion of journalists under the age of 25, 63% of the total sample.

Respondents whose job titles were classified as placing them in editorial management or as section heads made up 34% of the total sample. Only 13% of them were below the age of 25, while 40% of those between the age of 30 to 39, 44% of those between the age of 40 to 49, and 41% of those aged 50 or over had job titles falling into these categories (Journalism Training Forum 2002). The proportion of total men and women working as section heads was identical (6%), whereas 31% of men worked in editorial management compared to 25% of women. The Forum report concluded from this that (2002: 17): "There does not appear to be much evidence that women are not progressing to senior roles but there are more men than women in editorial management roles." Evidence cited earlier about the larger proportion of women enrolling on journalism courses since 1994 gives ground for hope that this will change. As more women make a career in journalism and experience, correlated to age, begins to count in their favor, we would expect to see greater numbers of women in editorial management.

Education and Qualifications

In 1995, 49% of British news journalists surveyed had a bachelor's degree of some kind, but only around 1% had a bachelor's degree in journalism, and around 9% had a postgraduate diploma in journalism awarded by a university or within a company or elsewhere (Delano 2001; Delano & Henningham 1995). University education continued to expand in Britain, and the Forum survey (Skillset 2006) found in 2001 that 7% of British journalists had an undergraduate degree in journalism, 62% an undergraduate degree in another subject, 27% had a postgraduate qualification of

Table 17.3   British Domiciled Students Enrolled Full-time at British
Universities in Journalism Programs

Academic Year	Undergraduates (first year)	Postgraduates
1995–1996	520	319
1996–1997	510	326
1997–1998	570	405
1998–1999	615	395
1999–1900	735	490
2000–2001	1,005	600
2001–2002	1,315	630
2002–2003	1,475	745
2003–2004	1,605	830
2004–2005	2,035	815
2005–2006	2,225	910
2006-2007	2,245	995
2007-2008	2,425	990

Source: Higher Education Statistics Agency (HESA 1997–2009) data shown is for undergraduate first year, full-time first degree students, and full-time postgraduates (who
include a small proportion of "research degree" students).

some kind in journalism, and 13% a postgraduate qualification in another subject. This increase in
the number of journalists with degrees in journalism can be expected to continue, following the
rapid expansion of journalism education as a subject field in British universities (Hanna & Sanders
2007, 2009).

Some journalism bachelor's degree programs in Britain have vocational education in at least
50% of their content (e.g., journalism news-writing and broadcast skills), and this proportion
(compared to that given to academic modules) is likely to be higher in most journalism postgraduate programs.

Some British universities are accredited by the national journalism training bodies: the
National Council for the Training of Journalists (NCTJ), the Broadcast Journalism Training Council (BJTC), and the Periodicals Training Council (PTC). By 2010, for example, 22 universities, as
well as a number of other educational institutes, were listed as having NCTJ accreditation for at
least one program (NCTJ 2010).

In 1995, 40% of news journalists held an NCTJ qualification (Delano & Henningham 1995).
In 2001, the Journalism Training Forum survey found that 58% of British journalists held a journalism training body qualification: three-quarters of those working on regional newspapers held
a qualification of this kind compared to 42% of those working in magazines (2002). Eighty-two
percent of all respondents considered that these qualifications represented relevant or very relevant skills training. A large proportion of respondents received their qualification from the NCTJ,
which accounted for 64% of accredited courses taken.

Career Training and Development

The Forum study had a particular focus on issues related to "post-entry" career training and
development (Journalism Training Forum 2002). It found in 2001 that 24% of British journalists

had not undertaken any kind of career training in the previous year. Of those that had, 85% found the learning activity useful, and 60% of all respondents considered that there were new or additional skills they needed to acquire to improve their work. Television journalists were most likely to make this claim (72%) and national newspaper journalists least likely to say this (50%). The most commonly mentioned areas in which new skills were thought necessary were information technologies, new media, media law, and shorthand writing. A subsequent survey found that the most common type of training provided by employers for career entrants in print and broadcast journalism sectors was in media law (Spilsbury Research 2006), a reflection of the fact that the British legal environment for the media (e.g., law relating to libel and contempt of court) is more restrictive (and therefore more financially punitive) than that of many other democracies.

Job Satisfaction

Most journalists who responded in 2001 declared that like most of their 1995 counterparts (Henningham & Delano 1998), they were content with their jobs. On a scale of 1 to 10 with 1 being "agree completely" and 10 "disagree completely," journalists were asked whether they agreed with the statement that "journalism is a job I enjoy doing." Seventy-eight percent responded between 1 and 2 and only 5% between 9 and 10. A majority also agreed with the statement that "journalism has lived up to my aspirations as a job" and that they intended to stay working in journalism (Journalism Training Forum 2002; see also Frith & Meech 2007).

Rewards and Conditions

The Forum survey found that the average working week for British journalists in 2001 was 41.6 hours as compared to 35 hours as an average for all occupations. Eighty-five percent of respondents considered these hours to be reasonable. Journalists were more divided about salary levels, with 50% expressing satisfaction with their salary and 48% expressing dissatisfaction. The median annual salary among respondents to the Forum survey (2002) was £22,500 (approx. U.S.$33,900). Salary levels varied largely in relation to sector (television and national newspaper journalists were paid the most and regional journalists the least) and length of experience.

The National Union of Journalists (NUJ 2010) says research has shown that nearly half of all British journalists earn less than the nation's average wage; that 80% cannot afford the average house mortgage; and that journalists' starting rates are at least £7,000 (U.S.$10,547) less than the median starting salary for graduates. NUJ data from 2005 showed that the starting annual salary for a trainee reporter with a weekly or daily newspaper outside London could be as low as £12,000 (U.S.$18,080), rising to around £17,000 (U.S.$25,613) after two years, and that the average salary for a magazine trainee reporter in or around London was £19,750 (U.S.$29,757) for staff employed for less than one year (2005a, 2005b). The Prospect careers Web site (2010) cited data from 2009 that a journalist's starting salary could still be around £12,000 (U.S.$18,080)—compared to an average 2008 graduate starting salary of £24,048 (U.S.$36,233)—but that the average salary of journalists with five to nine years of experience was between £21,700 (U.S.$32,695) and £35,000 (U.S.$52,735).

There is some evidence that working conditions have deteriorated in some newsrooms. The NUJ (2007), which in 2008 had around 28,000 full members, produced a report stating that three-quarters of journalists surveyed said that the introduction of new media technology had brought increased workloads, and in some cases rising stress and longer hours. Also, Lewis,

Williams, and Franklin (2008), in a study of journalism produced by national media in Britain, reported that journalists' reliance on public relations material and news agency sources was extensive, and concluded that most journalists operate under economic, institutional, and organizational restraints which required them to draft and process too many stories to be able to operate with freedom and independence.

Conclusions

Henningham and Delano (1998) produced valuable data on British journalists' views on news media roles and on the ethics of various reporting practices, using questionnaire formats pioneered in the United States in 1971 by Johnstone, Slawski, and Bowman (1976) and in comparative research by Donsbach (1983) and Kocher (1986). The Forum fieldwork in 2001 did not have such a focus, and nor has any subsequent survey of working British journalists. However, our recent studies of British journalism students' views and attitudes give us reason to believe that it is possible to discern some elements of the "gung ho," highly competitive, adversarial traits in British journalism culture that have been recorded by others (see Ball, Hanna, & Sanders 2006; Hanna & Sanders 2007, 2008, 2009; Henningham & Delano 1998).

But our surveys of postgraduate students (Hanna & Sanders 2008, 2009) and undergraduates (Hanna & Sanders 2009, 2010) also found that, compared to the generation of British journalists surveyed in 1995, British journalism students ascribed much less importance to adversarial roles, and to a varying extent less importance to other watchdog-type roles, and to the role that journalists should "concentrate on news which is of interest to the widest possible audience." These differences in views and attitudes between those journalists and the students could, as we noted, have arisen from a number of factors including generational differences in social outlook, the fact that the students are more likely to be from elite social backgrounds, or the fact that the students, compared to the journalists, had experienced much less newsroom "socialization."

It might be argued that some of the "gung ho" elements of British journalism culture should become extinct. We argue that it may be of concern to British journalism educators, and to those who care about democratic debate in Britain, if journalism students graduate with a lower level of support for watchdog roles, and ascribing less importance to concentrating on news of interest to the widest possible audience, as compared to an older generation of journalists. These findings about students can be set in the context of increasing market fragmentation and of consumption of "niche" news from the Internet, trends that may contribute to a decline in shared social understandings (Currah 2009). An overriding concern, in Britain as in other nations, is how much of the journalism industry will in years ahead be economically able to hire young journalists at all, let alone nurture them into becoming watchdogs.

References

Ball, Amanda, Mark Hanna, and Karen Sanders. 2006. What British journalism students think about ethics and journalism. *Journalism and Mass Communication Educator* 61(1):20–32.

Barnett, Steven. 2008. On the road to self-destruction. *British Journalism Review* 19(2):5–13.

BBC. 2005. At a glance: BBC job cuts. March 21. Retrieved from http://news.bbc.co.uk/2/hi/entertainment/4369221.stm

BBC. 2007. BBC cuts back programmes and jobs. October 18. Retrieved from http://news.bbc.co.uk/2/hi/entertainment/7050440.stm

BBC. 2010a. What is the BBC? Retrieved from http://www.bbc.co.uk/info/purpose/what.shtml.

BBC. 2010b. The BBC story. Retrieved from http://www.bbc.co.uk/historyofthebbc/resources/index.shtml.

BBC Trust. 2009a. Part one. Annual report and accounts 2008/09: The BBC Trust's review and assessment. Retrieved from http://downloads.bbc.co.uk/annualreport/pdf/bbc_trust_2008_09.pdf.

BBC Trust. 2009b. Part two: Annual report and accounts 2008/9: The BBC's Executive's review and assessment. Retrieved from http://www.bbc.co.uk/annualreport/.

Bolton, Paul. 2009. House of Commons student and graduate debt statistics. Retrieved from http://www.parliament.uk/commons/lib/research/briefings/snsg-01327.pdf

Currah, Andrew. 2009. Challenges: What's happening to our news? An investigation into the likely impact of the digital revolution on the economics of news publishing in the UK. Oxford: Reuters Institute for the Study of Journalism. Retrieved from http://reutersinstitute.politics.ox.ac.uk/fileadmin/documents/Publications/What_s_Happening_to_Our_News.pdf.

Delano, Anthony. 2001. *The formation of the British journalist 1900–2000.* PhD thesis, University of Westminster, London.

Delano, Anthony, and John Henningham. 1995. *The news breed: British journalists in the 1990s.* London: The London College of Printing and Distributive Trades.

Donsbach, Wolfgang. 1983. Journalists' conceptions of their audience. *Gazette* 32:19–36.

Foreign and Commonwealth Service. October 22, 2010. BBC World Service. Retrieved from http://www.fco.gov.uk/en/about-us/what-we-do/public-diplomacy/world-service

Frith, Simon, and Peter Meech. 2007. Becoming a journalist: Journalism education and journalism culture. *Journalism* 8(2):137–164.

Greenslade, Roy. 2010. Mirror national titles to lose 200 jobs as papers move towards digital future. June 10. Retrieved from http://www.guardian.co.uk/media/greenslade/2010/jun/10/trinity-mirror-job-losses

Hanna, Mark, and Karen Sanders. 2007. Journalism education in Britain: Who are the students and what do they want? *Journalism Practice* 1(3):404–420.

Hanna, Mark, and Karen Sanders. 2008. Did the education breed watchdogs? A study of British journalism students in graduate schools. *Journalism and Mass Communication Educator* 62(4):344–359.

Hanna, Mark, and Karen Sanders. 2009. *Should editors prefer postgraduates? A comparison of United Kingdom undergraduate and postgraduate journalism students.* Paper presented at *The Future of Journalism* conference, Cardiff University, September 9–10.

Hanna, Mark, and Karen Sanders. 2010. *Perceptions of the news media's societal roles: How the views of United Kingdom journalism students changed during their education.* Paper presented at the 2nd World Journalism Education Congress, Rhodes University, July 7–9.

Henningham, John, and Anthony Delano. 1998. British journalists. In *The global journalist: News people around the world,* edited by David H. Weaver, pp. 143–160. Cresskill, NJ: Hampton Press.

Higher Education Statistics Agency (HESA). 1994–2009. *Students in higher education institutions* [reference volumes for academic years 1994/5 to 2007/8]. London: Author.

Higher Education Statistics Agency (HESA). 2003–2004. Data purchased by the Association for Journalism Education. Retrieved from http://www.ajeuk.org, from the cy.

House of Commons Select Committee for Culture, Media and Sport. 2010. Future for local and regional media: Fourth report of session 2009–10, Volume II, Oral and written evidence.Retrieved from http://www.publications.parliament.uk/pa/cm200910/cmselect/cmcumeds/43/43ii.pdf

House of Lords Select Committee on Communications, 2008. 1st Report of Session 2007–8: The ownership of the news, Volume II, Evidence. London: The Stationery Office. Retrieved from http://www.publications.parliament.uk/pa/ld200708/ldselect/ldcomuni/ldcomuni.htm.

Johnstone, John, Edward J. Slawski, and William W. Bowman. 1976. *The news people: A sociological portrait of American journalists and their work.* Urbana: University of Illinois Press.

Journalism: Theory, practice and criticism. June 2009. *Special 10th anniversary edition—The Future of Journalism* 10(3).

Journalism Studies. August 2010.[Special issue] *The Future of Journalism* 11(4).

Journalism Training Forum. 2002. Journalists at work: Their views on training, recruitment and conditions. London: Self-published. Retrieved from http://www.skillset.org/uploads/pdf/asset_262.pdf?1.

Kocher, Renate. 1986. Bloodhounds and missionaries: Role definitions of German and British journalists. European Journal of Communication 1:43–64.

Lewis, Justin, Andrew Williams, Bob Franklin, and J. Thomas. 2008. *The quality and independence of British journalism.* Cardiff: Cardiff University.

Nat West. 2007. Student money matters. NatWest press release, August, 14. Retrieved from http://www.natwest.com/global/media/y2007/m-5.ashx.

National Council for the Training of Journalists (NCTJ). 2010. Accredited courses. Retrieved from http://www.nctj.com/custom/accredited/.

National Union of Journalists. 2005a. Pay rates—NUJ minimum pay rates 2005. Retrieved from http://www.nuj.org.uk/innerPagenuj.html?docid=333.

National Union of Journalists. 2005b. Pay rates—*London Magazine* Branch pay survey 2005. Retrieved from http://www.nuj.org.uk/innerPagenuj.html?docid=333.

National Union of Journalists. 2007. Shaping the future: NUJ Commission on multimedia working. December 16. Retrieved from http://www.nuj.org.uk/innerPagenuj.html?docid=605.

National Union of Journalists. 2010. End low pay. Retrieved from http://www.nuj.org.uk/innerPagenuj.html?docid=333.

Newman, Nic. 2009. The rise of social media and its impact on mainstream journalism: A study of how newspapers and broadcasters in the UK and US are responding to a wave of participatory social media, and a historic shift in control towards individual consumers. Working paper. Oxford: Reuters Institute for the Study of Journalism. Retrieved from http://reutersinstitute.politics.ox.ac.uk/fileadmin/documents/Publications/The_rise_of_social_media_and_its_impact_on_mainstream_journalism.pdf.

Newspaper Society. 2008. Analysis of the annual regional press survey findings for 2006. London: Newspaper Society. Retrieved from http://www.skillset.org/uploads/pdf/asset_11608.pdf?1.

Newspaper Society. 2009. Analysis of the annual local media survey findings for 2008. London: Newspaper Society. Retrieved from http://www.newspapersoc.org.uk/PDF/Industry-Survey-2008.pdf.

Newspaper Society. 2010. Locally connected. In print-online. Retrieved from http://www.newspapersoc.org.uk/Default.aspx?page=5530.

Ofcom. 2007a. New news, future news; the challenges for television news after digital switch-over. Retrieved from http://www.ofcom.org.uk/research/tv/reports/newnews/.

Ofcom. 2007b. A new approach to public service content in the digital media age. Retrieved from http://www.ofcom.org.uk/consult/condocs/pspnewapproach/.

Ofcom. 2009. The communications market report 2009. London: Ofcom. Retrieved from http://www.ofcom.org.uk/research/cm/cmr09/.

Office for National Statistics. 2009. Labour force survey: Employment status by occupation and sex (4 digit SOC). Retrieved from http://www.statistics.gov.uk/StatBase/Product.asp?vlnk=14248&Pos=&ColRank=1&Rank=272

Office for National Statistics. 2010. Population estimates. Retrieved from http://www.statistics.gov.uk/cci/nugget.asp?id=6

Periodicals Publishers Association (PPA). 2009. News release. Report on the January–June 2009 ABC release. August 13. Retrieved from http://www.ppamarketing.net/cgi-bin/go.pl/data-trends/article.html?uid=421.

Ponsford, Dominic. July 16, 2010. National press ABCs: Quality sales tumble. Press Gazette. Retrieved from http://www.pressgazette.co.uk/story.asp?sectioncode=1&storycode=45718&c=1

Press Complaints Commission. 2008. *The Review* [annual report for 2007]. Retrieved from http://www.pcc.org.uk/assets/80/PCC_AnnualReview2007.pdf.

Press Complaints Commission. 2009. *'08 The Review* [annual report for 2008]. Retrieved from http://www.pcc.org.uk/assets/111/PCC_Ann_Rep_08.pdf.

Preston, Peter. 2008. Damaged limitations. *Guardian* Online, February 9. Retrieved from http://www.guardian.co.uk/books/2008/feb/09/pressandpublishing.society.

Printing Industry Research Association (PIRA International). 2002. Publishing in the knowledge economy: Competitiveness analysis of the UK publishing media sector main report. Retrieved from http://www.publishingmedia.org.uk/download/02dti_competitive_analysis.pdf.

Prospects. 2010. Newspaper Journalist: Salary and conditions. Retrieved from http://www.prospects.ac.uk/p/types_of_job/newspaper_journalist_salary.jsp.

The Sector Skills Council for Creative Media (Skillset). 2004–2009. Employment census, 2004, 2006 and 2009. Retrieved from http://www.skillset.org/research/activity/census/.

The Sector Skills Council for Creative Media (Skillset). 2006. Mark Hanna's correspondence in March with Skillset, in relation to data gathered in research for, but not published in, Journalism Training Forum (2002).

The Sector Skills Council for Creative Media (Skillset). 2010. Mark Hanna's correspondence in January with Skillset about data collected for Skillset Employment Census (2009).

Spilsbury Research. 2006. *An audit of training arrangements for new entrants into journalism.* Retrieved from http://www. skillset.org/uploads/pdf/asset_11602.pdf?1.

Sutton Trust. 2006. *The educational backgrounds of leading journalists.* Retrieved from http://www.suttontrust.com/ reports/Journalists-backgrounds-final-report.pdf.

Thompson, Caroline. 2002. The future of public service broadcasting—An international perspective. Speech given at the Broadcast Magazine/Commonwealth Broadcasting Association Conference. January 29. Retrieved from http:// www.bbc.co.uk/pressoffice/speeches/stories/thomsoncarolinecbs.shtml.

Tryhorn, Chris. 2009. BBC must cut £400m from budget—Mark Thompson. *The Guardian* Online March 19. Retrieved from http://www.guardian.co.uk/media/2009/mar/19/bbc-budget-cut-mark-thompson.

Tunstall, Jeremy. 1996. *Newspaper power: The new national press in Britain.* Oxford: Clarendon Press.

Wilby, Peter. 2008. A job for the wealthy and connected. Media *Guardian* journalism training "special." April 7. Retrieved from http://www.guardian.co.uk/media/2008/apr/07/pressandpublishing4.

18 Journalism in Hungary

Maria Vasarhelyi

Until the beginning of the so-called systems change in 1988, there was no media market and no free press in Hungary. After the socialist dictatorship gave way to a democratic market economy, the nation's media conditions experienced radical transformation. Until 1988, all press products were owned, governed, and operated by the state. As a result, there was little variety in mediated public opinion. Opinions that criticized or questioned government could not be published, and content also had to conform to state directives. Although some secondary (*samizdat*) publications existed, they only reached a narrow circle of a few thousand intellectuals.

After the collapse of socialism, competition and freedom of expression quickly came to the Hungarian press. Censorship was terminated and media ownership rights no longer were controlled by the state. With the liberation of the market, dailies and weeklies mushroomed, while existing media were transferred to private ownership. Most papers were purchased by foreign proprietors. New genres appeared, including the tabloid press, which was immediately highly popular, and the so-called mixed-profile free papers, which were mostly controlled by foreign owners.

In the electronic media market, competition did not arrive until 1996 with the passage of the Media Act. Funded by a combination of subscription fees, public support, and commercial revenues, public service broadcasters began to compete with purely commercial and non-profit community media. To date, the country has three national, public-service television and radio channels, two national commercial TV and radio channels, and several regional or local TV and radio, mostly owned by local municipalities.

Although the conditions of market competition have been established in every segment of Hungarian media, there are few truly independent media outlets. The 1996 Media Act subjected the market to significant political influence. Parties delegate curators to oversee leading media organizations and to serve in agencies that distribute broadcast frequencies. In many cases, these party representatives favor political interests over objective professional criteria. When party loyalties clash, they frequently prevent compromise, and often lead to public service media operating without responsible leadership for a year or more. On the rare occasions when political bargains are struck, they regularly lead to unlawful decisions regarding frequency distribution, which later lead to court cases. Much of the printed press also is subject to political influence. Because of the small size and capital shortage of the market, governing parties can exert major pressure on revenues by controlling public advertisement orders.

Previous Studies

The first study of the social-economic status of Hungarian journalists was conducted in 1968 by Zsuzsa Ferge (1972). Because the survey was limited to only a few demographic indicators, the comparability of results is limited to those dimensions.

The next study (Angelusz, Ferenc, Márta, & János 1981, 1982) was sponsored by The Association of Hungarian Journalists (MUOSZ), and covered a wider range of topics. Along with social-economic situations, it examined general feelings and professional value preferences, views of the media world, ideological orientation, and information-gathering habits. This effort served as the foundation for four more MUOSZ-sponsored surveys in 1992, 1998, 2000, and 2006 (Vasarhelyi 1992, 1999, 2006). Despite the political changes in the 1990s that fundamentally changed how Hungarian journalists operate, efforts were made to retain as much of the 1982 study's design as possible to ensure longitudinal comparability.

Under dictatorial rule, Hungarian journalists were dominated by political considerations that determined placement, job preservation, and professional advancement. But the profession has had many consistent features across its systems, which make tracking developments in opinions both reasonable and worthwhile. Longitudinal data comparison is well-warranted for measuring changes in the social-demographic structure of Hungarian journalism, the degree of satisfaction with work conditions, professional values and ambitions, professional and general attitudes, and the restructuring of the "professional ethos."

Method

The latest survey of Hungarian journalists was performed in 2006 by the Communication Theory Research Group of the Hungarian Academy of Sciences, and commissioned by the National Association of Hungarian Journalists. Personal interviews, which lasted about 80 minutes each, were conducted with a representative sample of 940 journalists.

The sample reflects the actual proportion of journalists working for various media in Hungary. Twenty-four percent of those interviewed worked for dailies, 16% for weeklies, 15% in other print media, 16% in television, 15% radio, and 12% in online media. Fifty-two percent of respondents worked for national media, 28% for regional outlets, and 20% for local media. In terms of financing, 58% worked for privately owned commercial media, 32% for public service media, and 8% for non-profit organizations (see Table 18.1).

Table 18.1   Journalists' Age and Workplace in 2006 ($N = 940$, in %)

Workplace	<30 (N = 2 68)	31–40 (N = 264)	41–50 (N = 196)	51–60 (N = 212)	Total	N
National daily	29	41	14	16	100	94
Provincial daily	28	28	25	19	100	118
National weekly	28	26	21	25	100	107
Provincial weekly	34	23	20	23	100	57
Periodical	20	25	22	33	100	137
On-line media	38	26	19	17	100	115
National radio	9	21	37	33	100	46
Regional radio	45	26	21	8	100	87
National television	42	23	18	17	100	55
Regional television	38	26	20	16	100	87
Other	41	21	15	23	100	37

Table 18.2   Journalists' Age and Sex in 2006 (*N* = 940, in %)

Age Group	Male (N = 509)	Female (N = 431)	N
30 years or younger	50	50	268
31–40 years	55	45	264
41–50 years	52	48	196
51 and older	58	42	212

Findings

Basic Characteristics

The 2006 survey found that Hungarian journalists, as a group, are getting younger. This reverses a trend found in all of the previous studies. The number of young journalists also was on the rise, while the number of older journalists had declined. In 1997, 11% of Hungary's journalists were under age 30; by 2006, that figure had risen to 31%. In 1997, the average age of a Hungarian journalist was 44; nearly a decade later, it was 39 (see Table 18.2).

Lower average age is explained by several factors. First, the general employment rate of Hungarian youth has exceeded older generations for the past few decades. In 2001, the national employment rate of persons aged 20 to 40 was 64%, yet only 36% for those aged 40 to 62 were employed (Hungarian Central Statistical Office, 2001). This age-gap effect has increased with the emergence of newer commercial and online media, which especially appeal to younger generations.

The percentage of women in the profession also saw a substantial increase, from 31% in 1997 to 47% in 2006. The most noticeable change was a four-fold increase in unmarried men and women relative to 1997 (see Table 18.3). One of the main findings in 1997 was the high divorce rate of journalists. This tendency apparently has abated, as the divorce rate in 2006 fell by 2%. These changes are attributable to lower average age in this profession, the postponement of marriage, and radically new life-path characteristics of the people concerned. Additionally, more than three-quarters of journalists in the 2006 study married partners with the same level of education. Intra-professional marriages used to be scarce, with only one in 10 journalists marrying a colleague in 1997. By 2006, every fifth journalist married within the profession.

Another demographic finding was that the divorce rate shrunk for female journalists. In 1997, the divorce rate of women was almost twice that of men (14% vs. 26%); in 2006, the two indices had drawn closer together (12% vs. 19%). One explanation is that more divorced women than men live with a partner. For unmarried journalists, it was more typical of women (39%) to live with a partner than men (35%) in 2006.

Table 18.3   Journalists' Marital Status by Year (in %)

	1981 (N = 700)	1992 (N = 650)	1997 (N = 732)	2006 (N = 940)
Single	8	12	9	37
Married	79	66	63	43
Separated	—	3	6	3
Divorced	11	15	18	16
Widowed	2	4	4	1
Total	100	100	100	100

As a group, Hungarian journalists politically have shifted toward the center and the conservative end of the liberal–conservative axis. Yet, in line with findings from previous surveys, there were still more journalists in 2006 who identified themselves as liberal (47%) than conservative (35%). The rate of the latter, however, has dynamically expanded among journalists since the political system change.

Education and Training

Most journalists surveyed in 2006 had a university or college degree. Only 17% had no degree. Education levels have stabilized significantly since the mid-1990s after previous periods of great fluctuation. Since the 1990s, about 40% to 45% of journalists have acquired a degree. Previously, only about 12% to15% had done so. Likewise, there has been a great increase in the number of journalists who majored in journalism.

Among journalists surveyed in 2006, 32% held a university-level journalism degree, including most of the newer journalists. Journalism, media studies, and communications as a group has emerged as one of the three most popular majors in Hungary, with 8% of all higher education applicants in 2006 choosing such training at about 50 schools. Before the 1990s, there was no post-secondary journalism training in the country.

The data of our 2006 survey show that the journalists' foreign language skills improved significantly in the past decade. Since 1997, journalists who said they spoke no foreign languages fell from about 25% to 16%. Forty-two percent of respondents said they speak a foreign language fluently enough to use it for their work, an increase from 26% in 1997. The group of journalists who spoke two foreign languages was 27%, while 10% spoke more than two; both measures double the same findings from 1997.

Working Conditions

Data about satisfaction with work conditions and the workplace have been collected since 1981. This allows a comparison of how journalists in 2006 rated their working conditions to how such assessments may have developed and fluctuated for more than 25 years.

Among individual factors, Hungarian journalists most consistently are satisfied with the personal and professional qualities of colleagues and managers. Positive opinions also prevail regarding office atmosphere and workplace democracy. Journalists also were generally pleased with the material and physical conditions of work, especially the technical infrastructure. Other above-average marks were given to the chances of promotion and the amount of on-the-job training.

Out of 18 work satisfaction factors examined, journalists gave the worst ratings to opportunity for professional travel abroad. This finding is all the more noteworthy since journalism traditionally differs most from other professions in the mobility that is required. A journalist's ability to verify news on the scene plays a decisive role in the quality of information provided. So it is quite noticeable that travel is missing to a growing extent in Hungarian journalism. Instead, the press often relies on reports from news agencies, even if there is no physical obstacle to a reporter's presence. The survey suggests that the journalists themselves have identified this deficiency and that it is not so much journalistic initiative that is lacking as adequate travel support from most editorial offices.

Financial and social circumstances in the workplace generally earned average ratings. Journalists were mainly pleased with their level of income, but less optimistic about opportunities

Table 18.4   Journalists' Satisfaction with Working Conditions in 2006 (*N* = 940, in %)

	Completely satisfied	Rather satisfied	Mid-range satisfied	Rather dissatisfied	Completely dissatisfied	Total
Editorial office atmosphere	31	41	21	4	3	100
Interest in work	36	42	18	3	1	100
Number of ancillary staff	19	31	31	13	6	100
Physical conditions of work	22	35	26	12	5	100
Technical infrastructure of work	30	34	24	10	2	100
Human attitude of colleagues	33	45	18	3	1	100
Professionalism of colleagues	24	48	23	3	2	100
Level of income	7	29	34	16	14	100
Democracy at editorial office	23	41	22	8	6	100
Professionalism of the managerial staff	34	41	17	6	2	100
Human attitude of managers	37	39	16	6	2	100
Opportunities for professional advancement	16	35	30	12	7	100
Opportunities for financial advancement	4	24	38	21	13	100
Level of social allowances	11	27	32	18	12	100
Opportunities to travel abroad	10	18	21	22	29	100

for promotion. Average satisfaction rates, however, concealed major differences, as staff members employed in different positions in different media rated working conditions quite differently.

In a breakdown by media type, print media employees seem to be more satisfied with the conditions of their work than electronic media staff. Among print journalists, satisfaction is most widespread among those who work for non-dailies, which is probably related to the slower pace of work, lower stress levels, and greater possibility for thorough work. Overall, the most critical opinions came from employees of the television channels (see Table 18.4).

The survey contained five questions measuring work autonomy. Respondents said they had the most control over the choice of information sources, followed by the selection of human sources and how to approach story topics. Journalists faced the most obstacles in commenting on or evaluating events. As in 1997, decisions that carried more weight were less likely to be within the journalist's control. The autonomy indicators were combined into a scale for the purpose of a cluster analysis to further examine autonomy. The variable divided respondents into three groups—those with small, medium, and great autonomy.

Opinions of the state of freedom of the press have been rather diverse since democracy's arrival in Hungary. During the first few years of democracy, nearly half of journalists felt that the press was completely free. After five years, however, this number had diminished almost by half. In 1997, only one out of four journalists thought the field provided for the free expression of opinions. By 2006, the proportion who said the press enjoyed complete freedom rose to 38%. However, that number was still lower than the 45% who agreed in 1992. The percentage of journalists who believe there is no press freedom in Hungary, however, has remained steady at 4% in all three surveys (see Table 18.5).

Despite the 16 years that have elapsed since Hungary's regime change, 60% of journalists in the 2006 survey said there were still topics about which the public could not be honestly informed.

Table 18.5   Journalists' Assessments of Freedom of the Press in Hungary (in %)

	1992 (N = 650)	1997 (N = 732)	2006 (N = 940)
Press completely free	45	27	38
Press partially free	51	69	58
Press not free at all	4	4	4

Note.   Question: In your opinion, is the press completly free, partially free, or not free at all today in Hungary?

This increased from the early 1990s, when 53% said the same; yet it has decreased in the last 10 years, as 68% of journalists in 1997 mentioned taboo subjects about which the public could not be honestly informed.

Respondents also were asked if they had experienced external pressure to cover certain topics or prevent publication of certain information for political or economic reasons. Three-fourths said they had experienced this pressure, a finding that significantly correlates with concerns about press freedom in Hungary. Yet of the 80% who experienced such pressures, the majority said such attempts at influence were unsuccessful.

Probably the murkiest area of journalism, and the one that raises a growing number of unanswerable dilemmas, is that of professional and ethical norms. In Hungary, journalism ethics have traditionally been linked with the presentation of facts and social reality, but recent decades have seen shifts in such emphasis. A growing focus on entertainment and sensational issues, together with keener market competition, has prompted a disintegration of the established consensus and the softening of professional and ethical norms.

For the first time in this series of studies, a focus was placed on which professional and ethical norms have risen to the level of consensus—irrespective of media type and personal backgrounds—and which issues divided journalists.

Six scenarios were presented in which journalists could use newsgathering techniques that might violate traditional ethical norms. Journalists were asked whether they considered the use of each method acceptable in the interest of exposing the truth.

Their answers were instructive in several respects. Whereas the purchase of information was deemed acceptable by the majority, all other potential ethical violations were summarily rejected—even if the reporting could have helped serve a major public interest.

However, it is difficult not to notice many self-contradictions inherent in the answers, conflicts that also indicate the confusion surrounding journalism ethics. For example, while only one in 10 journalists considered cheating or misleading an interviewee generally acceptable, a much greater number found specific forms of cheating and misleading acceptable. Despite their similar means and ends, more journalists also rated the use of hidden cameras as more ethically acceptable than using hidden microphones. This disparity may be attributable to the "candid camera" being an established means of entertainment programming, whereas hidden microphones are often associated with criminal activities.

Differences in ethical opinions were found by age. In general, as Hungarian journalists age, they become increasingly rigorous about which ethical practices are acceptable. Whereas most under age 40 considered questionable reporting practices to be acceptable, almost two-thirds of those over age 50 categorically refused them. This reflects a shift in attitudes which is quite noticeable in everyday practice, and contributes to the softening of traditional norms. Generational gaps also existed in terms of defining who is a public figure and what is public information. Although younger journalists generally identified the scope of public information more widely, they interpreted the circle of public actors more narrowly than their older colleagues. Hungarian journalists generally agreed that politicians are public actors, but they held different views on whether heads of public institutions (local governments, hospitals, schools, etc.)—as well as journalists, media stars, and artists—are public actors or not. The most striking difference concerned the public role of journalists, who were regarded as public actors by only half of young respondents (less than 40 years old), but by 80% of older ones. The rate of journalists that defined themselves as public actors increased gradually with age. In the highest age brackets, it was twice the rate recorded in the lowest ones—60% compared to 30%, respectively.

There was broad consensus that information about public actors' infidelity was of no public concern; regardless of age, 9 of 10 journalists agreed. Yet there were significant generational differences concerning every other issue.

Four times as many younger journalists (20% to 25%) said that information about families of public actors concerned the public compared to the oldest ones (5% to 9%). Smaller differences were found concerning the newsworthiness of a public actor's sexual orientation (10% of the youngest journalists and 5% of the oldest) and addictions (40% of the youngest and 30% of the oldest). In general, journalists were more likely to agree that information about finances and property of public actors concerns the public (50% of the youngest and 37% of the oldest).

These findings illustrate that whereas younger journalists tended to adopt a more lenient attitude concerning the newsworthy parts of public actors' private lives, they interpreted the notion of "public actor" differently from their older colleagues—especially if it applied to them.

The opinions of both groups also differed with regard to the state of Hungarian publicity and the press. Although the majority of journalists (80%) were most concerned about the increasingly foul language of the press, older respondents were more pessimistic about it. There were also generational differences in whether journalists considered this problem as permeating the whole press (14% of young journalists, compared to 29% of older ones).

Older journalists were more critical of the general quality of the press and the sense of social responsibility among journalists. Concern that politics and political parties exert an excessive influence on the press increased proportionally with age. On average, 60% to 70% in the older age brackets expressed concerns about social responsibility—twice the rate of younger journalists. Older journalists also were more worried about the spread of foreign private capital in the press.

Although part of the difference in attitudes between younger and older generations is attributable to age-specific traits, these findings suggest that as a result of their different professional socialization, newer journalists have different ideas about the goals of the profession, its ethics, and about the role of the press. This finding is not simply related to generational differences that will level with time, but indicates a fault line that will transform the media world in Hungary fundamentally in the longer run.

Conclusions

This 2006 survey, which built on previous studies, indicates that Hungarian journalists are getting younger. They also are becoming more female, and are less likely to be married than in the past. Politically, Hungarian journalists have shifted toward the center and the conservative side, reflecting a somewhat marked rightward shift in the political preferences of Hungarian society.

Education levels of Hungarian journalists have stabilized, with the majority graduating from a university or college. There also was a notable increase in those who majored in journalism in college, and those able to speak a foreign language fluently enough to use it in their work. As for working conditions, Hungarian journalists—especially those who work for non-daily newspapers—were most consistently satisfied with the personal and professional qualities of colleagues and managers. They were least satisfied with professional opportunities to travel abroad. They were generally pleased with their income level, but less optimistic about opportunities for promotion.

Hungarian journalists say they have the most autonomy over which information sources they choose to use, and the least autonomy in commenting about events. Their opinions on the state of press freedom have fluctuated considerably since the beginning of democracy in Hungary. Whereas in 1992 nearly half felt that the press was completely free, five years later it was only one-fourth, yet by 2006 it had risen to nearly 40%. Still, 60% of the journalists in 2006 said there were topics about which the public could not be honestly informed, and three-fourths claimed to have experienced pressure to cover or not cover certain topics for political or economic reasons.

As is true elsewhere, professional and ethical norms of Hungarian journalism seem to have changed because of a growing focus on entertainment and sensational topics, as well as increasing market competition. Whereas paying for information was deemed acceptable by most Hungarian journalists, all other potential ethical violations were rejected by a majority. Differences were found by age and political ideology, with older and more leftist journalists less willing to use questionable reporting practices.

There was broad agreement that information about the infidelity of public actors is not of public concern, but younger journalists were more likely than older ones to think that information about the families of public actors was of public import. In general, younger journalists seemed more willing to consider the private lives of public actors as newsworthy. Older journalists were more critical of the general quality of journalism and the sense of social responsibility among journalists. These and other findings suggest that younger Hungarian journalists have notably different ideas about the goals, ethics, and roles of journalism than their older colleagues. These differences are likely to transform the news media world in Hungary in the longer run.

As Kovats (1998: 274) wrote, based on a 1992 survey of members of the Hungarian Journalists Association, "In this time of social upheaval, the journalists were confused between their different roles: the role of professional, the role of intellectual, and the role of citizen." This confusion, or at least disagreement, seems to have continued 14 years later.

References

Angelusz, Róbert, Békés Ferenc, Nagy Márta, and Tímár János. 1981. *They went to school of journalism*. Budapest: TK, Mass Communication Research Center, Hungary.

Angelusz, Róbert, Békés Ferenc, Nagy Márta, and Tímár János. 1982. *Journalist Research*. Budapest: TK, Mass Communication Research Center, Hungary.

Ferge, Zsuzsa. 1972. *The work of journalists*. Budapest: TK, Mass Communication Research Center, Hungary.

Hungarian Central Statistical Office. 2001. *Population census 2001*. Budapest: Author.

Hungarian Central Statistical Office. 2004. *Statistical yearbook 2004*. Budapest: Author.

Kovats, Ildiko. 1998. Hungarian journalists. In *The global journalist: News people around the world*, edited by David H. Weaver, pp. 257–276. Cresskill, NJ: Hampton Press.

Vasarhelyi, Maria. 1992. *The situation, ways of thinking and involvment of journalists*. Budapest: MUOSZ, Hungarian Association of Journalists.

Vasarhelyi, Maria. 1999. *Journalists, media workers and day laborers*. Budapest: Új Mandátum.

Vasarhelyi, Maria. 2006. *Profession: Journalist*. Budapest: MUOSZ, Hungarian Association of Journalists.

19 Journalists and Journalism in the Netherlands

Alexander Pleijter, Liesbeth Hermans, and Maurice Vergeer

"We are like the animal trainer in the circus, who tries to keep eight hungry tigers in check with his whip. And then suddenly the light goes out." This is how chairman Arendo Joustra described the state of journalism in the Netherlands at the 50th anniversary of the Dutch Society of Editors in 2009. "From all sides the threats come to us. We call them—very tough—opportunities and challenges, but we know that nowhere in the world has the solution yet been found."

This quote shows how desperate Dutch news organizations feel as they look at the substantial changes they have had to deal with over the past decade. These changes are very often framed in terms of crisis; Joustra even spoke in his speech about an "existential crisis." Key to these changes is the emergence of the Internet and digitization, which have had a major impact on media organizations and led to a series of trends. Newspaper readership continues to decrease and newspaper circulation has been caught in a downward spiral. Important sources of revenue, like classified ads, have moved to the Internet, and as new competitors appeared online, advertising moved to new online companies. As a consequence, traditional news organizations have been forced to implement cutbacks and to downsize their newsrooms. In addition, there are numerous changes that have led to struggles in the journalistic field; for example, journalists have had to learn how to work in a multimedia environment. How do journalists deal with this changing playing field? Does it affect their ethical standards and their journalistic role perceptions? And how does the adoption of new online tools change the way journalists work? In a longitudinal research project we track these developments in journalism in the Netherlands. In this chapter we focus on the demographics, the types of media journalists work for, and their professional activities and role perceptions.

Media Background

The Dutch media system has a long history of segmentation, many traces of which are still identifiable in today's media system, but this system began to erode in the 1960s. The daily press, for the greater part, followed the lines of the dominant ideological or religious segments in society. In 2010, there were five major (with a circulation of more than 100,000 copies a day) national newspapers left: *De Telegraaf* (popular, liberal; circulation of 653,000 in 2009), *Algemeen Dagblad* (popular, neutral; 445,000), *de Volkskrant* (left-wing; 258,000), *NRC Handelsblad* (liberal; 207,000), and *Trouw* (protestant, 108,000).

Until the late 1980s, broadcasting in the Netherlands was dominated by a monopoly of public broadcasters, which were funded but not controlled by the government, and commercial companies were not allowed to broadcast. This monopoly was first broken in 1989, when the Luxembourg-based commercial broadcaster RTL launched a television channel targeting a Dutch audience. Finally, in 1995, the Dutch-licensed commercial broadcaster SBS Broadcasting entered the Dutch television market with new news formats that focused on regional and soft news and competed with the more traditional public broadcasting news. As expected, the new commercial channels quickly decreased the audience share of the public broadcaster NPO. However, the advertising revenues of NPO remained relatively stable over the next decade (Dutch Media Authority 2001). The introduction of private broadcasters not only increased the number of television channels available in the Netherlands, but also raised the total hours of television news programs available to viewers. In 1988, Dutch television programming included 32 hours a week for news, current affairs, talk shows, and infotainment. In 1999, this had increased to 235 hours (Lohman & Peeters 2000).

Ultimately, television became the main medium for Dutch media audiences. In 1980, the average Dutch person spent about 1 hour and 45 minutes a day watching television (NOS-KLO 1994, 1995), but by 2009, this had increased to 3 hours a day (Dutch Audience Research Foundation 2010). The growth in news and education programs has been identified as a key reason for this increase in viewing time (Vergeer, Eisinga, & Franses 2012). Meanwhile, the radio audience decreased sharply from 130 minutes a week in 1975 to only 30 minutes a week in 2005. In 1975 the average person spent more than 150 minutes a week reading newspapers, which decreased to 90 minutes a week in 2005. Time spent reading magazines decreased from 90 minutes a week in 1975 to 45 minutes in 2005 (Breedveld, van den Broek, de Haan, Harms, Huysmans, & van Ingen 2006).

As in other countries, newspaper circulation in the Netherlands is declining. While this decline started in the early 1980s among regional newspapers, national newspapers actually gained circulation until the year 2000, after which they also show a significant downward trend in circulation. In 2008, the total circulation of daily newspapers was 3.5 million, which means only one newspaper for every two households (Bakker & Scholten 2009).

While regular newspaper circulations have decreased in the past 20 years, free newspapers have become popular among Dutch readers (Bakker 2008). In 1999, the first two free newspapers, *Spits* and *Metro*, were introduced, followed by *De Pers* in 2007. These free newspapers are distributed mainly at public train and bus stations in the Netherlands and have reached an impressive 1.6 million copies a day (Bakker & Scholten 2009).

Due to the declining circulation numbers in the last two decades, several reorganizations and mergers have taken place in the Dutch newspaper business. In 1980, there were 23 newspaper enterprises that published 43 independent titles; in 2000 only nine companies were left publishing 32 titles (Wijfjes 2004). In 2010, the Dutch newspaper market consisted of nine paid-for national newspapers, three free national newspapers, and 18 paid-for regional newspapers.

The diversity of the Dutch newspaper market suggested by the number of titles available is deceptive because regional newspapers collaborate extensively and use the same press agencies. People have little or no choice in newspapers, especially regarding local and regional news (Vergeer 2006). In 2008, the total newspaper market was dominated by three major publishers: TMG (Dutch, national and regional newspapers), Mecon (British, predominantly regional newspapers), and PCM (Dutch, predominantly national newspapers). Their respective market shares for 2008 were 27.5%, 20.3%, and 17.7% (Dutch Media Authority 2009).

Online news sites have become increasingly popular. The most popular site is Nu.nl, an online-only news site, which reaches one-third of the Dutch online population on a monthly basis—more than the Web sites of the most popular newspapers and the Web site of the Dutch national broadcasting company (Alexa 2010).

The expansion of media in the last decades has resulted in a sharp increase in the number of journalists working in the Netherlands. In 1980, the Dutch Association of Journalists (NVJ) counted 4,500 members, which had increased to more than 9,000 in 2000 (Wijfjes 2004). Assuming that the rate of unionization is about 60% (Wijfjes 2004), it can be estimated that the actual number of journalists has risen from 7,000 to 14,000. This growth can be attributed, for the most part, to an explosive increase in the number of broadcast journalists and freelancers. The number of freelancers in particular has increased five-fold from 293 in 1980 to 1,885 in 2000. During the same time period, the number of newspaper journalists has risen from 2,087 to 2,551. More recently, however, it seems that the number of journalists, especially in the traditional news media, is decreasing dramatically. Regional newspapers in particular had to cut their budgets and lay off journalistic staff to compensate. Exact numbers, however, are not available.

The increase in the number of journalists that was observed until 2000 went hand-in-hand with more journalism education programs in the Netherlands. In the mid-1960s, the first school of journalism in the Netherlands was launched in Utrecht, and in 1980 three additional schools made their debuts. In 1989, Erasmus University Rotterdam began offering journalistic training programs, followed two years later by the University of Groningen. Overall, there are now five master's programs in journalism at Dutch universities.

Recent developments in journalism (such as citizen journalism, online journalism, blogs, and user-generated content) have started discussions about journalistic norms, values, and ethics in the Netherlands and elsewhere. Critics state that the media increasingly hype particular events and present news in more sensational ways. They especially criticize new television formats, such as Reality TV with camera crews joining police or ambulance services, or programs that can be described as "ambush journalism" with camera crews forcing their way into companies and institutions to solve consumer problems.

The Internet has also put pressure on journalistic norms and values. Most influential has probably been the popular blog, *GeenStijl* (NoStyle), which has been most notable for its unusual and questionable journalistic methods and ethics. Discussions have taken place about whether or not to disclose names of crime suspects. While regular newspapers hold to their traditional approach to print only the initials of suspects, *GeenStijl* (and other blogs) publish the full names of crime suspects. It is important to note that the producers of *GeenStijl* do not consider themselves journalists and therefore do not recognize the authority of the Netherlands Press Council.

As a consequence of all these changes, in recent years the Netherlands has seen an increase in public debate about the role of media in society (RMO 2003), particularly about the alleged deterioration of the quality of journalism and the future of the press. Critics express their concerns that due to increasing financial pressure, quality journalism receives less funding. Both newspapers and magazines (print) are steadily losing readers and thus advertising revenue. The audience, especially younger consumers, turns increasingly to the Web for the news that supposedly is free.

At the same time, there are few successful journalistic business models for online news. In 2009, the Minister for the Media set up an advisory committee to investigate innovation and the future of the press. In its final report, the commission raised concerns about the diminishing social role of local and regional media (Tijdelijke Commissie Innovatie en Toekomst Pers 2009). Ultimately, the minister made available an €8 million grant (US$9.6 million) for press innovation, 50% of which will be spent on local and regional media. Moreover, the minister is trying to rejuvenate newspapers and news magazines by subsidizing jobs for young journalists.

Previous Studies

The Netherlands has no tradition of research on journalists. Journalism has been established as a serious field of research at Dutch universities only during the last 10 years. As a result, representative survey studies offering insight into professional characteristics of Dutch journalists in general are only available in small numbers.

The first national and (more or less) representative study of Dutch journalists was conducted in 1968 by Muskens (1968). He concluded that Dutch journalists, in general, want to be perceived as competent and influential in society. They see it as their job to bring about changes in society, which is a more activist approach than the common self-perception of being "neutral disseminators" of news.

In 1976, Kempers and Wieten (1976) conducted a survey of 1,485 Dutch journalists. This study focused on how media concentration (i.e., the merger of publishers) would affect the work of journalists. The authors concluded that most journalists had no formal say in the reorganization of newsrooms, but when they were consulted they were less negative about measures like the dismissal of journalists, compared to journalists who were not consulted.

Deuze (2002) collected data to profile Dutch journalists in 1999 and 2000. His telephone survey of 773 journalists aimed to research the characteristics of professional journalists in the Netherlands: how they regard their work; their professional norms, values, and ethics; and how they deal with their (changing) role in society. Deuze (2002) concluded that the average journalist had a somewhat left-wing political orientation, preferred analysis over news dissemination, had little contact with his or her audience, was attached to independence, and had pragmatic ethical principles.

One year later, in 2001, Pleijter, Tebbe, and Hermans (2002) conducted a mail survey on Internet use by Dutch journalists ($N = 685$). They concluded that the adoption of the Internet as a professional tool was nearly ubiquitous in 2001: 98% of journalists made daily use of the Internet for professional purposes and 60% used the Internet or e-mail for more than one hour a day. The main activities on the Internet were searching the Web for information and service information. Only a very small minority of journalists made use of communicative applications such as chat rooms, instant messaging, and newsgroups.

While nearly all journalists (85%) thought the Internet had made their work easier, only a minority (38%) thought the Internet had improved the quality of journalism as a whole. Furthermore, a small number of the interviewed journalists (15%) noted that they now leave the office less frequently to gather information for their reports and instead rely on the Internet. In fact, one-third of the journalists predicted a negative impact on journalism due to the introduction of the Internet, with special concern expressed for the potential damage to the credibility and thoroughness of journalism.

However, half of the journalists also noted that they now had more contact with the audience through the Internet. Finally, slightly more than half of the journalists (55%) thought the function of journalists was changing due to the fact that the audience is able to find relevant information on the Internet on its own. Therefore, journalists thought providing explanations of events and trends would become more important than simply distributing plain information or facts (Pleijter et al. 2002).

Comparing Results from Dutch Studies

Demographics.   Based on the above-mentioned studies, we can trace some significant changes in Dutch journalism between 1968 and 2002. First of all, it appears that the share of young journalists has decreased in past decades. In 1968, about one-third of journalists were under 30 years—a group that shrank to only 15% at the start of the 21st century (Deuze 2002; Muskens 1968; Pleijter et al. 2002). Presumably, this trend has to do with the fact that higher education has become increasingly important in the Netherlands before starting a career in journalism. In 1968, there was one journalism school, the School voor de Journalistiek Utrecht (plus separate courses at the universities of Rotterdam and Nijmegen). In those days, it was normal to start working in a newsroom as an apprentice and to learn all essential skills on the job. After the turn of the century, however, four out of five Dutch journalists held vocational or academic degrees (Deuze 2002; Pleijter et al. 2002), while only 6% were educated in the newsroom (Pleijter et al. 2002).

At the same time, more women entered journalism. In the late 1960s, only 5% of Dutch journalists were female. In 2000, Deuze (2002) found that one-third of journalists were female. However, despite this significant increase in the number of female journalists, women were less likely to reach higher positions within media organizations—only 4% of female journalists held an executive position in 2000, as compared to 15% of their male colleagues.

Media Types.   For a long time newspaper journalists dominated the journalistic profession. In 1968, 70% of all journalists worked at a newspaper (Muskens 1968). At the turn of the millennium, this number had dropped to 42%. At the same time, the number of journalists working for magazines increased from 4% to 15% and for national television from 3% to 11%. The number of online journalists increased slightly from only 1% in 2000 to 4% in 2002 (Deuze 2002; Pleijter et al. 2002).

Professional Role Perceptions.   The question of how journalists perceive their roles in society and how these perceptions might have changed over time is an important one. However, it is difficult to make inferences because questionnaires used in the aforementioned studies are not completely comparable. While Muskens (1968), for example, asked journalists about how they perceived their occupation, Kempers and Wieten (1976) asked about the "task" of journalists in society. Pleijter et al. (2002) on the other hand, only asked if journalists thought that due to the Internet, providing explanations has become more important than disseminating facts.

Despite these differences, some common findings have emerged. According to Deuze (2002), the biggest change in journalists' role perceptions is that they increasingly value news analysis and interpretation. While in 1976 only 1% thought the analytical role was important (Kempers & Wieten 1976), in 2000 this had risen to 87% (Deuze 2002). This finding is corroborated by Pleijter et al. (2002), who show that half of the journalists agree that providing explanations has become more important than disseminating facts. Providing entertainment and relaxation is also a widely shared role—approximately 50% of the journalists endorsed this role in 2000 (Deuze 2002). Unfortunately, previous studies did not ask for this role perception. These findings indicate how wide and pluralistic the field of journalism in the Netherlands had become at the end of the 20th century. Journalists nowadays not only consider themselves the bearers of the latest news, but also the interpreters of important developments, and a significant group also thinks that it is important to entertain the audience. This is not so strange because a lot of media use (like reading a magazine or watching television) represents a way of relaxing for the audience.

In the study we present here, we look further into developments in journalism in the Netherlands in the early 21st century (2006). We describe personal and professional characteristics, journalistic values, their perception of the audience, and finally, their role perceptions.

Method

This research project is part of an ongoing longitudinal project on Dutch journalism and the relationship between journalism practices and the use of the Internet in the Netherlands (Hermans, Vergeer, & d'Haenens 2009; Hermans, Vergeer, & Pleijter 2009; Pleijter, Hermans, & Vergeer 2007). The data were collected in the spring of 2006, using a random sample of 2,000 journalists from the Dutch Association of Journalists (NVJ) membership database. Of the approximately 14,000 journalists working in the Netherlands, about 9,500 journalists are members of the NVJ (Deuze 2002; Wijfjes 2004).

The sample was stratified to ensure a representative distribution across media types (e.g., newspaper journalists, broadcast journalists, freelance journalists) within the NVJ membership list. Sections that did not include journalists, such as student members and PR officials, were excluded. A printed questionnaire was sent to the home address of all selected journalists. The mailing included a stamped return envelope and, to further increase the response rate, a reminder was sent two weeks later. Ultimately, 642 journalists completed the questionnaire, resulting in a response rate of 32%.

In order to assess the basic demographic characteristics of journalists in the Netherlands, the survey included questions about gender, age, education, journalistic experience, journalistic education, and how many hours journalists work on a weekly basis.

The journalists' daily work practice was measured by asking where journalists were working and which activities they performed on the job. The actual place of employment was determined by asking journalists specifically for which media platform they worked (national newspaper, local newspaper, etc.), which resulted in a list of 17 different platforms. Journalists were also asked whether or not they had worked for these media platforms during the last year (multiple answers possible). These media platforms were then collapsed into five general media types (see Table 19.2). The journalists' daily activities, on the other hand, were measured with a list of seven journalistic activities that were included in the questionnaire (see Table 19.3). Because journalists are increasingly expected to be versatile, they were asked to indicate which activities applied to them (multiple answers possible).

To measure the journalists' role perceptions, the questionnaire included a list of 16 statements (see Table 19.4). Twelve statements were based on items from Deuze's (2002) Dutch study which used Weaver and Wilhoit's (1996) items from their U.S. study, such as "get information to the public quickly" and "provide interpretation and analysis." The Dutch questionnaire used in 2006 was augmented with four new items referring to new developments in journalism. We measured the role conception of journalists as translators of complicated issues with the statement "making complex information accessible for the public." The commercial role conception was measured with the statement "create a good environment for advertisers." The idea of journalists as orchestrators of public debate was measured with the statement "stimulate and facilitate discussion for the public." And finally, we measured the role of journalists as trend watchers with the statement "signaling new trends." The extent to which journalists agreed or disagreed with the statements was measured by a four-point scale (not important at all; not important; important; very important).

Journalists' perceptions of journalistic standards were measured by asking about the importance for them of the following traditional values in their work: autonomy, objectivity, hear both sides, checking facts, and neutrality. We also wanted to measure how journalists think about the formalization of these traditional values by capturing them in a code of conduct and by having them maintained by the Netherlands Press Council (a disciplinary tribunal where people can lodge complaints against journalists). So we asked the journalists the importance for them of a code of conduct and the Netherlands Press Council. In all these cases the journalists gave their opinion on a four-point scale (not important at all; not important; important; very important).

Because the Internet now enables people to select, produce, and distribute their own news, the relationship between journalists and the audience has changed during the past 10 years. To measure to what extent journalists take their audience into consideration in their work, we included

Table 19.1   Journalists' Demographic and Professional Background Characteristics

Demographic Characteristic	Percent
Gender (N = 643)	
Women	38%
Men	62%
Age (N = 636)	
>30	6%
31–40	31%
41–50	34%
51–60	25%
< 60	4%
Mean age	44
Median age	43
Education (N = 635)	
Post-academic	4%
University	26%
Higher vocational	52%
Intermediate vocational	4%
Secondary	13%
Other	1%
Journalistic Education (N = 606)	
University	6%
Journalism school	37%
On the job	15%
Nonspecific	42%
Working hours per week (N = 622)	
>24	9%
25–32	20%
33–40	41%
< 40	30%
Mean working hours per week	39

three statements: "Journalists serve their audience," "I take into consideration who my audience is," and "Comments of the audience are useful." All statements mentioned in this section were measured using one of two four-point scales ("not important at all," "not important," "important," "very important"; and "completely disagree," "disagree," "agree," "completely agree"). Subsequently, mean sum-scores were calculated, whereby a higher score indicates a higher degree of importance attached to the statement.

Findings

Background Characteristics

Dutch journalists in 2006 were predominately male (62%), with a mean age of 44 years, and worked on average about 39 hours a week. While about 8 in 10 journalists have a higher education degree (52% higher vocational; 30% university), only about 4 in 10 had attended a journalism school (37%) or a journalism program at a university (6%). This somewhat low percentage is due to the relatively late introduction of academic journalism education in the Netherlands. Thus, most journalists have either no specific journalism education (42%) or were trained on the job (15%).

Table 19.2   Types of Media Journalists Work For (in %)

Media Types	Percent[1]
Newspaper total	57
National newspaper	19
Regional newspaper	34
Free door-to-door newspaper	11
Regular news magazine	6
Broadcasting total	27
National public service broadcasting	13
Regional public service broadcasting	11
National commercial broadcasting	5
Local public service broadcasting	3
Online total	32
Web site	30
Web log	5
Magazines total	46
Professional magazine	29
General interest magazine	18
Corporate magazine	15
Associational magazine	10
News magazine	9
Other	12
Press agency	11
Cable newspaper	1

1 Journalists were allowed to indicate more than one media type and platform. The total percentage therefore exceeds 100%, indicating that journalists, on average, work for more than one media type and media platform.

Table 19.3   Journalists' Job Descriptions and Activities (in %, N = 643)

Jobs Descriptions	Percent
Writing texts or articles[1]	87
Editing texts	68
Producing reports	61
Managing/coordinating	48
Taking photo's	30
Presenting	20
Hosting a Web site	16

1 Journalists were allowed to indicate more than one activity. The total percentage
  therefore exceeds 100%, indicating that journalists, on average, perform more than
  one type of activity. Respondents were allowed multiple responses.

Occupational Characteristics

On average, Dutch journalists work for one to two different media types. This indicates that many journalists in fact worked for more than one news organization in 2006. The top three most important media types were newspapers (57%), magazines (46%), and online media (32%). Fewer journalists worked for broadcasting (27%) and other media platforms such as press agencies and cable newspapers (12%). Overall, these findings show that many Dutch journalists have been working across media types since 2006. Future research should look more closely into this development and provide more insight into how this trend might affect the practice of journalism.

Our findings also indicate that journalists increasingly take on multiple tasks in the process of news production. Table 19.3 shows that the average journalist performs three to four different activities in his or her daily work. However, journalists are still primarily concerned with textual activities: 9 out of 10 of the journalists interviewed say that they "write texts and articles," 68% "edit texts," and 61% "produce news reports." At the same time, almost half (48%) of journalists indicate that they also spend time with managing the newsroom or coordinating their editors' activities.

Journalistic Role Perceptions

Our findings show that journalists think that their most important roles are to make "complex information accessible for the public" (mean = 3.40), "provide interpretation and analysis" (3.23), "signal new trends" (3.20), and "get information to the public quickly" (3.12). Items that refer to a more critical journalistic role, such as investigating "suspicious issues" (2.80) or "government claims" (2.69) are seen as less important. Similarly, items that directly concern the public, such as "stimulate and facilitate discussion for the public" (2.80) or "give common people a chance to express their views" (2.68), also rank lower. In general, journalists do not think that their work should influence politics. "Exert an influence on the political agenda" scores rather low (2.33). On the other hand, looking at the critical role, journalists think it is important to "critically track down political developments" (2.90).

Finally, the results show that economic pressure has not yet influenced the role perceptions of journalists. "Providing entertainment and relaxation" for the audience is not very important (2.50). Even less important is it in their eyes to "create a good environment for advertisers" (1.91).

Table 19.4   Journalists' Role Perceptions (% saying "very important")

	Rank[1]	Very important	Mean[1]	SD	N
Making complex information accessible for the public	1	48%	3.40	0.667	629
Provide interpretation and analysis	2	37%	3.23	0.712	630
Signaling new trends	3	30%	3.20	0.627	628
Get information to the public quickly	4	33%	3.12	0.779	631
Develop social interests of the public	5	23%	2.94	0.797	630
Reach widest possible audience	6	24%	2.94	0.789	631
Critically track down political developments	7	26%	2.90	0.897	629
Track down abuses and make them public	8	24%	2.89	0.868	627
Investigate suspicious issues	9	20%	2.80	0.867	628
Stimulate and facilitate discussion for the public	10	19%	2.80	0.804	630
Investigate government claims	11	18%	2.69	0.907	627
Give ordinary people a chance to express their views	12	13%	2.68	0.805	630
Provide entertainment and relaxation	13	8%	2.50	0.777	629
Stand up for the disadvantaged	14	11%	2.37	0.908	630
Exert an influence on the political agenda	15	6%	2.33	0.808	627
Create a good environment for advertisers	16	4%	1.91	0.877	631

1   Means range from 1 = not important at all – 4 = very important. Ranks are based on means.

Table 19.5 shows that journalists still think that the traditional journalistic values of independence, objectivity, hearing both sides, checking information, and neutrality are very important in their daily work. All items scored 3.3 or higher on our 4-point importance scale. Thus, it seems that new developments, such as the rise of Internet, did not change these traditional journalistic values much. An ethical code or the Netherlands Press Council, on the other hand, were seen as less important. A possible explanation for this limited appreciation of the Council might be the fact that most journalists consider the Council's (non-binding) rulings a violation of their professional autonomy (Pleijter & Frye 2007).

Perceptions of the Audience

As our findings show, Dutch journalists have a somewhat ambivalent relationship with the audience (Table 19.6). While most journalists seem to indicate that they keep their audiences in mind

Table 19.5   Importance of Journalistic Values and Professional Code (% saying "very important")

	Rank[1]	Very important	Mean[1]	SD	N
Autonomy	1	72%	3.69	0.53	636
Objectivity	2	69%	3.68	0.51	633
Hear both sites	3	67%	3.64	0.57	635
Fact checking	4	61%	3.60	0.53	634
Neutrality	5	45%	3.31	0.73	628
An ethical code of conduct	6	22%	2.95	0.78	629
Council of journalism	7	12%	2.59	0.82	633

1   Means range from 1 = not important at all – 4 = very important. Ranks are based on means.

Table 19.6   Journalists' Perceptions of the Audience

	Rank[1]	Very important	Mean[1]	SD	N
I take into consideration who my audience is	1	50%	3.44	0.62	637
Comments of the audience are useful	2	46%	3.43	0.58	634
Journalists serve their audience	3	19%	2.85	0.77	628

1 Means range from 1 = not important at all – 4 = very important. Ranks are based on means.

in their work (mean 3.44) and also appreciate feedback from them (3.43), it is clear that fewer journalists believe that they actually should cater to their audience (2.85). Again, we believe that this reflects the fear that to do so would violate their autonomy and might threaten their position as indispensable gatekeepers of public knowledge and opinion.

Conclusions

A comparison of our findings with those compiled by Deuze (2002) in 1999–2000 shows that Dutch journalists have changed in the past few years. First, it is clear that the number of women working in journalism is still growing. In 2000, for example, about 32% of all journalists were women; six years later this percentage had increased to 38%. And while the average age of journalists remained at about 44, we observed that the group of younger journalists under 30 shrank from 12% in 1999 to 6% in 2006. This decline might be partly explained by the fact that younger journalists are less likely to be associated with the Dutch Association of Journalists, which served as the basis of our sample. Thus, we cannot be absolutely sure that there actually has been a decline in the number of younger journalists.

Despite our expectation that there would be more online journalists in 2006 as compared to 2000, we found no evidence of such a change. Overall, 30% of the journalists in 2006 indicated that they worked for online media and only 16% of the journalists were involved in hosting a Web site—very similar to what Deuze (2002) found in his earlier study of Dutch journalists. It is interesting to follow these developments as the process of convergence and multi-media newsrooms has started only recently in the Netherlands.

Our analysis of the journalistic role perceptions shows that Dutch journalists generally believe that their most important role is the "interpretation" of facts and events. Most journalists in our survey agree that it is not only important for journalists to make information accessible, but also to determine which information people actually need. These findings seem to support Weaver, Beam, Brownlee, Voakes, and Wilhoit's (2007) analysis of American journalists, which concluded that the "interpretative function remained the strongest perception among American journalists in 2002" (p. 141).

Our data show that Dutch journalists have a positive attitude toward their audience, which they take into consideration when doing their work and they find their audiences are useful. But on the other hand, they cling to their traditional role as gatekeepers of the public sphere. They do not feel it's very important to give the people a voice or the opportunity to contribute to the news. But that was in 2006. Now the participatory media culture has evolved enormously. People have become "prosumers" of media content; they produce, select, share, and distribute whatever they like or think is important. Social media have become very popular and play an important part in people's lives. These developments put a new pressure on journalists, as their role of gatekeepers is threatened as never before. How will they deal with the existential question of what the added value and the future role of professional journalists will be? Will the profession develop new role conceptions? These questions are clearly relevant for future research in this field.

References

Alexa. 2010. Top sites in the Netherlands. Retrieved from http://www.alexa.com/topsites/countries/NL

Bakker, Piet. 2008. The simultaneous rise and fall of free and paid newspapers in Europe. *Journalism Practice* 2: 427–443.

Bakker, Piet, and Otto Scholten. 2009. *Communicatiekaart van Nederland* [Communication map of the Netherlands]. Alphen aan den Rijn: Kluwer.

Breedveld, Koen, Andries van den Broek, Jos de Haan, Lucas Harms, Frank Huysmans, and Erik van Ingen. 2006. *De tijd als spiegel: Hoe Nederlanders hun tijd besteden* [Time as a mirror: How Dutch people spend their time]. The Hague: SCP.

Deuze, Mark. 2002. *Journalists in the Netherlands: An analysis of the people, the issues and the (inter)national environment.* Amsterdam: Aksant.

Dutch Audience Research Foundation. 2010. *Jaarrapport 2009* [Year report 2009]. Hilversum: SKO. Retrieved from http://kijkonderzoek.nl/images/stories/rapporten/ sko_jaarrapport_2009_def.pdf

Dutch Media Authority. 2009. *Dagbladenmarkt 2008* [Newspaper market 2008]. Hilversum: CvdM. Retrieved from http://www.mediamonitor.nl/content.jsp?objectid=9522

Dutch Media Authority. 2009. *Eigendomsverhoudingen Telegraaf Media Groep* [Ownership structure of the Telegraaf Media group]. Hilversum: CvdM. Retrieved from http://www.mediamonitor.nl/content.jsp?objectid=9839

Hermans, Liesbeth, Maurice Vergeer, and Leen d'Haenens. 2009. Internet in the daily life of journalists: Explaining the use of the Internet through work-related characteristics and professional opinions. *Journal of Computer Mediated Communication* 15:138–157.

Hermans, Liesbeth, Maurice Vergeer, and Alexander Pleijter. 2009. Internet adoption in the newsroom: Journalists' use of the Internet explained by attitudes and perceived functions. *Communications: The European Journal of Communication Research* 34(1):55–71.

Joustra, Arendo. (2009). Welkomstwoord tijdens de viering van het 50-jarig jubileum van het Genootschap van Hoofdredacteuren [Welcoming speech at the celebration of the 50th anniversary of the Dutch Society of Editors]. Retrieved from http://www.genootschapvanhoofdredacteuren.nl/organisatie/voordrachten-redevoeringen/voordrachten/welkomstwoord-arendo-joustra-tijdens-de-viering-van-het-50-jarig-jubileum-van-het-genootschap.html

Kempers, Frans, and Jan Wieten. 1976. *Journalisten en persconcentratie* [Journalists and media concentration]. Amsterdam: University of Amsterdam.

Lohman, Erik, and Allerd Peeters. 2000. Van schaarste naar overvloed: Nieuws en actualiteiten op tv [From scarcity to abundance: News and current affairs on TV]. In *De slag om het nieuws: Tv-nieuws en nieuwe technologie* [The battle for the news: TV news and new technology], edited by Wim Fortuyn, pp. 81–104. Den Haag: SDU.

Muskens, Gerard 1968. *Journalist als beroep: Een sociologische analyse van de leden van de Nederlandse Vereniging van Journalisten* [Journalism as a profession: A sociological analysis of the members of the Dutch Association of Journalists]. Nijmegen: Sociologisch Instituut.

NOS-KLO. 1994. *Jaaroverzicht continu kijkonderzoek—1993* [Annual report on continuous audience research—1993]. Hilversum: NOS-KLO.

NOS-KLO. 1995. *Jaaroverzicht continu kijkonderzoek—1994* [Annual report on continuous audience research—1994]. Hilversum: NOS-KLO.

Pleijter, Alexander, and Annemarie Frye. 2007. *Journalistieke gedragscode: Leiband of leidraad?* [Journalistic code: Leash or guidance?]. Nijmegen: Radboud Universiteit.

Pleijter, Alexander, Liesbeth Hermans, and Maurice Vergeer. 2007. De opmars van online nieuwsgaring in de Nederlands journalistiek van 2002–2006 [The rise of online news gathering in Dutch journalism, 2002–2006]. In *Journalistiek & internet: Technofielen of digibeten* [Journalism & the Internet: Technophiles or digital illiterates], edited by Erik van Heeswijk, pp. 27–46. Apeldoorn: Spinhuis.

Pleijter, Alexander, Frank Tebbe, and Liesbeth Hermans. 2002. *Nieuwe journalisten door nieuwe bronnen? Een landelijke inventarisatie van het internetgebruik in de Nederlandse journalistiek* [New journalists through new sources? A national inventory of the use of the Internet by Dutch journalists]. Nijmegen/Rotterdam: Katholieke Universiteit Nijmegen/ Bikker Euro RSCG.

RMO. 2003. *Medialogica: Over het krachtenveld tussen burgers, media en politiek* [Media logic: On the forces between citizens, media and politics]. The Hague: Author.

Tijdelijke Commissie Innovatie en Toekomst Pers [Temporary Committee on Innovation and the Future of the Press]. 2009. *De volgende editie* [The next edition]. Den Haag: Tijdelijke Commissie Innovatie en Toekomst Pers.

Vergeer, Maurice. 2006. *Lokale medialandschappen in Nederland 2005* [Local media landscapes in the Netherlands 2005]. The Hague/Nijmegen: Stimuleringsfonds voor de Pers/Radboud Universiteit.

Vergeer, Maurice, Rob Eisinga, and Philip Hans Franses. 2012. Supply and demand effects in television viewing: A time series analysis. *Communications—The European Journal of Communication Research* 37:79–98.

Weaver, David H., Randall A. Beam, Bonnie J. Brownlee, Paul S. Voakes, and G. Cleveland Wilhoit. 2007. *The American journalist in the 21st century*. London: Erlbaum.

Weaver, David H., and G. Cleveland Wilhoit. 1996. *The American journalist in the 1990s: U.S. news people at the end of an era*. Mahwah, NJ: Erlbaum.

Wijfjes, Huub 2004. *Journalistiek in Nederland, 1850–2000: Beroep, cultuur en organisatie* [Journalism in the Netherlands, 1850–2000: Profession, culture and organization]. Amsterdam: Boom.

20 The Journalists and Journalism of Poland

Agnieszka Stepinska, Szymon Ossowski, Lidia Pokrzycka, and Jakub Nowak

To understand the characteristics of contemporary Polish journalism, at least three crucial elements of its historical background need to be explained: (1) the three partitions of Poland at the end of the 18th century carried out by the Russian Empire, Kingdom of Prussia, and Habsburg Austria; (2) the post-World War II communist regime; and (3) a transformation of the media in Poland that started with the breakup of the Soviet Union in the late 1980s.

The first Polish newspaper was *Merkuriusz Polski Ordynaryjny*, which was launched in 1660 as a title closely related to the monarchy. Other newspapers that were published in the 17th and 18th century were either launched by monasteries or by political organizations. Thus, in the 17th and 18th century, writers, intellectuals, and politicians were acting as journalists (Łojek, Myśliński, & Władyka 1988).

The late 18th and 19th centuries were significant for the European press. The Polish–Lithuanian Commonwealth was annexed by Russia, Prussia, and Habsburg Austria, and the Polish state was divided into three "partitions" in 1772, 1793, and 1795. The invaders brought with them three different models of journalism that strongly affected Polish journalists and can still be recognized today among journalists from the three areas (Łojek et al. 1988).

The three occupying powers also made great efforts to slow down the professionalization of Polish journalism through censorship and political repression. As a result, the Polish press was either completely abolished or seriously censored during this period (Dziki 2000: 38–42; Habielski 2009: 13). However, despite imposing legal and political barriers to a free Polish press, illegal newspapers circulated frequently among Polish nationals (Łojek, Myśliński, & Władyka 1988). Thus, even under foreign rule, a traditional model of journalism with a focus on political, cultural, and social issues developed during the 19th century. Journalists, poets, and writers saw it as their responsibility to represent "the people without a state," support Polish cultural and national identity, and transmit this cultural knowledge from generation to generation during 123 years of invaders divesting the Polish population of its national character (Osica 2001: 27).

Once Poland gained independence in 1918, journalists faced numerous challenges that were a legacy of the long-lasting occupation: the technical underdevelopment of the previously illegal Polish media, the instability of three separate press markets, and the negative effects of commercialization (Dziki 2000: 44–47). Despite these problems, within the next 20 years the Polish media managed to develop their own identity, while still representing the political, social, and cultural diversity of the re-established country.

The progress of the Polish media was disrupted again by World War II. The only legal mass media under Nazi rule were those launched by the invaders. However, as in the previous occupation, about 2,000 illegal Polish underground newspapers and magazines were circulated between 1939 and the end of the war in 1945 (Lewandowska 1982).

The post-war period of the Polish media was characterized by a strong political dependence on the Soviet Union. Again, Polish journalists experienced censorship and political repression that was based on the idea of state-owned media. Some journalists agreed to co-operate with the regime, while others decided to join illegal anti-communist newspapers and magazines that were launched as early as 1944 (Habielski 2009: 198). While the electronic media were completely under communist control (Pokorna-Ignatowicz 2003), the Polish newspaper sector exhibited a bit more diversity. While some newspapers supported Marxist ideology and acknowledged the authority of the Communist Party (for example, *Trybuna Ludu* or *Sztandar Młodych*), other newspapers and magazines were associated with organizations of the Catholic Church (such as the high-quality weekly magazine *Tygodnik Powszechny*) (Dziki 2000: 49–54).

Overall, Polish journalists viewed themselves as social educators, with a strong sense of the political nature of their jobs, guided more by consideration of their social mission as defined by their political sponsors than by a story's attractiveness for the audience (Jakubowicz 1992). Furthermore, journalists were more likely than other white-collar workers to belong to the Communist Party. In 1985, about 53% of all Polish journalists belonged to the party, compared to 35% of white-collar workers in general (Centrum Badania Opinii Społecznej 1987; Jakubowicz 1992).

The transformation of the media in Poland was based on two crucial elements, a political breakthrough between 1989 and 1991 and a technological transformation that started in 1995. In particular, a few events should be mentioned here: (1) the abolition of press licensing in May 1989, (2) partly free parliamentary elections in June 1989, (3) the end of the communist press monopoly in March 1990, and (4) the abolition of censorship in June 1990. These developments had serious consequences for Polish journalism. Between 1989 and 1992, about 1,500 Polish journalists left their jobs (Bajka 2000: 45). Among them were journalists who previously supported the communist regime and those who were not able to respond to the technological changes and challenges. Some journalists experienced difficulties in adapting to a free-market economy and a commercial media system, while others suffered from political and social disorientation (Bajka 2000: 44–45).

At the same time, a new generation of journalists entered the profession. Some had previously worked for illegal, anti-communist newspapers and magazines, while others were recent university graduates with little professional experience and no interest in political involvement (Bajka 2000: 45–46). It is worth mentioning that along with the political and media transformation, more and more people graduating from high schools have been interested in studying political science and journalism. In 2009, media or journalism studies were offered by 42 public and private universities in Poland. Most journalism programs originally were part of political science departments and just recently have been formally converted into separate programs (Olszewski 2009).

The Print Media

Today there are no legal limitations regarding the establishment and distribution of private newspapers and magazines in Poland. Direct political influence on the printed press ended in 1991 along with the liquidation of *RSW Prasa*, the Communist Party's publishing house. Nevertheless, it is still possible to identify an informal political influence, mostly in the connections between the publishers' associations, the journalists' associations, and the political parties.

As elsewhere around the globe, the Polish press market has experienced a decline in newspaper and magazine circulation and a reduction of income from advertising in recent years. Publishers have responded with staff and publishing cost reductions, stronger connections between print and online versions of newspapers and magazines, lower subscription prices, and more special editions and inserts (Filas 2007).

In addition, foreign publishing groups began entering the Polish press market in the 1990s. By 2005, most of the Polish media market was controlled by publishing houses with foreign capital such as Wydawnictwo Bauer, Grupa Wydawnicza PolskaPresse, Axel Springer Polska, and Media Regionalne. Polskapresse, for example, owns nine Polish newspapers and magazines, while Media Regionalne owns 11 titles. These foreign investors not only brought capital to the Polish media, but also a market-oriented perspective. As a result, the number of local and regional newspapers declined in recent years, and several regional newspapers were closed completely. These changes have enabled media organizations to reduce the number of correspondents, editors, and regular journalists (Kopacz 2008).

This decline of the local press is a significant trend because about half of the Polish press titles are local newspapers. However, the structure of this media segment (of a total number of 2,500 to 3,000 titles) is still quite diverse. In 2002, 39% of the local newspapers belonged to the private owners, 36.5% to local governments, 14.4% to NGOs, 9.7% to the parish press, and 0.4% to the political parties. There were about 500 titles that had national reach and that were issued daily or weekly. The other publications were usually monthly magazines circulated in small local communities (Gierula 2002).

The most popular national daily newspapers in 2009 were the tabloid *Fakt* (modeled on the German *Bild* and owned by Axel Springer) and the quality newspaper *Gazeta Wyborcza* (owned by Agora, a Polish joint-stock media company). Both together had a 15% market share (Polskie Badania Czytelnictwa 2009). The two market leaders were followed by the free daily *Metro* (8%), the tabloid *SuperExpress* (7.5%); two quality newspapers, *Dziennik. Polska. Europa. Swiat* (4%) and *Rzeczpospolita* (4%); and the sports paper, *Przeglad Sportowy* (4%) (Polskie Badania Czytelnictwa 2009).

The Electronic Media

The Polish TV and radio sector has undergone radical transformation since the fall of the communist regime. As a result of the 1992 Broadcasting Act, a dual broadcasting model was introduced in Poland, which allowed both private and public TV and radio broadcasters (Mielczarek 2007). Polish public TV provides three terrestrial channels as well as a few satellite channels that include *TV Polonia* (for Polish viewers abroad), *TVP Kultura* (culture), *TVP Historia* (history), and *TVP Sport*. Furthermore, there are 16 regional stations that provide news to local and regional audiences.

The public TV broadcaster Telewizja Polska (TVP), which still commands more than half of the country's audience and advertising revenue, dominates the market more than any other public broadcaster in central European countries (Krajewski 2005: 275). In 2009, the market shares of the two public TV channels were about 27% (AGB Nielsen Media Research 2009). Public TV is also a leader in the ratings of news broadcasts in Poland. In fact, the newscast with the highest share ratings (41%) is *Teleexpress*, a 15-minute newscast which is broadcast at 5 p.m. for the public TVP1 station (AGB Nielsen Media Research).

At the same time, private broadcasters achieved large market shares (Godzic & Drzał-Sierocka 2009). Polsat (with 15% of the market share), TVN (13%), TV4 (2%), and Puls (1%) all managed to become major competitors in the Polish broadcast market. Poland is also the third-biggest cable television market in Europe (having about 4.5 million subscribers). The cable market is dominated by six operators with significant foreign capital involvement (Lara 2005).

In 2010, 58.4% of the Polish population had Internet access (Internet World Stats 2010). Despite the rapid growth in the number of Internet users in Poland since 2000, the number of broadband connections remains relatively low. The most active Internet users are those between the ages of 15 and 24 (Batorski 2009: 288–296; Gemius 2009).

Polish Journalists

The Polish press law defines a journalist as "a person who produces, edits or publishes press materials and who is employed by an editorial office or who undertakes such activities on behalf of and on the authority of an editorial office" (Ustawa Prawo Prasowe 1984, Article 7, Paragraph 2, Point 5). Furthermore, a journalist is "a professional who is obliged to serve the society and the country" (Ustawa Prawo Prasowe 1984, Article 7). There are no formal requirements for anyone to enter the profession.

It is worth emphasizing that the Polish Press Law Act was adopted in 1984 under the communist regime. Thus, despite several amendments, it is less than adequate for a modern, democratic state. For example, according to Article 10 of the Press Law Act, journalists must comply with the general principles of their publishers. Any violation of this provision can be a sufficient reason for dismissal. This regulation has caused considerable tensions in the relations between editors and journalists (Szot 2008).

Despite the fact that there is broad agreement among scholars, lawyers, and journalists that the current press law needs to be updated, none of the ideas presented since 1989 were accepted by all sectors of the media (Barć-Krupińska 2008: 82–83; Sobczak 2008; Stefanowicz 2007). The ongoing debates about a better press law also underscore the weakness of Poland's journalist associations. Although there are several organizations, none has managed to find support among all journalists for one shared concept to update the press law (Bajka 2000).

Previous Studies

Polish journalists have been the object of little systematic study. Although several academic institutions conduct studies on journalists and the media (for example, the Jagiellonian University in Cracow, the Warsaw University, the Adam Mickiewicz University in Poznan, the Maria Curie-Skłodowska University in Lublin, the University of Silesia, and the University of Wroclaw), many scholars have focused on regional and local outlets (for example, Kowalczyk 2008). While there are numerous essays on the state of journalism in Poland, actual surveys of journalists are rare and limited in scope.

The first qualitative and quantitative studies on Polish journalists were conducted by Zbigniew Bajka from the Press Research Center at the Jagiellonian University in Cracow in the 1980s. Bajka (1991), who mostly focused on relations between journalists and the government, found that journalists did not want to be perceived as "political officers," or related to the government in any way.

A decade later, Bajka (2000) conducted an Internet survey among 250 journalists at daily newspapers, magazines, and in electronic media. He found that most journalists (64%) made the decision to enter journalism on their own, while 19% followed their relatives or friends' suggestions, and 17% became journalists by chance (Bajka 2000: 51–52).

By comparing his newer study with findings from the older survey, Bajka also found that in the 1990s journalists most appreciated the opportunity to follow current affairs, meet interesting people, visit new places, learn new skills, and enjoy the prestige of the profession. At the same time, they were less enthused about having an opportunity to influence opinions and attitudes, or to help people solve their problems (Bajka 2000: 52–53).

Finally, Bajka studied journalists' autonomy and level of professionalization. He found that as many as 93% of respondents believed that although journalists expressed their own opinions in most cases, they had to occasionally promote the opinions of other actors. When asked which actors exerted pressure on journalists, 42% mentioned owners of the media organizations and editors, while 19% cited censorship by editors. Only 8% of journalists mentioned any political actor attempting to influence them (Bajka 2000: 55).

Subsequent surveys focused mostly on journalists working for local and regional media. Gierula (2006), for example, showed that journalists from the Silesia region most frequently experienced problems related to (1) the amount of professional obligations they had (34%), (2) access to information (31%), (3) the range of topics they had to cover (27%), (4) the work procedures in their editor's office (18%), and (5) the working and technical conditions (17.2%).

Pokrzycka (2008) continued exploring the issue of work-related problems with a survey of 100 journalists working for the local and regional press of the Lublin region. Her findings showed that journalists most frequently complained about (1) relatively low salaries in comparison to the degree of responsibility they had and the social roles they played, (2) understaffed editorial teams, and (3) a highly competitive media market. Some journalists also mentioned increased costs of living, official responses to criticism, the pressure of interest groups on media professionals, and the lack of job security as serious problems.

The question of the prestige of the journalist profession was also raised by Krawczyk (2006). The author interviewed 86 journalists and 451 citizens of the Katowice municipality (one of Poland's largest cities) with self-administered survey questionnaires. Surprisingly, his findings indicated that opinions about the journalistic profession were far more positive among the public than among journalists themselves. While only 22% of the interviewed journalists claimed that the prestige of their profession was high, as many as 69% of the general public expressed this opinion. The results of the study also showed that respondents with higher levels of education and those aged 50 or older were more likely to have positive views of journalists than younger respondents or those with less education (Krawczyk 2006: 43).

Method

Our study is based on 329 telephone interviews that were conducted with a random sample of Polish journalists in October and November 2009. The interviews, which lasted about 15 minutes each, were collected by Pentor Research International Poznan.

We defined journalists as media personnel responsible for the information content of several types of media: daily newspapers, weekly magazines, monthly magazines, news services (agencies), radio and TV stations, and online news media. Because a significant number of media personnel in Poland have limited employment contracts, we did not limit our sample to full-time employees. However, except for those journalists working for TV stations, most of the journalists surveyed in this study were full-time editorial personnel (editors, news directors, correspondents, columnists, and reporters). We excluded administrative personnel and those working as camera operators or sound technicians.

Table 20.1   The Survey Sample (*N* = 329)

	Designed Quotas Number	Percentage	Actual Quotas Number	Percentage
Daily newspapers	35	12.0%	46	14.0%
Weekly magazines	70	23.0%	46	14.0%
Monthly magazines	70	23.0%	112	34.0%
Press agencies	4	1.0%	5	1.5%
TV stations	46	15.0%	43	13.0%
Radio stations	50	17.0%	61	18.5%
On line media	25	9.0%	16	5.0%
TOTAL	300	100.0%	329	100.0%

Generating a good random sample of Polish journalists was a significant challenge. For example, we found it difficult to estimate the total number of journalists in Poland. Bajka (2000: 42) estimated this number to be around 25,000 in 2000, but, surprisingly, nobody has checked this number more recently. We quickly realized that there is no single official source that might provide us with the actual number of working journalists in Poland.

To gain a more current estimate, we decided to compile a list of all Polish news organizations with the help of the most recent *Media and Advertising Almanac* (*Almanach Mediów i Reklamy* 2007–2008). Based on the compiled list, we estimate that 12% of Polish journalists work for daily newspapers, 23% for weekly magazines, 23% for monthly magazines, 1% for news agencies, 15% for TV stations, 17% for radio stations, and 8% for the online media. Table 20.1 presents a breakdown of the final sampling frame, which was used to generate a stratified random sample of news organizations.

Although the actual numbers and percentages of journalists working for weekly and monthly magazines differ from those sampled, combining both groups in the sample makes this group fairly representative overall (46% and 48%, respectively). Thus, we decided not to make any other adjustments. We should note, however, that journalists working for online media and news agencies are underrepresented in our sample. We are aware of these shortcomings in the sample and will avoid drawing general conclusions based on the data coming from these two groups of respondents.

Findings

In the following pages, we present the results of our survey broken down by media sector. In some cases, the current data will be compared to the demographic profile of journalists provided by Bajka (2000). It is not strictly representative, but will serve as a valuable baseline nonetheless.

Table 20.2 traces the demographic profiles of Polish journalists by media sector. Our data suggest that the highest proportion of women work for news agencies (80%) and monthly magazines (48.2%), while the lowest percentage is found in online media (18.7%) and weekly magazines (30.4%). Overall, almost 41% of the journalists are women, a 6% increase in the number of female journalists compared to the 1990s (Bajka 2000). Journalists at TV stations are the youngest (29 years on average), while journalists working for news agencies and monthly magazines are the oldest (49 and 40 years, respectively). Those who work for TV also have fewer years of experience than those working for monthly magazines or daily newspapers.

Table 20.2   Demographic Profile of Journalists by Media Sector (*N* = 329)

	Dailies	Weeklies	Monthly Mags	Radio	TV	News Agency	Internet	Overall
Sex (% male)	67.4%	69.6%	51.8%	57.4%	58.1%	20%	81.3%	59.3%
Age (years)[1]	40	34	36	32	29	49	33	34
Married	60.9%	60.9%	64.3%	37.7%	44.2%	60%	56.3%	55.3%
Living in big cities	69.6%	65.2%	84.8%	36.1%	76.7%	100%	93.8%	71.1%
Experience (years)[1]	15	10	10	10	3	20	5	10
University degree	91.3%	84.8%	90.2%	70.5%	79.1%	80.0%	87.5%	84.2%
Journalism graduate	32.6%	30.4%	30.4%	21.3%	44.2%	40.0%	43.8%	31.6%
Total	46	46	112	61	43	5	16	329

1 Median

Interestingly, although most of the journalists in our sample were married (55.3%), television (37.7%) and radio journalists (44.2%) were much less likely to be married than other journalists. In comparison, most of the journalists in the 1990s were less experienced (80% worked for less than 10 years) and single (75%) (Bajka 2000).

The findings also indicate that most Polish journalists are highly educated. Overall, 84% of journalists have a university degree, but only about one-third of them had graduated from a university program in journalism. In the 1990s, 78% of the journalists had a university degree and 45% graduated from academic programs in journalism (Bajka 2000). Only 14% of the interviewed journalists belonged to either a journalist association or a trade union. The most organized journalists were found among those working for online media (31.3%), news agencies (20.0%), radio (18.0%), and daily newspapers (17.4%). The percentage of organized journalists in weekly (8.7%) and monthly magazines (11.6%), however, is significantly smaller.

The transformation of the Polish media has been strongly influenced by the type of employment most journalists have. Before 1989, most journalists were full-time media personnel (Bajka 1991). As Table 20.3 shows, two decades later we find that more than 20% of journalists overall, and almost 60% of TV professionals, are contract workers. Most either have time-limited contracts, or operate as independent media producers offering their work to TV stations. What makes this form of employment so popular among media organizations is the fact that the journalists rather than the employers have to cover the costs of social and health insurance.

The vast majority of the Polish journalists interviewed said they were either "very satisfied" (21.5%) or "fairly satisfied" (74.5%) with their current jobs (see Table 20.4). The highest satisfac-

Table 20.3   Structure of Employment by Media Sector (in %, *N* = 329)

	Dailies	Weeklies	Monthly Mags	Radio	TV	News agency	Internet	Overall
Full-time	69.6	78.3	69.6	72.1	27.9	100.0	56.3	65.7
Part-time	4.3	4.3	8.0	8.2	11.6	—	6.3	7.3
Contract	23.9	13.0	13.4	18.0	58.1	—	25.0	21.9
Volunteer	2.2	—	1.8	1.7	0	—	—	1.2
Unknown	—	4.4	7.2	—	2.4	—	12.4	3.9
Total	100.0	100.0	100.0	100.0	100.0	100.0	100.0	100.0

Table 20.4   Level of Job Satisfaction by Media Sector (*N* = 318)

	Dailies	Weeklies	Monthly Mags	Radio	TV	News agency	Internet	Overall
Very satisfied	15.6	17.8	24.8	27.1	5.0	20.0	46.6	21.5
Fairly satisfied	77.7	80.0	73.4	72.9	82.5	80.0	40.0	74.5
Somewhat dissatisfied	6.7	2.2	0.9	—	10.0	—	6.7	3.1
Very dissatisfied	—	—	0.9	—	2.5	—	6.7	0.9
Total	100.0	100.0	100.0	100.0	100.0	100.0	100.0	100.0

tion levels were found among journalists working for online media (46.6% "very satisfied"), radio stations (27.1%), and monthly magazines (24.8%). The lowest levels of job satisfaction were found among TV journalists (5% "very satisfied").

In addition to having the lowest level of job satisfaction, TV journalists also had the least positive views about how well their media organizations were informing the public (see Table 20.4). Only 7.1% of the TV journalists evaluated their organizations' performance as a source of information as "outstanding," while 23.8% described it only as "fair." Journalists in other media sectors tended to have more positive views. For example, 17.9% of the journalists working for monthly magazines and 15.6% of those working for weekly magazines stated that their media organizations did an outstanding job of informing the public.

When asked about how free they were to select stories to be covered, TV journalists again exhibited the lowest level of autonomy (see Table 20.6). While 20% of the TV journalists claimed that they only have "some freedom" in selecting stories, about one-third (31.7%) thought that they had "almost complete" freedom in that matter. In contrast, most journalists working for news agencies (60%) and weekly magazines (58.7%) said that they have "almost complete" freedom to choose the stories they write about.

We also asked respondents to judge the importance of various aspects of their jobs. Table 20.7 presents these aspects from the most important to the least important for Polish journalists. The results show that job autonomy and a chance to develop professional skills were considered very important by a majority of journalists in all media sectors (about 80%). For more than 60% of the journalists, not only are pay and job security very important, but also the chance to help people and the editorial policy of the organization. Interestingly, only one-third of journalists generally are interested in a promotion.

As before, it was mostly the journalists' employment situation that affected their views of their own media organizations. Again, TV journalists differed sharply from other journalists in their evaluations of the aspects of their job. First of all, almost half (48%) of the TV journalists

Table 20.5   Evaluation of Media Performance by Media Sector (*N* = 319)

	Dailies	Weeklies	Monthly Mags	Radio	TV	News agency	Internet	Overall
Outstanding	8.7	15.6	17.9	8.5	7.1	—	12.5	12.5
Very good	58.7	44.4	48.1	54.2	42.9	80.0	56.3	50.5
Good	19.6	33.3	27.4	32.2	26.2	20.0	12.5	27.0
Fair	13.0	6.7	6.6	5.1	23.8	—	18.7	10.0
Poor	—	—	—	—	—	—	—	—
Total	100.0	100.0	100.0	100.0	100.0	100.0	100.0	100.0

Table 20.6   Freedom in Selecting Stories by the Media Sector (*N* = 323)

	Dailies	Weeklies	Monthly Mags	Radio	TV	News agency	Internet	Overall
Almost complete	47.8	58.7	37.6	53.3	31.7	60.0	50.0	45.2
A great deal	39.1	26.1	43.1	35	43.9	40.0	31.2	38.1
Some	13.1	13.0	19.3	11.7	22.0	—	12.5	15.8
Not at all	—	2.2	—	—	2.4	—	6.3	0.9
Total	100.0	100.0	100.0	100.0	100.0	100.0	100.0	100.0

considered promotion to be "very important." This finding might be explained by the fact that the average TV journalist has spent less time in the profession than journalists in other media (see above), and may perceive promotions as a path to greater job security. Second, TV journalists also were less likely to say that job security is the "most important issue" for them (48%), as compared to 52.3% for newspaper, 56.6% weekly magazine, 61% monthly magazine, and 68% radio station journalists. However, almost 12% of all TV journalists refused to answer this question, which may indicate that the topic of job security is a sensitive one. Finally, because many TV journalists were not full-time employees, it is not surprising that they did not expect any fringe benefits in their jobs. As the analysis shows, those benefits were "very important" to only about 20% of journalists working for news agencies and TV stations. In contrast, a significant number of journalists working for newspapers (35%), radio (39%), and weekly magazines (50%) admitted that fringe benefits were very important for them.

The final set of questions was designed to find out more about how Polish journalists evaluate various key functions of the media. The list includes 14 typical media functions (adopted from Weaver, Beam, Brownlee, Voakes, & Wilhoit 2007) such as "getting information to the public quickly," "providing analysis and interpretation of complex problems," and "investigating claims and statements made by the government." Journalists were asked to indicate how important they considered each of the 14 functions for their own media organizations.

By comparing the exact numbers of answers listed as "very important," we are able to identify the priorities among Polish journalists (see Table 20.8). For Polish journalists, the top priority is providing information to the public quickly (81.7%), followed by acting as an adversary of public officials by being constantly skeptical of their actions (74.6%), and developing intellectual and

Table 20.7   Importance of Various Job Aspects (in %)

	Very important	Fairly important	Not too important	Percent	N
The amount of autonomy	86.2	13.5	0.3	100.0	327
The chance to develop professional skills	80.2	16.4	3.4	100.0	324
The pay	66.7	29.9	3.4	100.0	324
The chance to help people	66.0	29.6	4.4	100.0	324
Job security	61.0	30.5	8.5	100.0	318
The editorial polices of the organization	59.5	36.0	4.5	100.0	311
The chance to influence public affairs	58.3	35.3	6.4	100.0	326
Fringe benefits	41.4	45.5	13.1	100.0	314
The chance to get ahead in organization	35.9	46.6	17.5	100.0	320

Table 20.8   Importance of Media Functions (in %)

	Very important	Fairly important	Not too important	Percent	N
Get information to the public quickly	81.7	15.3	3.0	100.0	327
Be an adversary of public officials by being constantly skeptical of their actions	74.6	19.4	6.0	100.0	315
Develop intellectual and cultural interests of the public	74.2	22.1	3.7	100.0	326
Provide analysis and interpretation of complex problems	65.4	30.7	3.9	100.0	320
Point people toward possible solutions to society's problems	63.6	28.5	7.9	100.0	319
Give ordinary people a chance to express their views on public affairs	63.2	28.3	8.5	100.0	325
To set the political agenda	62.2	33.1	4.7	100.0	320
Concentrate on news that's of interest to the widest possible audience	60.5	32.4	7.1	100.0	324
Motivate ordinary people to get involved in public discussions of important issues	58.4	33.2	8.4	100.0	322
Discuss national policy while it is still being developed	46.6	41.9	11.5	100.0	320
Stay away from stories where factual content cannot be verified	42.8	42.0	15.2	100.0	264
Investigate claims and statements made by the government	42.6	40.1	17.3	100.0	317
Provide analysis and interpretation of international developments	42.0	43.3	14.7	100.0	319
Provide entertainment and relaxation	35.3	42.4	22.3	100.0	323

cultural interests of the public (74.2%). At the bottom of the journalists' priority list was: providing entertainment and relaxation (only 35.3% of the answers were "very important" and 22.3% of the answers "not too important"), as well as providing analysis and interpretation of international developments, and investigating claims and statements made by the government.

Conclusions

This chapter discussed the findings of the most extensive survey of Polish journalists conducted since the late 1990s. In general, Polish journalists are fairly satisfied with their jobs and have very positive perceptions of their media organizations as sources of information. Furthermore, most of the journalists display a deep sense of autonomy in their jobs and generally are happy with the level of freedom they have in selecting the stories they report. The findings also suggest that Polish journalists pay significant attention to job autonomy and opportunities to develop their professional skills, knowledge, and specialties. Moreover, most of them seem to appreciate the chance to influence public opinion.

The survey also found some systematic differences between journalists working for TV stations and journalists in other media sectors. One major difference was employment status. As our findings suggest, most TV professionals were contract workers, and fewer than one-third (27.9%) had full-time jobs. TV journalists also tended to be younger, single, less experienced, and more critical toward the media organization they work for. It is therefore no surprise that TV journalists tended to be less satisfied with their jobs, less likely to think that their media organization was doing a good job in informing the public, and less likely to feel that they have a great deal of autonomy in their jobs than journalists in other media sectors. Finally, they were less eager to discuss aspects of their professional situation such as job security, promotion prospects, or the media organization policy.

The aim of the last part of the study was to explore the self-perception of the profession, namely the roles journalists believe they should play. The results revealed that journalists across all the media sectors tended to perceive themselves as news providers rather than entertainment providers. They focused more on developing the public's intellectual and cultural interests than providing analysis and interpretation of complex problems, or serving in an adversarial role toward public officials by constantly being skeptical of their actions.

While much scholarship on Polish journalism examines local and regional news workers, less is known about journalists who work for media with a national scope. This study attempts to fill this gap by providing updated data not only on demographic profiles of Polish journalists, but also on their professional features, values, and standards.

References

AGB Nielsen Media Research. 2009. Rynek telewizyjny 2009—Podsumowanie [Television market 2009—A summary]. Retrieved from http://www.agbnielsen.pl/Rynek,telewizyjny,2009,-,podsumowanie,1455.html

Almanach Mediów i Reklamy 2007–2008 [Media and Advertising Almanac]. (2008). Wydawnictwo Grunder + Jahr Polska: Warszawa.

Bajka, Zbigniew. 1991. Dziennikarze (1981–1990). Komunikowanie masowe w Polsce–lata osiemdziesiąte [Journalists (1981–1990). Mass communication in Poland in the 1980s]. *Zeszyty Prasoznawcze* 1–2:149–159.

Bajka, Zbigniew. 2000. Dziennikarze lat dziewięćdziesiątych [Journalists of the 1990s]. *Zeszyty Prasoznawcze* 3–4:42–63.

Barć-Krupińska, Anna. 2008. Zmiany w prawie prasowym po 1989 roku [Changes in the press law after 1989]. In *Oblicza polskich mediów po 1989 roku* [The faces of the Polish media after 1989], edited by Lidia Pokrzycka and Beata Romiszewska, pp. 71–83. Lublin: Wydawnictwo UMCS.

Batorski, Dominik. 2009. Korzystanie z technologii informacyjno-komunikacyjnych [The use of information-communication technologies]. In *Diagnoza społeczna 2009* [Social diagnosis 2009], edited by Janusz Czapiński and Tomasz Panek, pp. 281–307. Warszawa: Rada Monitoringu Społecznego. Retrieved from http://www.diagnoza.com/pliki/raporty/Diagnoza_raport_2009.pdf

Centrum Badania Opinii Społecznej. 1987. Dziennikarze o sobie i polityce informacyjnej [Journalists about themselves and information policy]. Warszawa: Centrum Badania Opinii Społecznej.

Dziki, Sylwester. 2000. Prasa w rozwoju historycznym [Historical development of the press]. In *Dziennikarstwo i świat mediów* [Journalism and the media world], edited by Zbigniew Bauer and Edward Chudziński , pp. 32–58. Kraków: Universitas.

Filas, Ryszard. 2007. Prasa ogólnokrajowa po 1989 r. [Nationwide press after 1989]. In *Słownik wiedzy o mediach* [Media studies glossary], edited by Edward Chudziński, pp. 108–125. Warszawa-Bielsko-Biała: Wydawnictwo Szkolne PWN.

Gemius. 2009. Polski internet 2008/2009. [Polish Internet 2008/2009]. Retrieved from http://pliki.gemius.pl/Raporty/2009/02_2009_Polski_internet_2008_2009.pdf

Gierula, Marian. 2002. Znaczenie prasy lokalnej we współczesnym społeczeństwie polskim. [The role of the local press in a contemporary Polish society]. In *Rynkowe zachowania nabywców prasy* [The market-oriented behavior of the press consumers], edited by Jan Kania, pp. 43–50. Szczecin: Szczecin Expo.

Gierula, Marian. 2006. Dziennikarze współczesnej prasy lokalnej [Journalists of the contemporary local press]. In *Media i komunikowanie w społeczeństwie demokratycznym* [Media and communication in a democratic society], edited by Stanisław Michalczyk, pp. 76–90. *Szkice medioznawcze.* Sosnowiec: Wydawnictwo Wyższej Szkoły Zarządzania i Marketingu w Sosnowcu.

Godzic, Wiesław, & Aleksandra Drzał-Sierocka. 2009. *Raport o mediach audiowizualnych*: *Raporty o stanie kultury na Kongres kultury polskiej* [Report on the audio-visual media: Reports on a condition of the culture presented at the Polish Culture Congress]. Retrieved from http://www.kongreskultury.pl/title,pid,143.html.

Habielski, Rafał. 2009. *Polityczna historia mediów w Polsce w XX wieku.* [Political history of the media in Poland in the 20th century]. Warszawa: Wydawnictwo Akademickie i Profesjonalne.

Internet World Stats. 2010. Retrieved from http://internetworldstats.com/stats4.htm#europe .

Jakubowicz, Karol. 1992. From party propaganda to corporate speech? Polish journalism in search of a new identity. *Journal of Communication* 42(3):64–73.

Kopacz, Grzegorz 2008. *Bez odwrotu* [No retreat]. *Press* 4:10.

Kowalczyk, Ryszard. 2008. Media lokalne w Polsce: Prasa-Radio-Telewizja–Internet [The Polish local media: Printed press–radio–television–Internet]. Poznań: Wydawnictwo Wydziału Nauk Politycznych i Dziennikarstwa.

Krajewski, Radosław. 2005. *Organy ochrony prawnej. Zarys wykładu* [Legal protection authorities. A short lecture]. Płock: Wydawnictwo Naukowe Novum sp. z o.o.

Krawczyk, Dariusz. 2006. Prestiż zawodu dziennikarza w opiniach pracowników redakcji prasowych oraz mieszkańców aglomeracji katowickiej [The prestige of the journalism profession according to printed press journalists and press consumers in the Katowice catchment area]. In *Media a środowisko społeczne: Dylematy teorii i praktyki* [The media and milieu: Theoretical and practical dilemmas], edited by Stanisław Michalczyk and HalinaUlanecka, pp. 43–49. Katowice-Gliwice: Olpress.

Lara, Ania. 2005. Media landscape—Poland. European Journalism Centre. Retrieved from http://www.ejc.net/media_landscape/article/poland/

Lewandowska, Stanisława. 1982. Polska konspiracyjna prasa informacyjno-polityczna 1939–1945 [The Polish underground press 1939–1945]. Warszawa: Czytelnik.

Łojek, Jerzy, Jerzy Myśliński, and Władysław Władyka,. 1988. Dzieje prasy polskiej [The history of the Polish press]. Warszawa: Interpress.

Mielczarek, Tomasz. 2007. *Monopol, pluralizm, koncentracja. Środki komunikowania masowego w Polsce w latach 1989–2006* [Monopoly, pluralism, concentration. Mass media in Poland 1989 - 2006]. Warszawa: Wydawnictwa Akademickie i Profesjonalne.

Olszewski, Edward. 2009. Rozwój studiów politologicznych w uczelniach wyższych [Development of political science study programs at the universities]. In *Demokratyczna Polska w globalizującym się świecie* [Democratic Poland in the globalized world], edited by Konstanty A. Wojtaszczyk and Andżelika Mirska, pp. 201–221. Warszawa: Wydawnictwo Akademickie i Profesjonalne.

Osica, Janusz. 2001. Prasa lat zaborowej niewoli [Printed press during the partition occupation]. In *Prasa, radio i telewizja w Polsce:Zarys dziejów* [Printed press, radio and television in Poland: A brief history], edited by Danuta Grzelewska, Rafał Habielski, Andrzej Kozieł, Janusz Osica, Lidia Piwońska-Pykało, pp. 27–66. Warszawa: Dom Wydawniczy Elipsa.

Pokorna-Ignatowicz, Katarzyna. 2003. Telewizja w systemie politycznym i medialnym PRL. [Television in the political and media system of the Polish People's Republic]. Kraków: Wydawnictwo Uniwersytetu Jagiellońskiego.

Pokrzycka, Lidia. 2008. Problemy lokalnego dziennikarstwa—Analiza na przykładzie rynku prasowego Lubelszczyzny [The problems of a local journalism—A case study of the press market in a region of Lublin]. In *Oblicza polskich mediów po 1989 roku* [The faces of the Polish media after 1989], edited by Lidia Pokrzycka and Beata Romiszewska, pp. 205–212. Lublin: Wydawnictwo UMCS.

Polskie Badania Czytelnictwa [Polish readership research]. 2009. Retrieved from http://media2.pl/badania/52527-pbc:-czytelnictwo-prasy-w-kwietniu-2009.html

Sobczak, Jacek. 2008. Prawo prasowe: Komentarz [The press law: Commentary]. Warszawa: Wydawnictwo Wolters Khwer Polska.

Stefanowicz, Jan. 2007. Jakie prawo prasowe? [The press law: Like what?] Stowarzyszenie Dziennikarzy Polskich. Retrieved from http://www.spl.top.pl/dokumenty/jakie_prawo_prasowe.pdf

Szot, Lucyna. 2008. Status zawodowy dziennikarza w Polsce [Professional status of a journalist in Poland]. In *Oblicza polskich mediów po 1989 roku* [The faces of the Polish media after 1989], edited by Lidia Pokrzycka and Beata Romiszewska, pp. 175–190. Lublin: Wydawnictwo UMCS.

Ustawa z dnia 26 stycznia 1984 r. - Prawo prasowe, Dz. U. 1984, nr 5, poz, 24 [Press Law Act, January 26, 1984].

Weaver, David H., Randal A. Beam, Bonnie J. Brownlee, Paul S. Voakes, and G. Cleveland Wilhoit. 2007. *The American journalist in the 21st century: U.S. news people at the dawn of a new millennium.* Mahwah, NJ: Erlbaum.

21 Russian Journalists and Their Profession

Svetlana Pasti, Mikhail Chernysh, and Luiza Svitich

Russian journalism has seen many changes in the post-Soviet era. Beginning in the 1990s, with their newfound political freedoms media outlets celebrated in triumph after the collapse of communism and continued what began during *glasnost* and *perestroika* in the late 1980s. These unprecedented developments led to the journalism job market opening to anyone who wished to enter. New media laws adopted by the Russian Federation's reformist government freed news outlets from state control and made it possible for market-based media to emerge.

However, by the turn of the millennium, these positive reforms were partially reversed by several changes that impinged on those initial freedoms. A depressed economy and falling living standards reduced the buying power of Russians along with their information demand to a basic minimum. Readership of most papers and magazines declined, with their roles taken over by free televised programming and the Internet. In most cases, outlets had to seek financial support either from wealthy groups looking to use media to promote business interests, or from the state.

Within the past decade, the political freedoms of Russian media have gradually diminished in the face of increasing centralization of authority and state regulation (Nordenstreng & Pietiläinen 2010; Zassoursky 2004). Government authorities introduced their own media, created mixed-ownership alliances with commercial capital, and bought journalistic services by contract to ensure positive coverage. As a result, journalism leaned toward pro-state service in collaboration with market forces. The state and big business shared a strong media presence by combining their political and commercial interests of social control and profit. The result was a drift by Russian media toward an "etatist" ideology.

Although modern Russian journalism has transformed from being a state job (Soviet era) to a market freelance position (post-Soviet era), it is mostly unchanged in its political subordination. This paradox of market freedom and political non-freedom is a consequence of "guided democracy" or "simulation democracy" in which, as Dmitry Furman (2010: 11) explains, "democratic institutions and rules of law play a role of (fake) veneer, camouflage to hide the authoritarian system." This guided democracy prevails with the backing of a national consensus that became commonly approved after the social trauma of the 1990s—a social contract of stability and economic prosperity in exchange for political freedoms. By the end of 2010, half of Russia's population was disappointed with the market reforms, but conceded they should continue in order to strengthen the state's role in the economy and provide social security for the population (Levada Centre 2010a).

The fact that Russian media today directly or indirectly are in the hands of the government or government-controlled entities, negatively affects both the development of the market and the quality of its journalism. Nearly 80% of the press consists of non-market publications that are affiliated closely with financial-industrial groups and partially serve as a cloak for business, or state-owned organizations with financing from regional and local budgets. This is true even for

St. Petersburg, the second and so-called European capital of Russia. Among the 900 publications issued there, only 150 covered their expenses in business terms. The remaining 750 relied on various subsidies from the state, corporations, and solvent clients (Massmedia 2009: 269–272).

When journalists are forced to operate under such conditions, they cannot meet the public's needs and lose its trust. Erosion of credibility is evident in the media's slide in public opinion from Russia's fourth-most important social institution in 2001 and 2005 to eighth in 2010. Meanwhile, the president, government, financial institutions, and presidential administration retained the top positions. Political parties, intelligentsia, and trade unions have remained the most unimportant institutions throughout the 2000s (Levinson 2010). According to a recent survey by the Levada Centre (2010b), half of the Russian public thinks that contemporary news media are propaganda tools, and 66% of Russians say that government authorities or big business control the media.

Amid this financial chaos and struggle for credibility, the state is urging the media to adopt new technologies and promote the idea of "modernization." Journalists are asked to aid the growth of new communication technologies and become the "spearhead of modernization" (Medvedev 2009). In today's Russia, journalists must play conflicting roles while being placed in difficult positions, hence the need to study them and their profession.

This chapter uses data from a national survey of 800 Russian journalists in 2008 to explore who they are, how they operate, and how they perceive the current conflicted conditions of state political control and the welcoming neo-liberal approach of the market economy.

The Media in Russia

Russia's media market, ranked 10th largest in the world by economic indicators (Pankin 2010), operates at the intersection of state and business interests. In the past decade, Russian media have grown into a fashionable industry of entertainment, information, and advertising. Its rapid development has been triggered by societal changes, particularly increased consumption when income began to grow and public interest drifted from politics to private life.

The national media register Reestr SMI (www.reestrsmi.info) reported in 2010 that there were 66,032 print and electronic mass media outlets. This included 5,254 television stations, 3,769 radio stations, 28,449 newspapers, 21,572 magazines, 1,378 digests, and 5,610 other media. The sheer amount and diversity are amazing when compared to Soviet media of the mid-1980s, when Gorbachev began his political reform of *glasnost* and *perestroika* with five Central Radio services and eight Central Television services (Ovsepyan 1996).

Television remains the only really national mass medium and the most popular: 85% of the population watches TV every day with about 60% watching to keep track of events and relax (Federal Agency for the Press and Mass Communication of the Russian Federation [FARMC] 2010: 50). People do not have to pay to watch. Major national TV channels are transmitted from Moscow via terrestrial networks and satellites. The state operates the All-Russian State Television and Radio Company (VGTRK) including six television channels and more than 80 regional television and radio stations (GTRK). Another important player, Gazprom Media, owns the NTV and TNT channels. It is an affiliate of the state-commerical mixed owned Gazprom Company, which helps the state informally control private TV channels.

Radio is second in popularity. About half of the population listens to it at least once a week, and 77% of listeners prefer music (FARMC 2010). Radio comprises national networks and local radio stations. Two major national channels belong to the state (VGTRK): Radio Rossia, available for 66% of the population, and Mayak (55%).

Print journalism is third: 61% of the population read traditional newspapers, and 37% read magazines at least once a week. One-fifth of Russians do not read newspapers, and one-third do not read magazines. Among readers, 63% prefer information and analysis, and 32% of readers choose glossy entertainment magazines.

Finally, 39% of the population uses the Internet, and most users are young. Although the Internet is Russia's fastest-growing media segment, experts predict full national penetration only by 2040. In the global ranking of new information technology development for 2009, Russia ranked 74th among 134 countries, alongside Kazakhstan, Sri Lanka, and the Dominican Republic (FARMC 2010: 52). There is a big gap in Internet development (from 32% to 600%) between the urban centers of Moscow and St. Petersburg and the regions. The Russian language sector RuNet has grown rapidly. In 2009, it had 3,957 media sites (Rumetrika 2010). Mostly, users prefer news about sports, accidents, and social events.

The economic crisis of 2008 brought big losses among media. Almost a third of Russian journalists lost their jobs, and wages were reduced or frozen. The advertising market fell by more than 25% according to data from ZenithOptimedia, compared to more than 10.2% worldwide (FARMC 2010: 60–61). The crisis reduced consumer activity, which adversely affected the press—especially expensive glossy magazines, business, and advertising publications. People turned to cheaper periodicals and free press. Other changes included the closure of hundreds of unprofitable publications nationwide; revised structures, approaches, and methods of doing business; the training of new personnel; regular monitoring; and more attention to consumers than advertisers.

The crisis contributed to corporate mergers and takeovers with the trend of further market monopolization and redistribution in favor of leaders. As a whole, the Russian media market consists of 50 national media companies and about 100 inter-regional or regional media companies (FARMC 2010). Among them are three national leaders: VGTRK, the state company; Gazprom-Media, the state-commercial mixed-ownership company; and Prof-Media, a commercial company. The main trend of the last decade is the decrease of the commercial capital share and proportional increase of state capital and mixed (state and commercial) capital shares.

Lack of reliable statistics remains a problem as "no government agency today possesses exhaustive statistical data on the condition and dynamic of the national media market as a whole" (Vartanova & Smirnov 2010: 21). That is a result of the lack of transparency of Russia's economy and the media market in particular. Over-stated circulations of newspapers and magazines are common, along with falsified ratings of broadcasting channels, a wide disparity between registered media and issued media, and confusion over who really owns Russia's media.

Previous Studies

The first sociological studies of Soviet editorial offices appeared in the early 1920s with the aim of obtaining information on the social characteristics of post-revolutionary journalists. The Bolshevik party tried to dramatically increase the number of proletarian journalists who were party members (Svitich 1973). In 1929, a large-scale survey sampled 5,000 journalists at 374 editorial offices (Gus 1930). It found an increased number of journalists from working-class backgrounds. At first, labor specialization was studied, with researchers defining the following categories: literary, editorial, mass (worker-peasant correspondents and bureau of investigations), and printing.

During Khrushchev's thaw in the 1960s, sociologists gained more opportunities to study media, and new research on journalism and journalistic personalities appeared in Leningrad (Kuzin 1968) and Novosibirsk (Parfenov 1969). In 1968, a study headed by Grushin (Grushin & Onikov 1980) in the southern city of Taganrog explored information flow and public opinion in a midsized industrial city. Based on in-depth interviews, the findings showed that journalists mostly were interested in forming public opinion, but not expressing it (Shiryaeva 1969). From 1969 to 1972, the journalism faculty at Moscow State University studied local press (*rayonnaya*). Party officials, readers, and journalists were interviewed and a content analysis of newspapers was conducted. The study confirmed that journalists, like party leaders, saw newspapers' primary task as helping the party develop industry and collective farming goals (*Rayonnaya gazeta* 1977). These findings were confirmed in surveys between 1983 and 1986 in five regions with a sample of 700 journalists, publishers' representatives, and the audience (Svitich 1986).

Research at the end of the 1980s found changes in journalistic orientations that were related to Gorbachev's policies of *glasnost* and *perestroika*. For example, a 1988–1989 study on the multilingual press in Kirgizia (Tishin, Svitich, Tarasov, & Akulov 1990) found that Soviet journalists tried to better meet the needs of a wider audience, especially ethnic minorities. Nevertheless, government propaganda and limited topics that failed to account for ethnic minorities' interests dominated most Soviet journalists' minds. For the first time, this study also collected statistical data about the economic conditions of Soviet media and their employees.

By the early 1990s, dramatic political changes in the country and its journalism became obvious. A 1990 survey by Central Television and All-U.S.S.R. Radio journalists revealed the readiness of Soviet journalists for outlets to be economically independent and have more professional contact with foreign colleagues (Svitich & Shiryaeva 2007).

Economic factors and decentralization that occurred during the Soviet Union's final years gradually reoriented audiences to the regional press. A study of the regional press in 1991 and 1992 (Svitich & Shiryaeva 1994) found that most journalists (60%) felt fairly independent in their work. This was not too surprising, given the end of censorship and party control brought about by new media laws in 1991 (Richter 2002). Yet these newfound freedoms did not safeguard against new problems that emerged in the transitional period, such as excessive bias and political engagement of the press, vague concepts of newspapers, and economic dependence on new owners.

The first Russian–American comparative study of journalists occurred in 1991. The Russian survey included 1,000 journalists representing 34 national media outlets and 99 local media outlets in 10 geographic regions (Svitich, Shiryaeva, & Kolesnik 1995). It revealed similarities in the socio-demographic characteristics of journalists and their professional motivations, along with some differences. Russian journalists, for example, rated the creative character of their profession higher, whereas Americans mostly viewed journalism as an informational service. For Russian journalists, 1991 was a peak of unlimited freedom. Most had almost complete freedom to choose topics, and their work saw less editing by superiors. By contrast, American journalists described their working conditions as being more regulated. Yet both groups considered informing audiences quickly as the media's most important function. While this was nothing new for American journalists, it represented a radical reorientation for Russians.

The second Russian–U.S. project examined 610 journalists, again in 10 geographic regions (Zassoursky, Kolesnik, Svitich, & Shiryaeva 1997). It explored perceptions of controversial political and ethical activities within newsrooms. The study found that Russian journalists were oriented more toward regulation to address ethically complex problems, while American journalists preferred self-regulation and internal corporate ethical norms.

By the mid-1990s, the Russian press experienced successful journalistic reforms without censorship and ideological pressures. This was characterized by a diversity of media founders and an increased variety of publications and content. Yet surveys in 1994 and 1995 (Dzyaloshinsky

1996; Glasnost Defense Foundation [GDF] 1995) revealed serious economic problems, new forms of restrictions by local authorities and political groups, difficulties with information access, and a decline in professionalism. As a result, the early "euphoria" among professional journalists was slowly replaced by a greater degree of pessimism. Sociological centers and schools in St. Petersburg, Minsk, Kiev, Ljvov, Vladivostok, Rostov, Ekaterinburg, and other cities accumulated much knowledge and expertise in this area of research (Koltsova 2001; Korkonosenko 1997; Lozovsky 2001; Pasti 2007).

Method

The survey featured in this chapter was carried out as part of the "Media in a Changing Russia" project financed by the Academy of Finland (2006–2008) headed by Kaarle Nordenstreng. Data were collected in two stages. The first incorporated cases from the All-Russian Congress of Journalists organized by the Russian Union of Journalists in September 2008. Of the 620 journalists who attended the meeting, 260 participated in the survey. The second consisted of a nationwide survey of 536 journalists carried out in October and November of 2008 by the Institute of Sociology of the Russian Academy of Sciences.

The study's preparatory stage made it obvious that there was very limited information available from which to draw a random sample of Russian journalists. Official statistics cite figures for the entire community of media workers without reference to journalists as a distinct group. Available data on professional organizations such as the Union of Journalists reflected a membership that covered only about 20% of the entire community. Since primary data were lacking, the sample was spread across Russia to reach big-city journalists as well as those in smaller cities. The regional sample was drawn from 36 cities in three categories: large cities with 1 million or more people (319 respondents), mid-sized cities with 200,000 to 999,999 people (359 respondents), and small cities with fewer than 200,000 people (118 respondents). These cities represented all of Russia's six socio-economic zones (*okrug*) together with the metropolitan areas of Moscow and St. Petersburg.

Previous surveys of Russian journalists showed that a regular home-based interview might not always be possible. So interviewers were instructed to use any opportunity for an interview and seek breaks in journalists' schedules to accomplish the task. Interviews also had to be discreet, as some sensitive questions were involved. Journalists were asked to reveal their views on topics such as the level of editorial control, plagiarism, colleagues' illegal commercial activities, and censorship. The questionnaire's design was based on prior international research (Weaver 1998; Weaver & Wilhoit 1996; Wu, Weaver, & Johnson 1996).

The precondition of anonymity demanded that questionnaires had to be self-administered. However, the interviewers monitored the distribution of the questionnaires, checked them for omissions, and collected them after completion. If the respondents found it more convenient to meet in a public place such as a café, restaurant, or park, interviewers were asked to do face-to-face interviews.

Overall, 317 questionnaires were self-administered, 46 were based on personal interviews, 82 were telephone-based, and 91 were done through locally administered e-mail. For e-mail, respondents were first reached by telephone, agreed to participate in the study, gave their e-mail address, and received and returned the questionnaire online. To check data reliability, each questionnaire included a special request for respondents to be contacted later for verification purposes. This method produced few irregularities: seven cases were excluded because the respondent could not be reached for verification. In the end, 536 cases from the regular survey were merged with 260 cases from the study's first stage. Altogether, the data set includes interviews with 796 Russian journalists.

Findings

Demographic Background

Results are broken down by city size (large, mid-sized, or small), generation of journalists (Soviet: 1991 and earlier; transitional: 1992–1999; or post-Soviet: 2000 and later), and media type.

In the Soviet Union, journalism was an elite career. It was common for the political and economic elite to provide their children with an education and an opportunity to seek employment in the media. So it is not surprising that among journalists from large cities, more than one-third come from managerial families. In mid-sized cities, the number drops to about one-fourth, and in small cities it slips further to about one-fifth. While Russian journalists from large and mid-sized cities often have parents who are professionals, this was only the case for about 4% of journalists in this survey.

Table 21.1 shows that few journalists hail from the working class. Despite "affirmative action" for workers' sons and daughters during the Soviet era, only 16% of large-city journalists had such backgrounds. Apparently, working-class sons and daughters had better chances in smaller cities where they accounted for about half of all journalists.

In the last 20 years, significant changes have taken place in the social background of Russian journalists. For this analysis, journalists were split into generational groups depending on when they entered the profession. The first generation began prior to 1992, the second generation entered between 1992 and 1999, and the third generation began work in 2000 or later. While younger journalists tend to come from families of professionals, Table 21.2 shows that the proportion of journalists from managerial families did not change significantly through the generations. Yet journalists whose parents were professionals (not journalists) increased dramatically among those who entered the profession after 1992.

At present, 41% of Russian journalists are members of a journalist union. But there is a huge generation gap among the ranks. While about three-quarters of those who entered the profession

Table 21.1   Parents' Job by City Size (in %)

	Large city (<1 million)	Midsized city (200.000–999.000)	Small city (>200.000)	All Journalists
Top manager	8.4	7.2	4.3	7.2
Middle manager	25.3	18.2	17.2	20.8
Supervisor	3.4	6.1	4.3	4.7
Journalist or editor	4.4	4.3	0.9	3.8
Other professional	27.3	28.8	11.2	25.5
Clerk	8.8	8.6	9.5	8.8
Urban worker	12.1	17.9	27.6	17.1
Rural worker	4.0	5.2	20.7	7.1
Other	6.4	3.7	4.3	4.9

Table 21.2 Social Background of Journalists by Generation (in %)

	Soviet 1991 or earlier	Transitional 1992–1999	Post-Soviet 2000 or later	All Journalists
Top manager	7.4	6.3	8.4	7.4
Middle manager	22.3	20.4	19.5	20.7
Supervisor	5.5	6.3	3.1	4.9
Journalist or editor	3.1	4.2	3.8	3.7
Other professional	18.4	25.0	33.2	25.6
Clerk	10.2	8.8	7.6	8.8
Urban worker	19.5	19.6	12.2	17.0
Rural worker	10.2	5.0	5.3	6.9
Other	3.5	4.6	6.9	5.0
Females	50.2	61.5	67.4	59.7
Second job	42.3	47.8	47.1	44.3
Union membership	75.6	33.1	16.7	40.8
Journalistic education	50.5	37.1	44.1	43.1

before 1992 are union members, membership drops significantly for those who entered between 1992 and 1999 (33%) and those who did so afterward (17%).

The typical Russian journalist is female (60%), has a college degree (90%), and tends be middle-aged (41 years). The dominance of women in Russian journalism seems to be generational. While women are about equally represented among journalists who entered the profession during the Soviet era (1991 or earlier), those who entered in the transitional generation (1992–1999) increases to about 62%, and then jumps to 67% in the post-communist generation (2000 or later).

As Table 21.3 shows, the percentage of female journalists is especially high in news agencies (75%), press services (68%), and weekly newspapers (66%). While females represent the majority of Russian news workers, almost half the journalists at daily newspapers (46%), radio stations (44%), and online media (45%) are male.

Table 21.3 Proportion of Male and Female Journalists by News Medium (in %)

	Male	Female
News Agency	25.0	75.0
Press Service	32.0	68.0
Weekly Newspaper	34.5	65.5
Television	40.0	60.0
Weekly Magazine	41.7	58.3
Other Newspapers	42.1	57.9
Monthly Magazine	43.0	57.0
Radio	43.8	56.3
Online Media	44.7	55.3
Daily Newspaper	45.5	54.5
Other Media	46.7	53.2

Other findings show that younger journalists are more likely to hold a journalism diploma. In the youngest group (30 and under), 54% have a journalism diploma or are close to getting such a degree (three years or more of study via a journalism department). In the oldest group, 42% hold such a degree, while the smallest number can be found in the 40 to 49 age group (31%).

This composition reflects the volatile character of the labor market in the early 1990s. The expansion and liberalization of the media attracted men and women with a higher education regardless of their major. Among them, there were some who previously could not enter the profession because of their social or ethnic background, and were dissatisfied with the income, career prospects, and creative opportunities of their former jobs (Pasti 2005). The present media prefer to employ graduates of journalism schools.

Income

Although Russian journalists belong to a privileged professional group, many hold a second job. This tendency is especially high among journalists from large (51%) and mid-sized cities (47%), but even in small cities about one-third (30%) of the journalists have more than one job. In most cases, these moonlighters work in print media: 36% for weekly papers, 21% for daily papers, and 14% for monthlies. Broadcast journalists are much less likely to hold second jobs (12% among TV journalists and 6% among radio journalists).

The difference between print and electronic journalists in this respect is largely due to the number of relevant outlets and the level of competition between them. TV and radio stations insist upon exclusive commitments from journalists, while print media, which are often affiliated with larger corporations do not object to employees "honing" their talents with friendly publications. Another reason is that print journalists in Russia typically work alone and sell their materials as individual products as they see fit, whereas broadcast journalists collectively produce programs, performing as co-authors of a common product.

Because Russian journalists often have several employers and income sources, assessing their total earnings is extremely difficult. Survey questions about income are especially problematic among freelancers, who often are paid in cash and might want to keep their actual income secret. A further complication is that some income could be illegal. Russian journalists are known, for example, to promote commercial products and services in exchange for cash, a practice that allows many to substantially boost their regular income.

To estimate the degree of corruption among Russian journalists, the survey asked journalists whether they had produced a news piece in return for extra payments during the past 12 months. While journalists were expected to be somewhat reluctant to answer this question, an astonishing 52% admitted to this practice. It seems to be especially prevalent among younger journalists. More than half who entered the profession after 1992 admitted to producing news for outside money (57% of those entering between 1992 and 1999, and 55% of those entering in 2000 or later), while only 44% of those who became journalists before 1991 made such an admission.

Journalists across all three generations were fairly reluctant to disapprove of such activity. Among those who entered the profession in 1991 or earlier, only 22% disapproved of producing paid-for news. Younger journalists were even less likely to disapprove (10% of those who began between 1992 and 1999, and 14% of those who began in 2000 or later)—a clear indication that ethics in Russian journalism has declined over time. Overall, such findings of fairly widespread corruption indicate that any estimates of declared income should be read with caution.

On average, a Russian journalist is better off in material terms than many other workers with a higher education: 38% had an income between R10,000 and R20,000 per month (US$350–US$700). This level of income is not impressive by Moscow standards, but income levels and prices vary dramatically throughout Russia. In 2008, the average income nationwide was about R9,000 per month ($318), while in Moscow it was about R27,000 (US$954). One quarter (25%) of all respondents enjoy a monthly income that ranges between R20,000 and R30,000 (US$700–$1,350). However, a journalism career in Russia opens the possibility of an even higher income: 20% of the respondents have an income that exceeds R40,000 per month (US$1,400). A small group of elite journalists can land jobs that bring more than R80,000 per month (US$2,800). This group consists mainly of men (5%), with the proportion of highly paid women being much smaller (about 1%).

A Russian journalist's income depends largely on the type of media for which she or he works. Highly paid journalists (more than R40,000 a month) are most prevalent in TV (34%), news agencies (25%), and monthly magazines (28%) and less prevalent in daily papers (17%) and radio (13%). Higher income among TV journalists stems largely from the role they play in contemporary Russia. TV is increasingly treated by federal and local authorities as a tool to influence society and win support for their policies. Monthly journals carry privilege because of glossy magazines, which are the most prestigious segment of Russia's print media and the best vehicle for expensive advertisements.

Job Satisfaction

Most Russian journalists are fairly satisfied with most aspects of their jobs. As Table 21.4 shows, a clear majority of journalists are content with their independence to decide which stories to write (65%), their ability to help other people (64%), and the political orientation of the outlet for which they work (60%). Only about a third of Russian journalists are satisfied with their income (39%), their career opportunities (38%), their profession's political independence (37%), and extra privileges the job might offer (37%).

Table 21.4   Job Satisfaction by Generation (% saying "fully" or "mostly satisfied")

Reasons for satisfaction	Soviet 1991 or earlier	Transitional 1992–1999	Post-Soviet 2000 or later	All Journalists
Opportunity to decide what to write	70.7	62.7	61.2	64.7
Opportunity to help people	65.3	63.5	64.9	64.2
Media's political line	60.9	61.4	58.3	60.1
Job security, social security	43.4	52.1	59.7	51.6
Opportunity for better qualifications	50.2	48.7	55.1	51.1
Opportunity to influence society	46.5	46.9	53.8	48.9
Opportunities for second job	44.8	48.0	52.8	48.4
Opportunities to grow in the post	39.8	40.9	45.5	42.1
Income	42.7	40.0	34.4	38.8
Opportunity for other career via journalism	38.6	35.8	39.0	37.7
Political independence of the profession	34.0	32.4	44.9	37.1
Extra privileges	30.5	35.9	43.9	36.7

There are also notable differences in job satisfaction between the older and younger generations. Younger journalists are more enthusiastic about moonlighting prospects and more likely to be satisfied with the profession's political independence. They also feel more secure than their older colleagues, and they are happier with career perspectives and extra privileges than the older journalists.

In general, the younger generation seems to be the happiest and the most optimistic that journalism will meet their expectations for self-realization, creativity, and wide communication.

Job Constraints and Censorship

Journalists face limitations and constraints in most modern societies. In recent years, Russian journalists have faced growing government interference and instances of outright censorship. As Table 21.5 shows, threats to free speech in Russia are perceived to come from local authorities rather than the federal government—a view that seems most prevalent among Soviet-era Russian journalists (40.9%) and somewhat less so among the post-Soviet journalists (22.3%). About a quarter (23.9%) of these latter journalists also feels that significant constraints come from their editorial superiors, a concern that is shared among the post-Soviet generation as well (23.0%).

Ethics, on the other hand, seems primarily a concern among the older journalists. While about 18% of the Soviet-era and transition journalists consider ethics an important element in their profession, only 9% of the post-Soviet journalists share this sentiment. What these younger journalists consider more important than the older generations, however, are the effects of media specialization (21.5%) and advertisers (16.6%).

While censorship certainly has affected how Russian journalism is practiced it was somewhat surprising to see how much support there is for various forms of censorship. Only about one in 10 journalists (13%) thought "censorship is needed to select and ban harmful political content," yet about one in four (25%) agreed that "journalists should be controlled by society," and almost half (45%) said that "only editors should have the right to control content."

Overall, most respondents reported a high degree of autonomy in their work and conceded that the depth of editing is related to the material. But it was not clear what kind of editing is applied in each case, whether political or stylistic.

Table 21.5   Journalistic Constraints by Generation (in %)

Source of Constraints	Soviet 1991 or earlier	Transitional 1992–1999	Post-Soviet 2000 or later	All Journalists
Local authorities	40.9	25.0	22.3	29.4
Superiors in the editorial office	23.9	21.7	23.0	23.0
Audience	20.1	19.3	18.9	19.4
Ethics of the profession	18.1	17.6	8.7	14.6
Political position of medium	16.2	11.1	14.0	13.7
Special audience of media	10.8	17.2	21.5	16.5
Influence of federal authorities	10.4	8.2	2.6	7.1
Advertisers	8.5	18.0	16.6	14.5
Owners	8.5	11.5	9.8	9.9
Opinions of colleagues	2.7	2.9	4.2	3.4
Other	4.6	5.7	1.5	3.9

One-fifth of the journalists said that they can pursue their ideas "all the time," while 70% said they succeed in "most cases" and only about one in 10 journalists said that they are "not able to do what they want."

However, a decline of journalistic autonomy was found concerning the selection of news, topics, and problems that required coverage. Only one-fifth of the journalists said they were "fully independent," and one-third said they were "sometimes independent, sometimes not." Many Russian journalists make such decisions "depending on the situation."

Comparing these findings with the 1992 survey of Russian journalists (Svitich et al. 1995), one notices a decline in journalists' autonomy. Freedom to select news, topics, and problems decreased from 60% in 1992 to 20% in 2008 among "fully independent" journalists. The ability to emphasize ideas journalists believe are important dropped from 54% in 1992 to 22% in 2008. Yet for staff journalists—who were somewhat independent—freedom to select news, topics, and problems requiring coverage increased from 5% in 1992 to 29% of journalists in 2008, while the ability to stress important journalistic ideas rose from 6% in 1992 to 29% by 2008. These findings indicate that contemporary Russian journalists have adapted to changing conditions and tailor their behavior according to circumstances. Their editorial autonomy during the last 16 years has significantly decreased, yet they survive with the new rules of the game.

Perceptions of Media Performance and Reporting Methods

Most Russian journalists believe their employers are pretty good at delivering information to their audiences. While 10% say they are confident that the media do "an excellent job," 36% said they do "a good job," and 46% indicated they do the job "well, though not without certain deficiencies."

Journalists were asked who or what most affects their perception of what is newsworthy. As Table 21.6 shows, all age groups agree that professional judgment should be the chief determinant of news selection. Audiences were viewed as the third-best criterion, as some journalists believe readers and viewers have the right to guide what journalists cover. In particular, younger

Table 21.6   Acceptability of Influences on News Selection by Age (mean scores)

Age	Less than 30 years	30–39 Years	40–49 Years	50–59 Years	Total
Duration of work in the media	4.29	4.48	4.50	4.70	4.48
Professional skills, training	4.24	4.35	4.32	4.65	4.39
Audience, its preference	3.76	3.76	3.64	3.54	3.68
Other news sources	3.39	3.42	3.31	3.20	3.34
Internet	3.38	3.37	3.28	3.17	3.31
News agencies	3.45	3.38	3.20	3.10	3.30
Public opinion polls	3.29	3.34	3.08	3.34	3.28
Higher-ups	3.67	3.42	2.98	2.85	3.27
Colleagues	3.22	3.26	3.04	3.08	3.16
Competing media	3.12	2.93	2.73	2.69	2.89
Biggest players in the market	3.07	2.84	2.65	2.33	2.75
Friends, milieu	2.52	2.69	2.58	2.67	2.61

Note.   Scores displayed are mean scores on the basis of a 5-point scale where "1" means the lowest possible acceptability and "5" means the highest level of acceptability.

Table 21.7   Reporting Methods by Generation (% saying "acceptable depending on circumstances")

Reporting Methods	Soviet 1991 or earlier	Transitional 1992–1999	Post-Soviet 2000 or later	All Journalists
Payment for confidential information	42.6	52.3	51.7	48.6
Use confidential business or government info	43.5	42.7	42.1	42.6
Claiming to be somebody else to get information	32.6	40.7	40.4	37.8
Break promise not to expose a source	7.3	7.3	11.3	8.7
Pressure unwilling sources	19.5	37.9	41.0	32.8
Use personal documents without permission	9.0	15.6	21.8	15.6
Getting employed to get inside information	51.9	51.8	45.7	49.5
Use hidden cameras and microphones	56.9	51.2	51.3	53.2
Use actors for recreation of events	34.4	43.8	38.0	38.7
Disclose names of criminals	22.2	25.0	15.4	20.5
Disclose names of rape victims	24.7	27.0	22.2	24.5
Publish facts about private life without permission	38.8	55.7	52.6	48.9

journalists were more sensitive to audience reaction and the role of bigger market players. Unlike older journalists, they more often treat their job as a business and readily admit that audience size equates to economic success. Guided by years of acquired skills and news judgment, older journalists are more inclined to rely on their own "gyrocompass" in gauging newsworthiness.

About half (53%) of Russian respondents believe that, depending on the situation, a journalist has the right to use hidden cameras or microphones without warning the interviewee, while 49% agree that disparaging personal information can be divulged without prior consultation (see Table 21.7). One-third of Russian journalists believe that interviewees can be pressured to disclose key information, while about one-quarter (21% and 25%) feel that names of detainees and the accused, respectively, can be made public before a trial (generally the names of defendants are not published before a trial opens). In other words, when information is the ultimate goal, Russian journalists generally hold that certain boundaries of ethics and decency may be disregarded.

Conclusions

Like their country, Russian journalists are in the midst of a social and political transition. The values that are emerging seem to emphasize the need to survive in a highly competitive environment. The transition calls for a combination of mutually exclusive qualities: the ability to sustain group values, yet be an effective individual; the skill to be pragmatic and speak the language of the common good; the capacity to stay independent and adapt to the environment; and, most importantly, to sustain good relations with the ruling powers.

All of this separates the current form of Russian journalism from its predecessor. Soviet journalism was homogeneous, scrupulously administered, and functioned as a well-oiled propaganda and social organization. Today, new roles are emerging from the contradictions under which Russian journalism has evolved.

On the one hand, Russian journalism is a difficult and often dangerous profession. The sad statistics of violence against journalists include more than 300 killed (Russian Union of Journalists

[RUJ] 2011). Mortality is high because the news media cover human rights and social protest in a place where local courts are not independent from the authorities. As a result, many people seek justice in editorial offices. The Glasnost Defense Foundation (www.gdf.ru) regularly reports on violence against journalists and the numerous obstacles used to discourage their work. According to Reporters Without Borders (2010), Russia's press freedom is ranked 140 on a list of 178 countries.

On the other hand, the popularity of being a journalist has not declined, based on the growing number of journalism schools and large numbers of applicants, many from wealthy families. Young, well-educated, middle-class Russians seek media jobs because they provide opportunities for a fairly high income, along with the possibility of combining the main job with a second job in times of economic hardship (Pasti 2010). Being a journalist in Russia can bring influence and power, serve as a springboard for a political career, or can lead to fame, which can result in a higher social position or provide access to influential networks. Moreover, the technology used to produce modern media attracts young people, many of whom begin their careers in new forms of multi-media and online journalism.

Today, every third journalist in Russia belongs to the generation of news workers who started their careers in the 21st century. The profession has become younger. In 1992, every third journalist was under 35 years old. By 2008, every third journalist was under 30. However, this trend is true mostly for large cities, where journalists under 30 comprise 44% of the editorial staff. In small cities, they only account for 4% of the staff. Journalism school graduates tend to stay in the cities where they have connections and easily find jobs in large media, public relations, and advertising markets. Small cities with under-developed media and advertising markets are unable to attract young people, so editorial offices there typically are occupied by older workers—including the local intelligentsia. Russian journalism also has become increasingly female. In the younger generation, more than two-thirds are women.

In the largest cities, most journalists hail from elite and middle-class families. In small cities, half of journalists have working-class backgrounds. In large cities, media supervisors prefer to hire newcomers with a journalism education, while in small cities only 10% have a professional education. As a result, urbanization has produced gaps in the professional structure of Russian journalism. This differs from the Soviet days, when state media were filled with young, educated journalists without regard to regions or localities.

Two-thirds of today's Russian journalists are satisfied with their profession, due mostly to editorial autonomy, the opportunity to help people, and their conformity with media politics. Satisfaction levels are especially high among young journalists because of the job's creative aspects, potential financial success, and job security.

Younger journalists are more pragmatic and apolitical than their older colleagues. They enjoy a job that brings them wide contacts and opportunities for earnings and self-expression. Older journalists are more likely to believe that journalism is not an ordinary job, but a service to the people. However, these generational differences fade against the pressures of doing their jobs, dealing with authorities (especially in the small cities), and market forces (especially in large cities). Such pressures place personal well-being and media survival as the foremost goals of professional success.

Most Russian journalists are loyal to the political line of their media, which usually does not conflict with their commercial and often illegal activity in the profession. A second job and corruption have become common among Russian journalists, although in the theory of the profession they are signs of a loss of professionalism. At the same time, political control and censorship remain the main constraints to journalistic work. Increasingly, there is a growing and dangerous consensus in which journalism is viewed as a means of self-expression or the route to development of personal business, rather than as a public service. Given the satisfaction of most professionals with the current conditions under which they work, there is little reason to expect change.

One of the most intriguing questions concerning Russian journalism is how the impressive diversity of media outlets, their economic success, and the rise of new communication technology will influence professional development, particularly when it comes to political independence, which is a part of Russia's overall modernization. Twenty-five years ago, Soviet journalists enthusiastically supported Gorbachev's policy of democratization. Freedom became a key value in politics, economy, journalism, and private life. These new freedoms favored two new types of transformative Soviet state journalism: politically independent journalism and commercial journalism.

Yet by 2010, an increasing imbalance that favored commercial journalism over politically independent journalism had become obvious. The former increasingly substitutes for the latter and gives an illusion of freedom among journalists—but it is a freedom of the market, not of journalism as a profession.

The quality of Russian journalism is declining, and its reputation in society has suffered. The head of the Russian Union of Journalists said that the present media produce "no more than 15%" of news content, with the rest outsourced to public relations and political technologies instead of journalists serving as watchdogs (Bogdanov 2010). Russia is ranked 136th—between Yemen and Chad—out of 150 countries in the World Audit of Democracy (2011). Its ranking has decreased for 13 years from 106th to 136th. Russia is ranked 130th in press freedom and 127th in corruption.

Yet Russian society has shown only a weak interest in improved performance from its news media. Problems such as rising prices, growing unemployment, and poverty have taken precedence over freedom of expression (Levada Centre 2010c). Values of private life and survival prevail over political values—including free speech. Russia's transition into a consumer society has led to a tendency toward the bestowal of prestige upon an occupation increasingly connected with profit without regard for professional respect. At least one survey suggests that the short-term future for journalism in Russia looks promising from a market demand perspective (Malahova 2007).

How does one explain the paradox between the deterioration of democracy that has eroded media freedom in Russia and the growing satisfaction of its journalists? In the post-Soviet era, journalists were dissatisfied with their profession—in particular its low salaries, lack of social guarantees, returning political pressures, new forms of corruption, and deteriorating journalism (GDF 1995; Pasti 2004). Journalists began to excuse their venal practices by claiming a need to survive. They believed that after they became richer and joined the middle class, they would begin to think about democracy, their profession, and ethics. But this has not happened. During the 2000s, when Russia's economy and its media changed for the better, journalistic salaries rose drastically. Yet having a second job as a means of survival became a privilege and opportunity for advancement. Journalists became well-to-do people with influential contacts in government and big business.

As a result, Russian journalists work and live within the confines of a liberal-oriented market, whereas the institutions of media and journalism remain locked under an authoritarian state. However, when individual freedom accelerates institutional freedom, it does not mean free-market professionals adhere to democratic values. The submissive status of their profession and its tolerance for corruption erodes journalistic principles. Many journalists had predicted that material well-being would guarantee professional democratization, but that has not been the case.

The future of Russian journalism will depend on whether there is a change in the minds and ethics of its professionals and in society as a whole. Although independent journalists and media are not influential in Russia today, they still provide a "lifejacket" that safeguards the profession and offers hope for the possibility of true media freedom emerging in Russia.

References

Bogdanov, Vsevolod. 2010. Pressa dolzhna sluzhit tem, kem upravlayut, a ne tem, kto upravlyaet [Press must serve those who are governed, but not those who govern]. Interview of the Chair of the Russian Union of Journalists. *Rossia v ATR* [Russia in Asian-Pacific Region] 3(16):8–14.

Dzyaloshinsky, Iosif M. 1996. *Rossiiskaya zhurnalistika: Svoboda dostupa k informatsii* [Russian journalism: Freedom of access to information]. Moscow: Komissiia po svobode dostupa k informatsii.

Federal Agency for the Press and Mass Communication of the Russian Federation (FARMC). 2010. *Russian periodical press market 2009: Condition, trends, prospects—Annual report.* Moscow: Author. Retrieved from http://www.farmc.ru

Furman, Dmitry. 2010. *Dvizhenie po spirali: Politicheskaya sistema Rossii v ryadu drugikh sistem* [The spiral motion: The political system of Russia in a number of other systems]. Moscow: Ves Mir.

Glasnost Defense Foundation (GDF). 1995. *Zhurnalist i zhurnalistika Rossiiskoi provintsii* [The journalist and journalism of the Russian provinces]. Moscow: Nachala-Press.

Grushin, Boris A., and Leonid A. Onikov. 1980. *Massovaya informatsiia v sovetskom promyshlennom gorode* [Mass information in the Soviet industrial city]. Moscow: Politizdat.

Gus, Mikhail. 1930. *Za gazetnye kadry* [For the newspapers' personnel]. Moscow: Leningrad.

Koltsova, Olessia. 2001. News production in contemporary Russia. *European Journal of Communication* 16(3):315–335.

Korkonosenko, Sergei G. 1997. The "new politization" of Russian journalism. *The Global Network* 8:81–89.

Kuzin, Vladilen I. 1968. *Partiinyi komitet i gazeta* [The party committee and the newspaper]. Leningrad: Lenizdat.

Levada Centre. 2010a. Polovina rossiyan razocharovanny rynochnymi reformami [Half of Russians are disappointed with market reforms]. Retrieved from http://www.polit.ru/research/2010/11/25/reforms.html

Levada Centre. 2010b. Rossiyane ne veryat v nezavisimostj rossiiskih SMI [Russians do not believe in independence of Russian media]. Retrieved from http://www.polit.ru/research/2010/12/7/russiansmi.html

Levada Centre. 2010c. Trii chetverti rossiyan ne udovletvoreny urovnem morali i nravstvennosti v strane [Three-fourth of Russians are dissatisfied with the level of morality in the country]. Retrieved from http://www.polit.ru/research/2010/12/21/moral.html

Levinson, Alexei. 2010. Nashe "my": Lestnitsa kuda? [Our "we": Stairs to where?] *Vedomosti* February 9. Retrieved from http://www.vedomosti.ru/newspaper/print/2010/02/09/225046

Lozovsky, Boris N. 2001. *Chetvertaia vlast i obshchestvo: na ternistom puti k soglasiy* [The Fourth Estate and society: On the thorny path to agreement]. Ekaterinburg: Uralsky Gosudarstvennyi Universitet.

Malahova, Anastasia. 2007. Prestizh v tsene. [Prestige is valued highly]. *Ekspert.* Retrieved from http://www.expert.ru/authors/115414/

Masssmedia Rossiiskogo megapolisa: tipologia pechatnykh SMI [Mass media of the Russian megapolis: Typology of print media]. 2009. St. Petersburg: Faculty of Journalism, St. Petersburg University, Roza mira.

Medvedev, Dmitry A. 2009. Poslanie Presidenta Rossii Federaljnomu Sobraniy [The speech of the President of the Russian Federation to the Federal Legislative Assembly]. Retrieved from http://www.rg.ru/2009/11/13/poslanie-tekst.html

Nordenstreng, Kaarle, and Jukka Pietiläinen. 2010. Media as mirror of change. In *Witnessing change in contemporary Russia,* edited by Tomi Huttunen and Mikko Ylikangas, pp. 136–158. Helsinki: Aleksanteri Institute.

Ovsepyan, Rafail P. 1996. *Istoria noveishei otechestvennoi zhurnalistiki* [The history of modern Russian journalism]. Moscow: MSU.

Pankin, Alexei. 2010. Democracy is dangerous for the media. *The Moscow Times*, May 25.

Parfenov, Gennady S. 1969. Hekotorye resultaty issledovaniya problem zhurnalistskogo tvorchestva [Some findings of the study of the problems of journalistic creative work]. *Vestnik MSU* 10(2):43–53.

Pasti, Svetlana. 2004. Rossiiskiy zhurnalist v kontekste peremen: Media Sankt-*Peterburga* [A Russian journalist in the context of change: Media of St. Petersburg]. Tampere, Finland: Tampere University Press.[English publication under former surname of the author Svetlana Juskevits. 2002. *Professional Roles of Russian Journalists at the End of the 1990s: A Case Study of St. Petersburg Media.* Tampere: Tampere University Press. Retrieved from http://tutkielmat.uta.fi/pdf/lisuri00006.pdf]

Pasti, Svetlana. 2005. Two generations of contemporary Russian journalists. *European Journal of Communication* 20(1):89–115.

Pasti, Svetlana. 2007. *The changing profession of a journalist in Russia.* Tampere: Tampere University Press.

Pasti, Svetlana. 2010. A new generation of journalists. In *Russian mass media and changing values,* edited by Arja Rosen-holm, Kaarle Nordenstreng, and Elena Trubina, pp. 57–75. Routledge: London.

Rayonnaia gazeta v sisteme zhurnalistiki [The local newspaper in the journalism system]. 1977. Moscow: Moscow State University.

Reestr SMI. 2010. Reestr pechatnykh i elektronnykh smi Rossii' [Register of the print and electronic media in Russia]. Retrieved from www.reestrsmi.info.

Reporters Without Borders. 2010. *Press freedom index.* Retrieved from http://en.rsf.org/press-freedom-index-2010,1034.html

Richter, Andrei. 2002. Media regulation: Foundation laid for free speech. In *Russian media challenge,* edited by Kaarle Nordenstreng, Elena Vartanova, and Yassen Zassoursky, pp. 115–154. Helsinki: Aleksanteri Institute.

Rumetrika. 2010. *Runet:* Auditoria Internet-smi vyrosla na 31% za god. [RuNet: Audience of Internet media has grown over 31% for the year]. Retrieved from http://www.media-atlas.ru/items/index.php?id=15058

Russian Union of Journalists (RUJ). 2011. Database of deaths of journalists in Russia. Retrieved from http://journal-ists-in-russia.org/journalists

Shiryaeva, Alla A. 1969. Zhurnalist v sotsialisticheskom obshchestve [A journalist in a socialist society]. *Vestnik MSU,* 10(3): 33–42.

Svitich, Luiza G. 1973. Zhurnalistika 20-kh godov (Iz istorii sotsiologic-heskikx issledovanii) [Journalism of the 1920s: From the history of sociological studies]. *Vestnik MSU,* 10(6): 42–56.

Svitich, Luiza G. 1986. *Effektivnost' zhurnalistskoi deiatelnosti* [Effectiveness of journalistic work]. Moscow: MSU.

Svitich, Luiza G., and Alla A. Shiryaeva. 1994. Zhurnalist novoi pressy [The journalist of the new press]. *Vestnik MSU,* 10(3): 3–13.

Svitich, Luiza G., Alla A. Shiryaeva, and Svetlana G. Kolesnik. 1995. Rossiiskiy i Amerikanskiy zhurnalist [The Russian and American journalist]. *Vestnik MSU,* 10(1): 30–42, 2: 20–27.

Svitich, Luiza G., and Alla A. Shiryaeva. 2007. *Rossiiskii zhurnalist i zhurnalistskoe obrazovanie* [The Russian journalist and journalistic education]. Moscow: MSU.

Tishin, Alexei I., Luiza G. Svitich, Alexander B. Tarasov, and Vladimir F. Akulov. 1990. *Chitatel' i gazeta v zerkale sotsi-ologii* [A reader and a newspaper in the mirror of sociology]. Frunze: MSU.

Vartanova, Elena and Sergei Smirnov. 2010. Mapping contemporary trends in Russian media industry. In *Russian mass media and changing values,* edited by Arja Rosenholm, Kaarle Nordenstreng, and Elena Trubina, pp. 21–40. Routledge: London.

Weaver, David (ed.). 1998. *The global journalist: News people around the world.* Cresskill, NJ: Hampton Press.

Weaver, David, and G. Cleveland Wilhoit. 1996. *The American journalist in the 1990s: U.S. news people at the end of an era.* Mahwah, NJ: Erlbaum.

World Audit. 2011. World democracy in January 2011. Retrieved from http://www.worldaudit.org/publisher.htm

Wu, Wei, David Weaver, and Owen V. Johnson. 1996. Professional roles of Russian and U.S. journalists: A comparative study. *Journalism & Mass Communication Quarterly* 73(3):534–548.

Zassoursky, Ivan. 2004. *Media and power in post-Soviet Russia.* Armonk, NY: M.E. Sharpe.

Zassoursky, Yassen N., Svetlana G. Kolesnik, Luiza G. Svitich, and Alla A. Shiryaeva. 1997. Zhurnalisty o pravakh i svobodakh lichnosti i sredstv massovoi informatsii [Journalists on rights and freedoms of individuals and mass media]. *Vestnik MSU,* 10(3):20–36, 5:14–43.

22 Journalism in Slovenia

Peter Lah and Suzana Žilič-Fišer

In 1991, Slovenia declared its independence from the Socialist Federal Republic of Yugoslavia. In 2004, it joined the European Union and NATO, and in 2007, the Economic and Monetary Union (EMU) best known for its common currency, the euro. The period in which Slovenia exercised full sovereignty was marked by two processes. First, during its transition from an autonomous state within the Communist Yugoslav Federation into an independent democratic country, Slovenia had to establish new legal and administrative institutions while restructuring its economy along the lines of modern market principles. On the other hand, during the European Union accession process, the country needed to harmonize its laws and institutions with those of other EU member states. Consequently, all aspects of social and economic life underwent rapid and frequent changes. For example, between 1991 and 2005, the law concerning the nation's public broadcaster, RTV Slovenia, was rewritten or amended five times. In 2011, the coalition of "transition" parties failed to implement yet another change.

Background

Slovenia is a democratic welfare state with a population of two million people. The political landscape is shaped by two currents: The "transition" block, also referred to as the left, consists of political parties as well as labor unions and many associations whose origins, both institutional and personnel, date back to the communist regime (Social Democrats, Liberal Democrats, Zares, and Desus). The "spring" block, commonly referred to as the right, consists of parties that were founded around 1990 or after (People's Party, Nova Slovenija, and Democratic Party). With the exception of the four-year period between 2004 and 2008, the parliament as well as the government was dominated by the "transition" block.

The absence of a viable opposition to political parties and civil-society groups that evolved from the communist-dominated organizations has profound implications for the state of the media in Slovenia. At the interpersonal level, most journalists studied at the Faculty of Social Sciences at the University of Ljubljana. It is the same higher education institution where the vast majority of politicians had been trained since the 1960s. The underlying philosophy at this academic institution was, and continues to be, sympathetic to Yugoslav-style socialism and, more generally, the left. When the state of the media in Slovenia is assessed, it is important to understand the significance of personal ties between professional politicians, high-level administration figures, and journalists, and their shared philosophy.

Second, the transition of the communist-era institutions and leading cadres (e.g., parties, civil-society groups, managers, and universities) to democracy and a market economy assured their ownership and control of the media. Perhaps nothing illustrates this better than the case of Janez Kocijančič, chairman of the Council of Radiotelevizija Slovenija (RTV), the highest governing body of the public broadcasting corporation, between 1998 and 2006. Prior to 1991, he headed Slovenia's regional government and subsequently served as chief executive officer of Adria Airways, a major state corporation. From 1993 until 1997 he was chairman of (Združena lista socialnih demokratov [United list of social democrats] ZLSD), the Communist Party's successor, and a member of parliament between 1992 and 1996. In 1991 he became chairman of Slovenia's Olympic committee, a position he still held in 2010. It was in this capacity that he became member of the Council of RTV in 1998. He is a visible example of the transition or transmogrification of a member of the predemocratic political and economic elites. In the case of private media, those who had power in the 1980s successfully maintained their influence, either through state-controlled investment funds, or as owners of the newly privatized media organizations. It is significant that media organizations that have run afoul of the named elites have had a hard time attracting advertising. It is not a coincidence that the two "dissident," pro-"spring" weekly magazines, *Reporter* and *Demokracija*, have consistently failed to secure advertising from major state-controlled corporations.

Slovenia's Media Today

According to official statistics in 2010, there were currently 877 media outlets registered in Slovenia. There are eight daily newspapers with a circulation of about 263,000 readers. *Delo* and *Slovenske Novice*, both produced by the Delo Publishing Company, account for more than half of that figure. The company captures 35% of advertising expenditures on daily newspapers. *Dnevnik*, *Večer*, and *Primorske Novice* are regional dailies, while *Finance* is a business newspaper. *Slovenske Novice* is a tabloid, and *Žurnal24* is a free tabloid paper. *Reporter* and *Mladina* are political weekly magazines. *Mladina* started as a youth magazine well before 1990. It is considered sympathetic to the "transition" block. *Reporter*, founded in 2008, is the sole "pro-spring" independent weekly magazine.

There are three public service television channels and 35 commercial television channels in Slovenia. The public broadcaster, Radiotelevizija Slovenija (RTV), operates three: SLO 1, SLO 2, and SLO 3. The private broadcaster Pro Plus also operates three commercial channels: POP-TV, Kanal A, and TV Pika. Both are headquartered and have their main broadcast centers in Ljubljana. The third operator with nationwide coverage is TV 3. The remaining channels are all local or regional.

Approximately 73% of RTV Slovenia's revenues come from viewers' license fees (about US$13 for each household per month in 2010); the rest comes from advertising income. In addition to the main broadcast center in Ljubljana, RTV Slovenia also operates regional broadcast centers in Koper and in Maribor. They broadcast regional programs and a program for the Italian and the Hungarian minorities in Slovenia, respectively. Along with the growth of the Internet, since the late 1990s RTV Slovenia has developed an online, multi-media Web portal (www.rtvslo.si). RTV Slovenia, which is the only public service broadcaster in Slovenia, is obligated to fulfill public service requirements. As such, it is supposed to support national cultural productions and offer information that is in the public interest. While RTV Slovenia is financed by audience license fees, the Slovenian government determines the actual size of this fee and parliament appoints the RTV management, both reasons why RTV Slovenia is often regarded as a media institution that depends on national politics.

Slovenia has 81 radio stations, of which eight are part of the public service system. The remaining 73 can be divided into two groups. Seventeen are radio stations "of special significance" which gives them a semi-public status. In exchange for providing certain types of programs the fee is waived for using the network of antennas operated by RTV Slovenija. They also can apply for production subsidies. In order to be eligible, programs must address at least one of the media policy goals as defined by the 2006 media law, namely: safeguarding and enabling democratic discourse and culture; supporting a diverse culture; supporting and enabling the development of ethnic minorities; as well as filling quotas for educational programs and domestic (Slovenian as well as European) production (Lah 2009).

With the transformation of RTV Slovenia from state to public service broadcasting the policy for assigning the rest of the radio frequencies was adopted. Some radio and local broadcasters applied for special status to fulfill their public service requirements. They are subsidized by the state with support for certain media content, but a major part of financing comes from the advertising.

The second group of stations consists of 55 private commercial stations that depend almost exclusively on advertising. While they are held to some broad requirements in regard to content, such as quotas for domestic and European production, they are generally free to shape their programming. The media law in Slovenia does not impose regulations regarding content on commercial broadcasters' programing. Finally, Radio Ognjišče is a Catholic radio station with nationwide coverage. It is not-for-profit and has a status that makes it eligible for subsidies and reduces its operational costs. Its main sources of revenue are advertising and private donations.

There is little foreign ownership in the media. Among the major media organizations in Slovenia, only three are majority owned by non-Slovenian entities. POP-TV is owned by the Bermuda-based Central European Media Enterprises. It has media holdings in several central European countries. *Žurnal*, a free weekly newspaper, along with the online *Žurnal24*, is owned by Styria A.G. from Austria (Bašić-Hrvatin & Petković 2007). Styria also has a 25.7% stake in *Dnevnik*. The Bonnier Corporation of Sweden owns the business paper *Finance*. Foreign ownership is significant as it often introduces new styles and standards in the journalistic profession. As a system, Slovenian journalism has proven quite resistant to significant outside influences.

There are two main professional journalism organizations: the Union of Slovenian Journalists (Sindikat novinarjev Slovenije; SNS) and the Slovenian Association of Journalists (Društvo novinarjev Slovenije; DNS). In 2007, a third group, the Association of Journalists and Writers (ZNP), was founded to protest against what journalists perceived as the older associations' political alignment with leftist political parties. The Union of the Slovenian Journalists, which was founded in 1990, represents its members in relation to media management and owners, state institutions, and other organizations. In the last decade its activities have focused on defending wages. It provides free legal assistance and support to its members. In 2010 it was involved in about 230 employment-related court cases on behalf of its members. The Slovenian Association of Journalists was founded in 1905 by writers and journalists and currently has about 900 members.

According to the two main journalist associations (SNS and DNS) in Slovenia, more than 2,000 journalists are employed in print, television, and radio media. This figure is based on data from individual media organizations, associations, institutions' home pages, publicly available data, and similar sources. According to the latest data, 1,750 journalists are permanently employed. Another 420 are registered with the Ministry of Culture as freelance journalists. Some estimate that another 300 journalists are not registered with any of the journalist associations. The freelance journalists are registered with the Ministry of Culture because the freelance status enables them to make reduced payments to social security funds. However, journalists are not forced to register with any of the associations.

The "status" of journalists is conferred either by the media organization for which they work or by the Ministry of Culture. Formal recognition as a journalist is important for several reasons. First, concerning freedom of speech, the law offers protection to journalists and media from certain aspects of litigation. Second, freelance journalists enjoy certain privileges, such as reduced payments to social security funds (e.g., health insurance and retirement fund). Finally, it is necessary to carry identification as a journalist to gain access to certain events and institutions.

Previous Studies

Slovenian journalism has evolved within a central European political context. The development of journalism was limited by the values that were supported by the regime. For most of their history, ethnic Slovenians lived in separate territorial and administrative jurisdictions. Such circumstances were not favorable for the development of journalism. Under Habsburg rule (before 1918) and during the two Yugoslav periods (1918–1941 and 1945–1991), Slovenia was deemed a province and journalism was on the margins of societal influence. Consequently, its development lagged somewhat behind political and cultural centers such as Vienna, Trieste, Zagreb, and Belgrade (Amon 2004: 287). The relation between political centers and the province was important for the development of journalism. The centers enabled access to key political decisions and to sources that were relevant for major changes in society. Journalists in the province were far away from key decisions and major sources of information.

The experience of communist rule exerted a strong and lasting influence on the understanding and practice of journalism in Slovenia. Between the end of World War II and 1990, the Communist Party completely shaped journalism and the media according to its ideas and interests. In the federated multi-ethnic and multi-lingual Yugoslav state, individual states were in charge of day-to-day operation of media organizations. One notable exception was the Tanjug news agency, which was run by the federal government. All media activities were controlled by the government. As one prominent party official stated in the 1960s:

> It is not possible to think of a journalist who would not look at the problems of society in a socialist way ... if he is not [a socialist], then he cannot work in this profession.... [A journalist] is necessarily a public political worker who has to be politically active.... For the socialist press, there is only one basic and generally known freedom, that is, the freedom to propagate socialist ideas (Novak 1996, 11–12).

Top media managers were recruited from the ranks of the Communist Party leadership. Formal journalism training was done within the faculty of sociology, political science, and journalism at the University of Ljubljana. The communist-influenced Code of Journalism (1965, 1969, 1973, and 1982) defined the role of the journalist as a supporter of Marxism and Leninism, accountable to the state, constructor of the self-management economic system, and supporter of the socialist self-management political system (Poler Kovačič 2004). The revised Code of Journalism of 1988, however, ushered in some important changes in the understanding of journalism and the role of the journalist, namely, that the journalist is responsible to society rather than to the communist political elite (Košir 2003: 80).

In the 1980s, some journalists started criticizing the communist Yugoslav regime. Most vocal among them were op-ed writers who were not professional journalists (Amon 2004; Poler Kovačič 2004). Many of them were not employed by journalistic media, which were tightly controlled by the state during that period, but rather by universities and other organizations, which gave them a greater degree of freedom. Further, they tended to be better educated than professional journalists. Finally, in the late 1980s, they became very vocal in opposing the tendency of the Serbian leadership to centralize and in calling for democracy. Their involvement is consistent with an important trait of Slovenian journalism in all historical periods, namely, the drive to influence public opinion (Splichal 2000: 47–51). This trait places Slovenian journalism within Hallin and Mancini's (2004) North/Central European model. A study of professional values by one of the authors showed that journalists in 2002 maintained a strong sense of involvement with the political life of the country (Lah 2004a).

Research into journalism after 1990 revealed that professionalism continued to present a challenge. Today, pressures come from the commercial and sensational nature of media operations, rather than from oppressive communist ideology (Kalin Golob 2003; Košir 2003; Poler 1996; Poler Kovačič 2001). Some authors argue that the key elements of professionalism, especially autonomy and ethics, are in crisis (Poler Kovačič 2004: 290). Media professionals are accountable to media owners who often have close connections to political elites. Consequently, one of the main problems of mass media in Slovenia is the lack of transparency at all levels: ownership of private media, management of public broadcasting income and finances, circulation of print media, advertising and marketing, and relations between management, editorial, journalistic, and advertising departments (Bašić-Hrvatin & Kučić 2002; Milosavljevič 2004a).

A commercial approach to journalism has also provided fruitful ground for interference with the freedoms and rights of citizens. The commercial ideology that drives private broadcasters has started to seep into the values and choices of public service broadcasters who are competing for the same audience. RTV Slovenia found itself in the position of having to attract as many viewers as possible in order to increase its advertising revenue (Žilič-Fišer 2006, 2007).

Other studies suggest that the influence of public relations on Slovenian journalism is growing. Content analysis of television news reporting reveals an alarming lack of transparency in regard to sources of information, the latter often being press releases and other materials provided by public relations agencies and practitioners. Erjavec and Poler Kovačič (2004) found that between 1999 and 2000, the use of media sources attributed to public relations offices increased drastically. The research focused on the national daily media. It should not come as a surprise therefore that media credibility is decreasing and journalists are perceived to be lacking in talent, critical distance, and complexity of thought (Vreg interview; Milosavljevič 2004b).

Method

The total number of journalists in Slovenia is too small to warrant a sampling approach. Instead, we decided to reach out to all of them. Using publicly available data, primarily the registry of freelance journalists and Web sites of individual media, we were able to compile a list of close to 1,400 e-mail addresses. We further approached media and professional organizations with the request to forward to their employees and members our call to participate in research. Most of them were supportive of the initiative. The survey yielded 406 completed questionnaires, which represents a response rate of 29%.

We defined a "journalist" as anyone who earned more than half of his or her income through work for general-interest media in an editorial capacity (i.e., they were not technical staff, production assistants, and similar). We estimate the number of journalists who work for major national and regional media, not including RTV Slovenija, to be at least 700.

We decided to use an online survey based on the assumption that respondents would be more likely to participate online than in a telephone interview. The response rate was increased by allowing journalists to complete the questionnaire in more than one session. The questionnaire, which is based on Weaver and Wilhoit's (2007) study, was available to the journalists for five weeks in October and early November 2009. However, in the interest of keeping the questionnaire as short as possible (by which we hoped to increase participation), we decided to omit some questions from Weaver and Wilhoit's original survey that were not meaningful in Slovenia (e.g., civic journalism).

Findings

Basic Characteristics

Forty-seven percent of our respondents are male and 53% are female. The average age of the Slovenian journalists is 40 years (median=37), but the largest age groups are those between 30 and 40 years (39%) and under 30 years (22%). The fact that journalism is a relatively young profession in Slovenia is reflected in the fact that one-third of the journalists have worked in journalism for less than 10 years. Twenty percent report between 11 and 15 years of professional tenure, and another 18% between 16 and 20 years. Thirteen percent have worked in journalism for more than 30 years. The average time spent in journalism was 16 years (median = 14).

Forty-one percent of the journalists are married, 27% live with a partner, 21% are single, and 6% are divorced. For comparison purposes, the distribution in the general population aged between 20 and 60 years is: 57% married, 36% single, 2% widowed, and 5% divorced (Statisični urad Republike Slovenije [SURS] 2002).

The findings also indicate that Slovenian journalists are not a religious bunch. Slightly more than half say they do not belong to any church or religion, and another 9% declined to answer the question. All in all, 37% are Catholic, while a mere 2% indicate other religious affiliations. Forty-nine percent say they never go to church, while 12% indicate they attend religious services once a month or more often. This compares with 10% of the population that identifies themselves as atheists and 26% that declined to answer. Of those remaining, 56% are Catholic, 3% belong to other Christian denominations, and about 2% are Muslim.

When asked with which political party or movement they identified, three-quarters either declined to answer or reported "none." Among those who did indicate a party, 7% identify themselves with Zares, 6% with Social Democrats, 4% with Liberal Democrats, 7% with Democratic Party, and 2% with Nova Slovenija. This means that 17% of those one-fourth who responded see themselves aligned with left-leaning parties (i.e., Zares, Social Democrats, and Liberal Democrats) and 9% with more right-leaning parties. However, when asked to indicate their ideological leanings on a continuum between 1 (far left) and 10 (far right), most journalists cluster around 5 (middle) with a mean value of 4.5. Thus, Slovenian journalists see themselves pretty much in the middle of the ideological spectrum.

Education and Training

Most of the journalists (60%) say that they have an undergraduate degree and another 6% indicate that they hold a graduate degree. Twenty percent completed high school and 11% completed post-secondary or professional programs. Among those who have an undergraduate college degree, 57% name journalism as their field of study, while 34% say they studied social sciences. Thirteen percent studied liberal arts, 7% business and commerce, and 15% (combined) the liberal arts, education, technical and information technology, law, and natural sciences (percentages add up to more than 100% because some respondents had double majors).

The vast majority (84%) of the journalists expressed an interest in continuing education. Areas mentioned most frequently are language courses and professional growth. Seventy-one percent of the respondents had attended journalism workshops and seminars in the course of their career. Such training opportunities are typically organized by news organizations for their staff.

Working Conditions

The median net salary among the journalists in our sample is €1,200 per month (about US$1,464) with a mean of about €1,400 (US$1,700) (the median gross salary is about US$2,000). This compares with an average salary of €1,000 (US$1,220) in Slovenia in 2009 (SURS 2009). Four out of five journalists are either satisfied or very satisfied with their job. When asked about reasons for becoming journalists, "job autonomy" tops the list with nearly 95% saying it is important or very important (mean 3.6), followed by the "opportunity to help people" (mean 3.3), and a "chance to influence public affairs" (mean 3.2). Conversely, "pay" (mean 2.2), "job security" (mean 2.2), and "fringe benefits" (mean 1.8) rank lowest.

When one compares their expectations with current satisfaction, the rank order does not change, although the scores tend to be lower. One item that deserves attention is "editorial policies of the media organization." It ranks lowest together with "opportunities for advancement" and "pay" (see Table 22.1).

Slovenian journalists report a high level of interaction with audiences. Seventy-one percent communicate with their audiences about stories more than once a month. Possibly as a result of this interaction, nearly 75% of the journalists disagree with the statements that "audiences are gullible" or "not interested in social problems" (56%). About half the journalists believe that audiences are "more interested in breaking news than analysis," while 40% disagree with this statement.

Owners are perceived as primarily "interested in high audience numbers" (90%) and "above average profits" (86%) but not in "high staff morale" (57%). Nearly 70% of the journalists also say that resources are dwindling. They were split on whether emphasis on profits trumped quality journalism, though, with 46% agreeing and 43% disagreeing with the claim. Only 40% thought that the quality of journalism was improving, and 28% thought that their organization extensively polled audiences about their interests and needs.

Table 22.1   Journalists' Job Satisfaction (in %)

When you consider the following aspects of your job, how satisfied would you say you are?	N	*Not satisfied at all*	*Somewhat satisfied*	*Quite satisfied*	*Extremely satisfied*
Overall	389	3	14	70	12
Pay	393	13	35	49	3
Fringe benefits	325	10	35	52	4
Editorial policies	372	14	34	44	9
Job security	371	16	18	57	9
Training	372	16	39	40	6
Job autonomy	394	3	14	57	26
Advancement	370	15	38	41	6
Help people	369	2	13	64	20
Influence public affairs	355	3	21	63	13

Professionalism

Forty-five percent of the journalists say they are members of the Slovenian Association of Journalists and another 8% belong to other associations. Forty percent are union members. While two out of three journalists in our sample have full-time employment, 17% work as freelancers, and 13% are part-timers.

Professional Roles

Some interesting patterns emerged from journalists' responses to the standard items concerning professional roles (see Table 22.2). There is strong agreement, for example, that good journalism is about quickly providing information to an audience, providing analysis and interpretation, and keeping watch on the government. Somewhat less agreement is found on items such as "giving ordinary people a chance to express themselves," "motivate them to get involved in public affairs," and "pointing them toward solutions." Three-quarters agree that "providing entertainment and relaxation" and "concentrating on the widest possible audience" are important journalistic roles. A similar percentage thinks the same about "political agenda-setting" and "participating in the development of national policy."

Table 22.2   Journalists' Professional Roles (in %)

How important is it that the media......	Extremely important	Quite important	Somewhat important	Not important at all	N
Get information to the public quickly	58	41	1	—	404
Provide analysis and interpretation	57	41	1	—	403
Provide entertainment and relaxation	16	61	20	3	401
Investigate claims and statements by government	51	43	3	—	403
Provide analysis and interpretation of international development	32	59	6	—	404
Stay away from stories where factual content cannot be verified	24	56	14	2	402
Concentrate on news that is of interest to the widest possible audience	18	54	25	1	403
Discuss national policy while it is still being developed	20	54	18	4	403
Develop intellectual and cultural interests of the public	44	51	2	1	402
Be an adversary of public officials by being constantly skeptical of their actions	46	44	7	—	403
Be an adversary of businesses by being constantly skeptical of their actions	42	47	7	1	401
Set the political agenda	17	60	16	2	399
Give ordinary people a chance to express their views on public affairs	39	54	5	1	401
Motivate ordinary people to get involved in public discussions of important issues	38	53	7	1	399
Point people toward possible solutions to society's problems	39	52	6	1	401

The aforementioned items concerning professional roles were used to perform a factor analysis. Four profiles emerged, which account for 56% of variation. The first profile consists of the following items: "analysis and interpretation," "research and question government," "analyze and interpret situation abroad," "be adversary of government and business," and "cultivate intellectual and cultural interests in audiences." We labeled it "modernist journalist." It embodies the qualities of professional journalism as it developed in Western societies in the latter part of the 20th century (Hallin & Mancini 2004). The second profile is sharply defined by three items with the strongest loadings: "motivate audiences," "give opportunity to ordinary people to express themselves," and "point toward solutions." We labeled it "civic journalist." The third profile is defined by three items, namely: "provide quick information," "entertainment and relaxation," and "broad audience reach." It is negatively associated with "watchdog" and "agenda-setting" items. We labeled it the "entertainment journalist." The fourth profile consists of following items: "attract broad audience," "participate in public debate," and "agenda-setting." We labeled it "political journalist."

The four profiles indicate that journalism is a complex phenomenon. They can be compared to and contrasted with two normative classifications, namely, Siebert, Peterson, and Schramm's "Four Theories of the Press" (1956) and Hallin and Mancini's "Comparing Media Systems" (2004). Aspects of Sieber et al.'s libertarian theory can be found in our "modernist" as well as "political journalist" profiles. The social responsibility theory is most clearly expressed in the "modernist," "civic," and "political journalist" profiles.

Hallin and Mancini proposed three models of journalism: "Mediterranean," "North/Central European," and "North Atlantic." The second one clearly corresponds to our "civic," "modernist," and to some extent, "political journalist" profiles. This finding is consistent with the cultural and political traditions of Slovenia; specifically, its entrenchment in the central European cultural and political space that came to the fore in the late 1980s with the writers' active involvement in the processes of the country's democratization and independence.

Ethics

Journalists in Slovenia strongly support basic standards of professional and universal ethics (see Table 22.3). Only 1% of the respondents think, for example, that it is acceptable in certain circumstances to disclose the identity of a confidential source, and only 3% think the same about publishing the name of a rape victim. False identification, unauthorized use of private documents, and

Table 22.3 Journalists' Perceptions of Problematic Reporting Methods (in %)

Given an important story, which of the following, if any, do you think may be justified on occasion?	Justified on occasion	Would not approve	Don't know	N
Paying people for confidential information	17	69	12	404
Using confidential business or government documents	46	37	13	404
Claiming to be somebody else	11	85	3	404
Agreeing to protect confidentiality and not doing so	1	97	1	404
Badgering unwilling informants to get a story	20	74	5	404
Using personal documents without permission	9	86	4	402
Getting employed to gain inside information	21	68	9	403
Using hidden microphones or cameras	31	61	6	402
Using re-creations or dramatizations of news by actors	9	82	7	399
Disclosing the names of rape victims	3	93	4	403

Table 22.4   Sources of Influence on Journalists' Ethical Judgments (in %)

How influential have the following been in shaping your ideas of journalism ethics?	Not influential at all	Not really influential	Quite influential	Extremely influential
Teachers	20	34	37	7
Family upbringing	5	14	49	32
Religious training	50	29	4	2
Day-by-day newsroom learning	2	10	57	29
Senior reporters, editors, or news directors	2	9	55	32
Publishers, owners or general managers	27	51	17	2
Seminars on ethics for journalists	22	36	28	6
Web resources	18	39	34	4
Professional or trade publications	11	21	55	9
Experience on student media	22	38	28	6
Decisions of respected news organizations	10	26	54	6

dramatizing of news stories are deemed unacceptable by more than 80%. Roughly 70% disagree with paying for information, badgering sources, and getting a job for the purpose of obtaining confidential information. The unauthorized use of government documents is seen as unacceptable by 54% of journalists, while the use of hidden recording devices is rejected by 69%. The analysis also indicates areas in which there is less certainty. For example, 12% of the journalists are unsure whether paying for information or unauthorized use of government documents is ethically acceptable.

It is clear from the analysis that in journalists' minds there is a divide between actions that concern private persons and those concerning public figures or institutions. It is somewhat troubling that many respondents had few reservations about misleading others (e.g., using hidden recording equipment, seeking employment with the purpose of obtaining confidential information, and false identification). More than 80% say that family upbringing, respected senior journalists, and everyday experiences in the newsroom influenced their ethical judgment (see Table 22.4). In addition, more than 60% identify decisions of respected media and professional publications as sources of ethical judgment. Formal training in journalistic ethics, on the other hand, is seen as much less influential. Only 44% mention high school and college teachers, 34% student media, and 34% seminars on ethics as sources of influence.

Conclusions

At the end of the first decade of the 21st century, times are not good for Slovenian journalists. Slovenian society has undergone tremendous changes since 1990. Those journalists who are now in their late 40s or older were trained and started to practice journalism under the heavy hand of communist dictatorship. The fight for freedom and political independence promised greater respect for human dignity and professional autonomy. The process of privatization, which began in the early 1990s, dragged on for more than a decade. It had two important consequences in Slovenia. First, dispersed ownership made it difficult for foreign investors to enter the Slovenian market because they could not buy controlling shares in any media organization. Second, it created a less-than-transparent environment in which managers and others with ties to political decision makers gradually were able to concentrate ownership. However, for many years, a status quo has persisted in which journalists and editors enjoyed a considerable level of autonomy, in particular those working at RTV Slovenija and major newspapers. This autonomy, however, did not always translate into greater professionalism.

Around the turn of the millennium it became obvious that the new media owners could not be counted on for sympathy with the values of journalism. Investment funds and private corporations were following their political and economic interests. Tabloid media were an obvious consequence of the short-term economic gain sought by most owners. Unfortunately for journalists, the Slovenian media now are controlled by corporations which lack knowledge, experience, or interest in journalism. *Delo*, for example, is owned by a brewery, while *Dnevnik* is owned by a publishing company that recently has shown interest in expanding into the tourism industry. Unsurprisingly, journalistic quality tends to suffer in media organizations that are controlled by owners that lack experience and enthusiasm for a journalistic mission (Lah 2004a).

The discourse about media and journalism has focused on large organizations. Meanwhile, smaller media organizations, in particular local print as well as broadcast media, have struggled to survive. Many depend on subsidies by either local or national government for their continued existence. Through a subsidy scheme that was enacted by the Media Law of 2006, the Ministry of Culture disbursed €12.5 million (U.S.$5.25 million) to several hundred applicants between 2006 and 2009. The bulk of it went to small and mid-size, that is, local and regional, electronic media. These subsidies, while keeping smaller organizations just barely afloat, contributed little to their economic viability or quality of content. Furthermore, from the vantage point of autonomy, journalists (owners) who depend for their survival on subsidies will likely avoid issues that could irk the party that controls the Ministry of Culture.

Aside from structural issues there seems to be a crisis of professional leadership among news editors. One indicator of this is the failure to uphold professional ethical standards. The Slovenian Honor Court regularly chastises journalists for their mistakes. However, the court's findings seldom have consequences for the journalists involved. Many respondents expressed dissatisfaction with editors and managers whom they perceived as lacking competence and willingness (or ability) to stand up for journalistic values when faced with the demands from senior management.

Good regulatory regimes are those in which media effectively self-regulate. For that to happen, there need to be (1) owners and managers who value quality journalism, (2) a certain level of political civic culture, and (3) journalists who are committed to socially responsible, ethical journalism. The first and second factors are necessary, yet insufficient. It seems that the fate of journalism in Slovenia depends on the ability of the journalists to uphold the values of serving the public and to support the standards that guarantee their autonomy from politics and business alike.

References

Amon, Smilja. 2004. Obdobja razvoja slovenskega novinarstva. [Phases in development of Slovenian journalism]. In *Poti slovenskega novinarstva—Danes in jutri* [The paths of Slovenian journalism—Today in tomorrow], edited by Melita Poler Kovačič and Monika Kalin Golob, pp. 53–68. Ljubljana: FDV.

Bašić Hrvatin, Sandra, and Lenart J. Kučić. 2002. Monopoly—Družabna igra trgovanja z mediji [Monopoly—The social game in buying and selling media]. *Medijska preža/MediaWatch* 15 (Winter 2002): 4–12.

Bašić Hrvatin, Sandra, and Brankica Petković. 2007. *In temu pravite medijski trg?* [You call this a media market?]. Ljubljana: Mirovni inštitut.

Erjavec, Karmen, and Melita Poler Kovačič. 2004. *Rutinizacija slovenskog novinarstva u razdoblju društvene tranzicije* [Journalistic routines in times of social transition]. *Medijska istraživanja* 10(1): 5–21.

Hallin, Daniel C. and Paolo Mancini. *Comparing media systems: Three models of media and politics.* New York: Cambridge University Press.

Kalin Golob, Monika. 2003. *Stil in novinarski škandal* [Style and journalistic scandal]. *Teorija in praksa* 40(2): 229–244.

Košir, Manca. 2003. *Surovi čas medijev* [The era of brutal media]. Ljubljana: FDV.

Lah, Peter. 2004a. *Quality press and European integration: Social communication and commercialism in Slovenian and German newspapers.* Ph.D. dissertation, Northwestern University, Evanston, IL.

Lah, Peter. 2004b. *Media and communication landscape in Slovenia.* Bochum: Projekt-Verlag.

Milosavljevič, Marko. 2004a. Primanjkljaj javnega delovanja: (ne)transparentnost novinarstva in množičnih medijev v Sloveniji [A deficit in openness: (Lack of) transparency in journalism and mass media in Slovenia]. In *Poti slovenskega novinarstva—Danes in jutri* [The paths of Slovenian journalism—Today in tomorrow], edited by Melita Poler Kovačič and Monika Kalin Golob, pp. 139–155. Ljubljana: FDV.

Milosavljevič, Marko. 2004b. Uravnotežiti moramo teoretska in praktična znanja (Interview with France Vreg) [We need to balance theoretical and practical knowledge]. In *Poti slovenskega novinarstva—Danes in jutri* [The paths of Slovenian journalism—Today in tomorrow], edited by Melita Poler Kovačič and Monika Kalin Golob, pp. 279–284. Ljubljana: FDV.

Marja Novak. 1996. *The change from a socialist to a market-led media system in Slovenia.* Ph.D. Dissertation, University of Westminster.

Poler, Melita. 1996. Ethics and professionalisation of Slovene journalism. *Javnost/The Public* 3(4): 107–121.

Poler Kovačič, Melita. 2001. O novinarski odgovornosti [Responsibility in journalism]. In *Vatovec selected readings*, edited by Slavko Splichal, pp. 87–94. Ljubljana: Evropski inštitut za komuniciranje in kulturo ter FDV.

Poler Kovačič, Melita. 2004. Podobe (slovenskega) novinarstva: o krizi novinarske identitete [Images of (Slovenian) journalism: Identity crisis]. In *Poti slovenskega novinarstva—Danes in jutri* [The paths of Slovenian journalism—Today in tomorrow], edited by Melita Poler Kovačič and Monika Kalin Golob, pp. 85–112. Ljubljana: FDV.

Siebert, Fred, Theodore Peterson, and Wilbur Schramm (1956). *Four theories of the press: The authoritarian, libertarian, social responsibility and Soviet communist concepts of what the press should be and do.* Urbana: University of Illinois Press.

Splichal, Slavko. 2000. Novinarji in novinarstvo. [Journalists and journalism]. In *Vregov zbornik Vreg* [Selected readings], edited by Slavko Splichal, pp. 47–56. Ljubljana: Evropski inštitut za komuniciranje in kulturo ter FDV.

Statut Društva novinarjev Slovenije (Slovene Association of Journalits' Bylaws). 2006. *Društvo novinarjev Slovenije* [Slovene Association of Journalists]. Retrieved from http://www.novinar.com/dokumenti/statut.php

Weaver, David H., Randal A. Beam, Bonnie J. Brownlee, Paul S. Voakes, and G. Cleveland Wilhoit. 2007. *The American journalist in the 21st century: U.S. news people at the dawn of a new millennium.* Mahwah, NJ: Erlbaum.

Žilič Fišer, Suzana. 2006. Upravljanje radiotelevizije kot proces kompleksnega usklajevanja [Radio-television management as a complex harmonization process]. *Podjetje in delo* 32(5): 949–959.

Žilič Fišer, Suzana. 2007. *Upravljanje televizije* [Television management]. Ljubljana: FDV.

23 Journalists in Spain

Pedro Farias, Francisco Javier Paniagua Rojano, and Sergio Roses

The recent evolution in Spain's media system has been significant and has served as a model for other countries undergoing a transition from authoritarianism to democracy. In slightly more than 30 years, the country has moved from a situation where the media, journalists, and content were controlled by the Franco dictatorship to a period of freedom and openness.

This led to the emergence of private print and broadcast media, the professionalization of journalism, and an increased public awareness of the role of media in society. At the same time, Spanish media and journalists have modernized their techniques and working methods, and watched their presence and influence spread not only to the rest of the European Union (EU) but worldwide—particularly in Latin American countries that share the same language.

Compared to other European Union nations, Spanish audiences consumed low levels of media in 2010, with commercial television—and its clear focus on entertainment—being dominant while press readership was relatively low. The start of 2010 saw the beginning of a modest process to alter national public television, with advertising removed from the scheduling. However, this transformation was guided by commercial goals to promote advertising revenue distribution among private companies, rather than being a quest for excellence and independence concerning information content.

By focusing on entertainment and "showbiz" coverage, and tying advertising revenue to audience share, especially in electronic media, the result is a preference by media outlets for content that draws larger audiences, rather than stories or programs that offer genuine relevance and social impact. This often hinders the public from gaining knowledge that would aid them in making informed decisions regarding significant issues. Limited consumption of newspapers and information on current affairs also leads to an absence of media that champion freedom of expression, along with a lack of regulatory and self-regulatory structures within media systems.

Spain has been classified as a "polarized pluralist media system" (Hallin & Mancini 2004). It is significant that in recent years, the number of Spanish journalists who belong to trade unions and professional associations has increased (Farias et al. 2007: 79), yet they lack enough strength in negotiations with media corporations to resolve problems with their employment conditions.

Professional associations generally regulate and self-regulate media performance in Spain, act as platforms for social dialogue, promote journalistic training, and stimulate debate on the social responsibility of media in democratic life. Some segments of Spanish media reject regulation as a form of censorship and support the view that the best regulation is none at all. Meanwhile, the considerable polarization and politicization of Spain's media, another phenomenon characterizing the current state-of-affairs (Hallin & Mancini, 2004), had an excessive impact on content. A national poll of citizen attitudes about news credibility in 2009 found that 47.3% of Spaniards perceived that the line between information and editorial comment was too often blurred (Farias et al. 2009: 90).

Given such conditions, it seems paradoxical that Spain proportionally has the most academic institutions in the field of communication and journalism in Europe, and the largest percentage of journalists with a university degree in journalism (Farias et al. 2009: 114). One might assume such figures would vouch for the quality of information and its purveyors. Instead, the result is an over-abundance of labor that breeds instability in the job market. Because it reduces operating costs, companies often hire recent, lower-wage graduates to the detriment of experienced, higher-wage journalists, overlooking the limited returns as far as content quality is concerned. This is easy to accomplish because of the lack of employment regulation and the limited power of professional organizations to prevent such practices. Despite such conditions, Spain has a modern, stable media system with freedom of information guaranteed.

Previous Studies

Since 1990, several studies have examined Spanish journalism, mainly from a sociological point of view. They often employ surveys, fieldwork, and analytic tools commonly used by sociologists—in a balance of qualitative and quantitative research methods.

In 1994, Diezhandino, Bezunartea, and Coca surveyed 98 professionals whom they called "the elite of journalism." They asked about aspects related to teaching and journalism, their professional practice, and the training and profiles of journalists. In this study, 80% of journalists reported a very high degree of satisfaction, while 53% considered leaving their profession for various reasons, such as reducing stress (23.3%) or to spend more time with their families (23.3%). Indeed, more than half said that they had, at the most, three free hours a day, and 78.3% declared that their professional lives made their family lives more difficult.

In 1994, most journalists surveyed thought that society regarded journalism as a prestigious profession, mainly due to its proximity to power (20%), importance (36.7%), and the intellectual training of journalists (41.7%). At that time, journalists also were satisfied with the autonomy or independence of their job duties, and on a 10-point scale, valued the freedom they enjoyed in their work at 7.2. By the mid-1990s, 83% of respondents said that journalists' main obligation was to act as impartial intermediaries between the events and the public, while 36.7% believed that their mission was to control and keep watch on public powers.

In 2000, the Centro de Investigaciones Sociológicas (CIS) published two studies focusing on Spanish journalism (Canel, Rodríguez, & Sánchez 2000; Garcia de Cortázar & Garcia de León 2000). Through a survey of 600 journalists and 20 in-depth interviews, de Cortázar and de León found an increase in professional training and a rejuvenation of these professionals. Most had a university degree (76.1%, with 69.2% having a journalism degree), and their average age was 42.2 years old. It was surprising to see that journalism was considered a personal lifestyle by 33% of those surveyed—an aspect that weighed in favor of choosing journalism as their profession. Additionally, 80% were pleased with their jobs, and most mentioned the relationship between their profession and power, as in the 1994 study by Diezhandino and colleagues. Lastly, the 2000 study highlighted the disparity between women and men in journalism, especially the fact that women held just 18.7% of senior editorial management positions such as editor in chief.

Canel, Rodriguez, and Sanchez (2000) produced similar findings through a combination of survey ($N = 1,000$) and in-depth interviews. In their study, the number of journalists with professional degrees increased (92% had a degree in communication, while 75% had a degree in information sciences). Although 68.8% considered leaving the profession at some point, respondents held journalism in high regard as a profession. Half of the journalists worked between eight and

10 hours a day, and had little free time. Only 30% earned more than €1,800 a month in 2000, meaning, as often happens nowadays, young people had to survive on meager salaries. Concerning professional practice, Canel et al. also found that more than half of journalists did not receive training through their companies and that one in three journalists thought that the news agenda was conditioned by official and institutional meetings. Half were members of a professional association, with the Federation of Press Associations (FAPE) having the most members.

The most recent findings about conditions in Spanish journalism come from the Informes de la Profesión Periodística (Farias et al. 2005–2009), commissioned in 2005 by the Association of Journalists of Madrid ($N = 1,000$). One of the most surprising findings was the common concern with problems in the workplace: 40% worried about workplace instability, 22% were concerned about low pay, and 17% worried about unemployment. Journalists were more concerned about these issues than about ethical values, press freedom, or journalistic autonomy. The survey also included questions on such "intangibles" as self-esteem and professional identities that revealed journalists were pleased with their profession (48%), but found it necessary to reinforce their credibility. In 2004, 36% of journalists wished to work in another medium within journalism and 16% said they would like to leave the profession altogether. Almost 35% were satisfied with their salaries, while 32% believed that their profession had a good image in society compared to 20% who believed otherwise. A large majority (87%) considered the level of unionization and professional association membership among journalists inadequate.

Method

Since 2005, data for this study have been obtained from journalists throughout Spain for the Annual Report of the Journalistic Profession. These studies are published by the Madrid Press Association (Asociación de la Prensa de Madrid, APM) and directed and coordinated by this chapter's authors. The data were gathered through computer-assisted telephone interviewing (CATI). Active journalists belonging to the Spanish Press Association Federation (Federación de Asociaciones de la Prensa de España; FAPE) supplied participants for this study.

Random probability sampling was used to select 1,000 individuals from FAPE's list of 12,412 journalists. The field work was performed by the company Demométrica from September 8–22, 2009. This was the sixth consecutive year of using the same methods in the Spanish journalist survey. The survey has been funded by the APM since 2005, and the Spanish Government's Department of Science and Innovation and the European Union since 2008 (Project C502008–05125).

Findings

Basic Characteristics

About 54% of journalists in the sample were men and 46% women. The largest age category was 36 to 45 years of age (29.3%), followed by the youngest group aged 35 and under (27.5%), those between 46 and 54 (24%), and those 55 or older (19.2%). The median age was 43.

Most journalists completed communication studies at a university (86.1%), with a sizeable proportion having studied journalism (74.8%). Some 7.8% of journalists studied in other fields, while the remaining 6.1% had no form of university qualification. Two in 10 journalists interviewed completed either a doctorate (4.3%) or master's degree (18.9%).

Table 23.1   Medium of Employment (2009, $N = 1,000$, in %)

Medium	Percent
Press (newspaper)	31.0
Magazines	9.4
Radio	11.1
Television	22.3
Internet (digital editions)	3.6
Communication departments	14.9
News agency	4.3
Contributor/Freelance	2.4
Other	0.6
Don't know/refused	0.4

More than half worked in the print media (31%) or in television (22.3%). Some 14.9% were employed in a communications department or press office. Journalists working in radio accounted for 11.1%, followed by those employed at magazines (9.4%), news agencies (4.3%), and digital media (3.6%)—along with contributors or freelancers (2.4%) (see Table 23.1).

More than half of the journalists interviewed worked at a multimedia group (51.3%). This reflects the trend toward a concentration of communication companies in Spain. Likewise, more than half worked at a media outlet with more than 250 workers (55.8%). Journalists employed at small companies (between seven and 50 employees) made up 18.8% of the sample, followed by those at outlets with 51 to 249 employees (16.8%), and those with small outlets with fewer than seven employees (7.2%).

The mean number of years of professional experience was 20.01 ($sd = 11.27$). Most journalists had between 11 and 20 years of experience (32.6%), followed by those with 21 to 30 years (28.1%), 10 years or less (23.5%), and 31 years or more (15.5%).

Most media professionals surveyed were editors (37.9%). Other heavily represented groups included senior editors (13.6%), contributors or freelancers (11.1%), and heads of communication departments (8.1%). The least-represented categories (deputy editors, reporters, assistants, presenters, executives, etc.) were grouped together and comprised 15% of the sample (see Table 23.2).

Table 23.2   Employment Category (2009, $N = 1,000$, in %)

Type of Job	Percent
Senior editor	13.6
Editor	7.7
Head of department	8.1
Section head	6.4
Writer	37.9
Contributor/Freelancer	11.1
Others	15.0
Don't know/refused	0.2

Education and Training

Since the outset of communication studies at Spanish universities in 1971, changes in the approach to content and methods have been common in an attempt to adjust to social demands and needs.

Such studies were first offered at schools of journalism, radio, and television, which sowed the seeds for today's faculties of information and communication science. A study by the National Quality and Accreditation Evaluation Agency (Agencia Nacional para la Evaluación de la Calidad y Acreditación; ANECA) on communication graduate qualifications indicated that prior to this period, "we do find other initiatives laying the foundations for such studies, such as the course in journalism run by the university professor and journalist Fernando Araujo y Gómez at Salamanca University in 1887" (ANECA 2004: 99).

By the 1980s, with the democratic era underway, seven new faculties had been established. Twelve journalism schools opened their doors to students during the 1990s. Since 2000, journalism studies appeared at 13 more universities. By 2009, this major was offered at 36 Spanish universities, of which 55.6% were public and 44.4% private.

University studies throughout Europe are in the midst of reform. The European Higher Education Area (EHEA) aims to standardize university studies throughout the EU, valuing practice above theory, reducing the number of students per class, and supporting the learning of languages and new technologies. The ultimate aim is to encourage the international mobility of Europe's professionals across the 46 countries belonging to the EHEA. The new system was introduced in 2010 for all journalism courses in Spain. It includes the European Credit Transfer System (ECTS), which measures the volume of a student's workload. Along with teaching hours, this system tracks time dedicated to study, seminars, papers, work experience and projects, and all the hours required in order to achieve the objectives of a course.

Communication science studies in Spain can lead to three possible qualifications: journalism, advertising, or audiovisual. The new context of the EHEA establishes two training cycles for journalism studies: graduate and postgraduate. Graduate studies cover the first cycle of official university education and last for four years, or eight semesters. Postgraduate education is a second block and includes master's and doctoral courses.

The aim of journalism studies in Spain is to provide students with an analytical and critical capacity, a sound technical and professional background, experience in laboratory and professional work, reflections on the journalist's task, an openness to innovation, and the ability to adapt to change. Other objectives include professional work experience, mastery of foreign languages, a capacity for research and analysis, and familiarity with new technologies.

In addition, 14 journalism schools allow students to specialize in a specific area. Universities make it possible for students to combine journalism studies with other courses in communication (such as audiovisual communication, advertising, and public relations), or other fields such as law, economics, humanities, tourism, or political science, among others.

Farias and colleagues (2005, 2006, 2007, 2008, 2009) have performed annual analyses of the teaching of journalism using qualitative and quantitative methods. They found that Spanish journalism courses are characterized by a high level of admissions and a female majority in the lecture halls. In 2009, 70% of Spain's journalism graduates in Spain were women. This overview provides data which help us to understand the current situation of communication studies in Spain, such as the number of registered students, evolution in journalism graduate numbers, range of communication training, work experience at companies, and recruitment of new journalists.

Table 23.3   Journalism Students Compared with Students of Other Communication Subjects in all Spanish Universities (1998–2009)

	2004–2005	2005–2006	2006–2007	2007–2008	2008–2009
Journalism	17,090	16,365	16,449	18,278	18,470
Other communication subjects	43,604	43,786	44,192	30,052	30,162
% of journalism students	28.2%	27.2%	27.1%	37.8%	38.0%
Total no. of communication students	60,694	60,151	60,641	48,330	48,632

Journalism accounts for 38% of students registered in communication courses in Spain. In the 2008–2009 academic year, 18,470 students were registered in journalism courses. As Table 23.3 shows, the numbers of students signing up for journalism courses have increased since 2005.

In 2008–2009, 2,550 students completed their journalism studies. Since Spain's first journalism graduates were produced in 1976, 69,117 students have followed their lead. This figure corresponds to those holding a journalism graduate qualification, not the number of active journalists. Men accounted for 30.4% of new graduates in 2009, while women, as has been the trend, comprise the bulk of newly qualified journalists at 69.6%. Despite fluctuations, since 1994 more women have consistently graduated from journalism courses. The percentage of female graduates has remained between 58% (the lowest level) in 2002 and 70.2% (the high point) in 2008.

It is a widespread practice for journalism students to complete some work experience, often an internship, before entering the job market. According to the 2009 survey data, 79.3% of active journalists said they had gained work experience before entering the job market.

Most of this work was paid (70.1%) and highly rated by the great majority, receiving a positive assessment of 97.7%. During the 2008–2009 academic year, most students worked in print, newspapers or magazines (30%). For the first time since 2006 (the first year this question was asked) this was followed by communication departments at public institutions and private companies (21%), television (17%), and radio (14%). Electronic media came in last in terms of the number of university–company partnership agreements, resulting in the low number of TV and radio students gaining work experience.

Working Conditions

Journalists stated that their professional reputation and involvement in recruitment processes (20.6% and 20.1%, respectively) were the main routes by which they gained employment. In 2009, 17.7% of those surveyed were hired following a work experience placement at the company.

Contractual relationships between journalists and their employers remained fairly stable. In 2009, there was a preponderance of salaried contract employment (80.9%), but that figure had fallen from 86.9% in 2007. At the same time, the proportion of self-employed journalists rose from 12% in 2007 to 16.3% in 2009.

As a group, mobility seems to be the norm for Spanish journalists: 32.4% had worked at their current company for less than five years (24% from five to 10 years, 27.4% from 11 to 20 years, 12.2% from 21 to 30 years). Although most achieved stability within three years (40.2%), there is growing instability within the profession, as 38% stated that it took them more than 12 years to achieve a permanent contract (40.2% up to three years, 13.7% from three to eight years, 6.3% from eight to 12 years).

Nearly half of the journalists interviewed in 2009 (49%) were keenly aware of the impact of the economic crisis on their companies and their own employment conditions. Most affected by the

Table 23.4   Employment Aspects Affected by Economic Crisis (2009, $N = 1,000$, in %)

Employment Aspects	Percent Mentioned[1]
Economic/salary aspect	29.4
Redundancies/unemployment/hours cut	16.7
Less activity/less work	11.4
Reduced budget	11.2
Drop in advertising, advertising revenue	10.4
Staff cutbacks	10.0
More work/fewer staff	6.7
Instability/Insecurity	3.5
Less revenue, turnover	2.9
Fewer clients/loss of clients	2.4
Closure of companies	1.6
Fewer resources	0.6
Change in functions/job	0.4
Other	3.1
Don't know/refused	0.6

1 Respondents could give multiple responses.

recession were salaries (29.4% of those interviewed complained of salary cuts), with many in fact becoming unemployed as a result of staff reductions (16.7%), as Table 23.4 indicates.

The 2009 survey highlighted a growing conviction that job insecurity is a deep-seated problem for Spanish journalists. This was the opinion of 97.5% of those interviewed, compared to 96.2% in 2008. Journalists also agreed on the reasons for poor working conditions in their profession: corporate cost-cutting (mentioned by 95.7%), job devaluation (92%), excess labor supply (89%), organizational structure (84.8%), lack of experience and training (79%), and necessary sacrifices to develop professional careers (76.7%).

Meanwhile, most journalists stated that their training was appropriate for their job requirements (82.2%). The same applied to working hours (77.6%), tasks performed (76.8%), and type of contract (76.8%). Yet salaries were deemed appropriate by only 56.2% of journalists.

The 2009 survey saw more journalists wishing to move to a different outlet (40.8%, compared to 39.5% in 2008). When asked why, the journalists referred mainly to their promotion aspirations, although the importance of this factor fell in 2009 (38.5%, compared to 48.6% in 2008). In 35.8% of cases they also referred to financial aspirations, as Table 23.5 indicates. Other reasons included professional refreshment (13.2%) and limited satisfaction in the tasks they performed (9.1%).

Faced with low salaries compared to other professions, the average economic satisfaction of journalists stood at 5.4 on a 10-point scale (5.5 in 2008). The proportions vary depending on the medium in question. Those happiest with their pay worked in television (5.7), press offices (5.6), and radio (5.5). Moderate levels were found among print journalists (5.38), those in communication departments (5.35), and those at magazines (5.28). Journalists working at news agencies and on the Internet were least content with their pay (see Table 23.6 for actual income figures).

About 41% felt that unemployment and job insecurity were the main problems facing the profession in 2009, as Table 23.7 indicates. The hiring of unqualified employees, which until 2008 led the rankings, dropped to second place (18.5%). Only 6.8% felt that low salaries were their

Table 23.5   Reasons Why Journalists Want to Change Jobs (2009, N = 1,000, in %)

Reasons	Percent Mentioned[1]
For professional advancement	38.5
For financial reasons	35.8
For quality of life	18.1
For a change/for novelty	14.0
For personal interest/satisfaction/vocation	7.4
To have more free time	7.4
For prestige	14.2
Personal satisfaction/discontent	9.1
To learn/Train	13.2
Stability	4.7
Other	1.2

1 Respondents could give multiple responses.

Table 23.6   Net Monthly Income of Journalists (2009, N = 1,000, in %)

Income in euros	Percent
Less than 600€	2.0%
601 – 900€	3.0%
901 – 1,200€	10.4%
1,201 – 1,500€	13.6%
1,501 – 1,800€	13.5%
1,801 – 2,200€	16.7%
2,201 – 2,500€	8.7%
2,501 – 3,000€	9.0%
More than 3,000€	13.7%
Don't know/refused	9.4%

profession's main problem (17.8% in 2008). Other problems were mentioned by less than 5% of respondents (see Table 23.7).

As for reporting freedom, 42.5% stated that they had never been pressured in their professional activities, while more than half (57.5%) said they had experienced some form of pressure. Of these, 42.5% declared they had been pressured on several occasions, 38.5% on a few occasions, and the remaining 19% acknowledged that they had frequently been subject to pressure. Journalists who said they had been pressured identified the source as line managers (85.4%), politicians (31.1%), advertisers (16.3%), other companies (15.6%), and public institutions and other pressure groups (8.1%).

Journalists also were asked to assess the Spanish media's credibility on an odd-numbered scale from 1 to 5, with 5 indicating the highest credibility level. Radio outlets received the highest average rating with a score of 3.64 (sd = 89), followed closely by the print media at 3.42 (sd = .91), and lastly television, with an average score suggesting low levels of credibility (2.44, sd = .93).

In assessing the quality of Spanish media compared to media in other European countries (see Table 23.8), most journalists surveyed felt that Spanish newspapers were equal in quality to the

Table 23.7   Main Problems in Profession (in %)[1]

	N = 1,000 2007	N = 1,000 2008	N = 1,000 2009
Unemployment/Job instability	17.2	15.9	41.3
Unqualified entrants	25.5	29.8	18.5
Low remuneration (salary)	22.0	17.8	6.8
Students, internees performing professional tasks	3.7	8.7	4.5
Independence/Politicization/Objectivity	6.2	2.3	3.2
Lack of ethical codes	3.0	5.0	2.9
Education/Qualifications/Training	3.0	1.6	2.7
Prestige/Recognition	0.4	1.4	2.7
Limited freedom of expression	—	—	2.3
Commoditization/Too many journalists	1.0	1.8	2.1
Credibility	1.8	0.9	1.8
Lack of professionalism/Seriousness/Interest	1.9	2.0	1.8
Incompatibility with family life/Working hours	2.1	2.5	1.7
Inadequate professional structure	1.0	0.7	1.3
Job insecurity (under threat)	2.3	5.4	1.0
Focus on profits/Bottom line	—	—	1.0
Monopolies/Concentration of media	—	0.5	0.9
Inadequate workforce turnover and promotion	0.3	0.2	0.6
Sensationalism/Gossip/Celebrity	—	—	0.2

1 Respondents could give multiple responses.

press in other European countries (53.8%), whereas 28.1% believed they were of lower quality, and only 9.5% felt that the Spanish press was better than those in the rest of Europe. Television saw the poorest rating, with 43.8% indicating that Spanish stations were of lower quality than their European counterparts. As for the quality of radio, most held that it was equal to other European broadcasters (35.5%), although a considerable percentage believed that Spanish radio was better than elsewhere in Europe (31.2%). Only 8.2% felt that it was worse.

Professionalism

Journalists expressed a negative view of the independence of their profession in Spain. On a scale of 1 to 10, the average assessment was 4.56. More than two-thirds (69.5%) gave a negative assessment with a score of 5 or lower. This pessimistic view, constant since 2005, can only be interpreted as a direct criticism of the conditions under which those surveyed must perform.

Table 23.8   Perceived Quality of Spanish Media Compared to Media in Other European Countries (in %)

	N = 1,000 Daily Press	N = 1,000 Radio	N = 1,000 Television
Better	9.5	31.2	4.3
Same	53.8	35.5	38.0
Worse	28.1	8.4	43.8
Don't know/refused	8.6	24.9	13.9

When asked about professional practices among their peers, 68.2% felt that Spanish journalists were guilty of not citing their information sources. Likewise, 83.9% felt that in Spain, data provided by "trusted" sources were not sufficiently scrutinized.

The journalists also were asked to assess which journalism specialties most comply with professional ethical practices. Again, an odd-numbered scale from 1 to 5 was used, with 5 indicating the greatest compliance with ethics. Specialties ranked most in line with professional ethics were culture at 3.75, local news at 3.24, economy at 3.22, sports at 2.95, politics at 2.40, and society news at 2.13.

Conclusions

Journalism in Spain is a mature field that has established a high level of independence in recent years. Yet work is still required on improving such aspects as working conditions, the genuine independence of editorial teams, and the separation of editorials and news information at some public and private outlets.

In 2009, the Spanish media faced a professional crisis involving reduced working hours, temporary layoffs, staff reductions, falling circulation, new formats, all manner of promotions, transitions from paid to free content, and mergers to reduce costs. The global economic crisis proved particularly harsh. By November 2008, more than 30 media outlets in Spain closed, and more than 3,000 workers lost their jobs. Against this difficult economic background, some 17,000 journalists worked each day, withstanding the vicissitudes of the recession.

The excessive dependence on advertising demanded a quest for alternative business models that have yet to develop. As long as the advertising boom could support traditional media, the process of change was checked, indeed was almost in slow-motion. But it was there. Forecasts in Spain were for migrations to new business models to occur over 10 years. The economic crisis served to speed up the inevitable transition from a traditional paid information model to new formulae capable of achieving a financial return on content. This is the reason why conventional media, print newspapers and magazines, have suffered the most, and are the most information-laden

Yet alongside the business model, which affects journalists' employers, and the quest for the most appropriate platform, we must not overlook content. Aside from the formal quality of information (such as well-written texts and excellent design), the crucial ties of credibility and trust that had existed between the public and the media have gradually faded. To combat the crisis, companies in Spain have opted for the shortcut in the form of cost savings, primarily in their workforce, without properly considering the medium- and long-term consequences—a loss of trust in their content.

In Spain, as in the rest of the developed world, people have more forms of media from which to draw information. Yet in many cases, it is more superficial. The "dumbing down" of information fed by a new taste for lightweight, bite-sized information with less depth, threatens the health of a society that more than ever needs serious, professional reporters.

Spanish journalists must not shift away from the essence of their profession, namely the need to seek common ground with readers and viewers on the basis of reliability and trust. They need once again to take up the shield of journalistic reliability, which for decades was the hallmark of their occupation. To inform, one must reach the heart of a news story, and to do that—to effectively perform and shine a light for a public bewildered by the amount of information noise—professionals need better training, depth, and versatility. More than ever, citizens need to feel commitment from journalists. At the same time, journalists need at least basic stability to perform their jobs. This is what Spanish political and social structures should guarantee, but currently do not.

References

ANECA (National Quality and Accreditation Evaluation Agency). 2004. *Libro Blanco: Títulos de Grado en Comunicación* [White book. Degrees in communication]. Madrid: ANECA.

Canel, María J., Roberto Rodríguez, and José J. Sánchez (eds). 2000. *Periodistas al descubierto: Retrato de los profesionales de la información* [Journalists uncovered: A portrait of news professionals]. Madrid: Centro Investigaciones Sociológicas.

Diezhandino, Pilar, Ofa Bezunartea, and César Coca. 1994. *La élite de los* periodistas [The elite of journalists]. Bilbao: Ediciones de la Universidad del País Vasco.

Farias, Pedro (Director) et al. 2005. *Informe Anual de la Profesión Periodística* 2005 [Journalist profession annual report 2005]. Madrid: Asociación de la Prensa de Madrid.

Farias, Pedro (Director) et al. 2006. *Informe Anual de la Profesión Periodística 2006* [Journalist profession annual report 2006]. Madrid: Asociación de la Prensa de Madrid.

Farias, Pedro et al. (Director) 2007. *Informe Anual de la Profesión Periodística* 2007 [Journalist profession annual report 2007]. Madrid: Asociación de la Prensa de Madrid.

Farias, Pedro et al. (Director) 2008. *Informe Anual de la Profesión Periodística 2008* [Journalist profession annual report 2008]. Madrid: Asociación de la Prensa de Madrid.

Farias, Pedro et al. (Director) 2009. *Informe Anual de la Profesión Periodística 2009* [Journalist profession annual report 2009]. Madrid: Asociación de la Prensa de Madrid.

García de Cortázar, Marisa, and García de León, María Antonia (eds.) 2000. *Profesionales del periodismo: Hombres y Mujeres en los medios de comunicación* [Professionals of journalism: Women and men, in the news media]. Madrid: Centro de Investigaciones Sociológicas.

Hallin, Daniel C., and Mancini, Paolo. 2004. *Comparing media systems. Three models of media and politics.* Cambridge, UK: Cambridge University Press.

24 Swedish Journalists

Between Professionalization and Commercialization

Jesper Strömbäck, Lars Nord, and Adam Shehata

Swedish journalists are working in a media environment shaped by mixed ideological heritages. While journalistic traditions have been inspired by liberal ideas of press freedom and freedom of expression, they also have existed within a media system with linkages to different political groups in society and wide acceptance of state activities in the media sphere (Weibull 2007). Thus, Swedish news practices have developed under the cross-pressures of liberal ideas about freedom and social responsibility and ideas of diversity and equality.

This mixed heritage is also prevalent in most overviews and comparisons of national media systems (Hardy 2008; Hultén 2004), and Sweden is often referred to as a prototypical example of a "democratic corporatist" country characterized by a highly developed mass circulation press, a high degree of political parallelism, a high degree of professionalization, and strong state intervention in the media system (Hallin & Mancini 2004). In such a system, strong journalist unions, systems of institutionalized self-regulation, and general acceptance of a journalistic code of ethics encourage professional journalism, without excluding proactive media policies aimed at maintaining external or internal pluralism.

Today, Sweden's media system is highly developed with around 70 daily newspapers, 80 weekly newspapers, 65 national television channels (eight of which are public service broadcasters), and 103 national and local radio stations (14 public service). In 2006, 80% of the Swedish population aged 9 to 79 read at least one newspaper on a daily basis, 74% listened to radio, and 86% watched TV on an average day (Carlsson & Facht 2007). Additionally, Internet penetration is very high. Seventy-two percent of the Swedish population used the Internet more than once a week in 2009; among teenagers and highly educated Swedes the same figure was around 90% (Bergström 2010).

Swedish journalism is not only the product of historic perspectives on journalistic missions and roles but is also formed by current media developments and dramatically changing newsroom practices. To further explore Swedish journalism and how it is affected by changes in the media environment and the conditions under which journalists operate, we conducted a nationally representative survey of Swedish journalists in the fall of 2009. This chapter presents some of the most important findings.

Background

Freedom of information is guaranteed in Sweden; it is embedded in the Constitution. This legislation was originally written in 1766 and is the oldest of its kind in the world. It also guarantees citizens' rights of access to public documents and protection of journalists' sources.

Aside from a legal system with strong constitutional protection for freedom of information and freedom of speech, Sweden is characterized by a system of institutionalized self-regulation with respect to codes of ethics and newspaper journalism. The Swedish Press Council is a part of this structure but is not affiliated with the government. The council makes decisions concerning media ethics and also publishes regular reports with its considerations and explanations regarding its policy positions (von Krogh 2008).

Free and widely circulated newspapers played an important role in the democratization process in the early 20th century and have been a cornerstone in the formative processes of Swedish democracy and public opinion (Höyer 2005). Newspaper reading and sales per capita are still among the highest in the world (Shehata & Strömback 2011), and although the total circulation of newspapers is gradually declining, local and regional newspapers generally still hold a strong position in their markets (Carlsson & Facht 2007).

While Swedish press history is complex, it is reasonable to argue that journalistic traditions developed in interdependence with the political system (Höyer 2005). Party-affiliated newspapers were more common in Sweden than independent newspapers during the major part of the last century. The party press was not only defined by distinct party endorsements on editorial pages, but also by politicized owner influence, recruitment of politically loyal journalists, and politically shaped news coverage (Hadenius, Seveborg, & Weibull 1970). The party-press system was initially not imposed by the state, but the government's introduction of selective press subsidies from the state budget to second-ranking newspapers in 1971 was intended to strengthen the system, mainly by keeping alive second-ranking newspapers linked with the Social Democrats and the Centre Party (Hadenius 1992).

The political, although not partisan, influence over the media was even more evident with respect to the broadcast media sector. From the beginning of both radio and television broadcasting, a public service monopoly was institutionalized that was heavily inspired by the BBC. The governmental Broadcasting Complaints Commission supervised laws and regulations. The public service channels were, and still are, prohibited from broadcasting commercial advertising and are financed by mandatory license fees. These state regulations concerning the prevention of commercials in public service media also extend to activities in new media formats such as public service text-TV and public service Web sites.

The development of Swedish public service media imposed new ideals for journalists in this sector. Initially, journalists were expected to mirror societal conflicts and stay impartial and objective when covering current affairs. Gradually, however, public service journalists have become more independent and influential in setting the political agenda (Djerf-Pierre & Weibull 2008). Thus, public service broadcasting in Sweden is not the same as government or state controlled broadcasting.

Both radio and television remained heavily regulated areas and were monopolized markets until the early 1990s. Terrestrial television and local radio were deregulated in 1991 and 1993, respectively. Thus, despite the historically important role of partisan newspapers and politically regulated broadcast media, Sweden has witnessed a gradual weakening of political influence over the media. The current media system in Sweden is characterized by both high levels of journalistic professionalism and commercialization (Strömbäck & Nord 2008). The commercialization is most evident among the broadcast media, where deregulation and technological developments have resulted in a large number of new commercial local radio stations and TV channels. The increasing competition between private and public media, on the other hand, has gradually reduced audience shares for public service media, particularly with respect to television (Carlsson & Facht 2007; European Audiovisual Observatory 2008).

At the same time, newspapers have become more professional and less party-oriented. Most Swedish newspapers are now politically independent and not affiliated with any party (save for the partisan preferences expressed on the editorial pages). In addition, structural changes in the national, regional, and local newspaper markets have significantly affected the working conditions for journalists, because joint ventures and media mergers offer huge potentials for reducing staff, costs and improving editorial efficiency (Nygren 2007).

Finally, the growing importance of online media has brought significant changes to the media in Sweden, which has one of the world's highest penetration rates for Internet and broadband access. The most popular news sites on the Internet today are online services produced by leading national news media companies. Consequently, news production processes have become more oriented toward multi-channel publishing. In the new media convergence culture, journalists have to become more multi-skilled. Undoubtedly, these changes related to the development of new media have had profound effects on the working conditions of journalists and on the news production processes (Karlsson 2010; Nygren 2007).

Overall, trends of de-politicization, professionalization, and commercialization have strongly influenced the Swedish media system and the current working conditions for journalists. However, it is not clear whether these changes have increased the quality of journalism in Sweden. On the one hand, de-politicization and increasing journalistic professionalism have encouraged a more proactive, independent, and impartial style of news reporting. On the other hand, increasing competition for audiences and advertisers as well as growing economic pressures might result in a more superficial, cost-efficient journalism focused on capturing the largest possible audiences rather than on what are the most important issues.

Previous Studies

During the last few decades, media scholars have regularly surveyed Swedish journalists. However, attitudes and professional values among journalists have been discussed in non-academic works for an even longer time. In one of the first studies of Swedish journalists, done in 1955–1956, the importance of journalists' political affiliations was confirmed, and a majority of Swedish press journalists declared that they shared the political orientation of the newspaper where they worked (Ahrnstedt & Söderström 1958).

The first academic study of Swedish journalists was conducted in 1969. In that survey, 377 of 400 journalists in the sample were interviewed by telephone. In a supplementary study, journalistic work practices were studied at 19 media organizations. The two studies discovered an increasing professionalization among Swedish journalists; but there was a substantial generation gap with more professional values and role perceptions among younger journalists (Furhoff 1970).

A more comprehensive national survey of Swedish journalists was conducted by researchers at the University of Gothenburg in 1989. Based on a representative sample of 1,500 journalists (59% net response rate), the study focused on both journalist role perceptions and ethical considerations. Among many other things, the findings indicated that Swedish journalists had become more professionalized and socially homogenous, and that they perceived the watchdog function of journalism as the most important one (Weibull 1991).

During the same year, a similar study of journalists' attitudes was reported by a government-appointed committee entitled *Democracy and Power in Sweden*. This study, based on a representative sample of 1,500 journalists (62% net response rate), showed that about two-thirds of all Swedish media workers were men, that a majority had parents with an academic education, and that a majority supported left-leaning political parties (Petersson & Carlberg 1990).

Between 1990 and 1992, a comparative study of news systems analyzed political role perceptions of journalists in Great Britain, Germany, Italy, Sweden, and the United States. Roughly 275 Swedish journalists participated in this study, which was conducted by mail. The findings showed that Swedish journalists were more likely than journalists from other nations to say that a critical attitude defined their work. However, their function as critics of the government and society did not lead to a greater willingness to take part in partisan disputes (Patterson 1998).

A research team from the University of Gothenburg conducted follow-up surveys of their 1989 national survey in 1994, 1995, 1999, and 2005. The most recent one, conducted in 2005, was based on a sample of 2,000 journalists belonging to the Swedish Union of Journalists. The study confirmed a more widespread acceptance of professional norms and ethical guidelines with a continued strong emphasis on scrutinizing and controlling other powerful institutions in the Swedish society (Wiik 2007).

The 2005 study also indicated substantial changes in working conditions, with fewer journalists involved in newspaper production and about one-third of the work force occupied with online publishing (Edström 2007). The study indicated that ideological preferences among journalists deviated more than before from those of the general public, with journalists expressing stronger sympathies for parties on the left and the Green party than did the public. However, this trend was not as clear when journalists covering politics and business were studied; their political preferences were more in line with those of the public (Asp 2007).

Other recent studies have noted that Swedish journalists are much more supportive of investigative journalism than are politicians and citizens (Nord 2007), and that the latter two groups actually question journalists' claims of challenging the political establishment (Strömbäck 2004). However, both journalists and politicians in Sweden seem to agree that journalists have the ultimate power in framing the news (Strömbäck & Nord 2006).

Method

The data in this study of Swedish journalists are based on a national mail survey carried out between October and December 2009 and financed by the Centre for Political Communication Research at Mid Sweden University. The sample was generated in close collaboration with the Swedish Union of Journalists, which includes about 85% of all Swedish journalists. A sample of 1,200 journalists was randomly drawn from the Union's membership. Retired journalists who were still members of the union were identified and excluded from the sample. The exclusion of people who had left the profession or could not answer the survey due to illness resulted in a net sample of 1,187 journalists.

The working procedure was based on shared responsibilities. Union staff mailed the questionnaires to the respondents while research staff received and coded the answers. The research staff thus never saw the names of the respondents, while Union staff never saw the responses from respondents. Reminders were administrated by the Union and based on identification numbers on received questionnaires reported by the research center. Through this procedure, it was not possible to match the names and responses.

The survey went into the field on October 5, 2009, and after two reminders up to December 19, 621 out of the net sample of 1,187 journalists had returned their questionnaires. This corresponds to a response rate of 52%. The questionnaire included 38 questions divided into four sections.

Findings

In December 2008, the Swedish Union of Journalists had 8,367 female (48.9%) and 8,729 male (51.1%) members, in total 17,096 members (Svenska journalistförbundet 2009). Every year about 1,000 new journalists enter the workforce, while a number of journalists retire or leave for other work. To further describe the Swedish journalistic workforce, we turn to our survey findings.

In our survey, 49.6% of the respondents were female and 50.4% were male. Eighty-five percent were born in Sweden to Swedish parents, and the vast majority (78%) had completed a university degree. Forty-six percent had a university-level education in journalism, 6% another university education related to media or communication studies, and 26% some other university-level education. An additional 4% had studied journalism at vocational schools. Altogether, these results suggest that about 56% of Swedish journalists have some kind of higher education in journalism or media and communication. Other surveys of Swedish journalists suggest that the share might be even higher. According to the survey of journalists in 2005, 67% had some kind of journalism education (Edström 2007). The difference between surveys is likely due to different question wordings and response alternatives.

In terms of age, about 40% of Swedish journalists are younger than 40 years, 24% between 41 and 50 years, 26% between 51 and 60 years, and 10% are older than 60 years. Generally speaking, the younger the journalists are, the higher the probability that they have a university-level education. The correlation between age and educational level is significant (Cramer's $V=.212$, $p=.001$), and the difference between the youngest and the oldest journalists is the most pronounced (see Table 24.1).

One of the most widely discussed issues in journalism is the question of partisan bias. While those on the political left tend to perceive journalism as right leaning due to corporate ownership, those on the right tend to perceive journalism as left leaning due to the partisan preferences of journalists. While most research shows that the content of the Swedish media is politically neutral (Asp 2006; Petersson, Djerf-Pierre, Holmberg, Strömbäck, & Weibull 2006), there is little doubt that Swedish journalists stand to the left of the Swedish public (Asp 2007). A comparison of the party preferences of journalists with those among the public in October 2009 (when our survey was in the field) makes this clear. The Left Party, the Social Democrats, and the Green Party are left-wing parties, while the Centre Party, the Liberal Party, the Christian Democrats, and the

Table 24.1   Age and Education of Journalists (in %)

	Primary Education	Secondary Education	University Education	N
< 31 years	—	11	89	98
31–40 years	1	18	81	143
41–50 years	2	24	74	141
51–60 years	3	22	75	157
> 60 years	10	19	71	59
N	15	117	466	598

Note.   Percentages have been rounded to the nearest integer.

Table 24.2 Party Preferences of Journalists and Swedish Public (in %)

	Swedish Public	*Swedish Journalists*
Left Party	4.8	13.5
Social Democrats	34.6	22.5
Green Party	7.8	27.3
Centre Party	5.0	6.4
Liberal Party	7.8	12.0
Christian Democrats	4.7	1.3
Moderates	29.0	9.7
Swedish Democrats	3.9	0.2
Other	2.4	7.1

Note. Source for the public's partisan preferences: http://www.synovate.se/Templates/Page__195.aspx.

Moderates are center-right parties. The Swedish Democrats is a nationalistic, xenophobic party without representation in parliament at the time of this survey.

As shown in Table 24.2, whereas 47.2% of the public favors one of the left parties, the corresponding share among journalists is 63.3%. Thus, compared to the general public, Swedish journalists clearly are standing more to the left of the political spectrum. On a left-right ideological continuum, Swedish journalists also place themselves more toward the left. On a scale from 0 (extreme left) to 100 (extreme right), the mean is 41 and the median 40.

However, it should be reiterated that there is no evidence that the content of news journalism is shaped by journalists' partisan preferences (Petersson et al. 2006). The problem of Swedish journalism is not partisan bias, but rather structural biases (Strömbäck 2008).

Turning to Swedish journalists' working conditions and experience, the mean number of years working as a journalist in our survey is 17.5 years (median=15 years, SD=11.7 years). The most experienced journalist in our survey has worked in journalism for 50 years, while the least experienced has been in the business for only one year. Seventy-three percent have full employment, whereas 9% have temporary employment. Thirteen percent are working as freelancers, while 3% are currently unemployed.

Focusing on the fully employed, most are working for newspapers. As shown in Table 24.3, 50% work for local, regional, or national newspapers; 3% for free newspapers; and 18% for different

Table 24.3 News Organizations in Which Journalists Are Employed (in %)

News Organization	*Percent*
Daily newspaper	50
Free newspaper	3
Magazines	18
News agency	2
TV station (public service)	12
TV station (commercial)	4
Radio station (public service)	9
Radio station (commercial)	1
Other	1
N	407

Note. Percentages have been rounded to the nearest integer.

kinds of magazines. In all, 71% work as print journalists—although some of them might publish online as well. Most of the other journalists (21%) are working for public service TV or radio stations, while only 5% are working for commercial TV or radio stations. This is a reflection of the fact that public service broadcasting, which still is very strong in the Swedish media landscape, relies more on fully employed personnel than do commercial stations.

Most of the journalists in our sample are working as reporters: 40% describe themselves as reporters, 16% as managers, 7% as copy editors, 7% as Web editors, 5% as photographers, and 3% as editorial writers or commentators. The remaining 22% describe themselves as producers, researchers, or as working with other functions. In addition, a number of respondents (excluded here) gave more than one answer, suggesting that multi-job journalists have become increasingly common.

One major factor behind this development is the rise of digital media. Although only 7% describe themselves as Web editors, the number of journalists working with online publishing is significantly higher. In fact, 27% are working with online publishing on a daily basis, with an additional 20% working with online publishing several days a week. Only a quarter of the journalists say that they never work with online publishing. This suggests that online publishing and digital media have become heavily integrated in the daily news production and publishing processes. This suggests that journalists have become less rather than more specialized in terms of what media formats they work with.

Another aspect of specialization is the extent to which journalists cover specific beats or topics. Sweden is a small country with limited room for specialist publications or elite media, so it comes as no surprise that most Swedish journalists (70%) cover a variety of subjects and topics. In response to the question of what subject they mainly cover, politics and society was mentioned by 16%, sports by 7%, culture by 5%, economy and business by 5%, and entertainment by 4%. Based on these findings, it can be inferred that most Swedish journalists are generalists rather than specialists.

At the same time, most Swedish journalists have a rather high degree of autonomy in their daily work life. This is evident from the responses to questions about how much freedom they usually have in selecting the stories they work on and which aspects of the stories should be emphasized. The results are presented in Table 24.4.

Seventy-eight percent say that they have "almost complete" or "a great deal of freedom" in selecting the stories they work on. Similarly, 80% say that they have "almost complete" or "a great deal of freedom" in deciding which aspect of a story should be emphasized. In addition, when asked whether they are able to get a subject covered if they think it is important and should be followed up, 78% say that they "almost always" or "more often than not" are able to get the subject covered. These responses suggest that Swedish journalists have a great say over the content of the final news stories. Based on the responses to the question about how much editing their stories get from others, this indeed appears to be the case. While 24% say that their stories get a lot of

Table 24.4   Perceived Freedom to Select Stories and Aspects of Stories (in %)

	Almost complete	A great deal	Some	None	N
Freedom to select stories to work on	27	51	19	3	587
Freedom to decide which aspect of a story should be emphasized	27	53	16	3	586

Note.   Percentages have been rounded to the nearest integer.

editing from others, 62% say that they only get a little editing, and 14% note that their stories do not get any editing at all.

Taken together, these results suggest that Swedish journalists have significant autonomy and influence on the daily news production processes. If this is indicative of a high degree of journalistic professionalism, Swedish journalists should be described as highly professionalized. Perhaps this is the reason why most Swedish journalists are rather satisfied with their present job. Most journalists say that they are either "very" (29%) or "somewhat" (57%) satisfied with their present job, while only 14% say that they are either "not particularly" or "not at all" satisfied. Consequently, rather few Swedish journalists expect to leave journalism within the next five years. Excluding those who expect to retire, 71% of journalists expect to continue working in journalism, 15% think about changing their field of work, and 14% are undecided.

While most Swedish journalists are rather satisfied with their jobs, not all of them are happy with the performance of their news organizations. When asked about how well they think their news organizations are informing the public, most of the journalists think their own news organizations are doing either a "very good" (22%) or a "fairly good" job (57%). However, about one-fifth of journalists think that their organizations are doing "neither a good nor a bad" (17%) or a "fairly bad" job (4%).

To further investigate how Swedish journalists experience their news organizations and how changes have affected journalistic quality, respondents were presented with statements with which they could agree or disagree. The results show that a majority agree with the statement that "at their news organizations, profits are a higher priority than good journalism." A majority also agree that "newsroom resources have been shrinking at their news organization over the past few years." Based on this, it is somewhat surprising to find that almost identical shares agree and disagree with the statement that "the quality of journalism at my news organization has been rising steadily over the past few years." Thus, despite working at mainly profit-seeking news organizations where newsroom resources have been shrinking, one-third of Swedish journalists think that the quality of journalism has been rising steadily.

While this appears paradoxical, it might indicate that other factors than resources might determine the perceived quality of journalism in Sweden. One such factor might be the freedom journalists have to select which stories they cover and the aspects of the stories they emphasize. Thus, journalistic freedom and direct influence on the news production process might be perceived to offset the negative effects of decreasing newsroom resources. While this is only a speculation,

Table 24.5   Perceptions of Own News Organization (%)

	Strongly disagree	Somewhat disagree	Neutral	Somewhat agree	Strongly agree	N
At my news organization, profits are a higher priority than good journalism	18	16	15	33	18	579
The quality of journalism at my news organization has been rising steadily over the past few years	11	22	33	24	10	579
At my news organization, newsroom resources have been shrinking over the past few years	6	6	15	28	45	579
My news organization does a lot of audience research to learn what kinds of information our audience wants or needs	20	19	20	29	13	578

Note.   Percentages have been rounded to the nearest integer.

it is interesting to note that Swedish journalists do not seem to think that shrinking newsroom resources *necessarily* lead to less quality in journalism.

Professional Norms and Daily Work

Research on journalistic work practices has identified several factors that shape news media behavior. In general, journalists are always governed by a combination of pressures at various levels within and outside media organizations: professional norms, market pressures, information supply, etc. This section will look more closely at how Swedish journalists perceive their profession and the Swedish media in general.

Table 24.6 presents Swedish journalists' perceptions of how important various tasks are for the media *in general*. The tasks are presented in descending order from the most to the least important. Consensus among journalists is strongest when it comes to "get information to public quickly." Ninety-three percent of the Swedish journalists perceive this to be either "very" or "somewhat" important. All of the other tasks are perceived to be important by a majority of the respondents. Nevertheless, some tasks appear to be more important than others. For instance, to "concentrate on news that's of interest to the widest possible audience" and "provide entertainment and relaxation" are considered to be important by about three-fourth of the journalists, while only about half of them think that it is important "to set the political agenda" or "be an adversary of business."

The tasks discussed above can be seen as more general media practices that shape media content. The journalists were also asked to evaluate various *event properties* in terms of their influence on the likelihood of an event becoming news. In addition, the respondents were asked what importance they think these properties *should* have in a normative sense. The responses allow us to compare perceptions of actual media behavior with professional norms and ideals. Table 24.7 presents the mean scores of perceived actual and normative importance of each event property, which are measured on a five-point scale ranging from 1 = "no importance" to 5 = "great importance." The event properties are listed in descending order based on their actual importance score.

The following characteristics are perceived as having the greatest impact on what actually gets reported in the news—that the event is sensational and unexpected (4.68), that it is dramatic and

Table 24.6   Perceived Importance of Media Practices and Tasks (%)

	Percent	*N*
Get information to the public quickly	93	606
Concentrate on news that's of interest to the widest possible audience	79	597
Provide entertainment and relaxation	76	602
Give ordinary people a chance to express their views on public affairs	68	604
Provide analysis and interpretation of complex problems	66	604
Be an adversary of politicians and public officials by being constantly skeptical of their actions	63	600
Investigate claims and statements made by the government	61	600
Point people toward possible solutions to society's problems	57	604
Motivate ordinary people to get involved in public discussions of important issues	55	603
To set the political agenda	55	599
Be an adversary of businesses by being constantly skeptical of their actions	50	600

Note.   Percentages have been rounded, and reflect the share naming the tasks as either "very important" or "somewhat important."

Table 24.7   Actual and Normative Importance of Event Properties (mean values)

	Actual Importance.	Normative Importance.	Difference
That the event is sensational and unexpected	4.68	3.94	0.74
That the event is dramatic and thrilling	4.47	3.69	0.78
That it is an exclusive news story	4.33	3.45	0.88
That own media organization is first with reporting about the event	4.28	3.19	1.09
That the event is of interest to many people	4.24	4.23	0.01
That the event is about famous persons/organizations	4.08	2.55	1.53
That the event is about important persons/organizations	4.05	3.52	0.53
That the event has consequences for people's daily life	3.91	4.61	-0.70
That the event involves conflicts	3.82	2.80	1.02
That the information comes from an official, reliable source	3.81	3.46	0.35
That the event is of interest to the editorial managers	3.69	1.98	1.71
That the event increases people's awareness of problems in society	3.68	4.68	-1.00
That there are good pictures available	3.65	2.96	0.69
That the event is scheduled by the news department	3.58	2.23	1.35
That a single journalist is very interested in the topic	3.40	2.34	1.06
That the event increases people's insights and knowledge	3.22	4.60	-1.38
That there is a good press release available	3.17	1.68	1.49
That the event is easy to explain to the audience	3.14	2.22	0.92
That the event is inexpensive to cover	3.02	1.35	1.67

Note.   The scale ranges from 1 (no importance) to 5 (great importance).

thrilling (4.47), that it is an exclusive news story (4.33), that their own news organization is first with reporting the event (4.28), and that the event is of interest to many people (4.24). When asked how important different properties *should* be, on the other hand, most support is found for the following properties: that the event increases people's awareness of abuses in society (4.68), that the event has consequences for people's daily life (4.61), and that the event increases people's insights and knowledge (4.60). Obviously, there are some clear differences between what journalists think *is* and *should* be important when news decisions are made.

The last column in Table 24.7 shows the difference between perceived actual importance and normative importance for each event property. For instance, that an event "increases people's insights and knowledge" is perceived as having less influence when media organizations make news decisions than journalists think it should have. This is reflected in a negative difference score of -1.38. In contrast, the availability of a good press release is considered as having a larger influence than it should have (+1.49).

In some cases, there are large differences between perceived actual importance and normative importance. In other cases, the gaps are smaller. That an event is inexpensive to cover is perceived to have a greater influence than Swedish journalists think it should have. The same is true for events that are about famous persons or organizations, as well as events that are of interest to the editorial managers. That there is a good press release, that the news department has scheduled the event, and that their own news organization is first with reporting the event are also perceived as being more important than they should be.

There are also event properties that are perceived as being less important than they should be. These properties all share a common public interest orientation—that the event increases people's insights and knowledge, that it increases people's awareness of problems in society, and that the event has consequences for people's daily life.

Thus, it could be argued that the differences between the perceptions of what *is* and what *should be* important in deciding what is news occur mainly where news factors stemming from commercial pressures and media logic tend to be seen as more important than professional ideals of public service in everyday news production.

Professional Ethics and Perceptions of Power

Another aspect of journalistic professionalism and ethics is related to norms and values of appropriate behavior. To investigate this, journalists were asked whether they think a number of news-gathering techniques are justifiable means to gather information for an "important story."

As Table 24.8 indicates, some of the methods are clearly more acceptable to Swedish journalists than others. Fifty-six percent of the respondents think that it is never justified to "pay people for confidential information," while 25% believe it is justified on occasion. About half of the journalists believe it is appropriate to "use confidential information without authorization" or to "claim to be someone else," at least occasionally. "Getting employed in a firm or organization in order to get inside information," or "using hidden microphone or cameras," is supported by an even larger percentage of Swedish journalists. Thus, controversial information gathering methods seem to be more acceptable among Swedish journalists when they are based on professional working practices than resulting from economic transactions or involving personal documents.

Finally, Swedish journalists were asked about their perceptions of the influence of various media organizations on the public. A large number of studies have shown that the news media can exert a significant influence on public opinion. However, probably more important than the actual influence of the news media are the *perceptions* of their power (Tal-Or, Tsfati, & Gunther 2009). The fact that news media are perceived to be powerful can be important when other powerful actors (such as politicians) try to adapt, or at least pay attention, to the media.

Table 24.9 presents the journalists' perceptions of media power in descending order for each media organization. Unsurprisingly, Swedish journalists consider the public service broadcasting organizations as the most powerful or important entities that can influence the public. Swedish

Table 24.8   Support for Controversial Information Gathering Methods (in %)

	Justified on occasion	Never justified	Don't know	N
Paying people for confidential information	25	56	19	599
Using confidential information without authorization	52	33	14	603
Claiming to be somebody else	55	36	10	600
Badgering unwilling informants to get a story	51	39	10	601
Making use of personal documents such as letters and photographs without permission	17	70	13	602
Getting employed in a firm or organization to gain inside information	71	17	12	601
Using hidden microphones or cameras	85	10	6	602

Note: Percentages have been rounded to the nearest integer.

Table 24.9 Perceptions of Media Influence on Public

Media type	Mean (sd)	N
Swedish Television (SVT)	8.50 (1.36)	603
Swedish Radio (SR)	7.70 (1.71)	603
TV4	7.40 (1.77)	602
Metropolitan newspapers	7.35 (1.69)	599
Regional/local newspapers	6.86 (2.03)	599
Tabloids	6.71 (1.99)	600
Other commercial television channels	4.63 (2.13)	600
Commercial radio	3.83 (1.92)	603

Note: The scale ranges from 1 (no influence) to 10 (great influence).

Television (*Sveriges Television*) clearly is perceived to be the most influential. It is interesting to note that Swedish Radio (*Sveriges Radio*) is considered as more influential than the commercial channel TV4. Metropolitan newspapers are perceived to be fairly equal to TV4 in terms of influence on the public. Commercial radio and television channels other than TV4, however, are considered to have much less influence than the other media organizations.

Thus, while much has changed in the Swedish media landscape during the last decades, public service broadcasting media are still perceived as having the greatest influence on the public. Whether the Internet and social media will change this perception remains to be seen.

Conclusions

Swedish journalism as a profession has undergone profound changes during the last decades. As noted in the opening section of this chapter, the Swedish media system was once characterized by a strong party press with clear linkages between political parties and newspapers, but societal, technological, and economic developments have changed the circumstances of news production as well as the journalistic profession. Current trends in the Swedish media are perhaps best described in terms of de-politicization, professionalization, and commercialization, trends that ultimately shape the working conditions for journalists. But within these broad trends there is also evidence of significant stability within the Swedish journalistic profession.

Most Swedish journalists are highly educated, and most of them have university degrees in journalism or communication studies (Edström 2007). Not surprisingly, this is more common among younger journalists. The typical Swedish journalist is a generalist working for a daily local newspaper—a fact that reflects the character of the Swedish media system, which still is characterized by a strong newspaper market. Furthermore, the findings of this survey confirm results from previous studies showing that left-wing parties are over-represented among journalists when compared to the party preferences of the Swedish public (Asp 2007; Petersson et al. 2006).

When it comes to the daily work of Swedish journalists, the often contradictory cross-pressures of professionalism and commercial interests are clearly reflected in this survey of Swedish journalists. Perceptions of extensive autonomy in the daily news production dominate. An overwhelming majority of Swedish journalists say they have substantial freedom to select what stories to report and what aspects of a story to emphasize. Additionally, when Swedish journalists evaluate the newsworthiness of an event, they rely heavily on their own experience as well as judgments made by their closest colleagues and other news organizations. The reliance on colleagues and competitors reflects what Donsbach (2008) has called a social validation process in which other journalists, due to shared professional norms, are regarded as the only legitimate sources of influence in situations of uncertainty.

While a majority of the journalists agree that profits are more important to their news organizations than good journalism and that newsroom resources have been shrinking, this is not necessarily related to perceptions of lower journalistic quality. On the other hand, when evaluating the actual and normative importance of several news factors, Swedish journalists tend to think that professional public service oriented ideals have less influence in the daily news production than they should have. In this respect, the results indicate that commercial pressures tend to pull journalism in a direction not desired by Swedish journalists.

In sum, then, most of our findings suggest that the profession of journalism is resilient and still strong in Sweden. While increasing levels of professionalism once liberated journalists from their ties to political parties, they now face pressure from commercial forces. Apart from the growing importance of economic considerations, one of the most striking characteristics of Swedish journalists is their substantial degree of perceived autonomy from other actors, both individually and collectively. Coupled with a strong consensus about professional norms and news values, this makes Swedish journalists highly influential actors, both in terms of deciding what topics to cover and how, and in influencing the public. Whether further commercialization and new media will change this remains to be seen.

References

Ahrnstedt, Pelle, and Herbert Söderström. 1958. *Svenska dagstidningsjournalisters utbildning, rekrytering, attityder m.m* [Swedish journalists' education, recruitment, attitudes, etc.]. Uppsala: Uppsala Universitet.

Asp, Kent. 2006. *Rättvisa nyhetsmedier. Partiskheten under 2006 års medievalrörelse* [Fair and balanced news media. Bias during the 2006 election campaign]. Göteborg: JMG.

Asp, Kent. 2007. Partisympatier [Party Sympathies]. In *Den svenska journalistkåren* [Swedish journalists], edited by Kent Asp, pp. 221–239. Göteborg: JMG.

Bergström, Annika. 2010. Personligt och privat I sociala medier [Person and privacy in social media]. In *SOM-undersökningen 2009* [SOM National survey on politics, media and society], edited by Sören Holmberg & Lennart Weibull. Göteborg: SOM-institutet.

Carlsson, Ulla, and Ulrika Facht. 2007. *Medie Sverige 2007: Statistik och analys* [Media in Sweden 2007: Statistics and analyses]. Göteborg: Nordicom.

Djerf-Pierre, Monika, and Lennart Weibull. 2008. From public educator to interpreting ombudsman: Regimes of political journalism in Swedish public service broadcasting 1925–2005. In *Communicating politics: Political communication in the Nordic countries*, edited by Jesper Strömbäck, Mark Ørsten, and Toril Aalberg, pp. 195–214. Göteborg: Nordicom.

Donsbach, Wolfgang. 2008. Factors behind journalists' professional behavior. In *Global journalism research: Theories, methods, findings, future*, edited by Martin Löffelholz and David Weaver, pp. 65–78. Malden, MA: Blackwell.

European Audiovisual Observatory. 2008. *Television in 36 European states*. Frankfurt: Council of Europe.

Edström, Maria. 2007. Journalisters arbete och utbildning—omstrukturering pågår [The work and education of journalists—Restructuring in progress]. In *Den svenska journalistkåren* [Swedish journalists], edited by Kent Asp, pp. 55–66. Göteborg: JMG.

Furhoff, Lars. 1970. *Journalistkåren i Sverige* [Journalists in Sweden]. Stockholm: Aldus.

Hadenius, Stig. 1992. Vulnerable values in a changing political and media system: The case of Sweden. In *Television and the public interest. Vulnerable values in West European broadcasting*, edited by Jay G. Blumler, pp. 112–130. London: Sage.

Hadenius, Stig, Jan-Olov Seveborg, and Lennart Weibull. 1970. *Partipress* [The party press]. Stockholm: Rabén & Sjögren.

Hallin, Daniel C., and Paolo Mancini. 2004. *Comparing media systems. Three models of media and politics.* Cambridge, UK: Cambridge University Press.

Hardy, Jonathan. 2008. *Western media systems.* London: Routledge.

Hultén, Olof. 2004. Sweden. In *The media in Europe: The Euromedia handbook,* edited by Mary Kelly, Gianpietro Mazzoleni, and Denis McQuail, pp. 236–247. London: Sage.

Höyer, Svennik. 2005. The rise and fall of the Scandinavian party press. In *Diffusion of the news paradigm 1850–2000,* edited by Svennik Höyer & Horst Pöttker, pp. 75–92. Göteborg: Nordicom.

Karlsson, Michael. 2010. *Nätjnyheter. Fran slaten produkt till öppen process* [Online news. From a closed-off product to an open process]. Stockholm: Stiftelsen Institutet för Mediestudier.

von Krogh, Torbjörn. 2008. 'Constructive criticism' vs. public scrutiny: Attitudes to media accountability in and outside Swedish news media. In *Media accountability today…and tomorrow. Updating the concept in theory and practice,* edited by Torbjörn von Krogh, pp. 119–136. Göteborg: Nordicom.

Nord, Lars. 2007. Investigative journalism in Sweden. A not so noticeable noble art. *Journalism: Theory, practice & criticism* 5: 517–521.

Nygren, Gunnar. 2007. The changing journalistic work: Changing professional roles and values. Paper presented at the conference The Future of Newspapers, Cardiff University, Wales.

Patterson, Thomas E. 1998. Political roles of the journalist. In *The politics of news—The news of politics,* edited by Doris Graber, Denis McQuail, and Pippa Norris, pp. 17–32. Washington, DC: CQ Press.

Petersson, Olof, and Ingrid Carlberg. 1990. *Makten över tanken* [The power over people's thinking]. Stockholm: Carlssons.

Petersson, Olof, Monika Djerf-Pierre, Sören Holmberg, Jesper Strömbäck, and Lennart Weibull. 2006. *Media and elections in Sweden.* Stockholm: SNS.

Shehata, Adam, and Jesper Strömback. 2011. A matter of context: A comparative study of media environments and news consumption gaps in Europe. *Political Communication* 28:110–134.

Strömbäck, Jesper. 2004. *Den medialiserade demokratin: Om journalistikens ideal, verklighet och makt* [The mediatized democracy: On the ideals, realities and power of journalism]. Stockholm: SNS.

Strömbäck, Jesper. 2008. Swedish election news coverage: Towards increasing mediatization. In *Handbook of election news coverage around the world,* edited by Jesper Strömbäck and Lynda Lee Kaid, pp. 160–174. New York: Routledge.

Strömbäck, Jesper, and Lars Nord. 2006. Do politicians lead the tango? A study of the relationship between Swedish journalists and their political sources in the context of election campaigns. *European Journal of Communication* 2: 147–164.

Strömbäck, Jesper, and Lars Nord. 2008. Media and politics in Sweden. In *Communicating politics: Political communication in the Nordic countries,* edited by Jesper Strömbäck, Mark Ørsten, and Toril Aalberg, pp. 103–124. *Göteborg: Nordicom.*

Svenska Journalistförbundet. 2009. *Svenska Journalistförbundets verksamhet 2008* [The Yearly Report from the Swedish Union of Journalists, 2008]. Stockholm: Svenska Journalistförbundet.

Tal-Or, Nurit, Yariv Tsfati, and Albert C. Gunther. 2009. The influence of presumed media influence: Origins and implications of the third-person perception. In *The Sage handbook of media processes and effects,* edited by Robin L. Nabi and Mary Beth Oliver, pp. 99–112. London: Sage.

Weibull, Lennart. 1991. Svenska journalister 1989 [Swedish Journalists in 1989]. In *Svenska journalister—ett grupporträtt* [Swedish Journalists—A Group Portrait], edited by Lennart Weibull, pp. 176–184. Stockholm: Tiden.

Weibull, Lennart. 2007. Introduction. In *European media governance: National and regional dimensions,* edited by Georgios Terzis, pp. 55–62. Bristol: Intellect.

Wiik, Jenny. 2007. Granskningsidealet [The Watchdog ideal]. In *Den svenska journalistkåren* [Swedish Journalists], edited by Kent Asp, pp. 79–86. Göteborg: JMG.

25 Journalists in Switzerland

Structure and Attitudes

Heinz Bonfadelli, Guido Keel, Mirko Marr, and Vinzenz Wyss

Switzerland is a small, multi-cultural country in Western Europe with international ties but also a strong national and regional media landscape. Different historical, political, and cultural backgrounds have resulted in a series of regional characteristics that differentiate Switzerland not only from its neighbors, but also by the different language regions (French-, Italian-, and German-speaking) within the country. Typically, linguistic borders within a country also function as cultural borders. In Switzerland, these borders affect the social structure of journalists, their professional education, and their self-understanding vis-à-vis Swiss society (Marr & Wyss 1999; Wyss & Keel 2010).

Historically, the different regions have remained clearly separated despite increased mobility. For instance, cultural differences between the language regions are manifest in national referendums, where a harmonization of the political cultures can be observed but where clear differences still exist (Linder, Zürcher, & Bolliger 2008). Thus, any description of Swiss journalism culture needs to take into account these *regional differences* in order to render an adequate picture of the Swiss media.

The three regional media markets have been segmented into even smaller units by the federal structure of Switzerland, which has favored a high number of relatively small, local, and regional media products. In the past half-century, however, the Swiss media landscape has seen increased consolidation and concentration of media organizations and titles. In the last 20 years, the number of regional daily newspapers has shrunk by 40% to 76 titles (Kradolfer 2007: 8), while the overall circulation of these titles has diminished by only 13%. This trend has resulted in fewer newspaper titles with higher circulation numbers and the dominance of three large media organizations, Tamedia, Ringier, and Neue Zürcher Zeitung (NZZ). Further consolidation and cross-media concentration can be expected due to rapidly advancing convergence of the media in Switzerland (Trappel & Perrin 2006).

While the growing consolidation and concentration has reduced the variety of media in Switzerland, it also has led to a higher level of professionalization in journalism and an increase in the quality of news coverage (Blum 2003: 370). However, some media experts see these effects undermined by another trend in the Swiss media—media organizations increasingly define themselves as purely commercial businesses that have to produce profits. This shift in focus has resulted in a move toward tabloidization and commercialization of the Swiss media, with negative effects on the quality of the media overall (Blum 2009; Imhof 2009).

While new technologies have not had major consequences for the Swiss media yet, two trends have changed the media landscape in Switzerland in recent years. One is the emergence of free daily newspapers, which have proven to be the most profitable form of print journalism. After only a few years in existence, the free daily *20Minuten* has become the newspaper with the highest circulation and the largest advertising income in Switzerland. However, with increasingly stiff competition, several titles have already disappeared after only a few years of existence. The remaining free dailies not only siphoned off advertising revenue from regular newspapers but also undermined "regular" journalism by popularizing short, fact-oriented stories that lack depth and informational background. These free publications clearly favor a more audience-oriented journalism, addressing their readers as consumers, and focusing more on people and scandals and less on political and economic issues (Blum 2009).

The second development concerns the legal framework regulating the broadcast sector in Switzerland (Blum 2003). In 1983, the state licensed the first private FM radio stations, albeit only with local reach. Ten years later, in 1993, private TV stations were allowed to compete with the public broadcaster as well. However, the dominant player, especially in television, remained the Swiss Public Broadcasting Corporation, which is mostly financed by viewership fees, as compared to private broadcasters which finance themselves through commercials, and, to a much smaller extent, private membership fees. While the private radio landscape has flourished, private TV stations never gained much relevance in Switzerland and have a negligible market share. As a result, a revision of the Radio and TV Law in 2008 allocated a share of the public viewership fees to the private broadcasters. In turn, the private media were required to meet certain standards of journalistic quality in order to fulfill their public service function (Trebbe & Grossenbacher 2009).

Online news services started to appear around the turn of the millennium as new channels of existing print media. Today, the Internet is more important than radio or television and the prime source for daily news for most people in Switzerland (Meier 2009). Online news services have now reached a second stage where new forms of editorial organization and production are being developed to produce multimedia content for all media channels in integrated newsrooms. This trend has been accelerated by the global economic crisis and the loss of advertising revenue to new online media.

Previous Studies of Journalists

Until the late 1990s, no data were available about Swiss journalists or the state of journalism in Switzerland. In 1998, a team of media researchers from universities in Zürich and Berne conducted a survey to better understand who Swiss journalists are, how they work and think, and how they are organized professionally (Marr, Wyss, Blum, & Bonfadelli 2001). The survey was based on similar studies conducted in Germany (Weischenberg, Löffelholz, & Scholl 1993, 1994) and the United States (Johnstone, Slawski, & Bowman 1976; Weaver & Wilhoit 1986, 1996).

In the 1998 survey, the authors discovered that journalism and journalists in Switzerland were in many respects similar to their colleagues in other Western European and North American countries. Swiss journalists not only faced similar work and job conditions but also shared many of the journalistic role perceptions that characterize journalists in other industrialized countries. Moreover, they seemed to face the same changes brought about by technological and economic influences.

Nevertheless, some differences could be detected. The need and pressure to change, for example, seemed to be less dramatic and less acute than in neighboring countries. This difference may be explained by the strongly segmented Swiss media landscape and the emergence of media monopolies in small regions of Switzerland, which prevent direct competition between different media organizations.

Other differences concerned the basic characteristics of the Swiss journalists. The survey findings indicated that they usually started their media careers later than their colleagues in France,

Germany, or the United States and thus tended to be slightly older on average. And although the level of professionalization has increased, a formal journalistic education was still less common than in other comparable nations.

Finally, the study also found that while there is relative uniformity regarding the self-perception of the journalistic profession, there are significant differences between media in terms of education, salary, and work activities. Journalists working for weekend and weekly print media as well as for private radio stations showed a stronger orientation toward commercial interests. The researchers came to the conclusion that even though the international trends of change in the media had not yet significantly affected Switzerland, technological, economic, historical, and societal factors were the main forces that shaped and determined the situation of journalists in Switzerland at the end of the 20th century.

Ten years after this initial portrayal of Swiss journalists, the survey was repeated in 2008 by a team of researchers from universities in Winterthur and Zürich in order to determine how journalists and journalism in Switzerland had changed over the last decade, and how changes in the media and society had affected journalists in the country (Keel, 2011; Bonfadelli, Keel, Marr, & Wyss 2011). The data presented in this chapter are based on this national survey, which will use the 1998 survey to compare and describe these changes. In the following sections, methodological aspects relevant to this survey will be presented, followed by the results of the survey describing the Swiss journalists. We will finish with a series of conclusions about the current state of journalism in Switzerland, the changes it has been going through during the last decade, and the consequences of these developments for Swiss journalism, media, and society.

Methods

Our contribution is based on the latest data from three online surveys of Swiss journalists. The first survey contacted journalists working at private broadcasting stations and was carried out between November 2006 and January 2007 ($N = 449$, response rate: 39%). The second survey targeted Swiss journalists working in the public broadcasting corporation and was carried out between September and October 2007 ($N = 657$, response rate: 36%). Both surveys were supported by the Swiss Federal Communication Agency (*Bundesamt für Kommunikation* 2009) and were conducted by Heinz Bonfadelli and Mirko Marr at the Institute for Communication Science and Media Research at the University of Zürich.

The third survey interviewed journalists working in the print media and was conducted between June and July 2008 ($N = 1,403$; response rate: 19%). This survey was conducted by Vinzenz Wyss and Guido Keel for the Department of Applied Media Research in Winterthur at the University of Applied Sciences, Zürich. All three studies used comparable questionnaires, concentrating on aspects such as the journalists' employment situation, job realities, role definitions, job satisfaction, professional careers, and socio-demographics. Similar questions were also used in the first comprehensive survey of Swiss journalists conducted in 1998 (Marr et al. 2001).

The goal of both the 1998 and 2008 survey was to obtain a representative picture of Swiss journalists. As with similar research projects in other countries, the researchers were confronted with the problem that a complete sampling frame for the journalist population in Switzerland does not exist. Moreover, the definition of who is a "journalist" was also becoming less clear with the emergence of freelance journalists and bloggers. For the 1998 survey, the population was defined using the member lists of the three Swiss professional associations for journalists (Schweizer Verband der Journalistinnen und Journalisten, Schweizerische Journalistinnen und Journalisten Union, and

Schweizer Syndikat Medienschaffender). Membership in one of these associations is necessary to be officially registered as a journalist in Switzerland. The three membership lists resulted in a total population of 9,135 active journalists who were members of at least one of the three associations. A random sample of 5,404 was drawn proportionally to the membership structure of the three associations. Eventually, 2,020 completed questionnaires were used for further analysis and interpretation. The final sample was proportional to the overall population of journalists in terms of sex, form of employment, and language region.

For the 2008 survey, the methodological design was more complex. While to guarantee functional equivalence, the questionnaire was essentially the same, the sample was defined differently. First, while the print journalists received a printed questionnaire in the mail, journalists working for the private electronic media were asked to participate in an online survey. Moreover, the sample of journalists working in the private broadcast media was constructed differently from the sample of print journalists due to requests by the client of the study, namely the Federal Communication Agency. In order to determine the population of the private broadcast media, all private broadcasting organizations were asked to provide a list of their employees who earned at least half of their income or at least SFr12,000 a year with their journalistic work. This resulted in a total population of 1,155 journalists, of which 449 filled out the online questionnaire. About one-fifth of the sample consisted of journalists who would not have been included in the sampling method used in 1998. The journalists of the Public Broadcasting Corporation were sampled the same way, with a special focus on the exclusion of employees who were considered by their superiors within the respective organizations to have a more "artistic" than "journalistic" function (Bonfadelli & Marr 2008). The final population, which included journalists from all public radio and TV stations, consisted of 1,827 journalists, of whom 657 responded to the survey.

Journalists working in either or both print media and online editorial offices were selected the same way as the journalists in the 1998 survey. However, in 2008, only the members of the two journalism associations Impressum (formerly known as Schweizer Verband der Journalistinnen und Journalisten) and Comedia were approached, since the third association (Schweizer Syndikat Medienschaffender) organizes almost exclusively journalists from the electronic media. All 7,376 active members received a questionnaire by mail, which resulted in 1,403 completed questionnaires of print and online journalists. The sample represented the population of all print and online journalists proportionally. However, compared to the survey of the journalists working for the broadcasting media, the response rate was roughly 1.9 times lower, which is why a weighting factor was used for the print and online journalists. Overall, the combined samples of the 2008 online and mail survey resulted in a total sample of 2,509 respondents.

The analysis used a multi-layered analytical model (see Reese 2001; Scholl & Weischenberg 1998), to attempt to include organizational and societal context factors. However, due to the questionnaire-based research design, the source of all the acquired information remained the individual journalist.

Findings

Basic Characteristics

We estimate the total number of Swiss journalists in 2008 to be roughly 10,500. As pointed out above, this number should be considered with great caution, since the definition of who is a journalist and how journalists can be systematically counted have become less clear over the

Table 25.1   Sample of the 2008 Journalist Survey (in %)

	Total (N = 2,509)	Language region		
		German (N = 1,794)	French (N = 59)	Italian (N = 59)
Gender				
Female	35.2	35.4	35.1	31.0
Age				
Up to 35	26.4	27.6	23.5	22.8
35 to 44	31.5	29.7	36.1	36.8
44 and older	42.1	42.7	40.3	40.4
Form of Employment				
Freelancer	18.8	21.4	12.8	5.3
Employee	53.2	58.3	41.7	34.5
Hierarchical position				
Editor-in-chief	12.0	11.9	12.7	8.6
Sectional chief	28.3	29.3	26.2	22.4
Editor	48.4	46.4	52.3	62.1
Trainee	11.2	12.3	8.8	6.9
Media Type				
Paid daily newspaper	71.8	29.8	39.1	—
News magazine	17.0	15.4	22.3	—
Free daily newspaper	2.6	2.3	3.1	—
Trade press	8.5	10.2	4.9	—
Public broadcasting	17.8	18.3	13.4	—
Private Rradio	9.3	11.3	4.2	—-
Private TV	3.2	3.5	3.1	—
Online media	3.4	3.4	1.3	—
News Agency	4.4	3.9	6.2	—
Other	2.0	1.9	2.4	—

years. However, this estimate of Swiss journalists supports a conclusion from the 1998 survey: With roughly 136 journalists per 100,000 inhabitants, Switzerland has a relatively high number of journalists per capita.

In 2008, 35% of all journalists in Switzerland were women, a finding that supports previous studies that found that the proportion of female journalists in the country has been increasing steadily. In 1980, for example, the percentage of female journalists in the two large media regions—Zürich (German-speaking region) and Vaud (French-speaking region)—was only 17% (Saxer & Schanne 1981). In 1998, the percentage of female journalists throughout Switzerland stood at 32%. Today, the male bias is especially strong in private radio and daily newspapers and somewhat less pronounced among journalists at public radio and TV stations as well as in magazines and weekly newspapers.

The average age of Swiss journalists has slightly increased during the last 10 years, from 41 to 43 years. With an average age of 45, print journalists are even older. The average age among journalists working for private broadcasters, on the other hand, is considerably lower (32 for radio and

35 for TV). While only about 10% of all journalists working for the public broadcasting company are less than 30 years old, the figure for those younger than 30 at private broadcasters is 50%.

In Switzerland, foreigners make up roughly 20% of the population. This high share of foreigners is by no means represented in the media. Across all media types, more than 94% of all journalists are of Swiss nationality, and 92% say that they have grown up in Switzerland. This share is slightly higher in the French- and the Italian-speaking regions, but the representation of foreigners among the journalists remains below 10% in all language regions.

The religious background of the journalists was only included in the survey of the print journalists; however, there is no reason to believe that the data would be different for radio and TV. Here again, journalists reflect the general Swiss population, with one-third declaring themselves atheists and about one-third Catholic and Protestant, respectively. Less than 1% of the journalists belong to other religions such as Judaism or Islam.

Education and Training

As in many other countries, a formal journalism education is not required to become a journalist in Switzerland. At the same time, the growing complexity of journalistic work and the quickly changing media technologies make professionalization increasingly important. The educational systems in various Western countries have reacted to this need by establishing university-level degrees for journalism and journalism studies. Switzerland has been lagging behind in this development. Compared to neighboring countries, the Swiss have generally favored trade-related, non-university forms of education, and this trend is also found among Swiss journalists. For example, while two-thirds of German journalists had a university degree in 1998, only 44% of Swiss journalists had such a degree in that year. The gap in tertiary education has narrowed during the last 10 years with the establishment of new universities in Switzerland, which raised the share of university-trained journalists to 56% in 2008.

Besides the university courses, there are many other ways to receive a journalistic education. Typically, there are several journalism schools in all three language-regions of the country without university affiliation. They offer a more practical approach to the study of journalism. Usually, these courses are combined with internships and traineeships at media organizations. In the French-speaking part of the country, attendance at the journalism school is mandatory for all trainees who work for media organizations that are part of the Union Romand de Journaux (URJ), the media association of the French-speaking part of Switzerland. In the other language regions, no such obligations or requirements exist.

In 2008, 15% of all journalists said that they had no formal journalism education at all, but that they learned everything on the job instead. This number has remained stable over the last decade despite discussions about professionalization of journalism.

Even though fewer journalists do traineeships lasting longer than one year, internships and traineeships remain the most common way into Swiss journalism. Thus, despite the fact that some media organizations have reduced their number of traineeships due to financial pressure, one of three Swiss journalists got their journalism education from an internship of up to one year. However, the share of journalists who got their journalism education at a university has grown more than 20% in the last 10 years. The increase can be almost fully attributed to the new journalism degrees offered at universities. Finally, more than 40% of all journalists say that they acquired their journalistic skills in seminars and courses within their media organization, almost twice as many as 10 years ago.

Table 25.2   Trends in Journalism Education (in %)

	1998 (N = 2,008)	2008 (N = 2,506)
Internship lasting less than one year	33.5	35.4
Traineeship lasting more than one year	49.4	34.8
Long programs at journalism schools	25.8	29.7
Single classes at journalism schools	20.0	24.6
Internal courses	25.6	41.3
University	16.6	21.4
Other form of journalistic education	9.7	17.5
No journalistic education	13.2	15.8

Thus, despite the talk about better education opportunities for journalists to meet the growing challenges of their jobs, the extent of formal education has generally decreased in favor of shorter educational programs. When asked, 90% of all print journalists find their journalistic education adequate, and half of them even find their education "very adequate." Two-thirds of all journalists were satisfied with the opportunities they had to get further journalistic education in their work. This rate was significantly higher among journalists who work for public broadcasting than among those working for private broadcasting and the print media.

Working Situation

In the last few years, the media have been going through a fundamental crisis, facing enormous challenges from all sides. Advertisers re-shuffle their budgets in favor of online channels, and blogs and other journalistic formats challenge the information monopoly of the traditional news media. However, in 2008, almost 70% of all journalists say they would still recommend journalism as a profession, compared to 76% in 1998. The number is thus lower than in earlier surveys, but remains relatively high. There are significant differences between journalists from different media types: More than four in five journalists who work for public broadcasting recommend the job of a journalist, while less than half of those working for private radio or television recommend it. However, only one-third of all the journalists said that the climate in the media is good.

When asked what they appreciated most about their work, the aspect most mentioned was the variety and the interactions with their colleagues at work. More than 90% of all journalists stated that they were satisfied with these circumstances of their work. Next was the degree of satisfaction concerning the opportunity to work on one's own schedule. Two-thirds of the journalists found the workload, the time available to do research, and the job security satisfying. The aspects that were considered most dissatisfying were both of an organizational nature—the lack of career opportunities (especially among print journalists) and the low salaries—especially among journalists working for private broadcasters.

When addressing job satisfaction, Swiss journalists frequently pointed to the changing nature of the profession. New technologies and a changing media environment are fundamentally altering media production. However, when asked about the different tasks they perform during the day, the distribution between journalistic work, organizational duties, and technological work has remained surprisingly stable. In fact, the time journalists devote to technology has decreased to about 10% of the total working time as compared to 15% in 1998.

Organizational duties such as meetings make up 15% of the time, down from 20%. This decrease leaves more time for actual journalistic work: finding topics, doing research, producing articles or news items to be broadcast. One reason for this improvement in favor of journalistic tasks could be the journalists' perception of what "organizational tasks" and especially "technological tasks" involve. Transferring an article into the editorial software application, for example, was perceived as a technological task 10 years ago because the computer applications were a foreign aspect to the work and world of a journalist, but this task has become routine today. Thus, the way in which journalists deal with these new technological aspects of their work deserves a closer look.

No other technology has affected journalism so rapidly as has the Internet. Over the last decade several nationwide surveys have been conducted in Switzerland to find out how the Internet and, more recently, social networking, are influencing journalists and changing their practices (Bernet & Keel 2009). These surveys have shown that Swiss journalists are slow to adopt new online technologies compared to journalists in countries like the United States or Germany, or even compared to early adopters in Switzerland. However, the Internet has become the most important research tool for journalists in all types of media. In the 2008 survey, print journalists rated the Internet as the most important tool with which to acquire information, even after considering more important traditional methods of talking to sources face-to-face or on the telephone. This finding marks a clear change in the journalists' daily work when compared to only a decade ago.

Professionalism

Because print journalists in this study were selected based on their membership in a professional organization, we can discuss membership in professional organizations only based on answers from journalists working in radio or TV. Our findings show that about 45% of radio journalists and 50% of TV journalists are members of professional organizations.

The analysis of professional role perceptions has been a central aspect of journalist surveys around the world for the last 30 years, even though the validity of these responses has often been criticized. The key criticism is the question of what actually is measured when asking journalists about the importance of various professional roles in their work. It is reasonable to assume that the responses tell more about journalists ideals than actual behaviors influencing the daily work of journalists. While we believe that questions about the roles remain relevant, we also believe that responses have to be interpreted for what they are—ideas and concepts of what a journalist should do.

Similar to what was found in the 1998 survey, more than 95% of Swiss journalists thought that the most important journalistic role is that of a neutral reporter who tries to describe reality as objectively as possible. This is followed by the role of the analyzer who researches and dissects complex issues thoroughly. Some of the roles associated with service to the audience have grown in importance. More than four out of five journalists find important the role of a guide who helps the audience to find its way in an ever more complex world, more than the role of the critical watchdog that uncovers scandals and abuses of power.

For the majority of the journalists, their commercial role remains unimportant, even though some of these roles have gained a few percentage points over the last 10 years. More interesting in this context is the fact that more than twice as many journalists in private broadcasting find important the role of a creator of a suitable advertising environment or the efficient producer of a profitable product with high demand compared to their colleagues working for the public broadcaster. This finding must be seen as the need of private broadcasters to work toward these

Table 25.3   Importance of Journalistic Roles (in %)

	1998 Total	2008 Total	2008 Public Broadcasting	2008 Private Broadcasting
Neutral reporter who covers reality as objectively as possible	91.9	95.6	94.8	92.8
Analyzer who researches complex issues thoroughly	85.2	84.6	86.8	72.9
Guide who helps the audience to find its way in a complex world	77.8	81.2	78.9	79.9
Watchdog who unveils bad developments and problems	81.8	79.3	78.6	79.1
Service provider who satisfies the needs of the audience	63.9	72.3	78.9	81.7
Commentator who contributes to the public opinion making process	73.0	70.1	64.4	64.1
Intermediator Intermediary between different groups and actors in society	65.7	65.5	64.0	67.3
Advocate of the weak and disadvantaged	64.6	56.3	45.1	57.8
Animator who offers fun and relief for the audience	45.8	48.1	50.2	63.8
Cost-conscious information broker serving the media market effectively	32.1	34.5	32.8	46.5
Efficient salesperson of a profitable product in high demand	20.8	19.0	13.2	28.4
Salesperson creating a suitable advertising environment	12.7	13.8	5.8	22.2

goals in order to survive and not so much as a cultural difference between individual journalists, since many journalists working for a private radio or TV station later on change to the public broadcaster, leaving behind the commercial orientation of their preferred role.

In addition to a question about journalists' preferred roles, the 2008 survey asked journalists about the importance of various factors that influence their work. Answers to this question were assumed to reveal more information about the actual objectives or behaviors of the journalists at work. The comparison of these two questions shows that the journalists themselves seek to satisfy their audiences while adhering to certain general principles and values. A majority of the journalists (85.6%) believe that their organizations are trying to satisfy the audience, and almost as many (81.3%) believe their organizations are geared toward the public interest and related goals such as political information, societal integration, and education of the public. Half the journalists also believe that their organizations are equally influenced by factors such as powerful actors in society (53.2%) and the advertising market (48.2%), whereas 53.8% say that their organization is being guided by certain political or ideological views.

As for the journalists themselves, more important for most of them was the influence of the judgments of their colleagues, their personal friends, and the comparison with what other journalists do in other media.

Conclusions

Swiss journalists share many characteristics with their colleagues in other Western European and North American countries. One aspect of this is the fact that their situation shows more stability than change in a rapidly transforming media world, a finding in other countries as well (see, for example, Weaver, Beam, Brownlee, Voakes, & Wilhoit 2007: 239).

Despite fundamental changes in the media environment on an organizational level and in ways of media consumption, the basic characteristics of Swiss journalists have remained surprisingly stable with respect to aspects such as demographic composition, activities, educational professionalization, and importance of roles and values.

If any changes can be found in the decade between 1998 and 2008, they are minor, and they usually have two causes: a new generation of journalists entering the field, and more commercial media types such as private broadcasting programs and free daily newspapers gaining in importance.

Younger journalists consider the roles that are more closely associated with the public good (such as the commentator or the analyst) less relevant than roles that focus more on the particular service to the audience (such as entertainment or service provision). There is also a small generational effect concerning journalistic education—the share of younger journalists who have received journalism-specific training has increased. However, because the quality media have lost ground to free, entertainment-oriented media, the overall change in journalistic education is minimal. The share of journalists who say that they have not received any formal journalistic training at all has even slightly increased over the last 10 years, from 13.2% to 15.8%, or from 9.7% to 11.8% for journalists age 35 and younger. Furthermore, there has been a shift from internships lasting longer than a year to college degrees in journalism on the one hand, and shorter journalism training programs on the other.

Concerning organization, the share of freelance journalists has increased from 11.4% in 1998 to 18.8% in 2008. Interestingly, many of these freelance journalists work for only one or a few media organizations and usually have regular work assignments and hours. This leads to the conclusion that increasingly journalists work like regular staff but have freelance contracts.

The most striking change compared to 10 years ago is technology-related: The Internet has brought about the most fundamental changes in journalistic action in a very short time. Compared to 10 years ago, when the Internet was just starting to be used in newsrooms, it has nowadays become the central tool that is used constantly and in all aspects of the journalistic production including research of facts and people, confirmation of information, exchange with the audience, publication of content, and co-orientation with other media and their coverage.

Finally, a change can be noted concerning the job satisfaction of journalists. Overall, it is safe to conclude that it has decreased, and fewer journalists would recommend the profession in 2008 compared to 1998. Two factors that are responsible for this development are the increased workload for low pay, and job insecurity. They reflect a global media crisis, which goes far beyond Swiss media and their current economic problems, and poses much more fundamental questions regarding the way in which media function and the purpose they serve.

References

Bernet, Marcel, and Guido Keel. 2009. *Journalisten im Internet 2009*. [Journalists on the Internet 2009]. Winterthur/Zürich: Institute of Applied Media Studies.

Blum, Roger. 2003. Medienstrukturen der Schweiz. [Media structures in Switzerland]. In *Öffentliche Kommunikation* [Public communication], edited by Günter Bentele, Hans-Bernd Brosius, and Otfried Jarren, pp. 366–381. Wiesbaden: Westdeutscher Verlag GmbH.

Blum, Roger. 2009. Schweizer Medien: Bedenklicher Befund [Swiss media: Alarming findings]. *Klartext* 1: 24–25.

Bonfadelli, Heinz, Guido Keel, Mirko Marr, and Vinzenz Wyss. 2011. Journalists in Switzerland: Structures and attitudes. Zürich: Institut für Publizistikwissenschaft und Medienforschung. *Studies in Communication Sciences* 11(2):7–26.

Bonfadelli, Heinz, and Mirko Marr. 2008. *Journalistinnen und Journalisten im privaten und öffentlichen Rundfunk der Schweiz* [Journalists in private and public broadcasting in Switzerland]. Zürich: Institut für Publizistikwissenschaft und Medienforschung.

Bundesamt für Statistik. 2009. *Stimmberechtigte und Stimmbeteiligung seit 1990* [Voters and participation since 1990]. Retrieved from http://www.bfs.admin.ch/bfs/portal/de/index/themen/17/03/blank/key/stimmbeteiligung.html.

Imhof, Kurt. 2009. Fröhlich im falschen Leben [Happy in the wrong life]. *Neue Zürcher Zeitung*, November 17, 58.

Johnstone, John W. C., Edward J. Slawski, and William W. Bowman. 1976. *The news people: A sociological portrait of American journalists and their work*. Urbana: University of Illinois Press.

Keel, Guido. 2011. *Journalisten in der Schweiz. Eine Berufsfeldstudie im Zeitverlauf*. Konstanz: UVK.

Kradolfer, Edi. 2007. Pressevielfalt Schweiz: Ein Überblick [Press pluralism Switzerland: An overview]. Bern: Bundesamt für Statistik.

Linder, Wolf, Regula Zürcher, and Christian Bolliger. 2008. *Gespaltene Schweiz—geeinte Schweiz: Gesellschaftliche Spaltungen und Konkordanz bei den Volksabstimmungen seit 1874* [Split Switzerland—United Switzerland: Societal divisions and consensus in public referendums since 1874]. Baden: Hier & Jetzt.

Marr, Mirko, and Vinzenz Wyss. 1999. Schweizer Journalistinnen und Journalisten im sprachregionalen Vergleich [A language-regional comparison of Swiss journalists]. *Medienwissenschaft Schweiz* 2: 16–30.

Marr, Mirko, Vinzenz Wyss, Roger Blum, and Heinz Bonfadelli. 2001. *Journalisten in der Schweiz: Eigenschaften, Einstellungen, Einflüsse* [Journalists in Switzerland: Characteristics, attitues, influences]. Konstanz: UVK Medien.

Meier, Werner A. 2009. Das Mediensystem der Schweiz [The Swiss media system]. In *Internationales Handbuch Medien*, edited by Hans-Bredow-Institut, pp. 592–602. Baden-Baden: Nomos Verlagsgesellschaft.

Reese, Stephen. 2001. Understanding the global journalist: A hierarchy-of-influence approach. *Journalism Studies* 2:173–187.

Saxer, Ulrich, and Michael Schanne. 1981. *Journalismus als Beruf: Eine Untersuchung der Arbeitssituation von Journalisten in den Kantonen Zürich und Waadt* [Journalism as profession: A survey of the working conditions of journalists in the cantons of Zurich and Vaud]. Bern: Eidgenössisches Justiz- und Polizeidepartement.

Scholl, Armin, and Siegfried Weischenberg. 1998. *Journalismus in der Gesellschaft: Theorie, Methodologie und Empirie.* [Journalism in society: Theory, methods, and evidence]. Opladen: Westdeutscher Verlag.

Trappel, Josef, and Irène Perrin. 2006. Medienkonzentration in der Schweiz: Formen und Ausmass [Media concentration in Switzerland: Forms and dimension]. In *Medienkonzentration Schweiz*, edited by Heinz Bonfadelli, pp. 109–138. Bern: Haupt Verlag.

Trebbe, Joachim, and René Grossenbacher. 2009. *Qualität in Radio und Fernsehen: Die inhaltsanalytische Messung konzessionsrechtlicher Vorgaben für die Radio- und Fernsehprogramme der SRG SSR idée suisse* [Quality in radio and television: The content analysis of licencing requirements for the radio and TV programs of SRG SSR Idee Suisse]. Bern & Chur: Rüegger Verlag.

Weaver, David H., and G. Cleveland Wilhoit. 1986. *The American journalist: A portrait of U.S. news people and their work*. Bloomington: Indiana University Press.

Weaver, David H., and G. Cleveland Wilhoit. 1996. *The American journalist in the 1990s: U.S. news people at the end of an era*. Mahwah, NJ: Erlbaum.

Weaver, David H., Randal A. Beam, Bonnie J. Brownlee, Paul S. Voakes, and G. Cleveland Wilhoit. (2007). *The American journalist in the 21st century: U.S. news people at the dawn of a new millenium*. Mahwah, NJ: Erlbaum.

Weischenberg, Siegfried, Löffelholz, Martin, and Scholl, Armin. 1993. Journalismus in Deutschland [Journalism in Germany]. *Media Perspektiven* 1:21–33.

Weischenberg, Siegfried, Martin Löffelholz, and Armin Scholl. 1994. Journalismus in Deutschland II: Merkmale und Einstellungen von Journalisten [Journalism in Germany II: Characteristics and attitudes of journalists]. *Media Perspektiven* 4: 154–167.

Weischenberg, Siegfried, Maja Malik, and Armin Scholl. 2006. *Die Souffleure der Mediengesellschaft: Report über die Journalisten in Deutschland* [The prompters of the media society: Report on journalists in Germany]. Konstanz: UVK Medien.

Wyss, Vinzenz, and Guido Keel. 2010. Schweizer Journalismuskulturen im sprachregionalen Vergleich. Eine quantitative Längsschnittuntersuchung zu Strukturmerkmalen und Einstellungen [Swiss journalism cultures in a language-regional comparison: A quantitative longitudinal survey on structural characteristics and attitudes]. In *Medienkultur im Wandel*, edited by Andreas Hepp, Marco Höhn, and Jeffrey Wimmer, pp. 245–260. Konstanz: Universitätsverlag.

Journalists in North America

26 The Professional Creed of Quebec's Journalists in Canada

Marc-François Bernier and Marsha Barber

Canadian journalism is in flux. As in other areas of the world, a confluence of factors has affected how journalism is now practiced in Canada. According to the most recent census of occupations there are now more than 13,000 people in Canada who describe their profession as "journalist" (Statistics Canada Census 2006). They serve Canada's population of approximately 34 million people spread over the second largest country in the world in terms of land mass. While the country is officially bilingual, most journalists work in English. However, approximately a quarter of Canada's population is French-speaking, living mainly in the province of Quebec. That population is served by French-language media.

Many factors that have influenced American journalism have also affected Canada. The recent economic crisis has exacerbated the situation, but the Canadian media had begun their downward spiral before the crisis. Fragmented audiences, declining advertising revenue, and tough economic times have hit the sector hard.

As Dvorkin (2009) points out in an overview he wrote for the Canadian Media Research Consortium, the old business models have collapsed. More consumers of news are turning to the Internet. The problem is, in Canada as elsewhere, that the media do not understand how to take advantage of this development. Ironically, more Canadians read newspapers in some form, including online, than ever before (Dvorkin 2009). However, a business paradigm which allows news outlets to profit from their online operations has yet to emerge. As audiences fragment, turning to a number of different sources including the Internet, mainstream "legacy" media have yet to figure out how to turn new ways of consuming news to their economic advantage.

The impact is being felt across all sectors. The Canadian Association of Journalists (2009) reports that in the last year more than 1,200 full-time workers in Canadian news organizations lost their jobs. Newspapers have been especially hard hit. Several papers, including the *Halifax Daily News,* have closed shop. Other media groups have been forced to restructure. Canada's largest national newspaper, *The Globe and Mail*, offered early retirement to 10% of its staff and anticipates possible future layoffs (Dvorkin, 2009). Many media groups have been forced to restructure. Canwest Global, one of Canada's largest media conglomerates, has won an extension of bankruptcy protection so it can auction off publications in its insolvent newspaper division. As a result of these challenges, journalists are being stretched as never before, forced to do more with less. Career print journalists are being asked to file for media organizations' television and Internet operations, for example.

The situation is somewhat different in Quebec. According to a survey by the Centre d'études sur les médias, newspaper circulation has remained somewhat stable over the past eight years. Profit margins have declined 4% although advertising revenues have declined 23% in the same period. However, Quebec journalists interviewed for the Canadian Media Research Consortium say they feel the survival of their news operations is constantly under threat (Dvorkin 2009).

In the past, the government has made every effort to protect Canadian media. In contrast to the United States, Canadian regulatory influence has been encouraged. Government interventions have ranged from tax laws, which protect Canadian magazines, to regulations that stipulate percentages of national content on Canadian television. In addition, Canada's public broadcaster, the Canadian Broadcasting Corporation, is funded by tax payers.

A number of commissions and hearings have been initiated over the past four decades to explore media ownership and other issues. Strengthening indigenous Canadian media in the face of readily available media from Canada's southern neighbor, the United States, also has been a priority. Most recently, in 2009, the Canadian Radio-Television and Telecommunications Commission (CRTC), in charge of regulating Canadian television and telecommunications, began hearings into whether it should regulate the Internet in some way, seeing it as essentially another form of broadcasting. Federal broadcast officials eventually decided not to subject this new medium to the same rules as conventional media, arguing that regulation may discourage innovation.

Even in the face of recent economic challenges, Canada maintains a vibrant media sector. In 2009, it had 165 newspapers, 149 TV stations, and 733 radio stations (Marketwire 2009). To understand Canada's journalism, it is necessary to understand Canada's journalists. Research in this area is surprising sparse. Early surveys included one on former newspaper journalists, attempting to find out why they had left their employers (Wilson, 1966). Most cited low pay and lack of job satisfaction. In the 1970s, Donald Wright (1974, 1976) surveyed newspaper journalists in some of Canada's largest cities and private radio stations in Canada's most western province, British Columbia, to measure levels of journalistic professionalism. Wright found high levels of professionalism but somewhat low levels of job satisfaction. Between 1985 and 1995, George Pollard (1985) conducted several national mail surveys and concluded that broadcast journalists brought higher levels of professionalism to their work than those who worked on newspapers. He also found journalists enjoyed high levels of job satisfaction. In his 1990 survey, which included Francophones as well as Anglophones, Pollard (1995) concluded that newspaper journalists enjoyed high levels of job satisfaction due to a combination of intrinsic factors such as autonomy, authority, control of work, and extrinsic factors such as job security and income.

Other research focused on gender issues. Robinson and Saint-Jean (1998) studied newspaper and television journalists with the goal of understanding women's professional progress in Canadian media. They concluded that women have made substantial progress in the profession and "are now proportionately integrated in all but the highest ranks of both print and electronic news organizations" (370). Barber and Rauhala (2006) offered a less optimistic portrait when they surveyed Canadian news directors and found only 20% were female.

Pritchard and Sauvageau (1998) conducted an important study in which they obtained a demographic profile of Canadian journalists in all sectors. In addition to demographics, they measured job satisfaction and participants' evaluations of how different media sectors were performing, including each journalist's own organization. The authors investigated the participants' sense of the political orientation of their news organization and surveyed the journalists' own political beliefs. Finally, they measured which newspapers journalists read and journalists' views on the concentration of media ownership. The study concluded that Canadian journalists are fairly satisfied with their jobs, believe their organizations are doing a reasonably good job of informing the public, see themselves as more liberal than their news organizations, and are concerned media concentration may narrow the flow of ideas.

Pritchard and Sauvageau (1999a) also researched the professional values of Canadian journalists and monitored changes in Canadian journalists' views about the social and political roles of the news media. In 2005, Pritchard, Brewer, and Sauvageau published data on changes in Canadian journalists' views about the social and political roles of the news media. They found that three of five creed roles considered important by English-language journalists who had participated in the previous study had diminished significantly in importance: accurately reporting the views of public figures, providing analyses of complex problems, and giving ordinary people a chance to express their views. On the other hand, among French-language respondents, belief in only one role had declined significantly: getting information to the public quickly. The fifth role continued to be valued by both English and French-language journalists: that of investigating government and public institutions' activities.

Barber and Rauhala (2005) conducted surveys of Canada's senior broadcast and newspaper journalists. In a study of television news directors, those who make key newsroom decisions about what goes on air, they found that the news directors' political beliefs were in line with those of the general population. They also found these news directors were comfortably middle-class, had families, and tended to be involved in their communities. The news directors differed from those in the general population in one respect: they were somewhat more likely to have no religious affiliation and much less likely to attend a place of worship. Subsequent research on newspaper editors yielded a similar portrait.

In addition, Barber and Rauhala (2008) surveyed how Canadian news directors think about the journalistic roles of the journalists who work for them. They found that news directors have somewhat different priorities than their employees. They also found that senior television journalists in the private and public sectors have different values. Public news directors were less concerned about ratings and were much less likely than private sector journalists to believe their reporters were "providers of entertainment." In subsequent research, Barber (2008) explored how news directors' political beliefs and values are reflected in network electoral coverage. She found that in spite of critics' concerns that Canadian television networks exhibit bias in their political coverage, that bias was not evident. However, frontrunners (i.e., parties that polls predicted would do well) received more coverage than other parties, regardless of political stripe.

In the same year, Marcotte (2008) published a survey for the Centre d'études sur les médias, which aimed to define what journalists in Quebec see as quality journalism. The survey found that journalists were divided among "innovators," who embrace changes in the industry, and "traditionalists," who decry what they see as declining standards in the profession, such as the waning of "hard" news in favour of fluffier and lighter stories.

Other published surveys of Canadian journalists have focused on journalists in specific regions of Canada. Most have been written in French and have focused on Quebec. Pritchard and Sauvageau (1998) provide a good overview of these studies ranging from 1975 to 1995. They note that the majority assess demographics. However, one exception was Godin's research (1979), which gathered data on the political attitudes of senior Quebec journalists. Likewise, Langlois and Sauvageau (1982) documented the role conceptions of Quebec newspaper journalists.

Pritchard and Sauvageau (1998: 380) note that "scholars of journalism in Canada tend to speak only to the members of their own linguistic community." Few Anglophones cite research in French, and Francophones cite English studies less often than Anglophones do. This is a pity. As Pritchard and Sauvageau (1998: 380) argue, "This mutual ignorance not only impedes a full understanding of Canadian journalism but increases the likelihood that media scholars from one linguistic community will fail to grasp the richness and complexity of journalism in the other."

In this paper, we will explore the professional values of Quebec's journalists in a context of ownership concentration and media convergence. This research will add to knowledge about the state of Canadian media as well as the state of mind of Canadian journalists who have expressed concerns about media concentration in recent years.

The Professional Creed of Quebec's Journalists

In recent years, the field of journalism has experienced serious crises and profound changes. No Western country has been immune to this phenomenon. The causes are at once economic, technological, social, and cultural. Media companies have been forced to find and implement new strategies to ensure that they survive and their shareholders are satisfied.

Several of the issues raised by these crises and changes have caused concern among media observers, journalists, citizens, and even elected officials. Empirical research and theoretical studies have been devoted to investigating the impact of media ownership concentration and media convergence. Many authors have examined the effects of these transformations on the quality, diversity, and integrity of the information being produced (Alexander & Cunningham 2006; Bernier 2007, 2008; Bozonelos 2004; Huang, Rademakers, Fayemiwo, & Dunlap 2004; Kweon 2000; Lee & Hwang 1997; McCombs 1987; Mills 2005; Picard 2004; Pritchard 2001). The organizational challenges that journalism companies face as a result of these changes also have been studied (Daily, Demo, & Spillman 2003, 2005; Hammond, Patterson, & Thomsen 2000; Huang et al. 2007; Singer 2003, 2004). Moreover, elected members of the governments of Quebec (2001) and Canada (2003) have submitted reports to this effect, as have Canadian senators (2006).

For this study, we are particularly interested in documenting and having a better understanding of the concerns of journalists in Quebec. This Canadian province is home to 23% of the country's population. French is the most widely spoken language; English is also spoken, particularly in Montreal, the province's largest city. The work of Pritchard and Sauvageau (1999b) has previously demonstrated that there are few differences between the journalistic values held by Francophone journalists, who work primarily in Quebec, and their Anglophone colleagues, most of whom work in the other provinces and territories. Follow-up panel research conducted by Pritchard and Sauvageau (2003) brought to light various differences within a smaller sample of Anglophones and Francophones, but these differences did not affect their common adherence to the same basic journalistic values, which the authors referred to as the Canadian journalist's "creed."

Quebec's Francophone journalists can claim the highest rate of bilingualism in Canada (Pritchard & Sauvageau 1999b) and, together with their Anglophone counterparts, share journalistic values inherited from the Anglo-Saxon tradition (and not from the European tradition, as had long been the case).

Background

Media ownership is slightly more concentrated in Quebec than in the rest of Canada. New Brunswick is the sole exception; the Irving family controls virtually all of New Brunswick's private news media (Lord 2006).

Journalism in Quebec is dominated by three large media conglomerates: Société Radio-Canada, Quebecor, and Gesca. Radio-Canada is a public broadcaster and depends on public funds allocated by the federal government as its primary source of financing. It offers news and public affairs programming in both official languages (the Canadian Broadcasting Corporation, [CBC], is Radio-Canada's Anglophone counterpart), on television, radio, and the Internet. Pritchard and Sauvageau (1999b) observed that Radio-Canada was identified by Canadian journalists as one of their preferred sources for news, while we observed that the various media platforms of Radio-Canada are thought to offer the highest-quality news by the population of Quebec (Bernier 2009).

Quebecor is the more powerful of the two private media conglomerates. It controls the two most-read daily newspapers in their respective markets (*Le Journal de Montréal* and *Le Journal de Québec*) and owns the highest-rated private television station for both news and entertainment (TVA). It is also the dominant cable provider in the province (Vidéotron). Its other holdings include publishing houses, dozens of magazines, and a chain of book and music stores (Archambault).

The third major player in this field is Gesca, a company which belongs to the appropriately named Power Corporation of Canada. Owned by the Desmarais family, the Power Corporation is known to be influential in the halls of Canada's provincial and federal governments. In addition to producing entertainment television programs, Gesca owns seven of Quebec's 10 Francophone dailies. It is present in Montreal and Quebec and in various regions throughout the province.

As noted above, media convergence strategies and the concentrated ownership of the main news organizations have been the subjects of federal Senate committee reports, as well as parliamentary commission reports in both Quebec and Ottawa. Debate on these two subjects continues to this day.

It was in this context that we began our quantitative study in 2007. The subjects of this study were unionized journalists employed, for the most part, by the three media conglomerates outlined above.[1]

Method

A total of 1,780 unionized journalists employed by Quebec's main news organizations were asked to participate in this study. Most of the journalists were members of union locals affiliated with the Confédération des Syndicats Nationaux (CSN) [Confederation of National Trade Unions], through the Fédération Nationale des Communications (FNC) [National Federation of Communication Workers]. The FNC represents 1,580 of the journalists contacted for this study. The remaining 200 journalists were affiliated with the Fédération des Travailleurs et Travailleuses du Québec (FTQ) [Quebec Federation of Labour] through the Canadian Union of Public Employees (CUPE).

Of the 1,780 questionnaires sent to journalists through their union locals, 385 valid questionnaires were returned—a response rate of 21.6%. Each questionnaire was anonymous and confidential, and returned in a postage-paid envelope. An overwhelming majority of the journalists who returned the questionnaire (92%) were employed by one of the three main media conglomerates. Our sample was the largest ever used for the study of journalism in Quebec. In comparison, 554 Canadian journalists participated in the study led by Pritchard and Sauvageau (1999b) but only 50 were from Quebec.

Each questionnaire was numbered and accompanied by two letters: one from the journalist's union, and one from us inviting the journalist to participate in the study. More than one in five unionized journalists returned the questionnaire. This provides a usable sample of all unionized journalists in Quebec.[2] Prior to distribution, the questionnaire was pre-tested by several retired journalists. Their feedback allowed us to refine our questions.

Our main measurement tool was the 7-point Likert attitude scale. An answer of 1 indicated complete disagreement with the proposed question or statement, while an answer of 7 indicated complete agreement. Several questions used an ordinal scale, which proposed answers of varying intensity (very, quite, somewhat, not at all). Some questions were intentionally grouped together (those relating to the journalist's creed, for example); however, the order of presentation was left to chance to avoid creating a bias.

The use of an ordinal scale not only enabled us to obtain nuanced statistical data, but also allowed us to draw comparisons with previous studies where similar questions were asked. The graduated scale enables us to measure the intensity of an opinion within different groups, which in turn gives us a better understanding of the variables involved and allows us to reach more solid conclusions.

We have divided the results of this study into two parts. The first section compares the attitudes and opinions of journalists from each of the three major media conglomerates regarding the following question: How have concentration of ownership, media convergence, and the commercialization of news and information affected the quality, diversity, and integrity of the information being produced and disseminated?

The second part of our study reveals that, despite being employed by separate media conglomerates (each with different ownership characteristics, management methods, and target demographics), journalists in Quebec embrace the same creed. However, their employers are still a significant variable: the media conglomerates can either facilitate or limit each journalist's ability to produce and broadcast the kind of information he or she values.

Findings

Our sample was made up of a higher proportion of men (63%) than women (37%). As age decreases, the proportion of women in the sample increases, reaching 46.2% in the 18 to 25 age group. Only 15.7% of the journalists aged 55 and older were women. Nearly one-third of our sample (31%) was comprised of journalists aged 18 to 35.

The majority of our respondents were employed by Radio-Canada (45.4%), Gesca (30.6%), and Quebecor (15.6%). While the three media conglomerates accounted for more than 92% of respondents, journalists working for other media accounted for 7% of the sample (Cogeco, 2.6%; independent journalists, 2.3%; Radio-Nord, 1.6%; Corus, 1%; Astral, 0.3%; Transcontinental Media, 0.3%). A large majority of participating journalists indicated that they work in the traditional sectors of the news media, including daily newspapers (38%), television (28%), radio (18%), and weeklies (4%), while only 5% indicated that they work on the Internet.

When asked "In general, how satisfied are you in your current position?" 30% of the journalists said they were "very satisfied," while 50% were "quite satisfied." However, our research reveals that this high level of satisfaction coexists with very negative answers criticizing the impact of ownership concentration and media convergence on the freedom, quality, diversity, and integrity of information.

At the same time, a large majority of journalists in Quebec agree that new work methods made possible by advances in information and communication technology have had a positive impact on the quality of the content produced by their respective news organizations. Overall, 80% of the respondents said that in general these new work methods have had a *very positive* (19%) or *quite positive* (61%) impact on the quality of their company's product. This proportion rises to 96% among respondents aged 18 to 25, and hovers around 79% for all other age groups.

Perceptions and Attitudes Regarding Impact

Using the Likert scale, as described above (where 1 indicates complete disagreement and 7 indicates complete agreement), we measured the intensity of the journalists' attitudes and their perceptions of journalism in general. For example, the statement "Media convergence has a positive effect on journalism" garnered very little support (average score of 1.8 out of 7, $SD = 1.3$). There was no significant difference between journalists of different age groups, or between journalists from each of the three conglomerates.

Results were similar for the statement, "Media concentration has a positive effect on the public's right to quality information," with an average score of (2.2, $SD = 1.5$). In this instance, neither the respondents' ages nor their employers were determining factors. Results were identical for the parallel statement, "Media convergence has a positive effect on the public's right to quality information" (2.2, $SD = 1.5$).

The response to the statement, "The fact that a media outlet belongs to a press organization improves the quality of information" was also generally negative, but slightly more toward the middle of the scale (3.0, $SD = 1.7$). Quebecor journalists were more likely to disagree with this statement than their counterparts at Gesca. Journalists employed by Gesca, in turn, had a more favorable reaction to this statement than their counterparts at Radio-Canada; here again, the difference is statistically significant ($p < .05$).

The Journalist's Creed

The general hypothesis that we wish to verify is that journalists at Quebecor, Gesca, and Radio-Canada individually adhere, in more or less the same proportion, to the same journalistic values. To varying degrees, however, the different ownership characteristics, management practices, and convergence strategies of each conglomerate prevent them from staying true to this ideal.

Our study reveals that ownership characteristics influence journalists' ability to hold to their creed, whether public (Radio-Canada), private but publicly traded (Quebecor), or fully private (Gesca). We do so by comparing the importance journalists personally attach to each function with their assessment of the importance their news organization places on the same function.

A total of 14 statements were submitted for consideration by our sample, representing an equal number of journalistic functions. Our survey used the same journalistic functions proposed by Pritchard and Sauvageau (1999b) in their questionnaires from 1996 and 2003. However, we introduced two important changes that should be noted here. The first is that our attitude scale has seven degrees instead of four, which allows us to obtain a more nuanced response. In order to facilitate the comparison of data between our study and previous studies, we will convert the average values obtained by Pritchard and Sauvageau to make them compatible with our scale of seven (A = a x 1.75). However, it should be noted that there are limits to the effectiveness of this exercise and that Pritchard and Sauvageau conducted their survey by telephone, while our survey was in the form of a written questionnaire.

The second difference is more significant. We wanted to discover whether or not there is a deviation between a) how journalists personally hold to the creed, and b) how they perceive the media conglomerate they work for as holding to the creed. To us, this distinction was particularly important. Journalists regularly evaluate the quality, diversity, and integrity of the information being produced by their news organizations. It follows that they should be able to critically assess compliance with the journalist's creed.

We will present the results in descending order of importance, according to the significance that the journalists in our sample attach to each function. We will also show how they assess the importance that their respective news organizations place on the same function. This will allow us to calculate a journalist/media deviation score (J/MD) for each function. We can also compare our results with the results of Pritchard and Sauvageau, converted to a scale of seven.

The journalistic function that our sample deemed most important is the "**need to accurately report the views of public figures.**" The relevance of comparing journalists' personal opinions with their assessment of the importance their news organizations attach to each function is immediately apparent. The deviation between the two different scores (J/MD) reveals a discrepancy between the journalists' professional aspirations and how they assess their respective employers' priorities in regard to these functions. The J/MD is 1.08 for Quebecor, 0.32 for Gesca, and only 0.18 for Radio-Canada (see Table 26.1, first row).

Table 26.1 reveals the first major disparity concerning individual journalists' professional aspirations and their perceptions of their news organization's expectations. This function retains its status as the most important function in the journalist's creed, a position it also held in Pritchard and Sauvageau's (1999b) study. Quebecor journalists' average assessment of the importance their organization attaches to this function is statistically different ($p = < .05$) from the responses given by their counterparts at Gesca and Radio-Canada. This finding suggests that Quebecor's journalists have a considerably more negative perception of their news organization than their colleagues at the other two conglomerates. This result contrasts with the journalists' personal opinions: here, there is no significant difference in the importance journalists from all three conglomerates attach to this function, even though averages range from 5.5 at Quebecor to 6.55 at Radio-Canada (see Table 26.1, first row).

The second most important function, as indicated by our respondents, was the "**need to analyze and interpret complex problems.**" The rankings changed significantly since 1999 when this journalistic function was ranked fifth. Quebecor journalists again recorded the highest J/MD (1.46), while Radio-Canada journalists recorded the lowest J/MD (0.25). The J/MD for Gesca was 0.74 (see Table 26.1, second row). Once again, Quebecor journalists have a more negative perception of their news organization than those of the other organizations. The individual responses of Quebecor journalists are statistically different ($p = <.05$) from those given by their Radio-Canada colleagues, as are their assessments of their news organization. Quebecor journalists are less interested by this function than their colleagues at the public broadcaster, which are the most motivated by this "intellectual" function. In another survey, Barber and Rauhala (2008) found a full 95% of Canadian television news directors agreed this was a crucial function, with every news director in public broadcasting agreeing.

The importance of "**investigating the activities of government and public institutions**" also moved up in the rankings, climbing from fourth place to third in our study. As with many others, this social function is more important to the journalists than it is to their respective media conglomerates. The responses from Radio-Canada journalists are statistically different ($p = 05$) from those of their private-sector colleagues, on both the personal and media-assessment levels. This could be interpreted as a strong dedication to public affairs by the journalists of the public broadcaster, where their colleagues of private sector are less interested by this type of news which can be considered as dull. The low J/MD from Radio-Canada journalists suggests a similarity between their personal aspirations and the editorial policy of their news organization (see Table 26.1, third row).

Table 26.1 reveals a drastic change in the rankings: the importance of "**being skeptical of the actions of business**" leapt from ninth to fourth place. This is the first major change to the creed of 1999. The financial scandals that have been in the public eye in recent years could explain this change. Once again, journalists attach more importance to this function than their news organizations. The greatest deviation is at Gesca (1.47), whose journalists claim to be more vigilant than their counterparts elsewhere. Quebecor follows with a deviation of 1.32. Radio-Canada's

Table 26.1 Journalist/Media Deviation of the Journalist's Creed

Journalistic Function	Quebecor			Gesca			Radio Canada			Others			Total			1999
	For me	My org	Diff.	For me	My org	Diff.	For me	My org	Diff.	For me	My org	Diff.	For me	My org	Diff.	1999[1]
Accurately report the views of public figures	6.59	5.51	1.08	6.68	6.36	.32	6.73	6.55	.18	6.85	6.61	.24	6.68	6.71	-.03	6.34
Analyze and interpret complex problems	5.68	4.22	1.46	6.12	5.38	.74	6.38	6.13	.25	6.06	5.0	1.06	6.26	6.16	.10	5.51
Investigate activities of government & public institutions	5.71	5.08	.63	5.7	5.04	.66	6.23	5.88	.35	5.42	4.58	.84	6.44	5.92	.52	5.39
Be skeptical of the actions of businesses	5,42	4.08	1.34	6.03	4.56	1.47	5.78	5.09	.69	5.33	4.42	.91	5.46	5.76	-.30	4.72
Be skeptical of the actions of public officials	5.32	5.05	.27	5.91	5.17	.74	5.86	5.48	.38	5.39	4.79	.60	5.60	5.75	-.15	5.26
Get information to the public quickly	5.61	6.10	-.49	5.73	5.83	-.10	5.56	6.23	-.67	6.03	6.0	.03	6.56	5.66	.90	6.07

Note.   Scores are based on 8-point scales where 0 means complete disagreement and 7 means complete agreement with the proposition.
1 Pritchard and Sauvageu (1999)

deviation of 0.69 is minimal. The results indicate that Quebecor attaches the least importance to this function. Significant differences ($p = .05$) should be noted between the personal opinions of Gesca and Quebecor journalists, as well as between Quebecor and Radio-Canada journalists' evaluations of their respective news organizations. It seems that for Quebecor journalists, their media are considered as being more closely aligned with the business world than is the case for Gesca and Radio-Canada (see Table 26.1, fourth row).

The importance of "**being sceptical of the actions of public officials**" climbed from eighth place in 1996 to fifth in our study, once again changing the creed. As with the previous function, journalists appear to attach more importance to this role than their news organizations do. The largest deviation is at Gesca (0.74), while the smallest is at Quebecor (0.27). However, no significant differences were observed (see Table 26.1, fifth row).

In 1996, the importance of "**getting information to the public quickly**" was ranked the second-most important function in the creed by Canadian journalists. Our study sees this function drop to sixth place (see Table 26.1, sixth row). This drop can likely be attributed to the fact that journalists personally find this function less important than their news organizations. The rise in importance of the Internet may also be a significant factor here, as it has drastically increased the speed at which information can be transmitted. With this in mind, journalists may feel that their role is instead to analyze and explain the information, while offering informed commentary. The importance of "analyzing and interpreting complex issues" (ranked second in our study) would seem to support this hypothesis.

However, an analysis of journalists' personal responses that takes into account the kind of medium they work for (television, radio, magazine, etc.) shows no significant differences. It does not seem to matter whether the journalist works for a television news program or a weekly newspaper. Significant differences appear, however, when journalists are asked how much importance their news organization attaches to this function. Only then does it become clear that "getting the information out quickly" is less important for a weekly newspaper than it is for a television or radio station.

This is the first time that personal averages are lower than the scores attributed to the news organizations. As noted above, the numbers suggest that the function of "**getting information to the public as quickly as possible**" is not a professional role that is highly valued by the journalists in our sample. The greatest J/MD is for Radio-Canada (– 0.67), followed by Quebecor (– 0.49) and Gesca (– 0.1) (see Table 26.1, sixth row). Responses varied little by age group or media conglomerate. Once again, Barber and Rauhala (2008) found that television news directors, who often work in a management capacity in newsrooms, valued this function above all others.

Already we can conclude that the Québécois journalist's creed is different from the Canadian journalist's creed, because it includes six functions instead of five. As well, functions common to each creed are ranked in a different order of importance.[3]

The six functions that are very important to the journalists in our sample are listed below, followed by the percentage of responses with a value of 6 or 7 on our scale. "It is very important to... accurately report the views of public figures" (96.6%), "analyze and interpret complex problems" (80.5%), "investigate the activities of government and public institutions" (71.7%), "be sceptical of the actions of businesses" (70.6%), "be sceptical of the actions of public officials" (69.1%), and "get information to the public quickly" (64%). The creed has clearly changed, and a sixth, extremely important journalistic function has been introduced.

Table 26.2   Journalist/Media Deviation of the Journalist's Creed

Journalistic Function	2007 Ranking (1996)	J/MD Quebecor	J/MD Gesca	J/MD Radio Canada	J/MD Others	Scores 6 and 7
Accurately report the views of public figures	1 (1)	1.08	0.32	0.18	0.24	96.6 %
Analyze and interpret complex problems	2 (5)	1.46	0.74	0.25	1.06	80.5 %
Investigate activities of government & public inst.	3 (4)	0.64	0.66	0.35	0.82	71.7 %
Be sceptical of the actions of businesses	4 (9)	1.32	1.47	0.69	0.91	70.6 %
Be sceptical of the actions of public officials	5 (8)	0.27	0.74	0.38	0.60	69.1 %
Get information to the public quickly	6 (2)	− 0.49	−0.10	−0.67	−0.03	63.9 %
Total J/MD of the creed (sum)	—	4.28	3.83	1.18	3.60	—
IJ/MD of the creed (average)	—	.71	.64	.20	.60	—

Note: This table compares the respective rankings of 1996 and 2007 (years of the surveys). We can also see that journalists generally attribute more importance to the journalistic functions of their creed than their respective news organization, with the exceptions of being sceptical of the actions of public officials and getting information to public quickly. Remember we consider that a value of 6 or 7 means the function is very important to the respondent.

Average Index of the Journalist/Media Deviation for the Journalist's Creed

The following chart lays out the new ranking of the six journalistic functions in the francophone Quebec journalist's creed, in comparison with the Canadian journalist's creed. It also shows an average index of the J/MD for functions in the creed. This index (IJ/MD) is an overall average of the deviations observed for each function (J/MD1+J/MD2+…J/MD6=EJ/M total÷6 = IJ/MD of the creed). For each media conglomerate, the IJ/MD shows a considerable deviation between the importance that journalists personally attach to the creed's functions and the importance that, according to those same journalists, their news organizations attach to these functions.

Once again, Quebecor journalists stood out with a deviation index of .71. They attach greater importance to these six journalistic functions than their employers. These journalists are closely followed by their counterparts at Gesca, and those from the *other* media. Radio-Canada journalists indicated a low average deviation, which suggests that, on a professional level, they are relatively content—at least as far as the creed is concerned.

The numbers paint a different picture of private sector journalists: they suggest that these journalists and their employers do not attach corresponding levels of importance to the same journalistic functions. Thus, a professional malaise, as far as the creed is concerned, seems to be generalized amongst private sector journalists. However, this feeling appears to be most intense at Quebecor.

The numbers also show that, despite being judged very important by a large majority of the respondents, the function of "getting information to the public quickly" is less important to the individual journalists than it is to their news organizations—to the extent that this final function has barely managed to break into the creed.

Conclusions

Our study reveals that journalists in Quebec place more importance on their creed's journalistic values than their employers do. However, the deviation between journalists' personal evaluations and their evaluations of their news organizations was higher for Quebecor than for the other two conglomerates.

Meanwhile, information gathered in our quantitative study suggests that journalists at the dominant news organizations in Quebec are uncomfortable with media convergence and concentration of ownership. However, the situation differs from one media conglomerate to another.

Journalists at Quebecor are more critical and betray higher levels of dissatisfaction than their counterparts at Gesca and Radio-Canada in several different areas. For example, a majority of Quebecor journalists believe that the opinions and interests of their owners are regularly reflected in their news coverage. These same journalists also indicate that the interests and opinions of their owners have the most impact on what they write or revise. Private-sector journalists (at Quebecor and Gesca) are of the opinion that the need for advertising revenues influences the type of information being broadcast. They firmly believe that economic pressures and the need to meet the demands of shareholders are threatening the public's right to quality information. At the same time they do not believe, generally speaking, that the relationship between media owners and political decision-makers negatively influences the quality of information (data not reported here).

Our research reveals and documents a considerable professional malaise—perhaps even *professional distress*—among journalists at Quebecor. Meanwhile, their counterparts at Gesca might be characterized by a certain discomfort, and those at Radio-Canada by a relative serenity. Of all the journalists who have observed and experienced concentration of ownership and media convergence, those at Quebecor are the most critical of these actions, which are perceived as a threat to their journalistic freedom.

That having been said, the vast majority of journalists are worried about the impact of ownership concentration and media convergence on such essential aspects as the quality, diversity, and integrity of the information they produce. They strongly reject any suggestion that media concentration and convergence have a positive effect on the public's right to quality information. They also reject, though less strongly, the affirmation that being part of a press group improves the quality of the information being produced. They are firmly in agreement that sensationalism and entertainment news are increasingly threatening the public's right to quality information. The journalists in our sample are also leery of the dangers of mixing genres (such as news and opinion), although they are less firm on this subject.

In contrast, journalists in Quebec are very firmly opposed to the suggestion that media convergence encourages showing a diversity of views in the public arena. They are strongly in agreement that media concentration and convergence primarily serves the interests of media conglomerate owners and shareholders. Media competition is not generally seen as a threat to the dissemination of quality information, nor does it appear to encourage better quality in any significant way. The journalists in our sample fully agree that competition has become excessive in recent years.

Finally, it appears that ownership characteristics and management methods are factors that account for the differences observed between journalists working for a public broadcaster (Radio-Canada) or in the private sector (Gesca and Quebecor). It should be noted that Gesca is part of a corporation whose profits are largely made in the financial sector (primarily insurance and investments), and whose financial statements are not made public. Quebecor's media holdings, on the other hand, are part of a company whose principal sources of revenue are generated by its communication activities, and whose shares are publicly traded. Shareholder satisfaction is closely linked to media profits, which encourages more intense convergence and cross-promotional strategies than at Radio-Canada and Gesca. As a result of this situation, the total deviations reported by journalists at Gesca and Radio-Canada are lower than the deviations reported by journalists at Quebecor.

Notes

1. Our research was funded by the Fédération Nationale des Communications, the largest journalists' union in Quebec. However, journalists who belong to a union affiliated with the Fédérations des Travailleurs et Travailleuses du Québec also participated in the study.
2. There are an estimated 4,000 journalists in Quebec, many of whom are not unionized and were not included in this study. The Fédération Professionnelle des Journalistes du Québec (FPJQ) [Quebec Federation of Professional Journalists] has roughly 2,100 active members. Pritchard et al. (2005: 302) estimate that half of the journalists in Quebec belong to this professional organization.
3. If we refer to the criteria of "strong majorities" used by Pritchard and Sauvageau, the creed includes "very important" functions that the journalists are in strong agreement with (value of 6 or 7 on our scale). Remember that their scale only had four values: "very important, quite important, somewhat important, and not at all important." We consider that a value of 6 or 7 means the function is very important to the respondent.

References

Alexander, Peter J., and Brenda M. Cunningham. 2006. Diversity in broadcast television: An empirical study of local news. *The International Journal of Media Management* 6(3–4): 176–183.

Barber, Marsha. 2008. Getting the picture: Airtime and lineup bias on Canadian networks during the 2006 federal election. *Canadian Journal of Communication* 33(4): 621–639.

Barber, Marsha, and Ann Rauhala. 2005. The Canadian news directors study: Demographics and political leanings of television decision-makers. *Canadian Journal of Communication* 30(2): 281–292.

Barber, Marsha, and Ann Rauhala. 2006. The faces behind the scenes: Demographics and attitudes of news decision-makers in Canada. *International Journal of Diversity in Organisations, Communities and Nations* 5(3): 191–204.

Barber, Marsha, and Ann Rauhala. 2008. The Canadian news directors study: Role conceptions of television newsroom decision makers. *Electronic News* 2(1): 46–60.

Bernier, Marc-François. 2007. Protéger la dignité des justiciables dans les palais de justice du Québec: un cas de corégulation face à l'échec de l'autorégulation disciplinaire des journalistes [Protecting the dignity of litigants in Quebec's courthouses: A case of co-regulation considering the failure of self-regulation of journalists]. Paper presented at the annual meeting of the International Association of Communication and Media Research, Paris, July 23–25.

Bernier, Marc-François. 2008. Journalistes au pays de la convergence. Sérénité, malaise et détresse dans la profession [Journalists in convergence land, serenity, discomfort and distress in the profession. Québec: Laval University Press.

Bernier, Marc-François. 2009. Baromètre des médias 2009: Les médias et les journalistes du Québec sont crédibles, mais le public doute de leur indépendance face au pouvoirs politiques et économiques [2009 Media Barometer: News media and their journalists are credible, but the public has some doubts regarding their independence from political and economic powers]. Ottawa, Chaire de recherche en éthique du journalisme. Retrieved from http://www.crej.ca/barometre2009.pdf.

Bozonelos, Petty. 2004. The tension between quality journalism and good business in Canada: A view from the inside. *Communication* 29:77–92.

Canadian Association of Journalists. (2009). Press release, January 5.

Canadian Radio-Television and Telecommunications Commission. 2009. Press release, June 4.

Comité permanent du patrimoine canadien [Permanent committee on the Canadian heritage]. 2003. *Notre souveraineté culturelle: le deuxième siècle de la radiodiffusion canadienne* [Our cultural sovereignty: The second century of Canadian broadcasting]. Ottawa, House of Commons.

Comité sénatorial permanent des transports et des communications [Standing Senate Committee on Transport and Communications]. 2006. *Rapport final sur les médias d'information*, vol. 1. [Final Report on the Canadian News Media]. Ottawa, June.

Commission de la culture. 2001. *Mandat d'initiative portant sur la concentration de la presse*. Québec. [Mandate initiative on media concentration]. Secrétariat des commissions, Québec, Assemblée nationale du Québec.

Daily, Larry, Lori Demo, and Mary Spillman. 2003. The convergence continuum: A model for studying collaboration between media newsrooms. Paper presented at the annual meeting of the Association for Education in Journalism and Mass Communication, Kansas City, Missouri. July 30–August 2, pp. 428–457.

Daily, Larry, Lori Demo, and Mary Spillman. 2005. The convergence continuum: A model for studying collaboration between media newsrooms. *Atlantic Journal of Communication* 13(3):150–168.

Dvorkin, Jeffrey. 2009. State of the Canadian media. Unpublished manuscript.

Godin, Pierre. 1979. Qui vous informe? [Who are you informed by?] *Actualité*: 31–40.

Hammond, Scott C., Daniel Patterson, and Shawn Thomsen. 2000. Print, broadcast and online convergence in the newsroom. *Journalism and Mass Communication Educator* 55(2):16–26.

Huang, Edgar, Karen Davidson, Stephanie Shreve, Twila Davis, Elizabeth Buttendorf, and Anita Nair. 2006. Bridging newsrooms and classrooms: Preparing the next generation of journalists for converged media. *Journalism and Communication Monographs* 221–262.

Huang, Edgar, Lisa Rademakers, Moshood A. Fayemiwo, and Lilian Dunlap. 2004. Converged journalism and quality: A case study of the Tampa Tribune news stories. *Convergence* 10(4):73–91.

Kweon, Sanghee. 2000. A framing analysis: How did three U.S. news magazines frame about mergers or acquisitions? *International Journal of Media Management* 2(3–4):165–177.

Langlois, Simon, and Florian Sauvageau. 1982. Les journalistes des quotidiens québécois et leur métier [Journalists in Quebec daily newspapers and their craft]. *Politique* 1(2):5–39.

Lee, Tien-Tsung, and Hsiao-Fang Hwang. 1997. The impact of media ownership—How time and Warner's merger influence Time's content. Paper presented at the annual meeting of the Association for the Education in Journalism and Mass Communication, NEED CITY, Chicago, IL.

Lord, Marie-Linda. 2006. Les médias acadiens du Nouveau-Brunswick: entre monopole de presse et prise de parole citoyenne [Acadian Media in New Brunswick: Between press monopoly and citizen speech]. In *Médias et milieux francophones* [Media and French communities], edited by Michel Beauchamp and Thierry Watine, pp. 21–46. Montreal, Quebec: Presses de l'Université Laval, coll. CÉFAN.

Marcotte, Phillipe. 2008. *Quality in journalism as seen by news people* (tr. Marilyn Thompson). Quebec City: Centre d'études sur les medias/Canadian Media Research Consortium.

Marketwire Media Directory. 2009. Toronto, Ontario: Marketwire.

McCombs, Maxwell. 1987. Effects of monopoly in Cleveland on diversity of newspaper content. *Journalism Quarterly* 64:740–744.

Mills, Lisa. 2005. Too little too late: Network coverage of the FCC's 2003 media ownership rule changes. Paper presented at the annual meeting of the Association for Education in Journalism and Mass Communication, San Antonio, Texas. Retrieved from http://list.msu.edu/cgi-bin/wa?A2=ind0602B&L=AEJMC&P=R11681.

Picard, Robert G. 2004. Commercialism and newspaper quality. *Newspaper Research Journal* 25(1):54–65.

Pollard, George. 1985. Professionalism among Canadian news workers: A cross-media analysis. *Gazette* 36:21–38.

Pollard, George. 1995. Job satisfaction among news workers: The influence of professionalism, perceptions of organizational structure and social attributes. *Journalism and Mass Communication Quarterly* 72:682–697.

Pritchard, David. 2001. A tale of three cities: "Diverse and antagonistic" information in situations of local newspaper/broadcast cross-ownership. *Federal Communications Law Journal* 54:31–52.

Pritchard, David, Paul R. Brewer, and Florian Sauvageau. 2005. Changes in Canadian journalists' views about the social and political roles of the news media: A panel study, 1996–2003. *Canadian Journal of Political Science* 38(2):287–306.

Pritchard, David, and Florian Sauvageau. 1998. The journalists and journalism of Canada. In *The global journalist: News people around the world,* edited by David H. Weaver, pp. 373–393. Cresskill, NJ: Hampton Press.

Pritchard, David, and Florian Sauvageau. 1999a. English and French and generation X: The professional values of Canadian journalists. In *Canada: The state of the Federation 1998/99—How Canadians connect,* edited by Harvey Lazar and Tom McIntosh (pp. 283–306). Montreal, Quebec: McGill-Queen's University Press.

Pritchard, David, and Florian Sauvageau. 1999b. *Les journalistes canadiens: Un portrait de fin de siècle* [Canadian journalists: A picture at the end of the century]. Sainte-Foy, QC: Les Presse de l'Université Laval.

Robinson, Gertrude, and Armande Saint-Jean. 1998. Canadian women journalists: The "other half" of the equation. In *The global journalist: News people around the world,* edited by David H. Weaver, pp. 351–372. Cresskill, NJ: Hampton Press.

Singer, Jane B. 2003. The sociology of convergence: Challenges and changes in newspaper news work. Paper presented at the annual meeting of the Association for Education in Journalism and Mass Communication, Kansas City, Missouri, July 30–August 2.

Singer, Jane B. 2004. Strange bedfellows? The diffusion of convergence in four news organizations. *Journalism Studies* 5(1):3–18.

Statistics Canada. 2008. Occupation-national occupational classification for statistics 2006 (720), class of worker (6) and sex (3) for the labour force 15 years and over of Canada, provinces, territories, census metropolitan areas and census agglomerations, 2006 Census—20% sample data (table). Topic-based tabulation. *2006 Census of Population.* Statistics Canada catalogue no. 97-559-XCB2006011. Ottawa. Released March 4.

Wilson, C. Edward. 1966. Why Canadian newsmen leave their papers. *Journalism Quarterly* 43:769–772.

Wright, Donald K. 1974. An analysis of the level of professionalism among Canadian journalists. *Gazette* 20:133–144.

Wright, Donald K. 1976. Professionalism levels of British Columbia's broadcast journalists: A communicator analysis. *Gazette* 22:38–48.

27 U.S. Journalists in the Tumultuous Early Years of the 21st Century

Bonnie J. Brownlee and Randal A. Beam

The big news in the U.S. news environment in the early years of the 21st century is change—dramatic change. By the end of the first decade, ownership of news organizations had become increasingly concentrated in the hands of major corporations, which in turn struggled to settle on formulas both to remain profitable and to discharge their responsibilities as journalistic entities.

Changing technology continued to modify the means of gathering and disseminating the news and the way consumers accessed information. News organizations migrated to the World Wide Web, offering a vast amount of information in ever-innovative formats. Meantime, circulation at daily and Sunday newspapers continued to drop, viewership of network television news continued to decline, and news organizations continued to shrink their work forces as profits evaporated.

The 2010 "State of the News Media" report noted a number of employment trends. At daily newspapers, 13,500 full-time newsroom jobs were lost in 2009. That means that newsrooms had shrunk 25% in three years and just under 27% since the beginning of the decade. Advertising revenue at newspaper companies fell 23% in 2007 and 2008 and another 26% in 2009 (Pew 2010). Other estimates put the job losses even higher. Stock prices at newspaper companies fell 83% in 2008, and the owners of some papers were closing foreign and national bureaus. In some cases, what had once been among the nation's most profitable businesses began filing for bankruptcy (Beam, Weaver, & Brownlee 2009).

At the same time, journalism and mass communication programs across the United States actually grew, diversifying their offerings and graduating ever more professionals. By the end of the first decade of the 21st century, graduates were finding it difficult to land jobs, and salaries for those who did find work were stagnant.

The findings reported here suggest that even during what is a time of enormous change in the news business in the United States, much of what we have learned about the journalists themselves—their values, their perceptions of journalism's roles in society—are changing too, although perhaps not as much as some have suggested.

The main findings reported here come from the most recent American Journalist study, which was conducted in 2002 by the authors and their colleagues David Weaver, Paul Voakes, and Cleveland Wilhoit (Weaver, Beam, Brownlee, Voakes, & Wilhoit 2007). This survey followed similar studies in 1971, 1982–1983, and 1992 (Johnstone, Slawski, & Bowman 1976; Weaver & Wilhoit 1986, 1996).

The purpose of these studies has been to provide comparable data to record changes in journalistic work and journalists over time. As such, the methodology has remained much the same. We have supplemented findings from the main 2002 study with those from a smaller panel study conducted in 2007.

Method

Throughout the 40 years of these studies, journalists have been defined as those responsible for preparing or transmitting news stories or other timely information. They include full-time reporters, writers, correspondents, editors, news announcers, columnists, photojournalists, and other news people at U.S. news organizations.

To be able to compare across the decades, we closely followed the definitions of a journalist, the sampling methods, and the questions from the previous surveys (1971, 1982–1983, 1992). Our 2002 sample, the main probability sample, consisted of three stages. We first compiled a list of daily and weekly newspapers, news magazines, wire services, and radio and television stations. We estimated there to be 10,870 of such news organizations in the United States; from this, we used a systematic random sampling selection process that resulted in 515 news organizations, representing the six types of news organizations. The final sample consisted of 156 daily newspapers, stratified by standard circulation classifications; 120 weekly newspapers; 16 news magazines; 36 news service bureaus; 88 radio stations; 98 TV stations; one TV network operation. From these organizations we sought to obtain lists of all full-time journalists. Finally, from the lists of individuals, we drew systematic random samples. Our final sample attempted to reflect the actual percentages of workers in each of these organizations as a percentage of the working journalists in the country. That is, we wanted our sample to have roughly the same percentage of newspaper journalists, wire service journalists, etc., as were currently working in the U.S. media.[1]

The final sample consisted of 1,149 U.S. journalists selected using probability sampling. The adjusted response rate was 79%. A more detailed description of the sampling method can be found in *The American Journalist in the 21st Century: U.S. News People at the Dawn of a New Millennium* (Weaver et al. 2007). The Center for Survey Research at Indiana University conducted telephone interviews that lasted approximately 50 minutes with each of the selected respondents.

Results from the second study, which is summarized briefly at the end of the chapter, are based on a panel drawn from the main sample described above. The panel consisted of 400 of the journalists interviewed in 2002. They were interviewed again in 2007 by telephone for about 30 minutes. About 80% of the questions we asked of the panel were identical to the earlier questions, allowing us to compare responses from the same journalists across time. About 20% of the questions were new in 2007. The new questions focused on such factors as organizational change, new job duties, and perceptions about organizational goals or practices.

Findings

Basic Characteristics

Age and Gender.   The median age of U.S. journalists in 2002 was 41, older than in previous American Journalist studies. The number, though slightly higher than for the U.S. civilian workforce, follows the pattern of baby boomers progressing through the workforce. Gender proportions of journalists remained steady from the two previous studies, with 33% of the journalist workforce being women (see Table 27.1). This result is somewhat surprising, since women comprised about 64% of the enrollment in journalism and mass communication programs at the time (Becker, Vlad, Huh, & Mace 2003).

While the largest increase in women journalists occurred in the youngest age category (under age 25), as it has in past American Journalist studies, it is also true that there has been an increase

Table 27.1 Gender of Journalists (in %)

Gender	Journalists				U.S. Civilian Labor Force			
	1971[a]	1982–1983[b]	1992[c]	2002	1971[d]	1981[e]	1989[f]	2001[g]
Male	79.7	66.2	66.0	67.0	66.4	57.5	54.8	53.4
Female	20.3	33.8	34.0	33.0	33.6	42.5	45.2	46.6
Total	100.0	100.0	100.0	100.0	100.0	100.0	100.0	100.0

a From Johnstone, Slawaski, and Bowman, *The News People* (1976: 197).
b From Weaver and Wilhoit, *The American Journalist* (1986: 19).
c From Weaver and Wilhoit, *The American Journalist in the 1990s* (1996: 8).
d U.S. Department of Labor, 1971, Table A-2, p. 28.
e U.S. Bureau of the Census, Statistical Abstract of the United States (1982–1983, 103rd ed.: 379, cited in Weaver et al., 2007).
f U.S. Bureau of the Census, Statistical Abstract of the United States (1991, 111th ed.: 392, cited in Weaver et al., 2007).
g U.S. Bureau of the Census, Statistical Abstract of the United States (2002, 122nd ed.: 381, cited in Weaver et al., 2007).

since the 1980s in the percentage of women in the 55 to 64 age group. For those with 20 or more years of work experience, for example, only about a quarter of the U.S. journalist workforce was female. Still, that's better than the percentages in some other professions. The 2000 U.S. Census (cited in Weaver et al., 2007: 9) showed that the overall percentage of women lawyers and judges was 30%; physicians, 28%; architects, 23%; dentists, 19%; and engineers, 10%.

Our study found that the proportion of women was highest in news magazines (43%) and lowest in wire services (20%). The percentage of women in daily newspapers was 33%. As in earlier studies, women were less likely to be married (48%) than were men (67%) and less likely than men to have children living with them (33% vs. 46%).

Ethnicity. Each of the American Journalist studies has found the number of minorities in mainstream U.S. news media lags far behind the percentage of minorities in the U.S. population. Although the numbers have inched up over the years, in 2002, just about 4% of U.S. journalists were African American, a minority group that made up almost 13% of the U.S. adult population at that time. Hispanic journalists made up a little more than 3% of the journalistic workforce but a little more than 13% of the U.S. adult population. Overall, racial and ethnic minorities made up 9.5% of the total journalism workforce, if those who identified themselves as Pacific Islanders and "other" minorities were included. That compared with about 31% in the total U.S. population. Representation within the media showed that television news had the highest proportion of minority journalists (14.7%) and weekly newspapers had the lowest (5.6%) (see Table 27.2).

Although the overall percentages of minority journalists are small, the ratio of women to men among these groups differs from that of the non-Hispanic white journalists. In 2002, 54% of African American journalists were women, as were 56% of Asian American journalists, 46% of Hispanic journalists, and 39% of Native American journalists.

Political Views. U.S. journalists have tended to be more liberal than the U.S. population as a whole, and that remained the case in the 2002 study. About 40% of the journalists said they were "pretty far to the left" or "a little to the left" politically compared with only 17% of the population as a whole. About 41% of the U.S. population was "a little to the right" or "pretty far to the right" compared with only 25% of the journalists. One-third of the journalists said they were in the "middle of the road"; 38% of the U.S. population characterized itself this way.

The journalists' liberal leanings are also reflected in their political party identification. Compared with the U.S. population, journalists were about four percentage points *more* likely to iden-

Table 27.2   Racial and Ethnic Origins of Journalists Compared with Population (in %)

Ethnicity	Journalists				U.S. Population			
	1971[a]	*1982–1983*[b]	*1992*[c]	*2002*	*1970*[d]	*1981*[e]	*1990*[f]	*2002*[g]
African American	3.9	2.9	3.7	3.7	11.1	11.8	12.1	12.7
Hispanic	1.1	0.6	2.2	3.3	4.4	6.5	9.0	13.4
Asian American	—[h]	0.4	1.0	1.0	0.5	0.7	2.9	4.0
Native American	—[h]	—[i]	0.6	0.4	—	—	0.8	0.9
Jewish	6.4	5.8	5.4	6.2	2.6	2.6	2.4	2.0
Other (incl. Caucasian)	88.6	90.3	87.1	85.4	81.4	78.4	72.8	67.0
Total	100.0	100.0	100.0	100.0	100.0	100.0	100.0	100.0

a From Johnstone et al., *The News People* (1976: 26,198, 225).
b From Weaver and Wilhoit, *The American Journalist* (1986: 23).
c From Weaver and Wilhoit, *The American Journalist in the 1990s* (1996: 11).
d U.S. Bureau of the Census, Statistical Abstract of the United States (1972, 93rd ed.: 29, 33, 45, cited in Weaver et al., 2007).
e U.S. Bureau of the Census, Statistical Abstract of the United States (1982-1983, 103rd ed.:32, 33, 54, 55, cited in Weaver et al., 2007).
f U.S. Bureau of the Census, Statistical Abstract of the United States (1991, 111th ed.: 22, 56, cited in Weaver et al., 2007).
g U.S. Bureau of the Census, Statistical Abstract of the United States (2003, 123rd ed.: 15, 67, cited in Weaver et al., 2007).
h Not reported by Johnstone et al.
i Not reported by Wilhoit and Weaver (1986).

tify as Democrats (36% vs. 32%) but 13 percentage points *less* likely to identify as Republicans (18% vs. 31%). About one-third of the journalists and of the U.S. population identified themselves as political independents, with the rest either saying that they belonged to another party or refusing to give a party identification (see Table 27.3).

Education and Training.   The practice of journalism in the United States has never required any particular educational training or licensing. Those people with something to say and with the means to say it are free to do so. It is true, however, that the qualifications journalists bring to their jobs have changed significantly over the years. In the early years of the 20th century, there were few journalism programs and few graduates of them. Indeed, in 1910, there were only four four-year journalism programs in the United States (cited in Weaver et al. 2007: 32).

Table 27.3   Political Leanings of Journalists Compared with Population (in %)

Leaning	Journalists				U.S. Population		
	1971[a]	*1982–1983*[b]	*1992*[c]	*2002*	*1982*[d]	*1992*[e]	*2002*[f]
Pretty far to the left	7.5	3.8	11.6	9.0	—	—	3
A little to the left	30.5	18.3	35.7	31.1	21	18	14
Middle of the road	38.5	57.5	30.0	33.3	37	41	38
A little to the right	15.6	16.3	17.0	20.4	32	34	37
Pretty far to the right	3.4	1.6	4.7	4.5	—	—	4
Don't know/refused	4.5	2.5	1.0	1.7	10	7	5

a From Johnstone et al. (1976: 93).
b From Weaver and Wilhoit (1986:26).
c From Weaver and Wilhoit (1996: 15).
d From George H. Gallup, The Gallup Poll: Public Opinion (1983: 82).
e From Gallup Organization national telephone survey of 1,307 U.S. adults, July 6-8, 1992, and 955 U.S. adults, July 17, 1992.
f From Gallup Organization national telephone survey, September 2002. Question: "How would you describe your political views—very conservative, conservative, moderate, liberal or very liberal?"

That number grew to 54 in 1927 and to about 200 in 1971, when the first American Journalist study was conducted. By 1982, there were 304 colleges or universities with a journalism or mass communication program; 413 by 1992; and 463 by 2002. In that year, nearly 200,000 students were enrolled in those programs and just over 42,000 undergraduate degrees were granted.

The nature of journalism programs in the United States has evolved over the years, as has the focus of many of the programs' students. In 1982, 26% of the students in the nation's journalism programs studied a news-editorial curriculum. In 1991, that figure had dropped to 17%, and in 2002, the figure for news-editorial was 14%. The corresponding increases over the years have been in related fields such as advertising and public relations and in such other specialties as magazines, photojournalism, graphics and design, interpersonal communication, and media studies (Weaver et al. 2007: 33–34).

By 2002, a four-year college degree, although not necessarily with a major in journalism, was the most common educational attribute of those working in journalism and one that surely set journalists apart from mainstream Americans. Across all age groups, 89% of news journalists held a bachelor's degree of some sort. Among all adult Americans that figure was only 26%. Many working journalists hold graduate degrees—nearly 17% in the 2002 data.

Of all journalists younger than 25 a little more than three-quarters (76%) had majored in journalism or mass communication as of 2002. Overall, of the journalists with college degrees, 36% had majored in journalism.

Our study found differences among the news media in terms of the percentage of journalism graduates. Journalism majors were more likely to be found at daily newspapers and radio and television stations than at the wire services and magazines. Likewise, journalism majors were more likely to be working in the news media in the Midwest and West than in New England.

Working Conditions

Tasks in the Newsroom.   New communication technologies are refashioning journalistic work in the United States. Findings from the 2002 survey document just how thoroughly tasks involving the Internet, for example, are woven into newsroom routines.

Seven in ten journalists used the Web either daily or several times a week to read the online sites of other news organizations. About the same percentage reported searching for or receiving press releases via the Internet. The Internet also has become a tool that reporters and editors rely on regularly to find the names or addresses of sources (48%), to get background information for stories (62%), and to check facts (50%). And almost six in ten journalists said they routinely used e-mail to keep in touch with readers, viewers, or listeners.

Despite the Internet's potential for two-way communication, by 2002 it had not influenced one traditional reporting task: the interview. Though e-mail interviews might be convenient, only 7% of journalists said they used them daily or several times a week for that purpose. Other less common tasks included using the Web to search for story ideas (34%), downloading raw data from databases (19%), and analyzing government data with statistical software (5%).

The workplace tools that journalists use have changed significantly since the first American Journalist survey, as digital communication technologies have become fully integrated into newsrooms. But with the exception of editing or processing work, the division of core tasks has remained more or less the same. In the 1971 American Journalist study, about 79% of the journalists said that they did reporting regularly or occasionally. That percentage was the same in

2002 (though it was about ten points higher than in 1992). In 1971, about 65% said they edited the work of others "a great deal" or "some"; by 2002, that figure had grown to 77%, suggesting that over time editing has become a more common function. And about 42% of journalists in 1971 said that they supervised or managed the work of others. Again, the 2002 figure was almost identical.

Together, the findings reaffirm that multitasking has been a fact of work life in U.S. newsrooms for 30 years. The distinction between reporter and editor, or between supervisor and rank-and-file journalist, has never been absolute, and it is likely to remain that way. Although U.S. newsrooms have lost tens of thousands of journalists since the 2002 American Journalist survey, the range of tasks necessary to put out a newspaper or put on a newscast has not been shrinking. In fact, evidence suggests that it is growing (Deuze 2007; Wilson 2008). To accommodate, the smaller pool of journalists who remain in newsrooms will be expected, more than in the past, to be doing many different tasks.

Job Satisfaction.　The changing nature of news work may be influencing how journalists evaluate their jobs and careers. As U.S. journalists entered the new millennium, article after article in trade publications suggested that morale and job satisfaction were in free fall. "Low Morale—Is It Common in Newsrooms Across America?" a headline in the *Columbia Journalism Review* asked (Hickey 2001).

Journalists in our survey, however, have always reported being far more satisfied than dissatisfied with their work. In 2002, about 84% of the journalists were either very or fairly satisfied with their jobs. That figure was up about seven points from 1992 and was at roughly the same levels as in the 1982–1983 and 1971 surveys. Only a tiny percentage of journalists ever have said that they were very dissatisfied with their jobs.

Job satisfaction was relatively stable across different categories of journalists. It varied slightly by the age, gender, and race of journalists and by the types of organizations for which they work. In 2002, the journalists who were least satisfied with their jobs worked at news magazines (78% very or fairly satisfied) and daily newspapers (83%). The most satisfied were those at radio stations (91%) and news services (90%). Women were somewhat less satisfied than men (79% vs. 87%). Journalists under 25, who were new to the profession, were the most content in their work (91%), while the next older group, 25 to 34, was the least so (80%). The other age groups hovered at about 85%.

Findings from our 2002 national probability sample suggested that race was not correlated with job satisfaction. About 83% of minority journalists were either very or fairly satisfied with their jobs compared with 84% of non-Hispanic white journalists (see Table 27.4).

Table 27.4　Job Satisfaction by Year (in %)

	1971[a] (N = 1,328)	1982–1983[b] (N = 1,001)	1992[c] (N = 1,156)	2002 (N = 1,149)
Very satisfied	49	40	27	33.3
Fairly satisfied	39	44	50	50.6
Somewhat dissatisfied	12	15	20	14.4
Very dissatisfied	1	2	3	1.7

a From Johnstone et al. (1976: 238).
b From Weaver and Wilhoit (1986: 89).
c From Weaver and Wilhoit (1996: 100).

The most important clues to understanding journalists' job satisfaction are found in the perceptions that they have about their work environment. Analyses suggest that the following factors are particularly strong predictors of job satisfaction:

1. *Structural characteristics of the organization for which they work:*   Other things being equal, job satisfaction tends to be higher for journalists working for news organizations that are owned by a larger corporation, such as a newspaper or broadcast chain, and for organizations where the chief executive is a local resident.
2. *Organizational goals, priorities, or conditions:*   Journalists who perceive that their organization is doing a good job informing the public tend to like their work more, as do news workers who believe that the quality of journalism at their organization has been rising steadily. And, as might be expected, job satisfaction also is higher for journalists who say that keeping morale strong is a management priority at their news organizations.
3. *Individual characteristics and work-environment conditions:*   Years of experience and personal income are positively associated with job satisfaction, but the work environment is also critical. Journalists rate job satisfaction more highly when they feel that they have a lot of autonomy in their jobs and when they get a lot of feedback and comments from supervisors about their work.

Career Commitment.   A hallmark of professional work is that it is a lifelong pursuit. That has likely never been as true for journalists as for classic professions such as medicine and law. Nonetheless, journalists typically have demonstrated a strong commitment to their careers. That did not change in the 2002 survey, though the turmoil affecting the U.S. news media during the last part of the 2000s may be testing journalists' resolve.

In each of the last three American Journalist studies, respondents have been asked where they intended to be working in five years—in the news media or somewhere else. The percentage of journalists who plan to leave the field went from about 11% in 1982–1983 to 21% in 1992, before dropping to 17% in the 2002 survey. In 2002, about 5% intended to be retired or were unsure of their plans five years out. Another 77% said they intended to remain in the profession. Given the magnitude of staff cuts in 2008 and 2009, it is likely that some did not get that opportunity.

A multivariate analysis was used to evaluate the most important factors associated with journalists' career intentions. Almost 30 factors were considered. Years of experience turned out to be important, of course. As the length of a journalist's career increased, the likelihood of leaving the profession grew. Job satisfaction also was critical. Higher job satisfaction was associated with plans to stay in journalism. And journalists' perceptions about the profit goals of their news organizations also were linked to career plans. The more journalists believed that their organizations valued high profits over quality journalism, the more likely they were say that they intended to leave the profession. That finding suggests that the values of an employer may be an important predictor of career plans in the same way that they were a predictor of job satisfaction.

Income.   Though journalists downplay pay when asked about factors that are important to them in a job, income is nonetheless a key indicator of workplace conditions. As the news business deteriorated during the last few years, many news organizations responded by cutting salaries, which wiped out the salary gains that journalists made in the 1990s.

Those salary gains brought the 2001 median personal income of U.S. journalists to about $43,588. As in other professions, personal income varied widely. About one-fifth of journalists reported income of $70,000 or higher. Another fifth reported making $30,000 or less. The best-paid journalists could be found at news magazines and news services, where the median personal income was in the $70,000 range. The poorest-paid journalists worked for radio stations ($34,750) and weekly papers ($29,919).

The 1990s were a relatively prosperous time for journalists. Median personal income rose about 39% in the 1990s, about nine points above the inflation rate. Still, even with that healthy increase, the purchasing power of journalists was not as high as in the early 1970s, when the first American Journalist survey was conducted.

Many occupations, journalism among them, have a gender gap when it comes to pay. On average, women journalists earned only about 81% as much as men in 2001. That's about the same as in 1991 but much better than the 64% recorded for 1970 personal income. In addition to gender, other factors that predicted higher personal income were the size of the organization, education, years of experience, and a supervisory job.

Professionalism

Professional Autonomy.   Autonomy is a core characteristic of professional work (Beam, Weaver, & Brownlee 2009). During the last 30 years, the autonomy of reporters at U.S. news organizations has eroded steadily, at least as reflected in the responses that they have given to three questions about the amount of discretion that they have in the newsroom.

Two of the questions focus directly on constraints on their work. Reporters have been asked how much freedom they have to select the stories that they work on and to decide what to emphasize in those stories. Over time, the percentage saying that they have "almost complete freedom" to do those things has fallen by a third or more. In 1971, about 60% of the reporters said that they had almost complete freedom to select their own stories; by 2002, that figure had dropped to 40%. In 1971, about 76% of the reporters said that they were free to craft their stories as they thought best; by 2002, that figure had plummeted to 42%.

A third question assessed reporters' perceived ability to influence coverage at their news organization. In 1982–1983, they were asked for the first time how often they were able to get a story covered that they thought was important. In that year, about 59% said that they could "almost always" get an important subject covered. But by 2002, that figure had dropped seven percentage points, suggesting that reporters had become less influential in shaping coverage at their own news organizations.

To explore constraints on autonomy, reporters were asked to describe factors that limited their freedom at work. Most of their responses fell into four broad categories:

1. About 30% mentioned commercial constraints—basically limitations related to the profit goals or business needs of their news organizations. Those limitations came in various forms, ranging from getting pressure by advertisers who wanted to influence coverage to insufficient resources for news-gathering;
2. About 25% cited the policies, procedures. or customs of their news organizations. These obstacles included idiosyncratic rules imposed by news managers, organizational limits on story length, and various other institutional procedures that the reporters felt limited their freedom;
3. About 20% blamed outside agents, such as the government agency that refused to release essential information or the coach who refused to allow access to an athlete; and

Table 27.5   Indicators of Perceived Journalistic Autonomy and Influence by Year (in %)

Percentage who say...	*1971* (N = [b])	*1982–1983* (N = 794 [c])	*1992* (N = 806 [c])	*2002* (N = 912 [c])
They have "almost complete freedom" in selecting stories they work on	60	60	44	40
They have "almost complete freedom" to decide the aspects of a story to emphasize	76	66	51	42
They "almost always" can get a subject covered that they think should be covered	[d]	59	55	52

a Journalists who said they did reporting "regularly" or "occasionally" in the 1982–1983, 1992, and 2002 studies. Journalists "who did reporting" in the 1971 study.
b Weighted N of 4,084 reported in Johnstone et al. (1976: 222).
c Figures for earlier years from Weaver et al. (2007: 75).
d Comparable data not available.

4. About 10% believed that professional practices or customs limited their journalistic freedom (though not all considered that a bad thing). Objectivity as a professional practice was mentioned as a constraint, and some reporters even noted that ethical guidelines limited their freedom as journalists (see Table 27.5).

Journalistic Roles.   As in previous American Journalist surveys, the news workers were asked in 2002 for their views on the professional roles of the news media. The original 1971 study included questions about eight of these journalistic roles. By 2002, that list had expanded to 15 roles, which provide the foundation for four broad functions that Weaver and Wilhoit have identified for the news media: the interpretive function, the adversarial function, the disseminator function, and the populist-mobilizer function (Weaver et al. 2007; Weaver & Wilhoit 1996).

American journalists have been relatively consistent over time in their rankings of these journalistic roles. For example, "investigating government claims" has been ranked either first or second in importance in each survey since 1971. But the level of support for the roles, and for the functions associated with them, has shifted.

In the 2002 survey, the items showing the greatest support were associated with the interpretive and disseminator functions. More than half of the journalists considered it extremely important for the media to investigate government claims; to analyze and interpret complex problems; to get information to the public quickly; and to avoid stories where facts cannot be verified. Those were among the most important roles in the 1971 survey, too, though the magnitude of support in 2002 was somewhat less for the first two, which are associated with the interpretive function.

The mythology of journalism casts the press in the role of an adversary of the powerful. But the adversarial role has never been a particularly comfortable fit for journalists in these studies. The two items reflecting the adversarial function—being an adversary of public officials and being an adversary of business—have always received tepid support. That was true again in 2002. Only about a fifth of the journalists considered those roles extremely important.

The growth of new communication technologies like the Web or mobile phones appears to be depressing the importance of the disseminator function. About 59% of journalists still considered it extremely important to get information to the public quickly, but that figure declined ten points between 1992 and 2002. And support for the "mass" nature of the news media continued to erode. In 1971, about 39% of journalists considered it extremely important to produce news of interest to the widest audience. By 2002, that figure had dropped to 15%, the steepest decline in support for any of the journalistic roles. That decline parallels the rise in niche news media (magazines, radio, cable news channels, and Web sites) that do not try to cultivate large, heterogeneous audiences.

By looking at the proportions of journalists who considered the 15 roles extremely important, it was possible to group the roles and calculate general levels of support for each of the four functions of the news media. Here is what we found:

- About 63% of the journalists strongly supported the interpretive function in 2002. That's the same level of support as a decade earlier. This has consistently ranked as the most important of the functions.
- About 16% strongly supported the disseminator function in 2002. That declined substantially from 51% in 1992. The decline probably reflects the impact the Web and cable TV have had on news-media functions. Because these 24/7 media increasingly are the first to report breaking news, that function has become less important for print and traditional broadcast media.
- Roughly 10% strongly supported the populist-mobilizer function, which was about double the percentage from 1992. The civic-journalism movement, which emphasized giving citizens the tools they need to influence public policy, gained momentum during the 1990s.
- About 19% strongly supported the adversarial function, which was only one percentage point higher than in 1992.

In 1971, Johnstone et al. (1976) pointed out that journalists embrace multiple roles and functions for the news media, and that remains true. In 2002, about 80% of the journalists who

Table 27.6   Journalistic Role Conceptions by Year (% saying role was "extremely important")

	1971 (N = 1,313)	1982–1983 (N = 1,001)	1992 (N = 1,156)	2002 (N = 1,149)
Interpretive function				
Investigate government claims	76	66	67	71
Analyze, interpret complex problems	61	49	48	51
Analyze, interpret international developments	—	—	—	48
Discuss development of national policies	55	38	39	40
Adversarial function				
Be an adversary of public officials	—	20	21	20
Be an adversary of businesses	—	15	14	18
Disseminator function				
Get information to the public quickly	56	60	69	59
Avoid stories where facts cannot be verified	51	50	49	52
Concentrate on news of interest to widest audience	39	36	20	15
Provide entertainment, relaxation	17	20	14	11
Populist mobilizer function				
Give ordinary people chance to express views	—	—	48	39
Motivate ordinary people to get involved	—	—	—	33
Point people toward solutions to societal problems	—	—	—	24
Develop intellectual, cultural interests	30	24	18	17
Set political agenda	—	—	5	3

thought the populist-mobilizing function was very important also thought the interpretive function was very important. And about 80% of those who strongly endorsed the adversarial function were equally supportive of the interpretive function. The reality is that most journalists have a complex view of their professional roles and of the news-media functions associated with those roles. That finding was evident in 2002, as it had been in the previous studies (see Table 27.6).

Ethics.   Ethics are among the fuzziest aspects of journalistic practice. What is considered ethical behavior may depend on the personal values of the journalist, the customs of a news organization for which he or she works, the availability of accurate information about a situation, and the perceptions that reporters or editors have about the potential consequences of a decision. Because there are so many variables to consider, it is challenging to evaluate the ethical standards of journalists outside the context of a particular decision about a particular situation.

But to get a general sense of journalists' ethical values, our surveys have sought to track changes in their judgments about ten controversial reporting practices. The surveys have asked journalists to say whether each of those reporting practices was "justified on occasion" or "never approved under any circumstance."

Journalists' views on these reporting practices have changed more over time than many other facets of their professional culture. Our 2002 survey suggests that journalists are becoming more conservative in their ethical decision-making. The results showed relatively large declines since 1992 in support for two deceptive reporting techniques—getting a job in order to gain inside information and claiming to be someone else. We also found a lower rate of acceptance for using personal documents without permission and for disclosing the name of a rape victim.

Overall, acceptance of seven of the ten controversial practices either stayed at the same level or declined from the previous survey. Three increased, but only slightly. Very few journalists (8%) think that it is occasionally justified to break a pledge of confidentiality. Still, that was up three percentage points from a decade earlier. Journalists also were slightly more supportive of badgering an unwilling source to gain information and of telling a story with a re-creation or dramatization.

The reporting practices that were most acceptable involved surreptitious behavior but not lying or overt deception. Almost eight in ten journalists thought it was justifiable on occasion to use confidential business or government documents without authorization. About six in ten thought it was okay to use a hidden camera or microphone. Aside from breaking a confidentiality pledge, the least acceptable practices were using re-creations or dramatizations of the news (29% said it was justified on occasion), claiming to be someone else (14%), and paying for confidential information (17%) (see Table 27.7).

The American Journalist Panel Study

In the fall of 2007, a panel of 400 news workers who took part in the 2002 American Journalist survey was interviewed again. The five years following the 2002 survey had been a period of significant economic and technological turmoil in the news business (Beam et al. 2009). Many news organizations focused intently on beefing up their online presence. That change meant journalists had to learn new tasks. High profit margins, which had almost been a certainty for many news organizations for decades, came under pressure as the economy stumbled toward recession. Layoffs and buyouts became common ways to try to bolster profitability. Media companies, which had been such reliable money generators in the past, began to disappoint their owners, particularly

Table 27.7   Ethical Practices by Year (% saying behavior is "justified on occasion")

	1982–1983 (N = 995)	1992 (N = 1,154)	2002 (N = 1,136)
Paying for confidential information	27	20	17
Using confidential documents without authorization	55	82	78
Claiming to be somebody else	20	22	14
Breaking a pledge of confidentiality	5	5	8
Badgering an unwilling informant to get a story	47	49	52
Using personal documents without permission	28	48	41
Getting a job to gain inside information	67	63	54
Using hidden microphones or cameras	—	60	60
Using re-creations, dramatizations of news	—	28	29
Disclosing the names of rape victims	—	43	36

those whose stock was traded on public exchanges. These companies merged or shed assets to try to satisfy Wall Street money managers.

That was the context in which the first American Journalist panel study was conducted. The intent was to try to track changes over time among a subset of the journalists who had taken part in the 2002 study. Here is a summary of the changes that we found:

Political Views.   The panel journalists became less conservative and more moderate in their political leanings between 2002 and 2007. In 2002, about 40% of the panel journalists said they were either "pretty far to the left" or a "little to the left." That figure had edged up one percentage point by 2007. Another 29% said in 2002 that they considered themselves either "a little to the right" or "pretty far to the right." That figure had declined to 17% by 2007. Over the five years of the study, the percentage of participants characterizing themselves as "middle of the road" rose from 32% to 42%.

Tasks.   The Internet became even more integrated into work routines. The 2007 survey focused on eight of the online tasks about which journalists were asked in 2002. All were done more frequently five years later. Proportionally, the tasks that grew the most among the panel journalists were the use of the Web to check facts (from 50% daily or several times a week to 73%) and the use of e-mail to conduct interviews (from 8% to 21%).

Job Satisfaction and Career Commitment.   As a group, about 89% of the panel journalists were either fairly or very satisfied with their jobs in 2002. By 2007, however, that figure had dropped to 83%, still remarkably high job satisfaction given the uncertainties in their work environment. That figure may understate the journalists' growing disenchantment with their work, however. Over the five years, the job-satisfaction rating increased for about 17% of the panel journalists but declined for about 32%. The rating remained the same for the rest.

Career commitment also began wane. In 2002, about 15% of the panel journalists said they intended to be working outside the media in five years (after eliminating those who intended to retire or were unsure of their plans). By 2007, more than 22% of the panel said that they were planning to abandon journalism as a career.

Professional Autonomy.   Overall, reporters' perceptions about control over their work did not change dramatically between 2002 and 2007. The percentage of reporters who said that they had almost complete freedom to select stories or to decide which aspects of a story to emphasize increased slightly during the five years. But the percentage saying that they could almost always get important subjects covered declined from 55% in 2002 to 51% by 2007.

Additional analyses of the autonomy and influence questions pointed to one important concern: Reporters' autonomy declined at organizations that were under economic stress. These were organizations at which reporters said workloads had increased during the previous year, at which staff size had declined during the previous year, or at which layoffs or buyouts had been implemented in the last 12 months. Given that the end of 2007 marked the start of the deepest economic downturn in the United States since the Great Depression, it's likely that these factors, associated with reduced reporter autonomy and influence, have afflicted even more news organizations since.

Journalistic Roles.   Only modest changes occurred in the panel journalists' attitudes toward the professional roles that have been part of the American Journalist studies. Within the panel, journalists were slightly more likely to endorse the need to analyze and interpret complex problems; to be adversaries of public officials; and to help develop intellectual or cultural interests of the audience. They became more skeptical, however, of the need to analyze and interpret national developments or to discuss national policies. This finding may reflect a growing emphasis in U.S. journalism on producing local news, perhaps at the expense of national and international coverage.

Ethics.   The panel journalists became significantly more cautious between 2002 and 2007. Of the ten controversial reporting practices about which they were asked, the percentage who said they could be justified on occasion dropped for all of them. It declined significantly for paying for confidential information, for using confidential documents without authorization, for badgering unwilling sources to get a story, and for getting a job to gain inside information.

Conclusions

As we enter a second decade in the 21st century, the tasks and professional practices of journalists are being remolded by the economic and technological challenges confronting the U.S. news industries. Those challenges raise these issues for the U.S. journalist and for those who study these news workers:

1. Digital communication technologies allow journalists to more easily create customized content for niche audiences; to engage in two-way communication with the readers, viewers, and listeners; and to fashion stories that integrate text, audio, and moving images into a single "package" of content. For many, this means learning new skills and techniques, and that can be unnerving (Wilson 2008). It means a need for retraining at a time when newsrooms cannot afford to provide it. It means more work to do even as newsroom staffs are being downsized. We would not be surprised if these changes are affecting job satisfaction and career commitment. They also may be encouraging journalists to rethink their professional roles as they move from a situation in which they controlled the creation and distribution of content to one in which they may be sharing those chores with bloggers or so-called citizen journalists—the people "formerly known as the audience," as Rosen calls them (2005).

2. Journalistic functions may be changing. In the last American Journalist survey, the populist-mobilizer function was more important and the disseminator function was less important. Those trends may be likely to continue. The Web is a tool that can be used to create communities of interest. Journalists may become more aggressive in exploiting the Web's capacity to link, and perhaps help mobilize, people with common political, social, or economic interests. Simple dissemination may become less important for some news media, such as daily and weekly newspapers or news magazines. And if the news media become more partisan, the weakly supported adversarial function may grow in importance.

3. U.S. news workers continue to be strongly committed to public-service journalism. But the best public-service journalism—investigative or interpretive reporting—is expensive. The challenging economic environment for U.S. news organizations raises questions about whether they will be able to afford the costly investigative work that they have produced in the past.

4. Finally, it is a challenge for ongoing studies like ours to develop a suitable definition of a journalist. Over the last four decades, the American Journalist studies have defined news work organizationally. By that we mean that we have gathered information about individuals who worked full time creating content for formal organizations—typically commercial organizations—that distributed their work to large, heterogeneous audiences. Today, anyone with Internet access can produce and distribute "news." Some predict that the production of media content increasingly will be handled through temporary employment outside of formal organizational settings (Deuze 2007). Audience members already routinely supply content to news organizations like CNN. And, as commercial news organizations have downsized, universities and other not-for-profit organizations have stepped in to tackle public-affairs reporting. Scholars who study news work in the decade ahead may have to begin by answering a question that has seemed relatively straightforward in the past: Who is a journalist?

Note

1. Because this method resulted in very few people in several categories—news magazines and news services—we systematically oversampled from these groups. Likewise, we oversampled from two other groups: minority journalists (consisting of African Americans, Asian Americans, Hispanics, and Native Americans) and online journalists. Findings from the special samples of minority and online journalists are generally not included in this chapter.

References

Beam, Randal A., David H. Weaver, and Bonnie J. Brownlee. 2009. Changes in professionalism of U.S. journalists in the turbulent twenty-first century. *Journalism & Mass Communication Quarterly,* 86(2):277–298.

Becker, Lee B., Tudor Vlad, Jisu Huh, and Nancy R. Mace. 2003. Gender equity elusive, surveys show. Freedomforum.org, posted December 15. Retrieved from http://www.freedomforum.org/templates/document.asp?documentid=17784.

Deuze, Mark. 2007. *Media work.* Cambridge, UK: Polity.

Hickey, Neil. 2001. Morale matters: low and getting lower. *Columbia Journalism Review,* September/October: 37–39.

Johnstone, John W. C., Edward J. Slawski, and William Bowman. 1976. *The news people: A sociological portrait of American journalists and their work.* Urbana: University of Illinois Press.

Pew Project for Excellence in Journalism. 2010. The state of the news media: Annual report on American journalism: 2009. Retrieved from http://www.stateofthemedia.org/2010/

Rosen, Jay. 2005, March 17. Blogging, journalism and credibility. *The Nation.* Retrieved from http://www.thenation.com/doc/20050404/mackinnon

Weaver, David H., Randal A. Beam, Bonnie J. Brownlee, Paul S. Voakes, and G. Cleveland Wilhoit. 2007. *The American journalist in the 21st Century: U.S. news people at the dawn of a new millennium*. Mahwah, NJ: Erlbaum.

Weaver, David H., and G. Cleveland Wilhoit. 1986. *The American journalist: A portrait of U.S. news people and their work*. Bloomington: Indiana University Press.

Weaver, David H., and G. Cleveland Wilhoit. 1996. *The American journalist in the 1990s: U.S. news people at the end of an era*. Mahwah, NJ: Erlbaum.

Wilson, Kelly. 2008. High anxiety. *American Journalism Review*, February/March: 46–47.

Journalists in South America

28 Brazilian Journalists in the 21st Century

Heloiza Golbspan Herscovitz

Brazilian journalism operates in an ambiguous framework in tune with the country's ambivalence toward democracy. The Brazilian constitution guarantees freedom of expression and a harsh 1967 Press Law was abolished in 2009. Yet, attempts to control the media mushroom far and wide. Since 2009, a major daily newspaper has faced censorship for reporting on a corruption scandal involving well-known politicians. At the same time, the government has worked on a project that combines access to public information with increased state control over the airwaves, a demand for more national content on TV channels, and other mechanisms for "the social control" of the media (Freedom House, 2010).

These simultaneous and contradictory events that permeate Brazil's public sphere have caused further tensions between government and the news media. Former president Lula da Silva frequently complained of Brazil's media monopoly and the media's bias against his government and members of his political party during his eight-year term in office. In response, the news media, which avidly denounced cases of government corruption throughout Lula's two terms, condemned the president's Workers Party for its attempts to manipulate and hide information for almost a decade.

The path toward full democracy in the world's 10th largest economy, fifth largest country in geographical terms, and sixth most populous country is, therefore, an intricate one. Once defined by Austrian journalist and novelist Stefan Zweig (1942) as the "land of the future," for its tremendous potential for future development, Brazil has suffered from structural problems since its occupation by the Portuguese in 1532. Contrary to what happened in the Spanish and English colonies in the Americas, where books and newspapers have been published since the 17th century, the printing press arrived in Brazil with the Portuguese royal family only in 1808. After the country's independence from Portugal in 1822 and the end of the monarchy in 1889, a lively partisan press took root, evolving into a modern mass media system by the mid-20th century. In the process, Brazilian journalism instinctively abandoned a partisan press modeled by lawyers and politicians associated with the colonial aristocracy and replaced it with a professional attitude that supported the newspaper business's independence from government (Candiani 2009; Herscovitz 2000).

The Brazilian economy improved rapidly in the 21st century. Along with Russia, India, and China, the country became one of the largest emerging economies in the world (Kowitt 2009). At the same time, developments in Brazil's national media have been in tune with global trends. Formerly controlled by a group of nine wealthy families (Costa 1991), the Brazilian mass media have expanded into regional conglomerates over past decades, yet are still controlled by a small group of corporations. The growing concentration of media ownership and foreign investment brought significant changes to Brazil's media. In 2008, the Brazilian government approved the merger of Brasil Telecom and Oi, allowing telecommunication groups to hold concessions in more than one region of the country. Oi is now the country's largest telecommunication group controlling about

70% of Brazil's land-line market, 18.5% of the wireless market, and about 40% of broadband Internet services (Reuters 2008).

In 2002, Brazil's media law was revised to allow foreigners to own up to 30% of local television, radio, and print media businesses. Three years later, Portugal Telecom acquired 21% of the shares of Grupo Folha, owner of UOL, Brazil's largest Internet content provider along with *Folha de S. Paulo*, the nation's leading newspaper (Benson 2005). One year later, Naspers, a South African based global corporation, acquired 30% of Abril, Brazil's largest magazine publisher. In 2010, the Portuguese group Ongoing/Ejesa bought the Brazilian media company O Dia, based in Rio de Janeiro. O Dia, owned by the Tavares de Carvalho family, publishes three daily newspapers: *O Dia*, *Meia Hora*, and *Campeao*.

Despite the media concentration, Brazil is a media-rich country. Newspapers may be folding elsewhere, but in Brazil they are stable. The daily circulation of the 10 largest newspapers in 2008 reached 2.2 million, with an average daily individual circulation of 227,690 (National Association of Newspapers [ANJ] 2010a). These are small circulation numbers compared to those in well-developed countries, but for the Brazilian newspaper industry they represent an increase in readership and advertising revenue during the past few years, due partly to the country's rising literacy rate, the expansion of the middle class, and the rising number of college students. Currently, Brazil's national literacy rate is estimated at 87%, although in the poorest areas it reaches only 70% (Brazilian Ministry of Education, 2010). Furthermore, lower income students now have access to higher education, and 13.7% of people between 18 and 24 years old attend college—a victory for Brazilian standards (Anisio Teixeira National Institute of Research in Education [INEP], 2010).

Overall, Brazil has 673 daily newspapers—some of them published three days a week—with an estimated daily circulation of 8.5 million. Most of them are small; few have national recognition except for a couple of publications from Sao Paulo and Rio de Janeiro, Brazil's largest cities, and none has national circulation (ANJ 2010).

Brazil's magazine publishing is dominated by the Abril Group, the largest in Latin America (Donos da Midia 2008). Abril's publications includes *Veja*—considered to be the third largest weekly information magazine in the world—and 90 other titles, including the Brazilian versions of *Cosmopolitan*, *Elle*, and *Playboy*. Moreover, Abril owns a cable TV station and the exclusive rights to the MTV brand across multiple platforms, which include online, mobile, radio, and licensing (Abril 2010).

In a country still fighting illiteracy, broadcasting is by far the leading medium. Forty-one major groups operate hundreds of TV stations in Brazil, most of them private; the government controls several public stations, and many others are in the hands of politicians and religious groups (Donos da Midia 2008). They cater to a large audience—more than 175 million people watch television, 49.2% of them for over three hours a day, according to the Brazilian Institute of Geography and Statistics (Adnews 2010). The Globo network, Brazil's largest media conglomerate, owns 128 radio stations and 122 TV stations, most of them affiliates. Globo's 3,000 journalists produce over 62,000 hours of local journalism programming per year distributed to almost all Brazilian cities. Globo also owns 17 TV cable/satellite stations, several newspapers, and 27 weekly and monthly magazines.

As in most countries, the government controls the airwaves; however, the Brazilian Ministry of Communications routinely awards broadcast licenses to politicians in disproportionate numbers. More than 270 politicians are either owners or directors of 324 media companies, mostly radio and TV stations. Among them are 20 senators, 48 members of the Brazilian House of Representatives, 55 members of states' assemblies, and 147 mayors (Donos da Midia 2008).

In addition, broadcast licenses are frequently given to religious groups. Igreja Universal do Reino de Deus (Universal Church of the Kingdom of God; UCKG), one of the fastest-growing evangelical groups with churches and assets in several countries, owns TV Record, the third largest television network in Brazil. Its controversial leader, the self-appointed Bishop Edir Macedo, has been investigated since the early 1990s for charlatanism, tax evasion, and money laundering (Phillips 2009). Record owns more than 60 TV and radio stations, three newspapers, and an international company that distributes its TV programs in the United States, Canada, Europe, Africa, and Japan (Record 2010).

Brazil has been at the forefront of adopting new information and communication technologies. The country is home to almost one-third of all mobile subscribers in Latin America with a mobile penetration above 91%. Even in the Brazilian *favelas*, the lawless shantytowns located in the hills and on the periphery of major urban areas, citizens carry mobile phones and use Internet cafes. Overall, Brazil has more than 47 million Internet users and Portuguese is among the 10 top Internet languages. Moreover, *Brazil* has the largest number of text message users worldwide, as well as the most members in Orkut, the Google-sponsored social networking site that has captivated Brazilians and Indians (O'Leary 2008). Along with Russia, India, and China, Brazil registered the highest growth in online population in 2011 (Anatel 2009; Brazilian Institute of Public Opinion and Statistics [IBOPE] 2010; BuddeCom 2010; ClickZ 2007; Internet World Statistics 2008).

As Brazilians become more connected and networked, the mass media have expanded into new online formats and managed to stay relevant in the eyes of the public. News organizations were ranked in fifth place in the 2009 Social Confidence Index developed by the Brazilian Institute of Public Opinion and Statistics (IBOPE)—after family members, firefighters, churches, and the army. Public confidence in the media is far higher than confidence in the president, the public school system, banks, business, and the federal government. Overall, labor unions, political parties, and the Congress had the lowest credibility in Brazil (IBOPE 2009). These findings signal profound changes and improvements in the media considering that a 1997 national poll showed that most Brazilians mistrusted journalists and media owners (Antunes 1997).

The growing trust in the media coincided with legal improvements in media freedom. In 2009, the Supreme Court finally suspended 22 of the 77 articles of the 1967 Press Law, which violated constitutional guarantees of free expression and allowed authorities to censor media outlets and writers, to seize publications, and to impose prison terms of up to three years for violations. Nonetheless, defamation laws remain a concern and censorship orders issued by trial courts remain common. In the same year, Brazil ranked 13th on the Committee to Protect Journalists' (CPJ) *Impunity Index*, "a list of 14 countries in which journalists are killed regularly and governments fail to solve the crimes" (CPJ 2009). The country has a longstanding record of violence against the press, in particular against small newspapers and radio stations, which is sponsored by corrupt politicians and other public officials, who also file hundreds of criminal and defamation lawsuits against media outlets and seek disproportionately high damages. However, disregard for press freedom comes from federal courts as well. Since 2009 a federal court in Brasília, the nation's capital, prohibited the prominent daily newspaper *O Estado de S. Paulo* from publishing reports on a corruption scandal over questionable real estate operations involving the family of former President José Sarney, currently a Senate member. In addition, the court ruled that the media outlet would be fined $87,000 for every story published on the case. The ban extended to other news outlets, which were forbidden to reproduce or quote the newspaper's stories. *O Estado de S. Paulo*, one of the most prestigious daily papers in the country, was still under censorship in 2010 (Freedom House, 2010).

Previous Studies

Brazilian journalism as an occupation had not been the object of systematic studies until the 1960s, when the first analyses of Latin American journalists emerged. During that period, several groundbreaking comparative studies and surveys with small samples of journalists tried to define journalists' levels of professionalism (Day 1968; McLeod & Rush 1969; Menanteau-Horta 1967). After conducting a survey with less than 100 journalists working for metropolitan daily newspapers in Argentina, Mexico, and Bolivia, for example, Day (1968) concluded that Latin American journalism was a developing profession in a developing area of the world. Although these early studies had many drawbacks due to logistical difficulties and a lack of strategy to deal with national and cultural differences, they did pioneer the cross-national study of Latin American journalists.

The subject was revived when Donsbach (1981) compared McLeod and Rush's (1969) results on Latin American journalists with those obtained for German and Canadian journalists. However, his findings on how professionals influenced public opinion also were limited by small sample sizes, a lack of specificity about the groups surveyed, and a 12-year time gap between the two studies.

The first study involving Brazilian journalists was conducted a few years later by Ruótulo (1987). He compared dimensions of professionalism among 108 journalists working for elite newspapers in Brazil, Colombia, and Costa Rica, and found that Brazilians fared well in the public service dimension (high regard for objectivity and low desire for prestige) as well as in their vocational commitment to the profession, but were somewhat dependent on sources of information and on publishers to make a final judgment about what does or does not get published.

In the early 1990s, a series of qualitative studies by Brazilian researchers described journalists' professional traits (Travancas 1993) and their ethical dilemmas and routines (Chaparro 1994) with data gathered mostly through participant observation in newsrooms. Moving away from a focus on levels of professionalization and qualitative methods, Brazilian sociologist Adalberto Cardoso and I chose to draw a more comprehensive portrait of journalists by partially replicating Weaver and Wilhoit's (1986) work on American journalists with a mail survey of 355 Brazilian journalists conducted in 1994. Specifically, this study investigated Brazilian journalists' perceptions of media roles, job satisfaction, and ethical standards, among other aspects (Herscovitz & Cardoso 1998). The results indicated an ambiguous profile of journalists that reflected the contradictions of Brazilian society. By then, journalists lacked a clear idea of the role of the media in Brazil's emerging democracy and seemed to perceive the press as free from responsibility for the country's enduring social and political crisis. As much as they saw themselves as interpreters and investigators, journalists were not generally concerned with avoiding stories with unverified content.

In 1998, I conducted another survey with 402 journalists working for five daily newspapers, two weekly news magazines, four major magazines, three TV stations, and two news agencies of Sao Paulo, Brazil's main media hub (Herscovitz 2000). Results indicated that the typical Brazilian journalist then was a 38-year-old, white, middle-class, Catholic married male, politically left-leaning, underpaid but generally satisfied with the job, and with 15 years of professional experience. Women tended to be younger (34 years old) and had less professional experience (11 years).

A similar trend was identified in a follow-up study (Herscovitz 2004). Brazilians, who held a pluralistic view of media roles and perceived themselves as disseminators and interpreters of information, had a high tolerance for controversial journalistic practices and most of them ignored the journalism code of ethics. Thus, in the late 1990s, Brazilians were more concerned with discussing how the democratization process and the new technologies would affect their profession in the years to come. A special concern seemed to focus on how many jobs would be eliminated by computers and new information technologies.

More information enlightened the field with the study of the feminization of Brazilian journalism and its implications for professionalism (Rocha 2004). Since the 1990s, women have outnumbered men at journalism schools and filled newsrooms of magazines and TV stations. Nevertheless, journalism in Brazil is still a male-dominated profession, especially at newspapers and radio stations. Top positions at most newsrooms are occupied by men, whereas women tend to stay longer at less prestigious posts (Rocha 2004).

Method

Data for this study come from an online survey conducted among 506 Brazilian journalists in 2009. Journalists were defined as full-time or part-time newsroom personnel working for print, broadcast, or online news organizations. A journalist was considered a professional who held a journalism degree and a professional license registered at the Ministry of Labor as required by Brazilian law since 1969. While the Supreme Court overturned these requirements in 2009, the Brazilian Congress discussed the restoration of both the degree requirement and the professional licensing in early 2010 due to pressures from labor unions and journalism schools. Both unions and journalism schools continue to lobby for the restitution of the diploma and licensing in 2012. Therefore, this study upheld the definition since most people hired by news organizations had a professional license when this study was conducted.

Developing a traditional sampling procedure proved strenuous in such a large country (the world's fifth in territory with a population of 192.3 million). Moreover, Brazil's population is characterized by huge geographic disparities. More than half of the Brazilian population (57%) lives in the southeastern and the southern regions of the country, near the Atlantic coast, where most of the media are concentrated. The most populated cities are Sao Paulo, with 11 million, and Rio de Janeiro, with 6 million people. In the northeastern, northwestern (the Amazon area), and central western portions of Brazil, the number of media outlets is considerably smaller.

As in many other nations, it is impossible to establish the exact number of journalists working in Brazil due to lack of appropriate lists or other statistics. In addition, about 12,000 new journalists graduate every year in Brazil only to find that there are not enough jobs in the market. Since it was not possible to draw a traditional probability sample, I used a multistage sampling procedure instead, which started with a compilation of lists of organizations and their journalists provided by the National Association of Newspapers, the National Association of Television and Radio Stations, the National Association of Magazine Editors, the Brazilian Association of Investigative Journalism (Abraji), and the National Federation of Brazilian Journalists (Fenaj), along with private and public staff directories of news organizations. From this compiled list, I randomly selected 48 newspapers mostly from state capitals and large cities, 62 magazines with national and regional circulation, eight TV/radio networks, 25 Internet news portals and news agencies—altogether 143 organizations in 26 states.

Next, I contacted editors, coordinators, newsroom directors, or their assistants by e-mail and phone asking them to confirm the names of their staff members. In many cases, there were lists of current journalists available online. In other cases, representatives of news organizations e-mailed me their lists of working journalists. Corrections were made to update the final list and avoid duplications, eliminating news organizations that had folded or journalists who changed jobs.

While more Brazilian journalists have become familiar with surveys, the typical journalist in Brazil tends to distrust professional assessments. Consequently, many journalists refused to participate in this study because they did not know the researcher "in person" or were not sure how the data would be used. Local union leaders declined to distribute the survey among journalists because they would not be able to "control" the questions or the study's results. Additionally, many respondents wrote me about their frustration in answering multiple-choice questions and urged the researcher to conduct personal interviews instead. The majority, though, praised the initiative and recognized that Brazilian journalists know little about what the majority thinks of the profession.

In the end, I compiled a list of 1,576 journalists who fulfilled the study's conditions and definitions in the summer of 2009. Of those, 1,386 journalists had working e-mail accounts. All journalists with working e-mail accounts received an online questionnaire together with a letter asking for their participation in the survey. A total of 506 journalists completed the questionnaire, which represents a response rate of 36.5%. Overall, 54.7% of the respondents were male and 45.2% were female, which somewhat mirrors the gender distribution of Brazil's working population in metropolitan regions (53% male and 47% female; Dieese 2009).

Findings

Basic Characteristics, Education, and Training

Results of this survey can best be understood when placed in context. In 2009, about 30,000 journalists were registered with the Brazilian Ministry of Labor, by then a requirement for every journalist working in the field. While it is impossible to trace the growth of journalism in Brazil due to a lack of reliable statistics, it is clear that the profession has expanded greatly during the past decades. In the early 1950s, there were half a dozen journalism schools in four states: Sao Paulo, Rio de Janeiro, Bahia, and Rio Grande do Sul (Machado 2009). Five decades later, the number of schools has jumped to 433, according to the 2005 Higher Education Census. Of the 433 schools, 74 are housed in public universities and 369 in private universities (Moreira & Helal 2009).

Yet only a handful of these journalism schools enjoy a good reputation and credibility. For this reason, large news organizations located in Rio de Janeiro and Sao Paulo, the country's main media hubs, have established their own journalism short-training programs offered to young professionals who graduate from journalism schools all over the country. Entrance in these programs is highly competitive. While the best ones trained in those programs are usually hired, many of them don't last long in newsrooms troubled by frequent staff layoffs and high turnovers.

The data suggest that the typical Brazilian journalist is 39.8 years old, white (56.7%), married (46.1%), male (54.7%), with two children and with an average of 15.2 years of professional experience. Male journalists tend to be older (42 years) and have an average of 17.5 years of professional experience, while female journalists are younger (35.8 years) and have 13 years of professional experience. Self-employed journalists tend to be older (45 years) and have more years of experience (about 20 years), while journalists who work for online companies tend to be younger (37 years) and have fewer years of experience (about 13.4 years). Reporters tend to be the youngest in all newsrooms (30 years), while editors and special reporters are usually much older (43 years). Newsroom directors and columnists are also among the oldest in the field (45 and 53 years, respectively).

The majority of the Brazilian journalists hold a bachelor's degree in the field (required by law until mid-2009), but claim to have little time to pursue further formal education. About a third

Table 28.1 Demographic Profile of Journalists by Media Sector (in %)

	Dailies (N = 250)	Online (N = 68)	TV (N = 73)	Mag (N = 50)	Self[1] (N = 40)	Other[2] (N = 25)	Overall (N = 506)
Age (years)*	38.5	37.0	43.0	37.5	45.0	37.9	39.8
Experience (years)*	15.6	13.4	20.0	17.5	20.0	14.5	15.2
Males	54.8	60.2	46.6	46.0	65.0	64.0	54.7
Females	45.2	39.7	53.4	54.0	35.0	36.0	45.2
European descent	57.8	59.3	58.6	65.0	62.5	37.5	56.7
Mixed descent	33.2	33.3	36.2	32.5	31.3	50.0	36.0
African Brazilians	3.0	1.9	3.4	2.5	6.3	12.5	4.9
Left leaning	44.4	40.7	48.3	37.5	54.8	41.6	44.5
Center leaning	34.2	44.4	37.9	40.0	32.3	43.7	38.7
Right leaning	4.1	5.6	5.2	7.5	3.2	8.3	5.6
Graduate degree	30.2	27.8	22.4	22.5	34.4	31.2	28.2
Workshops, short courses	83.7	77.4	81.0	79.5	83.9	89.6	82.5
Fluency in English	80.0	72.2	79.3	82.5	59.4	58.3	71.8
Fluency in Spanish	49.2	42.6	44.8	45.0	53.1	43.7	46.4

1 Self indicates self-employed
2 Other indicates radio and news agencies
* Means

of the journalists hold a master's degree in related fields, while 13.3% of the women and 5.8% of the men were taking classes toward a graduate degree when they answered the survey. Almost 20% of the respondents said that they started a graduate program but dropped it later on. Yet, the majority indicated they frequently participate in workshops and courses of short duration (82.5%), and have found time to learn a second language (71.8% are fluent in English and 46.4% are fluent in Spanish).

Politically, Brazilian journalists position themselves as left (44.5%) and center-left leaning (38.7%), but currently do not subscribe to any political party (90.4%). Being politically positioned to the left of the center is a long-established tradition among Brazilian journalists, as previous studies have revealed (Herscovitz 2004; Herscovitz & Cardoso 1998). Brazil's historical lack of democracy, high levels of censorship, institutional corruption, and social disparities are some of the reasons that have kept journalists politically engaged throughout the 200 years of the Brazilian press. Nonetheless, party affiliation has dwindled.

Brazil has 27 political parties, but only 19 are represented in Congress and only two attract the interest of Brazilian journalists—the left wing Worker's Party and the center-left Brazilian Social Democratic Party (PSDB). A survey of journalists from major cities such as Sao Paulo, Rio de Janeiro, and Brasilia indicated that a third of the sample supported the leftist Workers' Party in 1994 (Herscovitz & Cardoso 1998). Another survey conducted with journalists in Sao Paulo in 1998 found that less than 20% supported the Worker's Party (Herscovitz 2000). In 2009, the majority did not support a political party (90.4%); only 6.1% of the respondents identified themselves as supporters of the Workers' Party, and 3.5% identified both with the PSDB and the Green Party.

Journalists have distanced themselves from professional organizations as well. The majority (80.5%) does not belong to professional organizations, which compares with 55% in 1994

(Herscovitz & Cardoso 1998). However, 38% are affiliated with the National Federation of Journalists.

Overall, 49% of the respondents work for daily newspapers. Another 14.4% work for television, 13.4% work for online publications, 9.8% for magazines, 7.9% were self-employed, 2.9% work for news agencies, and 1.9% for radio stations.

In fact, very few radio stations in Brazil actually employ journalists. Around the country, small radio stations in particular broadcast national newscasts distributed by communication conglomerates, leaving local news for commentators who may or may not be journalists. Interestingly, 7.9% of the respondents said they work independently. They own their own business alone or in small pools with other professionals who sell their work to different media.

Among survey respondents, about 27% of the respondents were reporters; 15.9% were editors; 6.2% were columnists; 6% were executive editors; and 5.6% were assistant editors, totaling 76.4% of the respondents. Other job titles for the remaining 23.6% were grouped in the category "other," which included foreign correspondents, managing editors, editorialists, anchors, or newscast producers. The majority (80%) worked full time, and 43.4% produced content for more than one medium owned by the company they worked for.

An equivalent number of male and female journalists worked as editors (28.3% and 28.4%, respectively), but more reporters were women (one-third of the sample as opposed to one-fourth of the sample in the case of males). In contrast, more men (8.6% vs. 2.1%) held positions as special reporters (generally, in charge of investigative journalism beats), columnists (9.3% vs. 2.9%), and newsroom directors (5.1% vs. 2.1%). The editors and foreign correspondents who answered the survey were all males. When broken down by media sector, the data show that more women than men worked for television and magazines, while more men worked for daily newspapers, online publications, and radio stations. In contrast, more men were self-employed or freelancers. Table 28.2 shows differences in the demographic profiles of male and female journalists. More women than men tend to be single, with mixed ethnicity, politically left-leaning, and Catholic.

Table 28.2   Demographic Profile of Male and Female Journalists (in %)

	Males (N = 277)	Females (N = 229)	Overall (N = 506)
Age (years)*	42.0	35.8	39.0
Professional experience(years)*	17.5	13.0	15.2
Married	54.5	37.1	46.1
Single	25.7	39.2	32.2
Political orientation (left)	42.5	47.0	44.5
Political orientation (center)	39.4	32.6	38.7
With graduate degree	30.4	31.3	30.8
European descent	59.1	54.6	56.9
Mixed descent	33.1	39.2	36.0
African Brazilians	3.5	2.9	3.2
Catholics	35.7	43.4	39.4
No religion	46.0	33.2	39.8
Parenthood	47.5	32.5	40.2
Union member	42.0	33.8	38.0

*Means

Table 28.3   Job Satisfaction by Media Sector (in %)

	Dailies (N = 250)	Online (N = 68)	TV (N = 73)	Mag. (N = 50)	Self[1] (N = 40)	Other[2] (N = 25)	Overall (N = 506)
Very satisfied	17.7	14.8	34.5	17.5	12.5	31.2	21.3
Fairly satisfied	43.4	59.3	37.9	55.0	31.3	39.6	44.4
Somewhat dissatisfied	27.8	20.4	17.2	12.5	28.1	18.7	20.7
Very dissatisfied	11.1	5.6	10.3	15.0	28.1	10.4	13.4

1 Self: indicates self-employed
2 Other indicates radio and news agencies

Working Conditions and Internet Use

Overall, 44.4% of the Brazilian journalists are "fairly satisfied" with their jobs but only 21.3% are "very satisfied." The group with the highest percentage of job satisfaction is television journalists (34.5%), while the least satisfied are self-employed journalists (28.1% said they were "very dissatisfied"). While male and female journalists share similar levels of job satisfaction, more men (24.6%) were very satisfied with their jobs than women (17.9%).

An open-ended question asked respondents which factors were responsible for their satisfaction or dissatisfaction with their jobs. Comments underscored journalists' passion for their profession: "I love what I do in spite of the problems" summarizes the thoughts of hundreds of respondents. But a content analysis of the 506 answers suggested a more complex pattern. The findings indicate that journalists' levels of job satisfaction mostly relate to low wages, a lack of recognition for their work, career advancements (many say they are stuck in their careers; others are happy to move up), concerns about the elimination of the diploma requirement,[1] lack of autonomy, long working hours, pressures in the work environment, lack of job security, benefits, editorial policies interfering with content, blogging—considered highly gratifying—the use of new technologies, and the requirement to develop multimedia skills (which scares the older journalists).

A large portion of the survey investigated the use and influences of new communication technologies. I was particularly interested in finding out how journalists perceive the Internet's impact on their work. The majority of the respondents acknowledge that the Internet has increased the speed in news delivery (98.1%), audience feedback (92.1%), news diversity (78.8%), and access to sources (65.1%). Conversely, the majority of the journalists feel that the Internet has lowered

Table 28.4   Influences of New Communication Technologies (in %, N = 506)

In your opinion, the Internet has increased…	Yes	No	Don't know
Speed in news delivery	98.1	1.7	0.2
Audience's feedback	92.1	5.6	2.3
Amount of opinion in the news	79.0	18.3	2.6
News diversity	78.8	17.3	4.0
Access to sources	65.1	29.0	5.9
Journalism accuracy	37.0	54.3	8.7
News analysis	33.2	62.8	4.1
Amount of investigative journalism	22.0	71.5	6.6
Journalism social responsibility	18.3	74.0	7.7
Journalism credibility	16.7	75.1	8.2
Journalism precision	16.3	76.0	7.6

journalism's level of precision (76%), credibility (75.1%) and social responsibility (74%). And most also think that the Internet has decreased the amount of investigative journalism (71.5%), news analysis (62.8%), and journalistic accuracy (54.3%). In addition, 79% of the respondents said that the Internet has increased the amount of opinion in the news.

A content analysis of 200 comments to the open-ended question on other perceived consequences of new technologies revealed a host of positive and negative factors that draw journalists' attention. On the positive side, journalists say that new technologies have opened a new path for independent journalism and the democratization of the news, including news segmentation and the ability to correct information quickly. Furthermore, journalists observed that new technologies have promoted a fierce competition among news organizations that operate online along with an intense revival of hot, swift scoops. On the negative side, journalists mentioned an excessive focus on entertainment news, the prevalence of news stories based on press releases as opposed to the "reality of the streets," and a surplus of snippets and short news stories that lack quality and depth. These elements, according to some professionals, seem designed to feed an audience with a short attention span. "Too much cut and paste is going on" was a common complaint.

In their daily use of Internet resources, Brazilian journalists focus on two main activities: reading other media (88.9%) and dealing with press releases (72.2%). About two-thirds of the respondents search for information online (64.2%), check names and addresses (65.4%), and look for online sources (66.2%). A little over half the sample search for story ideas (54.4%), but smaller percentages get audience feedback (47.2%), watch Web casts or online videos (20.7%), use spreadsheets (6.4%), or conduct interviews by e-mail (9.5%). Surprisingly, the latter is not a popular activity among Brazilian journalists. About 21% have never conducted an interview by e-mail, but most of them acknowledge that they have replaced face-to-face contacts with sources with phone conversations.

Although journalists do not make full use of Internet resources that could facilitate their work, Brazilian professionals show a growing interest in using social media and other new media applications. Half of the sample enjoys blogging (53.4%) and over two-thirds use Instant Messenger (63.8%) and social network Web sites (64.7%) such as Facebook or Orkut. Twitter is popular among Brazilian journalists as well—47.2% indicated that they use this application.

Table 28.5   Daily Use of Internet/Computer Resources (in %, N = 506)

	Dailies (N = 250)	Online (N = 68)	TV (N = 73)	Mag. (N = 50)	Self[1] (N = 40)	Other[2] (N = 25)	Overall (N = 506)
Read other media	86.3	88.9	89.7	87.5	87.5	93.7	88.9
Read press releases online	75.8	79.6	77.2	62.5	46.9	91.7	72.2
Search for information	63.6	69.8	77.6	60.0	56.3	58.3	64.2
Check names and addresses	63.3	70.4	63.8	47.5	75.0	72.9	65.4
Check online sources	57.1	77.8	68.4	45.0	65.6	83.3	66.2
Search for story ideas	51.3	62.3	62.1	42.5	50.0	58.3	54.4
Get audience feedback	41.9	64.2	34.5	37.5	65.6	39.6	47.2
Watch Webcasts, online videos	13.7	34.0	22.4	12.5	18.8	22.9	20.7
Use Excel spreadsheets	11.2	13.2	5.4	2.5	6.5	0.0	6.4
Conduct interviews by e-mail	6.6	13.2	10.3	5.0	21.9	0.0	9.5

1 Self indicates self-employed
2 Other indicates radio and news agencies

Table 28.6 Things Journalists Do Online by Media Sector (in %, *N* = 506)

	Dailies (N = 250)	Online (N = 68)	TV (N = 73)	Mag. (N = 50)	Self[1] (N = 40)	Other[2] (N = 25)	Overall (N = 506)
Messenger	71.4	81.5	43.1	77.5	53.1	56.2	63.8
Orkut, Facebook	61.7	68.5	62.1	72.5	65.6	58.3	64.7
Blogging	46.9	72.2	50.0	47.5	62.5	41.7	53.4
Twitter	38.3	59.3	53.4	52.5	40.6	39.6	47.2
Discussion lists	31.6	44.4	19.0	30.0	59.4	33.3	36.2
Chat rooms	15.3	22.2	25.9	17.5	34.4	25.0	23.3
LinkedIn	14.3	22.2	13.8	22.5	31.3	22.9	21.1
None	11.7	3.7	15.5	7.5	3.1	6.2	7.9

1 Self indicates self-employed
2 Other indicates radio and news agencies

Blogging is regularly used, mostly by online journalists (72.2%) followed by self-employed journalists (62.5%). Over half of the respondents agree that blogs offer information unavailable elsewhere (56.8%) and influence traditional media (55.1%). Less than half of the sample believes that blogs offer more analysis or that they generate better scoops than traditional media. And a little over one-third of the sample believes that blogs uncover traditional media's flaws or redefine the news.

As blogging becomes more popular in Brazil, over a third of the journalists (36%) in the sample have been encouraged by their news organizations to create their own blogs. While newspaper journalists (60.4%) were especially likely to have been asked to do so, journalists working for television (50.9%), radio, and news agencies (59%) said their employers did not particularly encourage them to create blogs.

Table 28.7 Perceptions of Blogs Produced by Journalists (% saying "believe so," *N* = 506)

Perceptions of Blogs	Percent
Offer information unavailable in traditional media	56.8
Influence traditional media	55.1
Offer more analysis than traditional media	49.7
Generate better scoops than traditional media	45.1
Uncover traditional media's flaws	36.8
Redefine what is news	35.7
Do none of these options	8.5

Table 28.8 Does Company Encourage Journalists to Blog? (in %)

	Dailies (N = 250)	Online (N = 68)	TV (N = 73)	Mag. (N = 50)	Self[1] (N = 40)	Other[2] (N = 25)	Overall (N = 506)
Yes	60.4	50.0	19.3	38.5	15.6	32.0	35.9
No	23.4	22.2	50.9	35.9	25.0	59.0	36.0
Don't know	7.6	5.6	7.0	10.3	0.0	0.0	4.3
Don't apply	8.6	22.2	22.8	15.4	59.4	9.0	22.9

1 Self indicates self-employed
2 Other indicates radio and news agencies

Professionalism, Media Roles, and Ethics

Brazilian journalists continued to embrace the interpretive and investigative media roles in 2009 as they did in the past (Herscovitz 2004; Herscovitz & Cardoso 1998). The 2009 study asked Brazilian journalists to rate the importance of 15 media roles, which can be compared to findings obtained in 1998 and 1994 (see Table 28.9). Overall, investigating government claims (79%) and providing analyses of complex national problems (72%) were the main roles mentioned by Brazilian journalists. Discussing national, regional, or local politics was the third most important role (63.4%). These results indicate that Brazilian journalists place a significant weight on proximity as a key news value, which mirrors findings of another study showing that most stories published by Brazilian major news portals focus on national and regional topics (Herscovitz 2009).

Two media roles became less important to Brazilian journalists over time—getting information to the public quickly and concentrating on the widest audience. While the speedy transmission of information to the public was considered extremely important by 70% in 1994 and 63.7% in 1998, only 38% of the journalists believed this role to be very important in 2009. Similarly, those who considered the role of reaching the widest audience possible shrank from 30% in 1994 to 22% in 1998 and, finally, to only 17.6% in 2009.

Coincidentally, these are two aspects of the Brazilian news media that have changed radically since the inception of the Internet in 1995, when a few daily newspapers put out their first online versions (Barbosa 2002). Since then, getting information to the public quickly has become effortless due to the Internet, and therefore a nonissue for most journalists. In addition, the media have become more segmented and niche-oriented, which may have affected the perceived importance of the concept of reaching the widest audience.

Table 28.9   Perceived Importance of Media Roles (% saying "extremely important")

	2009 (N = 506)	1998[a] (N = 402)	1994[b] (N = 355)
Investigate government claims	79.0	65.7	79.0
Provide analysis of complex national problems	72.2	59.7	67.0
Discuss national/regional/local politics	63.4	—	—
Provide analysis of complex international problems	54.8	59.7*	67.0*
Motivate citizens to discuss topics of public interest	51.4	—	—
Develop audience's intellectual/cultural interests	45.4	46.5	52.0
Suggest solutions to social problems	44.6	—	—
Avoid stories with unverified content	41.7	33.3	26.0
Get information to public quickly	38.0	63.7	70.0
Give citizens the chance to express themselves	37.6	—	—
Set the national/regional/local political agenda	28.4	—	—
Provide entertainment	19.9	16.2	30.0
Concentrate on widest audience	17.6	21.6	30.0
Serve as an adversary of government	14.6	22.4	55.0
Serve as an adversary of business	12.6	—	53.0

a Data compiled by Herscovitz
b Data compiled by Herscovitz and Cardoso
* The original questionnaires in 1998 and 1994 said "provide analysis of complex problems." In the 2009 survey, the question was split into national and international complex problems to test a trend toward hyper-localism.

Perceptions of other journalistic roles have changed as well. Serving as an adversary of government (14.6%) or of business (12.6%) seemed less important to journalists in 2009 than in previous years, especially in the early 1990s after the first free presidential elections in 1989 and the immediate launch of a major wave of media exposés of government corruption. In fact, in their open-ended comments, several journalists emphasized that today there is no adversarial role in the media, but a critical or skeptical role instead. The frequent censorship orders issued by the courts and the thousands of lawsuits filed by public officials and business people against journalists and media outlets (Committee to Protect Journalists 2010) may have impacted the diminishing adversarial role. At the same time, the consolidation of the Brazilian democratic process, initiated in 1985 after 21 years of military rule, and the professionalization of Brazilian journalists, now more integrated into a global culture of journalistic practices, may have contributed to a less belligerent stance on how to report on government and business.

During the first years of the democratization process, Brazilian journalists have reacted aggressively to the countless political scandals that have shaken the nation, including the impeachment of president Fernando Collor de Mello for his participation in a corruption ring in 1992 known as *Collorgate*, and the *Mensalao* (neologism for "big monthly payment") scandal, which almost brought down the government of President Lula da Silva in 2005, when an investigation found that that his key advisers made monthly payments to Congressional deputies to vote for legislation favored by the ruling Worker's Party.

Since then the adversarial role has taken a back seat, although politics and corruption remain entangled in Brazil. Journalists continue to denounce new scandals, but possibly under somewhat different terms as indicated by the findings. Avoiding stories with unverified content, for example, has gained more support (41.7%) among journalists compared to past studies (33.3% in 1998 and 26% in 1994). The eagerness to investigate government claims without caring to verify the content has declined due to complex and interrelated factors mentioned above. Fearing lawsuits and censorship, news organizations have avoided denouncing cases of corruption without proof and, sometimes even with enough proof. The most dramatic case was registered by mid-2009, when a federal district court prohibited the prominent daily newspaper *O Estado de S. Paulo* from publishing reports on a corruption scandal involving the family of former President José Sarney, currently a senator. The ban extended to other news outlets, which could not reproduce or quote the original reporting newspaper's stories. The newspaper was under censorship until the end of 2010 (SIP-IAPA 2009; Reporters without Borders 2010).

Findings indicate that press freedom is still a major issue in the country. About one-third of the journalists believe that there is press freedom in Brazil and almost 40% say that journalists practice self-censorship. Moreover, only 9% of the journalists surveyed believe that Brazilian news organizations follow ethical norms; 12% say that Brazilian journalism acts responsibly; and only 7% believe that news organizations are independent (all percentages are based on "strongly agree" responses).

Conclusions

Brazilian journalists have mixed feelings about the future of their craft, but, in general, are fairly satisfied with their jobs. Their uncertainty parallels similar feelings faced by journalists in other countries. They hope that the Internet does not wipe out the print media and that there are still jobs out there for those who write and report well. Furthermore, Brazilians cope with several internal dilemmas. The elimination of the college diploma in journalism as a requirement to enter

Table 28.10   Current Situation of Journalism (% saying "strongly agree")

	Dailies (N = 250)	Online (N = 68)	TV (N = 73)	Mag. (N = 50)	Self (N = 40)	Other (N = 25)	Overall (N = 506)
It follows ethical norms	9.6	5.6	15.5	2.5	12.5	8.3	9.0
There is press freedom	31.3	29.6	28.1	30.0	31.3	18.7	33.3
There is self-censorship	32.5	48.1	36.8	27.5	46.9	35.4	37.8
It is responsible	13.8	7.4	13.8	7.5	18.8	10.4	12.0
It is independent	7.1	5.6	10.3	5.0	6.5	8.3	7.1
It is sensationalist	0.2	14.8	22.8	17.5	25.0	20.8	18.1
It is superficial	15.4	16.7	20.7	22.5	40.6	12.5	21.4

the profession remains a major source of tension for journalists. Supported by media companies, the new ruling, which allows any person to be hired as a journalist, is criticized by unions, journalism schools, and professionals. Fifty-five percent of the respondents favor the diploma requirement. These professionals believe that salaries will shrink and journalism standards will drop if anybody can be hired as a journalist. Most of those who are against the diploma requirement (45%), though, believe that media companies will prefer to hire people who have a college degree in journalism.

Yet, the new ruling opening the entrance to journalism has already affected journalism schools in 2009 and 2010. More than 15 public schools lost applicants to their journalism programs in 2009. At the University of Sao Paulo, the most prestigious Brazilian university, journalism dropped from fourth to seventh place among the most popular courses in 2010, and at Universidade Federal de Santa Catarina, in southern Brazil, the prominent journalism school plunged from third in 2009 to tenth place in 2010 enrollment (Bonfim 2010; Porto 2009; Record 2009).

Other problems in the legal sphere supersede the diploma issue. Press laws and censorship have silenced journalists throughout Brazil's history. Although Brazilians enjoy more press freedom than ever, professionals and media companies as well as the government and civil organizations share distinct perspectives on how the media should operate next. One example was the controversial National Communication Conference, sponsored by the federal government in December of 2009, and organized by left-wing groups. The conference proposed, among many other things, the creation of a national communication council to oversee journalism activities, a new press law, the prohibition of media monopolies, the elimination of broadcast licenses to politicians, a reduction of foreign capital in national media companies from 30% to 10%, and limitations on advertising sponsorship in broadcasting. To nobody's surprise, the event was criticized by most media representatives such as the National Association of Newspapers, National Association of Editors, and the Brazilian Association of Radio and TV Stations.

There have also been fairly critical perceptions of how journalists and news organizations operate in Brazil. Brazilians are candid about the prevalence of self-censorship in newsrooms, and only a small fraction strongly agrees that news organizations follow ethical guidelines, are independent, and exercise the craft responsibly.

Ideological differences reinforce the notion of a profound divide between professionals and their companies, and may help explain why only 21.3% of the respondents are very satisfied with their jobs. In spite of disagreements between employers and employees, Brazilian journalists try to stay true to their ideals. The majority believes the most important media roles are investigating government claims, providing analysis of complex national problems, and discussing national, regional or local politics. Few support the adversarial role and, compared to past studies, more journalists are willing to avoid unverified content, which signals a path toward maturity after the first years of democratization, when overplayed exposés decreased the public's trust in the media.

Finally, the way Brazilian journalists deal with new technologies and how they perceive the transition to online mass media reveal a number of characteristics that help to delineate the complex frame of mind of the Brazilian professional. Journalists celebrate how the Internet has improved speed, feedback, and diversity, but believe that it has done little to increase accuracy, precision, and credibility so far. Professionals from many news organizations regret having to share computer stations with colleagues and complain about outdated software. Only a few journalists use e-mail for interviews or databases to produce investigative journalism, and most feel that they produce more information with less quality.

Brazilian journalists' state of mind is as complex as their craft. They are intense, have too many opinions, and would love to own the news organizations they work for. Asked why they became journalists, 403 respondents gave similar answers, some humorous, some nostalgic, from "I was stupid" and "Unfortunately, I love to write" to "I wanted to change the world and still do." Essentially, they pride themselves on being creative in tough circumstances, which is what journalism is all about in this transitional moment in Brazil.

Note

1. The elimination of the diploma requirement was the main reason why Brazil's journalists had mixed feelings about the future of the profession. The journalism diploma requirement has been a focal point regarding working conditions in Brazil. Journalists have passionately discussed the contentious decision by the Supreme Court in mid-2009 that declared unconstitutional the requirement for a university-level diploma as a condition to practice journalism. Since the ruling in June 2009, four proposals for a constitutional amendment (three in the House of Deputies and one in the Senate) have tried to reintroduce the requirement of a diploma (SIP-IAPA 2009). While practitioners fear that the end of the degree requirement may create legal uncertainty in a country with little tradition in protecting press freedom and respecting human rights, representatives of media companies argue that the new ruling is consistent with international standards of professional practice such as those of the United States. This survey included one question about the diploma. Results indicate that 55% of the respondents favor the diploma requirement, while 45% are against it, and a small percentage doesn't know. The diploma requirement is approved by the largest percentage of journalists who work for daily newspapers (55%). Likewise, more than half of those who are self-employed (53%) and the majority of those who work for other media (91.6%) favor the diploma. In contrast, about half the journalists working for television stations (51.7%) and magazines (55%) disapproved of the diploma requirement, whereas online journalists were somewhat split about the ruling: 48.1% disapproved and 44.4% approved it.

References

Adnews. 2010. *Brasileiros assistem mais de 3h de TV por dia* [Brazilians watch over three hours of television a day]. Retrieved from http://www.adnews.com.br/midia/101411.html.

Abril. 2010. Retrieved from http://www.grupoabril.com.br/estrutura/estrutura-10.shtm.

Anatel (National Agency of Telecommunications). 2009. Retrieved from http://www.anatel.gov.br/Portal/exibirPortalInternet.do#

ANJ (National Association of Newspapers). 2010a. *Data on journalistic industry.* Retrieved from http://www.anj.org.br/a-industria-jornalistica/jornais-no-brasil

ANJ (National Association of Newspapers). 2010b. *Jornais brasileiros vencem 28 categorias no prêmio Best of Newspaper Design* [Brazilian newspapers win 28 awards for Best Newspaper Design]. Retrieved from http://www.anj.org.br/sala-de-imprensa/jornais-brasileiros-vencem-28-categorias-do-best-of-newspaper-design.

Antunes, Americo. 1997. *Jornal do Jornalista* [The journalist's paper]. National Federation of Journalists. Retrieved from www.fenaj.org.br

Barbosa, Suzana. 2002. *Dos sites noticiosos aos portais locais* [News portals and local portals]. Paper presented at the 24th Congresso Brasileiro de Ciências da Comunicação- Intercom, Campo Grande, MS, Brazil, Retrieved from http://www.bocc.ubi.pt/pag/barbosa-suzana-jornalismo-online.pdf

Benson, Todd. 2005. Brazilian media group to reorganize with eye on stock sale. *New York Times*, January 5. Retrieved from http://www.nytimes.com/2005/01/05/business/media/05paper.html

Bonfim, Elias. 2010. *Medicina da UFSC tem 59,81 candidatos por vaga; veja concorrência do vestibular 2010* [Competition for college entrance in 2010]. Retrieved from http://www.formacaosolidaria.org.br/blog/vestibulares/medicina-da-ufsc-tem-5981-candidatos-por-vaga-veja-concorrencia-do-vestibular-2010

BuddeCom Telecommunications Research. 2010. *Brazil—mobile market—overview, statistics & forecasts*. Retrieved from http://www.budde.com.au/Research/Brazil-Mobile-Market-Overview-Statistics-Forecasts.html

Candiani, Herci R. 2009. Journalists and intellectuals in the origins of the Brazilian press (1808–1822). *Journalism* 10(1):29–44.

Chaparro, Manuel. 1994. *Pragmatica do jornalismo, buscas praticas para uma teoria da açao jornalistica.* [Journalism praxis, searching for a journalistic action theory.] Sao Paulo: Summus.

Clark, Andrew. 2009. Brazilian newspapers celebrate a rise in circulation: Print media booms in South America's biggest economy. *The Guardian,* October 12. Retrieved from http://www.guardian.co.uk/media/2009/oct/12/brazil-newspapers-circulation

ClickZ. 2007. Brazil, Russia, India and China to lead Internet growth through 2011. Retrieved from http://www.clickz.com/3626274

Committee to Protect Journalists. 2009. *Getting away with murder 2009.* Retrieved from http://www.cpj.org/reports/2009/03/getting-away-with-murder-2009.php

Costa, Caio T. 1991. *O relogio de Pascal, a experiencia do primeiro ombudsman da imprensa brasileira* [Pascal's clock, the experience of the first Brazilian ombudsman]. Sao Paulo: Siciliano.

Day, J. Lawrence. 1968. The Latin American journalist: A tentative profile. *Journalism Quarterly* 45:509–515.

Dieese, Inter-Union Department of Statistics and Socio-Economic Studies. 2009. Retrieved from http://turandot.dieese.org.br/icv/TabelaPed?tabela=2

Diniz, Laura. 2009. *O modelo é o Granma de Fidel* [Fidel's *Granma* is the model]. Veja.com. December 23. Retrieved from http://veja.abril.com.br/231209/modelo-granma-fidel-p142.shtml

Donsbach, Wolfgang. 1981. Legitimacy through competence rather than value judgments: The concept of journalistic professionalization reconsidered. *Gazette* 28:47–67.

Donos da Midia Database. 2008. Retrieved from http://donosdamidia.com.br/Estadao.

Freedom House. 2010. Retrieved from http://www.freedomhouse.org/template.cfm?page=251&year=2010

Grupo Abril. 2010. *Institutional profile.* Retrieved from http://www.grupoabril.com.br/IN/institucional/perfil-in.shtml

Herscovitz, Heloiza G. 2000. *Journalism as an occupation in Brazil: What journalists working for leading news organizations in Sao Paulo think about their profession compared to American and French journalists.* Doctoral dissertation, College of Journalism and Communications, University of Florida, Gainesville, Florida.

Herscovitz, Heloiza G. 2004. Brazilian journalists' perceptions of media roles, ethics and foreign influences on Brazilian journalism. *Journalism Studies* 5(1):71–86.

Herscovitz, Heloiza G. 2009. Brazilian news portals characteristics. *Brazilian Journalism Research* 5(1):99–122. Retrieved from http://vsites.unb.br/ojsdpp/viewarticle.php?id=219&locale=en

Herscovitz, Heloiza G., and Adalberto Cardoso. 1998. The Brazilian journalist. In *The global journalist*, edited by David H. Weaver, pp. 417–432. Cresskill, NJ: Hampton Press.

IBOPE (Brazilian Institute of Public Opinion and Statistics). 2009. November 26. Retrieved from http://www.ibope.com.br/calandraWeb/servlet/CalandraRedirect?temp=6&proj=PortalIBOPE&pub=T&db=caldb&comp=pesquisa_leitura&docid=A518AE36007849548325767A004C951B

Instituto Nacional de Estudos e Pesquisas Educacionais Anísio Teixeira (INEP). 2010. Report on Higher Education. Retrieved Oct. 10, 2010, from http://portal.inep.gov.br/indicadores-educacionais

Internet World Statistics. 2008. Retrieved from http://www.internetworldstats.com

Kowitt, Beth. 2009. For Mr. BRIC, nations meeting a milestone. *CNN/Fortune.* Retrieved from http://money.cnn.com/2009/06/17/news/economy/goldman_sachs_jim_oneill_interview.fortune/index.htm

Machado, Elias. 2009. Uma decisão histórica sobre o diploma [Historical decision about the diploma] *Observatorio da Imprensa,* March 31 Retrieved from http://www.observatoriodaimprensa.com.br/artigos.asp?cod=531DAC001

McLeod, Jack, and Ramona Rush. 1969. Professionalization of Latin American and U.S. journalists. *Journalism Quarterly* 46:583–590.

Menanteau-Horta, Dario. 1967. Professionalism of journalists in Santiago de Chile. *Journalism Quarterly* 44:715–724.

Moreira, Sonia Virgínia, and Carla Rodrigues Helal. 2009. Notes on media, journalism education and news organizations in Brazil. *Journalism* 10(1):91–107.

O'Leary, Noreen. 2008. The rise of Bric, How Brazil, Russia, India and China are reshaping the marketing world. *AdWeek,* February 1. Retrieved from http://www.adweek.com/aw/content_display/special-reports/other-reports/e3ibd2a4d5f94f9578bb5e64247c12ae3b1?pn=1

Phillips, Tom. 2009. Brazilian evangelical leader charged with fraud. *The Guardian,* August 13. Retrieved from http://www.guardian.co.uk/world/2009/aug/13/brazil-evangelical-leader-charged-fraud.

Porto, Joao. 2009. *Cai a procura por cursos de jornalismo nas universidades federais* [Interest for journalism courses drops at federal universities]. Retrieved from http://manualdosfocas.com/2009/12/cai-a-procura-por-cursos-de-jornalismo-nas-universidades-federais

Record News Portal. 2009. *Fuvest 2010: confira as mudanças na relação candidato/vaga.R7 Noticias,* May 10 [University Foundation 2010: Check changes on number of candidates per spot]. Retrieved from http://noticias.r7.com/vestibular-e-concursos/noticias/fuvest-2010-confira-as-mudancas-na-relacao-candidato/vaga-20091005.html

Record Network. 2010. Retrieved from http://rederecord.r7.com/

Reporters without Borders. 2010. *O Estado de São Paulo* approaching 200th day of ban restricting press freedom. February 10. Retrieved from http://www.rsf.org/O-Estado-de-Sao-Paulo-approaching.html

Reuters. 2008. Oi buys 947 mln reais in Brasil Telecom shares. July 22. Retrieved from http://www.reuters.com/article/idUSN2231560320080722

Rocha, Paula M. 2004. *As Mulheres Jornalistas no Estado de São Paulo: O Processo de Profissionalização e Feminização da Carreira* [Female journalists in Sao Paulo state: Professionalization and career feminization]. Doctoral dissertation, Centro de Educação e Ciências Humanas, Universidade Federal de São Carlos, Sao Carlos, Sao Paulo, Brazil. Retrieved from http://www.bocc.uff.br/pag/rocha-paula-melani-mulheres-jornalistas.pdf

Ruotulo, A. Carlos. 1987. Professional orientation among journalists in three Latin American countries. *Gazette* 40:131–142.

SIP-IAPA. 2009. IAPA condemns prior censorship of Brazilian news media. *Inter American Press Association,* August 3. Retrieved from http://www.sipiapa.com/v4/index.php?page=cont_comunicados&seccion=detalles&id=4232&idioma=us

Terra News Portal. 2009. *UFSC divulga concorrência do vestibular 2009* [Universidade Federal de Santa Catarina announces college entrance numbers for 2009]. Retrieved from http://noticias.terra.com.br/vestibular/interna/0,,OI3288991-EI8849,00-UFSC+divulga+concorrencia+do+vestibular.html

Travancas, Isabel. 1993. *O mundo dos jornalistas* [The journalists' world]. São Paulo: Summus.

Weaver, David H. 1998. *The global journalist: News people around the world.* Cresskill, NJ: Hampton Press.

Weaver, David H., and G. Cleveland Wilhoit. 1986. *The American journalist: A portrait of U.S. news people and their work.* Bloomington: Indiana University Press.

Weaver, David H., and Cleveland G. Wilhoit. 1996. *The American journalist in the 1990s: U.S. news people at the end of an era.* Mahwah, NJ: Erlbaum.

Zweig, Stefan 1942. *Brazil, a land of the future.* London: Cassell.

29   The Chilean Journalist

Claudia Mellado

Chilean journalists have developed their profession within a typically Western media system, where freedom of speech is guaranteed by the Constitution, and most of the media are privately owned. Unlike more developed nations, however, the media market in Chile is still somewhat small because of the economy of scale in which the media industry operates, the conservative advertising market, and the small size of the audiences.

One of the most pronounced characteristics of the country is its high level of centralization. With almost 17 million people, Chile is divided into 15 regions. Santiago, the capital, is located in the Metropolitana region and holds more than 40% of the nation's population. All of the media with national coverage are located in the capital, as well as the government and the corporate offices of the majority of national and international companies operating within the country.

The Chilean media system includes 58 daily newspapers (seven with national circulation), 10 weekly or biweekly newspapers, 1,985 radio stations, five national television networks, two cable news channels, and more than 80 regional and local television stations. There are also eight news magazines, a national newswire, and several international news services with branches in the country. However, the daily media agenda is mostly dominated by three television channels (TVN, Canal 13, and Chilevisión), two newspapers (*El Mercurio de Santiago* and *La Tercera*), and two radio networks (Radio Cooperativa and Radio Bío-Bío).

Paradoxically, the significant economic development that Chile has experienced in the last decades has generated less media diversity, which is reflected in the shrinking number of owners in each media sector. In fact, Chile registers the highest concentration rates in media ownership in Latin America (Becerra & Mastrini 2009; Mönckeberg 2009).

In the case of the press, the country faces a duopoly structure made up of the El Mercurio company, owned by the Edwards family, and Copesa (Consorcio Periodístico de Chile), belonging to the Chilean businessman Álvaro Saieh, both strongly linked to the country's political right. These companies manage almost 95% of the national newspaper circulation and receive 65% of the revenue generated by advertising in print media (ACHAP 2008).

The El Mercurio group controls different public corporations, making it the largest press conglomerate in Chile. It owns two national dailies, *El Mercurio de Santiago* and *Las Últimas Noticias*, an evening metropolitan newspaper, *La Segunda*, and at least 20 regional and local newspapers throughout the country. Copesa publishes the national dailies *La Tercera* and *La Cuarta*, a free morning metropolitan edition, *La Hora*, and the news magazine *Qué Pasa*.

Television is a mix of public and private undertakings. The national television networks include the public TV station Televisión Nacional de Chile (TVN); Canal 13, that used to belong to the Catholic Church, today is in the hands of the Luksic group, one of the most powerful families in the country; Megavisión is a private channel owned by the Claro group and the Mexican consortium Televisa; Chilevisión was previously owned by the right-wing businessman and Chilean President, Sebastián Piñera, and is now owned by Time Warner; and La Red, which is owned by the Mexican businessman, Ángel González. TVN and Canal 13, the country's oldest television networks, also have cable channels, as well as regional branches in almost the entire nation.

Radio is the most numerous media outlet, with 1,426 FM stations, 175 AM stations, 378 community stations, and six short wave stations. However, fewer than 10% of them have editorial and newsroom offices with journalists who dedicate themselves to news. Once considered a model of diversity and ownership dispersion, radio is now dominated by a small number of consortiums, such as the Spanish Prisa group and the Grupo Dial, which belongs to Copesa. Among the national networks, the Cooperativa and Radio Bío-Bío networks stand out, owning 48 and 51 radio stations, respectively. The Bío-Bío group also controls a regional television channel, and is associated with CNN Chile, a cable news TV station.

Almost all of the newspapers, TV channels, and radio stations have online versions, but there is only one exclusively digital newspaper, *El Mostrador,* and just three or four stable professional online news Web sites. The rise of new communication technologies and the various economic crises in Chile have led to a decrease in newspaper circulation and advertising revenue, generating massive layoffs and a relocation of the journalistic functions. Today, Chile's journalists face multifunctional roles and must perform many different tasks for the same pay. As advertising has become the main revenue source of the Chilean media, audience ratings and the subsequent sensationalism have become more important.

Background

Chile has experienced rapid economic growth and gradual political reform after the fall of military dictatorship in 1989. Today, the country is one of the most stable democracies in Latin America and has the region's best performing economy. Political parties, grouped into two dominant blocks—the Concertación, on the center-left side, and the Coalición por el Cambio (the former Alianza por Chile) representing the right side—have managed to coexist peacefully since the return to democracy.

During the past 20 years, the press had to readjust to a democratic system, slowly recovering its freedom and losing the fear it had under military repression. In structural terms, the media have also undergone important changes. While there has been a considerable increase in the number of media outlets, programming and competition for audience has grown as well.

Thus, despite the fact that Chile has a free press (Freedom House 2009), media concentration and a strong political parallelism have limited levels of information pluralism and put the media under constant pressure (Dermota 2002; Otano & Sunkel 2003). Of course, Chile does well when compared with other countries in Latin America. Chile has no problems with direct violations of freedom of speech such as those observed in Mexico, Colombia, and to some extent, Brazil. That is to say, no Chilean journalists have been beaten, murdered, or disappeared during the last 20 years.

However, from a legal point of view, there are many areas left unresolved. The current Ley de Prensa (press law), approved on June 4, 2001, is still far from guaranteeing media freedom. Although the law repealed a good part of the dictatorship's repressive legal apparatus that limited the practice of journalism in Chile, potential punishments for slander and defamation, as well as sanctions for secret recording of images or sound, are still part of the legal system.

Previous Studies

Despite the important role that the media have played in the country's political, economic, and social development, empirical studies of Chilean journalists are quite limited. A large part of the existing research is concerned with the labor market for journalists (Délano, Niklander, & Susacasa 2007; Gutiérrez & Lavín 2003; Mellado, Barría, Enríquez, & Besoain 2006; Mellado, Salinas, & Barría 2010) or journalism education (González 2003). However, some studies of sociodemographic profiles and professional roles and attitudes have been conducted since the 1960s. The majority of these studies have not been published in English-language journals or books, which has resulted in a limited awareness of Chilean journalism research beyond Latin America.

The first known study of Chilean journalists was carried out by Menanteau in 1967. He analyzed journalists' professionalization with a sample of 235 news people working in traditional media and public relations offices in Chile's capital, Santiago. His work is, coincidently, the first study of journalists done in Latin America. It was found that the journalists' objective occupational roles, as well as their own perceptions regarding their performance, came close to an evident professionalization. The results indicated that most of the journalists (78%) showed a favorable attitude toward the existence of journalism university programs, participated "always or very frequently" in professional organizations (69%), and would choose journalism as a profession again if they had the opportunity to do so (62%). Likewise, the majority of the journalists recognized that their motivation for entering journalism was because they had an authentic vocation. However, 6 out of 10 journalists said they would not encourage their children to enter journalism; rather, they would persuade them to study for another career.

During Pinochet's regime (1973–1989), only two empirical studies were carried out that focused on the professionalization of journalism. First, Planet (1981) surveyed 69 journalists from Santiago with the objective of describing their educational profile. He found that the majority of those who had senior positions in journalism had studied at a university, and had worked with an important nucleus of older journalists who were their teachers. In 1988, Arriagada and Saavedra (1990) studied 91 media organizations in the south of Chile. They surveyed 145 journalists from the press, radio, and television about different aspects of their jobs. Their study not only revealed that there was an acute shortage of journalists in each media outlet (on average, just 3.2 journalists at each), but also that many journalists worked both in the media and in public relations, thus undermining editorial independence and professional ethics. Unsurprisingly, the study also showed that the journalists surveyed generally believed that they had low levels of professional autonomy and independence.

In 1991–1992, Wilke (1998) carried out a comparative analysis of journalists from Chile, Ecuador, and Mexico. In the Chilean case, Wilke surveyed 116 journalists, and found that most were men (60%), under 40 years old (66%), and had studied at a university level (90%). They categorized journalism as their main occupation (83%), expressed high levels of editorial freedom (93% saying "always" or "nearly always"), although they had little professional experience in the media (38% had worked for only one to three years as a journalist). In terms of their conception of their journalistic role, Wilke's data describe Chilean journalists as neutral reporters and public entertainers, who are, however, in favor of criticizing abuses. Regarding the assessment of various methods of gaining information, the results indicated that Chilean journalists tend to approve certain controversial reporting practices, such as using secret state papers, pretending to have a particular opinion to arouse confidence in an interviewee, and putting an informant under pressure, while they reject broken promises of professional secrecy, the unexamined acceptance of information, and the publication of private documents without consent.

Gronemeyer (2002) analyzed Chilean journalists' autonomy and independence based on a mail survey that included 574 full-time and part-time news media workers. The study found that both groups gave very little importance to values such as obedience and neutrality, and great importance to such characteristics as veracity, critical thought, and independence within the practice of journalism. At the same time, the study revealed important differences between the levels of autonomy perceived by Chilean journalists and those perceived by editors, publishers, and executives, the latter being those who felt a greater degree of freedom in their work.

A few years later, Mellado and Parra (2008) conducted a survey with a stratified random sample of Chilean news people ($N = 240$) who had journalism degrees and worked in southern Chile. The objective of that study was very limited, as it only planned to profile demographic, labor, and educational aspects at a regional level. According to the results, the typical regional journalist was male or female, under 40 years old, Catholic, and from the political center left. They had no graduate studies, earned between $400 and $1,000 per month, and worked nine hours per day.

The latest study of the Chilean journalist was conducted in the context of the "Worlds of Journalism" project, a collaborative effort of journalism researchers from 18 countries. The study is based on face-to-face interviews with a nonprobabilistic quota sample of 100 journalists per country from 20 print media, radio, and television organizations with national and local coverage. In the case of Chile, the data showed that journalists give more support to the professional values of detachment and noninvolvement and to the functions linked to the watchdog journalism role. The findings also point to a relatively strong acceptance of the functions related to both the citizen-oriented approach, and the consumer-oriented approach of journalism (Hanitzsch et al. 2011; Mellado, Moreira et al. 2012).

Method

The profile of Chilean journalists reported in this chapter comes from a census ($N = 1,979$) and from an online survey of Chilean news media people ($N = 570$) in the most important cities of four regions in the country: Antofagasta, Bíobio, Araucanía, and Metropolitana. These four regions represent the north, center, and south of Chile, as well as 70% of the nation's population.

The objective of the census was to describe Chilean journalists' sociodemographic and employment characteristics, while the goal of the survey was to measure the journalists' perceptions regarding their working conditions, their professional orientations, and the influences on news work. The census and the survey were part of the national research project "Comparative Study of Chilean Journalists, Communication Professionals and Journalism Educators," financed by the Chilean National Fund for Scientific & Technological Development (Fondecyt).

Following Weaver and Wilhoit's (1986: 168) classic definition, a journalist was considered someone who has "editorial responsibility for the preparation or transmission of news stories or other information ... rather than those who created fiction, drama, art, or other media content." Because the objective of this research was to analyze the different types of news media journalists in the country, people working for "hard news," as well as "soft news" beats, such as sports and entertainment, were included. Unlike Weaver and Wilhoit, the studied population included not only full-time, but also part-time journalists who worked for any daily and weekly newspapers, news magazines, radio stations, television channels, newswires, and professional online media.

Journalists surveyed included reporters, news writers, commentators, columnists, copy editors, editors, publishers, news anchors, and producers of news. Photographers and cameramen were excluded, as were graphic designers, librarians, and audio technicians because they do not usually have direct responsibility for news content.

The data collection procedure was completed in two sequential stages. Since there was no official register that allowed an estimation of the total number of journalists, communication professionals, and journalism educators in Chile, we carried out a census of the four studied regions. For the purpose of this chapter, only the data from news media journalists will be reported.

Based on 10 official Chilean media registries,[2] we first built a list of the total number of existing media outlets in Chile. The personnel and human resource departments of all organizations were then contacted by e-mail, telephone, or in person. They were asked for the name, telephone number, and e-mail address of all of their part-time and full-time journalists. Each media outlet was contacted up to three times, requesting their collaboration, and assuring them of the confidentiality of the data.

After obtaining that information, each journalist was contacted via telephone and via e-mail, asking for their consent to answer questions about demographic background (age, sex, education), and employment situation (work day, contract type, number of jobs, and main job). Overall, information was obtained for 89% of the journalists who worked in the capital, and for 95% of the journalists from the other three regions. The remaining news workers participated in the census, but did not answer all of the questions. The census, which resulted in 1,979 identified journalists, was carried out between August 2008 and April 2009.

The second data collection strategy was a 47-question online survey given to all the journalists who were identified in the census. The questions were drawn from other journalist surveys conducted by Weaver and Wilhoit (1986, 1996; Weaver, Beam, Brownlee, Voakes, & Wilhoit 2007), Hanitzsch et al. (2007–2008), and Ramaprasad and Kelly (2003). However, due to cultural and social characteristics specific to Chile, some questions were eliminated, others were added, and still others were reworded, in order to explore important local issues.

The questionnaire had 10 sections: (1) job characteristics and journalistic routines, (2) professional orientations and job satisfaction, (3) professional roles, (4) epistemology and ethical standards, (5) professional autonomy, (6) influences on journalism, (7) membership in professional organizations, (8) education and training, (9) status of the profession and relationship with other communication professional cultures, and (10) demographics. Here, only a portion of the data will be described.

The survey was carried out during a five-week period in the Chilean spring of 2009. The research team e-mailed the journalists an invitation to participate in the study. Four days later, the link to the survey was sent to their e-mail address, instructing them to respond to the questionnaire at their convenience. The questionnaire asked subjects who had more than one job to only consider their most important workplace. The researchers waited two weeks for responses before sending a first follow-up e-mail to remind those who had not completed the questionnaire. During the three following weeks, a second, a third, and a fourth follow-up e-mail were sent to increase the response rate. Overall, a total of 570 usable questionnaires were completed, yielding a response rate of 29%.

With the objective of controlling nonresponse error, each sociodemographic, geographical, and work related variable—sex, age, level of education, region, media type, and full-time/part-time contract—was checked against the results of the census. According to the analysis, respondents and nonrespondents were quite homogeneous, with no significant differences among the groups in terms of gender ($\chi^2 = .22$, $p > .05$), education level ($\chi^2 = 6.81$; $p > .05$), media type ($\chi^2 = .99$; $p>.05$), or full-time/part-time positions ($\chi^2 = .75$; $p > .05$). The age variable presented significant differences between the sample and the population, but only in the 31 to 35 age group, which appeared to be overrepresented in the sample (Kolmogorov-Smirnov Test = .11; $p < .01$). Another important difference was observed in the sample's geographic distribution ($\chi^2 = 15.5$; $p < .001$). Although the representation of journalists from Santiago was almost perfect, journalists from the Bíobio and Araucania regions were overrepresented, while journalists from the Antofagasta Region were underrepresented. For the present analysis, the totals of these three regions were combined since no significant differences were observed between them.

In the next sections, we use the census data to present a general profile of the Chilean journalist population in terms of workforce size, geographical distribution, gender, age, education levels, employment contracts, type of work, and professional membership affiliation, while confining the survey to a description of their political attitudes, income, job satisfaction, journalistic role conceptions, ethical standards, and perceived influences on journalism.

Findings

Basic Characteristics of Chilean Journalists

According to the census, 1,979 Chilean journalists work in 186 news media organizations in the most important cities of the four regions studied. Given that the distribution of journalists throughout the country is similar to those in the four analyzed regions, with the exception of the capital, we estimate that there are a total of about 3,141 journalists working in Chile. More than half of all Chilean journalists work for the news media, both print and electronic (52.6%, including newspapers, news magazines, newswires, and professional news Web sites), while 27.4% work for television and 20% for radio. Due to the country's political and economic centralization, most Chilean journalists work in the capital, where 75.5% of the news workers have a job in different types of media (see Table 29.1).

Gender. The majority of Chilean journalists are men. However, women have obtained more jobs within the media in the last few years, and today they represent 39% of the total workforce. This number is similar to that reported by Wilke (1998) and Gronemeyer (2002) a decade earlier (40% and 37%, respectively), and it is much higher than the percentage found by Menanteau in 1967 (7%).

Table 29.1   News Media and Journalistic Workforce in Chile (in %)

Type of Medium	Geographic Distribution		N
	Capital	*Other regions*	
Radio stations	52.5	47.5	395
Network TV	82.3	17.7	480
Cable TV	87.3	12.7	63
Print newspapers	77.9	22.1	832
Internet	78.0	22.0	50
News magazines	93.2	6.8	88
Newswires	98.6	1.4	71

Table 29.2   Gender of Journalists by News Medium and Age of Journalists (in %)

	Male	Female	N
Medium			
Radio	70.9	29.1	395
Network TV	56.0	44.0	480
Cable TV	65.1	34.9	63
Print newspapers	60.2	39.8	832
News magazines	44.3	55.7	88
Newswires	67.6	32.4	71
Internet	58.0	42.0	50
Age			
23–29	18.0	31.2	458
30–40	59.0	58.5	1,164
41–50	12.9	7.8	216
50–64	8.4	2.1	117
65 or more	1.7	0.4	24

Men outnumber women in all media, with the exception of news magazines. At the same time, gender differences increase outside of the capital, where only 30.6% of journalists are women. Overall, the percentage of female journalists is slightly higher than the percentage of women in the general workforce (37.9%), according to the National Statistics Institute (2009) (see Table 29.2).

Age.   Chilean journalists tend to be young and, as a group, are getting younger. In the last four decades, the average age of Chilean journalists has decreased from 40 years at the end of the 1960s (Menanteau 1967) to 35.6 years in this study. According to our census, 78.5% of the journalists are under 40, and only 7.1% are over 50.

Female journalists are younger than their male counterparts. Our findings show that very few women over the age of 50 years still work for the Chilean media. The age difference and the strong predominance of men in the largest age groups can be explained by two factors. First, a significant number of women only began enrolling in journalism schools at the beginning of the 1990s. Second, according to Chilean law, women can retire when they turn 60, five years earlier than men.

According to our data, journalists who work for online newspapers and news Web sites are the youngest (mean age = 32 years). The average age for this group of journalists is two years lower than the overall population of journalists—94% of all online journalists are under 40 years old. Meanwhile, journalists who work in radio are the oldest (mean age = 36.5 years).

Political Attitudes.   The survey asked journalists to identify their political preference on a 7-point scale, where 1 represents the political "left" and 7 the political "right." They were also asked to place themselves on a similar scale in terms of their personal values and ideology, where 1 represented a "liberal" position and 7 a "conservative" position.

The findings suggest that most Chilean journalists consider themselves to be on the left side of the political spectrum with a fairly liberal ideological position. Almost 57% of the respondents position themselves closer to the left, and only 19.7% report sympathizing with the right, while about a quarter (23.7%) said they were politically neutral. This compares to 52% of the population that voted for the political right in the 2010 presidential election.

Table 29.3 Education Levels of Journalists by Medium (in %)

	Written Media (N = 1,041)	TV (N = 543)	Radio (N = 395)	% of total population (N = 1,979)
No university studies (N = 74)	0.6	0.6	2.5	3.7
Incomplete higher education (N = 76)	0.9	0.6	2.3	3.8
Complete higher education (N = 1705)	46.6	24.9	14.7	86.2
Master's degree (N = 120)	4.3	1.3	0.5	6.1
Doctoral degree (N = 4)	0.2	—	—	0.2
Total	52.6	27.4	20.0	100.0

In terms of ideological values, 70.5% of Chilean journalists expressed a more liberal stance and only 14% associated themselves with a conservative position. Surprisingly, important differences were not observed within rank levels, media sector, gender, or age of the journalist. However, journalists working in the capital considered themselves to be more "left" and held more liberal values than their counterparts in the rest of the nation.

Education and Training. In the mid-1960s, Menanteau (1967) reported that 50% of practicing journalists had attended universities. Nevertheless, very few of them had journalism degrees. It was at the beginning of the 1980s when journalism schools started to flourish in Chile, and journalists began to be educated at a professional level. In the 1990s, Wilke (1998) found that 80% of Chilean journalists had some sort of professional degree and 70% had a degree in journalism. Later, Gronemeyer (2002) reported that 77% of journalists had some type of study linked to journalism.

Although there is currently no law in Chile that restricts the practice to journalists with a degree in journalism, most Chilean journalists have at least an undergraduate degree. The census data show that 92.5% of news workers have at least a bachelor's degree, and 86.2% have studied journalism, but only 6.1% of all journalists hold a master's degree (see Table 29.3).

Working Conditions

Employment and Income. About 80% of Chilean journalists are full-time employees. About 60% of them possess long-term position contracts, 24% have fixed-term contracts, while the rest work without any formal contract. Remarkably, approximately 35% of the journalists also have between two and four other jobs, especially in areas associated with corporate communication and journalism education.

Another important observation is the fact that Chilean journalists' average income is very low. According to our survey findings, salaries vary between US$1,000 and US$2,000 per month. About 31.5% of the journalists earn less than $1,000, 16.3% between $2,000 and $3,000, and only 13% make over $3,000. The journalists with the highest salaries tend to be those who work in the capital, are men older than 40 years, have high level positions, work in either TV or newspapers, and have a graduate degree.

Type of Work. Chilean journalists can be classified by their managerial responsibilities. The census data show that 70.8% are nonmanagement staff, 20.4% are junior managers (department head, desk head, or senior editors), and 8.8% are senior managers (publishers, editors-in-chief, general managers, or executive producers). Among the first group, 56.1% are reporters or news writers, 6.8% are television or radio news producers, 5.6% are news anchors or news program hosts on radio stations, and 2.3% are commentators or columnists. Higher rank positions are dominated by men (72%), while journalists in junior and senior management positions are mostly between 35 and 55 years old.

The survey asked journalists for the percentage of time spent on different everyday activities. According to the results, they spend most of their time (45%) on news production (writing, producing, or editing) followed by reporting and gathering information (35%), and laying out news and editorial coordination (20%). However, a majority of journalists (61.2%) do not have a specific beat and report about different types of news instead.

Job Autonomy.   The survey included four items related to the journalists' perceived job autonomy on a five-point scale, ranging from "always" to "never." Almost 66% of the surveyed journalists claim that when they have a good idea for a subject, which they think is important to follow-up, they are always or almost always able to get the subject covered. Likewise, 65.3% perceive they have quite or a lot of freedom to select the stories on which they will work, and 67.5% perceive they have quite or a lot of freedom to decide which aspect of a story should be emphasized. However, only 42% indicate that their work is not edited by others. In order to estimate overall perceptions of job autonomy, the four items were then converted to a professional autonomy index (Chronbach's alpha = .74). The findings show that 62.3% of the journalists acknowledge a high level of freedom in making news decisions, while 27% report medium levels and 10.6% perceive low levels of autonomy.

Not surprisingly, journalists without managerial responsibilities perceive lower levels of autonomy than their superiors. The same situation is observed among women, journalists in the capital, those who have higher levels of education, and those who associate themselves with the political left.

Job Satisfaction.   Respondents were asked about their general satisfaction with their current job. Overall, more than half of Chilean journalists (51.1%) feel "fairly" or "very" satisfied, 34.2% are "somewhat" satisfied, and 14.7% are "unsatisfied" with their job. To get more specific answers, the survey asked respondents to rate 16 objective and subjective job aspects twice, once for importance and once for satisfaction, both on five-point scales (see Table 29.5). Even though all items were scored "high" or "very high" in perceived importance, satisfaction scores were much lower. Two of the three items scored as the most important are included in this group, and are the worst evaluated. While 56.5% believe that salary is an extremely important aspect of their job, only 2.8% of the respondents are very satisfied with their monthly income. This is to be expected, considering the low salaries of journalists in Chile. Results are similar regarding reconciliation of work with family. While 68.1% evaluate this aspect as extremely important, only 10.2% say that they are very satisfied. The long and demanding workdays that news workers tend to have, often without a well-defined schedule, could explain this figure.

To evaluate possible relationships between the relative importance and the relative satisfaction of the journalists, Pearson's correlation coefficients were calculated for the 16 item pairs. As Table 29.4 shows (see last column), there is no clear association between both aspects, since only 10 item pairs correlated significantly but none of them was particularly strong. This means that the journalists' job satisfaction has very little to do with the importance that they give to

Table 29.4   Perceived Importance of and Satisfaction with Different Job Aspects

Factors	Mean (How Important) [a]	Mean (How satisfied) [b]	Pearson's r
Working conditions			
Pay	4.50	2.96	-.17**
Fringe benefits	4.18	3.18	-.03
Job security	4.31	3.35	.01
Having a prestigious job	3.76	3.64	.23**
Conciliation of work/family life	4.60	2.96	-.05
Autonomy and professional development			
Editorial Policy	4.17	3.57	.16**
Autonomy	4.40	3.60	.09*
Developing a speciality	4.07	3.49	.06
Chance to advance	4.29	3.00	-.08
Influence on society			
Using all abilities and knowledge	4.41	3.67	.11**
Helping people	4.22	3.63	.22**
Influencing public affairs	3.98	3.54	.25**
Having a valuable job	4.13	3.68	.22**
Work environment			
Supervisors who appreciate abilities	4.31	3.42	-.02
Co-workers who make the job easy	4.32	3.73	.14**
Staff support	4.26	3.73	.13**

* $p < .05$; ** $p < .001$
a   Scale ranges from 1 = not really important to 5 = very important.
b   Scale ranges from 1 = totally unsatisfied to 5 = very satisfied.

certain attributes within their jobs. It must be closely related to other unknown factors, perhaps circumstantial, from their individual or collective reality.

Predictive Model of Job Satisfaction.   Using a total of 13 independent variables, including basic structural characteristics of journalists' news media, objective and subjective job attributes, as well as the journalists' personal characteristics, we ran a multiple regression predicting job satisfaction.

The multiple-regression analysis shown in Table 29.6 explains 46.8% of the variance, yet only six of the variables have significant effects. While the work environment characteristics were influential, neither the structural characteristics of the media nor the journalist's personal characteristics were significant. The fact that seven of 13 independent variables were not significant suggested the need to look for a more parsimonious model that only retained the significant variables. The reduced model explained 47.0% of the variance in job satisfaction. It presents a similar structure to the full model, with some differences in the regression coefficients' values which did not alter the order of importance of the predicting variables.

As Table 29.5 shows, the most important predictor of job satisfaction is satisfaction with pay. As expected, journalists who feel most satisfied with what they earn are more likely to be satisfied with their job compared to those who are less satisfied. This is particularly interesting given the fact that actual salary is controlled for in the equation and also is significant. As a matter of fact,

Table 29.5   Predictors of Chilean Journalists' Job Satisfaction

Predictors	Zero-Order Correlations	Full Model	Reduced Model
	Pearson's r	*Standardized Regression Coefficients*	*Standardized Regression Coefficients*
Personal Characteristics			
Gender (female)	—	.04	
Age	.11 *	.00	
Organizational Characteristics			
Region (capital)	—	.03	
Television[a]	—	.00	
Print Media[a]	—	.01	
Objective and Subjective Job Attributes			
Media experience	.12 *	-.08	
Income	.31 *	.14**	.11**
Management staff (yes)	—	.01	
Satisfaction with pay	.52 *	.34 **	.35**
Reconciliation of work and family life	.38 *	.19 **	.18**
Use all of their abilities and knowledge	.45 *	.27**	.27**
Level of perceived autonomy	.29*	.12 **	.11**
Belief journalists are respected professionals	.21 *	.13 **	.13**
Covers a beat (yes)	—	-.05	—
Adjusted R^2		.47	.47

* $p < .01$; ** $p < .001$, for two-tailed tests
a Dummy variables with radio chosen as the excluded group

the standardized regression coefficients indicate that the effect of the subjective evaluation of salary is much greater than the journalist's actual income.

The second and third most powerful predictors are the possibility of the journalists using all of their abilities and knowledge, and the reconciliation of their work and family lives. Controlling for the other factors, journalists who feel they are putting everything they know into practice, and those who consider that their family life is not negatively affected by their work routine, tend to be more satisfied. Other significant predictors are the level of perceived autonomy and the belief that journalists are respected professionals. Those who feel freer to make news decisions, as well as those who believe that journalists are respected professionals, are usually happier with their jobs. Interestingly, the journalists' job hierarchy level does not predict job satisfaction.

Professionalism

Membership in Professional Organizations.   Membership in journalism organizations is an important factor to be considered, especially in Latin America, where such organizations promoted the establishment of journalism schools in order to professionalize the trade.

The survey shows that only 13.5% of journalists belong to the Colegio de Periodistas de Chile, Chile's official journalist association, and only 14.5% say they are members of other professional journalism organizations. This might be explained by the fact that more than half of the members say they are dissatisfied with the association's effort to create a positive image of the profession and to improve journalists' working conditions.

Journalistic Role Conceptions.   Following previous studies, we asked the Chilean journalists to judge the importance of 28 functions that the news media should perform. The questions employed a five-point scale, ranging from "not important" to "extremely important."

According to our findings, Chilean journalists have a rather pluralist conception of media roles. Although none of the items were rated as extremely important by more than 45% of the journalists, the functions that showed greatest acceptance were related to the civic role of the press and the individual needs of the public.

As Table 29.6 shows, Chilean journalists believe that the most important media roles are to "provide the audience with the information that is most interesting," "provide citizens with the information they need to make political decisions," "develop the cultural and intellectual interests of the public," and "promote democracy." At the same time, journalists were found to be strongly supportive of "educate people about controversial and complex topics," "influence public opinion," and "act as a watchdog" of the government, political parties, and the business elite.

In contrast, "convey a positive image" of the economic and political leaders and "highlight the benefits of the current economic model" are rated as the least important media roles for Chilean journalists. Likewise, the classic professional values of detachment and noninvolvement were not rated as very important, unlike Wilke's (1998) results, and the Chilean data in the Worlds of Journalism project (2010).

Based on the results of a Principal Component Analysis (PCA), Chilean journalists' beliefs about various media roles can be grouped into five different dimensions.[3] The *watchdog role* is the main dimension, explaining 15% of the variance. Just as in Weaver's studies (Weaver & Wilhoit 1986, 1996; Weaver et al. 2007), this factor is related to journalists' monitoring function, serving as the fourth estate, with an ongoing surveillance of the government, as well as the political and economic powers. However, a new element was added: citizen vigilance.

The items that loaded in the second dimension can be called the *supportive or propagandist function*. This dealt with the positive image that the media can provide for the country's leaders, by defending the economic and social advances, as well as supporting the public policies that contribute to national development. In the Chilean context, this type of role conception also tries to develop national patriotism, emphasizing the country's triumphs over the rest of Latin America.

The *citizen-oriented journalism function* is the third dimension. This approach considers the public as a citizen rather than a consumer, and focuses on providing what the public "should know." This role is involved with educating and motivating people to participate in politics, as well as the promotion of just causes. Unlike the result of other studies, "developing the intellectual and cultural interests of the public" also belongs to this factor, possibly due to the elite and unpopular connotation that culture has for many sectors of the country.

The fourth dimension, the *consumer-oriented journalism function*, focuses on the logic of the market, where everyday life and consumerism are the most important issues. Reaching the largest audience possible, emphasizing what the public "wants to know," and entertaining, are fundamental aspects of this type of journalistic role.

The final factor corresponds to the *disseminator function*, and includes aspects typically found in Western journalism cultures, like being a passive observer who describes reality in a neutral manner without getting involved.

Table 29.6   Perceived Importance of Media Roles

Media roles	Mean [a]	SD	% saying "extremely important"
Watchdog function[b]			
Act as watchdog of the government	3.84	1.21	38.9
Act as watchdog of business elites	3.79	1.25	37.5
Act as watchdog of political parties	3.56	1.31	31.0
Act as a watchdog of citizens	3.33	1.30	24.0
Propagandist function[c]			
Give relevance to the country's advances and triumphs	3.23	1.15	14.4
Actively support government policy on national development	2.64	1.14	6.0
Cultivate nationalism/patriotism	2.24	1.19	5.1
Highlight the benefits of the current economic model	2.18	1.07	2.3
Convey a positive image of political leadership	2.04	1.00	2.1
Convey a positive image of business leadership	2.01	1.03	2.1
Citizen-oriented journalism function[d]			
Develop the intellectual and cultural interest of the public	4.11	.95	41.4
Promote democracy	4.01	1.08	41.1
Provide citizens with the information they need to make political decisions.	4.08	1.03	44.1
Educate people about controversial and complex topics	3.97	1.08	39.3
Motivate people to participate in civic activity and political discussion.	3.73	1.04	25.9
Ensure coverage of local issues	3.70	1.16	31.6
Advocate for social change	3.67	1.10	26.7
Consumer-oriented journalism function[e]			
Provide the audience with the information that is most interesting	4.20	.86	44.6
Give the audience concrete help to manage their everyday problems	3.77	.95	24.9
Concentrate on news that is of interest to the widest possible audience	3.49	1.04	18.7
Provide entertainment and relaxation	3.38	.97	11.2
Disseminator function[f]			
Be a detached observer	3.21	1.24	15.8
Be a passive observer	2.36	1.29	6.5
Other ungrouped roles			
Get information to the public quickly	4.10	.94	40.7
Influence public opinion	3.89	1.03	33.0
Set the political agenda	3.26	1.17	15.6
Promote ethical or moral values, either conservative or liberal	3.18	1.28	18.0
Debate and evaluate international policies that affect Latin America	3.47	1.17	22.2

a   Scale ranges from 1 =not important at all to 5 = extremely important.
b   Alpha = .85
c   Alpha = .83
d   Alpha = .84
e   Alpha = .71
f   Alpha = .75

The role conception that gets the most general support is the *citizen-oriented*, followed by the *consumer-oriented* and the *watchdog*. However, the greatest discrepancies among journalists were found within the *watchdog function*, especially between rank levels and those who have and do not have a beat. The items included in the *consumer-oriented function* have the lowest standard deviations among all of the items, indicating strong agreement among the respondents.

Taking into account the percentages of those who considered each dimension as very important or extremely important, 81% of the journalists were classified as favoring more than one function at the same time, 14% of the journalists were classified as supportive of just one, and 5% did not express noticeable preferences for any of them. The greatest overlaps were found between the watchdog and the citizen-oriented functions, and the citizen-oriented and consumer-oriented functions.

The analysis also showed that the *disseminator* and the *consumer-oriented* conceptions tend to be stronger among television journalists, while the *propagandistic* role conception is more likely to be found among print journalists. On the other hand, the *citizen-oriented* function was perceived as more important among radio and online journalists, and the *watchdog* function was also stronger within the last group.

Surprisingly, we found no significant relationship between age and professional roles. This contradicts the idea found by other national and international studies about the differences that exist among different age groups of journalists in countries that have experienced prolonged dictatorial periods (Canel & Piqué 1998; Manzi, Helsper, Ruiz, Krause, & Kronmüller 2003; Stange & Salinas 2009). In our case, there are no differences in professional attitudes between younger journalists (who did not work during the military regime, and who have higher education levels), middle aged journalists (who lived through a great part of the dictatorship inside the media), and older journalists (journalists by trade, who have experienced the country's different political, economic, and social periods over the last 45 years).

However, the data also show that journalists who lean toward the left consider the *watchdog and citizen-oriented* roles to be more important, while their colleagues on the political right believe the *consumer-oriented* and *propagandist* roles to be more important.

Ethical Standards.   While only a small number of journalists belong to a professional association that promotes ethical codes, most of them seem to support certain universal ethical values in their profession. For example, 43.3% of the surveyed journalists strongly agree that "there are ethical principles which are so important that they should be followed by all journalists, regardless of situational context," while just 11.8% consider that "what is ethical in journalism varies from one situation to another."

Nevertheless, Chilean journalists apparently do not embrace a highly idealistic approach to obtaining the truth. More than half consider that "there are situations in which harm is justifiable if it results in a story that produces a greater good," and only 26% agree that "reporting and publishing a story that can potentially harm others is always wrong, regardless of the benefits to be gained."

To obtain a better understanding of how journalists might apply ethics in their daily work, we also asked our respondents to describe the level of support they would give to seven controversial reporting practices. Table 29.7 shows that the majority of Chilean journalists justify most of these methods, especially those linked with "using confidential documents," "using hidden microphones or cameras," "claiming to be someone else," and "badgering an unwilling informant." Print and television journalists expressed significantly more support for these practices. The only reporting

Table 29.7   Attitudes Toward Various Reporting Practices by News Medium (in %)

Reporting Practice	Percentage saying "May be Justified"		
	Radio (N = 395)	Television (N = 543)	Print Media (N = 1,041)
Paying people for confidential information	30.3	32.2	29.4
Using confidential documents without authorization	73.2	63.8	78.5
Claiming to be someone else	40.2	44.2	47.7
Not protecting source confidentiality	—	3.3	4.0
Badgering unwilling informants to get a store	35.1	41.0	49.3
Making use of personal documents without permission	20.8	26.2	29.5
Using hidden microphones or cameras	64.6	75.5	54.7

practice that got almost total rejection among Chilean journalists (95.1%) is "disclosing confidential sources."

Perceived Influences on Journalism.   The questions of "What is newsworthy?" and "What forces shape the news?" have been discussed in the journalism scientific community for many years (Fishman 1980; Preston 2009; Shoemaker & Reese 1996; Tuchman 1978). Our survey listed 29 organizational, political, economic, professional, and procedural factors, as well as reference groups, as potential sources of influence on news work. Respondents were asked how important each of those sources is in their day-to-day job on a five-point scale (ranging from 1 = "lowest influence" to 5 = "greatest influence").

The data show that "the market and audiences" is ranked at the top (31.8%), followed by advertising considerations (29.3%), ownership of news organization (28.2%), profit expectations (27%), lack of material and human resources (26.5%), and news sources (26.0%). Peers and colleagues from other media (0.5%) and journalism unions (1.4%) are not perceived as influential on news judgments, nor is politics (4.7%). These findings resonate very well with the country's social changes, where the logics of the market and the economy are perceived by many as the most decisive factors when it is time to make decisions. The data also reaffirm the low credibility and weak power assigned by the journalists to their professional organizations.

Conclusions

The results of this study come from two complementary sources—a census of 1,979 news media journalists and an online survey of 570 journalists regarding their levels of professionalism, working conditions, perceived influences on journalism, and personal characteristics.

A summary of the findings obtained from both sources shows that the typical Chilean news media journalist can be characterized as male, less than 40 years old, working as a full-time reporter without a specific beat, poorly paid, and leaning toward the political left. The majority of journalists are located in the capital of Santiago, and more than half of them work in the print media. Although there has been a considerable increase in the participation of women within the media, they do not have high-ranking positions, and they retire from journalism earlier than do men.

This study also shows a positive development in the journalist's educational level—almost 90% of them have a degree in journalism—but low levels of specialization and low levels of membership in professional organizations, indicating a weak professional identity. Coincidently, the professional organizations, as well as the journalist's reference groups directly linked to the profession, are considered to have little influence on their day-to-day job behavior and on their judgment of what is newsworthy.

In terms of personal needs and satisfaction, journalists assign more importance to the labor aspects than to the professional aspects of their work. Although they are relatively satisfied with their jobs, both their interests and their biggest complaints are associated with their salary and with the possibility of reconciling their work and family lives. Within the professional aspects of their work, journalists especially value the possibility of using all their abilities and knowledge, as well as their freedom in the newsroom. Their perceived levels of autonomy are moderately high, although more than 30% of them feel several constraints in making news decisions, especially those who do not have editorial power and those who lean toward the left of the political spectrum.

Parallel to this, Chilean journalists have a very pluralist conception of their professional roles. They reject promoting and defending authorities and consider it fundamental to monitor society and the groups in power.

This situation, however, causes certain contradictions among what they should (or would want) to do, and their everyday practice. It is understandable that after years of political suppression, Chilean journalists deeply value the possibility of acting as watchdogs of the country's political parties, presidential administration, and the de facto powers in the country. Nonetheless, a large portion of the Chilean media outlets are in the hands of the political-economic elite, and many laws still deny journalists the right to exercise their watchdog role.

The fact that political influences in the newsroom are not perceived as very important by the journalists does not mean that they do not have power in their workplaces. Due to the strong association that Chilean politics has with the economy, the data suggest that the impact of the political factor is being hidden by economic factors such as audience ratings and advertising sales, and by the pressures caused by the everyday operations of each organization.

On the other hand, Chilean journalists consider it fundamental to focus on citizens and on topics that are really important for the public. At the same time, though, they support and defend the need to satisfy journalism's commercial needs, such as obtaining a larger audience and giving the public the trivial and entertaining content that helps them live day to day. The two objectives do not have to be contradictory, as they both aim to provide benefits to the audience. However, there is concern as to how the economic pressures and the potential tensions between the interests and benefits of the media, and the journalist's values and ideals, jeopardize the independence of Chilean journalism.

Another aspect of this study analyzed the news workers' ethical values. Although they mostly agree with following universal ethical principles, they do not widely support idealism as a value for seeking the truth. This way of thinking does not seem surprising in a country that has lived through serious conflicts where the press has had to use different methods to survive. But although ethical standards strongly depend on cultural and national contexts, these results are similar to those obtained from American journalists (Weaver et al. 2007).

In fact, if we compare Chilean journalists and their American peers, we can see that both groups share ethical standards and some professional orientations. However, Chilean news workers give greater importance to the watchdog role and distance themselves even more from the traditional disseminator role of the press.

The concentration of the media, market demands, and a strong political parallelism shape a great part of the Chilean journalism. The results of Chile's latest presidential election reaffirm this model. The manner in which journalists confront these pressures and struggle to defend the freedom of the press and information pluralism will determine the news media system's health during the coming years.

Notes

1. Research for this chapter received funding from Fondecyt Grant No. 1080066 (Chilean Fund for Development of Science and Technology). I would like to express my gratitude to Claudia Lagos (University of Chile), Gustavo González (University of Chile), Carlos Del Valle (University of La Frontera), Omar Barriga (University of Concepcion), Magdalena Saldaña (University of Concepcion), and Mary Hayes (Catholic University of the Holy Conception) for their meaningful ideas and comments on the first versions of this chapter.

2. Colegio de Periodistas de Chile (Chilean Journalists' Professional Society), Silver Guide, National Television Council (CNTV), National Press Association (ANP), Radio Association of Chile (ARCHI), Undersecretary of Telecommunication (Subtel), ARETEL (Regional Television Association), National Association of Community and Citizen Radio in Chile, Chilean Association of Advertising Agencies (ACHAP), and Business White Pages.

3. Cronbach's alpha obtained by a sixth factor (composed of two items and related to the press's influence on society and on the political agenda) indicated a very low reliability for the scale (less than .5), causing its elimination from the model. Likewise, three other items were excluded from the analysis—the first because it did not exhibit a theoretical tie with the rest of the items in the factor where it loaded, and the other two because it did not fit clearly with any of the factors. The final five dimensions account for 62.4% of the variance. The alpha indexes ranged from .71 to .85. Each dimension had eigenvalues over 1.0. In all cases, factor loadings above 0.5 were retained. Varimax rotation was used.

References

ACHAP. *Informe inversión publicitaria 2008* [2008 Advertising investment report]. Santiago: Asociación Chilena de Agencias de Publicidad *y* Megatime.

Arriagada, Eduardo, and Gonzalo Saavedra. 1990. Algunos problemas de información social en los medios del Sur [Some social information problems in southern media]. *Cuadernos de Información* 6:81–89.

Becerra, Martín, and Guillermo Mastrini. 2009. *Los dueños de la palabra: Acceso, estructura y concentración de los medios en la América latina del siglo XXI* [The owners of the word: Access, structure and Latin American media concentration in the 21st century]. Buenos Aires: Editorial Prometeo.

Canel, María José, and Antoni Piqué. 1998. Journalists in emerging democracies: The case of Spain. In *The global journalist,* edited by David. H. Weaver, pp. 299–319. Cresskill, NJ: Hampton Press.

Délano, Manuel, Karin Niklander, and Paula Susacasa. 2007. Los periodistas recién titulados y el mercado laboral [Recently graduated journalists and labor market]. *Calidad en la Educación* 27:205–234.

Dermota, Ken. 2002. *Chile inédito, el periodismo bajo democracia* [Unpublished Chile, journalism under democracy]. Santiago: Ediciones B.

Estadísticas Laborales: Cifras comentadas. 2009. [Labor statistics: Commented figures]. Santiago: Instituto Nacional de Estadísticas.

Fishman, Mark. 1980. *Manufacturing the news.* Austin: University of Texas Press.

Freedom House. 2012. *Freedom in the World 2012.* Retrieved from http://www.freedomhouse.org/sites/default/files/inline_images/FIW%202012%20Booklet_Final.pdf

González, Gustavo. 2003. Cincuenta años de periodismo universitario en Chile: Encuentros, desencuentros y desafíos [Fifty years of journalism education in Chile: Understandings, misunderstandings and challenges]. *Comunicación y Medios 14*: 13–26.

Gronemeyer, María Elena. 2002. *Chilean journalists: Autonomy and independence blocked by conformism and insecurity.* Ph.D. dissertation, School of Journalism and Mass Communication, University of North Carolina, Chapel Hill.

Gutiérrez, Fernando, and María del Carmen Lavín. 2003. *Mercado laboral para periodistas en Concepción. Informe 1998-2002* [Labor market for journalists in Concepción]. Concepción: Ediciones Universidad Católica de la Santísima Concepción.

Hanitzsch, Thomas. 2007. Deconstructing journalism culture: Toward a universal theory. *Communication Theory* 17:367–385.

Hanitzsch, Thomas. 2007–2008. *World of journalisms* project: Questionnaire for journalists. Retrieved from http://www.worldsofjournalisms.org/download.htm

Hanitzsch, Thomas, Folker Hanusch, Claudia Mellado, Maria Anikina, Rosa Berganza, Incilay Cangoz,...Edgar Kee Wang Yuen. 2011. Mapping journalism cultures across nations: A comparative study of 18 countries. *Journalism Studies* 12(3):273–293.

Manzi, Jorge, Ellen Helsper, Soledad Ruiz, Mariana Krause, and Edmundo Kronmüller. 2003. El pasado que nos pesa: la memoria colectiva del 11 de septiembre de 1973 [Regretting the past: The collective memory of September 11, 1973]. *Revista de Ciencia política* 23(2):177–214.

Mellado, Claudia, Salinas, Paulina, and Sergio Barría. 2010. Estructura del empleo periodístico y validación profesional de sus prácticas en el mercado laboral chileno [Structure of Journalistic Employment and Professional Validation of its Practices in the Chilean Labor Market]. *Innovar* 20 (36): 91 - 106.

Mellado, Claudia, Sergio Barría, Jorge Enríquez, and Felipe Besoain. 2006. *Balance 2006. Perspectivas profesionales y del mercado periodístico de la Octava Región, Chile* [2006 Balance: Professional and journalistic labor perspectives in the Eight Regions, Chile]. Concepción: Publicaciones Dirección de Docencia, Universidad de Concepción.

Mellado, Claudia, Sonia Moreira, Claudia Lagos, and María Elena Hernández. 2012. Comparing journalism cultures in Latin America: The case of Chile, Brazil and Mexico. *Gazette* 74(1):60–77.

Mellado, Claudia, and Elizabeth Parra. 2008. Indicadores de identidad y perfil del periodista regional en Chile [Identity and profile indicators of the regional journalist in Chile]. *Opción* 23:145–167.

Menanteau, Horta Darío. 1967. Professionalism of journalists in Santiago de Chile. *Journalism Quarterly* 44:15–23.

Mönckeberg, María Olivia. 2009. *Los magnates de la prensa. Concentración de los medios de comunicación en Chile* [Press magnates: Communication media concentration in Chile]. Santiago de Chile: Random House Mondadori.

Otano, Rafael, and Guillermo Sunkel. 2003. Libertad de los periodistas en los medios [Freedom of journalists and the media]. *Comunicación y Medios* 14(2):65–80.

Planet, Mario. 1981. La formación de los periodistas en Chile [The education of journalists in Chile]. In *La formación de los periodistas en América Latina (México, Chile y Costa Rica)* [Journalism education in Latin America: Mexico, Chile and Costa Rica], edited by José Valdivia, pp. 189–250. Mexico City: Nueva Imagen.

Preston, Pascal. 2009. *Making the news: Journalism and news cultures in Europe.* London: Routledge.

Ramaprasad, Jyotika, and James Kelly. 2003. Reporting the news from the world's rooftop: A survey of Nepalese journalists. *Gazette* 65(3):291–315

Shoemaker, Pamela, and Stephen Reese. 1996. *Mediating the message: Theories of influence on mass media content.* White Plains, NY: Longman.

Stange, Hans and Claudio Salinas. 2009. Prácticas periodísticas en Chile entre 1975 y 2005: Estudio de las huellas materiales en la noticia [Journalistic practices in Chile between 1975 and 2005: Study of material traces in the news]. Paper presented at the 13th Jornadas de Investigadores en Comunicación, Universidad Nacional de Córdoba, San Luis, Argentina.

Tuchman, Gaye. 1978. *Making news: A study in the construction of reality.* New York: Free Press.

Weaver, David H., and G. Cleveland Wilhoit. 1986. *The American journalist: A portrait of U.S. news people and their work.* Bloomington, IN: Indiana University Press.

Weaver, David H., and G. Cleveland Wilhoit. 1996. *The American journalist in the 1990s: U.S. news people at the end of an era.* Mahwah, NJ: Erlbaum.

Weaver, David, Randall Beam, Bonnie Brownlee, Paul Voakes, and G. Cleveland Wilhoit. (2007). *The American journalist in the 21st century: U.S. news people at the dawn of a new millennium.* Mahwah, NJ: Erlbaum.

Wilke, Jürgen. 1998. Journalists in Chile, Ecuador and México. In *The global journalist,* edited by David. H. Weaver, pp. 433–452. Cresskill, NJ: Hampton Press.

30 Journalists in Colombia

Jesus Arroyave and Marta Milena Barrios

From an outside perspective, Colombian news media largely resemble those of any other Latin American country. National and regional newspapers provide plenty of information and analysis. The radio and television broadcasting system offers instant coverage with a professional approach, and weekly magazines consistently supply their readers with investigative stories.

However, in Colombia, journalism also is characterized by complex and changing dynamics that have helped to forge a combative and unique configuration of news media. For instance, politics and journalism have long been closely tied in a special manner. The majority of Colombian presidents have been media owners, directors of newspapers, or journalists in their previous careers. For several decades, the most important news media outlets were affiliated with long-standing political parties. Likewise, some of the most important national television news stations used to belong to the families of political leaders. Similarly, most regional media used to belong to elite families who had close relationships with the government. Therefore, a tension between partisan and impartial journalism has been constant.

Additionally, political violence also has been a longstanding feature of Colombian history, which has had enormous repercussions for the country's news media. Accusations of media manipulation by many different sides of the armed conflict are common. The guerrillas as well as the paramilitary have been constantly accused of intimidating, kidnapping, and murdering journalists. Likewise, the Colombian Army and the government have been accused of manipulating or distorting information.

Drug trafficking is another of the factors that most highly affects the practice of journalism in Colombia. Bomb attacks, threats, kidnapping, bribery, exile, and murder have been very common responses to media coverage of drug dealers or organized crime. Perhaps the most important mobilization that has taken place in Colombia was when all the media closed for one day as a protest against the murder of the director of *El Espectador*, who was believed to have been killed by Pablo Escobar, the leader of the Medellin Cartel, in 1986.

Despite these negative influences on the culture of Colombian journalism, there also have been other positive developments that distinguish the country's news media tradition. For instance, there has been a long tradition of professional writers, poets, and novelists who have contributed to newspaper and magazine journalism, and influenced how a special style of features are written and presented in the country's media. Also, opinion journalism has been strong and carefully read. As a result, Colombian pundits have influenced both the country's public opinion and journalism style. Finally, Colombia's continuing struggle with large-scale social, economic, and cultural contradictions has led many journalists to develop a special style of advocacy reporting that goes beyond normal news coverage. Instead, journalists tend to take part in solving community problems, in some cases by pressuring public officials, and in other cases by asking the private sector for support.

To better understand the complex and multifaceted phenomena that have shaped Colombian journalism, we conducted several qualitative and quantitative studies at both the national and regional levels. This chapter presents the key findings of two national surveys and a third study of qualitative interviews of Colombian journalists from 2006 to 2008. In total, 543 active journalists, working in a variety of news media, participated.

Media in Colombia

The challenging task of describing the culture of Colombian journalism begins with the brief acknowledgment of its profound ties to the country's social and political development. One must also highlight more than two centuries of courageous reporting, and draw attention to the media's advocacy for literature and its partisan tendency in the country's sometimes accidental progress from colonialism to democracy. And without a doubt, a complete picture should also mention the facts and narratives of the brave people who disseminated Colombia's overwhelming social reality despite the persistent threat of political and violent reprisal.

From 1886 to 1994, 22 of 28 Colombia presidents had previously been employed as media directors, columnists, or newspaper owners (Herrán 1991). This tendency continues today. For example, the Colombian Vice President (2002–2010), Francisco Santos, and the most important defense minister of the past decade, Juan Manuel Santos (who was responsible for the legendary rescue operation of Ingrid Betancourt), used to be co-owners of *El Tiempo*, the country's most influential and widely read news outlet. Both of them continue to occupy leadership positions in the national spectrum. Francisco Santos is currently the director of RCN radio, one of the most prestigious radio stations in the country, while his cousin, Juan Manuel Santos, was elected president of Colombia for the 2010 to 2014 period.

In short, it has been very difficult to maintain a genuine independent press in Colombia.

The strong ties of journalism to everyday life in Colombia could also explain why more than 1,000 newspapers were founded during the 19th century, supporting both liberal and conservative ideas. Of the publications that arose during this period, two managed to stand out: *El Espectador*, founded in Medellin by Fidel Cano in 1887, and *El Tiempo*, founded in Bogotá in 1911. Both are still in circulation and feature national and international coverage. Their influence can be illustrated by how frequently and intensely their personnel and facilities have been the targets of violence. *El Espectador* director Guillermo Cano and reporter Roberto Camacho were murdered on December 17, 1986, after the newspaper featured critical coverage of Escobar's drug trafficking. And on September 2, 1989, a vehicle loaded with 121 pounds of dynamite exploded in front of the paper's offices, destroying most of the building, including the newspaper production machinery, and putting *El Espectador* out of circulation for eight days. It returned, functioning out of an improvised newsroom, with the headline "*¡Seguimos Adelante!*" (We move on!). Although the violence was commonly attributed to Escobar, no one has yet been found legally responsible.

El Tiempo also suffered the actions of drug lords who wanted to pressure the government in order to avoid their extradition to the United States. Francisco Santos, then serving as editor-in-chief, was kidnapped by Escobar in 1990. Part of his odyssey is recounted in Gabriel Garcia Marquez's *News of a Kidnapping* (1997). The violence of the 1980s affected more than 100 journalists who personally suffered the terrors of the war fought by the Colombian institutions against the drug cartels.

Unfortunately, sporadic episodes of terrorism against mass media are still present in the everyday life of Colombia. On August 12, 2010, 50 kilograms of dynamite exploded in an open parking lot in front of the offices of Caracol Radio and EFE news agency. As a result, nine people were hurt and approximately 500 houses and buildings were damaged but none of the media stopped their broadcasts. Authorities attributed the terrorist attack to the FARC, the 60-year-old guerrilla group. Caracol airs a program called *Voces del Silencio* (Voices of Silence) in which families of hostages detained by FARC, send messages of hope that are received in the midst of the forest.

In contemporary Colombia, informative media institutions have been linked to the construction of the nation, the formation of power relations among social actors, and the creation of an ideological public forum. In its course, Colombia's democratic and liberal tradition has much in common with the press's own tradition. Politicians, intellectuals, opinion leaders, and ordinary people have to turn to the press not only to express themselves, but to criticize government on the basis of failing to fulfill basic needs, provide social assistance, or prevent corruption.

From a narrative point of view, one has to acknowledge the great contribution of Colombian journalists to the development of feature writing (*crónica*) in Latin America as a mixed genre between literature and journalism. The *crónica* was the only journalistic genre conceived and fully developed in Latin America. Experts on feature writing highlight the importance of this genre "to understand a fundamental stage of Latin American culture" (Rotker 2005: 15). This was because during Modernism, as a cultural tendency, journalistic feature writing contained both poetry and fiction. Some of the founders of this genre were poets: José Martí, Manuel Gutiérrez Nájera, and Rubén Darió.

The *crónica*, which permits the professionalization of the writer and creates a new way to narrate, existed as a Latin American-specific genre long before Tom Wolfe, Norman Mailer, and Truman Capote diffused it under the name of New Journalism (Tomas Eloy Martinez, cited in Rotker 2005: 10). One of the most popular practitioners of this style was Gabriel Garcia Márquez; however, there were many less famous or anonymous reporters who continued to write wonderful *crónica* pieces in their everyday work.

Previous Studies

There is a growing body of literature that has explored various issues of Latin American journalism such as ethics (Herrán & Restrepo 1992), news media conglomerates (Larsen, 2005), digital newspapers (Barrios & Arroyave 2008; Franco & Guzman, 2004), sensationalism and tabloidization (Arroyave & Hughes 2004; Garcia 2003; Hallin 2000; Pedroso 1994), education (Fuentes 1992; Santoro 2000), and press freedom (Hughes & Lawson 2005; Inter-American Press Association 2005), but there are few studies analyzing the identities and practices of professional journalists (Arroyave, Gil & Blanco 2007). Among those few, there is one related to the issue of journalists' salaries (Pastran 2000); others related to their occupational profiles, such as in Venezuela (Aguirre 1990), Brazil (Vasallo de Lopes 1997), Mexico (Benassini 2001), and Chile (Mellado 2005); and others related to journalistic routines and customs in Brazil (Herscovitz and Cardodo 1998) and Argentina (Martini & Luchessi 2004).

Although it is possible to find essays and opinion pieces on the state and quality of Colombian journalism, there have been few systematic studies that ask active journalists about the work they do and the conditions under which they perform. The few attempts have methodological problems or do not provide enough information about methodological issues.

In a survey of Colombian journalists, Manrique and Cardona (2004) found that the typical Colombian journalist was "a young, inexperienced, and underpaid professional who worked more than eight hours a day" (p. 1). Manrique and Cardona also reported that it is difficult for journalists to pursue careers in any medium because most news organizations do not have consistent policies that compensate seniority or bonuses that stimulate extra work. Indeed, Colombian news media tend to prefer young professionals because they are willing to work longer hours for less pay. The compensation problem also reveals underlying gender discrimination. Colombian women are underrepresented in news organizations, and if they are hired, they are generally paid less than their male counterparts. In some regions, men make up 80% to 90% of the workforce in media organizations (Manrique & Cardona 2004).

In a longitudinal study, Gomez and Hernandez (2008) found that Colombian press freedom remains in a critical state after negative developments in the last 10 years. Aside from the traditional threats received from the guerrillas and paramilitaries, local, regional, and national members of the government have emerged as key actors who exercise pressure on the media. For instance, in a national survey that took place in 2007, journalists stated that the following security institutions exerted pressure on the way they did their job: National Police (55%), National Army (52%), Administrative Security Department (45%), National Navy (41%) and the Air Force (35%). According to the authors, the government has grown accustomed to making its own press releases and limiting the amount of journalistic investigation when it comes to newsworthy acts of violence by providing its own versions of the events.

Method

In this study, quantitative and qualitative methods were used in three different phases:

1. Focus Groups: Focus groups were used to provide an initial investigation into the daily experiences of Colombian journalists and to establish a platform for future research. This approach brought together professionals from different media on different career paths. These discussions served to reveal reactions and contrasts. They also allowed the opinion of one professional to act as a stimulant and activate the participation of others in the discourse (Flores & Alonso 1995; Frey & Fontana 1993; Krueger 1988).

Five focus groups were carried out in what are considered the five most important cities of Colombia: Bogota, Medellin, Cali, Barranquilla, and Cartagena. Participants were all active journalists, employed by media outlets, and with various years of experience. A total of 36 active journalists participated in the discussion sessions (see Table 30.1). There were 20 men and 16 women, reflecting the gender composition of most Latin American media. A psychologist with ample experience conducting focus group discussions was hired to serve as the moderator. He used a semistructured guide to lead the dialogues; however, in many cases there were comments and answers that triggered new topics.

The journalists were invited to participate on an individual basis, but in several occasions, groups were formed with the help of a particular association or journalist syndicate. In other regions, groups with diverse journalists and media permitted more varied compositions. Between six and eleven journalists participated in each group in the discussion activities. The five focus group discussions were taped and transcribed in their entirety, and served as the core of the analysis. The emergent categories were analyzed using the Comprehensive Data Treatment Method (Silverman 2001). The four leading categories for analysis were personal, formative, institutional (working conditions), and obstacle/threat issues. In order to strengthen the validity of the findings, the authors analyzed the transcriptions separately, and then compared findings.

2. Personal Safety Survey: One of the topics that produced the most vivid and profound discussions during the focus groups was related to journalists' personal safety. Due to the various

Table 30.1   Geographic Distribution of Journalist Sample (*N* = 300)

Cities	Inhabitants	Province	Percent	Total N
Bogotá	6,778,691	Cundinamarca	51	153
Medellin	2,223,078	Antioquia	17	51
Cali	2,068,386	Valle del Cauca	16	48
Barranquilla	1,380,437	Atlántico	11	33
Cartagena	895,400	Bolívar	5	15

and severe threats and obstacles, safety concerns have changed the way media operate and the way news is produced.

To investigate this important subject, the Interamerican Dialog NGO sponsored a national survey in 2006 of 300 active journalists using multistage cluster sampling. The five main Colombian cities (Bogotá, Medellin, Cali, Barranquilla, and Cartagena) were proportionately sampled based on population in the 2005 census. Table 30.1 shows the number of questionnaires completed in each city as a proportion of the population distribution.

Due to the fact that an updated national database of journalists is not available in Colombia, several regional databases containing the names of journalists who work for the main media outlets were used to establish the sampling frame. The main national and regional press (newspapers and magazines), broadcasting, and online media outlets in each of six cities were identified. In each city, we used clusters of media organizations and randomly selected journalists working for those media. A balance between male and female members was sought. Similarly, the sample included editors, coordinators, and reporters who were representative of the organizational and hierarchical composition of most Colombian media. Almost all of the surveys were conducted by telephone. Some journalists expressly asked to fill out the questionnaires online at their convenience. Of the 300 surveys completed, only 10% were completed online.

Results of the focus groups in the first stage of this study served as the basis for the survey questionnaire. Twenty local journalists participated in a pilot study aimed to test the validity of the questionnaire. The survey was also shared with scholars who work on journalism and media analysis, whose comments and suggestions were incorporated into the final questionnaire. Also, six questions related to the use of new technology in newsrooms were added to the final instrument. The final survey contained 25 questions that covered perceived personal security, use of new technology, and various demographic factors.

3. Formative, Institutional, and Personal National Survey: In the third phase we decided to further explore some key issues that emerged in the focus group discussions in a second quantitative survey in 2008. The same procedure regarding the sample frame used in the previous survey was followed in the quantitative study. Due to funding limitations, the final sample was composed of 217 active journalists working in the most important media outlets of the five most important cities of Colombia. The questionnaire was based on the four main categories that were identified in the qualitative study. The sampling procedure attempted to minimize bias by selecting respondents who were proportionately representative of the total population by basing the number of journalists on the population of each city (see Table 30.1). For example, Bogotá, the capital, has a larger population and more newspapers, radio stations, and television channels; therefore, more surveys were conducted in this city.

Findings

Data from the focus group and surveys are presented in this section. Findings regarding education are presented first, followed by those related to working conditions and use of new technology. The second set of results focuses on the impact of journalists' professional work on their personal lives. Finally, data related to obstacles, threats, and violence against journalists are presented.

Education

Education has always been a contentious issue of discussion among journalism and media professionals in Colombia. Although the first Latin American school of journalism opened in Argentina in 1934, for several decades most journalists learned on the job. In the 1960s, communication emerged as an academic major and found its natural place in most schools of journalism in Latin American universities. In the mid-1960s the social communication and journalism major (as it is generally known in most Latin American universities) was established. In the 1970s and 1980s the new major went through a steady growth. In the 1990s, in part due to advances in technology and media penetration, social communication and journalism became one of the growing fields of study in Latin America (Benassini 1999).

Today, there are more than 2,000 schools of journalism in South America (FELAFACS, 2009). In Colombia, there are about 70 schools with a focus on communication and journalism (AFA-COM). Today, most journalists are professionals with college degrees.

However, there are still many journalists who work in news media without university training, particularly in small cities and rural areas. Also, there is the popular perception that social communication and journalism is among the least demanding majors.

There are just two postgraduate journalism programs in Colombia, both of them in the capital, reducing the opportunities for further education in this field. Such tensions in regard to journalism training and education were evident in both focus groups and the national survey carried out in the main cities in Colombia. The following quote summarizes one of the most consistent ideas that showed up in the focus groups:

> A lot of people started studying journalism because they saw it as their last option if they couldn't handle law, medicine, or engineering. They went to communication because it was the option that didn't require any math.

Some journalists expressed concern that younger colleagues increasingly associate their field with entertainment, gossip, and appearing on television:

> There is a big fraud on the part of the universities ... a large number of people who want to study journalism because all of them want to be on television, all of them want to anchor entertainment programs. Journalism as a discipline should be fully structured due to the large degree of harm that it may cause if used incorrectly and because of the big responsibility it has as it helps create public opinion.

Quantitative data seem to support such ideas. Forty percent of the journalists surveyed strongly agree or agree that the social communication and journalism major doesn't have enough prestige in Colombia. Along similar lines, almost half of journalists agree or strongly agree (47%) that journalism should be taught at a graduate level, as shown in Table 30.2.

Table 30.2   Perception of Journalism Education (*N* = 219, in %)

	Strongly Agree	Agree	Undecided	Disagree	Strongly Disagree
I think the career of journalism does not have enough prestige in Colombia	13.2	26.9	18.3	32.0	9.6
Journalism should be considered a postgraduate program and not an undergraduate one	17.8	29.7	10.5	25.1	15.5

In general, journalists perceived that an undergraduate degree is not enough training to properly fulfill the duties of their demanding jobs. Likewise, concerns about this issue also emerged in the focus group discussions:

> I realized that reporters need a lot of education and have to be involved in the academic world in a very deep manner ... I think reporters do not have the tools that are needed to achieve success, so postgraduate studies are mandatory.

However, once they start working as active journalists in any medium they do not receive much training to improve their professional skills or continue their education. Forty-five percent of journalists never received any development courses promoted by their employer. Only about 20% said they had job-related training at least two or three times during the past year. Of those journalists who participated in job training (65.2%), the majority participated in short-term training sessions lasting only a few days (38.8%) or less than a week (11.4%). Training that lasted longer than a week was attended by only 15%.

Job Compensation and Satisfaction

Low satisfaction with pay has been a constant complaint from Colombian journalists. Different journalist organizations have fought for better salaries, especially in small cities. The national survey reveals that this is a key issue among journalists. Eighty percent of those surveyed agreed that their profession is poorly compensated, while only 1.4% disagreed.

Similarly, 95% of journalists agreed their employers should pay for overtime, which currently does not happen in most media outlets. And 51% agreed that their organization often offered no social security whatsoever. Almost 20% were undecided in answering this question, indicating a certain lack of knowledge concerning the existence of social security in their organizations.

Due to financial limitations, Colombian news organizations frequently force their employees to sell advertisements as an alternative form of income. Some companies pay the journalist a minimum wage and grant them a sales quota that allows them to sell airtime and collect money through their own advertising spots. Some other organizations don't even grant them a salary, and only pay based on advertising sales. In this scenario many professionals wonder: "Are we *journalists or salesmen?*"

In this regard, 62% agreed that the advertising sales quota system promotes doubtful ethics within journalism. This situation has strong ethical implications because it deals with their professional independence and the quality of their work. Some journalists testified as to how difficult it is to have to sell advertisements, apart from covering news stories, in order to make a living (see Table 30.3). One journalist expressed concern with this issue as follows:

In radio, we receive salary for the advertising spots, and many times a journalist's role becomes "news salesmen" in order to survive. This prevents one from being independent, because sometimes one has to sell information in order to fulfill one's basic necessities. For instance, if one sells a spot to Fábrica de Licores de Antioquia (Liquor Factory of Antioquia), one cannot say negative things about the company because they provide us with our supper.

Another focus group participant said:

We can't focus only on reporting, because we have to find time to look for advertising, send invoices, and collect the money. That prevents the journalist from dedicating time to research. The investigative process is supposed to be a routine part of daily journalism, but it is not accomplished because of the lack of time we have to delve into the social reality to construct journalistic exposés.

Since salaries are not good and some have to sell ads for wages, it is not unusual that journalists have to look for additional jobs. Forty-four percent of journalists said that they have to find other work outside the journalism profession. Among the most common are teaching (22.9%), business adviser (11.5%), and sales (7.3%). Other fields included public relations (4.2%), radio host (3.1%), graphic design (2.1%), and other nonmedia related jobs (24%).

Autonomy is another key issue for Colombian journalists. The pressure from the private and public sectors is felt in newsrooms, affecting journalism's independence. There is a long tradition in Latin American countries of public and private sector influence through advertising. Colombian journalism is no exception. More than one in every three journalists surveyed (35.2%) agreed that their superiors have suggested coverage of a news article involving owners or sponsors of their media. In turn, this reality suggests a bias in favor of certain entities or individuals.

Although there are many problems that journalists have to face as a result of difficult working conditions, the majority of them feel very satisfied (51.1%) or satisfied (43.4%) with their careers. Only about 2.8% said that they are either dissatisfied or very dissatisfied, and 2.7% said they were undecided. Even though there are many negative aspects, professional journalists who participated in this study clearly identified, with great satisfaction, the rewards they have obtained from the sacrifice they make in the daily practice of their jobs: "The satisfaction lies in obtaining an answer and knowing that you have contributed to improving the quality of life of a group of people."

Table 30.3   Journalists' Perceptions Regarding Institutional Practices in the Media Industry ($N = 219$, in %)

	Strongly Agree	Agree	Undecided	Disagree	Strongly Disagree
In Colombia, journalism is a poorly paid profession	40.2	40.2	11.4	5.0	1.4
The prestige of a journalist is related to the medium for which he/she works.	23.9	39.7	12.3	16.9	6.4
Often journalistic companies offer no social security to journalists.	12.8	37.9	19.6	16.9	10.1
In Colombia, the advertising system promotes journalism with dubious ethics.	27.4	34.3	21.0	10.1	4.6
Paying journalists extra hours worked should be an obligation.	58.5	36.5	1.8	1.4	0.9

"This profession comes from the gut, it is felt deep within, and whoever has the 'journalism worm' shouldn't avoid dealing with this job. You chose this career because you liked it."

New technologies such as the Internet have reached a critical mass among Colombian journalists. Almost all the journalists surveyed (99.7%) use the Internet in their jobs. Ninety-five percent use the Internet once or several times daily, indicating that it is becoming an essential tool in newsrooms. About 34% of the usage is for electronic mail, while 30% involves using search engines, and consulting institutional web pages for their work routines. Among the news genre, most journalists surveyed use the Internet for news stories (64.6%), reporting (12.7%), opinion columns (10%), feature writing (7%), and interviews (5.5%).

Personal Life

Very interesting answers emerged when Colombian journalists were asked about their perceptions of the effect of their careers on their personal lives. Table 30.4 shows that 28% agree or strongly agree that journalism has affected their love lives. Perhaps more worrisome, 58% strongly agree or agree that their jobs have influenced their eating habits.

Overall, 59% agree or strongly agree that journalism has negatively altered their personal lives. This finding reveals a critical aspect that should be taken into serious consideration. The all-consuming nature of the work affects the journalist's private sphere to a great degree.

In a similar fashion, journalists in all five focus groups complained about the implications of the career for their personal lives. One participant remarked:

> We leave home at 4:30 in the morning, and we never know at what time we are going to return…. I try to provide my people, my family, with quality time, but as time goes on they have come to understand that that's how a journalist's life is.
>
> One of the things that I have hated, and still hate, from reporting is that you have to give up your social life. One works Mondays through Sundays, and you are supposed to have a free day, but sometimes it is not possible. I didn't even have time to see my mom.

Journalists not only lack an appropriate space to share time with loved ones, but it also seems as though there is no time for satisfying individual necessities either. In the words of the participants in this research, "in journalism, there's no time for life." The Editor of one of the most important newspapers in Columbia remarked:

Table 30.4   Journalists' Perceptions of the Effects of Their Profession on Their Personal Life (*N* = 219, in %)

	Strongly Agree	Agree	Undecided	Disagree	Strongly Disagree
The practice of journalism has affected my relationships	7.6	20.6	15.5	34.7	18.7
I have been away from my social life due to the exercise of journalism	12.3	29.2	12.3	28.8	14.6
Journalism has affected my nutritional habits	24.2	34.3	9.6	20.1	9.1
I often don't enjoy my personal life due to the extensive work shifts	23.3	35.6	13.7	18.3	8.2
Journalism allows me to have enough free time to have a hobby	12.3	22.8	16.4	32.9	13.7

You're still in time. Don't make this serious mistake, this is not life. Study something else, this is not life. Every honest journalist will tell you this: I don't have a life; I have not had a life. I haven't slept well for a long time, 15 years more or less, because I lie down listening to news from radio stations, and then I wake up with the earphones listening to radio news. I started having larger ears....

Professional Security

Since violence has been a prominent issue in Colombian history and has affected journalism for decades, the topic deserves special attention. When exploring if journalists knew about any violent acts against any colleague or media, 86% responded affirmatively, an overwhelming majority. Likewise, 41% of journalists reported that they have received a threat as a part of their daily routine. Some journalists even reported being assaulted (11.3%) or kidnapped (5%). Things got worse when exploring violence exerted on colleagues. Forty-six percent of journalists were aware of other colleagues who have received threats, 17.3% knew of physical assaults, 7.7% knew of kidnappings, and 8.2% knew of specific murders.

When asked whom they considered the most responsible for violence against journalists, the first three choices were guerrillas (38.8%), paramilitary (19.6%), and drug traffickers and organized crime (18.2%). Interestingly, government officials (12.5%) and National Army and police (6.2%) were considered the fourth and fifth most prevalent choices. This finding is particularly disturbing since these are the institutions that should protect journalists and freedom of expression in the country.

Colombian journalists have had to devise unique strategies to deal with the security problems, such as not signing their stories or not showing themselves in front of the camera in order to protect their lives. In other words, they have had to become anonymous in their reporting to "survive in the middle of the battlefield." As a journalist explains:

> I have been here since *Telepacífico* started, and the audience doesn't know who I am. I began working in a TV station as a reporter when the authorities started seeking the members of the Cali drug cartel. After that I had to bear drug terrorism, paramilitary forces, and the FARC guerrilla actions in Cauca. Therefore, I feel that the more anonymous I can remain, the safer I can be.

Although violence against Colombian journalists seems to be high, there remains much skepticism about what the government is doing to condemn those who obstruct freedom of expression. The majority of journalists believe that investigations never (23%), rarely (41%), or only sometimes (24%) end in successful prosecutions. Very few journalists believe that successful prosecutions are frequently (10%) or always (2%) the case.

Conclusions

This chapter has presented the findings of the most extensive study of Colombian journalists to date. Three studies conducted from 2006 to 2008 in the country's most important media markets have provided a broader understanding of journalists' job conditions and perceptions. A total of 545 active journalists working in different media outlets participated in focus groups and two national surveys.

The complex picture that emerged showed that Colombian journalists continue to grapple with professional issues related to education, salary, and personal safety. These three areas of major findings are marked by paradoxes: While most journalists considered postgraduate training indispensable, there are just two specific graduate degree programs available in Colombia. While many journalists enjoy their work, the majority are very dissatisfied with their salaries and the obstacles to making a living wage. But although threats of violence continue to intimidate and limit Colombian journalists, they still carry out their duties and produce truly admirable news pieces.

In terms of the status of education, many Colombian journalists are disappointed with the lack of prestige of their profession and fear that an emphasis on entertainment and celebrity through appearing on television is harming public perceptions of journalism. One journalist remarked, "Many kids join the communications and journalism programs to study a profession that will allow them to be on TV; all of them want to be anchors of entertainment programs."

In regard to working conditions, important findings about journalists' payment and social security were revealed. Journalists were not only very dissatisfied with their salaries, but also with the lack of social security in their jobs. Similarly, the vast majority (95%) expressed dissatisfaction with the lack of overtime pay. As a result, it is not surprising that almost half of journalists (44%) said that they need to work more than one job.

Likewise, a system that results in journalists selling advertising for their wages has allowed public and private institutions to interfere with news reporting. This practice perpetuates a vicious cycle, since some public and private organizations have big advertising budgets used to manipulate local and regional news media outlets. Journalists are aware of this. Sixty-two percent agree that the system of selling advertising promotes doubtful ethics within journalism. Furthermore, 35% of journalists affirmed that their editor or director has suggested specific coverage of advertisers, thus affecting their journalistic autonomy.

In short, Colombian news organizations are not providing adequate conditions necessary for journalists to fully accomplish their jobs. As Manrique and Cardona (2004) also found, working conditions are so precarious that journalists find themselves looking for other options in order to survive. These structural problems create concerns in terms of journalistic output and the impact on public opinion. These findings cast serious doubts on the quality and content of some Colombian reporting. If information that comes through news media is influenced by public or private advertisers who control the journalists' salaries, there is no guarantee that such information is in the best interest of the public.

Such problems in the workplace also have an impact on journalists' personal lives. Journalism is so demanding that it has serious repercussions for journalists' social lives, not to mention their physical and mental health. Divorce, social isolation, eating disorders, and family problems were very common problems identified by journalists. As one journalist said, "So whoever practices 100% journalism ends up being an outcast from society."

Finally, findings indicate that Colombian journalists continue to face threats to their personal safety. Seven in ten journalists surveyed said that they had felt their lives were at risk, which is very alarming. Additionally, more than half of journalists who participated have hidden their identities in order to protect their lives. As a result, it is common to find anonymous news pieces and reporting in many media outlets. These concerns and approaches are quite understandable. In 2008, 162 cases of threats to freedom of expression were reported (Flip 2008). In the last two decades, 120 journalists have been murdered in Colombia. In turn, this country reports one of the highest number of journalists killed on the continent. Threats and obstacles limit reporting about any public issue, and thus independent reporting becomes a distant ideal in the country.

Although guerrillas, paramilitary groups, and drug traffickers were cited most frequently as responsible for violence against journalists, government officials also emerged as sources of restriction on news coverage. Along those lines, journalists perceived that the government has been highly ineffective in investigating attacks made upon professional reporters.

The different actors involved in Colombia's civil conflict have attempted to impose their versions of the story by manipulating the information provided to journalists. In some cases, the war information agenda was created not only by the government, but also by other countries that have great interest in the results. There are repercussions for the way journalists inform the public about the civil conflict because of the competition between these interests and their attempts to control the flow of information.

In the end, Colombian journalism is not easy to label. The complex and sometimes paradoxical findings in this chapter reveal the struggles of the profession. However, while it is evident that many different problems surround Colombian news media, the journalists' commitment, courage, and creative solutions continue to provide the country's citizens with much valuable information on a daily basis.

References

AFACOM. Asociación Colombiana de Facultades y Programas Universitarios de Comunicación Social [Colombian Association of Faculties and University Programs in Communication].

Aguirre, Jesus (1990). Perfil ocupacional de los periodistas de Caracas [Occupational profile of journalists in Caracas] Federal. *Revista Comunicación*, 69: 6–17. Caracas, VE

Arroyave, J., and I. Blanco. 2005. Como perciben los periodistas su profesión: entre el agotamiento y la fascinación. [How journalists perceive their profession: Between exhaustion and fascination]. *Investigación y Desarrollo* 13(2):364–389.

Arroyave, Jesus, Gill, Juliet, & Blanco, Iscar. 2007. Latin American journalists' perceptions of the profession: Between exhaustion and fascination. *Florida Communication Journal XXXIV*, 36, 2, Fall Issue, pp 67 - 76.

Arroyave, Jesus, and Sally Hughes (2004). Market-driven journalism and tabloidization of mainstream Mexican TV news. Paper presented at the International Congress of the Latin American Studies Association, Las Vegas, NV.

Barrios, Marta Milena, and Jesús Arroyave. 2008. Latin American digital newspapers between definition and frustration. Paper presented at the 26th World Congress of the International Association for Media and Communication Research (IAMCR), 2008. Stockholm, Sweden.

Benassini, Claudia. 2001. Escuelas de comunicación en México: Realidad o imaginario social? [Communication schools in Mexico: Reality or social imaginary?] *Diálogos de la Comunicación* 51: 42–51.

FELAFACS. 2009. *Federación Latinoamericana de Facultades de Comunicación Social* [Latin American Federation of Communication Schools].

Flores, Javier, and Cristina Alonso. 1995. Using focus groups in education research: Exploring teachers' perspective on educational change. *Evaluation Review* 19:16–29.

Franco, Guillermo, and Julio Cesar Guzman. 2004. The state of online journalism in Latin America: A continent wide newspaper survey reveals a disparity with print in pay and reputation. Retrieved from http://www.poynter.org/content/content_view.asp?id=64532#authors

Frey, James, and Andrea Fontana. 1993. The group interview in social research. In *Successful focus groups: Advancing the state of the art,* edited by D. L. Morgan, pp. 20–34. Newbury Park, CA: Sage.

Fuentes, Raul. 1992. El estudio de la comunicación desde una perspectiva sociocultural en América Latina [The study of communication from a socio-cultural perspective in Latin America]. *Diálogos de la comunicación* 32:12–26.

García Márquez, Gabriel. 1997. *News of a kidnapping.* Bogota, Colombia: Editorial Norma.

García de Jesús, Yomarie. 2003. *"Sensacionalistas" pero "objetivos": la encrucijada entre la información y el entretenimiento.* ["Sensational" but "objective": The intersection between information and entertainment].Web para Profesionales de la Comunicación Iberoamericanos. Año V, Vol.23. Retrieved on December, 2003, from http://www.saladeprensa.org/

Gómez, Juan Carlos, and Juan Camilo Hernández. 2008. Libertad de prensa en Colombia: La contradicción en la búsqueda de la verdad [Freedom of press in Colombia: The contradiction and the search for truth] Revista Palabra Clave, 17. Chía: Facultad de Comunicación de la Universidad de La Sabana.

Hallin, Daniel. 2000. La Nota Roja: Popular journalism and the transition to democracy in Mexico. In *Tabloid tales: Global debates and media standards*, edited by C. Sparks and J. Tulloch, pp. 267–284. New York: Rowman & Littlefield.

Herrán, Maria Teresa. 1991. *La industria de los medios de comunicación en Colombia* [The mass communication media industry in Colombia]. Bogotá: Fescol.

Herrán, María Teresa, and Javier Darío Restrepo. 1992. *Ética para periodistas* [Ethics for journalists]. 2nd ed. Santafé de Bogotá: Tercer Mundo Editores.

Herscovitz, Heloiza, and Adalberto Cardoso. 1998. The Brazilian journalist. In *The global journalist*, edited by David H. Weaver, pp. 417–432. Cresskill, NJ: Hampton Press,.

Hughes, Sally, and Chappell Lawson. 2005. The barriers to media opening in Latin America. *Political Communication* 22(1):9–25.

Inter-American Press Association. 2005. IAPA General Assembly issues conclusions on state of press freedom in the Americas. Retrieved from http://www.ifex.org/international/2005/10/14/iapa_general_assembly_issues_conclusions/

Krueger, Richard. 1988. *Focus groups: A practical guide for applied research*. Newbury Park, CA: Sage.

Larsen, Amy Jo. 2005. Media reform and social movements: Acting together in the public interest. Report Presented to the Faculty of the Graduate School of The University of Texas. Retrieved January 8, 2010 from http://21stcenturyproject.org/docs/media/LarsenPR.pdf in

Manrique, Alejandro, and Ivan Cardona (2004). La situación laboral de los periodistas en Colombia. *Revista El Pulso del Periodismo* [The labor situation for Colombian journalists]. Retrieved from http://www.pulso.org/Espanol/Nuevos/periodColo031204.htm.

Martini, Stella, and Lila Luchessi. 2004. Los que hacen las Noticias: Periodismo, información y poder [Those who make the news: Journalism, information and power]. Buenos Aires: Editorial Biblos.

Mellado, Claudia. 2005. Proyecto DIUC 205.174.002-1.0 *Realidad laboral, asociativa y profesional de los periodistas de la Octava Región* [Labor, associative and professional reality for the eighth region journalists].

Pastran, Adolfo. 2000. *Periodismo y salario mínimo en Nicaragua: Revista Pulso del Periodismo* [Journalism and minimum wage in Nicaragua]. Retrieved from www.saladeprensa.org/art155.htm

Pedroso, Rosa. 1994. Elementos para una teoría del periodismo sensacionalista [Elements for sensationalist journalistic theory]. *Comunicación y Sociedad* 21:139–157.

Riffe, Daniel. 2005. *Analyzing media messages using quantitative content analysis in research*. Mahwah, NJ: Erlbaum.

Rotker, Susana. 2005. *La invención de la crónica* [The invention of the chronicle]. México, City: Fondo de Cultura Económica.

Santoro, Ninetta. 2000. Communicative language teaching materials: A critical language perspective. *Prospect* 15(1):46–60.

Silverman, David. 2001. *Interpreting qualitative data* (2nd ed.). London: Sage.

Vasallo de Lopez, Immacolata. 1997. *Exploraçoes metodológicas num estudo de recepçao de telenovela. Temas contemporáneos em comunicaçao* [Methodological explorations in a study of the soap operas reception. Contemporary topics in Communication] pp. 151–167. Sao Paulo, Brasil: Edicon/Intercom.

31 Major Trends of Journalist Studies in Latin America

A Meta-Analysis of Five Decades of Research

Claudia Mellado

The pronounced technological, cultural, economic, and political changes that have taken place since 1990 have dramatically affected communication and journalism studies. The expansion of the field, the methodological approaches, and the most common and influential subjects all have been affected by these changes. Numerous academic studies have served to monitor and organize the scientific production of this discipline in many parts of the world (Chang & Tai 2005; Donsbach, Laub, Haas, & Brosius 2005; Kamhawi & Weaver 2003; Machill, Beiler, & Fischer 2006; Perloff 1976; Riffe & Freitag 1997; Schweitzer 1988; Shoemaker 1987; Wartella & Reeves 1985; Wimmer & Haynes 1978). In Latin American academic circles, however, the discussion about how journalism and communication research have changed does not seem to be a priority as evidenced by the lack of cross-national studies and systematic meta-analyses. In fact, the absence of these analyses actually prevents the discovery of characteristics that are shared by journalism and communication studies in Latin American countries. Such efforts, however, could support the identification of common methodological and theoretical frames that have been contextualized within Latin America's media environment.

Very few academic studies so far have analyzed the production of scientific knowledge within the field of Latin American communication studies (Fuentes Navarro 1992; Huesca & Dervin 1994; Jiménez 1982; Sánchez Ruiz 2002). Moreover, in countries such as Mexico, Brazil, or Venezuela, national issues have been investigated but without considering the regional contexts, thus limiting the impact of the most important findings for a broader understanding of commonalities and contrasts across Latin America (e.g., Aguirre 2007; Vassallo de Lopes & Romancini 2006; Fuentes Navarro 2003, 2007).

In light of these shortcomings, this chapter seeks to bridge the gap between current research and the rapid changes that have taken place among the Latin American media. The chapter is based on a meta-analysis of existing studies and will outline the empirical research about Latin American journalists conducted and published between 1960 and 2007. The analysis will identify the cycles and stages of academic development, as well as images and operational definitions of the journalism profession in Latin America. It will also discuss the analytical methods used, and then will conclude with suggestions for future studies.[1]

Previous Studies

A review of the trends in Latin American journalism and mass communication research suggests that scholarly work focusing on journalists has received little attention. McNelly (1966), for example, noted that up to the mid-1960s most Latin American media studies focused on the uses and effects of the mass media. Later, in a review that considered the period up to the 1970s, Beltrán (1976, 2000) reported that the most prominent research themes in the field of Latin American media studies were the history of journalism and press, communication policy, media structures and functions, message formats, media availability, message consumption, and message context.

In an examination of studies that have been carried out by Latin American and U.S. American communication scholars in Latin America, Gómez-Palacio (1989) noted 12 predominant themes: uses and effects of mass media; communication and development; communication and culture; political communication; mass media characteristics; alternative communication; history of communication; communication policy; mass media and ideology; Latin American journalism; and new information technology. Within these categories, new information technology, alternative communication, and Latin American journalism were, though important, found to be the topics that had received the least attention.

Pineda (2001: 81) identified six research topics that have been popular among Latin American communication scholars in the early 21st century: globalization and new communication technologies; audiences and critical reception processes; communication education; theoretical–methodological approaches and updated reviews in the field of mass communication; problems in communication management; and difficulties linked to the career and education of journalists. According to Pineda (2001), although there is interest in journalists and their profession among Latin American academics, most of the current studies focus on assessing academic programs or the media market, while ignoring other important factors that define the profession.

If we consider these studies from a historical perspective, it is clear that research about Latin American journalists has been very limited and that the topics of study have been primarily about the receiver, the media institutions, or the social construction of messages—rather than the producers of the messages. This conclusion seems to hold despite the fact that journalists are influenced and conditioned by the contextual realities that mediate their ability to produce content (Mellado 2009a).

Another problem in the analysis of Latin American journalist studies is that scholars themselves have not offered a clear definition of the journalism profession around the globe (Deuze 2005; Hanitzsch 2008; Josephi 2005; Wasserman & Beer 2009; Weaver 1998; Zelizer 2000). Splichal and Sparks (1994) propose two different options: First, due to cultural differences, journalism is so diverse that it can only be interpreted within the context of the specific nation in which it is analyzed. Second, due to general characteristics that are shared cross-nationally, journalism might become a universal profession that is not determined by particular national interests.

Based on these opposing views, it might be wise to acknowledge that each Latin American country is characterized by specific historic and cultural environments that need to be acknowledged for understanding the particular dynamics and developments of journalism in each of these nations (Mellado 2009b). Nevertheless, an effort should be made to identify common elements that define Latin American journalism due to similar social or cultural structures.

In this context, several Latin American scholars have noted that research so far has failed to formulate a comparative frame rooted in the particular experience of Latin American journalism. Instead, most studies have uncritically reproduced foreign research models without examining their conceptual and methodological applicability (Beltrán 1975, 1976; Fuentes Navarro 1992; Marques de Melo 1971). Josephi (2005: 576), for example, suggests that the evidence found by most recent comparative studies outside the North American orbit question the universal validity of those models, showing "the gap between theory and practice."

Considering these deficiencies within the current research on Latin American journalists, this chapter is based on the belief that a systematic analysis might serve as a guide for future comparative studies of journalism and communication in the region.

Methods

The objective of this analysis is to outline research on Latin American journalists and to describe the major trends within this line of study. We will investigate the structure of this research, its evolution in the last five decades, its methodological and conceptual characteristics, the relationships between scholars, and its influence on the conceptual and operational definition of the "journalist."

This chapter is based on a meta-analysis of all studies on Latin American journalists conducted and published between 1960 and 2007. For the purpose of this analysis, a "journalist study" is defined as quantitative or qualitative scholarly work that explores, describes, compares, or explains some personal, educational, labor, or professional aspects of journalists. Such studies must consider Latin American journalists as the main subject of the analysis and have a (implicit or explicit) conceptual framework that defines them. All studies published in scientific journals, books, research reports, conference proceedings as well as master's theses and Ph.D. dissertations were considered.[2] Journalism studies that focus expressly on the message, the channel, or on the audience were not considered. In addition, documents identified as book reviews and journalistic or literary texts were excluded.

The meta-analysis includes scholarly material written in Spanish, Portuguese, and English because the first two are the official languages of Latin American countries and the third one is the most influential foreign language in the region. Latin America included all Spanish or Portuguese speaking countries located in North, Central, and South America that are independent republics and have comparable political, social, and economic systems, despite obvious cultural differences (Mellado 2009b). These countries are: Argentina, Bolivia, Brazil, Chile, Colombia, Costa Rica, Cuba, Ecuador, El Salvador, Guatemala, Honduras, Mexico, Nicaragua, Panama, Paraguay, Peru, Dominican Republic, Uruguay, and Venezuela. Puerto Rico was also included in spite of its dependent relationship with the United States. This assumption makes it possible to recognize common elements as well as the specificities of the studies from a comparative perspective (Livingstone 2003).

One of the greatest challenges for this study was the lack of comparable databases that included a complete list of studies of Latin American journalists. The challenge was how to uncover the largest possible number of studies produced and published not only in different nations but also in different types of publications. As a result, the material for this study was the product of an extensive database search targeting all studies of Latin American journalists published between 1960 and 2007.[3] In addition, a variety of historical card catalogues were searched in order to find older studies that might not have been included in online listings.

In each of the catalogues and databases, several searches were conducted using both different and combined keywords such as *journalism, journalist, journalistic profession, journalism studies, Latin America, profession, professionalism, journalism education, gender studies, professional roles, work conditions, journalists labor market, journalist profile,* and *journalistic practices,* among others. The bibliography and the citations of each identified article, book, thesis, dissertation, or research report found were also scanned in order to ensure that titles not already included in the historic catalogues and databases would be included in this meta-analysis.

The unit of analysis used in this overview of research on Latin American journalists was a single study, understood as a collection of data obtained through research. The studies were systematically reviewed and then classified according to their authorship, approaches, methods, and theoretical perspectives. In order to identify research trends, we coded the year of publication, the identity, and nationality of the authors, the language of the study, the type of publication, the country of publication, and the geographic zones studied. Research content was identified by coding (1) the explicit or implicit definitions of journalist, (2) the research topic, (3) the theoretical perspectives mentioned, and (4) the bibliography used. To see which scholars were most often cited in research on Latin American journalists, the name citations in each study were recorded and then aggregated.

One of the most difficult categories to code was the use (or not) of a theoretical perspective in the studies. This was mostly due to the fact that many studies simply did not clearly indicate on which theory they were based (if on any at all). Nevertheless, we searched for theories that were explicitly named as well as conceptual orientations present in the theoretical framework of each study. When there was more than one theory or conceptual orientation present in the text, all of them were coded.

Finally, in order to understand the dominant research methods used in studies of Latin American journalists, all studies were categorized as either quantitative or qualitative. We considered a study to be "quantitative" if it included numeric calculations using statistical procedures to obtain results; it was considered to be "qualitative" if analytical and narrative techniques were used to explore and describe the reality as the respondents experience it. Studies were coded as mixed if they presented both methodological approaches.

To test the coding procedures, two independent research assistants coded 20% of the analyzed data. The results of the intercoder reliability test indicated that the coefficient of agreement (Krippendorf's alpha) was between .84 and .96, with an average of .92.

Results

We identified a total of 191 studies about Latin American journalists carried out between 1960 and 2007. During the first three decades under investigation, only a small number of studies were published (10.5%). This low number is partly due to the spread of military dictatorships in Latin

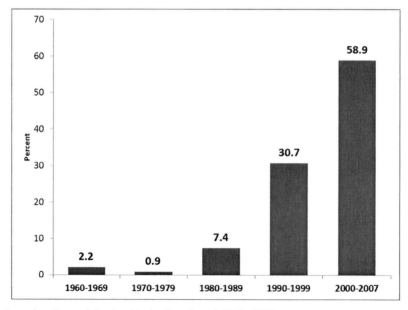

Figure 31.1 Journalism Research Productivity by Time Period (1960–2007)

America during the 1970s, which resulted in an oppressive environment that inhibited educational and academic development in the social sciences. But between 1990 and 1999, the number of publications about Latin American journalists increased dramatically (31%) and peaked in the new century with almost six in 10 studies published between 2000 and 2007.

Country of Publication

The analysis indicates that studies about Latin American journalists were published in 13 Latin American countries and three other nations. However, according to the consulted sources, seven Latin American countries did not publish any empirical research about local journalists: Paraguay, Dominican Republic, Nicaragua, Panama, El Salvador, Cuba, and Honduras.

Overall, scholars in Brazil (34%) are the clear leaders in the number of published studies about Latin American journalists, followed by communication researchers in Mexico (21%). Scholars in Venezuela (8%), Chile (6.5%), Spain (6%), and Colombia (3.5%) combined contributed about a quarter of all studies, while their colleagues in the United States contributed 11%. Media scholars from Costa Rica (3%), Argentina (2%), Peru (2%), and other nations (4%), contributed the remaining journalist studies.

An important context considered in our analysis was each country's educational infrastructure. During the last three decades, a general positive correlation is observed across all countries between the number of colleges and schools of journalism and mass communication (FELAFACS 2005; Ferreira & Tilson 2000; Nixon 1970), and the number of studies. But when comparing the number of studies with the number of schools within each time period in each nation, the data do not show an evident positive link between the two factors. Except for Chile, Brazil, Costa Rica, and Peru, more journalism schools did not automatically produce more research about journalists.

As shown in Table 31.1, Chile showed significant growth between 2000 and 2007 both in the number of journalism schools and the number of journalist studies published. In fact, Chilean media scholars published 11 times more studies in that time period as compared to the 1990s. Similarly, Brazilian scholars tripled the number of published studies between 2000 and 2007. The opposite relationship was identified in countries like Mexico and Venezuela, where the number of studies of journalists decreased, even though the total number of journalism schools increased considerably during the same time period. Hernández and Schwarz (2008) explain that due to the political and social changes that Mexico has undergone during the last decade, the development of journalism studies within the country has been focused more on the study of news production, and media coverage of the political-electoral processes and their association with journalism as an object of study, rather than the study of the journalists. In Venezuela, meanwhile, changes in public administration, political idealogical struggles, as well as the institutional deterioration of universities and organizations promoting journalism research, are possible explanations for the decline in productivity on the topic in favor of the analysis of journalistic discourses, the political economy, and public opinion studies (Aguirre 2007).

Scope

Not surprisingly, our findings suggest that there is a tendency among Latin American journalism studies to take local or national perspectives. While more than a third of the studies had a local focus, 28% analyzed national issues, 26% were case studies, and only 11% took a cross-national perspective. The most studied journalists were those from Brazil (39% of all studies), Mexico

Table 31.1   Journalism Schools and Studies of Journalists in Latin America (1960s–2000s)

	1960s		1970s		1980s		1990s		2000s	
	Journ. Schools	Studies	Journ. Schools	Studies	Journ. Schools	Studies	Journ. Schools	Studies	Journ. Schools	Studies
Venezuela	3	—	3	1	3	4	5	10	15	2
Mexico	2	—	7	—	42	3	89	20	321	16
Chile	1	—	5	—	7	—	27	1	54	11
Colombia	2	—	4	—	9	—	12	—	55	5
Argentina	2	—	16	—	21	—	18	3	55	2
Peru	2	—	8	—	10	—	12	1	32	3
Bolivia	—	—	1	—	2	—	7	—	29	1
Guatemala	1	—	1	—	1	—	2	—	7	2
Brazil	2	—	24	—	71	2	64	16	348	46
Costa Rica	2	—	1	—	2	1	2	2	6	3
Ecuador	2	—	2	—	4	—	9	1	31	—
Uruguay	—	—	—	—	2	—	2	1	5	—
Puerto Rico	—	—	—	—	6	1	6	—	16	—
Cuba	2	—	1	—	1	—	2	—	4	—
Dom. Rep.	—	—	2	—	1	—	5	—	10	—
El Salvador	1	—	1	—	1	—	2	—	10	—
Honduras	2	—	1	—	1	—	2	—	4	—
Nicaragua	—	—	1	—	1	—	1	—	9	—
Panama	—	—	1	—	1	—	2	—	6	—
Paraguay	—	—	2	—	1	—	2	—	8	—
Total	24	0	81	1	187	11	271	55	1025	91

Note.   Overall correlation coefficient (Spearman's rho) between the number of schools and the number of studies for each decade: 1960s: cannot be calculated because one of the variables is constant; 1970s: $\rho = .144$; n.s., 1980s: $\rho = .475$; $p = .034$; 1990s: $\rho =.594$; $p = .006$; 2000s: $\rho = .682$; $p = .001$

(27%), Venezuela (17.5%), and Chile (17.5%), which coincides with the distribution of studies according to country of publication. Meanwhile, the countries whose national journalist characteristics were least analyzed were El Salvador, Honduras, Dominican Republic, Panama, Puerto Rico, and Cuba.

Type of Publication and Authors

The studies on Latin American journalists can be classified by the following types of publication: journal articles (35%), master's theses (23%), books (11%), Ph.D. dissertations (11%), book chapters (9.5%), research reports (6.5%), conference proceedings (3%), and other types of publications (0.4%). Our analysis shows that compared to the 1990s, the number of journal articles doubled since 2000, while the number of masters theses increased by 94% and the number of dissertations increased by an astonishing 260% (see Figure 31.2).

Overall, 295 different authors or co-authors were identified in the studies on Latin American journalists. As expected, most of authors (93%) from Spanish-speaking countries published their results in Spanish—similar to most Brazilian authors (81%) who published in Portuguese. The

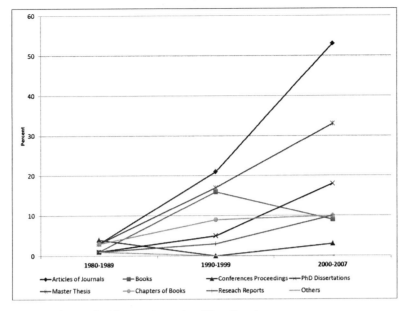

Figure 31.2 Evolution of Type of Publication During Last Three Decades

majority of studies (77%) were written by single authors. However, less than 4% of the authors have led more than one study and less than 2% kept producing on the same topic for more than a decade. In terms of university affiliation, there is not supremacy of some local or foreign academic institution. In other words, no individuals or group of researchers dominated the research productivity.

About three-quarters of the journal articles (77%) were published in Latin American journals (mostly in Mexico and Brazil) with the remainder appearing in journals located in the United States, Spain, and the Netherlands. The largest number of published articles in any single journal were found in the Venezuelan communication journal *Estudios Venezolanos* (6 articles), the Mexican journal *Sala de Prensa* (6), and *Journalism Quarterly* (6) from the United States. However, of the 191 articles analyzed for this study, only nine were published in journals that are indexed in the Social Science Citation Index (SSCI).

Typology of Studies

In terms of content, 10 different types of research studies were identified with journalistic practices and routines, occupational profiles and labor markets, and journalism education being the highest-ranking categories (see Table 31.2).

An analysis of the evolution of the different types over time indicates that studies of journalistic practices and routines have experienced the most growth since the 1990s, doubling in number between 2000 and 2007. In contrast, studies of occupational profiles and labor market conditions dropped almost by half during the same time. The lack of new studies on professional orientation and levels of professionalization in the last decade is noteworthy because it contradicts the lively conceptual debates that the topic has generated within the professional and academic world in Latin America. The lack of studies on gender, working conditions, representations, and worldviews during the 1970s and 1980s, on the other hand, coincides with the period of political and military oppression by the dictatorial regimes in Latin America.

Table 31.2   Research Topics of Latin American Journalist Studies (in %)

Research topic	Concentration 1960–2007	Percent of Change 1990–2007
Journalistic practices & routines	31.6	+135.2
Occupational profiles & labor markets	19.3	– 42.9
Journalism education	18.7	+72.7
Attitudes & professional roles	16.0	0
Working conditions & job satisfaction	15.5	+9.1
Representations & images of journalists	10.7	+116.7
Socio-demographic profiles	8.6	– 12.5
Professional memberships	5.3	0
Professional orientation & professionalization	3.7	– 100.0
Gender studies	3.2	+50.0

Note.   The total percentage is more than 100% because many of the studies address more than one research topic.

The Definition of "Journalist"

The findings confirm that a majority of studies define journalists as reporters or editors who produce news information for the media. Although 86% of the studies about Latin American journalists do not provide an explicit definition of journalists, about 65% rely on an implicit definition by including only those who hold a job in the mass media. The other studies define journalists as those working for the "mass media, corporate communication and journalism education" (24%), those working for "mass media and corporate communication" (6%), or those working for "corporate communication" only (5%). Most of the studies that employed broader definitions of journalists come from Mexico and Brazil, and to a lesser degree from Chile, Costa Rica, and Venezuela. It is important to emphasize, however, that most studies in all analyzed countries primarily define journalists as linked to the mass media.

This situation is somewhat contradictory, since most journalism schools and communication colleges in Latin America have focused since the 1970s on training journalists not only for jobs in the mass media, but also to work in public, private, and educational organizations. This focus has been promoted by the United Nations Educational, Scientific, and Cultural Organization (UNESCO) and the International Center of Superior Studies of Journalism for Latin America (CIESPAL), influencing strongly both the future of the field and of the profession (Ferreira 2006; Marques de Melo 1988, 1993; Rogers 1997).

Theories

Theoretical development is probably the main concern in the disciplinary evaluation of any field. In the case of studies about Latin American journalists, however, the use of theories was not very common. Only about one-third (34%) of the studies in our analysis made references to an explicit theory or conceptual orientation, while the vast majority simply did not mention any conceptual framework at all. The theories most often referred were theories related to the profession (19%), Bourdieu's concept of "habitus" (17%), attitudes and professional roles (15%), the production of news content (12.5%), social representations (10%), the press in general (6%), and the concept of gatekeeping (6%).

Citations

About one-quarter (27%) of the studies in this analysis did not cite any literature. Among the studies that actually cited some literature, 93% used only foreign references, with 58% of those sources coming from U.S.-based publications and 41% from European publications. A citation analysis revealed that 69% of the studies included in our analysis were never cited by any of the other studies in the analysis, and only 19% were mentioned by more than two different studies. In other words, almost three-quarters of the research on Latin American journalists has very little impact in the academic field of journalism studies.

Overall, only 31 different academic authors were cited in two or more studies and only nine were cited in at least three studies. The majority of the cited authors were of U.S. or European origin (listed in decreasing order): Pierre Bourdieu (French sociologist and university professor); Jack McLeod and Searle Hawley (American journalism professors); David Weaver and Cleveland Wilhoit (American journalism professors); Max Weber (German sociologist); Mauro Wolf (Italian journalism professor); Wilbur Schramm (American communication professor); Manuel Castells (Spanish sociologist and university professor); Raúl Fuentes Navarro (Mexican sociologist and university professor); and Elliot Freidson (American sociologist and university professor).

Methods

As shown in Table 31.3, the majority of studies (42%) carried out between 1960 and 2007 were based on quantitative approaches. However, these percentages present important variations, especially between the 1990s and now. The first qualitative studies began to appear in the 1990s and since then have grown to almost half (48%) of all studies published between 2000 and 2007. This contrasts with about 29% of the studies published between 2000 and 2007 that rely on quantitative methods and 23% that rely on mixed methods. Thus, most of the more recent studies of Latin American journalists present a qualitative rather than quantitative approach. This finding supports the so-called cultural turn of empirical analyses suggested by some communication scholars (Bonnell & Hunt 1999).

Certain countries tend to produce more qualitative research than others. This is the case for Brazil, where only 7% of the studies of journalists used quantitative methods and 20% used a mixed approach. However, the quantitative approach continues to dominate in countries such as the United States (64%), Venezuela (75%), Chile (67%), and Argentina (80%).

Among the studies using quantitative methods, surveys (55.5%) and content analyses (39.5%) constitute the majority of the research techniques used. However, while the use of content analysis has tripled during the past decade, the use of surveys increased only by about one-quarter (26%). Qualitative studies, on the other hand, are dominated by the use of in-depth interviews (75%). Compared to the 1990s, the use of this research technique has more than tripled between 2000 and 2007.

TABLE 31.3   Studies of Latin American Journalists by Research Method (1960–2007)

Method	1960–1969	1970–1979	1980–1989	1990–1999	2000–2007	Total
Qualitative	—	—	—	18	51	69
Quantitative	3	1	11	35	31	81
Both	—	1	5	11	24	41
Total	3	2	16	64	106	191

In both quantitative and qualitative analyses, the reproduction and adaptation of U.S. measurement instruments was found in more than 60% of the analyzed studies. Coincidentally, the above mentioned studies are the same as those that restrict the definition of journalists to those who work for the mass media. Unfortunately, the use of convenience samples in most of these studies prevents authors from generalizing their findings. For instance, 45% of both quantitative and mixed research designs include fewer than 100 respondents, and 92% include fewer than 500 subjects.

Discussion

This chapter traced the evolution in Latin American journalist studies between 1960 and 2007 with an emphasis on the structure, depth, and level of conceptualization in this scholarly field. The observed increase in the number of studies reaffirms the expansion that this area of study has had in the region. Nevertheless, this overview also documented a rather late growth beginning in the 1990s. Since many of the earlier studies closely mirrored those originating in the United States, the number of original studies and new scientific developments has been limited in Latin America. In addition, the long periods of dictatorships during the 1970s and the 1980s marked an important setback in the development of the communication and journalism field in the region.

At the same time, our analysis indicates a pattern of irregular growth and noticeable differences in the production of journalist studies throughout Latin America. While scholars from some South American countries have studied their journalists in diverse contexts, journalists working in Central America have been mostly ignored. We also noted that the observed increase in the number of colleges and journalism schools in several countries of Latin America did not necessarily encourage more studies of journalists.

This meta-analysis also shows that the way Latin American journalists have been studied has changed over time. The early studies in the 1960s and 1970s mostly focused on the professional orientation and the levels of professionalization of journalists. In the 1980s and 1990s, scholars shifted to a more quantitative approach to analyze the media market and professional roles of journalists. Finally, after the turn of the century, attention focused on journalistic routines and professional practices. The growing interest in the practical work of journalists has been associated with a similar growth in the use of qualitative research methods, such as in-depth interviews, participant or nonparticipant observation, and focus groups.

Among the most relevant findings of this meta-analysis is the fact that many Latin American researchers use "foreign" conceptual and methodological models to study Latin American journalists. As we have shown, academic studies of Latin American journalists often define journalists as those who work for the mass media (but not those who might work, for example, in public relations or government organizations). Moreover, the same studies that restrict the definition of journalists to those who work for the mass media are those that use "foreign" models to explain the work of Latin American journalists. While those models might be valid for the contexts in which they have been developed, some have not been adapted adequately to the local context.

As we have argued earlier, these "foreign" definitions and models might not apply in Latin America because many communication professionals who do not work in the mass media are still thought of as journalists. Part of the explanation is due to cultural, political, and historical factors as well as the approach used in Latin American journalism education in the last four decades, where there is a very strong link between journalism and communication studies. As a result, the conceptualization of journalists in the region faces a contradiction between the characteristics of the labor and educational sectors on the one hand (the practice), and the understanding of this occupation in empirical research (the theory), as Josephi (2005) has suggested. In this sense, the present study is a call to rethink the empirical and conceptual approaches of studies that focus on Latin American journalism.

Another important finding of this analysis is the apparent lack of impact that studies of Latin American journalists have had on journalism studies overall. Much of the empirical work identified in our analysis has not been cited by other researchers and therefore remains largely unknown even within the original authors' nations. One reason for this limited impact is certainly the fact that most studies have been published in Spanish or Portuguese and in local journals only, which has significantly reduced the potential audience for this type of work in North America and Europe. Other possible explanations for this lack of impact might be structural, such as limited access to bibliographical databases in many Latin American universities, limited distribution of scientific publications, or scarcity of places for academic interaction (such as conferences or regional meetings).

Overall, the methodological and conceptual weaknesses that still exist within Latin American journalism research, and the limited impact of this work in the rest of the academic field, might be responsible for (or reflective of) the shortage of research and the absence of leadership among Latin American scholars. These factors also might explain the lack of originality in the theories used to analyze Latin American journalists. Thus, in order to develop greater cognitive independence and local conceptual agreement with respect to journalist studies, Latin American scholars need to make an effort to communicate with each other and to participate in more collaborative research.

This work represents a first effort to systematize the research on Latin American journalists. Nevertheless, more systematic analyses need to be developed by the academic community to achieve conceptual agreements and to validate the theoretical bases and methodologies used in Latin American journalist studies.

Notes

1. The author wishes to thank David Weaver (Indiana University), Steve Wiley (North Carolina State University), Federico Subervi (Texas State University-San Marcos), and Kris Kodrich (Colorado State University), for their support and generosity as well as their comments on preliminary versions of this manuscript. Research for this article received funding from Fondecyt Grant No. 1080066 (Fondo Chileno de Desarrollo Científico y Tecnológico) and from the Fulbright Commission.

2. Though in both the North American and European contexts master's theses may not present major interest in the review of the knowledge within the field, for many Latin American countries these are considered valuable works of research, products of the still weak development of doctoral academic activity. Regional efforts are being made regarding the dissemination and visibility of these documents through the emergence of specialized data bases (Vassallo de Lopes & Romancini 2006).

3. Specifically, the present study used the following historic and online catalogues and databases: Worldcat (a U.S.-based catalogue of books, articles of journals, conference proceedings, research reports and world documents), library catalogues from Latin American universities, catalogues from Spanish university libraries, catalogues from Portuguese libraries, Communication and Mass Media Complete, ComAbstracts, Scientific Electronic Library Online (Scielo), Social Science Citation Index (SSCI), Proquest (theses and dissertations), TESEO (Database for Spanish dissertations), Latindex, Google Scholar, CC-DOC in Mexico, PORTCOM (Free access portal for production in Communication Sciences in Brazil), REDALYC (Scientific Journals from Latin America, the Caribbean, Spain, and Portugal), Infoamérica, Dialnet, ISBN, Cervantes Virtual Library, CIS (Sociological Research Center), Banco de Teses Coordenacao de Aperfeicomento de Pessoal de Nivel Superior (CAPES), Cybertesis, and REDIAL–TESIS.

References

Aguirre, Jesús María. 2007. Investigación venezonala sobre comunicación y cultura de masas. Panorama bibliográfico: 1994–2007 [Venezuelan research on communication and mass culture. A bibliographic panorama: 1994–2007]. *Revista Comunicación: estudios venezolanos de comunicación,* 140:88–97.

Beltrán, Luis Ramiro. 1975. Research ideologies in conflict. *Journal of Communication* 25(2):187–193.

Beltrán, Luis Ramiro. 1976. Alien premises, objects, and methods in Latin American communication research. *Communication Research* 3(2):107–134.

Beltrán, Luis Ramiro. 2000. *Investigación sobre comunicación en Latinoamérica. Inicio, trascendencia y proyección* [Research on communication in Latin America: Beginnings, transcendency and scope]. La Paz, Bolivia: Universidad Católica Boliviana y Plural Editores.

Bonnell, Victoria, and Lynn Hunt (eds.). 1999. *Beyond the cultural turn: New directions in the study of society and culture.* Berkeley: University of California Press.

Chang, Tsan-Kuo, and Zixue Tai. 2005. Mass communication research and the invisible college revisited: The changing landscape and emerging fronts in journalism-related studies. *Journalism & Mass Communication Quarterly* 82(3):672–694.

Deuze, Mark. 2005. What is journalism? Professional identity and ideology of journalists reconsidered. *Journalism* 6(4):442–464.

Donsbach, Wolfgang, Torsten Laub, Alexander Haas, and Hans-Bernd Brosius. 2005. Anpassungsprozesse in der Kommunikationswissenschaft: Themen und Herkunft der Forschung in den Fachzeitschriften *Publizistik* und *Medien & Kommunikationswissenschaft* [Processes of adaptation in communication research: Themes and origins of research in the journals *Publizistik* and *Medien & Kommunikationswissenschaft*]. *Medien & Kommunikationswissenschaft* 53(1):46–72.

FELAFACS. 2005. *La formación de los periodistas en las escuelas de comunicación de América Latina: situación actual, demandas labores y necesidades sociales* [The education of journalists in Latin American communication schools: Current situation, job demands and social needs]. Río Cuarto, Argentina: Universidad Nacional de Río Cuarto.

Ferreira, Leonardo. 2006. *Centuries of silence: The story of Latin American journalism.* London: Preager.

Ferreira, Leonardo, and Donn Tilson. 2000. Sixty-five years of journalism education in Latin America. *The Florida Communication Journal* 272:61–79.

Fuentes Navarro, Raúl. 1992. El estudio de la comunicación desde una perspectiva sociocultural en América Latina [Communication studies in Latin American from a socio-cultural perspective]. *Diálogos de la Comunicación* 32:16–27.

Fuentes Navarro, Raúl. 2003. *La investigación académica sobre comunicación en México. Sistematización documental 1995–2001* [Academic research on communication in Mexico: Systematic documentation 1995–2001] Mexico City: ITESO.

Fuentes Navarro, Raúl. 2007. Fuentes bibliográficas de la investigación académica en los postgrados de comunicación en Brasil y en México: Un acercamiento al análisis comparativo [Bibliographic sources of academic research on communication graduate studies in Brazil and Mexico: A comparative analysis]. *Matrizes* 1:165–178.

Gómez-Palacio, Carlos. 1989. *The origins and growth of mass communication research in Latin America.* Unpublished Ph.D. dissertation, Stanford University, Stanford, CA.

Hanitzsch, Thomas. 2008. Comparing journalism across cultural boundaries: State of the art, strategies, problems, and solutions. In *Global journalism research: Theories, methods, findings, future,* edited by Martin Löffelholz, and David Weaver, pp. 93–105. Malden, MA: Blackwell.

Hernández, María Elena, and Andreas Schwarz. 2008. Journalism research in Mexico. Historical development and research interest in the Latin American context. In *Global journalism research: Theories, methods, findings, future,* edited by Martin Löffelholz and David Weaver, pp. 221–224. Malden, MA: Blackwell.

Huesca, Robert, and Brenda Dervin. 1994. Theory and practice in Latin American alternative communication research. *Journal of Communication* 44(4):53–73.

Jiménez, José. 1982. *La ciencia de la comunicación en América Latina: Un caso de dependencia científica* [Communication science in Latin America: A case of scientific dependence]. UAM Xochimilco, Mexico: Cuadernos del TICOM n°13.

Josephi, Beate. 2005. Journalism in the global age: Between normative and empirical. *Gazette* 67(6):575–590.

Kamhawi, Rasha, and David Weaver. 2003. Mass communication research trends from 1980 to 1999. *Journalism & Mass Communication Quarterly* 80(1):7–27.

Livingstone, Sonja. 2003. On the challenges of cross-national comparative media research. *European Journal of Communication* 18(4):477–498.

Machill, Marcel, Markus Beiler, and Corinna Fischer. 2006. Europe-topics in Europe's media: The debate about the European public sphere: A meta-analysis of media content analysis. *European Journal of Communication* 21(1):57–88.

Marques de Melo, José. 1971. A pesquisa em comunicacao na America Latina: O papel do CIESPAL [Communication research in Latin America: The role of CIESPAL]. *Comunicacoes e Artes* 5:45–60.

Marques de Melo, José. 1988. Communication theory and research in Latin America: A preliminary balance of the past twenty-five years. *Media Culture Society* 10(4):405–418.

Marques de Melo, José. 1993. Communication research: New challenges of the Latin American School. *Journal of Communication* 43(4):182–190.

McNelly, John. 1966. Mass communication and the climate for modernization in Latin America. *Journal of InterAmerican Studies* 8(3):345–357.

Mellado, Claudia. 2009a. Orígenes, evolución y desencuentros en la investigación sobre el periodista latinoamericano [Origins, problems and disagreement over research on the Latin-American journalist]. *Innovar* 19(33):7–17.

Mellado, Claudia, 2009b. Periodismo en Latinoamérica. Revisión histórica y propuesta de un modelo de análisis [Latin American journalism: A review of five decades and a proposal for a model of analysis]. *Revista Comunicar* 17(33):193–201.

Nixon, Raymond. 1970. *Education for journalism in Latin America*. New York: Council on Higher Education in the American Republics.

Perloff, Richard. 1976. Journalism research: A twenty years perspective. *Journalism Quarterly* 53(1):123–126.

Pineda, Migdalia. 2001. ¿Qué investigar hoy sobre comunicación en America Latina? [What to research today on communication in Latin America]. *Diálogos de la Comunicación* 62:76–83.

Riffe, Daniel, and Alan Freitag. 1997. A content analysis of content analyses: Twenty five years of Journalism Quarterly. *Journalism & Mass Communication Quarterly* 74(4):873–882.

Rogers, Everett. 1997. Communication study in North America and Latin America. *World Communication* 26(3):51–60.

Sánchez Ruiz, Enrique. 2002. La investigación latinoamericana de la comunicación y su entorno social: notas para una agenda [Latin American communication research and its social setting: Notes for an agenda]. *Diálogos de la Comunicación* 64: 25–36.

Schweitzer, John. 1988. Research article productivity by mass communication scholars. *Journalism Quarterly* 65(2):479–484.

Shoemaker, Pamela. 1987. Mass communication by the book: A review of 31 texts. *Journal of Communication* 37(3):109–131.

Splichal, Slavko, and Colin Sparks. 1994. *Journalists for the 21st century.* Norwood, NJ: Ablex.

Vassallo de Lopes, María Immacolata, and Richard Romancini. 2006. Teses e dissertaçoes: Estudo bibliométrico na area da comunicação [Theses and dissertations: A bibliometric study of communication] In *Comunicação e produção científica: contexto, indicadores y avalidação* [Communication and scientific production: context, indicators and validation], edited by Dinah Aguiar de Población, Geraldina Porto Witter, and José Fernando Modesto de Silva, pp. 137–161. São Paulo, Brazil: Angellara Editora e Livraria.

Wartella, Ellen, and Byron Reeves. 1985. Historical trends in research on children and the media: 1900–1960. *Journal of Communication* 35(2):118–133.

Wasserman, H., and Arnold de Beer. 2009. Towards de-Westernizing journalism studies. In *The handbook of journalism studies,* edited by Karin Wahl-Jorgensen and Thomas Hanitzsch, pp. 428–438. New York: Routledge.

Weaver, David (ed.). 1998. *The global journalist: News people around the world.* Cresskill, NJ: Hampton Press.

Wimmer, Roger, and Richard Haynes. 1978. Statistical analyses in the *Journal of Broadcasting*, 1970–1976. *Journal of Broadcasting* 22(2):241–248.

Zelizer, Barbie. 2000. What is journalism studies? *Journalism* 1(1):9–12.

Journalists in the Middle East

32 Arab Journalists

Lawrence Pintak and Jeremy Ginges

"Journalist": In the Arab world, the definition of that term has been as malleable as that of "demo-crat." Indeed, the two are inextricably linked. Historically, the five Ws of journalism—who, what, where, when, and why—had more to do with Arab journalists themselves than the story they were reporting. Who did they work for, what was the political climate, where and when were they plying their craft, and why had they become a journalist in the first place? In short, was the system under which they toiled some semblance of a democracy or an Orwellian system where "democrat" meant precisely the opposite? This is what dictated whether the term "journalist" defined a person who functioned as a watchdog or as a lapdog, a check on power or a mouthpiece for those who abused it.

Background

In the early 1950s, a former U.S. diplomat in Beirut, Thomas McFadden (1953), surveyed journalists in Lebanon, Syria, Jordan, Iraq, and Egypt. It was a heady time for Arab journalism and Arab politics. The colonial era had come to an end. Arabs were seizing control of their own destiny. Journalism, which had played a key role in fostering Arab nationalism after the age of Ottoman Turkish rule, was experiencing a renaissance. The decade would see more than 270 newspapers and magazines founded in Syria alone as the country experienced "a golden age of pluralistic politics" (Ziadeh 2010). Much the same was true across the region.

In distributing his questionnaire in newsrooms, McFadden found an activist style of journalism even more critical than in most advanced democracies. "Arab editors believe the role of the press in society should be to fight for political causes. This is much more important, they think, than objectively to inform the Arab public," he reported (McFadden 1953: 67). Their priorities included the fight against imperialism, Zionism, government corruption and weakness, and the struggle for Arab nationalism, Arab unity, and, perhaps most importantly, the reform, modernization, and democratization of Arab society. With Arab media organizations shedding their dependence on political subsidies, McFadden confidently predicted that Arab journalism was entering an era of objectivity and independence.

The period described by McFadden proved to be a fleeting moment in history. The 1960s saw a wave of bloody coups and revolutions across the Arab world. The rise of the dictators meant the neutering of Arab journalism. Media became a weapon of politics and journalists the official scribes. Lebanon was the one notable exception. The political confrontations in that country, which would spawn decades of civil war as the internal conflicts of the Arab world were fought on the streets of Beirut, meant Lebanese news organizations gave voice to a plethora of views, depending on which faction or Arab government happened to be paying their bills at any given time (Pintak 2003).

Elsewhere, however, governments brooked no dissent; media were a tool for manipulating public opinion. In Egypt, for example, the regime of strongman Gamal Abdul Nasser used the Voice of the Arabs radio station to stoke the fires of conflict in the lead-up to the Six Day War with Israel in 1967, then continued to boast of Arab victories even as the Egyptian Air Force lay smoking in ruins and the Arab armies were in full retreat (James 2006). The fact that today, Mohammed Hassanein Heikal, the former editor of Egypt's powerful state-run *al-Ahram* newspaper, is considered by many Arabs to be "a legacy of journalism at its best" (Heikal 2007)—even though he doubled as Nasser's advisor, confidant, and mouthpiece—is emblematic of the profession's identity crisis.

Previous Studies

The level of government control of the news media varied across the region, but nowhere were journalists completely free of some level of direct or indirect government influence, even when newspapers and magazines were privately owned. In his classic study of the Arab media, first published in the 1970s, former U.S. diplomat William Rugh divided the Arab media into four main classifications: The "mobilization press," controlled by revolutionary governments like those in Libya, Syria, Iraq, and Sudan; the "loyalist press" of Saudi Arabia, the Gulf, and Palestine, which was largely privately owned but beholden to the government; and the "diverse press" of Lebanon, Kuwait, Morocco, and Yemen, which was relatively free and reflected a diversity of views, but was subject to more subtle pressures. Lastly, there was the offshore press, newspapers that had fled to London to escape the worst of the pressure. But these were mainly owned by Saudi interests and largely reflected Saudi policy (Rugh 1979).

The region's prisons, and cemeteries, were full of journalists who had strayed from the party line. The majority did as they were told, blurring fact and fiction as required; idealistic images of changing governments and society long-since abandoned. This self-perceived mouthpiece function was evident in a 1987 survey of Algerian journalists in which fully one-quarter of the respondents defined news as "[e]vents that have something to do with the government" while large percentages saw it as their job to "educate and form a modern Algerian citizen" (69%) and "enhance the objectives of the social revolution" (56%) (Kirat 1987: vii).

Along with support for the government, the propagation of Islamic values was ranked high by journalists in both Saudi Arabia and Kuwait (al-Rasheed 1998; Tash 1983). Only about 20% of Saudi journalists ranked freedom of the press as their most important need, and relatively few showed any enthusiasm for complete independence, emphasizing instead the requirement to balance the needs of the public and the needs of the government (Tash 1983). A separate survey of chief editors at Kuwait Radio and Television found that the majority avoided stories they considered against the interests of Kuwait, "friendly countries," or the Arab world (al-Anezi 2000), just as a 1988 study of editors at TV channels in four Arab countries found that "domestic news concentrated on the official and the positive" (Turkistani 1988: 288).

The elastic nature of professional identity among Arab journalists was reflected in a 2004 survey of 150 reporters and editors taking part in a BBC training workshop. There was strong agreement with the statement that journalism ethics are "mostly determined by the ideological and political inclinations" of the news organization that employed them (BBC World Service Trust Symposia 2004). The degree to which Arab journalists have traditionally been forced into an Orwellian world where normative values are in sharp contradiction with the empirical realities is evident in many of the surveys, as in the case of Algerian journalists, 45% of whom said it was important to criticize the government when needed, which the researcher noted "contradicts the realities of Algerian journalism in practice" (Kirat 1987: 163). Likewise, the code of ethics adopted by Egyptian journalists in 1972 called democracy "the only healthy and sound framework for practicing political liberties" (Arab Journalism Codes n.d.) even though the country was effectively a dictatorship.

Ironically, it was the launch of a government-financed television channel in 1996 that marked the beginning of the end of the professional schizophrenia that had defined Arab journalism for more than three decades. Al-Jazeera was the creation of the Emir of Qatar, the tiny oil- and gas-rich emirate protruding from the Arabian Peninsula. The emir had recently deposed his father and his goal was to propel his backward country into the 20th century and, in doing so, shift it out from the shadow of Saudi Arabia, which dominated the Gulf region politically and economically. What better way than to launch a pan-Arab television channel to directly challenge Saudi dominance of the region's cross-border media.

The emir hired a team of Arab television journalists who were refugees from a failed BBC-Saudi joint venture. Most of the reporters and editors had been trained in the BBC's ethos of fair, balanced, and independent journalism, and their marching orders were to create a pan-Arab news organization largely free of political interference. Operating under the motto "opinion and the other opinion," al-Jazeera proceeded to redefine Arab journalism, challenging governments, interviewing opposition leaders, and generally giving voice to those who had long been silenced. Much to the shock of viewers, this included interviewing officials of Israel—long such a pariah that it was usually referred to in the Arab media as "the Zionist entity." It was not long before virtually every Arab country expelled al-Jazeera's news teams or shuttered its bureaus at one time or another.

But as horrified as governments might have been at this new, pull-few-punches approach to journalism, reporters and editors at other news organizations across the region were energized. Al-Jazeera would later come under attack from the Bush administration for allegedly serving as a mouthpiece for Osama bin Laden and encouraging anti-American violence. Such criticisms largely missed the point: Arab journalists had found their voice; Arab journalism had begun to portray the world from an Arab perspective—and through an Arab lens—that largely ignored the wishes of Arab governments.

The draconian, top-down model under which journalists had long toiled was beginning to collapse. Even if they were still trapped within a news organization that did its government's bidding, journalists began to push the envelope. Just as American journalists of the 1970s were inspired by those like Woodward and Bernstein who had helped to bring down a president and end a war, Arab journalists awoke to the power and possibility of their profession.

Methods

A decade after the advent of this "al-Jazeera revolution," we set out to create a portrait of the shifting attitudes, values, and mores of the emerging new Arab journalist. At the time, more than 300 pan-Arab satellite channels crowded the broadcast spectrum. New semi-independent newspapers and websites, as well as activist bloggers, were also making their mark. And the Arab media were playing a pivotal role in shaping post-9/11 relations between the United States and the Arab world and the wider Muslim world.

The research tool for this study was a 48-question survey administered to Arab journalists in 14 countries, as well as Arab journalists based in the United States and Europe but working for news organizations in the Arab world (as opposed to émigré publications).[1] It was conducted between June 2005 and September 2006. Modeled on the Weaver surveys of American journalists (Weaver, Beam, Brownlee, Voakes, & Wilhoit 2007; Weaver & Wilhoit 1986, 1991, 1996), the questionnaire also drew on several other surveys of U.S. journalists (Hess 1981; State of the News Media 2004) and journalists in other parts of the developing world (Hanitzsch 2005; Ramaprasad 2001; Ramaprasad & Hamdy 2006; Ramaprasad & Kelly 2003; Ramaprasad & Rahman 2006; Romano 2003; Steele 2005), as well as several surveys of the public in the Arab world and Muslim-majority countries (Inglehart 2005; Moaddel 2000; Newport 2002; Zogby & Zogby 2004).

The survey, available in both Arabic and English, was administered in online and hard-copy versions in order to reach as broad a sample of modern Arab journalists as possible. The survey was directly e-mailed to 634 individuals in early summer 2005.[2] Journalist-researchers in Egypt, Lebanon, Syria, the West Bank of the Palestinian territories, Morocco, and the United Arab Emirates were hired to administer the hard-copy versions of the survey. There were two criteria for selection of target media for the sample. In the pan-Arab media, the top priority was the main print and television media. On the national level, the six to eight largest circulation newspapers in each country were the primary target. Since the goal was to paint a portrait of mainstream journalists, the estimated 63,000 bloggers in the Arab world (Dolan & Whitehouse 2006) and those working for avowedly Islamist media outlets were excluded.

The survey resulted in an aggregate usable response of 601 journalists. We estimate the total population of Arab journalists in the 20,000 to 25,000 range (Pintak & Ginges 2008), which puts the sample at more than 2% of the known population of Arab journalists. Thirteen percent of all respondents worked for the pan-Arab media, while the balance was employed by news organizations serving a particular country.[3] The geographic distribution of respondents was as follows: Gulf Cooperation Council countries (Saudi Arabia, Qatar, Kuwait, Bahrain, and Oman) and Yemen, 27%; Egypt, 25%; the Levant (Lebanon, Syria, Palestine, Jordan), 26%; North Africa, 17%; the United States and Europe, 4%; other, 1%.

Findings

Basic Characteristics

Journalists in the Arab world are overwhelmingly young and Muslim. Almost 80% of respondents were 40 years old or under. Sixty-one percent were male, half said they were married, the same percentage had at least one child, and only 3% had been divorced. Eighty-eight percent reported they were Muslim, 7% were Christian, and 4% chose "other," a breakdown that was representative of the overall Arab population. Thirty percent of the Muslims self-identified as "religious," 36% as "secular," and the balance did not declare.

Though they represented almost every Arab nation, the survey respondents' primary identification was with the Arab world, not their individual nation-state. When the respondents were asked, "To which geographical group do you belong first?" 32% chose Arab world, 25% said Muslim world, and 15% selected "nation," about the same percentage that chose "locality."

However, a second question on identity produced an interesting result. Asked to choose between five prompts in response to the statement, "Above all I am a …" half chose "journalist," with the other options falling well behind: "Muslim" (20%), "Arab" (9%), and "Egyptian/Saudi, etc." (9%).

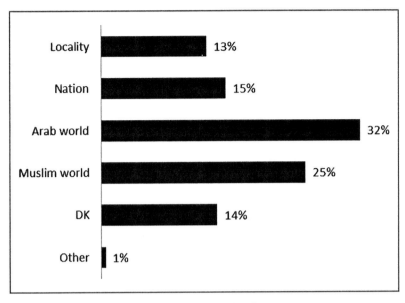

Figure 32.1 "To which of these geographic groups do you belong first?" (*N* = 562)

Education and Training

One-third of the respondents had been working in journalism for more than a decade, another 20% from five to 10 years, just under a quarter from three to five years, and the remainder less than two years. Almost 40% held a bachelor's degree and more than one-third had attended, but not graduated, from university; 17% had earned a master's degree and 2% held a doctorate. At the other end of the educational spectrum, 6% had only graduated from secondary school and a few respondents had only graduated from primary school. Of those who attended college, 62% took at least some journalism courses, though the reality is that, with a few exceptions, universities in the Arab world take a very theoretical approach to journalism. Less than a quarter of the sample (22%) said they held a journalism degree and about the same number (24%) had no professional training before being hired as a journalist.

Working Conditions

More than 70% of the respondents said they work full-time, 18% were freelancers, and 9% worked for more than one news organization. Journalists' need to work more than one job reflected the generally poor salaries in Arab journalism, a factor that also feeds corruption. For example, the starting newsroom salary at Egypt's largest newspaper, *al-Ahram*, is less than U.S.$100 a month, while over at state-run Egypt television and radio young reporters can expect just U.S.$35 a month (Dolan & Whitehouse 2006).

Our survey found a sharp disparity between the journalistic elite at the major satellite channels and pan-Arab newspapers and the majority of their colleagues. Almost three-quarters (72%) of our sample said they earned less than $1,000 a month, including 20% whose salaries were below $250. At the other end of the spectrum, 6% made between $5,000 and $7,499 and the elite 3% earned $7,500 or more. What that does not take into account, however, is the fact that top editors at some newspapers who officially earn only a few thousand dollars a year manage to live in

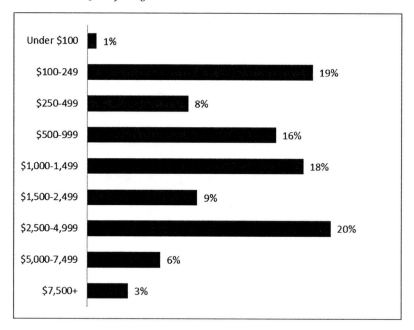

Figure 32.2 Journalists' monthly salary (*N* = 526)

expensive homes and drive flashy cars, which circles back to the issue of rampant corruption in the industry.

Professionalism

That issue of corruption was chief among the issues cited by Arab journalists for sobering views on their own profession. Fully half said that both the fairness and independence of the Arab media was poor, and almost as many (42%) gave the same poor rating to their industry's professionalism.

Asked about the greatest challenges to Arab journalism, significant majorities put the lack of professionalism, poor ethics, and journalistic corruption on par with government control, while

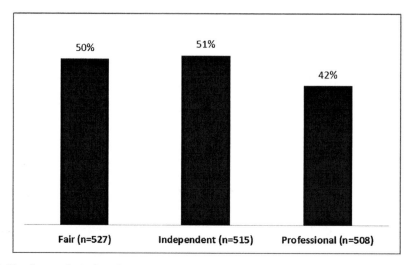

Figure 32.3 "Poor" rating for Arab media

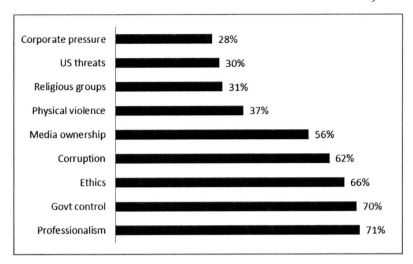

Figure 32.4 Most significant challenges to Arab journalism (*N* = 601)

more than half also cited problems with the ownership of media organs, since those individuals are usually closely associated with, or inseparable from, the totalitarian governments that dominate the region.

The so-called envelope culture in which journalists are given an envelope of "taxi money" to attend a news conference or write a favorable story is all-pervasive in the Arab world, and it occurs at both the individual and the institutional levels. News organizations often are provided with official or unofficial subsidies by governments, political parties, and powerful business people in return for following a particular political line. It is also common practice for editors to receive a percentage of advertising sales revenue, which skews coverage.

This issue of what, in the West, could be called "pay-for-play" journalism is an example of the many areas where the aspirations of Arab journalists diverge from the empirical reality. Survey respondents generally had a dim view of the role of money in shaping Arab journalism, with 81% rejecting the statement, "It is acceptable to take money to write favorable stories," three-quarters (74%) opposing the practice of writing favorable stories in exchange for advertising, and 60% saying it was never acceptable to take "travel money" from the subjects of stories.

During the period this survey was being administered, June 2005 to September 2006, Arab journalism was locked in a tense political environment, which resulted in several violent confrontations with the region's authoritarian governments. In its 2007 study, the Committee to Protect Journalists painted a grim picture of events in the previous year, reporting that "scores of journalists who challenged the political order were threatened by government agents, hauled before the courts, thrown in prison, or censored in media crackdowns that stretched from Algeria to Yemen" (Campagna 2007). Yet, at the same time, licenses for new newspapers were being issued, new satellite channels were being launched, and activist bloggers were emerging as influential voices that drove media coverage into areas previously off-limits.

Survey respondents implicitly acknowledged this inherent contradiction. Eighty-four percent completely or partly agreed that, on whole, the Arab media were becoming freer, and more than 50% completely or partly agreed that they were personally freer to do their jobs, even as they ranked media ownership, corporate pressure, and government control as the top challenges to Arab journalism.

Journalistic Mores

This ambivalence extended to the industry's performance. Only 29% said Arab post-9/11 coverage was "objective," although 60% said their own news organization was doing an "outstanding" job of informing the public. Tied into this self-evaluation are the fundamental questions of journalistic mores and mission.

Many Arab journalists opt for what has been called "contextual objectivity" (Nawawy & Iskandar 2002): the idea that objectivity must be evaluated in the societal context. The Saudi owned satellite channel al-Arabiya, for example, declares itself to be "an Arabic station, from the Arabs to the Arabs, delivering content that is relevant to the Arabs" (History of al-Arabiya 2010). For an Arab journalist reporting from an Arab city under siege by U.S. forces, speaking live to an audience across the Arab world as he shows the bodies of dead Arab children, objectivity becomes a relative term.

Almost 90% of respondents said journalists should be objective, but about the same number said they should also interpret events for their audience, and half (48%) said they should include their own opinion. Seventy percent said it was acceptable for journalists to participate in protests, and almost as many said journalists should be allowed to take part in political activities.

Notably, in societies where reporters can be jailed for insulting national and religious leaders, and where Western publications of what were considered highly insulting cartoons of the Prophet Muhammad set off a huge furor, 80% said journalists must balance the obligation to inform the public with the need to show respect for those being covered.

Journalistic Mission

As noted above, the Arab world is deep in the throes of a media revolution. Arab journalists believe that revolution should also extend to politics and society. The survey found that Arab journalists see their primary mission as that of driving social and political change. Three-quarters of the journalists surveyed said fueling "political reform" was the top job of an Arab journalist (see Figure 32.5). Only 2% of those surveyed said Arab society was not in need of reform; 64% said it must be gradually changed, while 32% said there was need for radical change.

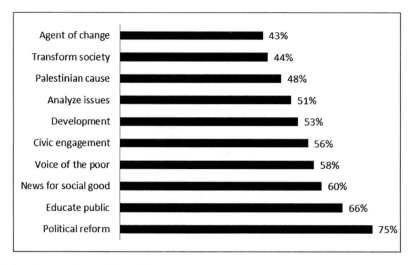

Figure 32.5 Top 10 journalist roles (*N* = 601)

Other journalistic roles cited by more than half the respondents included educating the public, using news for the social good, acting as a voice for the poor, encouraging civic engagement, driving development, and analyzing issues (see Figure 32.5). Roles traditionally ranked high by Western journalists, such as investigating the claims of governments (40%), fell far down on the Arab priority list.

This activist ethos could also be seen in the self-declared political identity of the respondents. Half described their political philosophy as "democrat,"[4] while just 15% selected Arab nationalist, 10% Islamist, and 8% as nationalist.

Although there are parallels with the perceived mission of journalists in other parts of the developing world, Arab journalists do not fall cleanly into any of the existing typologies identified in other studies of journalists, such as those proposed by Weaver et al. (2007), Rugh (1979), and Ramaprasad (2001; Ramaprasad & Hamdy 2006; Ramaprasad & Kelly 2003). We have therefore created a new set of typologies, which we believe are unique to Arab journalism. The activist functions fall within what we have labeled the "Change Agent" grouping, which brings together the dominant roles focused on political and social reform, elaborated above and in Figure 32.5. Closely associated with those roles is the grouping we call the "Guardian" function. Along with the dedication to driving social and political change is a perception among journalists that it is their duty to protect the region, its people, and its dominant religion in the face of outside threats (see Figure 32.6). This "Guardian" function includes support for the Palestinian people, which almost half of respondents said was an important task of Arab journalism, and a series of other roles identified by roughly one-third of respondents: foster Arab culture, enhance spiritual values, defend Arab interests), enhance pan-Arab unity, and protect Islamic traditions (see Figure 32.6). These underline the pan-Arab outlook of Arab journalists, which, the crosstabs indicated, is found whether they work for cross-border media or domestic news organizations.

Religion

The central role of Islam in Arab society was evident in the fact that 40% of respondents said it was necessary to believe in God to have good moral values, even though only about 25% said poli-

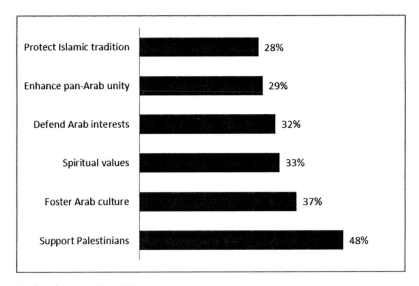

Figure 32.6 Guardian functions (*N* = 601)

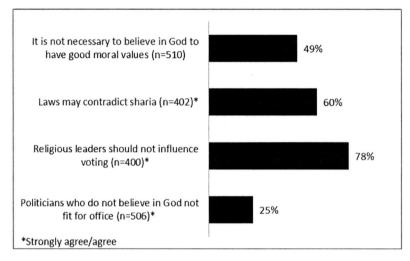

Figure 32.7 Religion and politics

ticians who do not believe in God are unfit for office. That latter view underscored the apparent desire among Arab journalists to separate religion and politics, and their critical view of Muslim clergy. Almost 80% said religious leaders should not influence voting, but 60% did not object to passage of civil laws that contradicted Islamic law (sharia). Even more telling, the majority did not believe Muslim clergy give adequate answers to the moral problems of the individual (57%), problems of family life (52%), or social problems (67%). Even on the question of whether clerics give adequate spiritual advice, they were split.

Attitudes toward the United States

In the years after 9/11, the Bush administration very effectively labeled al-Jazeera and the rest of the Arab media anti-American. "Arabic TV does not do our country justice," President George H. W. Bush said in early 2006. "They put out some kind—sometimes put out propaganda that just is—just isn't right, it isn't fair, and it doesn't give people the impression of what we're about" (Bush 2006).

The survey found that, while skeptical of U.S. policy, Arab journalists were not inherently opposed to all things American (see Figure 32.8). At the time of the survey, George W. Bush was still president, U.S. forces occupied Iraq and Afghanistan, and the so-called war on terror was at the top of Washington's agenda. An overwhelming proportion of respondents held an unfavorable view of U.S. policy (89%) and the United States (77%), but a clear majority held a favorable view of the American people (62%). Arab journalists simply did not appear to believe the Bush administration's statements about its good intentions toward Arabs. Asked whether a series of U.S. actions were a sincere desire to help or an effort to counter anti-Americanism, more than 60% of respondents said U.S. statements of support for Arab democracy, an independent Palestinian state, and even aid after the Asian tsunami were all just cynical efforts to curry Muslim favor.

Contrary to "conventional wisdom" in the West, hot-button issues like Palestine and Iraq fell well down on the Arab journalists' list of important issues facing the Arab world, behind political reform, human rights, poverty eradication, and education. Likewise, "lack of political change" was

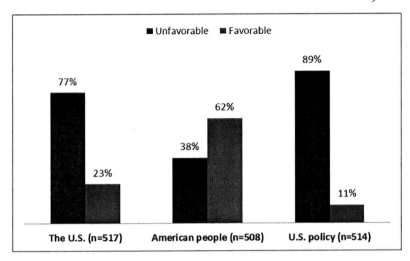

Figure 32.8 Attitudes toward the United States

virtually tied with U.S. policy as the greatest threat to the Arab world. Responding to the question of whether a series of events by al-Qaeda and the United States constituted acts of terrorism, the overwhelming majority labeled as "terrorism" the al-Qaeda related nightclub bombing in Bali (85%) and the execution of U.S. contractor Nicholas Berg in Iraq (73%), as well as the 2003 U.S. siege of Fallujah in Iraq (82%) and the 2002 Israeli siege of Ramallah (90%).

Conclusions

In several important ways, Arab journalism has come full circle. The freedom and sense of power that McFadden (1953) found among Arab reporters in the 1950s is beginning to return, as is the activist agenda in which the fight for political change trumped objectivity and helped shape the post-World War I Arab identity. Today, the "al-Jazeera effect" means journalists are re-discovering that passion, re-engaging with their own pan-Arab identity, and, in turn, re-shaping the sense of identity and political passions of the Arab public at large.

Arab journalists, the data show, are not the anti-American propagandists some in the West have painted them. But neither do they strictly adhere to the values and mores that, at least in theory, govern U.S. journalism. Like their counterparts elsewhere in the world, they are practitioners of an engaged form of journalism. After decades in which they were the propaganda arm of government, playing a role akin to the "development journalism" model of Southeast Asia, many Arab journalists now aspire to change the policies of those governments and in some cases, the governments themselves, as evident in the news media's role in the 2011 Arab Spring.

That is not to suggest Arab journalism is now free of political, economic, or physical pressures; far from it. Barely a week passes when an Arab journalist is not harassed, jailed, or worse. In 2009 alone, 14 Arab journalists were killed (Committee to Protect Journalists 2009); not a single Arab country was rated "free" on the Freedom House report on press freedom that same year (Freedom of the Press 2009); and in a 2010 speech prompted by news of Chinese cyber-spying on Google and other U.S. servers, Secretary of State Hillary Clinton singled out Egypt and Saudi Arabia, both close U.S. allies, for their attacks on Internet freedom (Clinton 2010).

Many Arab journalists do continue in the role of journalist-as-mouthpiece. Many news organizations remain government-owned or controlled by cronies of presidents, kings, and sheikhs. Self-censorship is rampant and fear stalks many newsrooms. But progress is being made. The survey shows that the mindset of Arab journalists is changing. In this new satellite-fed, Internet-laced landscape, there is a new sense of mission, a new hope for the future, and a new commitment to independence.

Arab journalists do not fit into any neat boxes. The data indicate that they defy the notion of a global set of journalistic values and mores. They do not aspire to be clones of their American counterparts or copy anyone else's template. They may share with their counterparts elsewhere a normative aspiration for fairness and balance, but they also see their craft as a weapon to be wielded on the battlefield of social and political change. Like journalists in other societies in transition, they feel a responsibility to the people they serve: against oppressive governments; and against threats from beyond the Arab world.

Pure objectivity can wait; for now, their views echo that of the late British correspondent Macdonald Hastings (1909–1982), who said during World War II, "Objectivity can come back into fashion when the shooting is over" (Humphries 1983: 57).

Notes

1. The countries, and sample size, included Jordan (17), Egypt (152), Lebanon (46), Syria (54), the West Bank of the Palestinian territories (39), Saudi Arabia (9), the United Arab Emirates (127), Bahrain (3), Qatar (17), Kuwait (2), Yemen (4), Sudan, Algeria (3), and Morocco (96). Eight attendees at a regional Arab media conference on Sudan did not identify their nationality on the survey instrument, but it is known that several were Sudanese. There was one respondent based in Latin America. Regional distribution: Gulf countries and Yemen (27%), the Levant (27%), Egypt (25%), and North Africa (without Egypt) (17%), U.S./Europe (4%), and unidentified (1%). Journalists working for pan-Arab media represented 13% of the sample.
2. These included the complete journalistic staffs at the satellite channels al-Jazeera and al-Arabiya and the pan-Arab newspapers *Asharq Alawsat, al-Hayat* and *al-Quds al-Arabi,* along with members of the Washington Arab Journalists Association. Twenty-eight were returned with undeliverable addresses, for a total e-mail distribution of 606.
3. The breakout by media type was as follows: Arabic-language print media (64%), television stations (25%), radio (7%), news agencies (3%), English-language print media (1%). Ownership of those outlets: Private (56%), government (23%), political parties (5%), individuals (6%), other (10%). Respondents by job category: Editors (64%), reporters (19%), assistant editors or producers (8%), television presenters (5%), and other (7%). Four percent were based outside the Arab world.
4. In the sense of supporters of democratic politics, not the U.S. political party.

References

al-Anezi, Khaled. 2000. *Factors influencing chief editors' news selection in Kuwait television and Kuwait radio.* Ph.D. dissertation, Southern Illinois University, Carbondale.

al-Rasheed, Anas. 1998. *Professional values: A survey of working journalists in the Kuwaiti daily press.* Ph.D. dissertation, Southern Illinois University, Carbondale.

Arab Journalism Codes.n.d. *Al-Bab.com.* Retrieved from http://www.al-bab.com/media/docs/arabcodes.htm.

BBC World Service Trust Symposia. April 14–16; April 18–20, June 23–25, 2004. Lebanon, Syria and Egypt. Data provided to the author by Juliette Harkin, BBC project manager, via e-mail April 12, 2005.

Bush, George Herbert Walker. 2006. *President's remarks at U.S. University Presidents Summit on International Education.* Washington, DC. Retrieved from http://georgewbush-whitehouse.archives.gov/news/releases/2006/01/20060105-1. html.

Campagna, Joel. 2007. May 9. Attacks on the press 2006: Middle East and North Africa. Retrieved from http://www.cpj.org/attacks06/mideast06/mideast_analysis_06.html

Clinton, Hillary R. 2010. *Remarks on press freedom.*, Washington, DC: The Newseum. Retrieved from http://www.state.gov/secretary/rm/2010/01/135519.htm.

Committee to Protect Journalists. 72 journalists killed in 2009/Motive confirmed. Retrieved from http://cpj.org/killed/2009/

Dolan, Theo, and Mark Whitehouse. 2006. Media sustainability index—Middle East and North Africa Washington, DC: IREX. Retrieved from http://unesdoc.unesco.org/images/0015/001520/152010e.pdf.

Freedom House. 2009. Freedom of the press [annual report]. Karin D. Karlekar (Ed.). Washington, DC: Freedom House. http://freedomhouse.org/template.cfm?page=470.

Hanitzsch, Thomas. 2005. Journalists in Indonesia: Educated but timid watchdogs. *Journalism Studies* 6(4):493–508.

Heikal's Enduring word. 2007. February 8–14. *Al-Ahram Weekly,* p. 3.

Hess, Steven. 1981. *The Washington reporters.* Washington, DC: Brookings Institution.

History of al-Arabiya TV. Retrieved from http://www.allied-media.com/ARABTV/AlarabiyaHIST.htm

Humphries, Lieutenant Commander Arthur A. 1983. Two routes to the wrong destination: Public affairs in the South Atlantic War. *Naval War College Review* 36(3):56–71.

Inglehart, Ronald. The worldviews of Islamic publics. 2005. Retrieved from http://www.worldvaluessurvey.org/wvs/articles/folder_published/publication_487/files/5_islamview.pdf

James, Laura M. 2006. Whose voice? Nasser, the Arabs, and "Sawt al-Arab" Radio. *TBS Journal* 16. Retrieved from http://www.tbsjournal.com/James.html.

Kirat, Mohamed. 1987. *The Algerian news people: A study of their backgrounds, professional orientation and working conditions.* Ph.D. dissertation, Indiana University, Bloomington.

McFadden, Tom J. 1953. *Daily journalism in the Arab States.* Columbus, OH: Ohio State University Press.

Moaddel, Mansoor. 2000. *In search of a sociopolitical community: The cases of Egypt, Iran, and Jordan.* Eastern Michigan University, Ypsilanti.

Nawawy, Mohammed E., and Adele Iskandar. 2002. *Al-Jazeera: How the Free Arab News Network scooped the world and changed the Middle East.* Boulder, CO: Westview Press.

Newport, Frank. Gallup poll of the Islamic world. 2002. February 26. Retrieved from http://www.gallup.com/poll/5380/gallup-poll-islamic-world.aspx

Pintak, Lawrence. 2003. *Seeds of hate: How America's flawed Lebanon policy ignited the jihad.* Sterling, VA: Pluto Press.

Pintak, Lawrence, and James Ginges. 2008. The mission of Arab journalism: Creating change in a time of turmoil. *The International Journal of Press/Politics* 13(3):193–227.

The POMED Wire. Retrieved from http://joshualandis.com/blog/?p=5011.

Ramaprasad, Jyotika. 2001. A profile of journalists in post-independence Tanzania. *Gazette* 63(6):539–555.

Ramaprasad, Jyotika, and Naila Nabil Hamdy. 2006. Functions of Egyptian journalists: Perceived importance and actual performance. *International Communication Gazette* 68(2):167–185.

Ramaprasad, Jyotika, and James D. Kelly. 2003. Reporting the news from the world's rooftop. *Gazette* 65(3):291–315.

Ramaprasad, Jyotika, and Shafiqur Rahman. 2006. Tradition with a twist: A survey of Bangladeshi journalists. *International Communication Gazette* 68(2):148–165.

Romano, Angela. 2003. *Politics and the press in Indonesia.* London: Routledge Curzon.

Rosentheil, Tom. 2004. The state of the news media. Washington, DC: Center for Excellence in Journalism. Retrieved from http://www.stateofthemedia.org/2004/index.asp

Rugh, Willliam A. 1979. *The Arab press: News media and political process in the Arab World.* Syracuse, NY: Syracuse University Press.

The State of the News Media (2004). A. Mitchell (Ed.). Washington, DC: Center for Excellence in Journalism.

Steele, Janet. 2005. *Wars within: The story of Tempo, an independent magazine in Soeharto's Indonesia.* Singapore: Equinox Pub./Institute of Southeast Asian Studies.

Tash, Adbulkader T. A. 1983. *A profile of professional journalists working in the Saudi Arabian daily press.* Ph.D. dissertation, Southern Illinois University, Carbondale.

Turkistani, Ahmad. S. 1988. *News exchange via Arabsat and news values of Arab television.* Ph.D. dissertation, Indiana University, Bloomington , IN.

Weaver, David H., and G. Cleveland Wilhoit. 1986. *The American journalist: A portrait of U.S. news people and their work.* Bloomington: Indiana University Press.

Weaver, David H., and G. Cleveland Wilhoit. 1991. *The American journalist: A portrait of U.S. news people and their work* (2nd ed.). Bloomington: Indiana University Press.

Weaver, David H., and G. Cleveland Wilhoit. 1996. *The American journalist in the 1990s: U.S. news people at the end of an era.* Mahwah, NJ: Erlbaum.

Weaver, David H., Randal A. Beam, Bonnie J. Brownlee, Paul S. Voakes, and G. Cleveland Wilhoit. 2007. *The American journalist in the 21st century: U.S. news people at the dawn of a new millennium.* Mahwah, NJ: Erlbaum.

Ziadeh, Radwan. 2010. Syria's democratic past: Lessons for the future. POMED Wire. Project on Middle East Democracy. Retrieved Jan. 10, 2010, http://pomed.org/blog/2010/01/pomed-notes-syrias-democratic-past-lessons-for-the-future.html.

Zogby, John, and James J. Zogby. 2004. *Impressions of America 2004.* Washington, DC: The Arab American Institute/Zogby International.

33 Journalists in Israel

Yariv Tsfati and Oren Meyers[1]

Israel is a young state that has rapidly changed and developed throughout its 64 years of existence. Zionist ideology that led to the establishment of Israel has played, and still plays, a fundamental role in shaping the political and professional worldviews of Israeli journalists; at the same time, Israeli journalism has been influenced by global values and trends. This holds both for the Israeli media systems, which down the years have become similar to Western capitalist media systems, and for the guiding professional ethos of Israeli journalists, shaped through constant contact with foreign journalism cultures.

Since Israel's 1948 Independence War and through its current military activities in Lebanon and Gaza, the coverage of national security themes has dominated the landscape of Israeli journalism. Moreover, living in an ongoing cycle of violent conflicts has shaped many aspects of Israeli public life and journalistic discourse that are not directly related to the conflict itself. At the same time, Israel is a vibrant democracy and its journalism extends far beyond mere coverage of the country's external conflicts.

Finally, Israeli journalism has been shaped by the development of social cohesion alongside the expansion of social rifts. Beside the deep involvement of Israeli journalism in nation-building endeavors, the varieties of Israeli journalism reflect a mosaic of competing and at times clashing ethnic and political affiliations. So while mainstream Israeli journalism appears in Hebrew, significant sectors of Israeli society—namely new and veteran immigrants and Israeli Palestinians—often consume local media that are printed and aired in Russian, Arabic, and other languages. Accordingly, one of the defining characteristics of the Israeli ultra-Orthodox Jewish community is its reliance on its own sectorial news outlets.

Background

Israeli journalism was not invented in 1948 with the birth of Israel. Rather, pre-state Hebrew journalism had a pivotal role in the establishment of the Zionist movement, which advocated the establishment of a Jewish state. In addition to the immediate involvement of Zionist parties and leaders in publishing politically affiliated newspapers, a more profound connection existed between the Zionist movement and the Hebrew language because Hebrew newspapers were the vehicle by which the ancient language was revived and disseminated (Soffer 2004).

In 1950, 17 dailies were published in Israel, 11 Hebrew dailies and six dailies in other languages (Naor 1998). Ten were affiliated with political parties, labor organizations, or the government (Limor 1999). Also, 38 weeklies and bi-weeklies were published in Israel at the time, catering mostly to specific audiences such as sports fans, children, and so on. Israeli television only began broadcasting in 1968, so the only available electronic medium during Israel's first two decades of existence was the radio—the state-owned Kol Yisrael radio station was directly supervised by the

Prime Minister's office, and Galey Tzahal, the army radio station, aired mainly music and greetings from soldiers to their families. Only during the 1960s did the two stations begin to broadcast more journalistic content (Naor 1999).

During Israel's first decades of existence very few Israeli journalists were able to position themselves as critical observers of the young state. This type of ideological commitment has characterized the journalistic cultures of many developing nations (Zelizer 2004: 168–169), and it held for Israeli journalists writing for the party-affiliated newspapers as well as for those who wrote for privately owned newspapers. The mainstream journalistic community of the 1950s was not just supportive of the Zionist ideal of building a Jewish homeland, but it also viewed itself as an integral part of its fulfillment. Hence, in most cases, publication policies were restrained and receptive to the authorities' requests (Nossek & Limor 1998). Moreover, the adoption of an ideological frame exerted a fundamental influence on how Israeli journalists distinguished good journalism from bad journalism. Of course, different journalists had very different ideas regarding what was actually good for the country. But it is important to note that in that era the ideological justification was an essential element in the journalistic debate on professional excellence (Meyers 2005).

Along with this strong ideological commitment, Israeli journalists of the formative era also engaged in initial efforts to define their independent professional identities. A salient manifestation of this tension was the development of competing institutions that guided, and to some extent still guide, the work of Israeli journalists. The most systematic means whereby Israeli journalists adhered without coercion to the wishes of officials was the institution of the Editors' Committee. It was first formed to coordinate a uniform journalistic response to the policies of the British Mandate, which restricted Jewish immigration to Palestine. After the establishment of Israel the committee decided it would continue its activities. Its original members were the editors of Israeli dailies, and later the editors of the electronic media joined as well. The editors usually met at the request of high-ranking officials such as the Prime Minister or the Minister of Defense. Often the officials revealed secret matters to the editors and asked them to make sure that the information was not published by their news organizations. Off-the-record information exchanges between sources and journalists are of course routine, but the Editors' Committee was unique in its institutionalization of concealment of information from the public through a formal mechanism and by making sure that all Israeli dailies were part of the agreement (Lavi 1998). In the late 1970s and after, the status of the committee greatly diminished.

Other processes of institutionalization reflected the first stages of the development of professional awareness. The Israeli Press Council was established in 1963 as a voluntary body made up of representatives of journalists' organizations, newspaper owners, and the public at large. The council's main goals are to guard the freedom of the Israeli press, to promote the quality of journalistic work, and to enforce the council's code of ethics (Caspi & Limor 1999). The council operates ethics courts that can sanction and condemn news organizations and journalists although it has no legal jurisdiction.

The aforementioned process by which the Editors' Committee lost its clout, while the Press Council became a relatively influential factor in Israeli journalism, demonstrates the enormous changes in the status and professional self-perceptions of Israeli journalists over the years. The operation of the Editors' Committee reflected a sense of co-operation between the press and official authorities, and it ignored the duty of both journalists and officials to publicly account for their decisions. In contrast, the operating principles of the Press Council are embedded within the concept of public accountability (Meyers 2005).

Through the 1970s and 1980s Israeli journalism changed in various significant ways due to shifts and crises in Israeli society, the development of new media, and the influence of the norms and practices of Western journalism. According to a number of self-reflexive journalistic accounts, the national trauma of the 1973 Yom Kippur War ended, in many respects, the era in which Israeli journalists yielded to the authority of generals and politicians and self-censored their criticism (Lev 1974; Shagrir 1974). The outcomes of this shift were sensed through the coverage of the 1982 Lebanon War in which journalists were far more willing to question the wisdom of political decisions and military operations. Following the same line, the 1977 rise of the Likud party to power, ending the decades-long hegemonic rule of the Labor party, contributed to the development of critical political reporting.

Developments in the media field in the 1970s and 1980s were characterized by the rise and dominance of the public Israel Television channel, which for more than two decades monopolized the realm of television news. Israel Television journalists sought to operate according to professional norms and the ideal of public service (Caspi & Limor 1999). Still, as the only source of television news in the country, they were constantly confronted with political pressures and threats. Another major development that characterized the media field in the 1970s and 1980s was the rise of the local (print) press. The growth of such newspapers marked the decentralization of national establishment power bases (Caspi 1986).

Through the last two decades the Israeli media system has further changed, in ways that make it far more similar to modern Western media systems. Since the early 1990s, state monopoly over electronic broadcasting has come to an end with the introduction of cable broadcasting (1990), two commercial broadcast television channels (Channel 2 [1993]; Channel 10 [2002]), local-commercial radio stations (1996), and satellite broadcasting (2000). Correspondingly, the surge in the number of commercial electronic outlets has moved Israeli media into a globalized era, in which viewers can choose among local channels that rely mostly on local programming, converted channels that give foreign channels a minimal local feel (for instance, the National Geographic channel), foreign channels, and more (J. Cohen 2005).

Additionally, Internet use has become seemingly omnipresent in Israel throughout the last decade. A 2008 survey revealed that 4 million Israelis aged 13 and older (55% of the entire Israeli population) surfed the Internet (M. Cohen, 2008). An earlier, 2004 survey showed that 72.8% of Israeli Internet users regularly read online news contents (Shwartz-Altshuler 2007).

The Israeli print press has naturally been influenced by these changes. The overwhelming dominance and success of the commercial media model has led to the nearly total elimination of the party press. The remaining commercial newspapers struggle to secure their status and profitability, as advertising budgets are increasingly diverted to television and the Internet. Furthermore, Israel's leading daily newspapers—the popular *Yedioth Aharonoth* and *Ma'ariv* (and to a lesser extent the elitist *Ha'aretz*)—are currently threatened by the growing popularity of the relatively new tabloid *Yisrael Hayom*, distributed for free.

The demographic and professional landscape of Israeli journalism during the last two decades has been characterized by several major trends. Increased ratings-driven competition between Israeli news outlets has led to the development of lighter crowd-pleasing "infotainment" journalism, which fails to serve the public as a serious source of information on current events. Moreover, the growing involvement of commercial conglomerates in the production of news has resulted, at least in some cases, in self-censorship that helps news outlets preserve their relations with advertisers and advances the financial interests of media owners (Tausig 2006).

The dominance of the commercial–capitalist media model has also changed the landscape of Israeli journalism through the sharp decline in the number of unionized journalists. During Israel's first four decades of existence the vast majority of Israeli journalists negotiated their salaries and hiring conditions collectively; nowadays most Israeli journalists are not unionized. This decline in union membership has opened a rift between a small number of "star" (mostly television) journalists, who are generously compensated for their work, and a large body of lower-ranking underpaid journalists. Furthermore, the collapse of organized labor eliminated the option of journalistic tenure, which made laying off journalists far easier. In turn, the decrease in the number of unionized journalists has increased the rapid turnover in the profession and increased journalists' vulnerability to internal and external pressures (Avrahamy 2005).

While this review focuses on the most popular news media in Israel that appear in Hebrew, it is important to note the parallel operation of non-Hebrew Israeli news media. In the course of the last century four types of Arab news media developed in Palestine under the British Mandate and later in Israel: outlets sponsored by the Communist Party, by nationalistic parties, by religious outlets, and by commercial companies (Kabha 2006). Other non-Hebrew news outlets developed, mainly in response to immigration waves. Hence in the 1950s, newspapers in German, Hungarian, French, English, and other languages served immigrants during their first years in the country. Correspondingly, through the last 20 years, various Israeli news media in Russian have catered to the needs of more than a million immigrants from the former Soviet Union.

Previous Studies

While survey research on Israeli journalists is relatively scarce, much research has examined the work of Israeli journalists using other methodologies, varying from newsroom studies investigating journalism through a focus on the social organization of news work (Roeh, Katz, Cohen, & Zelizer 1980), to institutional research examining the history of Israeli print and broadcast media, and analyzing the real-life operation of the "Israeli model" under changing circumstances (Caspi & Limor 1999). There have also been text-based studies using critical-cultural strategies and perspectives to examine the ways Israeli journalists cover the Arab–Israeli conflict that have pointed to a set of hegemonic limitations confining journalists' work to a consensual sphere (Liebes 1997; Neiger, Zandberg, & Meyers 2010).

The earliest existing survey work is the 1964 study of Israeli journalists by Shmuel Schnitzer, a prominent *Ma'ariv* journalist (Schnitzer 1964). This survey does not satisfy the usual methodological requirements, but it provides an interesting portrait of the professional community of the time. Later surveys of Israeli journalists were conducted in an academic context. Shamir's 1988 survey focused on the views of Israeli elite journalists on press freedom and its public responsibilities (Shamir 1988). And Reich's recent contribution to the international "Worlds of Journalism" research project is based on a survey probing Israeli journalists for the sources that influence their work and their perception of their influence (Hanitzsch et al. 2009).

In the last decade, we conducted three surveys covering large and diverse samples of Israeli journalists (Meyers & Cohen 2009; Tsfati 2004; Tsfati & Livio 2008; Tsfati, Meyers, & Peri 2006). The focus was on their working conditions, their professional values, the ethical dilemmas they encountered, and their perceptions of the influence of the Israeli news media. The integrated look provided in this chapter, based on the findings of all three surveys, enables us to offer a more comprehensive and generalizable account of Israeli journalists and the current situation of Israeli journalists as a professional community and as members of Israeli society.

Methods

The current exploration is based on three surveys of Israeli journalists conducted in 2002 (*n* = 209), 2004 (*n* = 200), and 2008 (*n* = 333) (Meyers & Cohen 2009; Tsfati 2004; Tsfati & Livio 2008; Tsfati, Meyers, & Peri 2006). The surveys were supported by different sponsors and conducted for different purposes. The 2002 and 2004 surveys were sponsored by the Israeli Democracy Institute (as part of the Israeli Democracy Index Project). The 2008 survey was sponsored by the Tel Aviv Journalists' Association and the University of Haifa. As in previous survey research, a journalist was defined as a person who works for a media organization and makes decisions that have a direct effect on hard news content (Donsbach & Klett 1993). This categorization includes reporters and editors, but excludes camerapersons, graphic editors, copy editors, and the like. Also excluded were journalists who concentrate on soft news, such as sports, travel, and fashion.

The 2002 and 2004 surveys used stratified sampling to build a diverse sample of reporters and editors. Journalists were sampled from every major Hebrew-language national news outlet. These included print (*Yediot Ahronoth, Maariv, Haaretz*), television (Channels 1, 2, and 10), and radio news outlets (*Kol Yisrael* and *Galey Tzahal*), and a sample of local newspapers and television stations. Each outlet was further stratified by respondents' seniority, to ensure that the sample included senior reporters and editors on the one hand, and more junior reporters on the other (financial, political, military, and foreign affairs correspondents of Hebrew language national news outlets were classified as senior reporters).

In the 2002 and 2004 surveys, a separate stratum was created for journalists from alternative media targeting specific populations (including news outlets in Arabic, English, and Russian, the financial press, and news media targeting religious and right-wing groups). The 2008 survey included a more exhaustive and inclusive sampling base and a more detailed strata system, with a separate stratum for journalists working for local radio stations, for outlets in Russian, Arabic, and English, for the financial press, for free newspapers circulated nationally, and for online outlets.

There is no national directory of Israeli journalists, and available lists (e.g., from journalists' professional organizations) are neither exhaustive nor updated, and contain many individuals who no longer work in journalism. Thus, our sampling base was initially composed of journalists' lists provided by the *Ifat* Media Information Center. The *Ifat* dataset is based on bylines and credits from current editions of news outlets, and thus encompasses only people currently practicing journalism. This list was updated and complemented through a cross-reference examination of bylines and credits appearing in Israeli media, lists provided by journalists' associations, and in a few cases lists provided by editors in various news media.

Apart from the more elaborate sampling frame used in 2008, the three surveys differed in several methodological respects. In 2002, due to budgetary considerations, half of the questionnaires were mailed to journalists who had previously been contacted and had agreed to participate in the study; other journalists were interviewed over the telephone. In 2004 and 2008 all journalists were interviewed over the telephone, except for 12 in 2008 who chose to fax or e-mail their answers. Data collection in 2002 and 2004 was conducted by the Dahaf Institute for Public Opinion Research; in 2008 the data were collected by the University of Haifa Survey Research Center. In 2002 and 2004, the survey company was instructed to reach a predetermined number of interviewees from each stratum (and was provided with a randomly ordered list of journalists that was at least double in size for each stratum, totaling 391 journalists).

In 2008, the survey company was provided with an extensive list of 756 journalists (constructed through the strata structure described above). The survey company attempted to randomly contact 702 journalists. After the completion of 150 interviews we compared the result-ing sample with the strata structure and found only minor differences with the exception of the over-representation of *Yedioth Tikshoreth* journalists, who were thus excluded from the sample from that point onwards. Phone interviews continued until we reached the pre-defined number of interviewees. Only minor differences were found between the resulting sample and the pre-defined stratified structure.

Because of the use of different sampling frames, survey procedures and survey methods (e.g., phone vs. mail and phone), the surveys differed in their response rates. In 2002 the response rate was 53.7%, in 2004 73.8%, and in 2008 47.4%. As reported below, results obtained from the three separate surveys were fairly similar, especially in terms of demography, but also on other survey items. Despite the impossibility of assessing how representative the samples were, given limited knowledge of population parameters, the similar results obtained from the three independent surveys are encouraging.

The differences in the sampling frames and methodologies are reflected in the composition of the samples—the 2008 sample contains a significantly higher proportion of journalists working for print media (70.0%) than the 2002 sample (60.8%) and the 2004 sample (57.0%), and a lower proportion of television journalists (13.8% compared with 17.7% and 26.5% in 2002 and 2004) and radio journalists (11.7% compared with 20.1% and 14.0%). Perhaps as a result of the develop-ments in the local online media market (which was reflected in the strata structure) the rate of online journalists rose from 0.5% in 2000 to 2.5% in 2004 and 4.5% in 2008. These differences among the samples were significant ($\chi^2(8) = 33.55$, $p < .001$)

Findings

Demographic Profile

Table 33.1 presents the demographic characteristics of the three samples. As the table demon-strates, Israeli journalists are predominantly Jewish (for the sake of comparison, the rate of Arabic-speaking Palestinians living in Israel is roughly 20%). Our sample was also much more secular than the Israeli population at large (the estimated rate of adult secular Israelis, both Jews and non-Jews, is approximately 60%). The proportion of Israeli-born journalists in the samples was much higher than an equivalent rate of 60.5% in a random sample of the adult Israeli population from 2008 (Tsfati & Livio 2008). Among Jewish respondents many more defined themselves as Ash-kenazim (Jews of European descent) than as Mizrachiyim (Jews of Middle Eastern descent). More than two-thirds of the journalists in all three samples were males, and the average age was around 40. Roughly 26% of the journalists surveyed in 2002 and 2004, and 31.4% in 2008, reported below average incomes. Tsfati and Livio (2008) compared their journalist sample with a sample of the Israeli adult population and found that with the exception of age, the differences between Israeli journalists and the Israeli public were all statistically significant. In sum, journalists in Israel tend to be significantly more secular and educated, with a much higher proportion of them being Israeli-born, Jewish, and male than in the population as a whole.

Statistical tests comparing journalists working for different media (print, radio, television, and online) revealed that television had a higher proportion of journalists with an academic degree and they tended to belong to a higher income group than journalists working in other media. Internet journalists were significantly younger (average age 31.2 years) than all other journalists. No other significant differences than these appeared in the demographic profile of journalists across media.

Table 33.1 Demographic Profile of Journalists by Year

	2002 N = 209	2004 N = 200	2008 N = 333
Sex (% Male)	67.6%	68.5%	70.3%
Ethnicity (% Arab)	3%	4%	4%
Religiosity (% Secular)	77.5%	79.0%	72.7%
Israeli born	91.2%	87.4%	—
Average age	39.40	40.98	38.63
Academic education	62.1%	69.7%	70.8%
Average years of schooling	15.24	15.95	15.46
Income (% below average income)	25.7%	25.5%	31.4%

Education and Training

As Table 33.1 shows, the average education of journalists in the three samples was 15.3 years as compared to 13.3 years in a 2004 sample of the Israeli public (Tsfati & Livio 2008). Academic degrees were reported as held by 62.1% of 2002 respondents and 70.8% of 2008 respondents. This trend reflects increasing college education of the Israeli workforce in the 1990s and 2000s, especially since the opening of academic programs in the areas of journalism and mass communication. In 2008, 23.9% of the journalists studied or had academic degrees in communication or journalism, while 6.6% had studied at professional schools of journalism, and 17.8% had studied or had academic degrees in areas related to their specific field (e.g., a financial reporter who had studied economics). The rest reported no academic education or academic education in areas unrelated to their journalistic work.

Working Conditions

As reported in Table 33.1, a large portion of Israeli journalists earned below-average incomes. Perhaps as a result, 23.4% of respondents in the 2008 survey reported having an additional part-time or full-time job to supplement their income from journalism. Only 8.4% of the 2008 respondents worked as freelancers, 73.1% were employed on the basis of a personal contract with the media organization, and only 14.8% were employed on the basis of a union-negotiated collective contract.

The respondents in 2004 were asked a series of questions about their working conditions and work environment (see Table 33.2). More than half of the respondents "felt pressured to meet expectations at any price," while only 37.6% disagreed with this statement. In response to the statement, "as a journalist I am exposed to harassment or to expressions of public hostility," 41.2% agreed, while 47.5% disagreed. There were statistically significant differences between males and females in response to this item—more than half (51.6%) of the female journalists agreed with it, compared to 36.5% of the male journalists. Almost 40% of the journalists sensed physical threats as part of their work from time to time, and 50.5% of the respondents disagreed with this statement.

Perhaps surprisingly in light of these data, 89% of the journalists agreed that they enjoyed getting to work, and 87.5% agreed that their superiors allowed them to operate freely. Similarly, 82.3% reported they had the tools to cover their beats, and 76.8% reported good interpersonal relationships in their work environments. Only a handful of respondents disagreed with these

Table 33.2   Working Conditions (in %, 2004 survey)

	Strongly Disagree	Disagree	Not Sure	Agree	Strongly Agree
I feel physical threats from time to time.	21.0	29.5	10.8	25.1	13.6
I am exposed to harassment/ public hostility.	16.5	31.0	11.3	28.6	12.6
I feel pressure to meet expectations at any price.	10.7	26.9	12.2	34.5	15.7
I feel I make a decent living as a journalist.	13.1	20.7	13.2	33.8	19.2
I feel secure about my workplace.	9.5	12.6	16.4	34.5	27.0
There are good interpersonal relations at my work.	4.5	8.6	10.1	41.4	35.4
I feel I have the tools to cover my beat.	1.5	6.6	9.3	35.2	47.4
I feel that my superiors allow me to operate freely.	2.0	2.0	8.5	36.2	51.3
I enjoy going to work every day.	4.1	1.0	6.0	37.6	51.3

statements. Although most respondents agreed with the items "I feel secure about my work place" (61.5%) and "I feel I make a decent living as a journalist" (53%), a substantial minority thought otherwise: about one-third of them (33.8%) reported they did not make a decent living as journalists, and 22.1% reported low levels of job security. These responses were significantly more frequent among journalists working for the local media. Responses to these items were statistically unrelated to sex, age, or education.

All three surveys included items measuring job satisfaction, but comparison over time was not possible as the surveys differed in their response categories. In 2002, 39.7% of the journalists responded that they were "very satisfied" with their work, 54% said that they were "somewhat satisfied," and 7.2% that they were "not so satisfied." One percent reported they were "not at all satisfied." In 2004, satisfaction significantly increased (50% very satisfied, 44.9% somewhat satisfied, 3.5% not so satisfied, and 0.5% not at all satisfied). In 2008 journalists responded to a similarly worded question on a 1 to 7 scale from "very unsatisfied" to "very satisfied." The mean response was 5.62 ($SD = 1.25$).

Journalists' high satisfaction was also expressed in the intention to continue to work in the field in the future. Of the journalists interviewed in 2008, 45.4% said that they were "very interested" in continuing to work as journalists in the future, 47.3% that they were "somewhat interested," 6.1% that they are "not so interested," and only 1.2% that they were "not at all interested."

Table 33.3 presents regression models predicting journalists' reports of their job satisfaction levels. Different independent variables were used in the different models, as the three different surveys contained different possible predictors of job satisfaction. The most consistent predictor was perceived autonomy—the more journalists felt autonomous, the more they reported being satisfied with their work. Higher satisfaction was also associated with the feeling that journalism was a respectable occupation (in 2008), with job security (in 2004), and with perceived audience trust (in 2002, but this association was not significant in 2008). In 2002 journalists were asked a series of questions about the importance they assigned to various aspects of their work. None of their responses was associated with job satisfaction, which was also unrelated in 2004 to journalists' reports of their working conditions (i.e., perceived hostility or threat, evaluation of interpersonal relationships, etc.).

Other factors did not emerge as consistent predictors of job satisfaction. Pay was a borderline significant predictor in 2002; relevant education (in journalism or communications or in fields related to their beat) had marginal significance associated with satisfaction in 2002; and working

Table 33.3　Regression Models Predicting Job Satisfaction (standardized coefficients)

	2002	2004	2008
Importance of chance to help people	.05 (.06)		
Importance of job security	.08 (.06)		
Importance of promotion possibilities	.03 (.07)		
Importance of pay level	−.10 (.07)		
Importance of sense of public service	−.09 (.07)		
Importance of chance to win public appreciation	.10 (.05)		
Perceived pressure to meet expectations		−.06 (.11)	
Job security		.16 (.03)*	
Perceived threat		.10 (.03)	
Perceived hostility		−.07 (.03)	
Have tools to cover my beat		.06 (.05)	
Good interpersonal relationships		.08 (.04)	
Perceived audience trust	.16 (.06)*		−.02 (.06)
Perceived influence on society		.03 (.04)	.07 (.06)
Perceived respectability			.41 (.06)***
Perceived autonomy	.34 (.08)***	.28 (.05)**	.27 (.05)***
Sex (female =1)	.11 (.10)	.05 (.10)	.08 (.14)
Age	.11 (.00)	.04 (.00)	.06 (.00)
Education (years)	.10 (.02)	.03 (.02)	−.06 (.03)
Relevant education (=1)	.13 (.08) #	.02 (.08)	.07 (.16)
Secular (=1)	−.07 (.11)	.01 (.11)	−.09 (.15)#
Income	.16 (.03) #	.04 (.03)	.10 (.05)
TV(=1)	−.03 (.11)	−.07 (.11)	.05 (.19)
Radio (=1)	.01 (.11)	−.07 (.13)	.09 (.20) #
Internet/wire (=1)	.00 (.58)	−.06 (.25)	−.02 (.30)
Working for local media (=1)	.22 (.11)**	−.12 (.13)	−.00 (.19)
R2	.31	.23	.33

Notes:　# p < .10, * p < .05, ** p < .01, *** p < .001. Numbers in parentheses are standard errors.

for a local outlet was significantly associated with satisfaction in the same data. Secular journalists reported marginally significant less satisfaction, and working for a radio outlet was associated with higher satisfaction levels in 2008.

Professionalism

Respondents in 2004 and 2002 were asked to rate the importance of a series of professional journalistic norms. The question was worded: "Please indicate whether you think each of the following is an important principle of journalism." Response categories were from "not at all important" (coded 1) to "very important" (coded 4; see Table 33.4). The most highly embraced professional principle in both surveys was fact verification. Keeping the publisher out of the newsroom was also consistently rated as an important principle. Not publishing rumors was also regarded as a relatively important practice in both surveys.

Table 33.4   Perceived Importance of Professional Principles in 2002 and 2004 (in %)

	2002		2004	
	Very Important	Somewhat Important	Very Important	Somewhat Important
Refraining from the use of first person	23.9	35.1	30.6	33.2
Keeping distance from the people you cover	46.4	39.2	33.0	48.0
Always remaining neutral	43.4	43.4	51.5	34.3
Taking into account what interests the public	25.6	58.9	26.5	59.5
Providing interpretation of news	53.4	38.9	46.7	40.7
Getting the story first	60.8	32.5	63.3	28.1
Getting both sides of a story	74.9	21.3	63.3	28.1
Not publishing rumors	78.8	17.3	69.7	24.2
Keeping the publisher out of the newsroom	82.8	13.9	81.0	14.9
Providing at least two sources to confirm a story based on anonymous sources	65.7	24.4	73.2	22.7

Corroborating stories based on anonymous sources, and getting both sides of the story, were perceived as "very important" or "somewhat important" by more than 90% of the respondents in both surveys. Neutrality, interpretation, taking into account the public interest, and keeping one's distance from the people one covers were somewhat less important (80–90% of respondents in both surveys ranked them as "very" or "somewhat" important). Refraining from the use of the first person in reporting was consistently perceived as less important. Only 59% in 2002 and 64% in 2004 ranked this category as "very" or "somewhat" important.

While lower-ranking and younger journalists were more likely to assign importance to neutrality, senior and older journalists were more likely to espouse fact verification, not publishing rumors, getting both sides of the story, and providing the audience with interpretation of news. Journalists working for local media were more likely to perceive neutrality as an important principle and interpretation as unimportant (Tsfati, Meyers, & Peri 2006: 162).

Interestingly, Tsfati, Meyers, and Peri (2006) compared journalists' perceptions of the importance of journalistic norms (as measured in the 2002 survey) with data collected from a representative sample of the Israeli public regarding their own perceptions of the importance of these norms. Neutrality and taking into account what interested the public were perceived as twice as important by the public as by the journalists, but fact verification, not publishing rumors, and providing interpretation were perceived as significantly more important by journalists. These authors also note that "by and large, younger journalists, junior journalists and journalists working for local outlets tend to be closer to the audience in their perceptions of what constitutes worthy journalism, whereas older journalists, senior journalists and those who work in national media are more likely to depart from the general public in those perceptions" (Tsfati, Meyers, & Peri 2006: 161).

However, the values held by journalists may be different from what they do and justify doing in practice. Journalists responding to the 2002 survey were asked whether several questionable reporting practices "may be justified on occasion" if the situation involved an "important story." The question wording and the list of practices were translated from the original questionnaire used by Weaver (1998). Responses are presented in Table 33.5. With the exception of revealing confidential sources, all practices were justified by a substantial majority of journalists. When

Table 33.5   Percent of Journalists Saying that Questionable Practices "May Be Justified on Occasion" (in %)

	"Justified on Occasion"
Getting employed in a firm or organization to gain inside information	79.2
Using confidential business or government documents without authorization	75.8
Paying people for confidential information	60.3
Claiming to be somebody else	60.0
Revealing confidential sources	9.7

compared to other countries in the Weaver 1998 book, Israeli journalists' support of problematic practices was generally among the highest. Logistic regression models predicting the answers to these questions yielded no significant effects of working for national versus local media, working for print versus electronic outlets, formal training, sex, age, years of schooling, and secularity. The only exceptions were that print journalists were more likely to justify getting employed to gain inside information ($p = .056$) and revealing confidential sources ($p = .097$).

The professionalism and ethical standards of Israeli journalists can be gauged not only by asking them about the practices they justify, but also more indirectly by asking them about problematic ethics violations they have encountered in their work. The 2004 respondents were presented with a list of such violations and were asked, "How frequently have you encountered each of the following, if at all?" Responses are presented in Table 33.6.

As the table shows, the most frequent violation concerns unfair coverage as a result of give-and-take relations between journalists and sources. Journalists' distortion of quotes also emerged as a frequent phenomenon. Influence by financial considerations and censorship and gag order violations were rather prevalent, but somewhat less frequent. Although a substantial portion of journalists had never encountered severe ethical violations (according to their own reports), a majority reported ever encountering such violations. Sheer invention of stories and interviewees was reported as relatively rare. The least often problematic phenomenon reported by respondents to our 2004 survey was eavesdropping. By and large, younger journalists and those employed by local outlets reported that they had encountered these practices less frequently.

Journalists' evaluations of the performance of Israeli media are also relevant in an assessment of the professionalism of journalism in Israel. When asked in 2002, "In general, how would you evaluate the Israeli news media today? What grade on a 1 (lowest) to 10 (highest) scale, would

Table 33.6   Problems Encountered by Journalists (in %, 2004)

	Frequently	Occasionally	Rarely	Never	Irrelevant
Unfair coverage due to give-and-take between journalists and sources	30.2	17.1	30.0	21.0	1.7
Journalists distorting quotes	29.8	23.2	28.5	17.2	1.2
Censorship and gag order violations	20.1	17.6	41.2	18.0	3.1
Influences of commercial considerations on news	16.1	13.1	34.2	27.6	9.0
Severe ethical violations	12.1	14.1	32.0	37.9	3.9
Journalists fabricating stories or interviewees	8.5	15.0	35.0	39.4	2.0
Eavesdropping	4.0	7.0	16.0	63.5	9.5

you give the Israeli media on its performance?" the average response was 5.85 (*SD* = 1.85). On the positive side, Israeli journalists tended to concur with the statement "The Israeli media are successful in uncovering corruption, abuse of power and misconduct" (1 = strongly disagree, 4 = strongly agree, *M* = 2.93, *SD* = .71, in the 2002 survey). When asked (in the 2008 survey) about the perceived influence of Israeli media on society (1 = very little influence, to 7 = very strong influence) journalists tended to perceive them as exerting an influence (*M* = 5.53, *SD* = 1.13) and to deem it slightly more positive than negative (*M* = 4.23, *SD* = 1.16, on a scale from 1 = very negative influence, to 7 = ery positive influence).

On the negative side, Israeli journalists tended to concur with the statements (measured in the 2002 survey on a scale from 1 = strongly disagree, to 4 = strongly agree); "Journalists are motivated too much by competition and too little by ethical considerations" (*M* = 2.89, *SD* = .81); "News reports in the Israeli media are full of factual errors and slipshod" (*M* = 2.63, *SD* = .89); and "The Israeli media are patriotic to a degree that compromises their professionalism" (*M* = 2.61, *SD* = .97). In general, no significant differences emerged between younger and older journalists, journalists with and without formal training, those working for national versus local media, and senior and junior journalists in their responses.

As journalists working in a society coping with continuous political and military conflicts, the respondents work for media outlets facing constant dilemmas regarding patriotism in coverage and a proper balance between security considerations and freedom of the press. Almost three out of four journalists (2002 survey) agreed that, in cases when media coverage may give rise to a threat to national security, the news media should apply self-censorship. However, when asked whether media coverage was beneficial or detrimental to Israel's national security, 25.4% replied that it was "very beneficial," 57.7% that it is "somewhat beneficial," 10% that it was "detrimental," and only 2.5% responded that the coverage was "very detrimental" to national security. About 25% agreed that "the media should exercise caution in issues that could damage Israel's image in the eyes of the world," 31.4% agreed that "the media should stress the positive aspects of the society and the state," but only 10% agreed that "the media should be careful with reports that could damage national morale."

Conclusions

Although there is no comprehensive list or directory of Israeli journalists, the demographic patterns found across the three surveys are consistent. All three surveys show that in comparison to Israel's general public, the community of Israeli journalists tends to contain larger proportions of Israelis of European or North American descent, Israeli-born and males, and that Israeli journalists are on average more educated than the general public. That said, we must remember that all three sampling bases under-represented or omitted journalists who are not publicly credited for their work. This demographic composition of Israeli journalists might offer an initial explanation for research findings demonstrating that news coverage of peripheral social groups in Israel (e.g., Arabs, Orthodox Jews, settlers, and residents of peripheral cities) tends to ignore these groups or portray their members negatively (Avraham 2003).

No comprehensive data exist on the working conditions of Israeli journalists of previous generations but from the accounts of veteran journalists, working conditions in the field seem to have deteriorated. About 25% to 31% of the respondents reported below-average salaries, about a third reported that they do not make a decent living as journalists, and a large minority reported low levels of job security and working in several jobs to make ends meet. Working through a union-negotiated collective contract (a more secure employment arrangement prevalent until the mid-1980s) seems to have ended almost entirely. These trends, and the decline in social status they entail, are probably the result of the changes in the Israeli media described above, in particular commercialization and privatization. These changes may also reflect wider social and economic changes, as similar patterns are evinced in other sectors of the Israeli workforce, especially those that have been aggressively privatized.

The results demonstrate problematic working conditions for many journalists: low pay, limited job security, and frequent encounters with pressures, threats, and harassment. Nevertheless, Israeli journalists reported surprisingly high levels of job satisfaction in absolute terms and in comparison with other countries. The explanation for this discrepancy might be rooted in the fact that people do not choose to become journalists on the assumption that they will get rich. Journalists who were more satisfied with their work tended to feel more autonomous and to feel that the Israeli audience trusts them; these are probably additional reasons for the high levels of satisfaction.

The Israeli journalistic community emerged from the results of the surveys as homogeneous demographically but also in its members' professional perceptions. Asked to rate the importance of central journalistic values, the journalists were less diversified in their responses than the Israeli public, even when controlling for the broader demographic array of the public. Journalists tended to stress the importance of verification of facts, and only to a lesser extent to perceive neutrality as a central value, while the opposite pattern was found among the general public. The fact that these patterns are stronger among older journalists working for national media may indicate that the homogenization of journalists' professional perceptions stems not from their formal education but from socialization and on-the-job training.

As mentioned, the journalists of Israel's formative era held the notion that their mission was to promote ideological ideals; later perceptions, evolving through the 1970s and 1980s, shifted toward adoption of the objective model (Peri 2004). The findings of the surveys, therefore, could be read as supporting evidence of a third phase in this process, in which a significant number of mainstream Israeli journalists question their ability to mirror reality objectively, or "as it is." Such journalists believe that their public mission is to balance the need to report the facts and the wish to contextualize these facts as involved interpreters.

High rates of respondents justified ethically controversial practices, especially compared with results from other countries as reported in Weaver's (1998) collection. While the reason underlying this pattern is unknown, we can suggest a speculative explanation: In contrast to Western cultures, Israeli culture does not view confidentiality and privacy as fundamental values. The higher rates of justifying reporting on confidential documents or paying for confidential information may reflect this cultural tendency or maybe the well-known Israeli audacity ethos (chutzpa: see Schejter & Cohen 2002).

Many journalists perceived the Israeli news media as overtly patriotic, to a degree that jeopardized their professionalism. At the same time, high rates of journalists supported self-censorship with regard to national security or military issues, and thought that journalists should be careful in their reporting of issues that could harm public morale. Thus within the context of the ongoing attempt to balance "nation and profession" (Zandberg & Neiger 2005), many of the fundamental dilemmas that characterized Israeli journalism of the formative era still dominate the collective journalistic consciousness.

Note

1. We are grateful to Oren Livio, Riva Tukachinsky, and Naftali Reznikovitch for their valuable help in collecting information on Israeli journalists. The 2002 and 2004 surveys were funded by the Israeli Democracy Institute and the 2008 survey was funded by the University of Haifa and the Tel Aviv Journalists' Association.

References

Avraham, Eli. 2003. *Behind media marginality*. New York: Lexington.

Avrahamy, Eyal. 2005. Journalism without coverage. *The Seventh Eye*. Retrieved from http://www.the7eye.org.il/articles/pages/article5703.aspx (in Hebrew)

Caspi, Dan. 1986. *Media decentralization: The case of Israel's local newspapers*. New Brunswick, NJ: Transaction.

Caspi, Dan, and Yehiel Limor. 1999. *The in/outsiders: The media in Israel*. Cresskill, NJ: Hampton Press.

Cohen, Jonathan. 2005. Global and local viewing experiences in the age of multi-channel television: The Israeli experience. *Communication Theory* 15:437–455.

Cohen, Mayan. 2008. 39% of Israeli internet users are registered in a social network. *The Marker*. Retrieved from http://it.themarker.com/tmit/article/2374 (in Hebrew)

Donsbach, Wolfgang, and Bettina Klett. 1993. Subjective objectivity: How journalists in four countries define a key term of their profession. *Gazette* 51:53–83.

Hanitzsch, Thomas, Rosa Berganza, Incilay Cangoz, Mihai Coman, Basyouni Hamada, Folker Hanusch, …Kee Wang Yuen. 2009. *Worlds of journalisms*. Retrieved from http://www.worldsofjournalisms.org/method.htm

Kabha, Mustafa. 2006. *The Arab press in Israel 1948–2006 as an apparatus in the identity-building process*. Tel Aviv: Herzog Institute of Communications, Tel Aviv University. (in Hebrew)

Lavi, Zvi. 1998. The editors' committee: Myth and reality. In *Media in Israel*, edited by Dan Caspi and Yehiel Limor, pp. 320–356. Tel Aviv: Open University of Israel. (in Hebrew)

Lev, Yigal. 1974. The press and the soldiers did not broadcast on the same wavelength. *Yearbook of the Association of Tel Aviv Journalists* 67–69. Tel Aviv: Association of Tel Aviv Journalists. (in Hebrew)

Liebes, Tamar. 1997. *Reporting the Arab-Israeli conflict: How hegemony works*. New York: Routledge.

Limor, Yehiel. 1999. The cruel fate of Israeli dailies. *Kesher* 25:41–51. (in Hebrew)

Meyers, Oren. 2005. Israeli journalism during the state's formative era: Between ideological affiliation and professional consciousness. *Journalism History* 31:88–97.

Meyers, Oren, and Jonathan Cohen. 2009. A contemporary self-portrait of journalists in Israel: Perceptions, positions and values. *Media Frames: Israeli Journal of Communication* 3(4):107–134. (in Hebrew)

Naor, Mordekhay. 1998. The press in the early years of the state of Israel. *Kesher* 23:80–87. (in Hebrew)

Naor, Mordekhay. 1999. Israel's army media. *Kesher* 25:52–62. (in Hebrew)

Neiger, Motti, Eyal Zandberg, and Oren Meyers. 2010. Communicating critique: Towards a conceptualization of journalistic criticism. *Communication, Culture and Critiques* 3(3): 377–395.

Nossek, Hillel, and Yehiel Limor. 1998. Military censorship in Israel: An ongoing compromise between clashing values. In *Media in Israel*, edited by Dan Caspi and Yehiel Limor, pp. 362–390. Tel Aviv: Open University of Israel. (in Hebrew)

Peri, Yoram. 2004. *Telepopulism: Media and politics in Israel*. Stanford, CA: Stanford University Press.

Roeh, Itzhak, Elihu Katz, Akiba A. Cohen, and Barbie Zelizer. 1980. *Almost midnight: Reforming late-night news*. Beverly Hills, CA: Sage.

Schejter, Amit, and Akiba A. Cohen. 2002. Israel: Chutzpah and chatter in the Holy Land. In *Perpetual contact: Mobile communication, public talk and public performance*, edited by James Everett Katz and Mark A. Aakhus, pp. 30–41. Cambridge, UK: Cambridge University Press.

Schnitzer, Shmuel. 1964. The Israeli journalist and his public image. *Yearbook of the Association of Tel Aviv Journalists* 44–46. Tel Aviv: Association of Tel Aviv Journalists. (in Hebrew)

Shwartz-Altshuler, Tehilla. 2007. Introduction. In *Online newspapers in Israel*, edited by Tehilla Shwartz-Altshuler, pp. 19–27. Jerusalem: The Israel Democracy Institute and Burda Center for Innovative Communications. (in Hebrew)

Shagrir, Micah. 1974. We were thrown into this war with no professional concepts. *Yearbook of the Association of Tel Aviv Journalists* 18–20. Tel Aviv: Association of Tel Aviv Journalists. (in Hebrew)

Shamir, Jacob. 1988. Israeli elite journalists: Views on freedom and responsibility. *Journalism Quarterly* 65(3):589–594.

Soffer, Oren. 2004. Paper territory: Early Hebrew journalism and its political roles. *Journalism History* 30:31–39.

Tausig, Shuki. 2006. Routine news. *The Seventh Eye*. Retrieved from http://www.the7eye.org.il/DailyColumn/Pages/article6219. aspx (in Hebrew)

Tsfati, Yariv. 2004. Exploring possible correlates of journalists' perceptions of audience trust. *Journalism and Mass Communication Quarterly* 81:274–91.

Tsfati, Yariv, and Oren Livio. 2008. Exploring journalists' perceptions of media impact. *Journalism & Mass Communication Quarterly* 85:113–130.

Tsfati, Yariv, Oren Meyers, and Yoram Peri. 2006. What is good journalism? Comparing Israeli public and journalists' perspectives. *Journalism* 7:152–173.

Weaver, David H. (ed.) 1998. *The global journalist: News people around the world*. Cresskill, NJ: Hampton Press.

Zandberg, Eyal, and Motti Neiger. 2005. Between the nation and the profession: Journalists as members of contradicting communities. *Media Culture & Society* 27(1):131–141.

Zelizer, Barbie. 2004. *Taking journalism seriously*. London: Sage.

34 Journalists in the United Arab Emirates

Mohamed Kirat

The media system of the United Arab Emirates (UAE) is still in its formative stage, which is a status befitting a rapidly developing nation. Established in 1971, the UAE continues to undergo a period of intense social change. The media workforce, composed mainly of expatriates from Arab, Asian, and European countries, covers the country's development and many other social issues.

Although the UAE is a small nation in terms of area and population (6 million), it has one of the best media infrastructures in the region for press, broadcast, and electronic media. The country has nine dailies in Arabic, seven in English, and more than 300 magazines of both general and specialized interest. The UAE also has several satellite television channels and radio stations. In addition, the UAE is home to a media zone—media city—which hosts over 750 news organizations from around the globe.

Furthermore, Internet penetration in the UAE is at 75.9% of the population (according to internetworldstats.com/me/ae.htm), which ranks first in the Arab world. In terms of advertising revenue, the UAE is first when controlling for population, and second overall, among Arab countries. Journalism education and training is also increasing rapidly with the establishment of 14 university departments of mass communication and public relations. Finally, there is great interest from government media officials in the localization of media job opportunities.

This chapter uses a survey, interviews, and observation to learn more about the identities of media practitioners in the UAE, such as their educational backgrounds, gender, and nationalities. The goal is to learn more about their job perceptions, their working conditions, their relationships with news sources, their conceptualizations of professionalism and ethical conduct, and, finally, how they approach their profession in a media system and country which is not theirs. The majority of media practitioners in the UAE (more than 80%) are foreigners, which is a rare situation in the world. These media practitioners come from a variety of countries with different backgrounds, cultures, schools of thought, educational systems, political systems, religious beliefs, and convictions, yet little is known about how they adapt and react to UAE media policies and practices.

Method

This study combined survey and in-depth interviews. First, from June to September 2000, an 80-item questionnaire was administered in both Arabic and English to journalists in person. Afterward, media managers, editors, and reporters were interviewed by the researcher to better understand those people in charge of the media industry in the country.

The questionnaire was patterned after similar surveys of journalists in other nations, including those done in the Arab world, the United States, and England (Johnstone, Slawski, & Bowman,

1973, 1976; Kirat 1993, 1998, 2000; Tash 1983; Tunstall 1977; Weaver, Beam, Brownlee, Voakes, & Wilhoit 2007; Weaver & Wilhoit 1986, 1996), while taking into consideration the conditions that make journalism in the UAE unique. A pre-test was administered to 20 journalists to ensure validity, reliability, adequacy of measures, and clarity of terms and language. The final questionnaire was distributed personally by the author to journalists and media managers, and also mailed to other news organizations and media practitioners.

The survey targeted a census of the population of UAE journalists, estimated at about 800, and covered the daily press, radio and television networks, the national news agency (WAM), and general-interest magazines and weeklies. Journalists working for specialized publications were not included in the survey. Despite skepticism on the part of journalists and media organization managers who declined to participate, the author collected responses from 160 journalists for a 32% response rate. Respondents represented 16 media organizations, including the national news agency, radio and television, the daily press (both Arabic and English language), and magazines.

UAE media organizations represented included Sharjah Television, Gulf News, Al Bayan, National News Agency WAM, Al Wahda, Al Ittihad, Dubai Television, Ajman Television, RAK Radio Station, UAQ Radio Station, Emirates News, Abudhabi Radio Station, Al Fajr, Al Khaleej, Durrat Al Emarat, and Dubai Radio Station. The daily press is represented by 75 journalists (46.8%); the television networks by 52 journalists (32.5%); the national news agency by 14 journalists (8.8%); the radio networks by 10 journalists (11.3%); and the weekly publications by one journalist (0.6%).

Findings

The findings from this survey offer a detailed and current picture of the demographics, education, job satisfaction, working conditions, roles, news values, ethics, professional orientations, and perceived impact on public opinion of this group of media practitioners.

Demographics

The journalists surveyed in this study are relatively young. They have a mean age of 36, and more than half (58.3%) fall in the 20 to 39 age bracket. This finding can be explained by the fact that older journalists are leaving the field for retirement or positions in other industries, and a new wave of media practitioners, including many recent university graduates, is entering the profession. One-fifth of journalists in the UAE are female (20%), which is an encouraging figure considering the modest number of working women in the country. Three-quarters of the journalists surveyed are married (75.6%), while 19.4% are single and have never married.

Only 20% of the surveyed journalists are UAE nationals. This fact is due mainly to the very young age of the country and its need for foreign workers. The bulk of foreign journalists working for Arabic-language media organizations in the country are from the Middle East, led by Egypt (19.4%), Sudan (8.1%), Syria (8.1%), Jordan (7.5%), and Algeria (4.4%). On the other hand, journalists working for English-language news organizations are predominantly Indian (70%).

Education and Training

More than half of the journalists surveyed (63.1%) hold a bachelor's degree, and 15.6% hold advanced degrees. A considerable percentage of those holding a bachelor's degree have a major in journalism (26.9%), while other majors include social sciences (19.3%), mass communication (11.9%), political science (8.8%), business (6.9%), natural sciences (3.8%), and humanities (3.1%).

Concerning continuing education, 63.1% of the surveyed journalists expressed interest in additional training in journalism. A majority of the respondents would like to have training in writing techniques (63.1%), followed by an interest in learning more about media technology (40%), multimedia (26.3%), broadcast media (16.5%), and training abroad (15.5%). The findings suggest that age and experience are the key factors in determining whether the journalist is interested in having more training and continuous education. Younger and less experienced journalists were more likely than older and more experienced journalists to opt for additional education. More than half of the surveyed journalists did not have any kind of journalism training before entering the profession (51.3%), and about half of that untrained group (48.1%) responded that they would like the opportunity to participate in training courses and workshops related to the profession.

Job Satisfaction and Working Conditions

More than half of the journalists (60%) were somewhat satisfied with their jobs, while 11.9% said they were somewhat dissatisfied, 17.5% said they were very dissatisfied, and only 2.5% said they were very satisfied. Three-quarters said their working conditions were either very good or good. In terms of work compensation, about 33% of those surveyed claimed to receive less than 4,500 AED per month (US$1,225), 28.8% receive between 4,500 AED to 6,500 AED (US$1,225–$1,770), 20.6% receive 6,500 AED to 8,500 AED (US$1,770–$2,314), and 9.4% receive 10,500 AED to 12,500 AED (US$2,859–$3,403). However, in recent years journalists in the country witnessed a substantial rise in their salaries.

Regarding journalists' attitudes about various aspects of their jobs, Table 34.1 shows that most journalists surveyed are satisfied or very satisfied with their job stability (83.8%), use of talents and creativity (75.1%), extent of freedom (76.2%), peer relationships (80%), and relationships with sources (63.1%). The attitudes of these media practitioners indicate that they are generally positive and happy about the job atmosphere and their working conditions, which is a good indicator of a healthy journalism practice in the UAE.

Independence and Freedom of Media Practitioners

For the most part, journalists in the UAE practice their jobs in an atmosphere of independence and freedom. In general, most journalists in the UAE responded that they have the freedom most of the time to cover subjects they regard as important (59.4%), and almost three-fourths (73.2%)

Table 34.1 Attitudes Toward Job-Related Issues (in %, N = 160)

	Very Satisfied	Satisfied	Dissatisfied	Strongly Dissatisfied	No Opinion	Total
Peer relationships	24.4	55.6	10.6	1.3	8.1	100.0
Relationship with sources	20.0	43.1	13.8	3.9	19.2	100.0
Use of talents & creativity	18.1	58.1	11.9	3.1	8.8	100.0
Attitude toward job	16.3	67.5	10.0	1.9	4.3	100.0
Stability in the job	13.8	61.3	9.4	3.1	12.4	100.0
Extent of freedom	13.8	55.0	13.1	1.9	16.2	100.0

Table 34.2   Interference in Jobs (in %, N = 160)

	Boss	News Organization	Ministry of Information	Others
Regularly	30.6	15.6	16.9	8.1
Occasionally	24.4	29.4	17.5	18.8
Seldom	13.8	11.3	18.8	12.5
Never	3.8	10.6	12.5	23.8
Not applicable	27.4	33.1	34.3	36.8
Total	100.0	100.0	100.0	100.0

responded that they have some or a great deal of freedom to select which stories to cover. However, many UAE journalists appear to be constrained when it comes to problems of getting access to sources (50%) and investigating corruption (53.1%) (see Table 34.2).

In terms of job interference, journalists were most likely to choose their bosses (editors or other media managers) as regular obstacles (30.6%), followed by problems with government officials (16.9%). However, the majority of respondents claimed only occasional, seldom, or no interference from their superiors, organizations, or other sources.

Table 34.3 displays the results of journalists' opinions about some common criticisms of the practice of journalism in the UAE. Results demonstrate that most journalists agree with most of the negative aspects and drawbacks of their profession expressed by critics and audiences. More than half of the journalists surveyed either agree or strongly agree that UAE journalism is too shallow and trivial with too much focus on entertainment (58.2%); too ephemeral with insufficient background information (62.5%); too selective in which news is covered (65%); too much of a spokesman for government (63.8%); too lacking in criticism and creativity (55.7%); lacking in investigative journalism (69.4%); too focused on routine government activities (72.5%); and too focused on urban centers to the detriment of covering the countryside and remote areas (54.4%).

Table 34.3   Journalist's Opinions about Criticism of UAE Journalism (in %, N = 160)

	Strongly Agree	Agree	No Opinion	Disagree	Strongly Disagree	Total %
Concentrates a lot on government routine activities	32.5	40.0	9.4	15	3.1	100.0
A spokesman of the government	29.4	34.4	16.2	13.8	6.2	100.0
Not enough hard hitting investigative journalism	26.3	43.1	9.4	16.9	4.3	100.0
Concentrates on urban areas and neglects countryside	22.5	31.9	9.3	22.5	13.8	100.0
Selectivity in news coverage	20.6	44.4	11.9	17.5	5.6	100.0
Manipulates public opinion on issues	18.8	33.8	14.4	26.3	6.7	100.0
Too ephemeral; not enough background information	18.1	44.4	6.2	21.9	9.4	100.0
Not enough respect for the facts	18.1	22.5	7.5	38.8	13.1	100.0
Lack of criticism and creativity	16.9	38.8	7.5	28.1	8.7	100.0
Too shallow and trivial, too much entertainment	14.4	33.8	11.9	26.3	13.6	100.0

Although these findings suggest that many UAE journalists enjoy freedom and independence on the job, they might also imply that journalists distance themselves from addressing sensitive issues to avoid any form of follow-up interventions and complications. These results also serve as confirmation of the widespread phenomenon of political control of the public and private sector media in Arab and other developing countries. Even though these findings reveal positive features such as satisfaction with jobs, organizations, and relationships between all media organization sectors, they also reveal the shortcomings and contradictions of the journalism profession in the UAE.

Media Roles

The data in Table 34.4 suggest that the journalists' definitions and philosophical views of media roles are compatible with the media policy of the UAE. The majority of UAE journalists agree that among the most important roles of the media in the country are to get information to the public

Table 34.4   Importance of Media Roles (in %, $N = 160$)

	Extremely Important	Quite Important	Somewhat Important	Not Really Important	No Opinion	Total %
Get information to the public quickly	88.1	8.1	3.1	0.7	—	100.0
Enhance the objectives of the union	75.6	13.1	3.8	3.1	4.4	100.0
Concentrate on news of interest to largest public	74.4	18.1	3.1	2.5	1.9	100.0
Educate and shape a modern Emirati citizenry	74.4	16.9	4.4	1.9	2.4	100.0
Enhance Islamic values among the population	71.9	10.6	10	2.5	5	100.0
Develop intellectual and cultural interests of the public	68.8	17.5	11.9	1.8	0	100.0
Analyze and interpret complex issues	68.1	21.3	8.1	0.6	1.9	100.0
Counterattack foreign propaganda	67.5	15.6	4.4	8.1	4.4	100.0
Investigate the government's claims and statements	61.9	19.4	14.4	2.4	1.9	100.0
Help achieve goals of development plans	61.3	17.5	13.1	4.4	3.7	100.0
Discuss national policy while it is still being developed	53.8	21.9	12.5	4.4	7.4	100.0
Should balance interests of government and public	53.8	19.4	13.1	10.6	3.1	100.0
Criticize official agencies of the government when needed	47.5	25	12.5	5.6	9.4	100.0
Avoid stories where factual content cannot be verified	44.4	16.9	12.4	10.7	15.6	100.0
Mobilize masses to enhance economic development	43.8	24.4	13.1	10	8.7	100.0
Provide entertainment and relaxation	35.0	30.6	29.4	4.4	0.6	100.0
Give public what they want, not what media think they need	34.4	33.8	15.6	19.3	6.9	100.0
Endorse government policies without any questions	17.5	15.6	14.4	36.3	16.2	100.0
Be skeptical of actions by public officials	12.5	11.9	8.1	51.9	15.6	100.0

quickly (88.1%), to enhance the objectives of the union (75.6%), to concentrate on news of interest to the widest public possible (74.4%), to educate and form modern Emirati citizens (74.4%), and to enhance Islamic values among the population (71.9%).

Such willingness to investigate and be critical reflects the growing culture of investigative and competitive journalism among journalists in the UAE (61.9% of the journalists agreed with these roles). These are encouraging figures when we consider that the practice of the press in the Middle East and the Arab world has not yet reached a level of investigative reporting and criticism of officials and government comparable to Western journalism except for very few countries and in very few news organizations.

Responses also indicate that UAE journalists show strong support for their roles as mobilizers and interpreters. Roughly three of four journalists agreed with the extreme importance of the "mobilizing" role, as indicated by four questions: the concentration on news of a wide interest (74.4%), the goal of enhancing Islamic values (71.9%), the goal of enhancing of union objectives (75.6%), and the goal of educating and shaping modern Emirati citizens (74.4%). Also, most journalists surveyed agreed with the "interpretive" role, as indicated by three questions: providing analysis and interpretations of complex problems (68.1%), developing intellectual and cultural public interests (68.8%), and avoiding stories in which facts cannot be verified (44.4%).

News Values

To investigate the influences of UAE journalists' conceptions of newsworthiness, they were asked to rate eight possible influences on a five-point scale, with five being the most influential. Table 34.5 shows that the journalists ranked news sources as most influential (47.5% rated this factor "very influential"), followed by journalistic training (35%), elite media priorities (31.9%), audience research (31.9%), and supervisors (28.8%).

Journalists also were asked for their definition of "news." The most popular choice defined news as events of interest to the people (35.6%), followed by events that have effects on the nation (21%), events that involve economic development (20.2%), and a tie between events involving government (14.4%), and issues that promote and strengthen unity and nation-building (14.4%). Again, these findings suggest that journalists in this study view news in a national context and along the lines of the policies in practice in the UAE. Our data show that more than half of the journalists reported changing their conceptions of news since they began their careers.

Table 34.5 Factors Influencing Journalists' Conception of Newsworthiness (in %, N = 160)

	1 Not At All Influential	2	3	4	5 Very Influential	Don't Know	Total %
News sources	3.1	5.0	14.4	27.5	47.5	2.5	100.0
Journalistic training	7.5	3.1	15.6	31.3	35.0	7.5	100.0
Audience research	10.0	5.0	16.9	28.8	31.9	7.4	100.0
Priorities of elite media	7.5	3.8	21.3	31.9	31.9	3.6	100.0
Public opinion polls	11.3	10.6	20.0	20.6	30.6	6.9	100.0
Supervisors	6.3	5.6	19.4	34.4	28.8	5.5	100.0
Friends & acquaintances	17.5	13.8	23.1	28.1	11.9	5.6	100.0
Peers on the staff	13.8	9.4	31.3	31.3	10.0	4.2	100.0

Ethics

Journalists in our survey were asked how influential various factors were on their perceptions of ethics. In terms of influence on the concept and meaning of journalism ethics, respondents found daily learning in the newsroom most influential (70%), followed by learning from senior reporters (47%), religious education (46%), and formal journalism education (43%). These findings indicate that a mixture of religious background and professional socialization has the greatest influence on the ethical attitudes and practices of UAE journalists.

Table 34.6 shows journalists' attitudes about controversial reporting practices that might generate ethical concerns. Respondents were asked whether they would not approve of the action, or whether it would be justified on occasion. Findings show that in all instances more than 70% of the surveyed journalists would not approve of the following: using personal documents without permission, using confidential business or government documents without authorization, using hidden microphones or cameras, re-creating or dramatizing news with actors, disclosing names of rape victims, getting hired under false pretenses to gain information, paying for confidential information, reneging on a promise of confidentiality, badgering unwilling informants for information, and claiming to be somebody else.

These findings reflect the commitment of journalists to a strong ethical stance, yet also their reluctance to engage in activities that may have undesirable consequences. In addition, the journalists' Arab-Islamic culture encourages them to avoid controversial and personal issues. However, these findings do not indicate that unethical practices never occur, although when they happen, they may differ from the examples we introduced.

Professional Orientations

Professionalism in the field of journalism and mass communication is an ongoing controversial issue in professional and academic circles. Studies of journalists such as those by Kirat (1993, 1998)

Table 34.6   Journalists' Attitudes toward Ethical Issues (in %, N = 160)

	Justified on Occasion	Would Not Approve	Not Sure	Don't Know	Total %
Paying people for confidential information	15.6	71.6	7.5	5.3	100.0
Using confidential business or government documents without authorization	13.1	78.1	3.8	5.0	100.0
Claiming to be somebody else	13.8	81.3	2.5	2.4	100.0
Agreeing to protect confidentiality and not doing so	12.5	67.9	3.3	16.3	100.0
Badgering unwilling informants to get a story	18.1	71.9	5.0	5.0	100.0
Making use of personal documents such as letters and photographs without permission	7.5	90.0	0.0	2.5	100.0
Getting employed in a firm or organization to gain inside information	13.1	81.9	2.5	2.5	100.0
Using hidden microphones or cameras	10.6	84.4	1.3	3.7	100.0
Using re-creations or dramatizations of news by actors	8.1	83.1	1.9	6.9	100.0
Disclosing names of rape victims	10.0	83.1	3.1	3.8	100.0

Table 34.7 Factors in Judging a Job (in %, N = 160)

	Very Important	Fairly Important	Not Too Important	Don't Know	Total %
Job security?	78.1	20.0	1.3	0.6	100.0
The chance to develop a specialty?	71.9	24.4	3.1	0.6	100.0
The chance to help people?	70.6	22.5	3.1	3.8	100.0
The pay?	63.8	32.5	3.7	—	100.0
The editorial polices of the organization?	61.9	30.6	1.9	5.6	100.0
The chance to get ahead in organization?	57.5	36.3	2.5	3.7	100.0
Fringe benefits?	56.9	37.5	5.0	0.6	100.0
The chance to influence public affairs?	55.6	33.8	4.4	6.2	100.0
The amount of autonomy you have?	53.8	38.1	4.4	3.7	100.0

and Weaver et al. (2007) have used indicators of journalistic professionalism such as membership in professional associations, journalism or mass communication degrees, subscriptions to professional journals, heavy media consumption, continuing education, and participation in workshops and training courses. Other indicators of professionalism include dedication to a news organization and its editorial policy, the search for independence and skills development, and a commitment to values such as impartiality and objectivity.

Table 34.7 shows that when evaluating a journalism job, the majority of respondents place most importance on the following factors: job security (78.1%), the chance to develop a specialty (71.9%), the chance to help people (70.6%), the pay (63.8%), the editorial policies of the organization (61.9%), and autonomy on the job (53.8%).

The data in Table 34.8 reveal the great extent of passion and professionalism of journalists in the UAE. Findings indicate a high degree of professionalism and dedication. More than two-thirds of the surveyed journalists consider the following factors as very important to their professional orientation: the opportunity to learn new skills and knowledge (77.5%), improving professional competence (77.5%), the prospect of using abilities and training (74.4%), security of the job the journalists hold (74.4%), being with people who are congenial (74.4%), having a job that is valuable to society (71.3%), opportunity for originality and initiative (70%), respect for the ability and competence of co-workers, having a job with a respected paper (68.8%), and excitement and variety the job provides (66.3%). Findings of the study also suggest that respondents chose to be journalists because of their love of journalism (81.3%) and the desire to serve their country and people (60.6%).

Another major indicator of journalist professionalism is media use among journalists. Our data show that journalists practicing in the UAE are relatively heavy media consumers compared to other countries. They watch local television news five days a week on average. UAE journalists' top television choices are Abu Dhabi TV (15.6%), followed by Middle East Broadcasting Center (14.4%), Dubai TV (11.3%), Egypt Satellite Channel (10.6%), and a tie among Sharjah (8.1%), CNN (8.1%), and BBC (8.1%).

Almost half of UAE journalists (41.9%) listen to radio news on a daily basis with an overall consumption rate of 4.1 days per week. The most popular newspapers and weeklies read by UAE journalists include *Al Khaleej* (38.1%), *Al Ittihad* (18.1%), *Al Bayan* (16.3%), and *Gulf News* (11.9%). Among foreign newspapers and weeklies, *Al Hayat* (12.4%) is most popular, followed by *Al Sharq Alawsat* (8.0%), *India Express* (7.1%), *Al Majala* (7.1%), *Al Wasat* (7.0%), *Al Qabas* (6.8%), *Newsweek*

Table 34.8   Professional Orientations (in %, N = 160)

	Very Important	Fairly Important	Important	Not Too Important	No Response	Total %
Opportunity to learn new skills and knowledge	77.5	12.8	3.6	6.1	0.0	100.0
Improving professional competence	77.5	14.4	6.9	1.2	0.0	100.0
Full use of your ability and training	74.4	12.1	6.7	6.8	0.0	100.0
Security of the job the journalist holds	74.4	17.5	7.5	0.6	0.0	100.0
Being with people who are congenial	74.4	12.5	8.8	4.3	0.0	100.0
Having a job that is valuable to society	71.3	14.4	13.8	0.5	0.0	100.0
Opportunity for originality and initiative	70.0	21.3	6.3	2.4	0.0	100.0
Respect for the ability and competence of co-workers	69.4	14.4	16.2	0.0	0.0	100.0
Having a job with a respected paper	68.8	16.3	9.4	5	0.5	100.0
Excitement and variety the job provides	66.3	21.9	10.6	1.2	0.0	100.0
Getting ahead in your organization	63.8	20.0	10.6	5.6	0.0	100.0
Supervisors who appreciate improvement	62.5	15.6	16.3	5.6	0.0	100.0
The chance to get ahead in the organization	60.0	21.3	13.7	5	0.0	100.0
Availability of support: working with people who support you	60.0	21.3	11.3	7.4	0.0	100.0
Enjoyment of what's involved in doing the job	56.9	24.4	13.1	5.6	0.0	100.0
Salary: earning a good living	53.1	31.9	11.9	3.1	0.0	100.0
Job that connects me with important people	52.5	26.9	13.1	7.5	0.0	100.0
Having an influence on important decisions	50.0	23.1	24.4	2.5	0.0	100.0
Opportunity to have influence on public	48.1	25.6	18.8	6.9	0.6	100.0
Freedom from close supervision of your work	40.0	36.3	16.9	6.2	0.6	100.0
Having a prestigious job in the organization	36.6	25.0	23.1	15.3	0.0	100.0
Having a job with prestige in community	34.4	25.0	25.0	15.6	0.0	100.0

(6.8%), *Washington Post* (6.1%), *Time* (5.5%), *India Today* (5.5%), *The Economist* (4.9%), *Al Wafd* (4.9%), and *Al Ahram* (3.7%).

Impact on Public Opinion

This study also explored the journalists' opinions about their audiences. Most UAE journalists agreed with the importance to their profession of understanding public opinion (92.5%), and most thought journalists know what the audience wants to read (65%). Most journalists felt that, most

Table 34.9 Journalists' Perceptions of Their Audience (in %, *N*=160)

	Somewhat Disagree	Strongly Disagree	Neutral	Somewhat Agree	Strongly Agree	No Response	Total %
Audience is interested in news more than analysis	13.8	10.6	9.0	36.6	29.4	0.6	100.0
Audience is not interested in routine news of government activities	23.8	16.9	11.9	31.9	15.0	0.5	100.0
Audience is interested in news that criticizes government policies	15.6	15.6	16.3	32.5	19.4	0.6	100.0
Audience is not interested in news about social problems	37.5	25	12.5	17.5	6.9	0.6	100.0
It is very easy to deceive the audience	47.5	20.6	7.5	13.8	10.0	0.6	100.0

of the time, the journalists and their audiences agreed on which issues are worth being covered (56.3%).

Table 34.9 shows that more than half of the journalists surveyed agreed somewhat strongly that the audience is interested in news more than analysis, and that the audience is interested in critical views in the news regarding development projects and government policies.

Journalists in this study believe strongly that the media are very influential in shaping and forming public opinion. Asked to rate the media's influence on a 10-point scale (with 10 indicating great influence, and 0 no influence at all), journalists scored a mean of 8 on the influence of the media on public opinion, a mean of 8.6 on how much media influence there should be on public opinion, and a mean of 7.8 on media influence on government. Asked to assess their own news organizations, journalists most often rated it as good (35%), followed by very good (29%), fair or poor (20%), and excellent (12.5%).

One of the disappointing findings of the study is the journalists' reluctance to use communication technology such as the Internet and databanks. About 72.5% of the interviewed journalists said they don't use these services at all. Only 3.5% of journalists claimed to use technology for their work on a daily basis, while 8.1% claimed to use it weekly. It can be argued here that with the rate of expansion of new information technology, journalists in the UAE tended in recent years to use it extensively in their work.

Conclusions

This study used survey data and in-depth interviews to draw a profile of journalists in the United Arab Emirates in terms of demographics (education, age, nationality) and opinions about professionalism, news values, ethics, working conditions, and impact on public opinion and society.

Eighty percent of UAE media practitioners are foreigners, coming mainly from the Middle Eastern countries and Southeast Asia, while native Emirati journalists constitute 20% of journalists. The mean age of journalists is 36, and 20% of journalists are female. Three-quarters of the journalists are married. More than three-quarters of journalists in the UAE hold a bachelor's degree or higher, and more than half of them have majored in journalism or mass communication.

More than half of journalists surveyed indicated a high level of job satisfaction, and three-quarters said that their job conditions are either good or very good. Journalists also expressed satisfaction with their freedom to practice their daily jobs.

However, more than half showed some dissatisfaction concerning their relations with sources when investigating sensitive issues. And those surveyed were unhappy with their news organization's policies toward continuing education and refresher courses. The majority of them have never been given the chance to enroll in training workshops, seminars and courses, although many expressed an interest in continuing education and training.

Among the interviewees, about three-quarters responded that they are either satisfied or very satisfied with their jobs, the stability of their jobs, the use of their talents and creativity, and their peer relationships. Overall, these findings suggest that journalists in the UAE are satisfied with their job conditions, which is a positive and healthy sign for media practice in the UAE and Emirati media organizations in general.

On the other hand, findings from the interviews revealed that journalists are aware of some weaknesses of Emirati journalism and common criticisms of it that can be made, such as lack of depth in reporting and journalists too often being viewed as spokespeople for the government. UAE journalists also were aware that they may be seen as concentrating too much on routine government activities, and they estimated highly their power to manipulate public opinion on some issues.

The findings confirmed that journalists in the UAE greatly value adhering to their standards of professionalism. Their beliefs and philosophies regarding the role of the media are compatible with the information policy of the country, which emphasizes national unity and national development.

Journalists practicing in the UAE are relatively heavy media users: they watch both local television stations and satellite television channels for an average of 5.2 days a week, and listen to radio news an average of 4.1 days a week.

In terms of media ethics, the study showed that the media practitioners learn mostly from day-by-day practice, from peers and colleagues, and from their family and religious upbringing. More than 70% of the surveyed journalists consistently objected to the use of a range of questionable methods to get news.

Journalists in this study also expressed strong support for the idea that the media are influential in forming public opinion and in influencing government decisions. These beliefs are reflected in and intersect with strong opinions on the mobilizing and interpretative roles of the UAE media.

Looking to the future of UAE journalism, these findings reveal the need for training and continuing education with specific concentration on modern technology such as databanks, multimedia, and the Internet. Findings show the journalists' general reluctance to embrace communication technologies (more that 70% do not use such reporting tools). Also, there is a need to concentrate on learning different languages, especially English, and Arabic for non-Arab journalists, to be able to communicate effectively in a multicultural media environment. Finally, more native Emirati citizens should be encouraged to enter the industry and become leaders in a media field currently dominated by foreign workers.

References

Johnstone, John W. C., Edward J. Slawki, and William W. Bowman. 1973. The professional values of American newsmen. *Public Opinion Quarterly* 36:522–46.

Johnstone, John W. C., Edward J. Slawki, and William W. Bowman. 1976. *The news people: A sociological portrait of American journalists and their work.* Urbana: University of Illinois.

Kirat, Mohamed. 1993. *The communicators: A portrait of Algerian journalists and their work.* Algiers: Office des Publications Universitaires.

Kirat, Mohamed. 1998. Algerian journalists and their world. In *The global journalist: News people around the world,* edited by David H. Weaver, pp. 323–348. Cresskill, NJ: Hampton Press.

Kirat, Mohamed. 2000. *UAE news people: A study of their professional orientations and working conditions.* Al-Owais prize winning studies for science and creation, vol. 2, 10th session, 1999, pp. 185–265. Dubai: Alshahama Commercial Printing. (in Arabic)

Tash, Abdulkader T. M. 1983. *A profile of professional journalists working in the Saudi Arabian daily press.* Unpublished Ph.D. dissertation. Southern Illinois University, Carbondale.

Tunstall, Jeremy. 1977. *Journalists at work: Specialist correspondents, their news organizations, news sources and competitor colleagues.* London: Constable.

Weaver, David H., Randal A. Beam, Bonnie J. Brownlee, Paul S. Voakes, and G. Cleveland Wilhoit. 2007. *The American journalist in the 21st century: U.S. news people at the dawn of a new millennium.* Mahwah, NJ: Erlbaum.

Weaver, David H., and G. Cleveland Wilhoit. 1986. *The American journalist: A portrait of U.S. news people and their work.* Bloomington: Indiana University Press.

Weaver, David H., and G. Cleveland Wilhoit. 1996. *The American journalist in the 1990s: U.S. news people at the end of an era.* Mahwah, NJ: Erlbaum.

Comparative Studies of Journalism

35 Worlds of Journalism

Journalistic Cultures, Professional Autonomy, and Perceived Influences across 18 Nations

Thomas Hanitzsch, Josef Seethaler, Elizabeth A. Skewes, Maria Anikina, Rosa Berganza, Incilay Cangöz, Mihai Coman, Basyouni Hamada, Folker Hanusch, Christopher D. Karadjov, Claudia Mellado, Sonia Virginia Moreira, Peter G. Mwesige, Patrick Lee Plaisance, Zvi Reich, Dani Vardiansyah Noor, and Kee Wang Yuen

Comparative research has clearly gained currency in the field of journalism studies. However, the cross-cultural inquiry into journalists' orientations and professional views is not a new area of research. With their comparison of journalists from the United States and Latin America, McLeod and Rush (1969) started a tradition that was taken further by, among many others, Patterson and Donsbach (1996), as well as Weaver (1998) with the first edition of *The Global Journalist*. While producing interesting insights into the variation of journalistic cultures across the globe, comparative journalism research suffered from a number of shortcomings (Hanitzsch 2009, for an overview). Journalism researchers often focused on Western countries at the expense of other world regions, most notably Africa, Latin America, and parts of Asia. Concepts and theories that underpinned much of the research primarily originated from the West and were not necessarily suited to non-Western contexts. Furthermore, the extent of methodological sophistication too often fell behind essential standards of sound comparative research.

The study *Worlds of Journalism* was set up to address some of these problems.[1] The project is an ongoing collaborative effort of journalism researchers from more than 20 countries from all over the world. Results from 18 countries will be reported in this chapter. Field research was conducted on three levels of analysis—the individual level of the journalists, the organizational level of newsrooms and media organizations, and the national level of media systems. The following account will focus on national differences across journalism cultures, professional autonomy, and perceived influences on news work.

Conceptual Background

In this section, we will briefly introduce our conceptualization of journalism culture, professional autonomy, and perceived influences. For a more detailed discussion we refer to other publications that discussed the theoretical framework in much greater detail (Hanitzsch 2007; Hanitzsch, Anikina et al. 2010; Hanitzsch, Hanusch et al. 2011).

Journalism Culture

One important starting point of our study was the individual journalist and the view that journalism cultures materialize in terms of the professional values journalists embrace. A journalistic culture is therefore constituted on the basis of a particular set of culturally negotiated professional values and conventions that operate mostly behind the backs of the individual journalists. There seems to be an ideological consensus, collectively shared by the journalists around the world, according to which journalism (1) is a professional service to the public that (2) is carried out in organizational contexts, (3) is mainly oriented toward facts, (4) provides timely and relevant information, and (5) requires at least some intellectual autonomy and independence (Deuze 2005; Kovach & Rosenstiel 2001).

The *Worlds of Journalism* study was less interested in these universals than in the elements that are likely to distinguish the various journalism cultures from each other. These "areas of disagreement" were conceptualized in terms of three separate domains: The area of *institutional roles* refers to the normative and actual functions of journalism in society (mostly referred to as "role perceptions"); *epistemologies* relate to the accessibility of reality and the nature of acceptable evidence; and *ethical ideologies* point to the journalists' responses to ethical dilemmas. The three domains can be further divided into seven dimensions:

- *Interventionism* reflects the extent to which journalists pursue a particular mission and promote certain values. The distinction between high and low interventionism tracks along a divide between two types of journalist—one involved and socially committed; the other detached and uninvolved.
- *Power distance* refers to a journalist's position toward loci of power in society. It distinguishes between an approach to journalism as "Fourth Estate" and "watchdog" on the one hand, and an opportunist, loyal, or collaborative mode toward power centers on the other.
- *Market orientation* accounts for journalists' perspective on the audience as either citizens or consumers. In the latter perspective, journalism cultures strongly submit to the market logic, while the former approach gives priority to the public interest and the creation of an informed citizenry.
- *Objectivism* marks the distinction between two fundamental beliefs: One claims the existence of an objective truth "out there" that can be reported "as it is"; the other concedes that news is an inevitably subjective representation of the world.
- *Empiricism* refers to the relative weight given to an empirical justification of truth—emphasizing observation, measurement, evidence and experience—and an analytical justification by accentuating reason, ideas, values, opinions, and analysis.
- *Relativism* marks the extent to which journalists believe that they should base their ethical decisions on universal ethical rules and moral absolutes or on the respective situational context.
- *Idealism* refers to the importance of (anticipated) consequences in journalists' reasoning about ethical dilemmas. Here, the division tracks along highly idealistic journalists who are means-oriented and those who are more goal-oriented in their reporting.

Professional Autonomy and Perceived Influences

Autonomy is conventionally assumed to be one of the most fundamental requirements for professional journalistic practice (e.g., McDevitt 2006; McQuail 1992). We mainly conceptualized professional autonomy as a construct that is situated primarily within the editorial organization and structures that govern news work. By professional autonomy we therefore mean the "latitude that a practitioner has in carrying out his or her occupational duties" (Weaver, Beam, Brownlee, Voakes, & Wilhoit 2007: 70).

From the perspective of the individual journalist, professional autonomy can be limited by a variety of forces that emanate from various levels. Drawing on a rich body of literature on influences on the news—including the work of Shoemaker and Reese (1996), Ettema, Whitney, and Wackman (1987), McQuail (2000), and Preston (2009)—we proposed five major levels of influences:

- The *individual level* refers to journalists' personal and professional backgrounds and orientations, as well as their specific roles and occupational characteristics within the news organization.
- The *media routines level* becomes manifest in the form of routinized investigation, news gathering and content presentation, as well as in the shape of limited resources.
- The *organizational level* involves technological imperatives, newsroom conventions, advertising considerations, as well as structures of editorial coordination and decision making.
- The *media structures level* refers to the economic imperatives of journalism which are especially relevant in commercial news organizations, but also in nonprofit and public service media.
- The *systemic level* of influence incorporates the relevant social, cultural, and ideological contexts within which journalists operate, most notably the political and legal conditions of news making.

These conceptual ideas have guided the development of measures that involved researchers from various nations. The research tools were geared toward capturing the variation in journalistic cultures and their driving forces in different cultural contexts. We also tried to avoid any normative starting point that suggested Western occupational values were generally "better" or "more professional" than others. Given that journalism has different social functions in different societies, we expected the extent to which journalists endorsed professional values to vary across countries. For this reason, Western professional values were not employed as a yardstick against which to measure the "success" or "failure" of non-Western countries to "catch up" with the West.

Methods

Selection of Countries and Samples

The *Worlds of Journalism* project was originally born out of a rather small-scale comparative pilot study set up in late 2006 that included seven countries: Brazil, China, Germany, Indonesia, Russia, Uganda, and the United States. As the project became better known in the scientific community, research teams from a number of additional countries joined in, and the study started to develop a dynamic structure of its own that itself attracted even more participants. In addition to the original seven countries, the final sample from which results are reported in this chapter included Australia, Austria, Bulgaria, Chile, Egypt, Israel, Mexico, Romania, Spain, Switzerland, and Turkey. The choice of countries cuts across democratic and authoritarian contexts, as well as developed and developing countries. One important practical consideration was the availability of qualified and committed researchers.

Within the various countries, sampling was carried out in two steps. We first selected 20 news organizations in every country following a common quota scheme (see Table 35.1). The choice of newsrooms was organized along four criteria: type of communication medium; reach (national vs. local/regional media); audience orientation for print media (quality vs. popular outlets); as well as ownership of electronic media (public, state-owned, or private channels). While the choice of

Table 35.1   Survey Sample

Media	Sublevel	National Media	Local Media	Total
1. Daily newspaper	quality: citizen-oriented	2 (10)	3 (15)	5 (25)
	popular: consumer-oriented	1 (5)	1 (5)	2 (10)
2. Weekly magazine or newspaper	quality: citizen-oriented	1 (5)	—	1 (5)
	popular: consumer-oriented	1 (5)	—	1 (5)
3. News agency		1 (5)	—	1 (5)
4. Television	state-owned/public	1 (5)	1 (5)	2 (10)
	private	3 (15)	1 (5)	4 (20)
5. Radio	state-owned/public	1 (5)	1 (5)	2 (10)
	private	1 (5)	1 (5)	2 (10)
Total		12 (60)	8 (40)	20 (100)

Note: Numbers in parentheses represent the total subsample of journalists in the respective media category.

popular print media was based on circulation, the quality outlets were selected according to their agenda-setting power.[2] Online newsrooms were omitted from the study, as the degree of their institutionalization still varied considerably across countries. All national research teams invested a great deal of effort in order to match the overall sampling scheme and, at the same time, achieve a reasonable approximation to the diversity that exists within their countries.[3] However, due to several idiosyncrasies in some countries, researchers sometimes had to make use of alternative options that were also provided as part of the sampling instructions.[4]

The sample size in every country was 100 respondents. We should note that with such relatively small numbers, it is hardly possible to provide representative pictures of news people in the 18 nations. However, considering the overall purpose of the study along with budget limitations, we decided to create "matched samples" that allow for comparison across countries (Hofstede 2001: 463). This means that samples are similar in terms of their internal composition (types of media, general ownership pattern, and audience) in order to ensure functional equivalence. If these conditions are met, Hofstede suggested minimal sample sizes of at least 20, preferably 50, respondents per country.

Journalists were defined as those who had at least some "editorial responsibility" for the content they produce (Weaver & Wilhoit 1986: 168). We tried to be as inclusive as possible in capturing the various domains of news work. Respondents were selected from both the traditional "hard news" beats, as well as from other areas of coverage such as sports, travel, and celebrities. Wherever possible, we selected five journalists in each newsroom. Within news organizations, journalists were further stratified according to the extent of their editorial responsibility. Ideally, one journalist was selected from the top echelon of the editorial hierarchy (e.g., chief editors and their deputies), one from the middle level of operational decision-makers (e.g., senior editors and desk heads), and three from the lowest level of the newsroom hierarchy (e.g., reporters). The selection of the journalists in each of these categories was based on random sampling. A description of the basic sample parameters is provided in Table 35.2.

Questionnaire and Data Collection

The research tools used in this study were collaboratively designed in order to guarantee a maximum degree of intercultural validity. A fully standardized master questionnaire was first developed

Table 35.2   Basic Sample Parameters

	Australia	Austria	Brazil	Bulgaria	Chile	China	Egypt	Germany	Indonesia	Israel	Mexico	Romania	Russia	Spain	Switzerland	Turkey	Uganda	USA
Female journalists (%)	40	35	45	64	61	46	36	25	33	41	30	65	51	40	33	36	31	42
Age (Mean)	38	41	39	36	36	32	43	43	36	38	38	32	30	40	41	35	32	47
Graduated college (%)	74	66	96	94	89	96	99	82	88	69	89	97	87	99	58	70	54	94
Worked as journalist (years, Mean)	15	17	17	12	12	9	20	16	10	13	15	8	9	17	15	12	8	23

in English and then translated into the relevant languages. A relatively simple wording was used in order to reduce potential translation problems. Translation usually involved an iterative translation/back-translation procedure or panels of bilingual experts in order to achieve a best possible approximation to the original master questionnaire.[5]

Data collection for the 18 countries included in this chapter took about 22 months and was completed in April 2009. In most countries the interviews were done by telephone. In Bulgaria, Egypt, and Indonesia, and also partly in China, we conducted face-to-face interviews, mostly because we expected journalists in these countries to not be accustomed to or highly distrustful of telephone interviewing. Turkey was the only case where journalists completed questionnaires on their own while a researcher was present.

The enthusiasm of journalists and newsroom managers for participation in the study varied from organization to organization and from country to country, sometimes substantially. Among the 356 newsrooms that were chosen in the first place, 22 refused to cooperate and were subsequently replaced. We also had to substitute 236 of the 1,800 originally selected interviewees due to refusal. All research teams invested a great deal of effort into convincing newsroom managers and journalists to cooperate, which was one of the reasons why the data collection took much longer than anticipated. In Switzerland, for instance, it took six months until the local researchers managed to get access to the newsroom of the public television SF.

Measures

The journalism culture measures used in this study were designed on the basis of the seven dimensions outlined above, as well as an extensive screening of the literature and previously used questionnaires. We compiled two lists of items that characterized unique aspects of the journalists' professional self-perceptions. A first list of 12 items was designed to measure the relative importance of institutional roles, and another list of 14 items was intended to capture the journalists' epistemological beliefs and ethical ideologies.[6] Professional autonomy was explored in a similar way by proposing two statements with which journalists could agree or disagree on a five-point scale.[7] Perceived influences were measured on the basis of 29 indicators, each referring to a distinct source of potential influence.[8] All scales were later reversed in order to make interpretations more intuitive, resulting in higher values to indicate higher importance, stronger agreement, and stronger influences.

Findings

Journalism Cultures

Institutional Roles.   With respect to the function and role of journalism in society, our findings indicate that journalists across the globe pay relatively high regard to detachment, as well as to providing political information and acting as a watchdog of the government (see Table 35.3). Providing the most interesting information ranks relatively high among the value priorities of journalists, as well as the potential of journalism to motivate the audience to participate in civic activity. The relatively low standard deviations point to a remarkable agreement among the surveyed journalists vis-à-vis the importance of noninvolvement and dissemination of political content. Altogether, these findings suggest that traditional Western role models that emphasize noninvolvement and a watchdog function seem to flourish among journalists around the world.

Table 35.3 Journalism Cultures—Institutional Roles (% "extremely" and "very important")

	N	Australia	Austria	Brazil	Bulgaria	Chile	China	Egypt	Germany	Indonesia	Israel	Mexico	Romania	Russia	Spain	Switzerland	Turkey	Uganda	USA	$\bar{x}$	SD	η^2
To provide citizens with the information they need to make political decisions	1,781	79.0	94.0	99.0	86.0	75.8	76.1	95.0	98.0	78.8	77.1	93.0	78.8	70.7	71.0	95.0	89.7	94.0	90.0	4.38	.92	.088
To be an absolutely detached observer	1,773	71.4	96.0	85.9	42.6	82.0	79.2	96.0	89.0	62.9	58.2	91.0	85.0	70.1	82.0	90.0	89.6	78.8	82.8	4.22	.96	.154
To act as watchdog of the government	1,782	76.0	81.0	89.0	68.7	64.0	83.2	96.0	88.0	80.8	57.7	72.0	47.5	56.7	58.0	65.0	90.6	87.0	86.0	4.05	1.11	.120
To provide the audience with the information that is most interesting	1,784	61.6	88.0	67.0	69.4	64.6	50.0	17.3	84.0	71.7	68.0	77.0	72.0	64.3	74.0	81.0	54.6	56.0	49.0	3.80	1.12	.205
To motivate people to participate in civic activity and political discussion	1,772	52.0	70.0	60.0	63.3	52.0	50.5	83.0	72.0	63.6	50.0	79.0	61.6	45.9	60.6	63.0	80.0	77.0	54.4	3.76	1.11	.068
To act as watchdog of business elites	1,767	67.0	59.6	51.0	35.1	58.2	57.4	76.0	72.0	60.2	40.2	58.0	25.3	32.3	44.0	56.0	74.5	57.0	71.7	3.47	1.29	.102

(continued)

Table 35.3   Continued

	N	Australia	Austria	Brazil	Bulgaria	Chile	China	Egypt	Germany	Indonesia	Israel	Mexico	Romania	Russia	Spain	Switzerland	Turkey	Uganda	USA	Total $\bar{x}$	SD	η^2
To advocate for social change	1,749	37.0	34.0	52.5	27.5	41.4	60.7	89.8	23.2	60.6	49.0	66.6	49.5	28.9	43.9	29.3	79.8	86.9	25.0	3.37	1.23	.206
To concentrate mainly on news that will attract the widest possible audience	1,781	40.0	39.0	19.0	41.8	50.0	69.1	66.0	36.0	71.4	44.2	43.0	31.3	52.5	30.0	37.0	52.6	61.0	31.0	3.37	1.12	.084
To influence public opinion	1,767	25.3	12.0	24.0	55.2	71.7	73.7	91.0	17.2	48.5	41.8	54.0	13.3	61.6	29.6	19.0	72.5	67.0	17.7	3.23	1.27	.280
To set the political agenda	1,767	25.0	19.0	24.2	19.8	49.0	45.1	43.4	21.0	41.4	39.2	43.0	26.8	35.1	18.0	23.2	54.7	51.0	11.0	2.94	1.17	.104
To support official policies to bring about prosperity and development	1,758	15.0	3.0	43.4	17.9	40.4	60.0	54.3	18.2	22.2	21.7	37.0	26.5	26.5	29.3	12.0	20.6	78.0	22.7	2.70	1.33	.256
To convey a positive image of political and business leadership	1,770	6.0	6.0	1.0	6.1	11.0	23.4	10.9	5.1	13.1	2.1	3.0	6.1	30.6	6.0	9.0	6.3	30.0	6.1	1.90	1.08	.164

Interventionist aspects of journalism, on the other hand, were much less supported by the respondents. Journalists in most countries tend to shy away from exercising influence on the political agenda and public opinion, or advocating social change. The greater standard deviations and Eta-squared values for some indicators, however, point to some disagreement among journalists in general and between countries in particular toward the role of intervention. Conveying a positive image of political and business leadership and supporting official policies to bring about prosperity and development also belong to this group of controversial items, though to a somewhat lesser degree. Of all 12 individual aspects of institutional roles, influencing public opinion and supporting official policies seem to be the most controversial ones in cross-country comparison. More than a quarter of the overall variation in journalists' responses to these items is due to national differences (28.0% and 25.6%, respectively). Opportunist values in journalism, such as supporting official policies, generally find little support among journalists in almost all nations. This is especially true for the favorable coverage of political and business elites.

The comparison of journalists' responses across the surveyed countries clearly shows that interventionism—that is, the active support of particular values, positions, group, and social change by journalists—is generally not a characteristic of Western journalistic cultures. Journalists from developing societies and transitional democracies, on the other hand, have a stronger tendency toward interventionism. It is especially the journalists in China, Egypt, and Uganda who stand out in this respect. About nine in 10 journalists in Egypt find it "very" or "extremely important" to influence public opinion and advocate for social change through their work. It remains to be seen if this strong interventionist impetus is a general trait among journalists in the Arab world.

Advocacy of social change is also highly regarded by journalists in China, Indonesia, Mexico, Turkey, and Uganda. To exert influence on public opinion is found to be a somewhat important role among journalists in Chile, China, Egypt, Russia, Turkey, and Uganda. Journalists in Western countries, on the other hand, score consistently low on these aspects of professional role perceptions. It seems that journalists are willing to intervene in social processes especially in contexts where political, economic, and social transformation occurs or is, at least, urgently needed.

With regard to power distance, our findings indicate that monitoring the political and economic elites is indeed a function of global currency. In Western contexts, both aspects—acting as a watchdog of the government and a watchdog of business elites—tend to go hand in hand. In other countries, however, the political appeal of journalism's watchdog role corresponds less strongly with skepticism toward business elites. This is the case in Brazil, Bulgaria, Chile, China, Egypt, Indonesia, Israel, Turkey, and Uganda. In these countries, the correlations between the two watchdog roles—being a watchdog of the government and business elites—are either nonsignificant, as in the case of Egypt, or fail to be of large magnitude (*Spearman's Rho* < 0.4).

The least vigilant and critical journalists seem to come from Romania, Russia, and Israel. Relatively little power distance, indicated by the willingness of journalists to provide support for official policies and to convey a positive image of political and business leadership, generally finds very little support in most investigated countries—with a few exceptions. We found the most opportunist or noncritical orientation among journalists in developing and transitional contexts. This is especially true for the more authoritarian contexts of China and Uganda, and, to some extent, also in Egypt where more than half of the journalists found it important to provide support for official policies. In Russia, just over 30% of the journalists said it is important to convey a positive image of leadership in their work. Again, Western countries score consistently low with regard to opportunist aspects of professional role perceptions.

China is an interesting case here, as 83% of the interviewed journalists found it important to act as a watchdog of the government. It is not the first time that communication researchers have encountered a surprisingly high regard for journalism's watchdog function among Chinese journalists (e.g., Chen, Zhu, & Wu 1998: 26). Such a relatively high score, we think, cannot be explained by social desirability alone. There is indeed some evidence of a critical attitude among Chinese journalists, especially toward local authorities, indicated by a number of investigative reports on corruption in municipal administrations in the local press (Bandurski & Hala 2010; de Burgh 2003).

Journalists in China, Egypt, and Indonesia have the strongest audience orientation. In these countries, about two-thirds or more of the respondents found it important to concentrate on news that will attract the widest possible audience. This is also true, though to a lesser extent, for their colleagues in Russia, Turkey, and Uganda. Providing the most interesting information tends to characterize European as well as Mexican and Indonesian journalism. This function is least supported by journalists in China, Egypt, Turkey, and the United States. Especially the Egyptian sample stands out in this regard, as only 17% of the interviewed journalists indicated that providing interesting information is important to their work. It is also notable that with the relatively low priority placed on providing interesting information, American journalists deviate considerably from their colleagues in the other Western countries.

The importance of the political information function of journalism remains relatively unchallenged across all investigated nations. At least three in four journalists in all the 18 countries found this aspect to be important. Russia and Spain are exceptions here as the percentages are relatively small. The motivational and participatory functions of journalism, indicated by the willingness of journalists to motivate people to participate in civic activity and political discussion, was least supported by journalists in China and Russia, and it also ranked low in Australia, Chile, and the United States. Given the long and lively discussion of public/civic journalism approaches in the United States, the American results came as a bit of a surprise, though they well correspond to findings from recent representative surveys of U.S. journalists (Weaver et al. 2007: 146). The emphasis on the motivational potentials of journalism is most pronounced among journalists in Austria and Germany, as well as among their colleagues in Egypt, Mexico, Turkey, and Uganda.

Epistemologies.   With respect to journalists' epistemological orientations, our results provide further evidence for the global importance of impartiality and neutrality standards within the profession, as well as for the significance of factualness and reliability (see Table 35.4). Furthermore, journalists around the world feel that personal beliefs and convictions should not influence their reporting. The role of subjectivity in news making, on the other hand, seems to be somewhat more controversial. A great deal of disagreement was prompted by the question of whether personal evaluation and interpretation should slip into the coverage. Cross-national differences loom especially large in this respect, accounting for a substantial 31.7% of the overall variance. Similarly, the journalists disagreed on the extent to which a journalist should provide the audience with orientation by making clear which side in a dispute, in the view of the journalist, has the better position.

However, the comparison of country scores does not reveal any consistent pattern. This is true for objectivism as well as for empiricism. There are considerable differences even between Western countries. Especially with regard to objectivism, it seems that the various aspects of this complex concept are cherished differently in different national contexts. Allowing the news to be influenced by personal beliefs and convictions is clearly disapproved of by journalists in Austria,

Table 35.4 Journalism Cultures—Epistemologies (% saying "strongly" and "somewhat agree")

	N	Australia	Austria	Brazil	Bulgaria	Chile	China	Egypt	Germany	Indonesia	Israel	Mexico	Romania	Russia	Spain	Switzerland	Turkey	Uganda	USA	Total $\bar{x}$	SD	η^2
I make claims only if they are substantiated by hard evidence and reliable sources	1,769	80.8	92.0	96.0	91.8	91.0	87.6	75.0	90.0	94.9	91.2	97.0	76.8	69.1	82.8	91.0	92.5	93.0	91.8	4.42	.83	.062
I do not allow my own beliefs and convictions to influence my reporting	1,775	69.0	81.8	81.8	63.9	77.8	74.7	85.0	72.0	87.8	62.6	81.0	81.0	76.8	80.0	75.0	68.0	86.0	76.3	4.09	1.02	.037
I remain strictly impartial in my work	1,774	68.7	79.0	78.8	64.3	81.8	94.8	93.0	75.0	69.4	60.4	84.0	89.0	69.8	74.0	64.0	69.1	88.9	73.2	4.08	.97	.076
I always stay away from information that cannot be verified	1,779	54.5	84.0	53.5	66.7	58.0	87.6	92.0	76.8	83.8	69.9	59.0	84.8	50.0	59.0	90.0	81.3	65.0	71.7	3.97	1.18	.088
I provide analysis of events and issues in my work	1,773	77.8	32.3	75.0	84.7	72.0	82.5	90.0	31.0	16.3	87.0	96.0	69.1	91.8	84.0	46.0	92.8	94.0	78.6	3.93	1.20	.317
I think that facts speak for themselves	1,772	63.0	66.0	66.7	78.0	66.0	83.5	75.6	60.0	72.7	62.2	76.0	67.0	50.5	48.0	63.0	68.8	87.0	72.7	3.90	1.04	.059
I think that journalists can depict reality as it is	1,762	56.3	39.0	76.5	68.4	60.6	62.1	54.2	35.0	80.6	60.2	63.0	59.6	33.0	50.5	50.0	68.4	78.8	68.4	3.62	1.17	.075
I always make clear which side in a dispute has the better position	1,734	14.1	19.2	20.2	23.5	34.0	30.5	59.4	13.1	32.3	18.9	25.0	34.4	25.3	18.4	16.0	10.4	56.1	9.4	2.61	1.24	.168

Brazil, Egypt, Indonesia, Mexico, Romania, Spain, and Uganda, while it is seen less critically by their colleagues in Bulgaria, Israel, and Turkey. Strict impartiality is paramount to journalists, especially in Chile, China, Egypt, Mexico, Romania, and Uganda, which indicates that impartiality is not, or at least not anymore, a distinct trait of Western journalists. It is notable that especially journalists working in the authoritarian contexts of China and Egypt have such extraordinarily high regard for impartiality. One reason might be the simple fact that a nonideological stance is the safest way to operate in an often difficult terrain, as it prevents journalists from getting into conflict with the state apparatus.

The news can depict reality as it is—at least this is believed by many journalists in the surveyed countries, though to a varying degree. More than two-thirds of the journalists in Brazil, Bulgaria, Indonesia, Turkey, Uganda, and the United States seem to adhere to this view, which sets their journalistic cultures apart from those in Austria, Germany, and Russia. Obviously, national differences in epistemological views cut across political and cultural boundaries. Although making clear which side in a dispute has the better position is consistently disapproved of by most journalists (with the exception of those in Egypt and Uganda), the extent of its disapproval varies. This aspect of subjectivity is generally more appreciated in developing and transitional contexts, and less pronounced in most Western journalism cultures.

A similar picture emerges from the analysis of aspects of empiricism. Journalists around the world strongly value the substantiation of facts by means of hard evidence and reliable sources. In most of the surveyed countries, at least nine in 10 journalists agreed on the importance of this particular aspect of empiricism. This was the case for Austria, Brazil, Bulgaria, Chile, Germany, Indonesia, Israel, Mexico, Spain, Switzerland, Turkey, Uganda, and the United States. Likewise, to stay away from information that cannot be verified is most respected by journalists in Austria, China, Egypt, Indonesia, Romania, Switzerland, and Turkey, but least valued by their colleagues in Australia, Brazil, Chile, Mexico, Russia, and Spain. Again, the political and cultural contexts of these countries do not seem to account for this pattern.

In a similar vein, journalists in most of the countries believe in the idea that facts do speak for themselves. There is not much cross-national variation, except for the fact that Russian and Spanish journalists seem to be somewhat more skeptical in this regard. For all of the above discussed aspects of journalistic empiricism, the differences between countries tend to be small, and the amount of variance that is due to cross-national variation is less than 10%. It seems that what we defined as the empiricism dimension is a rather psychological construct that is best explained at the individual level.

This is clearly different for the extent to which journalists provide analyses of events and issues. Here, our results mark a distinction between the various journalism cultures, with Australia, Austria, Germany, Spain, Switzerland, and the United States representing the least analytical journalism—and with journalists in Egypt and Uganda providing the most analytical reporting. However, no single contextual factor alone would sufficiently predict the national differences in the journalists' perceived importance of analysis in the news. This holds true, even though journalists in developing and transitional contexts tend to value more highly this aspect of professional epistemology.

Egypt is notably an interesting case across all epistemology-related items. The vast majority (93%) of Egyptian journalists has a high regard for impartiality, but at the same time they are among those who are most willing to provide analysis and orientation. This seems contradictory, but it might indicate that Egyptian journalists believe that providing orientation for the audience does not automatically mean that coverage is partisan or biased. Egypt is in fact an extreme case in a general trend across several developing countries where providing orientation in a political dispute does not necessarily conflict with an emphasis on perceived objectivity and impartiality.

Ethical Ideologies.   An overwhelming majority of journalists in the surveyed countries tend to obey universal ethical principles that should be followed regardless of situation and context (see Table 35.5). They also agreed on the importance of avoiding questionable methods of reporting, even if this means not getting the story. We found much less approval—although the extent of it varies between countries—for the idea that due to the inherent complexity of ethical dilemmas, journalists should have more personal latitude in solving these problems. This desire for flexibility also relates to the relative importance of means versus ends in professional contexts: According to the journalists' responses, there are situations in which many journalists would even justify inflicting harm upon other individuals if the result supports a greater public good.

Cross-national comparison shows that news workers in Western contexts exhibit a stronger tendency to disapprove of contextual and situational ethical practices, though this is also true for their colleagues working in Brazil, Mexico, Turkey, and Uganda. By contextual and situational practices we mean that ethical decisions are not based on moral absolutes but depend on the specific circumstances of the situation. Table 35.5 also indicates that it is especially the Chinese and Russian journalists who tend to be most open to situational ethical practices. A situational approach is also approved of by a majority of journalists in Indonesia and Uganda, while it is clearly disapproved of by news people in Brazil, Germany, Turkey, and the United States. Consistent with this finding, respondents in Western contexts showed relatively little support for the idea that journalists should be allowed to set their own individual ethical standards. Most journalists in Bulgaria, Chile, Indonesia, and Turkey, on the other hand, would like to retain some individual flexibility with respect to their ethical conduct. The relatively high importance of universal ethics and the openness to situational practices among journalists in China is an interesting contradiction that needs to be explored further.

Differences between journalists from Western and non-Western countries also exist with regard to idealism. Only in Bulgaria, Israel, and Russia was the use of questionable reporting methods rejected by a majority of the journalists. Although journalists in most countries generally avoid questionable methods of reporting, those working in Western contexts value this idea more than their colleagues who operate in a developmental and transitional environment. The picture is similar with respect to the acceptance of harmful consequences of reporting for the sake of a greater public good. About two-thirds of the interviewed journalists in most Western countries—but also their colleagues in Indonesia, Turkey, and Uganda—would like to keep all options on the table. Journalists in Chile and Egypt, and to some extent also in Bulgaria, China, Russia, and Uganda, on the other hand, exhibit a relatively strong normative orientation as they are less likely to accept harmful consequences no matter how important a story is perceived to be.

Professional Autonomy and Perceived Influences

Professional Autonomy.   Table 35.6 indicates that the levels of journalists' perceived autonomy depends primarily on political and legal forces that are usually seen as crucial parameters of the performance of media systems (Hallin & Mancini 2004). Only journalists in China and Russia, and to some extent also in Chile, do not share the otherwise relatively consistent perception of high professional autonomy. The United States scores exceptionally high on the two aspects of autonomy: to have control over the work and to take part in decisions that affect one's work. The

Table 35.5 Journalism Cultures—Ethical Ideologies (% saying "strongly" and "somewhat agree")

	N	Australia	Austria	Brazil	Bulgaria	Chile	China	Egypt	Germany	Indonesia	Israel	Mexico	Romania	Russia	Spain	Switzerland	Turkey	Uganda	USA	$\bar{x}$	SD	η^2
There are ethical principles which are so important that they should be followed by all journalists, regardless of situation and context	1,784	69.7	93.0	97.0	82.3	78.0	92.8	89.0	93.0	88.9	81.6	90.0	82.8	70.0	89.0	96.0	94.9	95.0	91.8	4.43	.88	.115
Journalists should avoid questionable methods of reporting in any case, even if this means not getting the story	1,758	62.6	88.7	75.8	42.3	61.2	64.2	60.0	77.0	69.7	45.3	70.0	59.2	35.7	77.1	76.5	70.2	62.0	82.1	3.83	1.16	.089
There are situations in which harm is justifiable if it results in a story that produces a greater good	1,734	56.0	68.0	55.6	32.7	54.1	20.0	62.9	72.0	76.8	65.6	41.4	57.0	39.4	47.9	80.2	69.3	75.0	60.0	3.51	1.23	.124
What is ethical in journalism varies from one situation to another	1,759	50.0	40.4	27.0	50.0	50.0	71.1	39.4	26.0	62.6	47.9	47.0	44.2	68.7	49.5	42.9	17.0	51.5	28.6	3.03	1.39	.116
Ethical dilemmas in news coverage are often so complex that journalists should be allowed to formulate their own individual codes of conduct	1,755	19.2	31.3	20.2	62.5	58.0	35.8	47.4	13.5	70.4	27.6	29.0	31.6	32.0	30.2	21.2	68.4	42.4	12.0	2.87	1.33	.172
Reporting and publishing a story that can potentially harm others is always wrong, irrespective of the benefits to be gained	1,750	16.3	19.4	24.2	37.9	51.5	45.7	64.6	12.2	25.3	20.8	32.3	34.0	42.9	26.0	15.5	17.6	39.0	14.3	2.76	1.34	.140

lowest professional autonomy was reported by the journalists in Russia where the political elites have put media freedom under pressure during the past 15 years (Simons & Strovsky 2006). Many Russian journalists may still remember the relative freedom they enjoyed during the early 1990s, and the loss of autonomy since then might contribute to their relatively negative assessments.

The remarkably high levels of perceived professional autonomy may seem somewhat counter-intuitive given that especially commercial imperatives and organizational limits are often seen to increasingly challenge journalistic autonomy. Perceived autonomy does indeed correlate nega-tively with the influence of organizational constraints (ownership, profit expectations, advertising considerations, and management) and external constraints (business people, advertisers, censor-ship, government officials, and politicians). Correlations are, however, not particularly large as the values for *Spearman's Rho* range between -.14 and -.25 (*p* < .001) for organizational influences and between -.15 and -.25 (*p* < .001) for external forces. These rather weak relationships may be interpreted in terms of a gap between normative ideas and empirical manifestation (Josephi 2005). Journalists often have noble professional ideals in mind when they speak about their work, and it may be difficult to admit that real practice does not meet these aspirations. Furthermore, the impact of external constraints on autonomy may largely go unnoticed by the average journalist who is most likely in a reporter role and therefore less involved in managerial decisions (Hanitzsch, Anikina et al. 2010). Another reason might be the fact that the external limits of professional autonomy often operate in the form of persuasive processes rather than forced compliance (Dons-bach 2004: 144). As a consequence of their internalization they may appear so natural to the jour-nalists that they are—at least partly—no longer perceived as "external" limits but as factors that inherently belong to the workings of journalism.

Perceived Influences.   An examination of the influences that journalists perceive in their day-to-day work shows both some common threads and interesting differences across the 18 countries in the study (see Table 35.7). Overall, influences from within the news organization were perceived as more influential than factors from outside the organization. Among the top 10 influences—news deadlines, conventions and ethics of the profession, news sources, supervisors and higher editors, conventions and ethics of the newsroom, shortages of news-gathering resources, procedures and standards of news production, news organization management, audience members, and new media technologies—only three come from outside the newsroom (professional conventions, news sources, and audience members).

Sources of influence that were believed to be "very" and "extremely influential" by a majority of the journalists in most of the countries studied include news deadlines (mentioned by a majority in 16 countries), conventions and ethics of the profession, conventions and ethics of individual news-rooms, news sources (14 countries), as well as supervisors and upper level editors (13 countries). These influences also tend to rise to the top three in each of the countries studied, with deadlines being listed as one of the top influences by journalists in Australia, Austria, Bulgaria, Egypt, Israel, Romania, Russia, Switzerland, and Uganda. Professional conventions rose to the top three among journalists in Austria, Brazil, Bulgaria, Germany, Indonesia, Israel, Mexico, Spain, Switzerland, Uganda, and the United States.

Generally speaking, it is the organizational, professional, and procedural influences that are seen to be the most powerful limits to the journalists' work. These influences originate from the journalists' immediate environment, and journalists have to deal with these forces almost every day. The impact of these factors seems to be much more evident and tangible to the journalists than

Table 35.6 Perceived Professional Autonomy (% saying "strongly" and "somewhat agree")

	N	Australia	Austria	Brazil	Bulgaria	Chile	China	Egypt	Germany	Indonesia	Israel	Mexico	Romania	Russia	Spain	Switzerland	Turkey	Uganda	USA	$\bar{x}$	SD	η^2
I have a lot of control over the work that I do.	1,778	87.0	79.0	82.0	76.0	61.6	52.1	76.0	75.0	79.4	86.7	89.0	70.1	43.8	73.0	77.0	70.5	65.0	95.0	3.94	.98	.092
I am allowed to take part in decisions that affect my work.	1,785	90.0	85.0	90.0	84.0	59.6	69.1	75.8	85.0	89.9	90.9	88.0	66.7	51.5	74.0	91.0	63.9	71.0	95.0	4.09	.99	.107

external and more abstract influences. Moreover, news organizations do in fact have a relatively strong grip on their staffs. While their struggle for autonomy alerts and, to some extent, protects journalists from certain external influences (such as politics and business), it leaves them fairly defenseless against organizational forces. The relatively strong importance of professional influences, on the other hand, may be seen as an indication of a global move toward professionalization and further consolidation of professionalism within the occupation of journalism.

The perceived influences that make up the bottom of the list all come from outside of the media, including religious leaders, friends and family, journalism unions, business people, media watch organizations, politicians, colleagues in other media, advertisers, government officials, and public relations. Among the sources of influence that were perceived to be of lowest importance, religious leaders was ranked the lowest in Switzerland, Romania, Brazil, Mexico, and Bulgaria. Other items that were rated the least influential included journalism unions in Germany and Russia; business people in Israel; media watch organizations in the United States; politicians in Germany; colleagues in other media in Spain, Turkey, and Uganda; advertisers in Australia; public relations in China, Indonesia, and Switzerland; and censorship in Austria and Germany.

The relatively moderate importance of political and economic factors comes as somewhat of a surprise, as their objective influence can hardly be denied. One reason for the low ranking of these sources of influence may be a potential difference between the true impact of the factors on news work and the way these limits are perceived by the journalists. Political and economic influences, we believe, are rarely experienced immediately by the average journalist. The power of these influences might be absorbed by news organizations and subsequently filtered, negotiated, and redistributed to individual journalists. News organizations may thus function as intermediaries of external interests and pressures rather than as a buffer.

Political and economic influences might therefore only *seem* to be less important because these factors are perceived as being less pervasive and much more remote by the journalists. Relatively few journalists have to deal with these influences in their everyday news work. In other words, the impact of political and economic factors may be less noticeable under the circumstances of routine news work, mostly because their significance is masked by organizational and procedural influences that have a stronger grip on journalists' everyday practice.

Differences between countries are most striking with respect to political influences (politicians, government officials, and censorship) and religious leaders. The Eta-squared values reported in Table 35.7 indicate that with regard to all these sources of influence, more than 20% of the overall variance is due to national differences. The influence of censorship is perceived most unevenly among the journalists, as disparities between countries account for 38% of the variance. The impact of censorship, government officials, and politicians is perceived to be especially pervasive by the journalists in China and Turkey. In addition to these countries, censorship is seen as an important source of influence also by news people in Chile, Egypt, Russia, Uganda, and notably, Israel. It comes as no surprise that journalists in democratic countries tend to see political influences as less important than their colleagues in less democratic societies. Religious leaders seem to have a profound impact on news work in Egypt, and to some extent also in Indonesia, Turkey, Uganda, and, interestingly, China. It is notable that especially Islamic societies, which often do not separate religion from the world of politics in the way Western societies do, are among those countries where the influence of religious leaders is felt most strongly by the journalists.

Table 35.7 Perceived Influences (% saying "extremely" and "very influential")

	N	Australia	Austria	Brazil	Bulgaria	Chile	China	Egypt	Germany	Indonesia	Israel	Mexico	Romania	Russia	Spain	Switzerland	Turkey	Uganda	USA	Total $\bar{x}$	SD	η^2
News deadlines	1,763	76.3	73.0	56.6	46.8	52.6	60.8	70.0	57.6	41.4	72.6	52.0	57.6	53.1	52.0	66.7	58.5	77.0	76.5	3.67	1.15	.056
Professional conventions	1,767	66.7	70.0	78.0	47.4	17.7	60.4	61.0	71.0	55.1	81.4	60.6	34.4	52.0	65.3	61.6	47.9	77.0	79.0	3.65	1.15	.127
News sources	1,762	71.4	71.7	69.7	46.4	53.1	71.9	70.7	60.4	24.2	67.0	65.0	60.0	36.1	67.7	57.7	41.2	76.0	69.7	3.62	1.16	.092
Supervisors and higher editors	1,732	73.4	63.2	79.4	46.3	44.2	80.4	60.6	51.0	29.3	46.3	60.0	46.9	52.1	67.3	52.0	47.3	75.5	80.4	3.59	1.09	.107
Newsroom conventions	1,750	72.4	62.0	79.6	40.9	29.5	56.5	58.0	62.2	56.6	69.5	64.0	36.1	52.6	49.0	59.0	61.3	74.0	81.4	3.59	1.14	.097
Shortage of resources	1,739	65.0	54.0	60.6	35.5	41.7	57.0	62.0	38.1	29.6	64.8	50.0	44.3	34.7	61.6	53.1	47.3	73.7	64.5	3.44	1.19	.066
Procedures and standards	1,744	63.3	51.0	58.6	39.3	49.0	52.1	58.0	43.9	53.5	53.7	53.0	40.8	19.1	53.1	29.6	59.4	76.5	58.3	3.42	1.15	.068
Management	1,738	39.2	15.0	55.2	42.6	57.9	81.4	58.0	15.2	31.3	32.2	55.0	40.6	66.0	50.5	24.5	54.5	74.7	61.9	3.27	1.29	.170
Readers, listeners or viewers	1,776	58.6	30.0	59.0	36.7	46.9	43.8	40.0	28.0	34.3	40.6	57.6	37.8	31.6	35.4	35.0	31.6	78.0	58.0	3.23	1.15	.089
New media technologies	1,724	55.3	42.0	57.9	33.0	37.0	40.4	68.0	33.0	24.2	38.3	55.6	34.4	11.7	43.4	33.3	26.1	73.0	74.5	3.22	1.19	.125
Media laws	1,763	50.5	31.0	32.3	32.0	12.5	57.4	57.0	24.0	27.3	55.8	35.0	29.9	44.9	28.6	30.6	77.3	77.0	38.5	3.12	1.24	.118
Ownership	1,654	16.9	16.1	35.9	40.4	63.2	76.4	55.1	10.7	30.3	21.4	36.5	37.4	61.5	43.2	15.1	58.1	63.3	23.4	2.98	1.42	.189
Sensibilities of the audiences	1,757	57.6	12.1	50.0	28.7	20.8	38.2	32.7	12.0	49.5	27.6	28.0	35.7	6.3	38.8	28.0	61.9	63.0	45.4	2.98	1.16	.141
Market and audience research	1,711	36.6	36.4	37.6	22.1	69.1	41.9	26.8	26.3	51.0	18.1	36.0	25.8	24.7	44.0	11.5	30.5	56.6	34.7	2.95	1.23	.139
Competing news organizations	1,774	42.0	23.0	37.0	25.8	31.3	46.9	35.0	27.0	25.3	31.3	24.0	25.3	13.3	27.0	29.0	24.7	63.0	48.0	2.89	1.16	.074

Profit expectations	1,657	32.5	16.2	28.4	22.0	56.7	33.3	18.6	13.1	22.7	16.3	26.8	28.0	28.6	26.8	20.0	56.3	55.1	26.7	2.64	1.33	.119
Peers on the staff	1,740	46.3	49.0	65.3	7.4	7.6	24.7	12.4	34.3	14.1	30.1	17.2	13.5	11.5	15.6	33.3	33.7	33.7	53.1	2.70	1.23	.199
Advertising considerations	1,645	21.7	10.1	21.3	26.9	49.5	27.2	25.0	5.8	19.4	11.2	20.6	22.3	24.4	23.7	4.4	47.5	55.8	10.5	2.41	1.30	.127
Censorship	1,751	19.0	0.0	6.0	7.1	34.4	74.2	39.8	0.0	8.1	34.0	15.0	12.8	37.6	9.1	7.1	71.3	46.5	9.4	2.31	1.38	.389
Public relations	1,754	22.2	7.0	7.0	14.7	11.5	6.3	19.8	4.0	4.1	5.3	21.0	7.1	14.9	14.0	0.0	13.8	46.0	12.1	2.26	1.08	.097
Government officials	1,764	10.1	2.0	9.0	8.2	17.7	56.8	34.3	1.0	8.1	3.2	11.0	8.1	22.8	9.1	3.0	64.2	40.0	10.1	2.19	1.22	.271
Advertisers	1,734	4.1	5.0	16.0	13.5	37.5	23.4	19.5	5.0	8.2	6.3	19.2	14.6	15.7	21.6	5.1	37.6	53.1	9.2	2.17	1.23	.160
Colleagues in other media	1,780	21.0	7.0	5.0	6.1	12.5	25.8	19.0	5.0	12.1	16.3	4.0	9.2	6.1	3.0	5.0	6.3	18.0	21.2	2.16	1.04	.097
Politicians	1,752	14.1	3.0	7.0	6.1	28.0	42.5	19.2	0.0	6.1	2.2	8.0	8.1	12.9	12.2	4.0	57.9	26.0	7.1	2.14	1.16	.220
Media watch organizations	1,610	12.1	4.1	9.0	3.3	14.9	25.0	16.3	2.0	27.3	15.1	8.0	6.1	12.4	5.3	-	19.8	39.4	3.1	2.09	1.14	.166
Business people	1,762	11.1	2.0	11.0	11.2	43.6	12.6	12.5	1.0	3.0	2.1	7.0	10.1	9.3	10.1	4.0	43.0	34.0	9.0	2.08	1.10	.187
Journalism unions	1,761	12.1	2.0	5.0	5.2	13.5	16.5	24.2	0.0	19.2	8.3	9.0	6.1	3.1	15.2	4.0	10.3	32.0	8.2	2.02	1.09	.156
Friends, acquaintances, family	1,781	16.0	7.0	7.0	8.1	8.3	10.3	18.0	3.0	9.1	7.2	6.0	4.1	10.2	7.0	7.0	6.2	18.0	11.0	2.01	1.04	.057
Religious leaders	1,740	5.1	1.0	2.0	2.1	10.4	17.1	29.8	1.0	17.2	3.2	2.0	1.0	7.4	8.2	0.0	16.8	20.0	6.2	1.88	1.04	.234

Conclusions

A few common trends emerged from a comparative analysis of the journalists' professional views as well as their perceptions of autonomy and influences. First, there is evidence pointing to the global primacy of journalistic role perceptions that are characterized by detachment and non-involvement. The watchdog role and political information also belong to the functions of journalism that seem to have universal appeal. Furthermore, the interviewed journalists agreed that their personal beliefs should not influence their reporting. Reliability and factual information, as well as impartiality, appear to be equally important to journalists around the globe. And in terms of the journalists' ethical conduct, there seems to be a relatively strong consensus regarding the importance of universal principles and the disapproval of questionable methods of reporting. Another general pattern is the relatively high level of perceived autonomy reported by the journalists in most of the countries, despite almost universal complaints about a constant decline in journalism's professional freedom, even in democratic societies. This finding was further corroborated by the fact that we found organizational, professional, and procedural influences to be perceived as more important than political and economic factors—at least from the subjective perspective of the individual journalist.

Interventionist aspects of journalism, on the other hand, are much less universally supported by the interviewed journalists. Similarly controversial is the role of subjectivity, even though cross-national comparison did not reveal any consistent pattern. Especially the various aspects of objectivism seem to play out differently in the analyzed national contexts. Among the factors that influence news work, it is the different perceptions of political forces that seem to play out most prominently in a comparative perspective.

The patterns of similarities and differences, however, are not neatly classifiable along common political or cultural dimensions. This conclusion from Weaver's (1998: 478) first edition of the *Global Journalist* still holds true. And yet, there are a few general tendencies in terms of how countries group together: One cluster consists of countries that represent a "Western journalism culture" in broad terms. In our study, this group includes Austria, Australia, Germany, Spain, Switzerland, and the United States. Brazil, Bulgaria, Israel, Mexico, and Romania form another cluster that could be described as "peripheral Western." It is composed of countries that are, in many ways, quite similar to the West. Finally, a third group largely consists of developing countries and transitional democracies, of which some tend to be authoritarian. This is the largest group and includes Chile, China, Egypt, Indonesia, Russia, Turkey, and Uganda.

Despite all its limitations, we think that the *Worlds of Journalism* study has demonstrated that comparative analysis is indeed a valuable tool that helps to put evidence from national surveys of journalists into proper perspective. It has also proven that large-scale collaborative research is a feasible and effective avenue in the field of journalism research. In fact, working on this project convinced us that collaboration is a key to future attempts of contextualizing our knowledge about the diversity of journalism cultures.

Notes

1. The study was funded by several institutions, including the German Research Foundation, Swiss National Science Foundation, Rothschild-Caesarea School of Communication at Tel Aviv University, School of Journalism and Communication at the University of Queensland, Australia, and the City of Vienna.
2. In every country, there exists a consensus among journalists and media scholars regarding the media outlets that are considered to drive the national political agenda. We therefore selected those quality outlets which were

commonly believed to have the greatest impact in this regard. For popular print media we chose the outlets with the highest circulation numbers. The selection of radio and TV stations was based on the ratings of their newscasts.

3. This was especially true for local media. Here, we sampled media outlets produced in various parts of the country—in urban centers and rural areas or, as in the case of Switzerland and Indonesia, in the regions inhabited by the country's major cultural populations.

4. This was the case in Austria, Egypt, and Uganda. Austria had no significant local TV station, so the number of national channels was increased. In the absence of local newspapers and private radio stations in Egypt, we decided to raise the number of national newspapers and state-owned radio channels. In Uganda, we increased the number of local radio stations to compensate for the lack of local TV stations.

5. The master questionnaire is available online at http://www.worldsofjournalism.org in the Download section.

6. The first list asked for "the things the news media do or try to do." The interviewed journalists could choose between five answer options: "extremely important," "very important," "somewhat important," "little important," and "not important at all." The second list dealt with "different approaches to news coverage." Here journalists could choose between "strongly agree," "somewhat agree," "neither agree nor disagree," "somewhat disagree" and "strongly disagree."

7. The two statements read as follows: "I have a lot of control over the work that I do" and "I am allowed to take part in decisions that affect my work."

8. Respondents were asked to identify the perceived importance of each single source of influence by choosing between five response options: "extremely influential," "very influential," "somewhat influential," "little influential," and "not influential at all."

References

Bandurski, David, and Martin Hala (eds.). 2010. *Investigative journalism in China: Eight cases in Chinese watchdog journalism.* Seattle, WA: University of Washington Press.

Chen, Chin Chuan, Zhu, Jian Hua, and Wei Wu. 1998. The Chinese journalist. In *The global journalist: News people around the world*, edited by D. H. Weaver, pp. 9–30. Cresskill, NJ: Hampton.

de Burgh, Hugo. 2003. Kings without crowns? The re-emergence of investigative journalism in China. *Media, Culture & Society* 25(6):801–820.

Deuze, Mark. 2005. National news cultures: A comparison of Dutch, German, British, Australian and U.S. journalists. *Journalism & Mass Communication Quarterly* 79(1):134–149.

Donsbach, Wolfgang. 2004. Psychology of news decisions: Factors behind journalists' professional behavior. *Journalism* 5(2):131–157.

Ettema, James E., D. Charles Whitney, and Daniel B. Wackman. 1987. Professional mass communicators. In *Handbook of communication science*, edited by Charley R. Berger & Steven H. Chaffee, pp. 747–780. Beverley Hills, CA: Sage.

Hallin, Daniel C., and Paolo Mancini. 2004. *Comparing media systems: Three models of media and politics.* New York: Cambridge University Press.

Hanitzsch, Thomas. 2007. Deconstructing journalism culture: Towards a universal theory. *Communication Theory* 17(4):367–385.

Hanitzsch, Thomas. 2009. Comparative journalism studies. In *The handbook of journalism studies*, edited by Karin Wahl-Jorgensen and Thomas Hanitzsch, pp. 413–427. New York: Routledge.

Hanitzsch, Thomas, Maria Anikina, Rosa Berganza, Incilay Cangoz, Mihai Coman, Hamada Basyouni, … Kee Wang Yuen. 2010. Modeling perceived influences on journalism: Evidence from a cross-national survey of journalists. *Journalism & Mass Communication Quarterly* 87(1):7–24.

Hanitzsch, Thomas, Folker Hanusch, Claudia Mellado, Maria Anikina, Rosa Berganza, Incilay Cangoz, … Kee Wang Yuen. 2011. Mapping journalism cultures across nations: A comparative study of 18 countries. *Journalism Studies* 12(3): 273 - 293.

Hofstede, Geert. 2001. *Culture's consequences: Comparing values, behaviors, institutions and organizations across nations.* 2nd ed. Thousand Oaks, CA: Sage.

Josephi, Beate. 2005. Journalism in the global age: Between normative and empirical. *Gazette* 67(6):575–590.

Kovach, Bill, and Tom Rosenstiel. 2001. *The elements of journalism.* London: Atlantic Books.

McDevitt, Michael. 2006. In defense of autonomy: A critique of the public journalism critique. *Journal of Communication* 53(1):155–164.

McLeod, Jack, and Ramona R. Rush. 1969. Professionalization of Latin American and U.S. journalists. *Journalism Quarterly* 46(3):583–590.

McQuail, Denis. 1992. *Media performance: Mass communication and the public interest.* Newbury Park, CA: Sage.

McQuail, Denis. 2000. *McQuail's mass communication theory.* Thousand Oaks, CA: Sage.

Patterson, Thomas E., and Wolfgang Donsbach. 1996. News decisions: Journalists as partisan actors. *Political Communication* 13(4):455–468.

Preston, Paschal. 2009. *Making the news: Journalism and news cultures in Europe.* New York: Routledge.

Shoemaker, Pamela J., and Stephen D. Reese. 1996. *Mediating the message: Theories of influence on mass media content.* 2nd ed. White Plains, NY: Longman.

Simons, Greg, and Dmitry Strovsky 2006. Censorship in contemporary Russian journalism in the age of the war against terrorism: A historical perspective. *European Journal of Communication* 21(2):189–211.

Weaver, David H. 1998. Journalists around the world: Commonalities and differences. In *The global journalist: News people around the world,* edited by D. H. Weaver, pp. 455–480. Cresskill, NJ: Hampton.

Weaver, David H., Randal A. Beam, Bonnie J. Brownlee, Paul S. Voakes, and G. Cleveland Wilhoit. 2007. *The American journalist in the 21st century: U.S. news people at the dawn of a new millennium.* Mahwah, NJ: Erlbaum.

Weaver, David H., and G. Cleveland Wilhoit. 1986. *The American journalist.* Bloomington: Indiana University Press.

36 Foreign Correspondents— An Endangered Species?

Lars Willnat and Jason Martin

Coverage of foreign news by the U.S. media has declined significantly in recent years as corporate owners sought increased profits and audiences grew more fragmented. Foreign affairs reporting is expensive, and many news organizations decided that shrinking budgets are best met by closing offices abroad and reducing the number of full-time foreign correspondents.

The public's changing media consumption habits and the instant availability of free online news have accelerated this trend. Similarly, a recent study by the Organisation for Economic Co-operation and Development (OECD 2010: 7) estimates that newspapers in 20 out of 31 OECD countries face declining readerships, with significant decreases for some (USA, 30%; UK, 21%; Italy, 18%; Spain, 16%; Japan, 16%; Germany, 10%). Especially damaging for the future of the press is that newspaper readership was found to be lower among younger people who tend to attribute less importance to print media.

At the same time, new communication technologies have transformed news gathering and its distribution, allowing for a more open and networked model of reporting international affairs through social media, news aggregators, and other online tools (Moore 2010). These technologies have given foreign correspondents quicker access to diverse news sources, but at the same time they have challenged the basic definition of journalism by empowering people, companies, governments, and other organizations who are able to participate directly in any public debate. This has placed the foreign press corps under extreme pressure to compete with alternative news makers and produce fresh, interesting news around.

To analyze these changes, this chapter will examine the state of foreign news in the United States, offer a critical review of research on foreign correspondents, and look at the future of foreign correspondence in the United States and worldwide.

Decline in Foreign News

The demand for international news has suffered from a series of economic, political, societal, and technological changes. These include the slow but continuing decline of newspapers; the end of the Cold War, which provided a clear framework and rationale for covering international affairs; the ensuing loss of attentiveness to foreign affairs among media audiences; the dominance of TV as the main news medium and its effect on news content; and an increase in inter-active media that enable people to select their information themselves (Moisy 1997).

Covering foreign affairs is expensive. According to some estimates (Carroll 2007), an average foreign newspaper bureau costs $200,000 to $300,000 a year, depending on whether a reporter's salary is included. Sambrook (2010) notes that revenues generated by foreign news have never sufficiently covered production costs. As a consequence, foreign news has always been subsidized by profits from other parts of a newspaper or broadcast company. As profits declined and pressures

495

grew to reduce costs, many news organizations closed their bureaus overseas in favor of sending local journalists or correspondents to global hot spots as events took place.

U.S. scholars also have argued that declining international news coverage can be attributed to a waning interest in foreign news (Gitlin 1980; Hallin 1986; Hess 1996; Moisy 1997; Schudson & Tifft 2005). A survey by the Pew Research Center (2008a) found that most Americans (53%) track international news when major developments occur, but far fewer (42%) consistently follow international events. Others found that U.S. audiences "show only a narrow interest in a limited category of news stories and are generally inattentive to events outside their immediate environment, especially those in the remote setting" (Tai & Chang 2002: 262).

Given such perceived disinterest, editors have cut back on foreign news. A Pew survey (2008b) of editors at 259 U.S. newspapers showed that international news was losing ground at greater rates than any other topic. Roughly two-thirds (64%) of newsroom executives said space devoted to foreign news had dropped during the past three years. Almost half (46%) said they had drastically cut resources devoted to foreign news, and only 10% considered foreign news "very essential."

So it is no surprise that U.S. media organizations have made deep cuts at their foreign news desks. Former correspondent Jill Carroll (2007), in a study for Harvard's Shorenstein Center, estimated in 2007 that small and mid-size U.S. newspapers have reduced their staffs of foreign correspondents by 30% since 2000. While larger newspapers have made smaller cuts, a recent census conducted by *American Journalism Review* found that the number of foreign correspondents employed by the 10 largest U.S. newspapers dropped 24% from 307 in 2003 to 234 in 2011 (Kumar 2011).

Media observer Jodi Enda (2011) vividly describes the consequences of these cuts for U.S. newspapers:

> The swift decline and, in some cases, wholesale disappearance of original foreign reporting at some of the nation's premier papers created a yawning journalistic void. Increasingly, big-city newspapers relied solely on wire services to provide foreign news. Space tightened again and again. Local, local, local became louder, louder, louder. No longer did papers have the space to run fascinating yarns about how people lived in remote, little-known villages thousands of miles away. They barely had the staff necessary to cover their own backyards. Neither did they have the resources to develop foreign stories that were not only interesting but also important stories that might explain a culture or a country in ways that either foretold or underscored key global developments in places like Pakistan, China or Congo.

U.S. television networks also have been closing foreign bureaus and, in many countries, only maintain an "editorial presence" with at least one representative, who may be a staffer, on contract, or a freelancer. As foreign correspondent Pamela Constable (2007) put it:

> In the 1980s, American TV networks each maintained about 15 foreign bureaus; today they have six or fewer. ABC has shut down its offices in Moscow, Paris and Tokyo; NBC closed bureaus in Beijing, Cairo and Johannesburg. Aside from a one-person ABC bureau in Nairobi, there are no network bureaus left at all in Africa, India or South America.[1]

The dramatic and sustained cutbacks in network resources and staffing have made it very difficult for TV journalists to cover world events, especially over any sustained period of time. According to the Tyndall Report (2010), which tracks the nightly newscasts of America's three main broadcast networks, international news coverage declined dramatically between 1988 and 2010. While NBC, ABC, and CBS featured more than 4,800 foreign news stories in 1989—the year the Berlin Wall fell and Chinese students protested at Tiananmen Square—such coverage dropped to about 2,700 stories in 2010, a decline of 56% overall.

Similarly, foreign coverage in U.S. newspapers declined dramatically between 1987 and 2010. According to content analyses by Pew (2011), the front page newshole for foreign affairs stories in major U.S. newspapers steadily shrunk from 27% in 1987 to 11% in 2010. During the 2008 U.S. presidential election year, such coverage reached an all-time low of 6%.

While it may be easy to dismiss these trends as American-only, there is some empirical evidence that this may not be the case. Content analyses of four British newspapers (*The Guardian*, *Daily Telegraph*, *Daily Mail*, and *Daily Mirror*) in 1979, 1989, 1999, and 2009 show that the percentage of foreign news stories in the first 10 pages have declined from 33% in 1979, to 27% (1989), 23% (1999), and 15% in 2009 (Moore 2010). Given the growing economic pressures on most Western media, it seems likely that a decline in foreign news can be found in Europe as well—at least among media that lack the luxury of public funding.

However, it would be short-sighted not to acknowledge that audiences today have unprecedented access to international news through the Internet and 24-hour news channels such as Al Jazeera, BBC World, France 24, China Central Television (CCTV), Deutsche Welle, and CNN amongst others. Internet scholar Evgeny Morozov (2010) writes that:

> We've never had faster access to more world news than we do today. Aggregators like Google News might be disrupting the business models of CNN and the *New York Times*, forcing substantial cutbacks in one particularly costly form of news-gathering—foreign correspondents—but they have also equalized the playing field for thousands of niche and country-specific news sources, helping them to reach global audiences.

While instant access to diverse news sources greatly benefits consumers of foreign news, "interactivity and engagement with diverse audiences is increasingly important in all areas of reporting—including international news" (Sambrook 2010: 56). Online media allow audiences to interact with journalists and, in some cases, even participate in producing news. CNNi Report, for example, accepts videos, photos, and audio from people who witnessed an event anywhere in the world, providing more diverse and possibly more authentic stories. By allowing audiences to access foreign news that is relevant to them and, at the same time, participate in producing such news, online media might be able to retrieve audiences that were lost to the constant dribble of entertainment and gossip so prevalent in today's media environment.

Despite the obvious benefits of instant and global access to foreign news, it is important to remember that fewer foreign correspondents working for traditional media also means less variety of foreign news consumed. Sambrook (2010: 31) argues that "digital newsgathering may be cheaper, but the additional productivity is soaked up by the expansion in channels and outlets, all reflecting a similar core agenda. An exponential growth in output rests on a reduced base of professional international newsgathering." In other words, the exponential growth of online news sources might blind us to the fact that more and more news is produced by fewer professional journalists every day.

This viewpoint is supported by a Pew (2006) study, which analyzed the news coverage of Google News during one entire day in May 2005. While Google News offered access to more than 14,000 stories on its front page that day, a deeper analysis showed they simply were accounts of the same

31 stories from different news sources. So audiences who rely on online news aggregators such as Google or Yahoo! are likely to encounter the same news stories from the same dominant media organizations. Only the most engaged and interested consumers of online news will encounter foreign news that is not produced by leading media conglomerates.

Defining Foreign Correspondents

Despite a significant body of literature on foreign correspondents and their work, precise definitions of who these journalists are cannot be found (Hahn & Lönnendonker 2009). Most studies done in the United States define foreign correspondents through publicly available lists such as the *Editor and Publisher International Yearbook* or the State Department's *Directory of Foreign Correspondents in the United States*, basically leaving the task of definition to others. Other studies have tried to compile lists by contacting media organizations and asking for lists of foreign correspondents they employ. Since the concept of what precisely constitutes a foreign correspondent is rather fluid (full-time, part-time, or freelancer?), such attempts did not produce representative lists.

Moreover, as Hamilton and Jenner (2004: 302) note, the definition of foreign correspondents "is based on an anachronistic and static model of what foreign correspondence is and who foreign correspondents are." They convincingly argue that economic pressures, inexpensive global communication, and faster and cheaper travel have undermined the traditional role of foreign correspondents stationed abroad. In addition, the growing globalization of commerce and culture has blurred the lines between foreign and domestic news. Similarly, Franks notes (2005: 100) that "the demarcation between home and abroad is dissolving as never before. This is not simply a matter of globalization, but the fact that domestic and foreign matters intersect in an ever more complicated way. A London commuter worries about safety on the tube, and this is linked to what is going on in Pakistan and elsewhere."

To account for the new media landscape, Hamilton and Jenner (2004) propose eight types of foreign journalists: (1) *traditional foreign correspondents* (full-time foreign correspondents who are nationals of the country that is home to their news organization); (2) *parachute journalists* (journalists sent to report short-term events, usually nationals of the country that is home to their news organization); (3) *native foreign correspondents* (foreign nationals who cover international news); (4) *foreign foreign correspondents* (foreign nationals who work for local news outlets); (5) *foreign local correspondents* (foreign nationals who work for foreign news organizations that make news available online); (6) *in-house foreign correspondents* (in-house journalists working online); (7) *premium service foreign correspondents* (full-time foreign correspondents who work for specialized media such as Bloomberg or Reuters); (8) *amateur correspondents* (unaffiliated, often untrained de facto journalists).

Others have called for a new breed of foreign journalists that report "global news." The assistant managing editor of the *Washington Post*, David Hoffman said in a recent interview: "What I am championing is a complete overhaul of the way we think of foreign news...to create [reporters] that are fully global, transnational correspondents. Some beats are organized as issues, ranging from climate change to technology to terrorism to pathogens" (cited in Carroll 2011: 11).

Current research has not yet caught up with these fast-moving changes. While it seems daunting to analyze a profession so closely linked to the unprecedented changes in modern journalism, foreign correspondents are at the forefront of this evolution and therefore deserve more attention from media scholars and other professional observers.

State of Research on Foreign Correspondents

Most research on foreign correspondents has focused on two main areas: surveys that generate demographic data and other details about who the correspondents are, and studies focusing on work routines and experiences. Such data is collected through surveys, content analyses, interviews, or observation.

Despite the social significance of such work, and more than a half-century of research about foreign correspondents, we still know relatively little about them. Formative research on the backgrounds of foreign correspondents performed between the 1950s and early 1990s produced mostly descriptive data derived from surveys, and focused almost solely on demographics, work experience, and use and access to sources. Most studies surveyed either the foreign press corps working in the United States, or journalists working abroad reporting international news for American media organizations.

Foreign Correspondents Working in the United States

Early surveys of foreign reporters working in the United States found them to be mostly male, middle-aged, highly educated, and having one to two decades of journalism experience. During this period, the foreign press generally relied on American media as their primary information source, partly because of difficulties with access to top-level U.S. government sources. This growing disenchantment with source access relative to their U.S. counterparts was a key finding that served as the basis for more sophisticated studies in the past 15 years.

Lambert (1956) was the first to analyze the work and demographic backgrounds of foreign correspondents in the United States using a mail survey of 217 foreign journalists from 37 countries. He found that most foreign journalists were well-educated males in their mid-40s who averaged about 18 years of professional experience.

Lambert found several important themes that formed the basis of subsequent studies. Along with foreign journalists relying primarily on U.S. newspapers to set their reporting agendas; they also believed they had a more interpretive role in reporting news than other types of journalists. Lambert also found they mostly were pleased with the cooperation of news sources, and that most had autonomy on what topics to report—so long as they were not censored back home. Lambert (1956: 356) concluded that "the people of the United States could feel confident that information sent abroad about this country was written by competent and trustworthy professional journalists" and that "these correspondents showed a devotion to truth and accuracy as journalistic ideals."

A study by Suh (1972) that closely followed Lambert's methods and findings renewed interest in foreign correspondent research nearly two decades later. His mail survey of 126 foreign journalists in the United States again found a prevalent interpretive role of foreign correspondents, the reliance on U.S. newspapers as their chief news source, and high satisfaction about cooperation with sources. The author also found that foreign journalists favored improved hiring standards, and believed strongly in professional autonomy as well as personal responsibility for their judgments and actions.

Mowlana's (1975a, 1975b) mail survey of 103 foreign journalists stationed in Washington, DC and New York City found the foreign press corps in the United States to be "a highly liberal, extremely well-educated, and socially unorthodox group" who filed mostly stories of general news coverage (1975b: 89). His studies also revealed that many foreign correspondents were unhappy that U.S. politicians or state officials usually were not interested in talking to them. The journalists in his studies averaged only about a dozen years of experience compared to about 20 years in studies by Lambert (1956) and Suh (1972).

Ghorpade (1984a, 1984b, 1984c) found that between the 1950s and 1980s, Washington-based foreign correspondents became younger and less experienced, but were better educated than their counterparts three decades prior. His mail survey of 317 journalists found the typical foreign correspondent to be a well-educated male in his early 40s, with about 18 years of experience. Differences in demographic characteristics based on home country were minimal.

Similar to previous studies, Ghorpade (1984b) found that foreign correspondents rated U.S. newspapers as their most important news sources. Official sources such as the White House, the Supreme Court, and the Pentagon were rated as least accessible and were used least often. Regardless of geopolitical origin, foreign correspondents also claimed less access to top government sources than U. S. journalists.

Nair (1991) carried out a mail survey of 117 Washington-based foreign correspondents, and as with similar studies, found them to be highly skilled, educated, and experienced reporters who made extensive use of U.S. media, mainly relying on major newspapers such as *The Washington Post, The New York Times,* or *The Wall Street Journal*; the major television networks, and CNN.

Nair's survey again found that foreign correspondents had less access to government sources than U.S. journalists, which some respondents attributed to "not wanting to deal with a foreigner with a shaky grasp of the language," or feeling "indifferent to what appears in the foreign press" (Nair 1991: 61). He also found that three-quarters of foreign correspondents reported a cooperative work climate with U.S. journalists, although contact with them was rare.

Willnat and Weaver (2003) built on these previous studies and other surveys of American and global journalists (Weaver 1998; Weaver & Wilhoit 1996) to look more in-depth at foreign correspondents' personal backgrounds and professional norms. Their mail survey of 152 U.S.-based correspondents from 52 countries found the average foreign correspondent to be a 45-year-old Caucasian male with a college education, more than two decades of journalism experience, and more than a decade as a foreign correspondent. On average, foreign correspondents were older, more educated, and more experienced than American journalists. Job satisfaction was fairly high relative to U.S. journalists due mainly to the autonomy the job affords, and the perceived interest that home audiences had in their work covering the United States.

Although most correspondents were somewhat or very satisfied with access to government information, a large majority cited difficulty in contacting government sources. Open-ended responses cited, among other reasons, perceptions of foreign coverage lacking importance and prejudice due to nationality (Willnat & Weaver 2003: 14).

The most comprehensive survey of foreign correspondents working in the United States was conducted in 1999 by Hess (2005). Based on a mail survey of 439 foreign correspondents, Hess found that the number of foreign correspondents in the United States increased substantially in the second half of the 20th century. In 1999, European correspondents accounted for 47% of correspondents in America, followed by Asian correspondents at 27%. The average foreign correspondent was about 42 years old and had been posted in the United States for about four years. Hess also found that full-time male correspondents outnumbered female correspondents three to one.

U.S. Foreign Correspondents Working Abroad

Journalists working abroad for U.S. media historically have shared a similar demographic profile with their foreign counterparts working in the United States. They have tended to be highly educated, highly paid middle-aged males with more than two decades of experience and about a decade as a foreign correspondent (Kliesch 1991; Yu & Luter 1964). U.S. foreign correspondents usually have been based in Europe, with London being the most popular location (Kliesch 1991).

Most surveys of U.S. foreign correspondents before the turn of the century found that 30% to 40% of U.S. reporters working abroad were foreign nationals (Hess 1996; Kliesch 1991). A more recent survey by Wu and Hamilton (2004) in 2001 found that foreign nationals working for American media has increased to 69%.

Estimates of how many U.S. journalists worked abroad after World War II are fairly vague. Anderson (1951), who conducted the first major global survey of foreign correspondents in 1950, showed only 293 such correspondents. The first systematic study of U.S. foreign correspondents was done by Maxwell (1956) in 1954 and based on a mail survey of 209 full-time correspondents. The study, which mainly focused on demographic data, concluded that most foreign correspondents (60%) held a college degree and that 80% of them were posted abroad before they were 35 years old. A similar study of 277 U.S. foreign correspondents stationed in Europe (Kruglak 1955) found that most correspondents were well-educated males in their 20s and 30s.

Wilhelm's (1963) "world census" of U.S. foreign correspondents identified 515 American journalists working for U.S. media in the early 1960s—mostly in London (14.2%), Rome (9.5%), Paris (9.3%), and Tokyo (9.1%). However, this count is slightly inflated because Wilhelm's study included a number of correspondents who did not work for the news media. A similar study by Yu and Luter (1964) estimated about 300 full-time journalists working abroad. Their survey of 140 U.S. correspondents stationed abroad found that the typical correspondent was a 41-year-old male with a college degree (57%) and about 10 years of experience as a foreign correspondent. Most were stationed in western Europe (47.9%), followed by Asia (23.5%), Latin America (12.1%), Canada (4.3%), Africa (4.3%), eastern Europe (3.6%), the Middle East (2.1%), and the Soviet Union (2.1%). A majority said they were "very" (24%) or at least "fairly" happy (53%) with their jobs and nine out of 10 would again choose the same profession if given a chance.

Bogart's (1968) study of 206 members of the Overseas Press Club focused on demographics and lifestyle of U.S. foreign correspondents. As in earlier studies, Bogart found that American correspondents were experienced, well-educated, and somewhat older reporters. Most U.S. correspondents also believed they had less access to official news sources where they worked than did foreign correspondents working in Washington.

No systematic surveys of U.S. foreign correspondents were done between 1967 and 1992. The few studies that focused on U.S. foreign correspondents during that period provided only basic counts of these journalists. Kliesch's (1991) second "census" of journalists working for U.S. media abroad, for example, found that the number of U.S. correspondents had jumped from an estimated 676 in 1975 to 1,734 in 1990. He also found that female journalists working for the American foreign press corps increased from 10% in 1975 to 25% in 1990.

In 1992, Hess (1996) continued the tradition of journalist surveys with a study of 404 U.S. correspondents working abroad, supplementing the effort with responses from 370 former foreign correspondents. While the average U.S. foreign correspondent still turned out to be a highly educated middle-aged male (mean age 43), Hess found higher education levels (97.8% holding college degrees) and more female journalists working abroad (29.2%) compared to Kliesch's study conducted in 1990. What made Hess's study unique was that it also checked the information U.S. foreign correspondents provided their audiences back home by analyzing 24,000 newspaper, wire service, newsmagazine, and television stories with foreign datelines. Hess concluded that U.S.

media, and TV news in particular, distorted the world geographically by under-representing many nations while focusing on those of interest to the United States.

Wu and Hamilton (2004) performed the most recent study of U.S. foreign correspondents in 2000. Based on a survey of 354 U.S. foreign correspondents, they found that most worked for magazines (42.5%), followed by newspapers (28.6%), wire services (24.0%), network television (19.4%), Internet (12.4%), cable TV (10.1%), and radio (7.5%). Similar to Hess's findings eight years earlier, the average correspondent in 2000 was a 44-year-old male (73.6%) with a college degree (82.4%), and about seven years of experience as a foreign correspondent. The authors also noted more foreign nationals working for the U.S. media abroad. While Hess (1996) found in 1992 that 77% of foreign correspondents were American citizens, Wu and Hamilton (2004) found eight years later that it had decreased to 69%. However, the authors found no differences in news values between citizen and non-citizen correspondents when deciding on what coverage to provide to their media organizations.

Studies of Foreign Correspondents' Work Routines and Performance

Scholars have investigated foreign correspondents' work routines and performance perceptions through a combination of surveys and interviews, along with content analyses and observation of work products and routines. While these studies generally are far behind comparable analyses of U.S. journalists (see, for example, Weaver & Wilhoit 1996), some early conclusions can be discerned.

Studies of foreign correspondents' perceptions of their journalistic roles have consistently shown that they embrace their function as information interpreters more than other types of journalists. Willnat and Weaver (2003) found that foreign journalists stationed in the United States rated the interpretive and analytical role as most important (73%), followed by investigation (56%) and getting information to the public quickly (55%). Foreign correspondents overall were much less likely to use questionable reporting tactics—such as using confidential information without authorization or secret recording devices—compared to regular U.S. journalists. Yet varied responses by the foreign press, depending on their home country, revealed few universal roles or norms beyond protecting identities of confidential sources.

Concerning geopolitical developments, Hahn and Lönnendonker (2009) conducted 27 in-depth interviews with U.S. foreign correspondents working for different American media outlets in Europe. The authors found that post-9/11 foreign coverage shifted in focus toward the Middle East, resulting in European-based U.S. correspondents reporting more about Muslim-related news in Europe to the exclusion of other topics. They also found a general and continuous decline in U.S. foreign news coverage from Europe.

Various other studies have used a mixture of methods to investigate the lives, habits, and work routines of foreign correspondents in specific places, such as those covering the Middle East (Ibrahim 2003; Nawawy 2001; Sreebny 1979); Australian correspondents covering Asia (Masterton 2009); and correspondents in China (MacKinnon 2007; Oksenberg 1994). The richest findings among these geographically focused studies have come from researchers who used a variety of methods or locations to produce greater knowledge. In their case study of London-based journalists, Morrison and Tumber (1985) used a mail survey, more than 150 in-depth interviews, and a range of observations to capture a full picture of their subjects' lives during the early-1980s.

German researchers have been particularly interested in learning more about the German foreign press corps abroad. Yet as with foreign press research in the United States, their work is mostly limited to surveys that produce descriptive or exploratory data (Gysin 2000; Hahn, Lönnendonker, & Schröder 2008; Junghanns 2004; Junghanns & Hanitzsch 2006; Kopper 2006; Kopper & Seller 2007). One exception is Marten's (1989) multi-method study in which he triangulated in-depth interview findings with newsroom observations and comparisons to poll results by the German Allensbach Institute.

More recently, scholars at the University of Dortmund conducted several EU-funded projects focusing on the work of foreign correspondents in Europe and other parts of the world. The first was based on in-depth interviews with 142 foreign correspondents from 11 countries working in Europe. The interviews were conducted in 2006 and center on the work routines and self-perception of foreign correspondents (AIM Research Consortium 2007). Similar interviews of 300 German foreign correspondents in 2006 examined working conditions and the influence of the home newsrooms on their daily work (Hahn et al. 2008). A third project conducted between 2004 and 2006 (see Kopper 2006) analyzed conditions of foreign news production among German correspondents stationed in the United States. Kopper (2006) concluded that German foreign correspondents have little direct access to U.S. sources, rely almost exclusively on leading U.S. media for information, and seldom alter reports to reflect more stringent journalistic norms and practices in Germany.

Hannerz's (2003, 2004) multi-site ethnography of foreign correspondents' social world is perhaps the most rigorous and triangulated qualitative investigation of its type. Between 1996 and 2000, Hannerz (2003) conducted in-depth interviews with about 70 American and European foreign correspondents stationed in Jerusalem, Johannesburg, and Tokyo. He also made extensive field and newsroom observations to paint a fuller picture of how these journalists navigate professional and cultural issues on a daily basis. Hannerz shows that foreign journalists' work is influenced by their on-site experiences, personal backgrounds, and interests of their home newsrooms.

One of the most recent attempts to provide a better understanding of foreign correspondents' work is Gross and Kopper's (2011) *Understanding Foreign Correspondence*. It provides a collection of articles on the work of European and American foreign correspondents, their professional norms and values, the impact of technology, and, most importantly, a discussion of theoretical frameworks that guide the study of international newsgathering. While the authors convincingly argue that media theories such as gatekeeping, agenda-setting, and framing can explain the social processes that influence how foreign news is created, such theories fail to explain the shifting values and norms of foreign correspondents and how they perceive their profession. What remains missing is a more integrative theory of "journalism culture" that explains the professional values shared by foreign correspondents across nations and cultures (see Hanitzsch et al., chapter 35 in this volume).

Other research has used content analyses of news coverage or popular media representations of foreign journalists to better understand their work routines and cultural impact. Such studies have included descriptive investigations of foreign coverage by *The Washington Post* (Lester 1994) and *The New York Times* (Berry 1990); regional American newspaper representations of Germany (Kleinfeld 1986); books by and about foreign correspondents (Starck & Villanueva 1992); and 20th-century movie representations of them (Cozma & Hamilton 2009).

Summary of Research Deficits

A review of related studies on foreign correspondents reveals several key areas of needed improvement, including: (a) more theoretical work; (b) more systematic empirical evidence; (c) more attention to methodological concerns; (d) more comparative studies that place findings in political, social, or cultural contexts; and (e) more consideration of foreign correspondence as a process, including attention to various contingencies such as economic and technological pressures.

Lack of Theory.   Prior research on foreign correspondents has been overly descriptive, usually atheoretical, or produced results that lacked contributions to theory building. As Hahn and Lönnendonker (2009) note, no coherent theoretical model for research on foreign reporting and foreign correspondents exists. The reliance on descriptive data stems from surveys of foreign correspondents and content analyses of their work. Too often, survey studies have focused on personal backgrounds of correspondents, assessments of work routines and pressures, and opinions about foreign news coverage that do not produce theoretical analysis. With a few exceptions (Hess 1996, 2005), most studies also have not linked analyses of *who* foreign journalists are with *what* they do. This reduces many surveys to descriptions of how foreign journalists view their profession without linking those perceptions to actual work.

When theory has been invoked, it serves as a referential framework, but the studies often fail to build on the theory cited. For instance, studies using Lasswell's (1948) theories of press functions as an influence on survey questionnaires have produced mainly descriptive data about roles that foreign correspondents prefer to self-identify (e.g., Nair 1991; Suh 1972; Willnat & Weaver 2003). Ibrahim (2003) used Shoemaker and Reese's hierarchy of influences (1996) as a framework for studying Middle East correspondents' work routines, but ultimately concluded that further empirical work was needed to form any systematic conclusions. Starck and Villanueva (1992) similarly proposed using cultural framing to study foreign correspondents, but never managed to show conclusively how culture might influence their work.

Given that the first studies on foreign correspondents appeared in the early 1950s, this is surprising. Yet studies of professional journalists have suffered from a similar lack of theory that would explain work and role perceptions. Only recently have scholars began to seriously consider theoretical foundations for their survey work on journalists (Hanitzsch 2007).

More Empirical Evidence.   One way theory may become more prominent in studies on foreign correspondents is by producing more systematic empirical evidence. As noted earlier, more studies are needed that link attitudes of foreign correspondents with their actual work. More consideration of the various influences on their work, including working conditions, routines, and news making processes, are needed as well. Specific concerns include economic and technological developments that have caused massive shifts in global journalism and affected how foreign journalists work. Hahn and Lönnendonker (2009), for example, note there is a need to study how online media and satellite technology affect foreign news coverage. Of particular concern is that traditional foreign correspondents stationed abroad might be replaced with "virtual" foreign correspondents. Overall, the number of studies on foreign journalists is surprisingly small and indicates a gap in the academic literature on professional journalism.

Another open question in research on foreign journalists is how their reports depict their host nation. For most people, the only (or most important) way to learn about foreign nations is through mass media. In turn, the way foreign correspondents describe a host nation will influence audience perceptions in foreign nations. Yet despite the obvious importance of such news reports for international understanding and peace, we know very little about how correspondents portray their host nations, why they cover certain topics rather than others, and how these depictions differ among journalists from countries around the world. Analyzing their work with theoretical concepts such as "globalization" or "domestication" of foreign news might help explain some of these questions and differences.

Methodological Concerns.   One of the biggest problems in researching foreign correspondents has been methodological flaws in the design of survey studies. Because of the transient nature of foreign correspondents and their ever-changing definition, attempts to identify the actual population have failed consistently. As a result, many studies are left to rely on incomplete lists as the sampling basis. Wu and Hamilton (2004), for example, relied on a list of 4,825 foreign correspondents compiled over several years by contacting news organizations and scanning newspapers for bylines. Since foreign correspondents often move to other assignments or were inaccurately counted, such lists usually are incomplete. Hess (2005), on the other hand, used various existing lists to identify nearly 2,000 foreign journalists working in the United States: the press gallery section of the *Congressional Directory*, the State Department's *Directory of Foreign Correspondents in the United States, Editor and Publisher International Year Book, Hudson's Washington News Media Contacts Directory, News Media Yellow Book,* and the membership directories of the Foreign Press Association of New York, the UN Correspondents Association, and the Hollywood Foreign Press Association. Although this is a fairly complete collection of foreign correspondent listings, most of these lists contain journalists that are long gone or just arrived in the United States.

While it is unfair to blame anybody for such shortcomings, media scholars need to generate better representative samples of foreign correspondents. Only then can something be said definitively about who foreign correspondents are and what they think about themselves and their profession. Of course, the first step in creating such a sample would be to define who actually qualifies as such a journalist, a task that becomes increasingly difficult as the nature of foreign news reporting evolves.

Lack of Comparative Studies.   Another concern is the lack of comparative studies that prevent placing foreign correspondent research in wider political, social, or cultural contexts. As previous chapters in this book have shown, comparative studies of journalists allow researchers to compare the norms and values of one group of journalists with those of other groups. The observed differences help us place findings outside normative frameworks into context and see them from a less culturally "biased" viewpoint. Stevenson (2004: 371) notes that "comparative studies do provide additional data points, but we do not see them very often. They are expensive and complicated, but without them, a large part of the body of comparative communication research continues to rely on traditional polemic, citing other polemics instead of evidence that challenges the conventional wisdom of critical research or even addresses the core questions." In other words, comparative research not only avoids narrow national perspectives, but allows scholars to incorporate and test the validity of new theoretical ideas and concepts across nations or cultures.

Overall, research needs to foster a more sophisticated understanding of foreign correspondents' work based on cultural differences in press systems, and the media climates where foreign correspondents are based as well as their home countries. Willnat and Weaver (2003), for example, suggest more focus on the influence of political systems and national cultures on journalists' roles and reporting methods.

Contingent Conditions.   Finally, as this review on foreign correspondent research has shown, there is a great need to address the latest economic and technological changes that have affected foreign affairs reporting. Economic pressures have forced many Western media organizations to reduce or eliminate their networks of foreign correspondents. Yet technological advances have allowed even small media organizations with limited news budgets to cover international events with "parachute" journalists or local stringers. How these paradoxical trends affect foreign correspondents' self-perception and foreign news production remains largely unknown. In addition, the growing concentration of foreign news reporting by a few large media corporations—coupled with the apparent surge of foreign news on the Internet—demands close attention from researchers concerned with diversity in international news. Foreign journalists play a key role in setting the international agenda and should be analyzed within a new framework of economic and political globalization.

The Future of Foreign Correspondents

As this chapter attempts to show, foreign correspondents are endangered and evolving. While media organizations have reduced the ranks of foreign journalists to trim costs, new media technologies have changed the process of foreign news production.

It seems likely that these economic and technological trends particularly will benefit media organizations with the resources to run global networks of news bureaus and foreign correspondents. Thus, powerful news agencies such as the Associated Press, which employs about 2,500 newsgatherers in more than 300 locations worldwide (Associated Press 2011) or Thomson Reuters with 2,800 full-time journalists in 200 bureaus around the world (Thomson Reuters 2010), will continue to provide the vast majority of professional foreign reporting. As Moore (2010: 43) points out, however, these organizations "are likely to come under increasing pressure to gather more news for more platforms in less time."

The Internet and an emerging global news audience have transformed foreign news in remarkable ways that remain poorly understood. Reese, Rutigliano, Hyun, and Jeong (2006: 256), for example, argue that "globalization and the Internet have created a space for news and political discourse that overrides geography and increases opportunities for non-mainstream, citizen-based news sources." Citizen journalists located anywhere in the world can post comments alongside stories written by professional foreign correspondents, add their information to stories, or even work directly with correspondents on stories that otherwise would go uncovered.

For example, citizen journalists played a crucial role during the "Arab spring" protests that rocked Tunisia, Egypt, Libya, Jordan, Yemen, and Syria in 2011. Mainstream media have relied extensively on bloggers, political activists, and involved citizens to provide information, pictures, and videos from protest sites that often were inaccessible to regular journalists. Media organizations also have increasingly used footage of natural disasters, accidents, crimes, and other unique events witnessed and recorded by such "accidental journalists." Social networking sites such as Facebook or YouTube accelerated this distribution of citizen-produced news by allowing global audiences to follow events without interference by local or foreign news organizations.

The global success of social networking sites also has changed the way many people receive and consume foreign news. A growing number of Facebook and Twitter users, for example, consume news sent to them by family, friends, or colleagues within their social network circle. While such a personalized distribution of foreign news might undermine the agenda-setting power of mainstream media, people are much more likely to pay attention to news forwarded by those they know. If that is the case, foreign news might experience a rebirth on social networks with a limited, but highly engaged audience.

Another trend in modern foreign reporting is a shift toward one-person bureaus. Small over-seas offices, staffed by a reporter with the latest digital-media technology that can record, edit, and send video, cost a fraction of what it takes to run a full-time bureau. Because of rapid advances in media technology, one reporter with a handheld digital video camera and a laptop can now cover a story that once required a correspondent, a producer, and a two-person crew. In 2007, ABC opened seven of these highly flexible and mobile "mini-bureaus" in Seoul, South Korea; Rio de Janeiro, Brazil; Dubai, United Arab Emirates; New Delhi and Mumbai, India; Jakarta, Indonesia; and Nairobi, Kenya. Altogether they cost about as much as the full-featured Paris bureau did when it was open (Gough 2007). While this new breed of foreign journalist is expected to write reports *and* gather audio, photos, and video during a typical reporting assignment, they are not totally alone. Their stories get edited by colleagues in London or New York and they often receive logisti-cal and technical support from stringers and ABC News partners such as the BBC (Dorroh 2008).

Even cheaper than journalists working alone abroad are "virtual foreign correspondents" who assemble news stories at home by relying exclusively on wire service reports, phone interviews, online news from abroad, and other sources accessed remotely by Internet. Thus, many "foreign" correspondents do not travel abroad anymore but report about international events right from behind their desks in New York or wherever their news organization is located. Although such news reports are much less expensive than regular foreign news stories, they are likely to be simi-lar to many stories published elsewhere. As Moore (2010: 44) notes, "they help fill the 'news hole' but are not distinctive and do not provide a competitive advantage."

Another interesting trend in foreign news reporting is the emergence of online sites that offer international news from freelancers or grant-supported journalists. The best-known example is probably GlobalPost (www.globalpost.com), launched in 2009 to provide "English-language read-ers around the world, with a depth, breadth and quality of original international reporting that has been steadily diminished in too many American newspapers and television networks" (GlobalPost 2001). It features reports from 100 to 120 freelancers worldwide who pay special attention to geographic areas that have been under-reported by mainstream U.S. media. In addition, 50 to 60 reporters on contract write at least one story a week (Sambrook 2010). GlobalPost earns most of its money through advertising, but also syndicates its content to newspapers, Web sites, radio stations, and television networks in the United States and abroad. Another revenue source is mem-bership, which costs about $30 a year and allows readers to access additional content and interact with correspondents (Enda 2011).

The nonprofit International Reporting Project (www.internationalreportingproject.org) was founded in 1998 to financially support journalists working on foreign news stories unlikely to be reported elsewhere (Enda 2011). Since the program's start, the International Reporting Proj-ect has supported more than 300 U.S. journalists with travel grants to more than 85 countries to work on stories to be featured their IRP news site. The reporters usually can stay five weeks abroad, then have another four weeks to work on their projects in Washington (Enda 2011). Yet despite the fact that such a non-profit, grant-based model fills an important niche by focusing on stories too expensive to cover for most mainstream media, many of those stories will appeal only to a small core audience. The same is true for profit-oriented efforts such as GlobalPost. Such cov-erage is extremely valuable and will add to the diversity of foreign news in the United States, but it will only appeal to audiences already interested in foreign news. As a consequence, growth of such online news sites beyond traditional foreign news audiences seems unlikely.

Ultimately, the contemporary state of foreign correspondence is marked by an intriguing contradiction: fewer journalists defined in the traditional sense are reporting abroad, and they produce a smaller stream of news with less variation, and yet technological developments also have effectively shrunk the globe for international journalism, expanded the range of outlets through which such news is available, and opened channels for many who would not have contributed or been defined as journalists under the older model. Meanwhile, researchers continue to struggle to understand not only the nature of these changes but also their impact on the foreign correspondent's profession and identity, the international news they produce and distribute, and what their impact holds for an increasingly interconnected world.

Note

1. The exception to this trend is National Public Radio (NPR), which increased the number of its foreign bureaus from six to 17 in the past decade, and has part-time correspondents in two more. Thirty percent of what NPR broadcasts in reports from its correspondents and on-air interviews is international in scope (Enda 2011).

References

AIM Research Consortium. 2007. *Reporting and managing European news—Final report of the Project "Adequate Information Management in Europe" 2004–2007.* Bochum/Freiburg: Projekt Verlag.

Anderson, Russell, F. 1951. News from nowhere: Our disappearing foreign correspondents. *The Saturday Review of Literature* 34:10–12, 80–81.

Associated Press. 2011. Facts & figures. Retrieved from http://www.ap.org/pages/about/about.html

Berry, Nicholas O. 1990. *Foreign policy and the press: An analysis of The New York Times' coverage of U.S. foreign policy.* New York: Greenwood.

Bogart, Leo. 1968. The overseas newsman: A 1967 profile study. *Journalism Quarterly* 45(2):293–306.

Carroll, Jill. 2007. Foreign news coverage: The US media's undervalued asset. Joan Shorenstein Center, Harvard. Retrieved from http://www.hks.harvard.edu/presspol/publications/papers/working_papers/2007_01_carroll.pdf

Constable, Pamela. 2007. February 18. Demise of the foreign correspondent. *Washington Post.* Retrieved from http://www.washingtonpost.com/wp-dyn/content/article/2007/02/16/AR2007021601713.html

Cozma, Raluca, and John Maxwell Hamilton. 2009. Film portrayals of foreign correspondents: A content analysis of movies before World War II and after Vietnam. *Journalism Studies* 10(4):489–505.

Dorroh, Jennifer. 2008. December/January. Armies of one. *American Journalism Review.* Retrieved from http://www.ajr.org/Article.asp?id=4443

Enda, Jodi. 2011, Dec./Jan. Retreating from the world. *American Journalism Review.* Retrieved from http://www.ajr.org/article.asp?id=4985

Franks, Suzanne. 2005. Lacking a clear narrative: Foreign reporting after the cold war. *The Political Quarterly* 76(supplement S1):91–101.

Ghorpade, Shailendra. 1984a. Foreign correspondents cover Washington for world. *Journalism Quarterly* 61:667–671.

Ghorpade, Shailendra. 1984b. Foreign correspondents and the New World information order. *Gazette,* 33:203–208.

Ghorpade, Shailendra. 1984c. Sources and access: How foreign correspondents rate Washington, D.C. *Journal of Communication* 34:32–40.

Gitlin, Todd. 1980. *The whole world is watching: Mass media in the making and unmaking of the new left.* Berkeley: University of California Press.

GlobalPost. 2001. Mission statement. Retrieved from http://www.globalpost.com/mission/mission-statement

Gough, Paul J. 2007, October 3. ABC News opening one-man foreign bureaus. Reuters. Retrieved from http://www.reuters.com/article/2007/10/05/industry-abcnews-dc-idUSN0344510720071005

Gross, Peter, and Gerd G. Kopper. 2011. *Understanding foreign correspondence.* New York: Peter Lang.

Gysin, Nicole. 2000. *Der direkte Draht zur Welt? Eine Untersuchung über Auslandskorrespondentinnen und -korrespondenten deutschschweizer Printmedien* [A direct line to the world? A study of foreign reporters and correspondents of Swiss-German print media]. Bern, Switzerland: Institut für Medienwissenschaften, Universität Bern.

Hahn, Oliver, and Julia Lönnendonker. 2009. Transatlantic foreign reporting and foreign correspondents after 9/11: Trends in reporting Europe in the United States. *International Journal of Press/Politics* 14(4):497–515.

Hahn, Oliver, Julia Lönnendonker, and Roland Schröder. (eds.). 2008. Deutsche Auslandskorrespondenten—Ein Handbuch [German foreign correspondents: A handbook]. Konstanz, Germany: UVK-Verlagsgesellschaft.

Hallin, Daniel C. 1986. *The "uncensored war": The media and Vietnam*. New York: Oxford University Press.

Hamilton, John Maxwell and Jenner, Eric. 2004. Redefining foreign correspondence. *Journalism*, 5(3): 301–321.

Hanitzsch, Thomas. 2007. Deconstructing journalism culture: Towards a universal theory. *Communication Theory* 17(4): 367–385.

Hannerz, Ulf. 2003. Being there … and there … and there! Reflections on multi-site ethnography. Ethnography 4(2):201–216.

Hannerz, Ulf. 2004 *Foreign news: Exploring the world of foreign correspondents*. Chicago: University of Chicago Press.

Hess, Stephen. 1996. *International news and foreign correspondents*. Washington, DC: The Brookings Institution.

Hess, Stephen. 2005. *Through their eyes: Foreign correspondents in the United States*. Washington, DC: Brookings Institution.

Ibrahim, Dina. 2003. Individual perceptions of international correspondents in the Middle East: An obstacle to fair news? *International Communication Gazette* 65(1):87–101.

Junghanns, Kathrin. 2004. *Merkmale und Selbstverständnis von deutschen Auslandskorrespondenten.* [Characteristics and self-understanding of German foreign correspondents]. Thesis, Ilmenau University of Technology, Germany.

Junghanns, Kathrin, and Thomas Hanitzsch. 2006. Deutsche Auslandskorrespondenten im Profil [Profile of German foreign correspondents]. *Medien and Kommunikationswissenschaft* 54(3): 412–429.

Kleinfeld, Gerald R. 1986. Das Deutschlandbild in der regionalen amerikanischen Presse [Germany's image in the regional American press]. In *Das Deutschland—und Amerikabild* [Germany— and the image of America], edited by Klaus Weigelt Melle, pp. 54 - 60. Germany: Knoth.

Kliesch, Ralph E. 1991. The U.S. press corps abroad rebounds: A 7th world survey of foreign correspondents. *Newspaper Research Journal* 12(1):24–33.

Kopper, Gerd G. (ed.). 2006. *"How are you, Mr. President": Nachrichtenarbeit, Berufswirklichkeit und Produktionsmanagement an Korrespondentenplätzen deutscher Medien in den USA* [News Jobs, career reality and production management for German media correspondents in the U.S.] Berlin: Vistas Verlag.

Kopper, Gerd G., and Lisa Seiler. 2007. Der Arbeitsplatz von US-Korrespondenten für deutsche Medien—Ermittlungsschritte [The job of U.S. correspondent for the German media-determination process]. In *"How are you, Mr. President": Nachrichtenarbeit, Berufswirklichkeit und Produktionsmanagement an Korrespondentenplätzen deutscher Medien in den USA* [News Job, career reality and production management for German media correspondents in the U.S.], edited by Gerd G. Kopper Berlin: Vistas Verlag.

Kumar, Priya. 2011. December/January. Foreign correspondents: Who covers what. *American Journalism Review.* Retrieved from http://www.ajr.org/article.asp?id=4997

Lambert, Donald A. 1956. Foreign correspondents covering the United States. *Journalism Quarterly* 33:349–356.

Lasswell, Harold. 1948. The structure and function of communication in society. In *The communication of ideas*, edited by Lymon Bryson, pp. 37–51. New York: Institute for Religious and Social Studies.

Lester, Elli. 1994. The collectible other and inevitable interventions: A textual analysis of the Washington Post's foreign reporting. *Argumentation* 8:345–356.

MacKinnon, Rebecca. 2007. *Blogs and China correspondence: How foreign correspondents covering China use blogs. Paper presented at the World Journalism Education Conference, Singapore.*

Marten, Eckhard. 1989. *Das Deutschlandbild in der amerikanischen Auslandsberichterstattung: Ein kommunikationswissenschaftlicher Beitrag zur Nationenbildforschung* [The image of Germany in American foreign reporting: A contribution to the communication of scientific research regarding the nation's image]. Wiesbaden, Germany: Deutscher Universitäts-Verlag.

Masterton, Murray. 2009. A clash of cultures for foreign correspondents. *Pacific Journalism Review* 15(1):19–30.

Maxwell, J. William. 1956. US correspondents abroad: A study of backgrounds. *Journalism Quarterly* 33:346–348.

Moisy, Claude. 1997. Myths of the global information village. *Foreign Policy*, 107:78–87.

Moore, Martin. 2010. Shrinking world: The decline of international reporting in the British press. Media Standards Trust. London. Retrieved from http://mediastandardstrust.org/wp-content/uploads/downloads/2010/11/Shrinking-World-FINAL-VERSION.pdf

Morozov, Evgeny. 2010, May/June. Think again: The Internet. Foreign Policy. Retrieved from http://www.foreignpolicy.com/articles/2010/04/26/think_again_the_internet

Morrison, David E., and Howard Tumber. 1985. The foreign correspondent: Date-line London. *Media, Culture, & Society* 7:445–470.

Mowlana, Hamid. 1975a. September/October. Typewriter ambassadors: Explaining America to the world. *Intellect*.

Mowlana, Hamid. 1975b. Who covers America? *Journal of Communication* 25:85–91.

Nair, Murlai. 1991. The foreign media correspondent: Dateline Washington D.C. *Gazette* 48:5–64.

Nawawy, Mohammed. 2001. Culture and conflict in the Middle East: Western correspondents' perceptions of the Egyptian and Israeli cultures. *Online Journal of Peace and Conflict Resolution* 4(1). Retrieved from www.trinstitute. org

Oksenberg, Michel. 1994. The American correspondent in China. In *China's media, media's China*, edited by Chin-Chuan Lee, pp. 205 - 224. Boulder, CO: Westview.

Organisation for Economic Co-operation and Development. 2011. *OECD working party on the information economy, the evolution of news and the Internet*. Retrieved from http://www.oecd.org/dataoecd/30/24/45559596.pdf

Pew Research Center. 2006. *State of the news media 2006: Content analysis*. Retrieved from http://stateofthemedia. org/2006/online-intro/content-analysis/

Pew Research Center. 2008a. *Key news audiences now blend online and traditional sources*. Retrieved from http://people-press.org/2008/08/17/key-news-audiences-now-blend-online-and-traditional-sources/

Pew Research Center. 2008b. *The changing newsroom: What is being gained and what is being lost in America's daily newspapers?* Retrieved from http://www.journalism.org/files/PEJ-The%20Changing%20Newspaper%20Newsroom%20 FINAL%20DRAFT-NOEMBARGO-PDF.pdf

Pew Research Center. 2011. The state of the news media. Retrieved from http://stateofthemedia.org

Reese, Stephen D., Lou Rutigliano, Kideuk Hyun, and Jaekwan Jeong. 2006. *Mapping the blogosphere: Professional and citizen-based media in the global news arena*. Retrieved from http://journalism.utexas.edu/sites/journalism.utexas. edu/files/attachments/reese/reese-rutigliano-8-3-B-copy.PDF

Sambrook, Richard. 2010. *Are foreign correspondents redundant?* Reuters Institute for the Study of Journalism. Oxford University. Retrieved from http://www.scribd.com/doc/44988203/Are-Foreign-Correspondents-Redundant-Text

Schudson, Michael, and Susan E. Tifft. 2005. American journalism in historical perspective. In *The press*, edited by Geneva Overholser and Kathleen Hall Jamieson, pp. 17–47. Oxford: Oxford University Press.

Shoemaker, Pamela, and Stephen D. Reese. 1996. *Mediating the message*. New York: Longman.

Sreebny, Daniel. 1979. American correspondents in the Middle East: Perceptions and problems. *Journalism Quarterly* 56(2):386–388.

Starck, Kenneth, and Estela Villanueva. 1992. *Cultural framing: Foreign correspondents and their work*. Paper presented at the annual meeting of the Association for Education in Journalism and Mass Communication, Montreal.

Stevenson, Robert L. 2004. Problems and pitfalls of comparative research in political communication. In *Comparing political communication: Theories, cases and challenges*, edited by Frank Esser & Barbara Pfetsch, pp. 367–383. New York: Cambridge University Press.

Suh, John C. W. 1972. 126 foreign correspondents talk about work in America. *Editor & Publisher* (April 15): 27–30.

Tai, Zixue, and Tsan-Kuo Chang. 2002. The global news and the pictures in their heads. *Gazette*, 64(3):251–265.

Thomson Reuters. 2010. *Reuters—The facts*. Retrieved from http://thomsonreuters.com/content/financial/pdf/ news_content/reuters_news_factsheet.pdf

Tyndall Report. 2010. *Year in review*. Retrieved from http://tyndallreport.com/yearinreview2010/international/

Weaver, David H. (ed.). 1998. *The global journalist: News people around the world*. Cresskill, NJ: Hampton Press.

Weaver, David H., and G. Cleveland Wilhoit. 1996. *The American journalist in the 1990s: U.S. news people at the end of an era*. Mahwah, NJ: Erlbaum.

Wilhelm, John R. 1963. The re-appearing foreign correspondent: A world survey. *Journalism Quarterly* 40:147–168.

Willnat, Lars, and David Weaver. 2003. Through their eyes: The work of foreign correspondents in the United States. *Journalism* 4(4):403–422.

Wu, H. Denis, and John Maxwell Hamilton. 2004. U.S. foreign correspondents: Changes and continuity at the turn of the century. *Gazette: The International Journal for Communication Studies*, 66(6):517–532.

Yu, Frederick T. C., and John Luter. 1964. The foreign correspondent and his work. *Columbia Journalism Review*, 3(1):5-12.

37 Political Journalists

Covering Politics in
the Democratic-Corporatist Media System

Arjen van Dalen and Peter Van Aelst

The democratic functions of the media are at the center of discussions about the societal role of journalists (e.g., McNair 2009; Strömbäck 2005). These democratic functions, like the information, watchdog, and expression function are laid down in legal texts (Graber 2003) and ethical codes (Sonnenberg 1997) and are part of the core values of the occupational ideology of journalists (Kovach & Rosenstiel 2001).

Journalistic cultures differ across countries (Hanitzsch 2009; Weaver 1998), but also within countries the journalistic profession is divided into different beats, each with its own "micro-culture" (Ericson, Baranek, & Chan 1989: 34), and "its own rules and values" (Van Zoonen 1998: 124). The role of the media in democracy and the normative demands connected to that role are of special importance for political journalists, who are the prime intermediaries between politicians and citizens. Understanding the particularities of the political beat will, therefore, help us to better grasp the mediating role of journalism in politics.

Because the democratic functions of the media become most apparent in the work of political reporters, political journalism has been described as the "most sacred part" of journalism (Neveu 2002: 23). This places political journalists in a privileged position compared to other media workers and gives them a certain amount of prestige within the profession (Hess 1981; Tunstall 1970). On the other hand, political journalists are also in the line of fire from scholars, politicians, and media watchdogs. Politicians accuse journalists of being too powerful because they can make and break political careers and often dominate the political agenda (Van Aelst, Brants, van Praag, de Vreese, Nuytemans, & van Dalen 2008). Scholars charge political journalists with over-emphasizing negativity and presenting a cynical picture of the world of politics (Patterson 2000). Media critics accuse political journalists of being out of touch with the public and too close to those in power (see Schudson 2003). To sum up: political journalists play a central but contested role in democracy and, therefore, deserve our special attention.

This chapter discusses how political journalists perceive their role and position in democracy based on a comprehensive survey of eight Western European countries. The institutional contexts in which political journalists work in Western Europe have strong similarities because they all are parliamentary democracies with high levels of press freedom, a strong tradition of public service broadcasters, and a pluralistic media landscape (Kelly, Mazzoleni, & McQuail 2004). However, the historical, political, and cultural settings in which Western European political journalists work also show important differences (Hallin & Mancini 2004; Patterson & Donsbach 2004; Pfetsch 2004).

The media systems approach by Hallin and Mancini provides the starting point for our country comparison. Our core focus is on six countries belonging to the democratic-corporatist media system: Norway, Sweden, Denmark, Germany, Belgium, and The Netherlands. These countries will be compared to one country belonging to the liberal media system (the United Kingdom) and a country belonging to the polarized–pluralist media system (Spain). Our interest is in describing differences and similarities of political journalists across countries, rather than testing hypotheses based on Hallin and Mancini's model.

The data presented in this chapter are the result of a comparative survey among 960 journalists who report about national politics.[1] These surveys were conducted between 2006 and the beginning of 2009 and resulted in response rates that varied between 31% and 74%. In our comprehensive overview of political journalists in Western Europe, we will present data on their socio-demographic and ideological profile, relations with sources, role conceptions, and perceptions of their political power. We will first provide some historical background regarding the position of political journalists in countries belonging to the democratic-corporatist media system followed by a brief discussion of the main research themes and findings in studies of political journalists.

Political Journalism in Democratic-Corporatist Countries

Political journalists in northwestern Europe function in what Hallin and Mancini (2004) describe in their seminal work as the democratic-corporatist media model. This model differs from the liberal model consisting of Anglo-American countries and the polarized–pluralist model that covers Mediterranean Europe. The relationship between media and politics in the democratic-corporatist countries is traditionally characterized by three co-existences (Hallin & Mancini 2004: 144–145). First, an early development of the mass press co-existed with political parallelism in newspapers, mirroring the divisions in society along religious, ideological, and linguistic lines. Second, a formal link between newspapers and political parties co-existed with high levels of professional autonomy, guaranteed by self-regulatory measures. Third, elevated levels of press freedom co-existed with an influence of the state on how the media are organized, in the shape of press subsidies, and a strong tradition of public service broadcasting.

Traditionally, political journalists started out as political supporters, who served the interests of the political parties they were associated with. In those days journalists generally worked according to a partisan or political logic, where politicians set the terms. Over the years, political journalism has increasingly become politically autonomous due to developments in society such as an increasingly volatile electorate, a decline in membership of political parties, and developments within the media, such as increased professionalization, the introduction of commercial television, and increased competition between media outlets (Brants & Van Praag 2006). Journalistic values like neutrality, objectivity, and balanced reporting have spread from the United States to other media systems. Today, in the democratic-corporatist countries, a partisan bias is increasingly perceived as contradictory to the standards of journalistic professionalism.

Even though the relationship between the media and politics in all of the three media systems has become increasingly similar over the years, the particularities of the media systems still have an influence on the setting in which political journalists do their work. Convergence toward the liberal media model does not imply that this model is copied without adaptation. In the democratic-corporatist countries, the strong partisan bond between media and politics has almost completely evaporated (Petersson, Djerf-Pierre, Holmberg, Strömback, & Weibull 2006), but previous party color is occasionally visible in newspapers, for instance in the coverage of election campaigns in Norway (Allern 2007) or in the political preferences of newspaper readers in Denmark (Hjarvard 2007). According to Brants and Van Praag (2006), the strength of a public service tradition and a political culture of consensus modify the convergence to the liberal media model. Differences between a media-driven American and politically motivated German political communication culture are a consequence of different political systems and the varying degrees of polarization of the media market (Pfetsch 2001).

We expect the Spanish journalists in particular to stand out in comparison to the journalists in Northern Europe. The polarized pluralist media system in Spain has long been characterized by lower levels of professionalization and by more influence from politicians and other actors from outside the media (Hallin & Mancini 2004). How different the British journalists are from the political journalists in the democratic-corporatist countries is an empirical question. Although the United Kingdom resembles the democratic-corporatist media system to some extent (with a strong public service broadcaster), it belongs, according to the Hallin and Mancini typology, to the liberal media system that is dominated by commercial media and market mechanisms (like non-institutionalized self-regulation and heavy competition in the media market).

Main Issues

With a few exceptions (e.g., Patterson & Donsbach 1996; Pfetsch 2001), most studies based on surveys or interviews with political journalists are single country studies, mostly originating from an Anglo-American context. In this section, we present the main research themes and findings of previous studies.

Traits. The socio-demographic and ideological profile is a recurring element of comprehensive studies of political journalists. Central to these accounts is the question whether the traits of political journalists represent those of society. The assumption behind this interest in representation is often that the socio-demographic background of journalists influences their work and that a press corps which forms a mirror representation of society leads to more diversity in the news (Deuze 2002). On the other hand, scholars have pointed out that in daily practice professional roles and socialization within organizational structures and goals have more influence on the news than the personal characteristics of individual journalists (Gans 1979; Henningham 1995; Shoemaker & Reese 1991; Weaver 1998).

The United States has a long tradition of studies of political journalists, going back to Rosten's (1937) *The Washington Correspondents*. Based on a comprehensive survey among journalists covering politics in Washington, Hess (1981: 90) comes to the following conclusion; "If there is an average Washington reporter and an average American, they do not look like each other; the average influential Washington reporter looks even less like the average American" (Hess 1981: 90). Jeremy Tunstall (1970) presented similar findings for the Westminster Lobby correspondents, who were predominately male, had an average age of 42, and mainly came from a middle-class background.

As a possible antecedent of bias in political coverage, several studies looked into the self-placement of political journalists on an ideological left–right scale. A comparative study by Patterson and Donsbach (1996) showed that journalists who report about politics in the United States, Great Britain, Germany, Italy, and Sweden position their political leaning left of the center, without taking extreme positions.

Relations with Sources. The relationship between journalists and their sources, mainly politicians, is characterized by mutual dependence between "mutually adaptive actors, pursuing divergent (though overlapping) purposes" (Blumler & Gurevitch 1995: 32). Politicians need the news media to get their message across and to reach out to voters and colleagues. The political journalist needs to know what is going on in the world of politics, needs this information fast, and prefers to have it first-hand. This marriage *de raison* is most often portrayed as a dance, a tango even, with almost intimate interactions between both partners (Gans 1979). A long tradition of studies in (political) communication and media sociology and case studies of journalists have given us insight into how the bargaining process of political information takes place. Such studies almost always focus on how (political) journalists deal with politicians in a certain country, mostly the United States and the United Kingdom (for an exception see Mancini 1993; Strömbäck & Nord 2006).

Several (participatory) case studies of journalists (e.g., Crouse 1974; Jones 1995; Rosenstiel 1993) and surveys among political journalists and politicians (Davis 2009; Van Aelst, Shehata, & van Dalen 2010) show that most political journalists have frequent and informal interactions with their sources due to the mutual dependency. However, these close and often personal contacts do not guarantee a harmonious relationship because in some cases, distrust and conflicts take the upper hand (Brants, de Vreese, Möller, & van Praag 2010). This tension is no recent phenomenon, but rather an inherent, though variable, characteristic of the relationship. In his study of U.S. press–government relations more than 40 years ago, Nimmo (1964) distinguished between three kinds of patterns in the relationship, referring to different degrees of harmony. The relationship can range from *co-operative,* characterized by common goals and low conflict, to *compatible,* with increasing tensions, to *competitive,* guided by mutual suspicion and mistrust.

It is clear that both partners benefit from the co-operative pattern characterized by a high degree of informality. For political journalists it means easy and fast access to political information that, on the basis of the trust in the relationship, can be considered highly reliable (Tunstall 1970). Furthermore, the journalist often receives not only information about policy outcomes and plans, but also about how these were established. The journalist becomes a first-hand observer of political "behind the scenes" struggles and intrigues. This being said, a very close relationship might also create problems and raise normative questions (see also Van Aelst & Aalberg 2009). Journalists are supposed to be politically independent and keep their sources at a certain distance in order to perform their role as public watchdogs (Blumler & Gurevitch 1981, Schudson 2003). Journalists who are too intimate with their sources are accused of losing their independence and with it their ability to hold politicians to account.

Journalistic Roles and Political Power.   While our knowledge of the demographics and source relations of political journalists is mostly based on single country studies, we have more comparative knowledge about differences in their journalistic approaches and role conceptions. Discussions about the political roles of journalists are generally related to their autonomy vis-à-vis politicians. The journalistic self-conception can range from a passive approach, where journalists function as a mouthpiece of politicians, to an active approach, where journalists intervene in the messages of politicians by "shaping, interpreting, or investigating political subjects" (Donsbach & Patterson 2004: 265).

Prior research suggests that (political) journalists in the democratic-corporatist countries take an autonomous position toward politicians. Compared to journalists in Italy and the United Kingdom, journalists in Germany and Sweden have a more active journalistic approach (Donsbach & Patterson 2004). Weaver (1998: 465) concludes that journalists in countries with a democratic tradition generally attach more importance to being a watchdog of government than journalists in countries without such a tradition. Content analysis has shown that journalists in Spain (Strömbäck & Luengo 2008) and in France (Esser 2008) have a passive, non-interventionist approach when covering national elections compared to journalists in Northern Europe and the United States.

Country differences in journalistic role conceptions can have consequences for the power of the media to influence the political and public agendas. Several scholars have investigated the power balance between journalists and politicians and not only asked whether journalists follow the agenda put forward by politicians, but also whether the media influence the political agenda (Strömback & Nord 2006; Walgrave & Van Aelst 2006). While longitudinal studies comparing media coverage and political activity generally conclude that the mass media affect the political agenda only to a moderate extent (Tan & Weaver 2007, 2009), surveys among politicians and journalists generally show that these "privileged witnesses" perceive a more than moderate influence (Davis 2007; Walgrave 2008).

Methods

Our comparative analysis of political journalists is based on self-completed questionnaires, which were filled out by 960 journalists from Norway, Sweden, Denmark, Germany, Belgium,[2] The Netherlands, the United Kingdom, and Spain.

We defined political journalists as individuals who regularly report on or analyze national politics and work for national and regional newspapers, commercial and public service broadcasters, news agencies, or weekly magazines. Also a small number of political journalists working for online media are included. This definition includes beat journalists who cover the day-to-day work of government and parliament, as well as journalists who are specialized in a certain policy field, like the environment or employment. These populations were defined as members of unions of parliamentary journalists, members of journalistic unions with national politics or a specific policy field as their area of expertise, or journalists who are accredited to parliament. Considering the relatively small size of the populations under study, we opted for surveying the whole target group rather than taking a sample. To improve the comparability of the populations in the different countries after the surveys had been completed, we filtered out those journalists who were not regularly in contact with politicians and did not regularly report about politicians.[3]

We conducted the survey in each of the eight countries between February 2006 and January 2009. Questions were translated by native speakers and discussed with political scientists who were familiar with political communication in each of the countries. The journalists were invited via letter and email to fill out the questionnaire either on paper or online. We used several strategies to increase the response rate such as incentives, personalized letters and emails, and multiple follow-up contacts. In Spain and the United Kingdom, additional phone calls were made to increase response, which was falling behind. Response rates of the targeted population ranged from 31% in the United Kingdom to 74% in Denmark (see Table 37.1).

Because we surveyed whole populations, the distribution of journalists working for different media types differs somewhat from country to country. In Spain, for example, there are more journalists working for radio and news agencies and in Norway and Sweden more journalists working for print media. In the tables we present the results per country only. Relevant differences between journalists working for different media outlets are discussed in the text.

Findings

Demographic Background

Table 37.1 gives an overview of the age and gender of the political journalists in our study. The mean age varies between 41 in Denmark, Spain, and Belgium and 46 in Sweden and Ger-

Table 37.1   Characteristics of Political Journalists by Country

	BE	NL	NO	SE	DK	DE	UK	ES
	February–March 2006	September–December 2006	February–April 2007	November 2007–March 2008	November 2007–January 2008	April–July 2008	September 2008–January 2009	October 2008–January 2009
Response rate	66%	61%	57%	52%	74%	32%	31%	57%
Sex (% female)	23%	19%	27%	43%	28%	29%	23%	41%
Mean age	41	42	44	46	41	46	44	41
Median age	42	41	43	45	37	46	43	40
Mean political leaning*	4.1	4.9	4.1	4.5	4.9	4.4	4.5	3.6
	(1.63)	(1.60)	(1.68)	(1.69)	(1.43)	(1.36)	(1.58)	(1.28)
Mean political leaning of medium*	5.1	5.4	5.1	6.1	5.8	5.4	5.0	5.4
	(1.45)	(1.55)	(1.66)	(1.60)	(1.63)	(1.37)	(1.27)	(1.77)
N	147	102	181	110	71	200	85	64

Note: BE = Belgium; NL= The Netherlands; NO= Norway; SE = Sweden; DK= Denmark; DE= Germany; UK = United Kingdom; ES= Spain.
*Scale from 0 (completely left leaning) to 10 (completely right leaning); standard deviation in parentheses.

many. These differences in age can be partly explained by the time at which journalists join the political beat. German journalists join the political beat later than their colleagues in smaller democratic-corporatist countries. In Germany, less than 10% of the political journalists are below the age of 35, while in Denmark and Belgium, more than 40% are in this age group. The place of the political beat in the career path of journalists in different countries also explains some of the age differences. In Denmark, the political beat often functions as a stepping-stone in the journalistic career (Carlsen & Kjær 1999), where journalists gain experience and move on after a couple of years. In other countries, like the United Kingdom, journalists tend to stay on the political beat longer.

More than 30 years after the studies by Tunstall (1970) and Hess (1981), political journalism is still a predominantly male profession. In the Netherlands, male political journalists outnumber their female colleagues four to one. Sweden and Spain are the only two countries where more than 40% of the political beat is female. This is mainly due to the age group 30 to 40, where female reporters in these two countries outnumber male reporters. Across the countries, the gender division is more equal in the younger age groups than among older generations.

To measure political leaning, the political journalists were asked to position themselves and the media organization they work for on a scale ranging from 0 (completely left leaning) to 10 (completely right leaning). Comparable to the findings by Patterson and Donsbach in 1996, the political leaning of journalists who report about politics can best be described as slightly left of center (Table 37.1). In the six democratic-corporatist countries, the majority of political journalists position themselves on or immediately next to the neutral middle position, with a mean score within one point left of the middle position. Only a small minority described themselves as completely left leaning. The average political leaning of British journalists and their media is comparable to the average of the democratic-corporatist countries. In Spain, journalists on average have a more left political leaning than their colleagues in Northern European countries.

The center-left self-placement of journalists is balanced by a center-right placement of the media they work for. As Table 37.1 shows, across countries political journalists describe the media organization they work for as on average slightly right of center. The more right-leaning position of the Swedish media, for example, is mostly the result of print journalists who position their media organization more on the right than in other countries. It is worth noting that the political leaning of the print media has a higher standard deviation than the leaning of television. This can be explained by the fact that, in all Western European nations, political leaning remains an important means for newspapers to position themselves, while broadcast organizations profile themselves with a more neutral position.

So, are political journalists a special breed of journalists? The difference between the demographic profile of political journalists and general reporters is a difference of degree rather than of kind. Surveys of the general populations of journalists in the past have shown that journalists are more often male than female and tend to have a left political leaning (Weaver, 1998). For political journalists, these features are more profound in the case of gender and less profound in the case of the political leaning. The gender division is more skewed among political reporters than among general reporters as surveyed by Deuze (2002) and Skovsgaard et al. (see chapter 13 this work). This confirms that the political beat is more a male beat than other genres (Van Zoonen 1998). Overall, the over-representation of political journalists with a left political leaning is smaller than among general reporters, especially in The Netherlands and in Denmark.

Relations with Sources

Because of the mutual benefits, the relationship between political journalists and politicians is characterized by frequent interactions. On average, nearly half of all political journalists reported contacts with politicians almost every day (45%), and another 30% said they met with politicians at least a few times a week. The high number of contacts can also be seen as a consequence of the services or institutions that are created in or around the parliament to facilitate the interaction process between political journalists and politicians. This can be a place in the parliament where journalists are able to work and invite politicians for interviews or more informal places such as bars and restaurants. All countries have at least some of these meeting places in and around parliaments.

Overall, political journalists who work for television have less frequent contacts with politicians than those who work for the print media, but the difference is limited and does not hold in all countries. More important are the substantial country differences. In Belgium, Sweden, and especially Germany, daily contacts are not the norm for most journalists, although two-thirds have at least a few contacts a week. Spain and the United Kingdom do not differ from the democratic-corporatist countries in this respect. The outlier in the number of contacts is Denmark, where almost all journalists meet with their main sources on a daily basis. The intense relationship in Denmark might be explained partly by the high mutual trust and low levels of suspicion. Earlier research has shown that Danish political journalists have less cynical opinions about politics than their colleagues in Spain, United Kingdom, and Germany (Van Dalen, Albaek, & de Vreese 2011).

The most important ways of contact between journalists and politicians are over the phone (67% at least a few times a week), interviews (37%), in the corridors of parliament (32%), and press conferences (25%). Again, these overall percentages hide some significant country differences. For instance, the majority of Swedish political journalists report hardly any contacts in the corridors of parliament. A different pattern of types of contacts is shown in Spain. Three of four Spanish political journalists meet politicians at press conferences several times a week, but on the other hand, hardly one of 10 reports frequent interviews with politicians. This means that Spanish journalists tend to follow the communication agenda of their political sources instead of pursuing their own.

This is also shown by the answers to the question of who mostly initiates those contacts (see Table 37.2). In the standard situation, journalists initiate these contacts. Only in Spain, less than half of the political journalists state that they take the initiative most of the time. This can be explained by the position of the mass media vis-à-vis political actors, which is less autonomous in Spain than in Northern Europe (Hallin & Mancini 2004).

In general, frequent contacts with sources are seen as a valuable asset for journalists. However, at the same time, an overly close relationship with these political sources can endanger their role

Table 37.2   Journalists' Contact Initiation with Politicians by Country (in %)

	BE (N=140)	NL (N=101)	NO (N=168)	SE (N=110)	DK (N=71)	DE (N=199)	UK (N=83)	ES (N=64)
Most of the time me	60	82	72	85	79	57	66	45
About equally divided between the two	31	18	24	14	18	40	31	52
Most of the time the politicians	9	0	4	1	3	3	3	3

Table 37.3 Characteristics of Informal Relationships Between Political Journalists and Politicians by Country (in %)

	BE (N=124)	NL (N=101)	NO (N=157)	SE (N=105)	DK (N=70)	DE (N=178)	UK (N=84)	ES (N=64)
How often do you have lunch with politicians?								
Daily	—	1	1	—	1	1	4	—
Weekly	16	24	10	1	17	22	36	31
Monthly or less	70	63	47	33	64	67	49	62
Never	14	12	42	66	17	11	12	6
How often do you give politicians advice on their job?								
Often	4	2	—	1	1	—	6	—
Sometimes	25	25	14	5	7	12	28	22
Seldom	30	32	30	15	34	36	31	33
Never	41	42	56	79	58	52	35	45
Do you consider any politician to be your friend?								
Yes	25	23	27	12	7	30	58	37
Do you give your mobile phone number to politicians?								
Yes	86	96	94	54	93	90	96	75

as public watchdogs (Schudson 2003). Journalists who become too intimate with politicians might lose their critical position or end up "in their pockets" as Blumler and Gurevitch (1981) put it. Following Van Aelst and Aalberg (2009), Table 37.3 gives an overview of four indicators of the personal nature or intimacy of the relationship between journalists and politicians in our eight countries.

In general, political journalists easily exchange phone numbers, but a majority of them seem reluctant to give advice to politicians or frequently have lunches with them. On average, only one of four considers one or more politicians to be a friend. As we lack a clear benchmark, it is difficult to determine how "normal" this is, but overall these relationships really cannot be called informal. Although the personal nature of these relationships is comparable in most countries, Swedish and British journalists differ from the overall picture.

In the United Kingdom, 40% of political journalists have frequent lunches with politicians and almost 60% consider at least one politician as a friend. These findings confirm the work of Davis (2009) based on in-depth interviews with politicians and journalists working at Westminster. As a consequence of the daily contacts, the frequent social activities, and the long working experience of most political journalists, the British politician–reporter relations have become "fairly institutionalized and socially integrated" (Davis, 2009: 210). Because political journalists tend to stay on the political beat over a longer period, they tend to develop closer and more stable long-term relations. Our survey shows that the informality among British political journalists working for television is much lower than the (partly partisan) print media, where journalists and politicians still co-operate on certain issues or campaigns.

The close relationships between British journalists and politicians contrast with the nature of these contacts in the democratic-corporatist countries in general, but the absolute counterpart of the "informal" British journalist is the far more formal Swedish journalist. Two-thirds of them never lunch with politicians, hardly one of five gives politicians advice, and even fewer have friends among politicians. Earlier research has shown that Swedish politicians, more than their colleagues in other democratic-corporatist countries, have a personal assistant who deals with the media (Van Aelst, Shebata, & van Dalen 2010). These spokespersons might function as go-betweens who nurture the relationship with journalists. However, this tentative explanation needs to be addressed in further research.

Journalistic Roles and Political Power

Political journalists have a clear preference for non-revenue goals of journalism (see Table 37.4). Only a small minority of the respondents believe it is very important to address the audience as consumers and provide entertainment and relaxation. Together with reporting the news fast, political journalists in the democratic-corporatist countries see it as their most important task to give context to what is reported. This is an indication of an active role conception. On the other hand, in none of the countries under study, do journalists consider investigating claims by the government and setting the political agenda as the most important roles. Within countries, journalists working for print media and broadcasting have different preferences, which are in line with the different characteristics and target groups of these media. Setting the political agenda is more important to print journalists, while broadcast journalists value the quick delivery of information more. Journalists who work for commercial television, on the other hand, find providing entertainment more important than journalists working for public service stations.

Across the democratic-corporatist countries, the relative ranking of roles is quite similar, but two countries stand out. Compared to their colleagues abroad, Norwegian political journalists are more preoccupied with setting the agenda. There is a lot of prestige within the profession related to setting new issues on the agenda, and Norwegian journalists are convinced they determine the campaign agenda during elections (Allern 2001). The other country that stands out is Germany, where political journalists attach more importance to providing analysis and interpretation and investigating claims by the government than in other countries.

How do these role conceptions of political journalists in the democratic-corporatist countries compare to the conceptions of their colleagues in the United Kingdom and Spain? Political journalists in Spain consider the speedy distribution of information as their main role, but so do the Swedes. The Spanish journalists, who are generally considered to be less autonomous in their work, have lower scores for the "active roles" than the Germans and the Brits (investigating claims

Table 37.4   Role Conceptions of Political Journalists by Country (% saying "very important")[1]

	BE (N=135)	NL (N=97)	NO (N=161)	SE (N=109)	DK (N=70)	DE (N=197)	UK (N=85)	ES (N=62)
Get information to the public quickly	34	30	41	69	32	36	44	73
Provide analysis and interpretation	48	53	15	25	32	73	47	32
Investigate claims by the government	22	34	12	23	27	44	34	19
Set the political agenda	2	5	19	6	3	9	12	10
Provide entertainment and relaxation	2	1	5	7	—	2	6	3

1   Question wording: How important are the following goals for you when you report on national politics? (Five point scale from "completely unimportant" to "very important")

Table 37.5   Journalists' Perceptions of Media Agenda-Setting Power by Country

	BE (N=127)	NL (N=97)	NO (N=161)	SE (N=109)	DK (N=68)	DE (N=195)	UK (N=84)	ES (N=59)
Agenda-setting by media[1]	3.7	3.5	3.8	3.8	4.0	3.7	3.9	3.6
Agenda-setting by politicians[2]	3.6	3.4	3.5	3.4	4.0	3.9	4.1	4.0
Main agenda-setter[3]	Balanced	Balanced	Media	Media	Balanced	Politicians	Politicians	Politicians

Note: Scale ranges from 1 = never to 5 = very often.

1   Mean scores; combined scale of: how often do the following actors manage to place new issues on top of the political agenda: print media; audiovisual media.

2   Mean scores; combined scale of: how often do the following actors manage to place new issues on top of the political agenda: the Prime Minister (or equivalent); ministers; Members of Parliament.

3   "Media" or "politicians" indicates differences are significant at p < .05; "Balanced" indicates differences are not significant at p < .05.

by the government and providing analysis and interpretation), but these scores are comparable to the scores in the Nordic countries. The goals of Spanish political journalists do not stand out in comparison to political journalists in other European countries (for a similar finding, see Algarra & Gaitano 1998). However, in light of the relationship with their sources reported earlier, it is questionable whether Spanish journalists actually put the roles they value into practice.

The ranking of roles for British journalists shows a pattern similar to the ranking in the democratic-corporatist countries. The percentage of British political journalists who believe that investigating claims by government is very important is comparable to the percentage in The Netherlands and below that of the Germans. Almost half of the British journalists see the entertainment role as important, which is considerably more than in the democratic-corporatist countries.

Despite the low number of political journalists who believe it is their "role" to set the political agenda, many believe the media often have the power to do so (see Table 37.5). In all countries, more than half of the respondents believe both the print media and television often or very often place issues at the top of the political agenda. In Norway and Denmark, two-thirds of the journalists believe this to be true. In Belgium, The Netherlands, Norway, and Sweden, the audiovisual media are considered more influential than the print media. In Denmark, Germany, Spain, and the United Kingdom, the print media are considered most influential.

The finding that journalists believe their work influences the political agenda to a large extent, while setting the political agenda is not an important role, seems paradoxical. Political journalists seem to consider this agenda-setting influence as a side effect of what they perceive to be their main tasks: reporting the news and giving context to what they report.

To put the agenda-setting power of the media in perspective, we also asked how these journalists perceive different political actors' agenda-setting power. When we compare the agenda-setting power of the media and of politicians, we see how impressive the perceived political power of the media is in the small democratic-corporatist countries. In Belgium, The Netherlands, and Denmark, the relation is balanced, while in Norway and Sweden, political journalists perceive themselves as more influential than politicians in setting the political agenda. These findings resonate with a study by Van Aelst and Walgrave (2011) among members of parliament in these countries, which confirms the strong impact of the media on the political agenda. These politicians often see the media as the top political agenda setter, in some cases even outweighing the prime minister.

While in the smaller democratic-corporatist countries the agenda-setting power of the media is similar or larger than that of politicians, the opposite is true in Germany, Spain, and the United Kingdom. In these countries, the perceived influence of the media is somewhat smaller than that of politicians. We believe this different power balance is not so much the result of a different role conception or a perceived smaller influence of the mass media, but rather of a stronger grip of politicians on the political agenda. The explanations might lie in the differences in political institutions and political culture between these countries and the smaller Nordic countries (Lijphart 1999; Pfetsch 2004).

Conclusions

Based on a comparative survey of political journalists conducted in eight Western European countries, this chapter provided an overview of the main demographics, source relations, and role conceptions of political journalists, with an emphasis on the situation in the democratic-corporatist countries. The cross-national comparison provided insight into the universal characteristics of political journalism that apply across countries and highlighted some of the national particularities, which can be traced back to the structural characteristics of the media system, the political communication culture, or the political system.

Do our comparative data show a particular profile of political journalists in the democratic-corporatist countries Norway, Sweden, Denmark, Germany, Belgium, and The Netherlands, that is distinct from journalists in the United Kingdom and Spain? In terms of demographics and ideological orientation, political journalists in the democratic-corporatist countries hardly differ from their colleagues in other media systems.

The role conceptions of journalists also were relatively similar. For example, Spanish and Swedish political journalists assigned almost similar weights to the different roles. Also, the journalists' opinions regarding the agenda-setting power of the media were highly comparable across countries. The fact that Spanish, British, and German political journalists on average are slightly less impressed by the media's agenda-setting influence compared to the political actors seems to be due to the political constellation in these countries rather than the actual position of political journalists.

This does not mean that the modus operandus is identical. When we asked journalists about the routine contacts with sources, we could, in a few cases, conclude that Spanish or British political journalists really differ from their colleagues in the six democratic-corporatist countries in this study. In practice, the less autonomous political journalists in Spain have a more passive approach toward their main sources, as they rely strongly on forms of contacts (such as press conferences) where politicians rather than journalists take the initiative and control the event. Political journalists in the United Kingdom, especially from the print media, have a more informal relationship with politicians. Furthermore, even within the democratic-corporatist countries, we find considerable differences in the daily working practice. Danish journalists, for instance, are more often in contact with their sources than their colleagues in neighboring countries, while Swedish journalists have a more formal relationship with politicians.

These findings show that despite the fact that demographics and role conceptions of political journalists are largely similar across countries, national contexts continue to matter for the work they do. The dimensions behind Hallin and Mancini's (2004) media systems alone are not enough to explain variations in the relations with politicians and perceived influence of the media on politics. Political communication culture and political institutions seem to be influential as well.

The descriptive, cross-national comparisons of political journalists presented here have generated new hypotheses and research questions. Future research will have to test our often tentative explanations, going beyond the description of national particularities and moving closer to the ideal of developing generalizable theories (Norris 2009). We see mainly two research strategies that would contribute to such an effort. First, such projects will benefit from incorporating a longitudinal perspective, to see how national contexts moderate international trends like commercialization or professionalization. Second, studying these survey-based findings in combination with the content these journalists produce would further reveal how role conceptions translate into practice. A gap between theory and practice is inevitable when one compares what journalists aim for with what they actually do (Mancini 2000).

Notes

1. The data were collected by the following research teams: For Belgium: Michiel Nuytemans, Stefaan Walgrave (University of Antwerp) and Peter Van Aelst (Leiden University); Norway: Toril Aalberg and Ann Iren Jamtøy (Norwegian University of Science and Technology); Sweden: Jesper Strömbäck and Adam Shehata (Mid Sweden University); Netherlands: Kees Brants, Philip van Praag, and Claes de Vreese (ASCOR, University of Amsterdam); other countries: Arjen van Dalen, Erik Albaek (Center for Journalism, University of Southern Denmark), Claes de Vreese (ASCOR, University of Amsterdam).The authors wish to thank these scholars for generously making their data available for this chapter.
2. When we speak about Belgium in this chapter, we actually mean Flanders. This is the Dutch-speaking part of the country containing 60% of the Belgian population.
3. For all countries, journalists who reported never being in contact with politicians were excluded. In Sweden, Norway, and Belgium, where we had to rely on a less narrowly defined target population, we included an extra control question. We asked: "In how many of the last ten articles/news items you wrote was a party or politician of your country mentioned?" Journalists who answered "three articles or more" were included in the analysis.

References

Algarra, Manuel Martín, and Norberto González Gaitano. 1997. The political role of the Spanish journalist. *Political Communication* 14:481–495.

Allern, Sigurd (2001) *Flokkdyr på Løvebakken. Søkelys på Stortingets presselosje og politikkens medierammer* [Herd journalism? Spotlight on the Norwegian parliamentary press lobby and the media's framing of politics]. Oslo: Pax.

Allern, Sigurd. 2007. From party press to independent observers? An analysis of election campaign coverage prior to the general elections of 1981 and 2005 in two Norwegian newspapers. *Nordicom Review* 28:63–79.

Blumler, Jay G., and Michael Gurevitch. 1981. Politicians and the press: An essay on role relationships. In *Handbook of Political Communication*, edited by Dan D. Nimmo and Keith R. Sanders, pp. 467–493. Beverly Hills, CA: Sage.

Blumler, Jay. G., and Michael Gurevitch. 1995. *The crisis of public communication.* New York: Routledge.

Brants, Kees, and Philip van Praag. 2006. Signs of media logic; half a century of political communication in The Netherlands. *Javnost—The public* 13(1):25–40.

Brants, Kees, Claes H. de Vreese, Judith Möller, and Philip van Praag. 2010. The real spiral of cynicism? Symbiosis and mistrust between politicians and journalists. *The International Journal of Press/Politics* 15(1):25–40.

Carlsen, Erik Meier, and Peter Kjær. 1999. Diagnoser af den politiske journalistik—indtryk fra en interviewrunde [Diagnosis of political journalism—Impressions of a round of interviews]. In *Magt og fortælling; hvad er politisk journalistik?* [Power and narrative, what is political journalism?], edited by Erik Meier Carlsen, Peter Kjær, and Ove K. Pedersen, pp. 44–59. Forlaget Ajour.

Crouse, Timothy. 1974. *The boys on the bus.* New York: Ballantine Books.

Davis, Aeron. 2007. Investigating journalist influences on political issue agendas at Westminster. *Political Communication* 24:181–199.

Davis, Aeron. 2009. Journalist-source relations, mediated reflexivity and the politics of politics. *Journalism Studies* 10(2):204–219.

Deuze, Mark. 2002. *Journalists in the Netherlands.* Amsterdam: Aksant.

Donsbach, Wolfgang, and Thomas E. Patterson. 2004. Political news journalists: Partisanship, professionalism, and political roles in five countries. In *Comparing political communication: Theories, cases and challenges,* edited by Frank Esser and Barbara Pfetsch, pp. 251–270. Cambridge, UK: Cambridge University Press.

Ericson, Richard V., Patricia M. Baranek, and Janet B. L. Chan. 1989. *Negotiating control: A study of news sources.* Milton Keynes, UK: Open University Press.

Esser, Frank. 2008. Dimensions of political news cultures: sound bite and image bite news in France, Germany, Great Britain, and the United States. *The International Journal of Press/Politics* 13:401–428.

Gans, Herbert J. 1979. *Deciding what's news: A study of CBS Evening News, NBC Nightly News.* New York: Pantheon.

Graber, Doris. 2003. The media and democracy: Beyond myths and stereotypes. *Annual Reviews of Political Science* 6:139–160.

Hallin, Daniel, and Paolo Mancini. 2004. *Comparing media systems: Three models of media and politics.* New York: Cambridge University Press.

Hanitzsch, Thomas. 2009. Comparative journalism studies. In *The handbook of journalism studies,* edited by Karin Wahl-Jorgensen and Thomas Hanitzsch, pp. 413–427. London: Routledge.

Henningham, John. 1995. Political journalists' political and professional values. *Australian Journal of Political Science* 30(2):321–334.

Hess, Stephen. 1981. *The Washington reporters.* Washington, DC: The Brookings institution.

Hjarvard, Stig. 2007. Den politiske presse; En analyse af dankse avisers politiske orientering [The political press: An analysis of the political orientation of Danish newspapers]. *Journalistica* 5:27–53.

Jones, N. 1995. *Soundbites and spin doctors: How politicians manipulate the media and vice versa.* London: Cassell.

Kelly, Mary, Gianpietro Mazzoleni, and Denis McQual. 2004. *The media in Europe: The Euromedia handbook.* 3rd ed. London: Sage.

Kovach, Bill, and Tom Rosenstiel. 2001. *The elements of journalism.* New York: Crown.

Lijphart, Arend. 1999. *Patterns of democracy: Government forms and performance in thirty-six countries.* New Haven, CT: Yale University Press.

Mancini, Paolo. 1993. Between trust and suspicion: How political journalists solve the dilemma. *European Journal of Communication* 8:33–51.

Mancini. Paolo. 2000. Political complexity and alternative models of journalism. In *De-Westernizing media studies,* edited by James Curran and Myung-Jin Park, pp. 265–278. London: Routledge.

McNair, Brian. 2009. Journalism and democracy. In *The handbook of journalism studies,* edited by Karin Wahl-Jorgensen and Thomas Hanitzsch, pp. 237–249. London: Routledge.

Neveu, Erik. 2002. Four generations of political journalism. In *Political journalism; new challenges, new practices,* edited by Raymond Kuhn and Erik Neveu, pp. 24–44. London: Routledge.

Nimmo, Dan D. (1964). *Newsgathering in Washington: A study in political communication.* New York: Atherton Press.

Norris, Pippa. 2009. Comparative political communications: common frameworks or babelian confusion? *Government and Opposition* 44(3):321–340.

Patterson, Thomas E. 2000. *Doing well and doing good: How soft news and critical journalism are shrinking the news audience and weakening democracy—and what news outlets can do about it.* Cambridge, MA: John F. Kennedy School of Government, Harvard University.

Patterson, Thomas E., and Wolfgang Donsbach. 2004. News decisions: Journalists as partisan actors. *Political Communication* 13:455–468.

Petersson, Olof, Monika Djerf-Pierre, Sören Holmberg, Jesper Strömbäck, and Lennart Weibull. 2006. *Media and elections in Sweden: Report from the democratic audit of Sweden.* Stockholm: SNS Forlag.

Pfetsch, Barbara. 2001. Political communication culture in the United States and Germany. *International Journal of Press/Politics* 6(1):46–67.

Pfetsch, Barbara. 2004. From political culture to political communication culture: A theoretical approach to comparative analysis. In *Comparing political communication: Theories, cases, and challenges,* edited by Frank Esser and Barbara Pfetsch, pp. 344–366. Cambridge, UK: Cambridge University press.

Rosenstiel, Tom. 1993. *Strange bedfellows: How television and the presidential candidates changed American politics 1992.* New York: Hyperion.

Rosten, Leo. 1937. *Washington correspondents.* New York: Harcourt Brace.

Schudson, Michael. 2003. *The sociology of news.* New York:. Norton.

Shoemaker, Pamela J., and Stephen D. Reese. 1996. *Mediating the message*. New York: Longman.

Skovsgaard, Morten, Erik Albæk, Claes H. de Vreese, and Peter Bro (forthcoming). Danish journalists. In *The Global Journalist*, 2nd ed., edited by David Weaver and Lars Willnat. Malden, MA: Routledge.

Sonnenberg, Urte. 1997. Regulation and self-regulation of the media. In *Organising media accountability: Experiences in Europe*, edited by Urte Sonnenberg, pp. 17–22. Maastricht: European Journalism Centre.

Strömbäck, Jesper. 2005. In search of a standard: Four models of democracy and their normative implications for journalism. *Journalism Studies* 6(3):331–345

Strömbäck, Jesper, and Óscar G. Luengo. 2008. Polarized pluralist and democratic corporatist models: a comparison of election news coverage in Spain and Sweden. *International Communication Gazette* 70:547–562.

Strömbäck, Jesper, and Lars W. Nord. 2006. Do politicians lead the tango? A study of the relationship between Swedish journalists and their political sources in the context of election campaigns. *European Journal of Communication* 21(2):147–164.

Tan, Yue, and David H. Weaver. 2007. Agenda-setting effects among the media, the public, and congress, 1946–2004. *Journalism & Mass Communication Quarterly* 84(4):729–744.

Tan, Yue, and David H. Weaver. 2009. Local media, public opinion, and state legislative policies: Agenda setting at the state level. *International Journal of Press/Politics*, 14(4):454–476.

Tunstall, Jeremy. 1970. *The Westminster lobby correspondents: A sociological study of national political journalism*. London: Routledge & Kegan Paul.

Van Aelst, Peter, and Torril Aalberg. 2009. Between love and hate. A comparative study on the informality of the relationship between politicians and political journalists in Belgium, Norway and Sweden. Paper presented at annual meeting of the International Communication Association, Chicago, Illinois.

Van Aelst, Peter, Kees Brants, Philip van Praag, Claes H. de Vreese, Michiel Nuytemans, and Arjen van Dalen. 2008. The fourth estate as superpower? An empirical study of perceptions of media power in Belgium and the Netherlands. *Journalism Studies* 9(4):494–511.

Van Aelst, Peter, Adam Shehata, and Arjen van Dalen. 2010. Members of Parliament, equal competitors for media attention? An analysis of personal contacts between MPs and political journalists in five European countries. *Political Communication* 27(3):310–325.

Van Aelst, Peter, and Stefaan Walgrave. 2011. Minimal or massive? The political agenda-setting power of the mass media according to different methods. *International Journal of Press/Politics* 16:295–313.

Van Dalen, Arjen, Erik Albæk, and Claes H. de Vreese. 2011. Suspicious minds. Explaining political cynicism among political journalists in Europe. *European Journal of Communication* 26(2):147–162.

Van Zoonen, Liesbet. 1998. A professional, unreliable, heroic marionette (M/F): Structure, agency and subjectivity in contemporary journalisms. *European Journal of Cultural Studies* 1(1):123–143.

Walgrave, Stefaan. 2008. Again the almighty mass media? The media's political agenda-setting power according to politicians and journalists in Belgium. *Political Communication* 25(4):445–459.

Walgrave, Stefaan, and Peter van Aelst. 2006. The contingency of the mass media's political agenda setting power: Toward a preliminary theory. *Journal of Communication* 56:88–109.

Weaver, David H. (ed.). 1998. *The global journalist: News people around the world*. Cresskill, NJ: Hampton Press.

Conclusions

38 Journalists in the 21st Century
Conclusions

David Weaver and Lars Willnat

Comparing journalists across national boundaries and cultures is no easier now than it was in the late 1990s when the first *Global Journalist* book was written. In fact, it is more complicated, given the dramatic changes in journalism during the past decade. In addition to the many characteristics, attitudes, and behaviors that could be said to depend on the specific situation, there has been a blurring of the boundaries between journalism and other forms of public communication, and between journalists and those formerly known as media audiences. This makes it even more difficult, though not impossible, to look for general patterns and trends. There are still similarities that seem to cut across the boundaries of geography, culture, language, society, religion, race, and ethnicity, as well as differences that are not easily explained.

Keeping in mind that many of the comparisons here are rough and post hoc, rather than carefully preplanned and controlled, this chapter focuses on the similarities and differences in the basic characteristics, working conditions, and professional values of journalists from more than 30 societies represented in this book.

This task is made easier by the fact that many of the studies reported in these pages have borrowed questions from our original questionnaire (Weaver, Beam, Brownlee, Voakes, & Wilhoit 2007; Weaver & Wilhoit 1986, 1996), which was modeled on the 1971 study of U.S. journalists done by sociologists at the University of Illinois at Chicago (Johnstone, Slawski, & Bowman 1976). But some of the surveys employ their own questions and measures, or modify the original wordings somewhat. And there is, of course, always the slippage in meaning involved in translating from one language to another, and in the changing meaning of words over time.

The point of trying to draw comparisons of journalists in these different areas of the world is the hope of identifying some similarities and differences that may give us a more accurate picture of who journalists are, where they come from, how they think about their work and occupation, and where the differences and similarities are as we begin this second decade of a new century. The major assumption is that journalists' backgrounds and ideas have some relationship to *what* is reported (and *how* it is covered) in the various news media around the world, in spite of various constraints, and that this news coverage matters in terms of world public opinion and policies.

A Profile of Global Journalists

Backgrounds and Demographic Profiles

In our latest study of U.S. journalists, conducted during the summer and fall of 2002, we concluded that the statistical "profile" of the typical U.S. journalist was much like that of 1992. The typical U.S. journalist then was a White Protestant, married male in his 30s with a bachelor's degree. In 2002, this average journalist was a married White male just over 40, less likely to come from a Protestant religious background, and slightly more likely to hold a bachelor's degree (Weaver et al. 2007). This demographic profile of U.S. journalists is similar in some ways to the profiles of journalists in other areas of the world, but there are some notable differences as well.

Gender.   For example, men were more typical than women in newsrooms in 23 of the 29 countries or territories reporting gender proportions (see Table 38.1), although in some countries women were almost as numerous as men (Australia, Brazil, Britain, Denmark, Hong Kong, Hungary, Spain, and Sweden), whereas in others women lagged far behind (Belgium, Israel, Japan, Korea, and the United Arab Emirates). The average proportion of women journalists across these 29 countries and territories was 41%, an increase from the 33% reported as an average in the first edition of *The Global Journalist* in 1998. However, the U.S. figure did not change from 1992 to 2002, in spite of all the women enrolled in U.S. journalism programs.

Age.   Another similarity between the United States and the rest of the world as represented here is that journalism tends to be a young person's occupation, with most journalists between 25 and 45 years old. The average age of journalists ranges from 32 to 53 in the 29 surveys reporting it, with the youngest journalists coming from Australia, Britain, Chile, China, Hong Kong, Indonesia, Malaysia, Poland, Singapore, Taiwan, and the United Arab Emirates (UAE), where the average age is from 33 to 36, and the oldest from Japan, where it is 53.

In most places, journalists are younger on average (39 years old) than is the work force in general. In many countries, young people become journalists to gain some experience before leaving for more lucrative and stable jobs in other fields, especially public relations. This seems to be a fairly common pattern around the world.

Education.   Although most U.S. journalists hold a four-year college degree, this is not the case in several countries, as Table 38.1 indicates. The locations with the lowest proportions of college graduate journalists are Finland, Germany, Hong Kong, Israel, New Zealand, Slovenia, and Switzerland—all below three-fourths. Those with the highest are Brazil, Japan, Korea, and Taiwan—all above 95%. Only one country (Finland) reports less than half of its journalists holding a four-year college degree, and the average for all 28 countries reporting this figure is 82%, so it is far more common than not for journalists to be college graduates in this group, although the variation across countries is substantial.

It is less typical for journalists to be graduates of journalism programs in college, however. Of the 25 nations reporting this figure, the average is 42.5%. Only eight countries reported more than half of their journalists had concentrated on journalism in college. In the other 17 countries or territories reporting this proportion, most did not exceed one-third, with the lowest figures from Finland, France, Israel, Japan, Korea, and Switzerland.

Thus whatever journalistic benefits or deficiencies are attributed to journalism education must be tempered by the fact that most journalists are not graduates of college-level journalism programs in this sample of nations.

Marital Status.   Only 14 countries reported the proportion of journalists who were married, and Table 38.1 indicates a fairly wide range—from 39% in Chile to 76% in the United Arab Emirates. Only six countries reported figures above one-half, and the average for all 14 reporting is 50%, making it impossible to conclude, as in the United States, that the typical journalist tends to be married.

Table 38.1 Basic Demographic Characteristics of Journalists

	Average Age	% Female	Total No. of Journalists	% Married	% Minorities	% Holding College Degree	% Majoring in Journalism
Asia							
China	33.1	52.9	700,000	—	—	93.4	—
Hong Kong	32.0[b]	48.1	—	—	—	71.7	56.8
Indonesia	35.0	33.0	23,000	—	—	87.8	53.5
Japan	53.3	2.1	21,103	—	—	95.6	15.0
Korea	38.6	17.8	35,300	48.6	—	97.1	21.9
Malaysia	35.0	55.0	2,500	42.6	55.0	91.2	30.4
Singapore	35.0	60.0	1,500	54.9	20.6	88.9	—
Taiwan	35.9	42.5	—	50.3	—	96.5	29.5
Australasia							
Australia	35.0[a]	45.0	4,200	—	16.0–24.0[f]	80.0	35.0
New Zealand	39.0[a]	—	4,000	—	12.9	68.0	—
Europe							
Belgium	42.0	27.8	4,500	43.5	4.0[f]	90.4	58.03
Denmark	45.0	46.0	6,000	—	1.0[f]	88.0	70.0
Finland	—	56.7	14,794	—	—	38.0	25.0
France	42.2	43.8	37,811	—	—	—	14.8[c]
Germany	41.0	37.0	36,000	44.0	—	69.0	31.0[d]
Great Britain	34.0	49.0	60–70,000	59.0	4.0	—	—
Hungary	39.0	47.0	5,500	43.0	—	83.0	32.0
Netherlands	44.0	38.0	14,000	—	—	82.0	43.0[c]
Slovenia	40.0	53.0	2,000	41.0	—	66.0	57.0
Poland	34.0[a]	40.7	—	55.3	—	84.2	31.6
Spain	43.0	46.0	25,000	—	—	93.9	74.8
Sweden	44.5	49.6	17,096	—	15.0[e]	78.0	46.0
Switzerland	43.0	35.2	10,500	—	6.0[f]	56.0	21.4
Russia	41.0	67.4	—	—	—	90.0	44.1
North America							
Canada	—	37.0	4,000[g]	—	—	78.7	—
USA	41.0[a]	33.0	116,148	60.0	9.5	89.0	36.0
South America							
Brazil	39.8	45.3	30,000	46.1	4.9	100.0	100.0
Chile	35.6	39.0	3,141	39.4	—	92.5	86.2
Colombia	41.8	—	—	—	—	—	—
Middle East							
Israel	38.6	29.7	—	—	4.0	70.8	23.9
UAE	36.0	20.0	800	75.6	80.0[f]	78.7	26.9
Overall Means	39.2 yrs	41.3%	47,444	50.3%	18.2%	82.1%	42.5%

a Median reported; b Estimate based on age groups; c Includes professional school degrees; d Includes journalism & media studies; e parents born outside present home country; f noncitizens/not born in present home country; g Quebec only.

Race and Ethnicity.   Only 13 of the countries and territories represented in this study reported a figure for racial and ethnic minority journalists. Table 38.1 shows that the reported figures are mostly small, except in countries where journalists are likely to be noncitizens from other countries, such as the United Arab Emirates. The figures for the other 11 countries reinforce the conclusion of the 1971 U.S. study by Johnstone et al. (1976) that journalists come predominantly from the established and dominant cultural groups in society. This seems to hold true especially in Belgium, Brazil, Denmark, Britain, and Israel, where the figures for minority journalists are all below 5%. Switzerland is close behind, with only 6% minority journalists.

Size of Workforce.   The estimated number of journalists working in the 25 different countries and territories reporting this figure varies tremendously, as one would expect given the great differences in the sizes and populations of these places (see Table 38.1). The countries with the largest populations—Brazil, Britain, China, France, Germany, and the United States—have the most journalists, as one would expect, but it is surprising that Brazil has so few considering the size of its population.

Some of these differences are undoubtedly due to different methods of estimating the total number of journalists, and some may reflect different definitions of who qualifies as a journalist. It does seem that those countries most advanced economically and most democratic politically tend to have larger numbers of journalists as compared to population.

Thus, in terms of demographics, the journalists from the various countries and territories were fairly similar in average age, but varied considerably in gender, percent of ethnic/racial minorities, level of education, and whether they concentrated on journalism in college. They also varied substantially in representation based on population.

Working Conditions

Obviously the working conditions of journalists also differ widely in the nations represented in this book, not only in terms of material resources but also in professional autonomy, political pressures, and norms and traditions of journalism that affect the subjects and approaches taken in reporting the news of the day. One of the most important indicators of the working conditions of journalists is their level of job satisfaction, which in some cases is linked to their perceived autonomy or freedom. In the United States, for example, declining levels of job satisfaction and perceived autonomy have gone hand-in-hand since the early 1970s (Weaver et al. 2007).

Job Satisfaction.   The proportions of journalists considering themselves "very satisfied" with their jobs varies greatly among the 22 studies that reported this, as Table 38.2 indicates. Those countries or territories with the smallest percentages of very satisfied journalists were Chile, Hong Kong, Japan, Korea, Taiwan, and the United Arab Emirates, with Singapore and Slovenia not far behind; those with the largest were Britain and Finland. Some countries with relatively high percentages—such as Finland, Colombia, and Israel—reported relatively high figures for perceived autonomy as well. The average for all 22 countries that reported "very" satisfied figures was 27.5%, below the U.S. figure of 33%.

Perceived Autonomy.   The journalists with the most perceived autonomy were from Australia, Belgium, Canada, and Finland, where more than three-fourths claimed to have a great deal of freedom on the job, as the leftmost column in Table 38.2 shows. Those countries with the fewest journalists claiming a great deal of freedom were Chile, Hong Kong, Korea, and Taiwan.

Table 38.2   Working Conditions and Job Satisfaction

	Perceived Autonomy (% Saying "Very Satisfied")	Job Satisfaction (% Saying "Very Satisfied")	Commitment to Journalism (% Saying "Want to Stay in Journalism")
Asia			
China	—	—	—
Hong Kong	2.5[c]	4.5[d]	—
Indonesia	24.2[e]	—	—
Japan	—	4.8	—
Korea	5.7	7.8[f]	—
Malaysia	16.3	18.1	71.1
Singapore	54.7[g]	12.2	55.5
Taiwan	7.8	5.5	57.0
Australasia			
Australia	82.0	38.0	70.0
New Zealand	—	—	—
Europe			
Belgium	79.1	—	87.8[a]
Denmark	—	—	—
Finland	86.0	84.0	—
France	—	38.0[b]	67.0
Germany	42.0	—	—
Great Britain	—	78.0	—
Hungary	56.0	36.0	—
Netherlands	—	—	—
Slovenia	26.0	12.0	—
Poland	44.4	20.7	—
Spain	—	—	—
Sweden	27.0[h]	29.0	61.0[a]
Switzerland	—	—	—
Russia	27.8	19.1	—
North America			
Canada	79.3	30.0	—
USA	40.0	33.0	77.0
South America			
Brazil	—	21.3	—
Chile	17.3	7.4	—
Colombia	59.4	51.1	—
Middle East			
Israel	51.3[j]	51.3[k]	—
UAE	22.5[i]	2.5	62.0
Overall means	9.5%	27.4%	67.6%

Notes: a Stay in journalism for next 5 years; b "Very happy" to be a journalist; c Those scoring 10 on a 10-point satisfaction scale; d Those scoring 5 on a 5-point Likert scale; e "Strongly agree" to "I am allowed to take part in decisions that affect my work"; f Those scoring 9 and 10 on a 11-point satisfaction scale; g Percentage of people saying they have "almost complete freedom" (8.3%) and "considerable freedom"(41.7%); h Those saying "almost complete freedom" to "How much freedom do you usually have in selecting the stories you work on?"; i People saying "almost completely free" to select a story to cover; j "Strongly agree" to "I feel that my superiors allow me to operate freely"; k "Strongly agree" to "I enjoy going to work every day."

Table 38.2 also shows that the proportions of journalists perceiving a great deal of freedom are correlated with the proportions claiming to be very satisfied with their jobs in several countries or territories, including Chile, Colombia, Finland, Hong Kong, Israel, Korea, Malaysia, Russia, Sweden, Taiwan, and the United States. This is not the case in Australia or Canada, however, where high percentages for perceived freedom were associated with low proportions of those who claimed to be very satisfied. These findings suggest that other factors besides perceived freedom in these countries contributed to job satisfaction, and Table 38.3 confirms this for Australia, where editorial policy was a stronger predictor of job satisfaction than perceived autonomy.

In the case of the least satisfied journalists, Table 38.3 shows that in Chile the strongest predictors of job satisfaction (or lack of it) were pay and the chance for journalists to use all of their abilities and knowledge. In Japan the best predictors were the journalists' evaluations of the practices of their news organizations and their relationships with the government. In Korea, it was job autonomy (almost none claimed to have a great deal) and service to the society. In Malaysia, job benefits, job security, and pay were the leading predictors. In Singapore, it was journalists' ratings of their organizations and ability to cover a subject of interest, but in Slovenia, the chance to help people was most prominent, followed by autonomy on the job. In Brazil, low pay and lack of recognition were the most important predictors of job dissatisfaction. In Taiwan, pay and journalists' rating of their organizations were the best predictors, and in the United Arab Emirates, it was job security and the chance to develop a specialty. In only four countries was perceived freedom on the job ranked as the most important predictor of job satisfaction—Finland, Korea, Poland, and Russia.

Another indicator of job satisfaction among journalists is their commitment to the occupation. Although only nine countries reported this, Table 38.2 shows that the greatest commitment was among journalists in Belgium (88%), followed by the United States, Malaysia, and Australia, all with 70% or more. The least commitment was found among journalists in Singapore and Taiwan, where slightly more than one-half wanted to continue working in journalism.

In contrast to the great differences in perceived autonomy and job satisfaction levels, the proportions saying they wanted to remain working as journalists did not vary as widely, and they did not seem to be systematically related to levels of perceived autonomy or job satisfaction (except for Australia and Belgium, where high levels of perceived autonomy were correlated with high levels of commitment to journalism), as Table 38.2 indicates. Apparently journalists have other reasons for wanting to stay in journalism besides perceived freedom and job satisfaction. One key consideration is likely to be the attractiveness of alternative jobs, in terms of pay, fringe benefits, privileges, and opportunities for advancement.

Professional Values

The definition and measurement of journalists' professional values, including roles and ethical standards, has been debated by scholars and commentators for at least a century. Some of these debates center on whether journalism *is* a profession (Beam 1990; Lawrence 1903; Splichal & Sparks 1994; Weaver & Wilhoit 1986) and some on whether journalism *should be* one (Bowman 1996; Glasser 1992).

The often stated view that journalism is not a true profession is similar to that expressed by Weaver and Wilhoit in the first *American Journalist* book. They wrote that "American journalists are unlikely ever to assume a formal professional status" because of their skepticism of institutional forms of professionalism such as certification or licensing, membership in organizations, and readership of professional publications (Weaver & Wilhoit 1986: 167).

Table 38.3 Three Best Predictors of Journalists' Job Satisfaction

	1. Predictor	2. Predictor	3. Predictor
Asia			
China	—	—	—
Hong Kong	—	—	—
Indonesia	Number of friends who are journalists	Secondary employment	Position in editorial hierarchy
Japan	Journalists' rating of their organization	Relationship with government	—
Korea	Job autonomy	Service to the society	Editorial policy
Malaysia	Job benefits such as meeting people, travel, etc.	Job security & pay	Opportunity to learn new skills
Singapore	Journalists' rating of their organization	Ability to cover a subject	Freedom in selecting stories
Taiwan	Pay	Journalists' rating of their organization	Perceived autonomy
Australasia			
Australia	Editorial policy	Job autonomy	Ability to help people
New Zealand	—	—	—
Europe			
Belgium	—	—	—
Denmark	—	—	—
Finland	Job autonomy	Job security	Chance for self-expression and self-fulfilment
France	—	—	—
Germany	—	—	—
Great Britain	Pay	Ability of superior	Sense of achievement at work
Hungary	—	—	—
Netherlands	—	—	—
Slovenia	Chance to help people	Job autonomy	Opportunity to influence public opinion
Poland	Job autonomy	Personal & professional development	Pay
Spain	Job security	Pay	Flexible work-time
Sweden	—	—	—
Switzerland	—	—	—
Russia	Job autonomy	Opportunity to help people	Political line of their media
North America			
Canada	—	—	—
USA	Rating of own institution in informing the public	Personal influence on subjects covered	Pay
South America			
Brazil	Pay	Professional recognition	Possibility for promotion
Chile	Pay	Conformity with the power to use all of their abilities and knowledge	Reconciliation of work and family life
Colombia	Pay	Obstacles of the journalism profession	Media status
Middle East			
Israel	Chance to help people	Job security	Possibility for promotion
UAE	Job security	Developing a specialty	Helping people

Looking across 22 countries, Splichal and Sparks (1994) noted that their initial hypothesis was that similarities across countries should prevail if journalism is really becoming a profession. They concluded that their major finding was a striking similarity in the desire of journalism students for the independence and autonomy of journalism. In addition, they didn't find evidence that journalism education and professional socialization were necessarily a function of politics or dominant societal ideology.

Based on these findings, they argued that some universal ethical and occupational standards were emerging in journalism, but Weaver (1998) found in comparing journalists from 21 nations that there were still many differences on a variety of possible measures of professionalism (perceived roles, reporting ethics, membership in professional organizations, perceived importance of different aspects of the job, and images of the audience). The difference in these conclusions may be due to the lack of specific questions about journalism roles, reporting practices, or ethical dilemmas in the Splichal–Sparks questionnaire.

There probably is a fairly universal desire for more freedom among journalists in various parts of the world, although the findings on the importance of this job aspect in 1998 and this present book are mixed, but that does not necessarily signal the emergence of any universal standards in journalism. A look at more specific professional roles or values, as well as reporting practices, may help to more precisely define the areas of agreement and disagreement among the more than 29,000 journalists from 31 societies represented in this book.

Roles. Our analysis of six possible journalistic roles shows that "reporting the news quickly" had the highest mean score (53% of 21 countries rated it extremely important), followed closely by "reporting objectively" (51%) and "providing analysis of events" (49%). The "watchdog" role was fourth (39%), followed by "providing access for the public" (36%) and finally by "providing entertainment" (19%). It is noteworthy that the average ranking of these roles by journalists in most countries differed substantially from that of U.S. journalists, who were much more likely to consider the watchdog of government role the most important (71%). Only in Australia did more journalists (90%) consider this role extremely important than in the United States.

Among the 21 countries or territories reporting on the role of getting information to the public quickly, there was a very wide range, with only 2% in Denmark rating this role as "extremely important" and 93% in Sweden doing so. In most cases, as Table 38.4 indicates, one-half or more of the journalists agreed that it was extremely important, except in Brazil, Canada, Chile, Denmark, Germany, Japan, Korea, Netherlands, and Taiwan. In all cases but two (Denmark and Korea), a third or more of the journalists thought this role was extremely important. Still, there was notable variation in the percentages of journalists who thought this role was very important. Possible reasons for this include competition from other news media, especially various Web sites, the type of medium the journalist worked for, and the norms and traditions of journalism in different countries.

On investigating government claims (or being a watchdog of government) the range was not quite as wide as it was for reporting news quickly, but it was still great (from 7% in Germany to 90% in Australia) with journalists most likely to consider this role very important coming from the more democratic countries of Belgium and the United States.

Those least likely to see this watchdog role as very important were from Brazil, Germany, and Japan, possibly because of the closer ties between journalists and government officials in these countries, and the increased acceptance of a larger role for government in these societies. Koecher (1986) argued in her article that German journalists tend to be "missionaries" rather than "bloodhounds."

Table 38.4 Professional Roles (% saying "extremely important")

	Report News Quickly	Provide Analysis of Events	Be Watchdog of Gov't	Provide Access For Public	Provide Entertain-ment	Report Objectively	Freedom House Score
Asia							
China	—	—	—	—	—	—	84
Hong Kong	51.0	36.2	23.3	—	16.1	—	33
Indonesia	—	9.0	39.0	—	—	29.6	52
Japan	33.5	6.2	2.5	—	9.6	—	21
Korea	17.5	23.4	40.0	16.0	13.6	40.8	30
Malaysia	78.3	62.2	21.0	43.4	27.2	48.0	64
Singapore	58.6	45.0	35.6	40.1	23.8	—	68
Taiwan	47.2	43.1	32.9	—	25.5	71.0	25
Australasia							
Australia	80.0	72.0	90.0	43.0	20.0	—	22
New Zealand	52.0	—	—	—	—	19.0	14
Europe							
Belgium	80.0	93.0	69.0	39.0	40.0	99.0	12
Denmark	2.0	55.0	56.0	28.0	4.0	—	11
Finland	—	—	—	—	—	—	10
France	—	—	—	—	—	—	23
Germany	42.0	40.0	7.0	12.0	13.0	55.0	17
Great Britain	—	—	—	—	—	—	19
Hungary	—	—	—	—	—	—	23
Netherlands	33.0	37.0	18.0	13.0	8.0	—	14
Slovenia	58.0	57.0	51.0	39.0	16.0	24.0	25
Poland	81.7	65.4	42.6	63.2	35.3	42.8	24
Spain	—	—	—	—	—	—	24
Sweden	55.0	32.0	22.0	28.0	31.0	—	10
Switzerland	—	36.9	26.9	14.6	11.9	63.8	13
Russia	80.5	77.8	53.0	68.8	24.8	—	81
North America							
Canada	37.9	51.7	45.2	30.9	6.2	81.6	19
USA	59.0	51.0	71.0	39.0	11.0	52.0	18
South America							
Brazil	38.0	72.2	14.6	37.6	19.9	—	43
Chile	40.7	—	38.9	—	11.2	15.8	30
Colombia	—	—	—	—	—	—	60
Middle East							
Israel	—	—	—	—	—	—	29
UAE	88.1	68.1	61.9	60.0	35.0	71.0	71
Overall Means	53.0%	49.2%	39.2%	36.2%	19.2%	51.0%	

Note. Source for Freedom House scores: Freedom of the Press 2010, Table of global press freedom rankings. Countries scoring 0 to 30 are regarded as having "Free" media; 31 to 60, "Partly Free" media; and 61 to 100, "Not Free" media. Available at: http://www.freedomhouse.org/uploads/fop10/Global_Table_2010.pdf

Considerable differences also were found for the perception of the analytical function of news media, or "providing analysis of complex problems." Among the 21 countries or territories where this role was measured, journalists in Japan (6.2%) and Indonesia (9%) were least likely to consider it very important. The countries where this role was most likely to be considered very important included Australia, Belgium, Brazil, Malaysia, Poland, Russia, and Sweden—a diverse mix of older and newer democracies (see Table 38.4).

Another role where there was some disagreement was the extent to which journalists should give ordinary people a chance to express their views on public affairs. Although only 17 countries reported the importance of this role, compared to other journalistic roles this one was not seen as important by more than two-thirds of the journalists in any location. Only in Poland, Russia, and the United Arab Emirates did more than half of the journalists consider this a very important role, as Table 38.4 shows. And only in Korea, Germany, the Netherlands, and Switzerland did fewer than one-fifth of the journalists consider this a very important role. Thus the range of opinions for this role was not as great as for the previous ones considered here.

There was more disagreement on the importance of providing entertainment among the 21 countries or territories reporting this role. Those journalists least likely to consider this very important were from Canada (6%) and Denmark (4%), whereas those most likely were from Belgium (40%). Most of the other countries were closer to the overall average of one-fifth considering it very important. Clearly, this is one role where national differences in journalistic values are in sharp evidence, especially in Europe.

There was also some disagreement on the importance of reporting accurately or objectively, with those journalists least likely to say so from Chile (16%) and New Zealand (19%), and those most likely from Belgium (99%) and Canada (82%). Although only 14 countries reported data on this role, its overall mean of 51% was the second highest of any of the six roles examined here.

Thus, there was considerable variation among journalists from different countries regarding the importance of most of these professional roles. No role was considered extremely important by more than 53% of all journalists on average, although there were very wide ranges for most of them, especially reporting the news quickly, being a watchdog of government, and providing analysis of events and issues, as Table 38.4 illustrates.

Clearly, there was more disagreement than agreement over the relative importance of these journalistic roles considered together, hardly evidence to support the universal occupational standards mentioned by Splichal and Sparks (1994). The reasons for the disagreement are difficult to specify for so many possible comparisons, but a secondary analysis of the data from journalists in China, Taiwan, and the United States by Zhu, Weaver, Lo, Chen, and Wu (1997) suggests that political system similarities and differences are far more important than cultural similarities and differences, organizational constraints, or individual characteristics in predicting the variance in perceptions of three roles (timely information, interpretation, and entertainment) by journalists in these societies.

To analyze whether there might be a relationship between press freedom and journalists' perceptions of their professional roles across nations, we correlated the press freedom scores of Freedom House[1] with the percentages of journalists who consider a journalistic role "extremely important." The Freedom House scores, which range from 0 to 100, are based on how much influence each country's legal, political, and economic environment has on its press. Countries with scores from 0 to 30 are considered having a "free" media, scores from 31 to 60 indicate "partly free" media, and scores from 61 to 100 identify "not free" media (see last column of Table 38.4).

The correlation analysis shows that journalists in countries with less press freedom are more likely to believe that "reporting news quickly" ($r = .46$, $p < .001$, $N = 21$) and "providing access to the public" ($r = .64$, $p < .01$, $N = 17$) are important roles of journalists. However, the perceived importance of journalistic roles such as "being the watchdog of the government" ($r = .04$, $p > .05$, $N = 20$), "providing analyses of events" ($r = .20$, $p > .05$, $N = 21$), and "providing entertainment" ($r = .37$, $p > .05$, $N = 21$) did not correlate significantly with press freedom scores. This was especially true for the watchdog role, where there was virtually no correlation.

While such correlations at the aggregate level cannot indicate whether journalists are actually influenced by the level of press freedom in their respective nations, the findings do show some interesting patterns. First of all, it seems that journalists in countries with less press freedom advocate traditional—yet uncontroversial—journalistic roles such as reporting the news quickly and providing access to the public. Surprisingly, journalists in more democratic societies are *not* more likely to believe in the importance of the "watchdog" function of the press, despite the fact that this is assumed to be the classic role of journalists in countries with high levels of press freedom.

One explanation might be the perception among journalists in countries with little press freedom that the news media cannot act as a watchdog of the government without running into restrictions—but that they can report the news quickly and offer access to the public without inviting censorship. Possible examples might be Singapore and Malaysia, where only a small percentage of journalists consider the watchdog function of the press a very important role, while a clear majority thinks that reporting the news quickly is important. In countries such as Germany, the Netherlands, Sweden, and Switzerland, on the other hand, journalists might be more trusting of their governments and therefore less likely to think that the media should act as watchdogs.

Overall then, it seems that at least some journalistic role perceptions are associated with levels of press freedom across nations. It is clear, however, that any such association will heavily depend on a country's political, social, and cultural system.

Ethics of Reporting Methods. Our surveys of U.S. journalists included questions about the acceptability of questionable reporting practices that were first asked in a 1980 study of British and West German journalists (Donsbach 1983; Koecher 1986) and also in public opinion surveys in the United States during the 1980s (Weaver & Daniels 1992; Weaver & Wilhoit 1986, 1996; Weaver et al. 2007).

For example, a majority of U.S. journalists in 1982, 1992, and 2002 said that getting employed to gain inside information may be justified on occasion. But a national survey of 1,002 American adults conducted in 1985 found that only 32% approved of journalists not identifying themselves as reporters (Gaziano & McGrath 1986), as did 32% in a 1981 Gallup national survey and 38% in a 1989 Indiana statewide survey (Weaver & Daniels 1992). The questions were somewhat different, but it is likely there was a considerable gap between the U.S. press and public on the acceptability of undercover reporting.

Another gap with the public appeared when U.S. journalists' opinions about the use of hidden microphones or cameras were compared with those of the public. Only 42% of the 1985 national sample of the public (and 46% of the 1989 Indiana sample) approved of using hidden cameras in 1985, compared with 63% of journalists in 1992 who said this practice might be justified. Again, the questions were not identical, but a gap seemed likely.

One practice that was approved by fewer journalists than the United States public was paying for information. Only 20% of the journalists in our 1992 study (and 17% in 2002) said this might be justified (Weaver & Wilhoit 1996; Weaver et al. 2007), compared with 30% of the 1985 national sample and 33% of the 1989 Indiana sample who approved. On this score, then, U.S. journalists seemed less permissive (or more ethical) than the public at large.

If journalists are becoming more professional (or at least in more agreement about the ethical standards of journalism) around the world, we should expect their views on the acceptability of various reporting practices to also become more similar.

In our earlier 1982 study of U.S. journalists, we found considerable differences between United States, British, and German journalists on whether certain practices might be justified. The German journalists were much less likely to approve of badgering or harassing sources, using personal documents without permission, and getting employed to gain inside information than were the U.S. and British journalists. The British journalists were especially likely to say that most of the questionable reporting practices could be justified, with the U.S. journalists in between the British and the Germans on most practices (Weaver & Wilhoit 1986).

When journalists from different areas of the world are compared, Table 38.5 shows considerable differences in the proportions saying that some reporting methods might be justified, as well as some agreement on other practices. But overall, the differences in this table are not as large as the differences in the proportions of journalists considering various roles to be very important, as illustrated in Table 38.4.

For example, on revealing confidential news sources, journalists from 9 of the 13 countries or territories measuring this were very reluctant to say it might be justifiable (15% or less said so in Australia, Chile, Germany, Hong Kong, Indonesia, Japan, Korea, Russia, Singapore, Slovenia, Taiwan, and the United States). On this practice, then, there was a high level of agreement among all journalists, suggesting a near-universal professional norm of protecting confidential sources. The overall average was 8% who thought that this practice might be justified in the case of an important story.

On other reporting methods, however, Table 38.5 shows some fairly large differences of opinion. With regard to paying for information, the range is from 6% in Japan who think this might be justifiable to 67% in Indonesia who think so. On undercover reporting (claiming to be someone else), the range is from 2% in Japan to 70% in Indonesia who might find this practice justifiable. For badgering or harassing news sources the percentages vary from 12% in Germany to 66% in Korea, and for using personal documents without permission from 2% in Japan to 49% in Korea.

As for using business or government documents without permission, the range of those who might approve runs from 13% in the United Arab Emirates to 81% in Australia and 78% in the United States. And finally, getting employed to gain inside information was seen as possibly justifiable by as few as 5.5% of journalists in Japan and as many as 80% in Israel.

Given these very large differences in the percentages of journalists who think that different reporting methods may be acceptable, it is clear that there are strong national differences that override any universal professional norms or values of journalism around the world, except in the case of revealing confidential sources, where there is overwhelming agreement that this should never be done.

Aspects of the Job.   Another possible indicator of professionalism of journalists is which dimensions of their jobs they consider most important. Some would argue that salary, job security, and chance to advance are less professional aspects of an occupation than editorial policies, ability to develop a specialty, autonomy, and helping people (Beam 1990; McLeod & Hawley 1964; Windahl & Rosengren 1978).

Table 38.5   Reporting Methods (% saying "may be justified")

	Reveal Confidential Source	Pay For Secret Information	Claim To Be Someone Else	Badger Or Harass News Sources	Use Personal Doc.Without Permission	Use Business or Gov. Doc. Without Permission	Get Employed To Gain Inside Information
Asia							
China	—	—	—	—	—	—	—
Hong Kong	10.3	23.1	26.3	57.9	24.6	—	—
Indonesia	8.1	67.3	70.2	17.6	29.2	31.7	62.1
Japan	2.1	6.0	1.7	14.6	2.2	55.8	5.5
Korea	15.1	15.9	44.2	66.2	48.8	48.8	33.6
Malaysia	—	38.6	26.8	—	—	39.4	—
Singapore	15.5	32.8	29.5	46.3	27.2	37.0	31.1
Taiwan	15.5	35.4	38.9	29.9	19.3	36.3	37.4
Australasia							
Australia	3.0	25.0	11.0	40.0	44.0	81.0	41.0
New Zealand	—	—	—	—	—	—	—
Europe							
Belgium	—	45.7	26.0	51.8	24.3	57.4	76.1
Denmark	—	—	—	—	—	—	—
Finland	—	—	—	—	—	—	—
France	—	—	—	—	—	—	—
Germany	3.0	27.0	32.0	12.0	8.0	59.0	49.0
Great Britain	—	—	—	—	—	—	—
Hungary	—	55.0	39.0	—	—	—	—
Netherlands	—	—	—	—	—	—	—
Slovenia	1.0	17.0	11.0	20.0	9.0	46.0	21.0
Poland	—	—	—	—	—	—	—
Spain	—	—	—	—	—	—	—
Sweden	—	25.0	55.0	51.0	17.0	—	71.0
Switzerland	—	—	—	—	—	—	—
Russia	8.7	48.6	37.8	32.8	15.6	42.6	49.5
North America							
Canada	—	—	—	—	—	—	—
USA	8.0	17.0	14.0	52.0	41.0	78.0	54.0
South America							
Brazil	—	—	—	—	—	—	—
Chile	3.0	30.4	45.2	44.4	27.0	73.6	—
Colombia	—	—	—	—	—	—	—
Middle East							
Israel	—	60.3	66.0	—	—	75.8	80.0
UAE	12.5	15.6	13.8	18.1	7.5	13.1	13.1
Overall Means	8.1%	1.7%	31.9%	37.0%	23.0%	50.8%	43.7%

Table 38.6 shows that there are wide disagreements among journalists from different countries on which aspects of the job are very important. Journalists in Australia, Colombia, Germany, Poland, Slovenia, and the United States were more likely to emphasize freedom on the job than pay, job security, and chance to advance. This was not the case in Indonesia, Malaysia, Spain, or the United Arab Emirates where journalists were generally more likely to say that pay, job security, and chance to advance were very important, most likely because journalists' pay in these countries is relatively low. Journalists in Chile, Korea, Russia, and Singapore were about equally likely to think that all aspects of the job (professional and nonprofessional) were very important.

Looking at Table 38.6 first by the "nonprofessional" job aspects, it's clear that Indonesian journalists were most likely to rate pay very important (78.5%), probably because of the low pay in that country, followed by Polish (66%) and UAE journalists (64%). Surprisingly, journalists in Slovenia (3%) and Russia (6%) were least likely to say so. Whatever the reasons for these differences, there is not much agreement across countries on the importance of pay.

For job security, journalists in Indonesia were most likely to consider it very important (84%), followed by those in the United Arab Emirates (78%) and Malaysia (66%). Those least likely to say so were from Slovenia (8%) and Russia (17%), most likely reflecting the economic situations in their countries and illustrating a considerable range of disagreement across countries.

As for the chance to advance or to be promoted, those most likely to rate it very important were from the United Arab Emirates (57.5%), Chile (48%), and Malaysia (46%), again likely reflecting the economies of their countries. Those least concerned about advancement were from Germany (7%) and Korea (8%), perhaps because their economies were strong at the time these surveys were done.

On balance, then, the journalists from Indonesia and the United Arab Emirates were most likely to emphasize the "nonprofessional" material aspects of the job of journalist, and those from Slovenia and Russia were among those least likely to rate these aspects very important. There are striking differences in the proportions of journalists from the different countries considering these aspects of their work as very important, suggesting little support for any universal views of journalists regarding their jobs.

Turning to the more "professional" job aspects, Table 38.6 shows that journalists from Australia (67%), Indonesia (73%), and the United States (69%) were most likely to rate editorial policy as very important, whereas those least likely to do so were from Germany (21%), Korea (19.5%), and Russia (22%). The range for this aspect of the job was smaller than those for the nonprofessional aspects, suggesting more agreement on this aspect of the job across countries. As for developing a specialty, journalists in Poland (79%) and the United Arab Emirates (72%) were most likely to rate it very important, whereas those from Slovenia and Spain (both 16%) were least likely.

Even on perceived freedom on the job, a journalistic norm that Splichal and Sparks (1994) identified as strikingly similar among the journalism students from 22 different countries, there were notable differences among the journalists interviewed in the studies reported here. Those from Poland (86%) were most likely to say that freedom on the job is very important, followed by those in Australia (64%) and Slovenia (63%), whereas those in Spain (25%), Russia (28%), and Korea (29%) were least likely. There does seem to be more agreement on the importance of this aspect of the job than on others, as Splichal and Sparks (1994) argue, but there is still considerable variance between countries.

And, finally, on the journalistic norm of helping people, those journalists most likely to consider this very important were from the United Arab Emirates (71%), Poland (65%) and the United States (63%). Those least likely were from Korea (16%) and Russia (27%), demonstrating a wide range of opinion on the importance of this indicator of professionalism.

Table 38.6   Important Job Aspects (% saying "very important")

	Pay	Job Security	Chance to Advance	Editorial Policy	Developing a Specialty	Job Autonomy	Helping People
Asia							
China	—	—	—	—	—	—	—
Hong Kong	—	—	—	—	—	—	—
Indonesia	78.5	84.1	55.6	73.1	62.1	61.6	41.5
Japan	—	—	—	—	—	—	—
Korea	20.7	33.7	8.2	19.5	27.2	28.9	15.8
Malaysia	57.5	66.3	45.8	58.1	53.3	33.9	52.2
Singapore	36.8	38.4	35.4	45.9	44.9	43.1	40.3
Taiwan	—	—	—	—	—	—	—
Australasia							
Australia	19.0	52.0	43.0	67.0	50.0	64.0	61.0
New Zealand	—	—	—	—	—	—	—
Europe							
Belgium	—	—	—	—	—	—	—
Denmark	—	—	—	—	—	—	—
Finland	18.0	47.0	—	—	—	—	—
France	—	—	—	—	—	—	—
Germany	12.0	21.0	7.0	21.0	—	42.0	—
Great Britain	—	—	—	—	—	—	—
Hungary	—	—	—	—	—	—	—
Netherlands	—	—	—	—	—	—	—
Slovenia	3.0	8.0	18.0	—	16.0	63.0	43.0
Poland	65.7	59.0	35.0	56.2	79.0	85.7	65.0
Spain	42.8	61.0	35.0	—	16.2	24.8	—
Sweden	—	—	—	—	—	—	—
Switzerland	—	—	—	—	—	—	—
Russia	5.8	17.0	13.9	21.8	19.2	27.8	26.7
North America							
Canada	—	—	—	—	—	—	—
USA	17.5	57.8	35.3	69.2	40.5	56.4	63.1
South America							
Brazil	—	—	—	—	—	—	—
Chile	56.5	47.4	47.7	39.1	34.2	48.2	40.5
Colombia	40.1	—	—	—	—	59.4	—
Middle East							
Israel	—	—	—	—	—	—	—
UAE	63.8	78.1	57.5	61.9	71.9	53.8	70.6
Overall Means	35.8%	47.9%	33.6%	48.4%	42.9%	49.5%	47.2%

On balance, then, the Korean and Russian journalists were least likely to emphasize the importance of the more altruistic aspects of the job, and the Spanish journalists were not far behind. Journalists from Australia, Poland, and the United States were most likely. As with most other indicators of professionalism, there appears to be no widespread agreement on the importance of these aspects of journalistic work.

Conclusions

Whether one thinks that journalists are becoming more alike, professionally or otherwise, around the world depends on the measures used. A variety of measures reviewed here suggest that there are still many differences among journalists from the 31 countries and territories represented in this book. Even though these are not a representative sample of all countries or territories in the world, they do include some of the largest and most influential, and they are located in most of the major continents and regions.

Further analysis is needed to uncover some of the reasons behind these observed differences. Many of them seem to reflect societal influences, especially cultural and political system differences, more than the influences of media organizations, journalism education, and professional norms. The patterns of similarities and differences are not neatly classifiable along some of the more common political or cultural dimensions, however, lending some support to the conclusion of Splichal and Sparks (1994) that professional socialization is not necessarily a function of politics or dominant societal ideology.

In the end, it seems more important to discover who journalists are, where they come from (including their educational experiences), and what they think about their work, their roles, their methods, and their ethics than to try to classify them firmly as professionals or not.

The findings from the studies included in this book suggest that the typical journalist is still primarily a fairly young college-educated man who studied something other than journalism in college, and who came from the established and dominant cultural groups in his country. In several countries women are as well-represented as men in journalism (China, Finland, Malaysia, Russia, Singapore, and Slovenia), which is a notable change from a dozen years ago when there were no countries where women were as numerous as men in journalism. The average proportion of women in the countries included in this book has risen to 41% from 33% in 1998. The average proportion of racial and ethnic minorities also has risen, which seems to indicate that they soon will be better represented in journalism.

Job satisfaction of journalists in many countries is linked to pay and job security as well as perceived autonomy, but other conditions are also important, especially journalists' perceptions of how well their news organizations are doing in informing the public and their relationships with their supervisors and peers on the job. Intention to stay in journalism seems more dependent on the attractiveness of alternative jobs.

The professional roles that most journalists agree on are the importance of reporting objectively and accurately, getting information to the public quickly, and providing analysis of events and issues. Especially journalists in countries with less press freedom tend to think that reporting news quickly and providing access to the public are important functions of the press. There is less agreement on the importance of being a watchdog on government and providing access for members of the public to express themselves. Beyond these roles, there is much disagreement over how important it is to provide entertainment.

Although there is no tendency for more journalists in democratically governed countries to consider the watchdog role very important, this is not an entirely consistent pattern. In one less democratic country, the United Arab Emirates, there is a relatively high proportion of journalists rating the watchdog role very important, perhaps because they know about cases of abuse of power that they think should be reported to the public. But, as others have pointed out, what journalists in a survey say is sometimes inconsistent with what they do in daily practice, so it is important to distinguish between the two.

Journalists also sharply disagree on whether some ethically questionable reporting practices might be justified in the case of an important story. The only practice that seems almost universally agreed upon is not revealing news sources who have been promised confidentiality. There are large differences of opinion on whether it might be justifiable to pay for information, to pose as someone else, to badger or harass news sources, and to use personal documents without permission. There is more willingness overall to use business and government documents without permission and to get employed to gain inside information.

These differences in perceptions of acceptable reporting methods are not easily explained in terms of geography. They probably have more to do with the cultural norms and journalistic traditions of each country than with region of the world or differing political systems, in contrast to journalistic roles, which seem to be more closely linked to political system than to culture.

In sum, it seems that the similarities and differences among the journalists analyzed in this book do not follow geographic, political, and cultural patterns. It is therefore difficult to say whether journalists around the world are becoming more similar or different in their views about professional roles and ethics. What seems certain, though, is that a culture of global journalism has not yet emerged.

The Future of Comparative Research On Journalists

Just as the first edition of *The Global Journalist* concluded more than 13 years ago, the second edition found little evidence of a trend toward a global journalism culture. The number of studies on journalists has grown during the last decade, and most of the research reviewed in this book shows that journalistic values and norms depend heavily on social, political, and cultural contexts. Yet while survey research on professional journalists has become more theoretically and methodologically sophisticated, the prevalent focus on journalistic norms and values has limited the value of these studies. As scholars who have conducted their own share of such studies, we acknowledge that this line of research provides valuable insights and should be pursued in the future with more comparative surveys. However, we also would like to point out that eventually, a singular focus on journalistic norms and values will run into the famous "so what" question.

So far, media scholars have done an impressive job of analyzing how journalists consider their profession and their daily work. They also have successfully compared such views across nations and have contemplated possible reasons for these perceptions, norms, and values. What they have not done, however, is investigate whether and how these beliefs influence the work of journalists around the world.

The reason for this gap in research is a simple one: such studies are enormously complex. Linking attitudes, beliefs, and behaviors always has been a difficult task for empirical researchers—and matching journalists' values and norms with their work products is even more challenging. Thus, it is no surprise that most survey studies on journalists have ignored the question of how their attitudes and beliefs influence media content. However, after more than two decades of survey research on journalists' norms and values, we think it is time to start analyzing the consequences of such beliefs and attitudes.

In these next few pages, we would like to offer some thoughts about possible theoretical and methodological issues that future studies should consider. We know that some of these suggestions may be difficult to implement, but we hope they will provide some help toward designing new studies that can increase our knowledge about the work of global journalists.

More Theory That Links Professional Values with Behavior

Throughout this book, most survey studies of journalists have been descriptive, focusing on demographics and professional values and norms. Moreover, many were conducted in one nation only, which limits the findings to a particular political or cultural context. While there has been some progress with comparative analyses of "journalistic cultures" in recent years (see chapter 35), these studies have been limited mostly to explaining societal, organizational, or individual factors that shape journalistic norms and values in each nation. As previously suggested, there is a clear need for theories that could explain whether and how these attitudes affect journalistic work. Such theories could be borrowed from psychology, for example, which has a rich tradition of analyzing potential links between attitudes and behaviors. A theory-based analysis of such links between professional attitudes of journalists and their work products also would encourage more comparative research into how journalists work in different national or cultural contexts.

The need to test such links between attitudes and behaviors can be observed, for example, among journalists in Hong Kong, who work under extreme political pressures from mainland China. As seen in chapter 3, a simple analysis of their norms and values would confirm that "despite the change in power structure since the handover in 1997, there is no significant decline in journalists' emphasis on the importance of the media disseminating truthful information to the public and criticizing the government and other power holders." However, as the authors point out, such findings "only show some general or theoretical acknowledgments of the importance of journalistic roles." To really understand whether their support of traditional journalistic roles influences their work, a content analysis of their work would be necessary. Given Hong Kong's charged political situation, it also would seem important to analyze the journalists' psychological state of mind. Journalists who experience some form of political fear or anxiety, for example, might be less inclined to pursue a story critical of the Chinese government—despite what they believe about the function of the press in their city.

In short, future studies of journalists should move beyond descriptive analyses by (1) explaining the potential causes of journalistic norms and values within a political or cultural context, (2) considering how these norms and values may interact with psychological dispositions that also might explain such behavior, and (3) checking media content for reflections of these norms, values, and psychological factors.

More Inclusive Definitions of Journalists

Defining who is or is not a journalist never has been easy. In many nations, journalists do not need an official permit or license to do their work, so anybody who wants to be a journalist can be one. This democratic tradition has promoted diversity in the media, yet hindered scholars who prefer clearly defined and complete lists of journalists from which they can draw samples. In the past, researchers in countries where such lists were not available often resorted to multistage sampling by asking media organizations for lists of journalists they employ. However, the growing number of freelancers and journalists who work part-time for multiple outlets has undermined this procedure's effectiveness. As the journalism profession becomes increasingly complex, new and internationally applicable definitions of who is a journalist should be developed. Definitions that vary by nation will make cross-national comparisons problematic, so any benchmarking efforts should be considered carefully by the international research community.

More Comparative Studies with Representative Samples

Obtaining samples that reflect the profession is one of the biggest problems in conducting survey research on journalists. Representative samples are essential because only they allow reliable and accurate statements about who journalists are and what they think. Any other type of sample— such as quota samples, convenience samples, or other varieties—might lead to conclusions that have little in common with reality.

As mentioned earlier, complete lists of working journalists are unavailable in many nations, which forces researchers to approach media outlets for lists of their employees. Yet many media organizations are reluctant to disclose employee lists because of privacy concerns and other less rational worries (for example, the fear of disclosing how small their permanent staff has become). But even if the media do cooperate, freelancers and part-timers often are excluded from lists because they are not considered part of the company. In such cases, it is the researcher's responsibility to ensure that the names of all "professional journalists" (however defined) are included.

Once samples are drawn, the next problem for researchers usually is that journalists do not like to participate in surveys. In some nations, constant survey requests from academics, students, and commercial companies clearly have dampened journalists' enthusiasm for participation. This situation differs from country to country, of course. But response rates among U.S. journalists, for example, have declined significantly. Such reluctance also reduces the usefulness of online surveys, which are cheaper than telephone surveys but usually have low response rates. Consequently, researchers who cannot hope for much cooperation from journalists are forced to employ more expensive methods, such as telephone surveys or personal interviews.

A final issue is the need for a better representation of journalists across all nations. While this book represents more or less a complete collection of all journalist surveys conducted during the past 10 years, some important areas of the world are not represented. We were unable, for example, to track down any representative surveys of journalists in Africa and South Asia. Given the large number of journalists in these parts of the world (not to mention the more than 2.2 billion people in general), the lack of studies from these regions represents a fundamental research gap. Thus, future studies should make a special effort to include African and South Asian media scholars. The still existing differences in research traditions between the West and these two world regions, which have contributed to the scarcity of studies, could be overcome with more and better networking and an emerging generation of young media scholars from Africa and South Asia.

More Comparative Studies with Standardized Questionnaires

Another way to improve research on journalists is the use of standardized questionnaires that can be compared cross-nationally. As this book demonstrates, most studies on journalists occur within national borders with little regard for possible comparisons to other nations. This has made it difficult to evaluate journalistic norms and values in a broader, international context. The recent cross-national study of journalists by Hanitzsch et al. (see chapter 35) provides a good example of how a standardized questionnaire can generate data that allow more sophisticated analyses and more meaningful conclusions.

While standardized questionnaires allow empirical tests of theoretical concepts across nations, it should be noted that not all abstract concepts have similar meanings worldwide. Press freedom, for example, is a fluid concept heavily influenced by political and cultural values. As a consequence, journalists are likely to define press freedom within their own socio-political context, based on varied associations and thoughts. While the analysis of such differences is the goal of comparative research, most survey studies are not designed to investigate respondents' conceptualization of such abstract concepts.

One way to avoid this problem is to not use the concept verbatim in the questionnaire. Weaver et al. (2007), for example, tested the perceived importance of the classic "media watchdog" role by asking journalists to indicate their agreement with the following three statements: "(1) Investigate claims and statements made by the government, (2) Be an adversary of public officials by being constantly skeptical of their actions, and (3) Be an adversary of businesses by being constantly skeptical of their actions." Agreement with these statements tapped journalists' thoughts related to the idea of "watchdog" without risking that the concept was misunderstood or not understood at all.

Consequently, the design of comparative questionnaires requires input and feedback from native scholars who can verify how questions and theoretical concepts are understood in their respective countries. This also applies to answer categories, which often are developed in Western survey studies and may be understood differently in non-Western societies. Asians, for example, often avoid extremes in scales that offer extreme opposites and instead tend to choose the middle categories (Harzing 2006).

Overall, we believe that the time has come for more comparative studies of journalists that are based on representative samples and standardized questionnaires. To fund and coordinate such studies will be a challenge, but they will help us to better understand the persistent differences between journalists around the world and the causes and consequences of these differences.

More Research Links with Other Academic Disciplines

Another weakness of journalist survey studies is their relative isolation from other disciplines, such as sociology, political science, and psychology. This has encouraged descriptive research without theoretical models that could explain journalists' attitudes and behaviors across nations. As previously mentioned, theories borrowed from psychology could clarify how norms and values shape the work of professional journalists. Similarly, the vast number of studies on professionals such as doctors and lawyers, found mostly in sociology and organizational research, could lead to more sophisticated models that explain how journalists perceive and maintain their professionalism. Interesting parallels are found, for example, in studies that investigate attitudes of medical doctors toward patients who use medical Web sites to question their diagnoses (see, for example, Ballas 2001). Just as such patients challenge a physician's professional status by questioning his or her monopoly of specialized knowledge, citizen journalists challenge professional journalists by claiming to do the same work as they do.

Linking research on journalistic norms and values with research on cultural or religious values also promises new insights. Studies of Asian values in journalism (Masterton 1996; Xiaoge 2005), for example, have examined whether the media in countries such as Singapore and Malaysia reflect the frequent demands of their governments to act as nation-building partners. While such a normative view of the press might be politically driven, it seems important to probe whether specific sets of cultural values do in fact influence the work of journalists. For example, this might be the case in predominantly Muslim nations, where religion strongly influences all aspects of society. Such a focus on cultural values also would support research that avoids simple comparisons of journalists across nations—a strategy that has become less useful for analyzing an increasingly global media.

Given the interdisciplinary roots of media studies, the theoretical isolation of survey research on journalists is somewhat surprising. While it is understandable that media scholars rely mostly on methods and approaches with which they are familiar, research that taps the values, norms, and actions of journalists across nations must be more open to theories that can explain links between these concepts. We therefore recommend more interdisciplinary approaches in studies of global journalists.

More Comparative Research on Journalistic Practice

While research on journalistic norms and values provides fascinating insights into the minds of media workers, especially when done cross-nationally, we think the time has come for a broader research focus. As previously discussed, journalistic norms and values vary widely across nations and there is little indication this will change anytime soon. Clearly, the various social, political, and cultural factors that might explain these differences need more research. However, we now need to know whether and how these norms and values shape the *work* of the world's media practitioners. We therefore hope that future comparative studies will employ content analyses that test the potential impact of journalists' attitudes and beliefs on their work. An early example of such an approach is the Weaver and Wilhoit (1991) study that asked U.S. journalists in 1982 to provide researchers with examples of their best news stories. Assuming that such self-selected news stories might reflect the journalists' norms and values, Weaver and Wilhoit concluded that the media roles that journalists endorsed were present in similar proportions in the stories they submitted, but only those who clearly favored the interpretive role were more likely to actually write stories that reflected their views on the importance of this media role. They also found that even though U.S. journalists placed great value on the investigation of government claims, very few of them reported such stories as their best work.

In some ways, the current state of journalist survey studies compares with research on television violence conducted in the 1960s and early 1970s. Hundreds of descriptive studies documented and tracked the type and level of violence on TV, and many scholars speculated about its potential harm for children and young adults. By the early 1980s, empirical studies finally began testing the effects of TV violence on audiences and provided a more sophisticated view of how TV content might influence behavior. We believe studies of journalists are ready to take this additional step as well.

More Comparative Research on New Technologies and Changing Audiences

Technological changes in the newsroom have had profound effects on journalism practice in most nations. Journalists increasingly rely on the Internet to do their research and interviews. A rapid move to online publishing has forced especially older journalists to learn how to publish news stories across different media platforms. Finally, the way audiences receive news has become more interactive thanks to blogs and social media that allow immediate feedback and production of original content. Yet, most survey research on journalists has ignored these trends so far—and ignoring them any longer would risk making this type of research obsolete.

Studies on how new technologies affect journalistic practice could be easily combined with comparative research on journalistic norms and values. More studies are needed, for example, to analyze how journalists are affected by access to an almost unlimited number of competing news sources on the Internet. This question is especially relevant in international news reporting (see chapter 36). Research on how the pressures of multiple-platform reporting have affected the quality of work among online journalists is lacking as well, especially from a cross-national perspective.

The success of online journalism also has challenged the concept of "professional journalists" because more and more media workers have multiple employers and do not need permanent offices anymore. The loss of a permanent workplace has blurred the line between "professional" journalists who work from home for a media organization, and bloggers who also work from home but earn their income by running successful Web sites. An analysis of how such developments affect the self-perception of journalists from different nations promises to be an interesting and fascinating research topic.

More Comparative Research on the (Western) Crisis in Journalism

The final and most obvious deficiency in comparative survey research on journalists is the need for more studies on the potential effects of declining advertising revenues and shrinking audiences experienced by most Western media. While this "crisis" has not affected all Western media with the same severity, there is no doubt that budget cuts and staff reductions have affected journalists' daily work. It is also reasonable to assume that these cuts have influenced how journalists think about their profession, especially in terms of work environment, stress levels, quality of work, and overall job satisfaction.

Since the slumping economy has primarily affected Western media, it would be interesting to compare the perceptions of journalists in nations such as India, where media are booming, with journalists in countries such as the United States or Great Britain, where media are suffering. Because of different funding models, a comparison of journalists employed by private media organizations with those who work for large public broadcasters also would be interesting.

Overall, comparative survey research on journalists has only begun to investigate the various issues that determine how media operate worldwide. Journalists are fascinating research subjects and future survey studies will help us to better understand who they are, what they think about their profession, and how these perceptions influence their work. Undoubtedly, scholars who take a closer look at this profession will face high methodological hurdles and need an extra dose of patience and persistence. Yet journalists are crucial to any democratic society and must be the center of our attention no matter how elusive they might be.

Note

1. According to the Freedom House, the scores that reflect press freedom in each country are based on "23 methodology questions and 109 indicators divided into three broad categories: the legal environment, the political environment, and the economic environment. For each methodology question, a lower number of points is allotted for a more free situation, while a higher number of points is allotted for a less free environment. Each country is rated in these three categories, with the higher numbers indicating less freedom. A country's final score is based on the total of the three categories: A score of 0 to 30 places the country in the Free press group; 31 to 60 in the

Partly Free press group; and 61 to 100 in the Not Free press group." See Freedom of the Press 2010. Methodology. Retrieved from http://www.freedomhouse.org/template.cfm?page=350&ana_page=368&year=2010

References

Ballas, Marc (Mourad) S. 2001. The impact of the Internet on the healthcare industry: A close look at the doctor–patient relationship, the electronic medical record, and the medical billing process. *Einstein Quarterly Journal of Biology and Medicine* 18:79–83. Retrieved from http://www.einstein.yu.edu/uploadedFiles/EJBM/Impact_Internet_79-83.pdf

Beam, Randal A. 1990. Journalism professionalism as an organizational-level concept. *Journalism Monographs* 121:1–43.

Bowman, James. 1996. A pretense of professionalism. *New Criterion* 15(4):55–61.

Donsbach, Wolfgang. 1983. Journalists' conceptions of their audience. *Gazette* 32:19–36.

Gaziano, Cecilie, and Kristin McGrath. 1986. Measuring the concept of credibility. *Journalism Quarterly* 63:451–462.

Glasser, Theodore L. 1992. Professionalism and the derision of diversity: The case of the education of journalists. *Journal of Communication* 42(2):131–140.

Harzing, Anne-Wil. 2006. Response styles in cross-national survey research: A 26-country study. *International Journal of Cross Cultural Management* 6(2):243–266

Johnstone, John W. C., Edward J. Slawski, and William W. Bowman. 1976. *The news people.* Urbana: University of Illinois Press.

Koecher, Renate. 1986. Bloodhounds or missionaries: Role definitions of German and British journalists. *European Journal of Communication* 1:43–64.

Lawrence, Arthur. 1903. *Journalism as a profession.* London: Hodder & Stoughton.

Masterton, Murray. (Ed.). 1996. *Asian values in journalism.* Singapore: AMIC.

McLeod, Jack, and Searle Hawley Jr. 1964. Professionalization among newsmen. *Journalism Quarterly* 41:529–538, 577.

Splichal, Slavko, and Colin Sparks. 1994. *Journalists for the 21st century.* Norwood, NJ: Ablex.

Weaver, David H. (ed.). 1998. *The global journalist: News people around the world.* Cresskill, NJ: Hampton Press.

Weaver, David H., Randal A. Beam, Bonnie J. Brownlee, Paul S. Voakes, and G. Cleveland Wilhoit. 2007. *The American journalist in the 21st century: U.S. news people at the dawn of a new millennium.* Mahwah, NJ: Erlbaum.

Weaver, David H., and LeAnne Daniels. 1992. Public opinion on investigative reporting in the 1980s. *Journalism Quarterly* 69:146-155.

Weaver, David H., and G. Cleveland Wilhoit. 1986. *The American journalist: A portrait of U.S. news people and their work.* Bloomington: Indiana University Press.

Weaver, David H., and G. Cleveland Wilhoit. 1991. *The American journalist: A portrait of U.S. news people and their work.* 2nd ed. Bloomington: Indiana University Press.

Weaver, David H., and G. Cleveland Wilhoit. 1996. *The American journalist in the 1990s: U.S. news people at the end of an era.* Mahwah, NJ: Erlbaum.

Windahl, Swen, and Karl Erik Rosengren. 1978. Newsmen's professionalization: Some methodological problems. *Journalism Quarterly* 55:466–473.

Xiaoge, Xu. 2005. *Demystifying Asian values in journalism.* Singapore: Marshall Cavendish.

Zhu, Jian-Hua, David Weaver, Ven-hwei Lo, Chongshan Chen, and Wei Wu. 1997. Individual, organizational and societal influences on media role perceptions: A comparative study of journalists in China, Taiwan, and the United States. *Journalism & Mass Communication Quarterly* 74(1):84–96.

About the Authors

Erik Albæk is Professor at the Centre for Journalism, University of Southern Denmark. Professor Albæk has been visiting professor at MIT, Harvard University, Vilnius University (Lithuania), Potsdam University (Germany), and the University of Amsterdam. He has been chairman of the Danish Social Science Research Council and the Nordic Political Science Association. He has published articles in journals such as *Journalism & Mass Communication Quarterly, Journalism, Political Communication, Journal of Communication,* and *Party Politics.* Professor Albæk received his Ph.D. in political science from the University of Aarhus in 1988. Email: eri@sam.sdu.dk

Maria Anikina has been a Senior Lecturer, Faculty of Journalism, Moscow State University Lomonosov, Russia since 2007. Her teaching and research interests include theory of journalism and media sociology, mass consciousness and audience studies, competition of new and traditional media. She has published several book chapters and articles on Russian media and journalists. She received her Ph.D. from Moscow State University in 2006. Email: maria-anikina@yandex.ru

Jesus Arroyave is Associate Professor and Director of the School of Communication, Universidad del Norte, Barranquilla, Colombia. His teaching and research interests include media and journalism studies, communication for development and social change, and health communication. He has published book chapters and articles in journals such as *Investigación y Desarrollo, Revista Diálogos de la Comunicación,* and *Florida Communication Journal.* He has presented papers at research conferences in countries such as Germany, Sweden, Canada, Argentina, Puerto Rico, Cuba and the United States. Professor Arroyave received his Ph.D. in communication from the University of Miami in 2007 and his master's in communication and information studies from Rutgers University in 2002. Email: jarroyav@uninorte.edu.co

Marsha Barber is a Faculty Teaching Chair, and Professor in the School of Journalism at Ryerson University. Before that, Professor Barber was an award-winning documentary producer, and a senior producer for the Canadian Broadcasting Corporation. She trains journalists in Canada and internationally. Her research interests include election news coverage, gender representation in the media, journalistic values of newsroom leaders, and methods of effective teaching and training. She has published book chapters and research articles in journals such as the *Canadian Journal of Communication, Electronic News, International Journal of Learning, International Journal of Diversity, International Perspectives on Training and Learning* and a wide range of other publications. Email: m2barber@ryerson.ca

Marta Milena Barrios has been Professor in the School of Communications and Journalism, Universidad del Norte in Barranquilla, Colombia since 1996 and now is a doctoral candidate in social science. Before joining academia, she worked as a television reporter, press writer, and host of radio programs. Her research has been published in journals such as *Diálogos de la Comunicación, Razón y Palabra, Global Media Journal, Perspectivas de la Comunicación,* and *Investigación y Desarrollo.* She has participated in international conferences in Sweden, Puerto Rico, and the United States as well as being an international consultant. She received her master's degree in social development from Universidad del Norte and a master's in sciences de l'éducation from Université Paris XII. Email: mbarrios@uninorte.edu.co

Pedro Farias Batlle is a Professor of Journalism, Department of Journalism, University of Málaga, Spain. He received his Ph.D. in information science from the Universidad Complutense de Madrid, in 1996. He was a member of the Communication Group of the Spanish UNESCO Commission (1999–2005), Academic Secretary of UNESCO, Chair of Communication at the Universidad Complutense (1999–2003) and Deputy Director (2007) and Academic Secretary for Press Freedom of the UNESCO Chair at the Universidad de Málaga (2007 to the present). He is director of "Credibility of Information and Its Impact on the Public," Spanish Government National Research Project CSO2008-05125 (Department of Science and Innovation), and since 2005 has been the editor of Spain's *Informe Anual de la Profesión Periodística.* He has taught at the Universidad Complutense de Madrid and Universidad de Málaga, and been a visiting lecturer at a number of European universities. He is currently Vice President of Communication and International Projection at the Universidad de Málaga.

Randal A. Beam is Professor, Department of Communication, University of Washington. Professor Beam previously was on the faculty of the School of Journalism at Indiana University and the School of Journalism and Communication at the University of Oregon. His research focuses on journalists, professionalism, and social and economic influences on the news. He was a co-author of *The American Journalist in the 21st Century: U.S. News People at the Dawn of a New Millennium.* His research has appeared in *Journalism & Mass Communication Quarterly, Journalism Studies, Journalism Practice,* and the *Newspaper Research Journal.*

Rosa Berganza is a Professor, Department of Communication, University Rey Juan Carlos, Spain. Her teaching and research interests include communication theory, political communication, public opinion, and gender studies. She has published articles in journals such as *European Journal of Communication, Journal of Political Marketing,* as well as *Journalism & Mass Communication Quarterly.* She received her Ph.D. in mass communication from the University of Navarra, Spain in 1998. Email: rosa.berganza@urjc.es

Marc-François Bernier is Professor, Department of Communication, University of Ottawa (Canada), where he holds the Chair of Research in Journalism Ethics. Before joining UO in 2000, Professor Bernier was a professional political reporter, mainly in Québec City newspapers. His teaching and research interests include the ethical and sociological aspects of journalism. He has published books, book chapters, and articles in journals such as *Communication, Cahiers du Journalisme, Canadian Journal of Communication, and Canadian Journal of Political Science.* He is frequently called upon as an expert witness in civil defamation cases. Professor Bernier received his Ph.D. in political science from Université Laval in 1998. Email: mbernier@uottawa.ca

Heinz Bonfadelli is Professor for Mass Communication, Institute of Mass Communication and Media Research, University of Zurich. His research interests are uses and effects of mass communication, journalism research, science, and environmental communication. Email: h.bonfadelli@ipmz.uzh.ch

Peter Bro, Ph.D, is Professor, Head of Studies, and Director at the Center for Journalism, Department of Political Science, University of Southern Denmark. He has previously worked as press secretary in the Danish Parliament and as communication advisor in a PR-consultancy firm before he started his research career. He writes primarily about journalism, communication, politics, and democracy. His work has appeared in journals such as *Journalism Studies; Journalism Theory, Practice and Criticism;* and *Journalism Practice.*

Bonnie J. Brownlee is Associate Professor of Journalism at Indiana University. She has been on the faculty since 1981 and served as the Associate Dean for Undergraduate Studies between 2000 and 2009. She has long been involved with faculty governance issues and committees at IU and serves ACEJMC as a member of accreditation teams. She is currently a member of AEJMC's Teaching Committee and a member of *Journalism Educator*'s editorial advisory board. Her teaching interests include international communication and journalism ethics. She is co-author (with Dave Weaver, Cleve Wilhoit, Randy Beam, and Paul Voakes) of *The American Journalist in the 21st Century.* She holds A.B. and A.M. degrees from Indiana University and a Ph.D. from the University of Wisconsin-Madison. Email: brownlee@indiana.edu

Incilay Cangöz, Ph.D, is an Associate Professor, Department of Journalism, Anadolu University, Turkey, where she is also Director of the Women's Studies Center. She has been a visiting researcher at New York University. Her teaching and research interests include news sociology, mass communication theories, cultural studies, gender and media, children rights, and the media in Turkey. She received her Ph.D. from Anadolu University in 1999. Email: icangoz@anadolu.edu.tr

Joseph M. Chan is Professor of Journalism and Communication, School of Journalism and Communication, the Chinese University of Hong Kong, where he formerly served as chairman. His research interests lie at the intersection of international communication, political communication, and journalism studies. His publications have appeared in the *Journal of Communication, Communication Research, China Quarterly, Journalism and Mass Communication Quarterly,* among other journals and books. He was awarded the Changjiang Chair Professorship by the Ministry of Education, PRC, for which he was affiliated with Fudan University. He serves on the editorial boards of various international journals, and he was the founding chief editor of the Chinese Journal, *Communication & Society.*

Mikhail F. Chernysh graduated from the Moscow Linguistic University in 1977, and enrolled in a graduate course at the Institute of Sociology, Soviet Academy of Sciences in 1981. In 1985 he completed the graduate course and began work as a junior researcher at the same Institute. Currently he is Doctor of Sociology and Head of Department, Institute of Sociology of the Russian Academy of Sciences, and Chair at the State University of Humanities. He is also an expert and member of the Scientific Council of the Department of Sociology at the Higher School of Economics in Moscow. His main research interests are inequality and media in contemporary Russian society. He is author of 123 publications including two monographs *Social Institutions and Mobility in Contemporary Russia* (2005), and *Development of the Managerial Class in Russian Society* (2000). Email: mfche@yandex.ru

Jihyang Choi is a doctoral student in the School of Journalism at Indiana University. She was a journalist at the *Hankookilbo*, a national newspaper in Seoul, Korea before starting a doctoral program. She holds a bachelor's degree in history from Yonsei University, Seoul, Korea and a master's degree in journalism from Indiana University. Email: choi20@umail.iu.edu

Mihai Coman is the founding Dean of the School of Journalism and Mass Communication Studies at the University of Bucharest, Romania. He is the author of *Pour une Anthropologie des Medias* (2003) and co-editor of *Media Anthropology* (2005). He has also published and edited several books on mythology and mass media anthropology, as well as numerous articles in journals and edited volumes dedicated to the transformations in the mass media in post-communist countries. He graduated from the University of Bucharest and holds a Ph.D. in letters (1985). Email: mcoman53@yahoo.com

Jeroen De Keyser is a senior researcher in the Department of Communication Sciences, Ghent University (Belgium), where he is also a member of the Center for Journalism Studies. He received his Ph.D. in communication studies in early 2012. His research interests include the impact of emerging Internet technologies upon news content, as well as the related changing relationship between journalists and their publics. He has published several book chapters and articles in *Journalism Studies* and *First Monday*. Email: Jeroen.DeKeyser@UGent.be

Claes H. de Vreese is Professor and Chair of Political Communication and Scientific Director of The Amsterdam School of Communications Research (ASCoR), Department of Communication Science, University of Amsterdam. He is also Adjunct Professor of Political Science and Journalism, University of Southern Denmark. He has published more than 60 articles in international peer-reviewed journals, including *Communication Research*, *Journalism Studies*, *Political Communication*, *Journal of Communication*, *International Journal of Public Opinion Research*, *Public Opinion Quarterly*, *Scandinavian Political Studies*, *European Journal of Communication*, *West European Politics*, *EU Politics*, *Journalism & Mass Communication Quarterly*, *Mass Communication & Society*, and *European Journal of Political Research*. Email: c.h.devreese@uva.nl

Suzana Žilič Fišer is a Senior Lecturer at the Institute of Media Communication, University of Maribor. She holds a master's degree in political sciences from the Central European University, Budapest and a Ph.D. from the University of Ljubljana. Her research focuses on broadcasting, particularly public service broadcasting, public interest in media, social responsibility in media, and political communication in media. Professor Fišer is author of the book *Broadcasting Management, Public Service Broadcasting on the Market* (2007) and has published in a variety of international journals. She spent 10 years in the media industry as a journalist, executive producer, and chief editor. Between 2006 and 2008, she was president of the Commission on Media Pluralism that was established by the Ministry of Culture of the Republic of Slovenia. In 2009, she was a member of an expert commission for organizing media regulation in Slovenia. Email: suzanazf@uni-mb.si

Mitsuru Fukuda is Professor of Social Psychology, Graduate School of Journalism and Media and the Institute of Journalism and Media Studies, Nihon University, Tokyo, Japan. Professor Fukuda received his master's degree from the Graduate School of Sociology, University of Tokyo. His research interests include media effects on news coverage, media and terrorism, risk communication and intelligence studies. Professor Fukuda was a visiting scholar at the Arnold Saltzman

Institute of War and Peace Studies at Columbia University (2008–2010). He was an adjunct lecturer at Keio University, Sophia University, and Meiji University. He has published the book *Media to Terorizumu* (*Media and Terrorism*, Tokyo: Shincho Sha). Email: fukuda@law.nihon-u.ac.jp

Cherian George (Ph.D. from Stanford, 2003) is Associate Professor at Wee Kim Wee School of Communication & Information, Nanyang Technological University, Singapore and Adjunct Senior Research Fellow at the Institute of Policy Studies. He researches journalism and politics, including censorship and alternative media. He is the author of *Contentious Journalism and the Internet: Towards Democratic Discourse in Malaysia and Singapore* (2006), and *Singapore: The Air-Conditioned Nation* (2000). He runs a website on Singapore journalism issues (www.journalism.sg). Before joining academia, he was a journalist with *The Straits Times*. Website: http://www.cheriangeorge/net

Jeremy Ginges is an Associate Professor of Psychology and Director of the Laboratory of Social and Political Psychology at the New School for Social Research in New York City. He received his Ph.D. in psychology from Tel Aviv University in 2004. Prior to his current position he was on faculty in the Research Center for Group Dynamics, University of Michigan (2003–2006) and held a field research fellowship at the Solomon Asch Center for Study of Ethnopolitical Conflict, University of Pennsylvania (2001–2002).His work explores the role played by moral reasoning in binding people together to form meaningful social groups and the way moral reasoning, particularly over sacred values, influences the trajectory of cultural, political, and violent conflicts. Email: gingesj@newschool.edu

Manimaran Govindasamy is an editor with *The Malaysian Insider*, an independent news portal. He earned his doctoral degree in communication from Universiti Putra Malaysia. He has been in the media sector since 1991. For the past two decades, he served at three main media houses in Malaysia, both newspaper and online news portals, where he covered various political events, and social and economic issues. He also applies his vast journalism experience in the academic field. Email: gmani_maran@yahoo.com

Basyouni Ibrahim Hamada is Professor of Mass Communication and Public Opinion, Cairo University, Egypt. He is the Secretary General of the Global Communication Research Association and Chair of the Islam & Media Working Group, International Association of Media and Communication Research. He is the author of several books and articles published in both Arabic and English. His research interests include political communication, new communication technologies, development communication, media laws and ethics, media regulation, and international communication. Email: basyouni_hamada@yahoo.com

Thomas Hanitzsch is Professor of Communication, University of Munich, Germany. A former journalist, his teaching and research focuses on global journalism cultures, crisis and war communication, tabloid and celebrity news, as well as comparative methodology. He was the founding Chair of the Journalism Studies Division of the International Communication Association and is the co-editor of the *Handbook of Journalism Studies* (2009) and the *Handbook of Comparative Communication Research* (2012). He received his doctoral degree in communication and media studies from the Ilmenau University of Technology, Germany in 2004. Email: hanitzsch@ifkw.lmu.de

Mark Hanna is a Senior Lecturer in Sheffield University's Department of Journalism Studies. He joined it in 1996 after 18 years in journalism, mostly as a crime or investigations reporter. His research interests include media ethics and court reporting. He has published articles in *Journalism & Mass Communication Educator, European Journal of Communication,* and *Journalism Practice.* He co-authored *Key Concepts in Journalism Studies* (Sage, 2005), and *McNae's Essential Law for Journalists* (Oxford University Press, 2009). He chairs the media law examinations board of the National Council for the Training of Journalists. He graduated from Oxford University in 1978. E-mail: M.Hanna@sheffield.ac.uk

Folker Hanusch is Lecturer in Journalism, School of Communication, University of the Sunshine Coast, Australia. His main teaching and research interests include news representations of death and dying, comparative journalism practices, and lifestyle journalism. He is currently co-authoring a book examining journalism across cultures, and has published articles in journals such as *International Communication Gazette, Journalism & Mass Communication Quarterly*, and *Journalism Studies.* He received his Ph.D. in journalism from the University of Queensland in 2006. Email: fhanusch@usc.edu.au

Xiaoming Hao (Ph.D. from Missouri, 1993), a former journalist with China's Xinhua News Agency, is Professor at the Wee Kim Wee School of Communication & Information, Nanyang Technological University of Singapore. His research interests include international communication, comparative media systems, social impact of new communication technologies, audience studies and media effects. His publications have appeared in *Asian Journal of Communication, Communication Law and Policy, Gazette, Intercultural Communication Studies, Journal of Broadcasting & Electronic Media, Journal of Communication, Journalism and Mass Communication Educator, Journalism and Mass Communication Quarterly, Journal of Popular Film and Television, The Information Society* and *The Public* among others.

Ari Heinonen, Ph.D., is Senior Lecturer, Journalism, Department of Journalism and Mass Communication, University of Tampere, Finland. He is also Docent of Journalism both at the University of Tampere and University of Jyväskylä. Heinonen's teaching and research interests include the changing journalistic profession, journalism and new media, and journalism ethics. He has directed and participated in several national and international research projects on the changing nature of journalism in the Age of the Net. For several years he was the director of Tampere Journalism Research and Development Centre.

Liesbeth Hermans is Assistant Professor, Department of Communication Science, Radboud University, Nijmegen. Her field of research is journalism studies and political communication. Her interests in journalism include the influence of digitization on the news process, role perceptions of journalists, journalistic routines and conditions that change through new technology, and the changing relationship with the audience. She is coordinator of the project, "Journalists in the Digital Age," a longitudinal study of trends in Dutch journalism. Email: L.Hermans@maw.ru.nl

Heloiza Golbspan Herscovitz is Associate Professor, Journalism Department, California State University, Long Beach. Before joining CSULB in 2006, she taught at Florida International University in Miami, where she coordinated its Spanish-Language master's in Investigative Journalism program, and at two other Brazilian universities, UFSC and PUC-RS. A veteran Brazilian journalist with extensive experience as a reporter and editor for several publications in her birth country, such as the daily newspaper *Estado de S. Paulo and Nova* and Cosmopolitan's Portuguese version, she was a Fulbright Scholar at the University of Florida, where she earned her Ph.D. in mass communications in 2000. Her research interests include newsroom culture, news values, media roles, professional routines, global news media, and research methods. She has published several academic articles and book chapters on these topics. Email: heloiza.hersovitz@csulb.edu

Dedy N. Hidayat was Professor at the Graduate Program, Communication Department, University of Indonesia, Jakarta. He graduated from the College of Communications, University of Wisconsin, Madison, where he taught the political-economy of communication, media economics, and social statistics. Among his last publications is "Community Radio in Indonesia: A Reinvention of Democratic Communication" in *Javnost: Journal of the European Institute for Communication and Culture*. Vol.15, No.3 (2008), which is co-authored with Ed Hollander and Leen d'Haenens. Professor Hidayat died unexpectedly in 2010 and will be missed by his friends.

James Hollings fell in love with newspapers at the age of nine when delivering them on his Raleigh 20 in the hills around Wellington, New Zealand. After 18 years as a journalist for newspapers and radio, and a stint making film documentaries, he now teaches journalism at Massey University, still in Wellington. He has published on his experiences covering the Asian Tsunami in 2004, on media and children, and on surveys of New Zealand journalists. He recently completed a Ph.D. in communication on the decision-making process of reluctant and vulnerable witnesses and whistleblowers.

Beate Josephi coordinates the master's courses in the School of Communications and Arts, Edith Cowan University, Perth, Western Australia. Her research interests are in journalism, journalism education, and political communication. She is the editor of *Journalism Education in Countries with Limited Media Freedom* (2010) and has contributed book chapters to international volumes on journalism. Her articles have appeared in journals such as *International Communication Gazette*, the *Australian Journalism* Review, and *Communications: The European Journal for Communication Research*. Email: b.josephi@ecu.edu.au

Jyrki Jyrkiäinen has been Senior Lecturer, Department of Journalism and Mass Communication, University of Tampere, Finland since 1980. His teaching and research interests include media institutions and structures. He received his Ph.D. at the University of Tampere in 1994 with a study of concentration of newspapers. He was head of the department between 1998 and 2004. He conducted sections on the media economics, content, and diversity project of the Academy of Finland 1999–2002). He has published articles and book chapters in academic journals, course books, statistical publications of Statistics Finland, and in the Nordic Media Trends series published by Nordicom. He was the national correspondent in the EU Study on *Indicators for Media Pluralism in the Member States: Towards a Risk-based Approach*. He has recently published a survey on Finnish journalists. Email: jyrki.jyrkiainen@uta.fi

Christopher D. Karadjov is Assistant Professor, Department of Journalism and Mass Communication, California State University, Long Beach, USA. He is interested in researching consequences of the third-person effect, agenda-setting, framing, priming, as well as issues in international communication, and journalistic values and practices. He has published articles on attitudes of journalists and public relations practitioners, and currently studies Eastern European online discussion forums and blogs. He received his Ph.D. in mass communication from the University of Florida in 2007. Email: ckaradjo@csulb.edu

Guido Keel is Lecturer and Managing Director, Institute of Applied Media Studies (IAM), Zurich University of Applied Sciences. Before joining IAM, Keel worked as a journalist and PR consultant for various companies and agencies in Switzerland. His teaching and research interests include journalism research, online communications, and media quality management. Guido Keel received his Ph.D. in communication science from the University of Zurich. Email: guido.keel@zhaw.ch

Sung Tae Kim is Associate Professor and former Associate Dean, School of Media and Communication, Korea University. Before joining Korea University, he was a professor in the Department of Communication, DePaul University, Chicago, USA. His current research interests include the political impact of the Internet, online agenda-rippling, and new media industrial change. He teaches courses on political communication, Internet communication, and digital society. He has published about 50 research articles in academic journals, such as *Journalism & Mass Communication Quarterly, International Communication Gazette, New Media & Society*, and *Newspaper Research Journal*. He is now a recognized name in *Who's Who in Social Sciences Academia*. He received his Ph.D. in mass communication from the School of Journalism, Indiana University (Bloomington) in 2001. Email: sutkim@korea.ac.kr

Mohamed Kirat (Ph.D. Indiana University, 1987) is Professor, College of Communication, University of Sharjah, United Arab Emirates. His primary areas of research are the practice of public relations in the Arab world, media globalization and its impact on developing countries, the sociology of the communicators, press government relationships, and media ethics. He is the author of *The Communicators: A Portrait of Algerian Journalists and Their Work* (O.P.U., 1993), *Media and Society: Stakes and Challenges* (2001), *Contemporary Issues in Mass Media* (2006), *Public Relations in the United Arab Emirates: The Status of the Profession and the Practitioners' Characteristics* (2006), and *Construction of Social Consciousness: The Role of the Mass Media in Constructing Reality and Manufacturing Public Opinion* (2007). Professor Kirat has published over 50 journal articles about international communication, journalism, and public relations. Email: mokirat@sharjah.ac.ae

Peter Lah (Ph.D. in Communication Studies, Northwestern University, 2004) is Assistant Professor, Faculty of Media, Ljubljana, Slovenia. Between 2004 and 2007 he taught courses in interpersonal communication, mass media, communication ethics, and research methods at St. Louis University. His research interests include ethics of journalism and media regulation. Between 2006 and 2008 he was member of the Expert Commission on Media Pluralism that was established by the Ministry of Culture of the Republic of Slovenia. Since graduate school he has been a regular contributor to several newspapers in Slovenia, including the business daily *Finance* and the Catholic weekly *Družina*.

Geoff Lealand grew up with the smells and noise of the newspaper industry, with his father operating a Cossar Flat-Bed newspaper press for *The Hawera Star*. Educated in New Zealand and the United States, he now views the news media from the other side of the fence, through his teaching, research, and writing, in Screen and Media Studies at the University of Waikato, New Zealand. Interests include children and media, media education, national cinema, contemporary music, blogging, and television studies, and he has published extensively on these subjects in New Zealand and overseas journals.

Francis L. F. Lee (Ph.D., Stanford University, 2003) is Associate Professor, School of Journalism and Communication, Chinese University of Hong Kong. His research interests cover journalism, political communication, public opinion studies, and media economics. His work on journalism and politics has appeared in such journals as *Journalism & Mass Communication Quarterly, International Journal of Press/Politics, International Journal of Public Opinion Research, Communication Research, New Media & Society*, and the *China Quarterly*, among others. He co-edited the book *Media and Politics in Post-handover Hong Kong* (2008), and is currently working on a book about the relationship between the news media and the pro-democracy protest movement in Hong Kong since 2003.

Ven-hwei Lo is Professor, School of Journalism, Chinese University of Hong Kong. Before joining the Chinese University, he taught at the National Chengchi University, Taipei, Taiwan for 24 years. He holds a bachelor's degree in journalism from the National Chengchi University, a master's degree in journalism from the University of Oregon, and a Ph.D. in journalism and mass communication from the University of Missouri-Columbia. His research interests include news media performance and the effects of mass media. He is the author of seven books and his recent publications have appeared in the *Asian Journal of Communication, Communication Research, Journalism and Mass Communication Quarterly, Journal of Broadcasting & Electronic Media, International Journal of Public Opinion Research, Media Psychology, The Chinese Journal of Communication, The Harvard International Journal of Press/Public, Studies in Media & Information Literacy Education*, and *Mass Communication Research*. E-mail: loven@cuhk.edu.hk

Maja Malik is Assistant Professor, Institute of Communication Science, University of Muenster, Germany. From 2003 to 2006 she worked as research associate in the Journalism Department of Hamburg University. Her teaching and research focus is on media occupations and professions, the coverage of social issues, media journalism and self-criticism, journalism theories, and theories of public relations. She has published books and book chapters on journalism in Germany, on media criticism, and survey methods in journalism research. Maja Malik received her doctorate in communication science from the University of Muenster in 2003. Email: maja.malik@uni-muenster.de

Mirko Marr is head of methodology and data integration at the Corporation for Media Research in Berne, Switzerland. He graduated from the University of Leipzig (Germany) and earned his Ph.D. in communication science at the University of Zurich (Switzerland), where he later worked as an Assistant Professor at the Institute for Mass Communication and Media Research. Email: mirko.marr@mediapulse.ch

Jason Martin is an Assistant Professor of Journalism, College of Communication, DePaul University. His teaching and research interests include political communication during election campaigns, media effects on civic participation, and issues of media law regarding public affairs journalism. He has published articles in journals such as *Communication Law & Policy, Journal of Media Law & Ethics*, and *Newspaper Research Journal*. Professor Martin received his Ph.D. in Mass Communications from Indiana University. Email: jam15@indiana.edu

Aralynn Abare McMane is Executive Director for Young Readership Development at the World Association of Newspapers and News Publishers (France and Germany) and a member of the Advisory Board of the European Journalism Centre. She has taught at Indiana University and at the University of South Carolina in the United States, and at the Centre de Formation des Journalists (France) and, as a Knight International Press Fellow, at the American University of Bulgaria. She has published several articles in journals and book chapters on French media and journalists and worked as a journalist in the United States and France. She received her Ph.D. in mass communications from Indiana University in 1989. Email: aralynn.mcmane@wan-ifra.org

Claudia Mellado is Associate Professor, School of Journalism, University of Santiago, Chile. Before joining USACH in 2010, she taught at the University of Concepcion in the same country. She received her doctoral degree in communication from the Pontifical Pontificia University of Salamanca, Spain in 2004. During 2007–2008, she did her postdoctoral work at the School of Journalism, Indiana University. Her research focuses on the study of Latin American journalism, professional cultures, journalistic practices, journalism education, and comparative studies. She has led and collaborated in important journalism research projects at national and international levels, such as the Comparative Study of Chilean Journalists and JMC Educators, Worlds of Journalism, and the Global Report on the Status of Women in the News Media. Email: claudia.mellado@usach.cl

Oren Meyers is a Senior Lecturer, Department of Communication, University of Haifa. Meyers received his Ph.D. from the Annenberg School for Communication, University of Pennsylvania in 2004. His teaching and research interests include journalistic values and practices, collective memory and popular culture. He has published articles in journals such as *Journal of Communication*, *Journalism*, *Journalism Studies*, *Media, Culture & Society*, and *The Journal of Popular Culture*. Email: omeyers@com.haifa.ac.il

Sonia Virginia Moreira is Associate Professor, Social Communication Faculty, Rio de Janeiro State University, Brazil. Her research focuses on the broadcasting industry in Brazil, journalism, and regional and international communication. She is the author of several articles and book chapters on journalism and communication-related topics and served as president of the Brazilian Society for Interdisciplinary Studies in Communication. She holds a doctoral degree in communication sciences from the University of São Paulo. Email: soniavm@gmail.com

Peter G. Mwesige is Executive Director of the African Centre for Media Excellence in Kampala, Uganda. He was previously in charge of newsroom training in East Africa at Nation Media Group, the region's biggest multimedia company. A former Executive Editor of Monitor Publications and Political Editor of *The New Vision* newspaper in Kampala, he also served as Head of the Mass Communication Department, Makerere University, where he was a senior lecturer. He received his doctoral degree in mass communications from Indiana University, Bloomington in 2004. Email: mwesige@acme-ug.org

Dani Vardiansyah Noor is Executive Development Program Director, Esa Unggul University, Jakarta, Indonesia. He served as Dean of Faculty of Communication at the same university from 2000 to 2008. His teaching and research interests include media effects on political attitudes and public opinion formation. He has published several books in Bahasa Indonesia, including *Introduc-*

tion to Communication (2004) and *Philosophy of Communication* (2005). Email: dani.vardiansyah@esaunggul.ac.id

Lars W. Nord is Professor and Chair of Political Communication and he is also Director of the Centre for Political Communication Research, Mid Sweden University. His research interests include political journalism, media policy, and political communication. He has published several books, book chapters, and articles in journals such as *The International Journal of Press/Politics, Journalism, European Journal of Communication* and *Media, Culture & Society*. Professor Nord received his Ph.D. in Journalism from Stockholm University in 2001. Email: lars.nord@miun.se

Jakub Nowak, Ph.D., is a Lecturer, Journalism Department, Faculty of Political Science, Maria Curie-Skłodowska University, Lublin, Poland. His scientific interests include: modern media systems, communication theory, and political communication. E-mail: nowakkuba@gazeta.pl

Shinji Oi is Professor of Journalism, Graduate School of Journalism and Media and the Institute of Journalism & Media Studies (IJ&MS), Nihon University, Tokyo, Japan. Professor Oi was President of the Japan Society for Studies in Journalism and Mass Communication (2007–2009), and also trustee of the Newspaper Foundation for Education & Culture (2008–2010), operating NEWSPARK (the Japan Newspaper Museum). His teaching and research interests include normative theory of journalism, journalism history, and the principle of journalistic objectivity. He has published a number of book chapters and articles in academic journals, including *Journalism wo Manabu Hito no tameni (An Introduction to Journalism Studies,* Kyoto: Sekai Shiso Sha), edited by Shinji Oi et al., "Nihon no Journalist Zo" (The Profile of the Japanese Journalist), *Asahi Soken Report* 202 (2007), and "Hikaku Journalism Gaku no Shiza" (An Introduction to Comparative Journalism Studies), *Journalism & Media,* 2 (2009). Email: shinoi@law.nihon-u.ac.jp

Szymon Ossowski, Ph.D., is Assistant Professor, Faculty of Political Science and Journalism, Adam Mickiewicz University, Poznan, Poland. His research interests include ethics in politics, theory of liberal democracy, as well as public relations, political marketing, mass media, and e-governance. He has published a book and almost 30 book chapters and journal articles. Since 2003 he has been serving as an editorial assistant to the Central European Political Studies published by the Faculty of Political Science and Journalism at the Adam Mickiewicz University in Poznan. E-mail: szymon.ossowski@amu.edu.pl

Svetlana Pasti (Juskevits) is a postdoctoral researcher at the University of Tampere. She graduated from Leningrad State University in journalism and has worked as a journalist and editor at Murmansk Radio. She earned her doctoral degree in social sciences at the University of Tampere in 2007. She has been a researcher in various projects of the Academy of Finland, the Finnish Ministry of Education, and the European Union related to media and journalism in Russia and Central Europe. Her research and teaching interests focus on post-Soviet changes in journalism and the professional culture of journalists as well as political traditions in Russia. She has authored the books *A Russian Journalist in a Context of Change: Media of St Petersburg* (2004) and *The Changing Profession of a Journalist in Russia* (2007). In addition, she has written several book chapters and published articles in the *European Journal of Communication* and *Nordicom Review*. Email: svetlana.pasti@uta.fi

Steve Paulussen, Ph.D., is Lecturer in Journalism and New Media at the University of Antwerp and the Erasmus University College Brussels. He is also Senior Researcher at the IBBT research group for Media & ICT (MICT), Ghent University (Belgium), where he is involved in different projects that relate to issues of media production and media use in a convergence culture. Since 2006, he has also been a member of the Center for Journalism Studies. Most of his publications focus on different aspects of online journalism, participatory journalism, and newsroom convergence. He is co-author of the book, *Participatory Journalism: Guarding Open Gates at Online Newspapers* (2011). Email: steve.paulussen@ugent.be

Lawrence Pintak is Founding Dean of The Edward R. Murrow College of Communication, Washington State University. He is a veteran of more than 30 years in journalism and the media business on four continents who now writes and lectures on America's relationship with the Muslim world, the role of the media in shaping global perceptions and government policy, and the future of journalism in a digital/globalized world. Prior to WSU, Pintak served as director of the Kamal Adham Center for Journalism Training and Research at The American University in Cairo. A former CBS News Middle East correspondent, Pintak has reported for many of the world's leading news organizations. His books include *The New Arab Journalist* (I.B. Tauris, 2010); *Reflections in a Bloodshot Lens: America, Islam & the War of Ideas* (2006); *Seeds of Hate* (2003); and *Beirut Outtakes* (1988). He holds a Ph.D. in Islamic Studies from the University of Wales.

Patrick Lee Plaisance is Associate Professor, Department of Journalism and Technical Communication, Colorado State University, USA. A former journalist, he teaches media ethics, reporting, and communication theory. His research focuses on journalistic values, newsroom socialization, media ethics theory, and moral psychology. He is the author of *Media Ethics: Key Principles for Responsible Practice* (2008) and has published several book chapters as well as articles in journals including *Communication Theory, Journalism & Mass Communication Quarterly, Journal of Mass Media Ethics,* and *Journalism Studies*. He received his Ph.D. from Syracuse University in 2002. Email: Patrick.Plaisance@ColoState.EDU

Alexander Pleijter is Assistant Professor, Center of Journalism Studies, University of Groningen. Previously he worked in the Department of Journalism and New Media, Leiden University and the Department of Communication Science, Radboud University, Nijmegen. His research interests include the adoption of new technologies by journalists, changing journalistic norms and values, online journalism, blogging, and news making routines. Pleijter wrote his dissertation on *Types and Logic of Qualitative Content Analysis in Communication Research* and received his Ph.D. in 2006 from Radboud University, Nijmegen. Email: a.pleijter@gmail.com.

Lidia Pokrzycka, Ph.D., is a Lecturer, Journalism Department, Faculty of Political Science, Maria Curie-Skłodowska University, Lublin, Poland. She is a certificated journalist (post-graduate studies at Warsaw University) and a scholar who specializes in local journalism. She has published four books and 100 articles about local media and situations of Polish journalists. She received a Ph.D. in mass communication from the Maria Curie-Sklodowska University in 2004, e-mail: lpokrzyc@wp.pl

Karin Raeymaeckers is Professor, Department of Communication Sciences, Ghent University (Belgium). She is Director of the Center for Journalism Studies and a member of the Euromedia

Research Group. Her teaching and research interests include media structures and media policy, journalism studies and political communication. She has published books on the development of the media landscape in Belgium and chapters in books on media policy and journalism studies. She has also published several articles in journals such as *Journalism Studies, Journalism Practice, European Journal of Communication*, and *International Communication Gazette*. Email: Karin.Raeymaeckers@ UGent.be

Sony Jalarajan Raj, Ph.D., is a Lecturer in Journalism, School of Arts and Social Sciences, Monash University. Before becoming a Lecturer, he worked as a journalist for NDTV, Doordarshan, Asianet News, All India Radio, and Hindu Business Line. His research interests include communicative rationality, information flow, digital divides, and the News Media influences on the public sphere. In 2008, he was a Thomson Foundation (UK) Fellow in Television Studies with the Commonwealth Broadcasting Association. He has lectured at Mahatma Gandhi University, Kannur University, University of Kerala, and Curtin University of Technology. He has published research articles in *Journal of Communication Studies, Journal of Science Communication*, and *Mass Communicator*. Email: sonyjraj@gmail.com

Zvi Reich is a Lecturer, Department of Communication Studies, Ben Gurion University of the Negev, Israel. A former newspaper editor, his teaching and research interests include journalism studies, news sources, news practices, journalism and epistemology, journalism and authorship, and the use of communication technologies among journalists. He is the author of "Sourcing the News" and has published articles in journals such as *Journalism & Mass Communication Quarterly, Journalism Studies,* and *Journalism: Theory, Practice & Criticism.* He received his Ph.D. in communication and political science from the Hebrew University in 2003. Email: zreich@bgu.ac.il

Ian Richards is Professor of Journalism, University of South Australia, Adelaide, Australia. His research interests include journalism and communication ethics and he has published many book chapters and journal articles in this field. He is the author of *Quagmires and Quandaries: Exploring Journalism Ethics* (2005) and since 2003 has been editor of *Australian Journalism Review,* Australia's leading refereed journal in the academic field of journalism. A former newspaper journalist, he has worked and studied in Australia and the United Kingdom. Email ian.richards@unisa.edu.au

Francisco Javier Paniagua Rojano holds a graduate degree (1996) and doctorate (2004) in journalism from the Universidad de Málaga, where he has taught business and institutional communication since 2003. He is the Deputy Director of R&D+i Project "Critical Analysis of the Media System: Credibility and Impact on the Public," Department of Science and Innovation, and since 2005 has been the editing co-ordinator of the *Informe Anual de la Profesión Periodística,* published by the APM. He has been an invited lecturer at the Department of Political Communication of the Instituto Universitario Ortega y Gasset in Madrid. His key works include his book, *Comunicación Política y Elecciones: Nuevas Prácticas en el Escenario Español* (2004). He is currently Director of Communications at the Unversidad Internacional de Andalucia, Spain.

Sergio Roses is a researcher in the Department of Journalism, University of Málaga, Spain. His research is focused on studies of journalists and on trust in news media. Dr. Roses has been involved in research projects funded by the Spanish government concerning trust in media, and also by private institutions including the Madrid Press Association (APM). Since 2006, he has been a co-author of the Spanish *Informe Anual de la Profesión Periodística* [Journalist Profession Annual Reports]. Email: sergioroses@uma.es

Shinsuke Sako is Associate Professor of Sociology and Media Studies, Department of Journalism and the Institute of Journalism & Media Studies (IJ&MS), Nihon University, Tokyo, Japan. His teaching and research interests include media discourse analysis, journalistic fields, the relationship between ICT and surveillance society, and the theory of governance of social and communication spaces. He has published book chapters in *Television Polyphony* (Kyoto: Sekai Shiso Sha), edited by Mamoru Ito and Mafumi Fujita, in *Kukan Kanri Shakai* (*Governance of Social Spaces*, Tokyo: Shinyo Sha), edited by Kiyoshi Abe and Hiroshi Narumi, in *Media no Henbo to Mirai* (*The Transformation and Future of the Media*) (Tokyo: Yachiyo Shuppan), edited by Shinji Oi and the Department of Journalism at Nihon University. Email: sakou@law.nihon-u.ac.jp

Karen Sanders is Professor of Communication, CEU San Pablo University (Madrid) and Chair of its Department of Advertising and Institutional Communication. She is also visiting professor at IESE Business School. She is a specialist in political communication and ethics and journalism, publishing *Ethics and Journalism* (Sage, 2003) and *Communicating Politics in the 21st Century* (Palgrave Macmillan, 2009) as well as numerous articles and chapters. In 2002 she co-founded the Institute of Communication Ethics. Together with other colleagues in Spain, in 2006 she launched the Association of Political Communication (ACOP). She previously taught at the University of Sheffield's Department of Journalism Studies. Email: kbfsanders@gmail.com

Armin Scholl is Professor, Institute for Communication Science, Münster, Germany (since 1998). From 1994 to 1998 he worked as Assistant Professor at the Free University of Berlin. In his dissertation (1991) he combined methodological and epistemological aspects of surveys. His research and teaching focus is on communication theory, journalism research, and empirical methods. In 1993 (together with Siegfried Weischenberg and Martin Löffelholz) and in 2005 (together with Siegfried Weischenberg and Maja Malik) he conducted two representative surveys on "Journalists in Germany." He has published several articles and book chapters on theoretical and methodological aspects (*Journalism Studies, Constructivist Foundations, Communications*) and on empirical results in journalism research (*Web Journal of Mass Communication Research, Global Journalist,* edited by David Weaver). Email: scholl@uni-muenster.de

Josef Seethaler works as a Senior Scientist at the Commission for Comparative Media and Communication Studies (CMC), Austrian Academy of Sciences. He also lectures at the universities of Vienna and Salzburg. His research focuses on political communication (with special emphasis on election coverage), the role of the media in international relations, and the development of media systems. He is co-author and co-editor of several books and has written numerous articles on the relationship between media and politics. He received his doctoral degree in Media and Communication Studies from the University of Vienna in 1984. Email: josef.seethaler@oeaw.ac.at

Adam Shehata is Assistant Professor in Political Communication, Department of Media and Communication, Mid Sweden University. His current research focuses on media effects during election campaigns, political learning, and the relationship between media systems and political engagement. He has published articles in journals such as the *European Journal of Political Research, International Journal of Press/Politics, Journal of Communication,* and *Journalism Studies.*

Elizabeth A. Skewes is Associate Professor, School of Journalism and Mass Communication, University of Colorado at Boulder, USA. A former newspaper reporter and magazine editor, her research focuses on media sociology and news practices, the media's role in electoral politics, factors that influence media content about political campaigns, and politics in popular culture. She is the author of *Message Control: How News Is Made on the Presidential Campaign Trail*, and the author or co-author of several book chapters and journal articles. She received her Ph.D. in mass communications from Syracuse University in 2001. Email: elizabeth.skewes@colorado.edu

Morten Skovsgaard is Assistant Professor at the Center for Journalism, Department of Political Science, University of Southern Denmark. He holds a bachelor's degree in journalism (2001) and worked as a journalist for some years before receiving a master's degree in journalism (2007). He is currently completing his dissertation based on a survey of Danish journalists. Email: skh@sam.sdu.dk

Clement Y. K. So is Professor in the School of Journalism and Communication, the Chinese University of Hong Kong. He was deputy editor-in-chief of Vancouver's *Ming Pao Daily News* and a reporter for *World Journal*, and marketing researcher of HK-TVB. He received a Ph.D. degree from the Annenberg School for Communication, University of Pennsylvania. His major research interests include: Hong Kong press, news sociology, citation analysis, and development of the field of communication. His major publications include *Global Media Spectacle: News War over Hong Kong*, *Press and Politics in Hong Kong: Case Studies from 1967 to 1997*, *Mainland, Hong Kong and Taiwan Journalists in Changing Contexts*, and *Television Program Appreciation Index: Hong Kong Experience, Sichuan Earthquake: Reflections from Hong Kong Journalists*.

Young Jun Son is Associate Professor, School of Communication, Kookmin University, Seoul, South Korea. His teaching and research interests include the relationship between media coverage and public opinion, media sociology, journalism theories, and journalism issues. He has published book chapters and articles in journals such as *Korean Journal of Journalism and Communication Studies*, *Korean Journal of Broadcasting and Telecommunication*, *Korean Journal of Political Studies*, *Korean Political Communication Studies*, and *International Journal of Public Opinion Research*. Professor Son received his Ph.D. in mass communication from Indiana University in 2003. Email: yoson@kookmin.ac.kr

Agnieszka Stepinska, Ph.D., is Assistant Professor, Faculty of Political Science and Journalism, Adam Mickiewicz University, Poznan, Poland. In 2001–2003 she participated in an international doctoral program, Europa Fellows, at the European University "Viadrina" in Frankfurt (Oder), Germany. Her teaching and research interests include international news flow, political communication, and intercultural communication. She has published more than 50 book chapters, journal articles, and conference papers. Her current research is focused mostly on exploring the content of the news media. Currently, she is participating in several international projects, including foreign news on TV, investigating the appearance of foreign news in domestic TV newscasts. E-mail: agnieszka.stepinska@amu.edu.pl

Jesper Strömbäck (Ph.D., Stockholm University, 2001) is Professor in Media and Communication and Lubbe Nordström-Professor and Chair in Journalism, Mid Sweden University, where he is also research director at the Centre for Political Communication Research. He has published more than 25 articles in various communication and political science journals, and more than 10 books on different aspects of political communication. Among his most recent books are *Global Political Marketing* (co-edited with Jennifer Lees-Marshment and Chris Rudd, Routledge 2010), *Handbook of Election News Coverage Around the World* (co-edited with Lynda Lee Kaid, Routledge 2008), and *Communicating Politics. Political Communication in the Nordic Countries* (co-edited with Mark Ørsten and Toril Aalberg, Nordicom 2008).

Linsen Su is Lecturer in the College of Cultural Communication, China Institute of Industrial Relations, Beijing, China. His teaching and research interests include media economics, audience analysis, and public opinion analysis. He has published book chapters and articles in journals in China and has presented papers at conferences such as AEJMC and ICA. He received his Ph.D. in mass communication from the School of Journalism and Communication, Renmin University, China in 2009. Email: linsensu@126.com

Luiza G. Svitich is Doctor of Philology, Honored Science Worker of the Lomonosov Moscow State University, the author of 170 scientific publications, 25 books and learning aids including *Fenomen zhurnalisma, Effektivnostj zhurnalistskoi deyatel'nosti, Professia zhurnalist, Vvedenie v zhurnalistiku, Sotsiologia zhurnalistiki, Tselinnaya zhurnalistika vremen Khrushchevskoi ottepeli, Zhurnalistskoe obrazovanie: vzglyad sotsiologa, Rossiiskii zhurnalist i zhurnalistskoe obrazovanie: sotsiologicheskie issledovania*. In the faculty of journalism of the MSU she gives courses on "Methodology and Methods of Journalism Research"; "Actual Problems of Contemporary Science and Journalism"; "Sociology of Journalism"; and "Journalism as Synergetic System." Her research interests lie in philosophy, sociology, and theory of values (*aksiologia*) of journalism. She participated in big national and international sociological projects including *Global Journalist*. She is one of the authors of the state standards in education in specialty journalism. Email: svitich@list.ru

Ezhar Tamam is Associate Professor of Communication, Department of Communication, Faculty of Modern Languages and Communication, Universiti Putra Malaysia, Serdang, Selangor Malaysia. Currently, he serves as Deputy Dean (Research and Innovation) at the faculty. He received his master's from Michigan State University and Ph.D. from the University of Oklahoma. His research interest includes the role of communication in development. Email: ezhar@fbmk.upm.edu.my

Yariv Tsfati is Associate Professor, Department of Communication, University of Haifa. Tsfati received his Ph.D. from the Annenberg School for Communication, University of Pennsylvania (2001). His research focuses on various facets of public opinion, in particular on trust in media, the third person effect, and campaign effects. He serves as chair of the Political Communication Division of the International Communication Association. His research was funded by the Israel Science Foundation, the German-Israel Foundation, and other institutes. Email: ytsfati@com.haifa.ac.il

Peter van Aelst is Associate Professor of Political Science at the University of Antwerp, Belgium, and one of the founding members of the research group "Media, Movements and Politics (M2P)" www.M2P.be. He also has a research position at Leiden University in The Netherlands and has published on social movements, agenda-setting, and elections in such journals as the *European Journal of Political Research, Comparative Politics,* and the *Journal of Communication*. His current research focuses on the relations between politicians and political journalists in comparative perspective. Email: peter.vanaelst@ua.ac.be

Arjen van Dalen, Ph.D., is Assistant Professor at the Center for Journalism/Department of Political Science, University of Southern Denmark. He wrote his dissertation on political journalism in comparative perspective. His research interests are in comparative communication research, particularly journalistic cultures and the relations between journalists and politicians. He has published about these topics in the *European Journal of Communication, Poltical Communication, Press/Politics,* and other journals.

Mária Vásárhelyi is Senior Researcher, Research Group for Communication Studies, Hungarian Academy of Sciences. Her main fields are media and communicator research and public opinion polls. In the media area, her research focuses mainly on the development of media market pluralism, the relationship of the media and politics, and the specifics of the operation of the public service media. Furthermore, since the system change (1990), she has headed several research projects designed to explore the social position of journalist society and the special features of its professional ethos and social role. In polling, her main lines of interest are the characteristics of public thinking on history and of social judgement on the change of the economic and social regime. She holds seminars on media ethics and on the development characteristics of public opinion at several Hungarian higher education institutions. She received her Ph.D. in 1996. She is the author of eight volumes of her own and of many book chapters and scientific papers. She regularly writes columns for Hungarian dailies and weeklies.

Maurice Vergeer is Associate Professor, Department of Communication Science, Radboud University Nijmegen, the Netherlands and visiting professor at the YeungNam University, Gyeongsan, South Korea. Before returning to academics, he worked at the Dutch Media Authority conducting research on media concentration and diversity. His research and teachings focus on consumption and production on the Internet by professionals and laypeople, broadcasters' programming strategies on television, local media landscapes, analysis of media concentration and diversity, and research methodology (in particular quantitative research methods). He is director of the pan-European project on political parties' use of the Web for election campaigning for the European Parliament election in 2009. He has published in journals such as *Journal of Computer-Mediated Communication, European Societies,* and *Javnost.*

David Weaver is Distinguished Professor and Roy W. Howard Research Professor Emeritus in the School of Journalism, Indiana University-Bloomington, where he was on the faculty since receiving his Ph.D. in mass communication research from the University of North Carolina at Chapel Hill in 1974. His teaching and research interests have focused on studies of journalists, media agenda setting, voter learning from news media, foreign news coverage, and newspaper readership. He has published a dozen books on these subjects, as well as many articles and chapters. He is a past president of AEJMC and MAPOR, and a Fellow of ICA. Email: weaver@indiana.edu

Siegfried Weischenberg holds the Chair in Journalism and Communication Studies at the University of Hamburg where he has worked also as head of the Institute for Journalism and Mass Communication, as director of the Centre of Media Communication, and as Academic Director of the Journalism Department at the Hamburg Media School since 2001. Educated in social sciences and mass communication at Bochum University where he received his Ph.D., he has been working for more than 35 years as an editor and freelancer for dailies, journals, broadcasting stations, and news agencies. From 1999 to 2001 he was chairman of the German Federation of Journalists. From 1979 to 1982 he was Professor of Media Production at Dortmund University, and until 2000 he was Professor of Communication Science and Head of the Journalism Department at Muenster University. Weischenberg has published more than 20 books and numerous articles on mass media and journalism. His main research areas are journalism, political communication, media ethics, media economy, communication technologies, and news production. Email: siegfried.weischenberg@uni-hamburg.de

Lars Willnat is Professor in the School of Journalism at Indiana University. Before joining IU in 2009, Professor Willnat taught at the George Washington University, Washington, DC and at the Chinese University of Hong Kong. His teaching and research interests include media effects on political attitudes, theoretical aspects of public opinion formation, and international communication. He has published book chapters and articles in journals such as *Journalism & Mass Communication Quarterly, International Journal of Public Opinion Research, Political Communication, Journalism,* and *International Communication Gazette.* Professor Willnat received his Ph.D. in mass communication from Indiana University in 1992. Email: lwillnat@indiana.edu

Vinzenz Wyss is Professor of Journalism Studies and Media Research as well as Head of Research, Institute of Applied Media Studies (IAM), Zurich University of Applied Sciences. His research interests are journalism theory, journalism research, news organization research, and quality management. Email: vinzenz.wyss@zhaw.ch

Edgar Kee Wang Yuen is Associate Professor, United International College, China. A former journalist and currently columnist, his teaching and research area is on news writing and media ethics. He received his B.A and M.Phil degrees from universities in Canada and Hong Kong. He is expecting his Ph.D.. degree from Peking University in 2011. Email: yuenkw1958@yahoo.com.cn

Hongzhong Zhang is Associate Professor, School of Art and Communication, Beijing Normal University. His teaching and research interests include audience measurement, the behavior of media audiences, impact of new media technologies on Chinese society, and media credibility. He has conducted 29 audience surveys in the past 10 years in China and has published two books and various journal articles. He received his Ph.D. in mass communication from the School of Journalism and Communication, Renmin University, China (2005). Email: zhanghz9@126.com

Author Index

Subject Index

Printed by Publishers' Graphics Kentucky